This book present
nirvana? Part 1 dis
tive thought in the I
and Southeast Asia,
both, and setting n
felicities. Part 2 ex
topias, "good place
Buddhist utopianis
utopian writing. Th
Vessantara Jātaka, w
ascetic quest for clo
demands of ordinar
these issues in relat
ogy in premodern c
vision of Buddhist h
the outside of texts

CAMBRIDGE STUDIES IN RELIGIOUS TRADITIONS 12

NIRVANA AND OTHER BUDDHIST FELICITIES

CAMBRIDGE STUDIES IN RELIGIOUS TRADITIONS

Edited by John Clayton (Boston University), Steven Collins (University of Chicago), and Nicholas de Lange (University of Cambridge)

1. LOUIS JACOBS
Religion and the individual: a Jewish perspective

2. ANNE-HUNT OVERZEE
The body divine: the symbol of the body in the works of Teilhard de Chardin and Rāmānuja

3. NIKKY-GUNINDER KAUR SINGH
The feminine principle in the Sikh vision of the Transcendent

4. FRIEDHELM HARDY
The religious culture of India: power, love and wisdom

5. TESSA BARTHOLOMEUSZ
Women under the Bō tree: Buddhist nuns in Sri Lanka

6 OLIVER LEAMAN
Evil and suffering in Jewish philosophy

7. DAVID SMITH
The dance of Siva: religion, art and poetry in South India

8. *edited by* SARAH COAKLAY
Religion and the body

9. RAYMOND BRADY WILLIAMS
Christian pluralism in the United States: the Indian immigrant experience

10. KEVIN TRAINOR
Relics, ritual and representation in Buddhism: rematerializing the Sri Lankan Theravāda tradition

11. JULIA CHING
Mysticism and kingship in China: the heart of Chinese wisdom

12. STEVEN COLLINS
Nirvana and other Buddhist Felicities: utopias of the Pali imaginaire

NIRVANA AND OTHER BUDDHIST FELICITIES

Utopias of the Pali imaginaire

STEVEN COLLINS
Professor in the Department of
South Asian Languages and Civilizations
University of Chicago

CAMBRIDGE
UNIVERSITY PRESS

CAMBRIDGE UNIVERSITY PRESS
Cambridge, New York, Melbourne, Madrid, Cape Town, Singapore, São Paulo

Cambridge University Press
The Edinburgh Building, Cambridge CB2 2RU, UK

Published in the United States of America by Cambridge University Press, New York

www.cambridge.org
Information on this title: www.cambridge.org/9780521570541

First published 1998
This digitally printed first paperback version 2006

A catalogue record for this publication is available from the British Library

Library of Congress Cataloguing in Publication data

Collins, Steven, 1951–
Nirvana and other Buddhist felicities: utopias of the Pali
imaginaire / Steven Collins.
p. cm. (Cambridge studies in religious traditions: 12)
Includes bibliographical references and index.
ISBN 0 521 57054 9 (hardback)
1. Nirvana. 2. Utopias – Religious aspects – Buddhism.
3. Buddhism – Doctrines. I. Title. II. Series.
BQ4263.C65 1997
294.3′423 – dc21 97-1147 CIP

ISBN-13 978-0-521-57054-1 hardback
ISBN-10 0-521-57054-9 hardback

ISBN-13 978-0-521-57842-4 paperback
ISBN-10 0-521-57842-6 paperback

In memory of my father
Patrick Collins
February 1909–March 1964

and of my teacher
Colin Macleod
June 1943–December 1981

Contents

Preface and acknowledgments

The origins of this book lie quite some time in the past. In 1979 it was fortunate for me that Clifford Geertz, who happened to be spending that year in Oxford, agreed to act as an examiner for my D.Phil. thesis. In the oral examination, he asked me whether I thought Buddhists were trying to escape from life or from death. I gave a text-bookish, doctrine-oriented answer: that although *saṃsāra*, what Buddhists aspire to escape from, is most often called the "round of rebirth," in fact it involves – necessarily – repeated death as well as repeated birth, and so nirvana is the transcendence of both life and death (cp. 1.1.a on *punarmṛtyu*, repeated dying). That seemed to do the trick at the time (I got the degree), but I was and have remained unhappy with it. It is not that there is a better conceptual, doctrinal answer; what I said is, I still think, adequate on that level. But the thrust of the question calls for a kind of reflective thought about Buddhism of which I was then quite incapable. It is for readers to decide whether or not that is still the case. This book is not a direct, one-thing-or-the-other answer to Geertz's question (I do not believe that either possibility, *simpliciter*, would take us very far, or that he thought it would), but it is a response to what I feel were some of its underlying concerns. Is to end suffering to live without suffering? Or is it finally to end, suffering?

In the early eighties, serendipity of more than one sort pushed my thinking in the direction which has led to this book. In 1983, Bristol University hosted a Colston Research Symposium on Utopias, the papers from which were published as P. Alexander and R. Gill (eds.) *Utopias* (Duckworth 1984). This introduced me to the link between monasticism and utopias, and to the work of J. C. Davis. In 1984 S. J. Tambiah published a review article in *History of Religions* (24, 1: 73–81) about Frank and Mani Reynolds'

(1982) translation of *Traibhūmi-kathā*, which characterized that text as proposing three sorts of utopia. This short piece, along with parts of Chesneaux's (1968) article, which relies on the useful but in some ways flawed work of Sarkisyanz (1965) on Burma, are the only materials I am aware of to have broached the subject of utopianism generally in relation to Theravāda Buddhism, as opposed to the common perception that anticipation of the future Buddha Metteyya (Maitreya) is "millennial." Some preliminary results of my own work in the area – along with those of earlier research on friendship which also led to Collins (1987) – were published as (1988) "Monasticism, Utopias and Comparative Social Theory." I can no longer recall how or when the ideas about nirvana to be found in Part 1 of this book began to take shape; but I know I was greatly aided – and still am – by a talk given on the BBC's Radio Three on 9 September 1984 by Eric Griffiths, called "Breathing Your Last." He kindly agreed to send me a script of the broadcast (Griffiths 1984ms.); excerpts from it were printed in *The Listener* (Griffiths 1984), and some of the material later appeared in Griffiths (1989: 123–41), "Breathing Immortally." In the talk, he reflected briefly but tellingly on the contrasting reactions to Proust's work and to his death on the part of his housekeeper and of Samuel Beckett; on what he saw as Proust's own "creative uncertainty about life after death"; on philosophy and poetry as differing "styles in which people think and speak"; and on "the moral drama of wishing to die and wishing to survive death" (1989: 128) in Tennyson's *In Memoriam*, written after the death of his friend Arthur Hallam.

> The life out of which we desire immortality we know only as a life of change, and it's impossible to know how to want another kind of life, cruel though the final change of death may be. These contradictions of desire could induce what Arthur Hallam called "that mood between contentment and despair, in which suffering appears so associated with existence that we would willingly give up one with the other, and look forward with a sort of hope to that silent void where, if there are no smiles, there are at least no tears, and since the heart cannot beat, it will not ever be broken"... [Tennyson] was susceptible to such moods, particularly in his exceptional feeling for the kinship of immortality to insomnia, of the similarity between living for ever and not ever being able to get to sleep. Perhaps the idea that personal immortality was a form of eternal insomnia came to Tennyson from the way in which it's possible to speak of death as "rest" or "sleep"; whatever the reason, he often expressed the

dreadfulness of his deepest hopes for survival in the anguished image of being perpetually awake. These contradictions, which bedevil thinking on the matter of immortality, on whether immortality is possible for beings who are in part matter, may be stilled by poetry though they prove an endless riddle for philosophical argument, "stilled" in the sense of "calmed" and also "preserved." (Griffiths 1984 ms.: 3–4; cp. 1984: 15).

Much of the context here is not relevant to what I have to say about Buddhism, notably the Christian background to Hallam's and Tennyson's ideas about "personal immortality," and Griffiths' own concern with the unique ability of poetry to respond to the fluctuating moods and attitudes embodied human beings have towards the fact of their mortal embodiment (though I do stress the need to set Buddhist narratives alongside its systematic thought, its stories next to its doctrine). But what he says is highly relevant both to particular concerns of mine about nirvana in Part 1 – for example: eternity as endlessness or timelessness (Introduction to Part 1), the "desire" for nirvana (1.4), the aporias of nirvana and the differing relation of concepts and images to them (2.2 and 2.3), and what I call the textualization of time (3.4) – and also to the way in which the book as a whole tries to respond, in its prosaic, analytical way, to Geertz's question, a challenge to which only poetry, perhaps, could ever properly respond. One thing I think I have learnt, since 1979, is the need to historicize: it now seems to me crucial that, although the inevitability of death remains the same, the "life" from which premodern Buddhists may or may not have been trying to escape was very different from that led by most moderns (at least, by anyone likely to read this book). But at the same time (perhaps better, *in* the same time: see 3.1), while it is true that the past is a foreign country, it is also true that human beings lived there: and as with any foreign country nowadays, learning and thinking about it requires moments of reflective equilibrium amid changing perceptions of sameness and difference.

As did *Selfless Persons* (cf. Collins 1982: 26), this book attempts to speak to a number of audiences. First, I hope to have provided specialists in the area, Buddhologists, Indologists, historians, anthropologists, and others, with a new account of some very familiar notions, and one which treats the material exhaustively. With the prima facie exception of Johansson (1969) – a work whose main argument clearly fails in my opinion (see 1.2.a, n.35), but which does usefully gather together relevant passages from the canonical texts, as also does Harvey (1995), whose overall strategy is essentially the same as Johansson's – I know of nothing said about nirvana which is genuinely new and valuable, ever since the fierce debate between La Vallée Poussin and Stcherbatsky came to an unresolved end in the early 1930s (Welbon 1968). Readers must decide whether what I have to say here is valuable; it is, I think I can say, new. Second, I have also aimed to provide non-specialists with a detailed and multilayered account of the world of traditional Pali literature, and of its place in history, one which does not presuppose any previous knowledge of Buddhism or of South and Southeast Asia. Those interested in the study of utopianism constitute one obvious specific audience, for whom I hope Part 2 of this work will help in extending their conversations beyond European and American tradition; but I would like to think that what I have to say here can be accessible, and perhaps also of interest, to any educated reader.

Part 1 extends and adds to the argument of my article 'Nirvāṇa, Time and Narrative' (Collins 1992a). The first version of that was written in Mahabaleshwar, Maharashtra in late December 1986 and early January 1987, and presented as a talk later that month at the Universities of Bristol and Michigan; it was also given at the Universities of Concordia (Montreal), Maine and Chicago. All five audiences made helpful comments. Preliminary versions of an Introduction and Chapters 1 and 2 were written in 1990–1. The first complete draft was written between June 1993 and June 1994, when it was first submitted to Cambridge University Press; a much expanded General Introduction was written in Fall Quarter 1995, and a second draft of Parts 1 and 2 during Winter and Spring Quarters 1996; the final version was completed between June and September of 1996. Parts or all of it have been read, sometimes in more than one draft, by the following friends and colleagues, to whom I am profoundly grateful for their comments (which were sometimes favorable, sometimes rigorously but always usefully critical): Anne Blackburn, Claude Grangier, Paul Griffiths, Charles Hallisey, Andrew Huxley, Krishan Kumar, Sheldon Pollock, Frank Reynolds, Lambert Schmithausen, and Jonathan Walters. The second draft was discussed by students in a graduate course at the University of Chicago in Winter 1996, and by some participants in a National Endowment for the Humanities Summer Seminar for College Teachers held there in Summer 1996. I am grateful to all of them for their questions and comments; individual suggestions which I have incorporated into the book are acknowledged in footnotes.

In 1991 I was very pleased to join the Department of South Asian Languages and Civilizations at the University of Chicago. I am certain that it would have been impossible for me to have written this book in the way I have done without having benefited from the extraordinarily stimulating and challenging intellectual milieu at Chicago, in the Department, in the Committee on Southern Asian Studies and the Chicago Humanities Institute, and throughout the Divisions of the Humanities and Social Sciences. I hope that my colleagues will find it an expression, however inadequate, of solidarity.

The following materials are used with permission of the publishers, whom I thank. Some passages in Chapter 3 are from "*Nirvāṇa*, Time and Narrative" (*History of Religions* 31, 3: 215–46), (c) 1992 the University of Chicago Press. The translation of the *Aggañña Sutta* in Appendix 5 is from "The Discourse on What is Primary" (*Journal of Indian Philosophy* 21: 301–93), and some passages in 6.5.c are from "The Lion's Roar on the Wheel-turning King: A Response to Andrew Huxley's 'The Buddha and the Social Contract'" (*Journal of Indian Philosophy* 24, 4: 421–46), both reprinted by permission of Kluwer academic publishers. Chapters 4 and 7 make extensive use of the translation of the *Vessantara Jātaka* in M.Cone and R.F. Gombrich (1977), *The Perfect Generosity of Prince Vessantara: A Buddhist Epic*, by permission of Oxford University Press.

Finally, some notes on terminology and style: what is meant by "the Pali *imaginaire*" is explained in the General Introduction II.e. The Pali textual tradition (ibid. II.b and d) has been carried by the Theravāda tradition of Buddhism (ibid. II.c); and I have sometimes used that qualifying adjective. But it would be tedious, and sometimes misleading, to add it on every occasion when the word "Buddhism" appears. When "Buddhism" appears without a qualifier, unless otherwise stated what is said should be taken to apply in the first instance only to the Theravāda tradition, with the question of its application to other kinds of Buddhism left open. In many cases what is said is true of other kinds; in others not. I use the unitalicized word "nirvana" without diacritics throughout, since it has become an English and American word, appearing in dictionaries (albeit often misunderstood). Chapter 2.1.a discusses the word itself, Sanskrit *nirvāṇa* and its Pali equivalent *nibbāna.* I have faced a quandary in choosing between the historical past tense, appropriate for the book's overall focus on the premodern world, and the present tense used by convention in academic discussions of literature. I have, I fear, not been entirely consistent; but I hope this will not cause misunderstanding. The General Introduction II.e and the General Conclusion attempt to make explicit what kind of historiography I think this book can be taken to be. Capital letters indicate technical terms: when the Pali term is not used see the Index and Glossary. All translations are my own unless otherwise specified.

Abbreviations

Abbreviations are those of the Critical Pali Dictionary. Only those post-canonical Pali texts which are cited in this book are given. Numbers in square brackets refer to the list of texts below. Each text cited in the book may thus be approximately dated.

Pali texts are referred to by the conventions found in PED and CPD: that is, the abbreviation for the text is followed, where appropriate, by the volume number in Roman numerals and the page number in Arabic numerals. In the case of the *Visuddhimagga*, two references are given, joined by "="; the first is to the page number of the PTS edition of the text, the second to the chapter and section numbers as given in the HOS edition.

A	*Aṅguttara Nikāya* [9]
Abhidh-s	*Abhidhammatthasaṅgaha* [73]
Anāg	*Anāgatavaṃsa* [85]
Ap	*Apadāna* [35]
Ap-a	*Apadāna-aṭṭhakathā= Visuddhajanavilāsinī*
As	*Atthasālinī* [42]
Att	*Hatthavanagalla-vihāra-vaṃsa* [63]
Bu-up	*Buddhaghosuppatti* [65]
Bv	*Buddhavaṃsa* [37]
Bv-a	*Buddhavaṃsa-aṭṭhakathā= Madhuratthavilāsinī* [38]
Cha-k	*Chakesadātuvaṃsa* [67]
Cp	*Cariya-piṭaka* [39]
Cp-a	*Cariya-piṭaka-aṭṭhakathā= Paramatthadīpanī VII* [40]
D	*Dīgha Nikāya* [3]
Dasab	*Dasabodhisatta-uddesa* [77]
Dasav	*Dasavatthuppakaraṇa* [79]
Dāṭh	*Dāṭhāvaṃsa* [61]
Dbk	*Dasabodhisattuppattikathā* [76]
Dhātuk	*Dhātukathā* [45]
Dhn	*Dhammanīti* [96]
Dhp	*Dhammapada* [13]
Dhp-a	*Dhammapada-aṭṭhakathā* [14]
Dhs	*Dhammasaṅgaṇi* [41]
Dīp	*Dīpavaṃsa* [55]

Gv	*Gandhavaṃsa* [97]
It	*Itivuttaka* [17]
It-a	*Itivuttaka-aṭṭhakathā* = *Paramatthadīpanī II* [18]
Ja	*Jātaka* [29] + [30]
Jinac	*Jinacarita* [86]
Jinak	*Jinakālamālī* [66]
Jināl	*Jinālaṅkāra* [84]
Kbv	*Kosala-bimba-vaṇṇanā* [75]
Khp	*Khuddakapāṭha* [11]
Kkh	*Kaṅkhāvitaraṇī* [69]
Kv	*Kathāvatthu* [47]
Kv-a	*Kathāvatthu-aṭṭhakathā* = *Pañcapakaraṇa-aṭṭhakathā* [48]
Ext Mhv	'Extended *Mahāvaṃsa*' [58]
Ln	*Lokanīti* [96]
Loka-n	*Lokaneyyapakaraṇa* [78]
Loka-p	*Lokapaññatti* [92]
M	*Majjhima Nikāya* [5]
Mhbv	*Mahābodhivaṃsa* [60]
Mhn	*Mahānīti* [96]
Mhv	*Mahāvaṃsa* [56]
Mhv-ṭ	*Mahāvaṃsaṭīkā*= *Vaṃsatthapakāsinī* [57]
Mil	*Milinda-pañha* [53]
Moh	*Mohavicchedanī* [74]
Mp	*Manoratha-pūraṇī* [10]
Mth-v	*Māleyyadevathera-vatthuṃ*[82]
Nett	*Nettipakaraṇa* [52]
Nidd I	*Mahāniddesa* [31]
Nidd II	*Cullaniddesa* [31]
Nidd-a I	*Mahāniddesa-aṭṭhakathā*= *Saddhammapajjotikā* [32]
Pajj	*Pajjamadhu* [88]
Pañca-g	*Pañcagatidīpanī* [90]
Paññāsa-j	*Paññāsa-jātaka* [81]
Paṭis	*Paṭisambhidāmagga* [33]
Paṭis-a	*Paṭisambhidāmagga-aṭṭhakathā*= *Saddhamma-pakāsinī* [34]
Paṭṭh	*Paṭṭhāna* [50]
Peṭ	*Peṭakopadesa* [51]
Pj I	*Paramatthajotikā I* [12]
Pj II	*Paramatthajotikā II* [20]
Pp	*Puggalapaññatti* [46]
Pp-a	*Puggalapaññatti-aṭṭhakathā* = *Pañcapakaraṇa-aṭṭhakathā* [46a]
Ps	*Papañcasūdanī* [6]
Pv	*Petavatthu* [23]
Pv-a	*Paramatthadīpanī IV* [24]
Rn	*Rājanīti* [96]
S	*Saṃyutta Nikāya* [7]
Sacc	*Saccasaṃkhepa* [91]
Sadd	*Saddanīti* [94]
Saddh	*Saddhammopāyana* [87]
Saddhamma-s	*Saddhammasaṅgaha* [64]
Samantak	*Samantakūṭavaṇṇanā* [89]
Sās	*Sāsanavaṃsa* [68]
Sīh	*Sīhalavatthuppakaraṇa* [80]
Sn	*Sutta Nipāta* [19]
Sp	*Samantapāsādikā* [2]
Spk	*Sāratthapakāsinī* [8]
Ss	*Sārasaṅgaha* [95]
Sv	*Sumaṅgalavilāsinī* [4]
Sv-pṭ	*Sumaṅgalavilāsinī-purāṇa-ṭīkā* [4a=72]
Tel	*Telakaṭāhagāthā* [83]
Th	*Theragāthā* [25]
Th-a	*Theragāthā-aṭṭhakathā*= *Paramatthadīpanī V* [26]
Thī	*Therīgāthā* [27]

Thī-a	*Therīgāthā-aṭṭhakathā*= *Paramatthadīpanī VI* [28]
Thūp	*Thūpavaṃsa* [62]
Ud	*Udāna* [15]
Ud-a	*Udāna-aṭṭhakathā*= *Paramatthadīpanī I* [16]
Upās	*Upāsakajanālaṅkāra* [92]
Vibh	*Vibhaṅga* [43]
Vibh-a	*Vibhaṅga-aṭṭhakathā*= *Sammohavinodanī* [44]
Vin	*Vinaya* [1]
Vism	*Visuddhimagga* [70]
Vism-a	*Visuddhimagga-aṭṭhakathā* =*Paramatthamañjusā* [70a]
Vv	*Vimānavatthu* [21]
Vv-a	*Vimānavatthu-aṭṭhakathā* =*Paramatthadīpanī III* [22]
Yam	*Yamaka* [49]

TEXTUAL CHRONOLOGY

Dates given here, which are in many cases speculative, follow Norman (83). Publication details for texts and translations not in the Bibliography here are in Norman (83); and also in the Pali Text Society's "List of Issues". Numbers in square brackets refer to those in the List of Abbreviations above.

1. CANONICAL TEXTS (c. fourth–third c. BC) and their COMMENTARIES (fifth–sixth c. AD, some perhaps later)

TEXT	TRANSLATION TITLE/ TRANSLATOR	COMMENTARY (with translator and translation title where available)
Vinaya-piṭaka		
Vinaya [1]	*Book of the Discipline* Horner (38–66; 5 vols.)	*Samanta-pāsādikā* [2] [partial translation in Jayawickrama (62) *Inception of the Discipline*
Sutta-piṭaka		
Dīgha Nikāya [3]	*Dialogues of the Buddha* T. W. and C. A. F. Rhys Davids (1899–1921, 3 vols.)	*Sumaṅgalavilāsinī* [4] [the subcommentary, the *Sumaṅgalavilāsinī-purāṇa-ṭīkā* [4a=72]
Majjhima Nikāya [5]	*Middle Length Sayings* Horner (54–9; 3 vols.)	*Papañcasūdanī* [6]
Saṃyutta Nikāya [7]	*Kindred Sayings* C. A. F Rhys Davids and Woodward (17–30; 5 vols.)	*Sāratthapakāsinī* [8]
Aṅguttara Nikāya [9]	*Gradual Sayings* Woodward, Hare (32–6; 5 vols.)	*Manorathapūraṇī* [10]
Khuddaka Nikāya		
Khuddaka-pāṭha [11]	*Minor Readings and Illustrator* (text and commentary) Ñāṇamoli (60)	*Paramatthajotikā I* [12] Ñāṇamoli (60)
Dhammapada [13]	[many versions available]	*Dhammapada-aṭṭhakathā* [14] Burlingame (21; 3 vols.) *Buddhist Legends*; Carter and Palihawadana (87) *The Dhammapada*
Udāna [15]	*The Udāna* Masefield (94)	*Paramatthadīpanī I* [16] Masefield 94–5; 2 vols.) *Udāna Commentary*
Itivuttaka [17]	*Verses of Uplift and Itivuttaka* Woodward (35)	*Paramatthadīpanī II* [18]

Sutta Nipāta [19]	*The Group of Discourses II* Norman (92a)	*Paramatthajotikā II* [20]
Vimānavatthu [21]	*Minor Anthologies IV* Horner (74)	*Paramatthadīpanī III* [22] Masefield (89) *Vimāna Stories*
Petavatthu [23]	*Minor Anthologies IV* Gehman [in Horner 74]	*Paramatthadīpanī IV* [24] Kyaw and Masefield (80)
Theragāthā [25]	*Elders' Verses I* Norman (69)	*Paramatthadīpanī V* [26]
Therīgāthā [27]	*Elders' Verses II* Norman (71)	*Paramatthadīpanī VI* [28]
Jātaka [29]	*Jātaka or Stories of the Buddha's Former Births* [with part of commentary: see Norman (83: 77–84)] Cowell et al. (1895–1907)	*Jātakāṭṭhakathā* [30] = *Jātaka or Stories of the Buddha's Former Births* Cowell et al. (1895–1907)
Niddesa [= *Mahāniddesa* and *Culla-niddesa*] [31]		*Saddhammapajjotikā* [32]
Paṭisambhidāmagga [33]	*Path of Discrimination* Ñāṇamoli (82)	*Saddhammapakāsinī* [34]
Apadāna [35]		*Visuddhajanavilāsinī* [36]
Buddhavaṃsa [37]	*Minor Anthologies III* Horner (75)	*Madhuratthavilāsinī* [38] Horner (78) *Clarifier of the Sweet Meaning*
Cariyapiṭaka [39]	*Minor Anthologies III* Horner (75)	*Paramatthadīpanī VII* [40]
Abhidhamma-piṭaka		
Dhammasaṅgaṇi 41]	*Buddhist Psychological Ethics* C. A. F. Rhys Davids (1900)	*Aṭṭhasālinī* [42] Maung Tin (20) *The Expositor*
Vibhaṅga [43]	*The Book of Analysis* U. Titthila (69)	*Sammohavinodanī* [44] Ñāṇamoli (87, 91; 2 vols.) *Dispeller of Delusion*
Dhātukathā [45]	*Discourse on Elements* U. Nārada (62)	
Puggalapaññatti [46]	*Designation of Human Types* Law (22	*Pañcapakaraṇa-aṭṭhakathā* [46a: printed with 46]
Kathāvatthu [47]	*Points of Controversy* Aung and C. A. F. Rhys Davids (15)	*Pañcapakaraṇaṭṭhakathā* [48] Law (40) *Debates Commentary*
Yamaka [49]		*Pañcapakaraṇa-aṭṭhakathā*
Paṭṭhāna (2 vols.) [50]	*Conditional Relations* (translation of *Tikapaṭṭhāna* only) U. Nārada (69, 81; 2 vols.)	*Pañcapakaraṇa-aṭṭhakathā* [50a: *Tikapaṭṭhāna* commentary printed with no.50 vol.2]

2. POST-CANONICAL TEXTS

TEXT	DATE	TRANSLATION	TRANSLATOR
(i) Early prose texts			
Peṭakopadesa [51]	before 5th c. AD	*Piṭaka Disclosure*	Ñāṇamoli (64)
Nettipakaraṇa [52]	before 5th c. AD	*The Guide*	Ñāṇamoli (62)
Milinda-pañha [53]	between 2nd c. BC and 5th c. AD	*Milinda's Questions*	Horner (63–4; 2 vols.)
Vimuttimagga [54]	before 5th c. AD	*The Path of Freedom*	Ehara et al. (61)
(ii) Chronicles (Histories) (all dates are henceforth AD)			
Dīpavaṃsa [55]*	after 4th c.	*Dīpavaṃsa*	Oldenburg (1879)
Mahāvaṃsa [56] *	after 4th c.	*Mahāvaṃsa*	Geiger (12)
Vaṃsatthapakāsinī (commentary on [56]), [57]	8–9th c.		
Mahāvaṃsa (from Cambodia, 'Extended *Mahāvaṃsa*') [58]*	12th c.		
Cūḷavaṃsa (also called *Mahāvaṃsa*) [59]*	[see Norman (83: 140–1)]	*Cūḷavaṃsa*	Geiger (29)
Mahabodhivaṃsa [60]	10th c.		
Dāṭhavāṃsa [61]	13th c.	*Dāṭhavāṃsa*	Law (25)
Thūpavaṃsa [62]	13th c.	*Thūpavaṃsa*	Jayawickrama (71)
Hatthavanagalla-vihāra-vaṃsa [63]	13th c.	*The Attanagalu-Vaṃsa* [sic]	d'Alwis (1866)
Saddhammasaṅgaha [64]	14th c.	*A Manual of Buddhist Historical Traditions*	Law (41)
Buddhaghosuppatti [65]	14th c.	*Buddhaghosuppatti*	Gray (1892)
Jinakālamālī [66]	16th c.	*Epochs of the Conqueror*	Jayawickrama (68)
Chakesadātuvaṃsa [67]	19th c.?		Law (52)
Sāsanavaṃsa [68]	19th c,	*The History of Buddha's Religion*	Law (52)
(iii) Commentarial texts and scholastic treatises			
Kankhāvitaraṇī [69] (commentary on the *Pātimokkha*)	4–5th c.		
Visuddhimagga [70] [commentary =70a]	4–5th c.	*Path of Purification*	Ñāṇamoli (75)
Abhidhammavatāra	6th c.		

[71] *Dīgha-nikāy-atthakathāṭīkā* [72]=[4a]	between 6th and 10th c.		
Abhidham-mattha-saṅgaha [74]	11–12th c.	*A Manual of Abhidhamma*	Nārada Thera (75)
Mohavicchedanī [73]	12–13th c.		
(iv) Story literature (prose)			
Kosala-bimba-vaṇṇanā [75]	13–14th c.	*Kosala-bimba-vaṇṇanā*	Gombrich (78)
Dasabodhisatt-uppattikathā [76]	12–4th c.	*Birth Stories of the Ten Bodhisattas*	Saddhātissa (75)
Dasabodhisatta-uddesa [77]	12–14th c.	*Dasabodhisatta-uddesa* (French)	Martini (36)
Lokaneyya-ppakaraṇaṃ [78]	before 14th c.		
Dasavatthu-ppakaraṇa [79]	before 15th c.	*Dasavatthu-ppakaraṇa* (French)	ver Eecke (76)
Sīhalavattu-ppakaraṇa [80]	before 15th c.	*Sīhalavattu-ppakaraṇa* (French)	ver Eecke (80)
Paññāsa-jātaka [81]	15–16th c.	*Apocryphal Birth Stories*	Horner and Jaini (85), Jaini (86)
Māleyyadevathera-vatthuṃ [82]	15–16th c.	*The Story of the Elder Māleyyadeva*	Collins (93b)
(v) Poetic works (in verse)			
Telakaṭāhagāthā [83]	between 10th and 13–14th c.		[see Norman 83: 156 n.206]
Jinālaṅkāra [84]	12th c.	*Jinālaṅkāra*	Gray (1894)
Anāgatavaṃsa [85]	12–13th c. [? – see 5.2.b]	*The History of the Future*	Section 5.2.b of this book
Jinacarita [86]	13th c.	*Jinacarita*	Rouse (5),
Saddhammopāyana [87]	13th c.	*Saddhammopāyana*	Hazlewood (88)
Pajjamadhu [88]	13–14th c.		
Samantakūṭa-vaṇṇanā [89]	13–14th c.	*In Praise of Mount Samanta*	Hazlewood (86)
Pañcagatidīpanī [90]	14th c.	*Pañcagatidīpanī*	Hazlewood (87)
(vi) Miscellaneous			
Sacca-saṃkhepa (scholastic verse) [91]	6th c. [?]		
Lokapaññatti (cosmology) [92]	11–12th c.	*Lokapaññatti* (French)	Denis (77)

Upāsakajanālaṅkāra (advice to laity) [93]	12th c.
Saddanīti (Pali grammar) [94]	12th c.
Sārasaṅgaha (anthology) [95]	13–14th c.
Dhammanīti, Lokanīti, Rājanīti, Mahāranīti [96]	14–15th c.
Gandhavaṃsa (bibliography) [97]	17th c.

* Note that GPD refers to both *Mahāvaṃsa* [56] and *Cūlavaṃsa* [59] (which some writers abbreviate to Cv) as Mhv; and to the 'Extended *Mahāvaṃsa*' [58] as Ext Mhv. For these names see Norman (83: 140–1).

Other abbreviations

BD	The Book of the Discipline (*Vinaya*, translated by I. B. Horner)
BDict	Buddhist Dictionary, Nyanatiloka (3rd edn., revised and enlarged by Nyanaponika, Colombo: Frewin, 1976)
BHSD	Edgerton's Buddhist Hybrid Sanskrit Dictionary, Edgerton, F. (New Haven: Yale University Press, 1953)
CG	M. Cone and R. F. Gombrich (1977)
CPD	Critical Pali Dictionary
CV	*cakkavatti* (Skt *cakravartin*)
DPPN	Dictionary of Pali Proper Names, G. P. Malalasekera (London: Pali Text Society 1938)
EB	*Encyclopedia of Buddhism*
ER	*Encyclopedia of Religion*, ed. M. Eliade (1987)
ERE	Hastings' Encyclopaedia of Religion and Ethics
EV I and II	K. R. Norman (1969) and (1971)
HOS	Harvard Oriental Series
JPTS	*Journal of the Pali Text Society*
KRN	K. R. Norman (1990–96), *Collected Papers*
MIA	Middle Indo-Aryan
MW	Monier-Williams' Sanskrit–English Dictionary
OED	Oxford English Dictionary
PED	Pali Text Society's Pali–English Dictionary
PTC	Pali Tipiṭikaṃ Concordance
SBB	Sacred Book of the Buddhists
Skt	Sanskrit
VJ	*Vessantara Jātaka*

General introduction Buddhism and civilizational history I structures and processes

This general introduction sets out a very broad framework, both historical and methodological, for the account of nirvana and other Buddhist felicities to be offered in the main part of the book. It raises a large number of heterogeneous, complex and difficult issues, making connections between my approach to them and those of other scholars. I hope that both what it says, and the point of saying it, will become clear during the course of the book. What I have to say falls into three parts:

(i) the first outlines a model for thinking about Theravāda Buddhism from the perspective of world history in general, and the history of civilizations in particular. It offers an analytical account of ideology and power in premodern agrarian states, and of the processes of culture-making in them which produced texts such as those of the Pali *imaginaire.*[1] What is said here about the discursive enunciation of order and the cultural logic of asceticism provides an essential part of both the conceptual and the sociological grounding for the Buddhist discourse of felicity, and for the particular role of nirvana within it.

(ii) The second part discusses the provenance of the ideas, images and stories dealt with in Chapters 1 through 7. It situates that imagined world in the real world of South and Southeast Asian history and historiography,[2] aiming to bring about a kind of double vision: one which will hold in view, throughout the book, both the inside and the outside of these texts at the same time.

[1] The sense in which I use this term, henceforth as a non-italicized English word, is explained in section II.e.

[2] For the sake of brevity I refer hereafter to "Southern" Asia, which for my purposes refers to what is now the Indian subcontinent, the island of Sri Lanka, and the territory occupied by the nation-states of Burma (Myanmar), Thailand, Cambodia, and Laos.

(iii) The third part introduces the specific topics addressed and my approach to them. This approach argues against what is a very widely held consensus in the study of Buddhism, shared by historians and ethnographers alike, by decentering nirvana within what is usually called "Buddhist doctrine," and recentering it in the perception of "Buddhism in practice" (by one and the same argument); and thus aims to present a new perspective from which to understand Buddhism as a phenomenon of history and culture.

In this Introduction, I adopt the wide-angle view of the *longue durée*, to locate the texts of the premodern Pali imaginaire in their natural habitat – the premodern world – and the readers (and writer) of this book in theirs – the modern world. In this way I hope to suggest how both the book and its subject matter are located in a common but mutually distanced historical space. One of the purposes of the book is to provide historians and theorists of the modern and (if such a thing exists) postmodern worlds with an alternative vision of the cultural possibilities of premodernity. The Pali imaginaire is only one part of Southern Asian Buddhism, and a fortiori of Southern Asian civilization; but it is a specific imagined world which, although produced in what I depict, ideal-typically, as the universal conditions of pre-industrial, agrarian society, has for modern scholarship the advantage of differing markedly and profoundly, in certain crucial respects, from that imagined in medieval European Christianity. (It would be wrong to assume, however, that it differs in every possible respect.) The apparently cosmopolitan conversation about modernity in contemporary scholarship is often, it seems to me, hampered by the fact that many who take part in it – not only westerners – tend to assume in practice that the societies from which the change to modernity is to be plotted are culturally comprehensible in the terms of medieval European Christianity. It is to Max Weber's very great credit that as a sociologist and social historian of modern Europe he set out to understand other premodernities in an empirical-historical manner, even if the questions he took with him, along with the state of scholarship available at that time, in large measure determined what he could see there. It is striking – and unfortunate – that many discussions in this genre still refer to Weber not only for his own ideas, which remain important, but also for the information he gives about Southern Asia and

Buddhism, which we now know to be very often either very misleading or simply wrong.[3] I hope, *inter alia*, that this book will provide the conversation about modernity with a more accurate and usable example of what LaCapra (p. 42 below) calls the "processing of primary material," from one tradition, in one part of the globe. It is not, however, a book about premodernity which takes Buddhism as an example; it is a book about Buddhism which finds it necessary to think about the conditions of premodernity if it is to arrive at the kind of understanding it seeks.

I. SOME CONCEPTS AND MODES OF ANALYSIS

I.a. Ideology and power in agrarian/tributary states

Historians seeking to delineate stages of world history have often done so from the teleological viewpoint of European triumphalism, or at least from a presupposition that "the rise of the West" is the principal world-historical *explanandum*. It may seem to some readers that the ideal-typical, generalizing kind of historiography to be found in this and the following sections necessarily does the same thing. I think, naturally, that this is not the case, and I try to describe exactly what are the historiographical intentions of this book in section II.e below: but for the moment the risk of being misunderstood as proposing ahistorical, structural-functionalist social matrices is one that has to be run. Later in the book I have much to say about two kinds of thought, which I call systematic and narrative. The distinction is applicable here: in systematic historiography of the sort I will be presently engaged in, one is looking to isolate in ideal-typical form deliberately simple categories of analysis, not to provide precise descriptive tools for a narrative historiography of specific times and places. If one confuses the two then the goal of elegant simplicity in an analytical model, intended to apply to a wide range of differing actual cases, will result in a woefully simplistic, even absurd failure to write chronologically and geographically detailed history. In discussing the concept of modernity in Buddhist Southern Asia in section II.c below, I have recourse to a particular, because to me particularly

[3] This book owes much to Weber; but it tries to make some radical revisions to a Weberian approach. A balanced assessment of Weber on South Asia can be found in D. Gellner (1982).

telling narrative history of late-eighteenth- to nineteenth-century Thailand, which illustrates clearly that one can indeed talk of the arrival of modernity at that time and place. The analytical scheme introduced in these first sections cannot, in itself, capture the specificities of such localized *histoire événementielle*. But both forms of thought and writing can be genuine and informative modes of historiography.

Any form of historical periodization, clearly, is contestable, and better seen as a tool of analysis which can be more or less useful, than as a descriptive matrix which might be more or less true. The most pervasive contemporary western form – ancient, medieval, and modern – is an invention of the seventeenth century, deriving from earlier Italian humanists (Green 1992, 1995). In world history what Gellner calls trinitarianism (1988: 16–29) is particularly common, and perhaps such tripartite divisions are plausible in part because they reproduce the narrative structure of beginning, middle, and end. Nonetheless, the model adopted here, in common with many others, posits three stages, whose distinguishing criterion is the mode of acquisition and/or production of food and resources; from this one can trace differences in the corresponding forms of social organization, and the conditions for the production of culture. Further subdivisions and transitional stages may of course be necessary for certain purposes. My purpose here is to bring out some features of the second, agrarian stage, which has characterized most human societies throughout most of human history, and in which what we call "civilization" emerged. This is the stage in which the Pali imaginaire was created and transmitted as a plausible whole. The three stages are:

(i) The *pre-agricultural:* usually referred to as that of hunter-gatherers, but also called communal (Amin 1980), family- or kin-ordered (Wolf 1982: 73ff.; Stavrianos 1992; Johnson and Earle 1987). At this stage food is for the most part gathered by women, supplemented by some hunting, which is done mostly by men. (Thus one might follow Mann 1986 in referring rather to "gatherer-hunters.") There may also be, to a greater or lesser extent (on which see below) some horticulture. Society consists only in small-scale families; disputes within and between such kin-groups occur, naturally, but anything serious enough to warrant, at a later stage, physical conflict and/or long-term submission of one group to the other is solved by the whole or part of a group simply moving to another area where they can gather and hunt untroubled.[4]

(ii) The *agrarian*: although the transition to settled agricultural life must have been gradual, and there is no agreed narrative of it, most theorists concur on the main features of this stage.[5] Food, obviously, now requires co-ordinated and co-operative agriculture; people living in settled abodes require new forms of conflict resolution. (The picture is complicated, but for my purposes not fundamentally changed, by the presence, in different times and places and to a greater or lesser degree, of nomadic pastoralism and/or merchant commercialism.) Society is organized in increasingly large-scale groupings, passing through family societies, local groups with or without leaders termed Big Men, chiefdoms, to agrarian states as regional and trans-regional polities, kingdoms and empires. In Southern Asia, as elsewhere, sociopolitical formations oscillated back and forth over this continuum (it being an "evolutionary" sequence only in ideal-typical terms[6]). At the largest end of the spectrum are found rulers called in Pali "Wheel-turning Kings," or "Emperors"[7] (*cakkavatti*-s). The political form of agrarian states is constituted by some mixture of routinized and bureaucratized military and/or political power. Defining features of the state include: a monopoly over the means of violence in a given area, taxation, the right, or at least the capacity to draft corvée labor and an army, the enforcement of some form of articulated law, and perhaps – although this is debatable – some ideology

[4] The features of this stage are arrived at by means of archaeological reconstruction of the past and extrapolation from contemporary peoples, obviously a procedure not without problems, as everyone working in the area realizes. But there is no alternative, apart from an all-purpose, self-defeating skepticism.

[5] Sanderson (1995: 34–51) gives an overview of the hypotheses so far suggested for the transition; and on pp. 94–133 surveys the characteristics of agrarian states once established.

[6] These ideal-typical categories are useful for an analysis which focuses on the question of overall historical development. Historians and anthropologists looking for accurate descriptive terms for spatio-temporally located circumstances may well find such a categorial sequence inadequate (see Bentley 1986: 297–8).

[7] Translators and historians often refer to Buddhist rulers as "emperors," although with important exceptions such as Aśoka in the third century BC, few governed territory as large as those normally called "empires." I use the word "king." In modern times the concept of kingship or emperorship has been scaled down to apply to rulers, monarchical and other, of ethnically plural nation-states.

which "justifies" or "legitimizes" the social status quo.[8] The agrarian stage, and the societies and states within it, are sometimes called "tributary." The term was first used of a world-historical stage by Samir Amin, to describe a mode of production in the Marxist sense (1976: 13ff.; cp. Wolf 1982: 73–100); but he and others have since generalized it, to depict "Formations" (Amin 1980), "Ideology," "Culture" (Amin 1989) and "Societies" (Stavrianos 1992). "Tribute" here refers to food, goods, services and eventually cash extracted by a ruling elite[9] from peasant-cultivators and herdsmen, directly by military or political means, and indirectly (but on this see below) by means of ideologies which normalize and so justify the extraction process. Society, hitherto egalitarian, is split into two main groups, the tribute-givers and the tribute-takers, and so Giddens (e.g. 1981, 1987) speaks of societies under these conditions as "class-divided."[10]

(iii) The *modern*: this is characterized by capitalism and industrialization, although there is dispute as to whether both are necessary, and if not, which is the more important. For those who emphasize changes in the mode of production it is the capitalist stage; that is, the stage at which the ruling elite not only extracts tribute from primary producers but also controls their access to the means of production, leaving them only the power to sell their labor. For others, such as Gellner (1988), this stage is better described as that of industrial society, where the production of food becomes the occupation of a minority, and most people manipulate the enormously increased capacity to produce wealth enabled by science and technology. And of course it is only now that one can speak of the beginnings of nations and the nation-state system, developing

[8] The narrative of this process is, of course, widely debated and contested, as are the criteria for what constitutes a "state." Overviews are given by Johnson and Earle (1987) and Sanderson (1995: 53–94). Claessen and Skalnik (1978) is a standard collection of articles; cp. also Carneiro (1988), replying to the critics of his influential (1970) article.

[9] The word "elite," unless otherwise specified, refers in this book only to a class defined socioeconomically. The word can be used differently, of course, as when it refers to those who are more sophisticated in terms of literacy and education. To conflate these two meanings, for example, would make it a priori impossible for anyone to be both rich and stupid – which would be an unfortunate restriction on one's historical vision.

[10] It is sometimes said that one should speak of "peasants" only where there is such subjection to a tribute-extracting class, for example by Wolf (1966); cp. Redfield (1989[56]: 19–20), agreeing with an earlier article by Wolf, on peasants as the "rural dimension of old civilizations."

in conjunction with the world-system colonialism of modern Europe (to use the terminology of Wallerstein, e.g. 1974). Previous "world systems" existed, in the sense of extensive trading networks;[11] South India, Sri Lanka and Southeast Asia were at the confluence of Roman, (later) Arab trading routes from the West, and Chinese from the East, from at least the beginning of the first millennium AD. Exactly when and how one can place the concept of modernity in Southern Asia is a complex question, addressed in the note in section II.c below.

Any analytical system can be further complicated. How horticulture fits into the transition from the hunter-gatherer to agrarian stages, for example, remains contested. Woodburn (1980, 1982) makes a helpful distinction between immediate-return and delayed-return hunter-gatherers (cf. Testart 82 on "non-storing" and "storing" kinds). The former acquire, with relative ease, only enough food and other requirements for a few days, avoiding long-term commitments in the production and storing of food, and in other forms of labor; the latter are part of a larger category of "delayed-return systems," which includes both hunter-gatherers of various kinds[12] and farmers. Only the former can be sharply contrasted with tribute-paying "peasants" cultivating food and/or rearing domestic or herd animals; and only they might have constituted the pre-agrarian, egalitarian, "original affluent society" made popular by Sahlins (1972; cp. Bird-David 1992). In the transition from agrarian to modern stages (which has occurred, where and when it has, in different places at different times and at different speeds), one can ask: did the modern begin with fifteen- to sixteenth-century merchant capitalism, whose historical course coincided – not coincidentally – with that of European colonialism, but which predated industrial society? If scientific technology and industrial production are the crucial factors, do we date modernity from the seventeenth century, when modern science as a system of thought, a form of knowledge, began, or should we follow Jacques LeGoff in arguing for what he calls "an extended

[11] See, inter alia, Abu-Lughod (1989), Amin (1991), Frank and Gills (1993), Chase-Dunn and Hall (1994a and b), Chase-Dunn and Grimes (1995), Peregrine and Feinman (1996).

[12] Examples given by Woodburn (1980: 98–9) are: part-time hunters; sedentary or semi-sedentary hunters and gatherers; fishermen who invest; trappers who invest.

Middle Ages," lasting until the nineteenth century, since it was only then that "modernity was fully embraced," in the sense that the conditions of industrial society, along with the mass education it requires, were not until then fully instantiated throughout society, at least in Europe (1988: 18–23; and cp. Gellner 1983)? And in this case are the still non-industrialized parts of the world "non-modern"? Important though these issues are, for my purposes they do not need to be addressed, although it is certainly crucial to recognize that the conditions of modernity – notably the political form seemingly required by the industrial or capitalist stage, the nation-state, and the facts of European colonialism – have affected both Buddhist ideology and western knowledge of it. It was under these conditions in the nineteenth century. that western knowledge of Buddhism arose, and from these conditions now that both western scholars and modern Buddhists look back at the premodern world and write their histories.[13] But my concern in this book is with the nature of society, the state and the production of culture in the agrarian stage, as an – ideal-typical, systematic – historical context for exploring the imaginaire of Pali texts.

The idea of delayed-return, storing hunter-gatherer systems undoubtedly helps clarify the possible nature of the transition from pre-agricultural to agrarian stages; but this development cannot – if we are concerned with the emergence of tributary systems in the full sense – be regarded as a natural, inevitable occurrence in the "evolution'[14] of human societies. The transition was, rather, an intensification of delayed-return cultivation propelled – perhaps inaugurated – by the incipient tribute-taking class, an intensification which could both rise and fall in any given place at different times. The process is often called the extraction of a surplus, but one might well recall here what John Berger says about the phenomenology of peasants: that for them the meeting of "enforced social obligations" – taxation and the like – is more likely to present itself as a preliminary obstacle,

[13] On Buddhist modernism, see Gombrich and Obeyesekere (1988); on western knowledge of Buddhism see de Jong (1987), Almond (1988), Carter (1993: 9–35), Scott (1994), Lopez (1995a).

[14] On the use of this contentious term in this regard see Johnson and Earle (1987), Sanderson (1995), and for a dissenting view Layton et al. (1991), who regard hunting-gathering and cultivation as alternative strategies which respond to climatic and other changes.

after which they can begin to work for the needs of their own families (1992[1979]: xiii). That is, the surplus needs to be produced first. Such "surplus" extraction was no doubt pursued by the tribute-takers for their own ends; but it also had benefits for the tribute-givers (as the takers were prone to point out), notably in the provision of what Peter Brown (1995: 53), speaking of the Roman Empire, nicely calls the "'gentle violence' of a stable social order." This is a theme explored in considerable detail later in this Introduction and in Chapters 6 and 7; but it is an ambivalent and very difficult issue relevant to the book as a whole, which is worth introducing here briefly.

Violence and other forms of coercion, both internal and external, would seem to be universal, indeed necessary preconditions for the hierarchical human societies which produced premodern civilization. When population density is sufficiently large (which can be brought about by coercion, as it was repeatedly by kings in mainland Southeast Asia) and the economic arrangements of agrarian society are sufficiently complex, the provision of internal dispute resolution, social order and eventually the administration of an impersonally conceived justice by greater degrees of centralized control produce the fact, or at least the rhetoric, of peace and prosperity which enables the production of an extractable surplus. Eckhardt (1995: 92; cf. 1992) summarizes his and others' quantitative research in premodern history by saying that "at both the global and regional levels, civilizations, empires and wars were significantly related to one another, tending to rise and fall together." Violence, exploitation and inequality entered into the very constitution of the agrarian states in which Buddhist felicities were produced as objects of human aspiration, including the utopian discourse that wished such things away. This affects both how one interprets these felicities taken singly (especially what Chapter 6 calls the "Perfect Moral Commonwealth"), and one's grasp of what I call in section III of this Introduction and *passim* the Buddhist discourse of felicity as a whole. That is to say, this is a theme of importance for understanding not only some particular products of the work of Buddhist culture, but also the conditions under which the work of Buddhist culture could take place at all.

Two further aspects of the agrarian state may be mentioned at this point. First, tributary relations vary along what Wolf calls "a continuum of power distributions." "It is possible to envisage two polar situations: one in which power is concentrated strongly in the hands of a ruling elite standing at the apex of the power system; and another in which power is held largely by local overlords and rule at the apex is fragile and weak" (1982: 80). These two situations correspond to what have been called – very imprecisely, to be sure, in the Southern Asian case – the Asiatic and Feudal modes of production respectively. Oscillation between strong/centralized and weak/diffused power – but with a long-term linear trend toward centralization – was characteristic of the sociopolitical circumstances of Theravāda Buddhist ideology throughout its premodern history. Second, the word "agrarian" does not exclude cities – on the contrary they were central, in more ways than one and increasingly so, in the agrarian stage, and are implied in the very idea of civilization. Marshall Hodgson's terminology is useful if rather ungainly: he saw civilization as a product of "agrarianate citied society" or "citied agrarianate communities" (1974: 107; 1989: 46). Cities were vital to the production of culture, as to economic, military and political power. In some places (as in insular Southeast Asia) they could develop into city-states based primarily on trade, but the fundamental organization of premodern civilization, and the framework of plausibility for Buddhist ideology, was that of agrarian social order.[15] In a valuable discussion of "The Politics of Aristocratic Empires," Kautsky (1982: 23) in my view unnecessarily restricts himself by defining "a pure traditional aristocratic empire as a political entity that contains an aristocracy and is unaffected by commercialization." He then has to exclude from his purview the classical Greek and Roman Empires, for example, since they were highly commercialized. It seems better, at least from the point of view adopted here, to say that premodern agrarian states, and certainly the political formations in which the traditional Pali imaginaire was of cultural significance, were predominantly agrarian in their demographic constitution, but contained, to varying degrees in varying times and places, urban *milieux*, which were important economically, culturally and otherwise. (To jump forward briefly: this perspective

[15] This is clear, for example, from the writings of Aung Thwin (1979, 1980) and Lieberman (1980, 1987, 1991) on premodern Burma, despite their disagreements about the importance of trade through coastal outlets, and other economic processes. (See further section II.e.)

will be useful in Chapter 2, when interpreting the textual trope of "the city of nirvana.")

The preceding is a preliminary sketch of agrarian states in world history. To begin to think, again ideal-typically, about the distribution of ideology and power in such societies, I want to start from models proposed by Gellner (1988) and Mann (1986). To start with Gellner: he accepts the three stages of world history outlined above, and considers not only the different means (or their absence) of producing, accumulating and storing food and resources, but also the forms of coercion and legitimation which accompany them (as well as, in the second and third stages, the social distribution and varieties of cognition they encourage[16]). "Agricultural society is defined by the systematic production and storage of food, and in a lesser measure of other goods. The existence of a stored surplus inevitably commits the society to some enforcement of the division of that surplus, and to its external defense. Hence violence, merely contingent amongst hunters, becomes mandatory amongst agriculturalists".[17] The surplus of agrarian societies is small, when compared to that of industrial society, but compared to that of hunter-gatherers it is sufficiently large and stable that such societies "tend to develop complex social differentiation, an elaborate division of labor. Two specialisms in particular become of paramount importance: the emergence of a specialized ruling class, and of a specialized clerisy (specialists in cognition, legitimation, salvation, ritual)" (1988: 17). (As mentioned earlier, the ruling class may in fact have emerged before or during the transition, encouraging if not initiating it.) These two groups he calls kings and clerisy, warriors and priests, or most simply thugs and legitimators.

This analysis is relevant to two classic themes in South Asian history. First, given that the two specialisms are only possible because of agriculture and the surplus it produces, a tripartite structure of workers, warriors and priests (he depicts the three

[16] Gellner's account of cognition and society in the agrarian stage (1988: 70–112 and *passim*) is extremely useful, but for my purposes he places too much reliance on literacy, the role of which in Southern Asia remains to be clarified, but was certainly less decisive than in Europe. He also concentrates too much on other things specific to the European past, notably the idea of a jealous God and Protestantism.

[17] (1988: 275; cp. also 1995: 34–5, 160–72); cf. R. Collins (1990: 125–31 and 1992) on "agrarian-coercive societies."

elements as production, coercion and cognition) is not so much a special feature of Indo-European society and culture, as Dumézil and his followers claim, but a structural feature of any agrarian economy producing a small but reliable surplus, as Gellner is aware (1988: 86). Second, "thugs and legitimators," where they are different, must, since they exercise related forms of coercion, come to some sort of mutual *modus vivendi*: thus the complex and multivalent relations between kings and priests, kṣatriya-warriors and Brahmins – which Dumont (1980, et freq.) saw in terms of a difference between power and status, a view which has occasioned much discussion – are again not specific traits of Indian society and culture but general features of the agrarian order.

For his purposes – which include as a central concern the search for possible explanations for the rise of industrial society in Europe, an issue which does not concern me here[18] – Gellner's dichotomy is adequate, but if one wants to accommodate more social and historical specificity more complex models are necessary. To acknowledge trade, as a source both of material wealth and of the prestige deriving from luxury goods brought from afar (and from association with the foreign and distant *per se*: Schneider 1977; Helms 1988), one may make economic power a separate category. Amin (1989: 1–2) is perhaps right in saying that before the modern era the realities of commerce were clear to everyone, whereas capitalism has mystified economic relationships, so that they now require a science of economics to be understood. But even if the facts were clear the capacity to influence trade was not direct. Kings could and did extort taxes and protection money from traders by direct coercion; but long-term royal income from mercantile wealth obviously could not be either generated or secured that way: it required indirect manipulation or persuasion. In a similar way, if one wants to differentiate the kind of power exercised by state bureaucratic and judicial apparatuses from the merely physical capacity to threaten and coerce, one can separate political power as an autonomous category, albeit that a standing army is probably also a necessary condition of statehood. To acknowledge these factors the fourfold model of Mann (1986) – whose general applicability as an analytical device can be separated from the tone of European triumphalism which pervades his

[18] For a valuable historical critique of Gellner (1988), see McNeill (1990).

work as a whole – is useful: power takes Ideological, Economic, Military and Political forms (his "IEMP model"). This model may be usefully set alongside Giddens' almost identical division of four "types of institution" (1981: 46–7): symbolic orders/modes of discourse, political institutions, economic institutions, and law/modes of sanction, each of which has a particular relation to the forces of signification, domination and legitimation. Greater attention to social and historical differentiation would require more complex models again.

In historical reality, of course, all four of Mann's forms of power combine and overlap with each other, and none more easily than the ideological. The main part of this book is concerned with texts produced by the Buddhist clerisy, whose most significant other is the king, and so the main focus, especially in Part 2, is on the relations between ideological and military-political power. But it is well known that trade was a very important feature of the early Buddhist social world, and of support for Buddhism, so the interaction between ideological and economic power was also important. For much of this General Introduction, and of the book as a whole, Gellner's simpler dichotomy between kings and clerisy is adequate, although complications are introduced by the existence of what he calls "rival elements within the wider clerisy" (1988: 156), and their varying relationships with the political and military power of kings and the ruling class.

Note: on the concept of ideology in the premodern world

It may be helpful to take a moment here to focus directly on the difficult issue of how, if at all, the concept of ideology may be used in premodernity. Who believed what? What does the term mean? It is certainly used, speaking generally, in a bewilderingly large number of senses.[19] There is, first, what Geuss (1981: 5) calls the "broad and rather unspecific" descriptive sense: this, he says, typically includes "such things as the beliefs the members of the group hold, the concepts they use, the attitudes and psychological dispositions they exhibit, their motives, desires, values, predilections, works of art, religious rituals, gestures, etc." Applied to the Pali texts which are my concern, this sense of the word does little

[19] As shown by Eagleton (1991), amongst many others.

more than refer in general to the ideas or doctrines of psychology, cosmology, ethics, etc. found in them. Many reject such a broad (and bland) sense, insisting that to be useful a concept of ideology must retain some connection with power, with the domination of one social group or groups by others: in Anthony Giddens' work, "'ideology' refers only to those asymmetries of domination which connect signification to the legitimation of sectional interests" (1984: 33; cp. 1979: 165–97). This would point to the ways in which Pali texts supported the status quo of tribute-extraction, notably in what is for an outsider the naturalization of contingent social hierarchies through the doctrine of karma (cp. 1979: 195–6, 1984: 25–6), in the homologies between kings and Buddhas, and in the often close connections between *Ethics, Wealth and Salvation*, as the title of Sizemore and Swearer (1990) has it. (One should also stress, as discussed further in this Introduction and in Chapter 6, that they can also contest the values of hierarchy and wealth.)

The Pali Theravāda tradition has had a major civilizational role in the hierarchical, agrarian/tributary states and empires of premodern Southern Asia, existing in what Gunawardana (1979: 344) called "antagonistic symbiosis" with kings. Analogously, for LeGoff (1988: 21) the European Middle Ages were "dominated by Christianity . . . which was at once a religion and an ideology and therefore enjoyed a very complex relation to the feudal world, which it both contested and justified." Many writers have commented on the evident connection between kings and inequality. Wyatt says of the *sakdi na* system of social ranking introduced by the Siamese (Ayudhya) king Borommatrailokanat (1448–88), who at one point abdicated in favor of his son, to become a Buddhist monk temporarily:

> If a peasant committed assault on a powerful official, it was much more serious than an assault on a slave, for the crime was an affront to social order and to the king from whom the official derived his status. The paramount concern of royal authority, as expressed in the law, was to regulate natural human inequality for the sake of the proper functioning of social order. (1984: 73, 78)

Geertz's choice of phrase in regard to Bali, where there was a comparable system of social statuses, is apposite: "the state drew its force, which was real enough, from its imaginative energies, its semiotic capacity to make inequality enchant" (1980: 123). And

Hagesteijn (1989: 145), writing of Buddhist Southeast Asia as a whole, generalizes the point further: "all types of political leadership are in fact based on the same structural principles: protection, maintenance of order, distribution of material means, and the embodiment of inequality."

What role did Buddhist ideology have in the constitution and maintenance of agrarian states and empires? Functionalists would point to the internalization of norms: thus for Parsons, "the core of a society, as a system, is the patterned normative order through which the life of a population is collectively organized. As an order it contains values and differentiated and particularized norms and rules, all of which require cultural references in order to be meaningful and legitimate" (1966: 10). In this spirit also is at least part of Bendix's statement and resolution of the problem: premodern societies, he says

> were marked by a concentration of wealth, status, and authority in the hands of the governing class, which comprised between 1 and 2 percent of the population but appropriated at least one half of the society's income above bare subsistence. To us, widespread inequality may suggest unremitting coercion and continuous, latent rebellion. But for many centuries, the vast mass of people acquiesced in the established order out of religious awe, a desire for peace and security, and the inability to unite in a common political action. In those earlier times, the rule of the privileged few appeared to the many as if it were a force of nature; it was to be enjoyed when it was benign and endured when it was not. (1978: 5–7)[20]

This way of understanding society and culture, whether in non-literate "primitive" situations, premodern civilizations or modern (lately globalized) conditions, has been subject to both empirical and theoretical criticism.[21] The empirical criticisms, which are based on historical data and modern ethnography, hold either that we can know that peasants and/or the working class did not share the ideology of the dominant class, or that it should be assumed that they did not unless there is positive evidence that they did. Theoretically the unwarranted, or at least unproven dominance or hegemony of ideology is part of what Archer (1988:

[20] Cp. the extraordinary figures given in Kautsky (1982: 80 n. 2, citing Lenski), claiming that in eighteenth-century France the aristocracy comprised 0.6 percent of the population, in China 1.3 percent.

[21] See Abercrombie et al. (1980), Archer (1988), Rösener (1992, 1993), Ludden (1985), Scott (1976), (1985), Shanin (1987), Wolf (1966).

1–21) calls the "Myth of Cultural Integration," held by functionalists and others: the "archetype of culture(s) as the perfectly woven and all-enmeshing web . . . the perfectly integrated system," which is not only presumed to be internally consistent but also to hold uniformly over a given social domain. Giddens, an implacable opponent of functionalism, claims that "it is . . . an error to suppose, even within the most cohesive of non-modern states, that the rationalized religions followed by those in the dominant class have much purchase over the day-to-day lives of the majority of their subject populations" (1987: 75). Sanderson (citing Giddens) states baldly that "agrarian societies are held together not by any sort of ideological consensus or common world-outlook, but by military force" (1995: 97).

The defects of the Myth of Cultural Integration are apparent, but formulations of Sanderson's kind surely move too far to the other extreme. The practical realities of military control over large distances in premodern times meant that a king, at the center of what is often called in relation to Southern Asia a *maṇḍala* (circle) of client kings,[22] had to exercise power through them, both politically and militarily (Mann 1986: 137–76). These local power-holders might control a small area by force alone, but a group of such "thugs" could not be held together under a king or emperor that way. And this helps clarify what was the role of ideologies such as the Buddhist: as Abercrombie et al. say (1980: 3) in their critique of the Marxist "Dominant Ideology Thesis," "in general, ideology has importance in explaining the coherence of the dominant class, but not in the explanation of the coherence of a society as a whole." Mann (1986) similarly speaks of religious ideologies in premodern societies, and especially in empires, as a matter of the cohesiveness and morale of the ruling class. So while one might accept, as so much modern ethnography suggests, that the significance to peasants of Buddhist ideology, at least in its more rarefied forms, has always been limited, if not non-existent, it seems a plausible hypothesis to suggest that it provided a "discursive arena" (Giddens 1987: 75) for ruling elites both to propagate the Grand Narratives of society and soteriology which articulated their power, and to exclude others from that arena,

[22] The term is ancient in Southern Asia; it was first used in this sense in western scholarship by Wolters (1968, 1982); cp. Mabbett (1977), (forthcoming), C. Reynolds (1992, 1995), Chutintaranond (1990).

making what he calls alternative "fields of opposition" impossible (cp. Archer 1988: 214–15).

The point here can be clarified by considering two interpretations, strong and weak, of Marx's famous remark in *The German Ideology* that "the ideas of the ruling class are in every epoch the ruling ideas: i.e., the class which is the ruling *material* force of society, is at the same time its ruling *intellectual* force" (1976: 67; cp. Abercrombie et al. 1980: 7–8; Archer 1988: 52). The stronger holds that there cannot be any other culture than that of the dominant class, that all classes are incorporated into the mental world constructed by it; the weaker that only the ideas of the ruling class are visible to an observer, especially in historical hindsight, since other classes lack the means and institutions to give lasting expression to their culture. Historiography and ethnography have shown that the stronger interpretation is false; the weaker, however, may well be true, and it is in this sense that I speak of Buddhist ideology in this book. This formulation of the issue has the significant advantage, in my view, of leaving the question of the actual influence of ideology in a given time and place open to empirical solution (in the rare cases where, for the premodern world, we have anything like enough data to come to one). It seems no more than common sense to think that the extent to which Buddhist ideology might permeate the mass of the population, if at all, would differ from place to place and from time to time. But my use of the term in the sense suggested by Giddens, where it refers to "asymmetries of domination which connect signification to the legitimation of sectional interests," does not depend on any empirical hypothesis of this sort; it requires only that those, in civilizational settings, who wielded military and/or political power should live in antagonistic symbiosis with those who wielded ideological power.

There remains, in this perspective, a historical story to tell. What follows in this paragraph is a hypothesis, but one which I think is well grounded in the past/historical and present/ethnographic facts: it is the general historical picture which this book assumes, although nothing essential to my argument depends on its truth. Early Buddhism, in so far as we can say anything about it, was adopted largely by the elite in ancient India (Gombrich 1988: 55ff., 78ff., Chakravarti 1987), and the Theravāda form of it was certainly introduced into Sri Lanka and Southeast Asia with the support of kings. The nature of early Buddhist and Theravāda history thus supports the view that these were indeed civilizational traditions of the ruling class. But at some point Buddhism was transformed from what Hallisey and Reynolds call a "civilizational religion" to a "cultural" one: that is, from an "international" phenomenon of society and culture where a monastic elite interacted with imperial elites in urban centers, to a more localized Monastic Order interacting with state elites also mostly in urban centers. This began when "the civilizational structure suffered increasingly severe disruptions" in the fifth century AD, and was completed between the ninth and thirteenth centuries (1989: 8ff., quote from p. 15). Keyes suggests that in the eleventh and twelfth centuries, when Theravāda first spread from Sri Lanka to mainland Southeast Asia, it was "the religion of a small number of virtuosos and a small number of elite lay persons . . . practiced in only a few centers, mainly urban," whereas from the thirteenth century it became a "popular" religion at the village level in the countryside as well (1995[77]: 80–90). I would be less sure about the possibility of dating this change either so early or so confidently as these authors (we will probably never have enough evidence to tell the full story), but whatever chronological narrative is given, I assume that it will recount, increasingly for the last two centuries, a version of what Gellner (1983) calls the downward spread of a "high culture," which is particularly characteristic of the rise of nationalism in the modern world. The contemporary ethnography of Theravāda, which is extensive, must be read in this light: as the culmination of a long development. In a recent ethnography of the Shan in northern Thailand, to which the General Conclusion returns, Tannenbaum describes Buddhism as "a marker of civilized identity [and] a rhetoric of justification," which distinguishes, in her case, lowland Shan from the neighboring hill-tribes, whom they regard as "uncivilized" (95: 10), and shows that the historical process in which Buddhism has spread downwards from the elite and outwards from urban centers is still not complete.

The Pali imaginaire was a discursive, textual world available to the imagination of elites, and gradually others, in the premodern agrarian societies of Southern Asia, and was an ideology in the sense given above. It would be wrong, however, to see the ideological power of Buddhism simply in terms of coercion, simply a matter of naturalizing social and historical contingencies. Passages from Foucault and Giddens are useful here:

If power were never anything but repressive, if it never did anything but say no, do you really think we should manage to obey it? What gives power its hold, what makes it accepted, is quite simply the fact that it does not just weigh like a force which says no, but it runs through, and it produces things, it induces pleasure, it forms knowledge, it produces discourse; it must be considered as a productive network which runs through the entire social body much more than a negative instance whose function is repression. (Foucault 1979: 36)

At the heart of both domination and power lies the *transformative capacity* of human action, the origin of all that is liberating and productive in social life as well as all that is repressive and destructive. (Giddens 1981: 51)

We should not suppose that religion, even "state religion", is a wholly conservative force; rather, religion is a framework of thought and social organization through which many aspects of life in traditional states may be filtered, including innovative forces and schismatic ones. (Giddens 1987: 75)

The rest of this first section explores the way in which the Buddhist monkhood, as holder of ideological power, was capable of both co-operating with those who held political, military and economic power, and of challenging them. Buddhist ideology helped justify the extraction of tribute by ruling elites; but it could also confront those elites with values (notably of asceticism) which they could not share. The Pali Buddhist discourse of felicity in the premodern world, in its articulation of an authoritative imaginaire, encompassed the affective and cognitive aspirations – happiness and wisdom – of both celibate virtuosos and laity. The ascetic quest for the felicity of nirvana was set at the summit of a (rhetorical) hierarchy, but the outside interpreter, I argue, should not reproduce this hierarchy in his or her analysis. The discourse of felicity as a whole is a form of ideological power, in Foucault's terms saying "yes" as well as "no," running through the social body (of the elite) inducing pleasure and forming knowledge – materially and imaginatively – of both non-ascetic and ascetic kinds.

I.b. Transcendental visions: the autonomy of ideological power

The idea that a "transcendental breakthrough" took place in an "Axial Age," dated to various times BC, is usually attributed to Karl Jaspers.[23] The idea has been taken up by many, including Hodgson (1974: 112). Reynolds (1972: 8) was the first to use it of Buddhism, to my knowledge, and it has been developed most in recent years by Eisenstadt (1981), (1982), (1986), in a generally Weberian approach, who includes Buddhism in a list of what he calls in different places "Civilizations," "World Religions" or "Great Traditions." Some aspects of this suggestion should be dropped (not least Jaspers' own "spiritual" attitude to history). The notion of a significant and mysterious chronological coincidence is of no use – it was always imprecise, and it is obviously impossible to accommodate Muhammad and Islam into any version of the BC time frame. Much of the vocabulary, moreover, such as "this world," and the "other-worldly," is misleadingly tied, like much else in the Weberian social science lexicon, to its provenance in Christian theology (Collins 1988: 103–6).[24] This book deliberately refrains from using this idea of "the world" and what opposes it, both in the cosmological sense and in the sociological schema of "inner-" or "this-worldly" versus "outer-" or "other-worldly" behaviors and motivations. Unless carefully defined and controlled (and sometimes even then), these terms almost always cause more confusion than clarity. The idea of transcendentalism is nonetheless useful as a descriptive category for certain cultural structures or processes, in certain societies. Not all societies have such a thing even now; and where it does occur one can trace the history of its production and deployment. On occasion, therefore, the complementary opposition between the transcendental and mundane is used in this book; but only in the specific sense outlined here, as a tool of civilizational history and sociological analysis.

A *transcendental* vision is a rationalizing, holistic analysis of life in the here-and-now, both individual and social, based ethically on a

[23] Jaspers (1965). Gunder Frank (1992: 23) cites a similar idea in Teggart (1939).

[24] One could, however, for purposes other than my present one, trace an explicit distinction between "this world" and the "other world" in Pali texts, as a dichotomy between life here-and-now and "after death" in a non-specific sense, which is somewhat different from the standard rebirth-versus-release picture (perhaps surviving from pre-Buddhist times). Compare Gombrich (1971b) on Buddhism and Jaini (1991) on Jainism.

realm of values and metaphysically on a locus of aspiration structured independently of and differently from the here-and-now. Schwartz, introducing a collection on "Wisdom, Doubt and Revelation: Perspectives on the First Millennium BC" (1975: 3–4) describes it as "a kind of standing back and looking beyond – a kind of critical, reflective questioning of the actual and a new vision of what lies beyond." Eisenstadt, following Weber, traces the idea of salvation and the quest for it to "the chasm between the transcendental and mundane orders," and "consciousness of death and the arbitrariness of human actions and social arrangements" (1986: 3). The capacity of clerics, as it were, to specialize in death – or at least, in representations of what it means and what follows it – makes them, as purveyors of transcendentalism, permanently able to display one-upmanship over kings. LeGoff remarks (1984) apropos the birth of Purgatory in Europe, that kings control many things, but not what happens after death. Neither their own post-mortem fate nor anyone else's could be affected by the coercion they employed for terrestrial power, a fact that Christian clerics, naturally, were not slow to affirm.

Physical coercion applied in the here and now cannot – apart from the extreme and un-generalizable case of torture – determine what people think, and certainly not what ideas of and aspirations to wisdom and happiness they might entertain. This, on the contrary, is the clerics' forte. They can, as it were, cross the boundary of the body and enter into people's minds, at least potentially: not only do they provide resolutions of the problems of suffering, evil and ultimately of meaning in life (what Weber called the problem of theodicy, in a wider sense of the term), but they can also elaborate visions of happiness which are, in one way or another, not subject to the threat posed, rhetorically and actually, by aging and death. (They can also, of course, elaborate visions of the punishments which await those who do not follow their rules, an activity to which traditional Buddhists devoted themselves with every bit as much enthusiasm as medieval Christians.) As mentioned earlier, we cannot know how far elite ideologies of death, wisdom and happiness were actually internalized by the majority in premodern societies: but we do know that they were given sufficient social prestige by those with military-political power that alternative discourses were suppressed. Examples are the Albigensians in Europe up to the fourteenth century (Ladurie

1979) and the still mysterious Ari of Burma, suppressed – though perhaps not completely crushed – when Anawrahta introduced Theravāda Buddhism, with its Pali textual tradition, into Upper Burma in the eleventh (Duroiselle 1916; Than Tun 1959; Mendelson 1961b: 576–7).[25] Their support was not wholly disinterested. "In 1209 the barons of the north of France organized a crusade against the Albigensians [in Languedoc]. The armies marched southwards in answer to an appeal by the Pope . . . [Thus] the King of France extended his power over the south and [annexed] Languedoc *de facto* in 1229" (Ladurie 1979: ix). And Anawrahta's conquest of the Mon city of Thaton in 1057, whence he imported Theravāda to Pagan, was also a constitutive act in making Pagan the center of the first imperial formation in Burmese history (Hall 1992: 240–1, Taylor 1992: 165).

What I call a *soteriology*, in Weberian style (cf. Gombrich 1988: 25ff., and *passim*), is an intellectualist attempt to find a reflective, rationalized ordering of life, and death, as a conceptual and imaginative whole, and to prescribe some means of definitively (if only imaginatively, so far as a non-believer can tell) escaping suffering and death, and achieving a "final" happiness. It is because this activity is necessarily the work of only a few members of society that, as the title of Eisenstadt (1982) puts it, "the emergence of transcendental visions" is also "the rise of clerics" as a social group. These clerics are textualists, self-conscious transmitters of an objectified *tradition*. That is to say, a transcendental vision is not merely a more or less systematized collection of ideas about the way things are. All human groups have this in some measure, since all, or almost all human activity involves culture, in the sense that it involves linguistic and other forms of representation and exchange; and everyone is capable of asking the kinds of simple question – where did the world come from? What happens after death? Why do good people often suffer and bad prosper? – to which a transcendental vision gives complexly articulated answers. The reference is not to culture and reflection as traits of human life, but to the creation and maintenance of a determinate, externalized, publicly recognized form of tradition which answers

[25] If the *Nikāya-saṅgraha*, a fifteenth-century Sinhala chronicle is to be believed (Fernando 1908), a preoccupation of Sri Lankan kings was the burning of nefarious books owned by opponents of the Mahāvihāra monastic lineage.

such questions (and determines, in part, whether and how they are asked), in one or more prestige languages, whose status depends in part on the very fact of its perceived traditionality. Halbwachs (1992[52]: 120–66), speaking of what he calls the social frameworks of memory, remarks that especially but not only in premodern societies, part of the social status of an elite is its claim (true or false) to preserve an ancestral heritage which has value for the society as a whole. The Pali Theravāda form of Buddhism, extensively oriented to the passage of time (as Chapter 3 tries to show), is one such heritage in the civilization(s) of Southern Asia.

To support such a class and such an activity, which is carried out through stories and concepts, in narrative and systematic thought,[26] a society must have reached a certain level of material and cultural complexity: indeed the presence of what is being called here a transcendental vision might be made into a defining condition of "civilization," which only some premodern human groups had, as opposed to culture, which all did, as do all human beings.[27] In this regard it is almost always paired with the presence of writing, and clerics as the privileged possessors of it (e.g. Giddens 1981 and Gellner 1988), but the case of Southern Asia shows that this is not necessary. The transcendentalism of both the Upaniṣads and early Buddhism emerged before the introduction of writing, or at least before the use of writing for cultural materials rather than for recording commercial transactions and the like (Hinüber 1990); and subsequent traditions continued to be oral, in many senses of the word (Collins 1992b).

Leaving the important and difficult issue of literacy aside, it seems to me important to emphasize not only what transcendental visions represent conceptually and narratively, but also what are their institutional requirements and consequences. The notion of the "transcendental" is by itself too idealist: one might better say that in social circumstances where clerics are distinguishable as a

[26] Cp. Gellner (1988: 77): "Concepts had always been confirmed by *stories* within which they figured. Now [after the rise of a literate clerisy] they were confirmed by well-articulated doctrine. . ."

[27] This distinction between "culture" and "civilization" is made solely for the present purpose – which is to distinguish between the universal human production of meanings and the elite production, in particular social contexts, of heritage-conscious traditions, which can function as ideology in the sense outlined. The two words, and the opposition between them, have of course been used in countless different ways: brief accounts and summaries of earlier studies are given in Dampierre (1961) and Starobinski (1993: 1–35).

separate group, maintaining a tradition of the kind just described, ideological power has attained a degree of autonomy.[28] In postulating a locus of value and aspiration beyond the here-and-now, but locating access to it in the tradition it is their job to preserve, clerics thus form a discrete social group – indicated clearly in the Buddhist case, as elsewhere, by the social fact of celibacy – capable of both endorsing the status quo in the here-and-now and criticizing it, in LeGoff's terms justifying it and contesting it: antagonistic symbiosis between kings and priests is a tension built into the very structure of this kind of social and civilizational arrangement. If one posits a spectrum of co-operation/conflict between those subdivisions of the elite in the premodern world whose primary power, analytically speaking, was military and political, and the wielders of ideological power – both groups possessing and interacting with economic power – one might set at one end the "theocracies" of ancient Mesopotamia, and Tibet from the early modern period; at the other, the constant struggle between church and state in medieval and early modern Europe. In the Theravāda case, aside from one or two possible exceptions in the early modern period (cf. the Critical Discussion in Chapter 5), a full overlap between kings and clerics was never attempted, although in the trope of the king as future Buddha (5.2.d), and related notions (6.5.b), the two dimensions were certainly fairly close to one another. (Buddhist clerics could, of course and did support one military-political faction against another.) At the other end of the spectrum one can find all manner of Theravādin clerical conflict with kings, from opposition through irony to indifference.

As well as the antagonistic symbiosis of kings and clerics in society, there is another tension, this one within the discourse of the clerics' own ideology, which it is important to notice. This is between the necessary absence of the transcendental from the actual – this is given in the very nature of transcendentalist visions – and the practical need for it to be in one way or another present in the actual: every marketing operation, one might say, needs retail outlets. If the locus of value is entirely absent from the here-and-now it will become irrelevant to it, and so unnecessary. (This was arguably the case in Puritan Christianity, which thus brought about its own demise: Wilson 1982.) In Buddhist Studies in the last

[28] This is perhaps clearer in Eisenstadt (1981) than in his later writing on this subject.

twenty-five years there has been some discussion of the "presence" of the Buddha in statues and relics of him.[29] The language here, again, I find to be a little too Christian-theological for comfort, but in general one might say, adapting Bergson's remark about societies (that they are "machines for generating gods"), that transcendental visions are machines for generating presence-absence discourse. It may be that "in the concept of nirvana Theravāda Buddhism maintains a far more elevated transcendentalist perspective than any other religion" (Wilson 1982: 74), but for traditional Buddhism there had to be some way for nirvana and Buddhahood to be immanent in the here-and-now, both through objects such as statues, relics and books (stage-props in the Buddhist socio-religious theater) and imaginatively, as something "good to think".[30] This book tries to show how nirvana was thought, as a concept, an image, and as a syntactic element of closure, structural and narrative, in the Buddhist discourse of felicity, implicit in any and every form of imagined well-being.

I.c. Stretching the here-and-now: soteriology and the state, time and tradition

Section I.a, describing societies before and in the agrarian stage of world history, referred to a sequence (neither inevitable nor irreversible) of social types: kin- or family-ordered, local groups with Big Men, chiefdoms, agrarian states as regional and trans-regional polities with kings and/or emperors. These developments, including the initial impetus for the transition from the hunting-gathering to agrarian stages, may have been encouraged, if not inaugurated, by the coercive force of ruling, tribute-taking groups. I referred also not only to what Brown calls the "gentle violence" of a stable social order, but also to the historical role of kings in creating and enforcing inequality. It is possible to focus on this aspect of the matter and equate kings with criminals, as was done explicitly and regularly in the aphoristic "wisdom" literature of South Asia, and in a number of Buddhist stories (examples of both

29 See, e.g., Gombrich (1971a), Tambiah (1984a), Schopen (e.g. (1987, 88), Eckel (1992) and Trainor (1997).

30 I do not mean to imply that the "transcendentalist" concept of nirvana was historically prior to its immanence in objects, etc. The reverse is just as likely, and just as speculative.

are given in Chapter 6). As Dirks puts it, there is a "structural relationship between banditry and kingship," such that, in his case, families in South India in the last few centuries have moved from being bandits to having "local level political authority," in part through "their capacity to enforce the rule of law by means little different from those exercised against it" (1987: 204–5; cp. Tilly 1985). There are obvious possibilities for clerical (especially ascetic) criticism of kings here, as direct condemnation or in the milder form of satire and irony, all of which can be found easily in Buddhist texts.

But to focus on this aspect alone would be to fail to see a number of things. In the first place, as mentioned, there are, tribute-extraction or not, real advantages to the provision of dispute resolution and peaceable, if inegalitarian, social life; this is a theme illustrated throughout Johnson and Earle's (1987) overview of "The Evolution of Human Societies." Kingship is in this perspective both an achievement and an index of social development. Crone (1989: 53–4), describing "Pre-industrial Societies" in general, offers a vivid picture of the violence involved in tax gathering, of the dangers lurking in the many areas which escaped state control such as forests, mountains, marshes, and deserts, and then adds:

> But even well-governed areas had their share of violence, and policing was always deficient. Every town had its pickpockets, thieves, burglars, swindlers, murderers, assassins and protection-racketeers, just as every road had its highwaymen and every sea its pirates. Private war and local feuds, riots and rebellion, marauding soldiers and brigandage, all these and other forms of disorder were commonplace in most societies most of the time.

No wonder, then, that the aspiration to any degree of order had its attraction; and the larger the area over which order was proclaimed, with whatever degree of truth, the more impressive the achievement, real and/or rhetorical. The local representatives of the distant king – judges, tax collectors – might well be as corrupt and rapacious as bandits, but the king himself could still be thought of as benevolent and just. As Dirks again puts it:

> however close the position and activities of bandit and king, the nature of violence and coercion effected by the two differs fundamentally. The violence of the bandit is illegitimate; it represents and causes disorder. Banditry is defined as such because it is exercised from outside

> the central institutions of rule and culturally mandated positions of authority.
>
> Kingship, of course, is just the opposite. Kings are not only legitimate, they define the realm of the legitimate. (1987: 242–3)

He uses an idea from Foucault: "the king has the enunciatory function over the discursive formation of order itself" (1987: 245).[31] I take this to mean that the king does not so much refer to a pre-existing realm of order and its rules as bring that realm into being; but at the same time "the king" here is not an empirical subject outside and previous to that realm, but a subject position, a status, defined by the elite discourse of order itself. Although one might quarrel with this somewhat in relation to polities which had both Theravāda Buddhist ideology and a strong tradition of written law,[32] where defining legitimacy seems to have been a more contested field than in Dirks' South Indian case, his Foucaultian formulation usefully opens up the issue of kings as emblems or icons of the very idea of order.

The issue of order leads to a second, more fundamental aspect of the civilizational *longue durée* which would be missed by concentrating on the maleficence of kings, or by taking the analytic separation within the tribute-taking class between kings and clerics, "thugs and legitimators," to be a description of two mutually exclusive groups. This is the fact that, in socially institutionalized traditions, the discursive formation of social order ("politics") over which the king has the enunciatory function, and the conceptual ordering of the universe, time and death ("religion"), in which the cleric has the iconic voice, are complementary elements of an overall civilizational work of articulation.[33] Both are involved in the construction of a hierarchized order at whose apex is set a generic, location-free wisdom and happiness, however much the internal nature of that hierarchy might evaluate action and involvement in or "outside" the social order, as when ascetics claim that salvation is found through celibacy. To construct and transmit

[31] Like others (Quigley 1993) he sees colonial and post-colonial dominant castes as continuous with the pre-colonial king: "the dominant castes strive for the enunciation as well as the enforcement of order" (1987: 179).

[32] Notably Burma: see Huxley (1995).

[33] To say this is not to say anything new: Bentley (1986: 293), for example, notes that "the interrelation of cosmic and political order has been a prominent theme in studies of Southeast Asian kingdoms," citing numerous studies; and it was clearly stated in F. Reynolds (1972).

a soteriological form of imagined order is also to construct and transmit an objectified textual picture of the (ideal) social order in which, or from which, such a soteriology can take place, a cosmology (though not in the Buddhist case a cosmogony, since the universe of space and time is beginningless), and what Chapter 4.1 calls a cosmo-geography.

More is said about the local and trans-local in this Introduction, especially in section III.c when opposing *soteriology* to *localized supernaturalism.* Here I make some general remarks on the way premodern military-political and cultural-religious trans-localism mirror each other structurally, as well as marching hand in hand historically. Military-political trans-localism aimed at a single state or empire, covering ever-larger areas, even "the world"; in European terms this is the *oikumenē*, the "world inhabited" by peoples seen as relevantly similar.[34] In Southern Asia this took the form of monarchic power radiating outward in a trans-local, trans-ethnic and trans-linguistic circle. Seeing the *oikumenē* as a governable single world was made possible by – better, was part and parcel of – the aspiration to cultural universalism, which replicated the political in a different register. The military-political center pushed out towards an ordered system of power focused on a single person or lineage, set against constant fissiparous tendencies to localism; the cultural/religious aimed to think the world in large-scale, *Weltgeschichtliche* narrative and other discursive frames, to situate agency and identity in an overarching construal of the everyday. A Wheel-turning King is not a jumped-up thug with a biggish backyard, but an emperor serenely presiding over human nature. In the Buddhist case, military-political universality and unity was achieved, ideologically, in this figure of the Wheel-turning King, conquering the four islands around Mt. Meru on which human beings and some gods live (4.1 and 6.5.a). Cultural-religious universality and unity was achieved in the religious ordering of the universe, in explanatory and descriptive schemata of unlimited applicability, such as the fundamental explanatory language of karma; the subsumption of all ills in the category of *dukkha*, suffering or unsatisfactoriness; and the central conceptual category of *saṅkhārā*, conditioned things/events, along with its

[34] This was always, of course, smaller than the real world, in the sense of the planet as a spatio-temporal whole: see section I.d p. 40, II.d p. 66 below.

negation or contradictory – the unconditioned, i.e. nirvana – as a necessary corollary, which together represent and account for everything that exists. Here as usual the coin of universalism had individualism as its reverse side, since the "realization" of this truth – both the understanding of it and the making of it real, as a matter of experience – took place within the individual's consciousness, disembedded from ordinary social life and placed in the abstract, intentional community of the monkhood.

Military-political and cultural-political universalism sought to conceive the time-space continuum as an ordered totality. Space was ordered as the cosmo-geography of the four islands around Mt. Meru, conquered and ruled by the Wheel-turning King. The ordering of time is more complex. To discuss it I use some of Giddens' terminology, but without adopting all of his theoretical commitments. He suggests that there are "three 'layers' of temporality involved in the analysis of the structuration of social systems":

(i) "the temporality of immediate experience, the continuous flow of day-to-day life";

(ii) "the temporality of *Dasein*, the life-cycle of the organism," which involves "the contingency of life in the face of death, and of biological reproduction"; and

(iii) "what Braudel calls the *longue durée* of institutional time." "Institutions are practices which 'stretch' over long time-space distances in the reproduction of social systems" (1981: 18–19, 28).

But just as the military-political imaginaire is not content until it has stretched out to the four corners of the earth, so the cultural-religious must stretch out as far as possible in time. Ultimately in Buddhism, as is seen in Chapters 3 and 5, the temporality of the universe stretches beginninglessly into the past and endlessly into the future, with felicitous appearances of Buddhas from time to time. All three of Giddens' social temporalities are encompassed in the trans-individual (but not collective) time of *saṃsāra*, the sequence of lives and deaths brought about by *karma*, and ended only by individuals' nirvana.

Giddens' "stretching" is also "time-space distanciation," by which term he means "to get at the processes whereby societies are "stretched" over shorter or longer spans of time and space" (1981: 90). Like Gellner, and many students of civilization, he argues that writing is the major factor in "the retention and control of information or knowledge," which brings about the greater time-space distanciation of agrarian civilizations, and that cities are "a distinctive feature" of all such societies (1981: 94–5). It is obvious, he says, "that societies differ greatly in terms of the extent of time-space "stretches" which they span; and we can ask how this comes about" (1981: 90). It comes about, in part at least, through the greater or lesser salience – thanks to objectification and textualization – of tradition. According to Shils (1981: 14), "Tradition means many things. In its barest, most elementary sense, it means simply a *traditum*; it is anything which is transmitted or handed down to the present." In the broadest sense a civilization is constituted by many forms of tradition, not only by shared texts (visual, aural-musical, written, oral), handed on as external objects like batons in a relay race: it is a repertoire of linguistic and other behaviors, styles of dress and cuisine, shared memories (of events or things or times or places), learned bodily habits (etiquette and commensal conventions, particular task-skills, ritual regularities, and so forth), the preservation of material objects, and other non- or only partly discursive practices, all of which are handed down from past to present to future (Connerton 1989). Giddens is right to say that "tradition . . . is the most elemental form of social reproduction, [and] involves a particular type of time-consciousness" (1981: 93). In the form of traditionality involved in premodern civilizations, textual (especially narrative) traditions would seem to have had a particular importance. Given oral as well as written textualities one might best speak of "heritages of objectified and transmittable discourse," which embody, extend, order and signify the passage of time, individual, trans-individual, and collective.

Chapter 3 argues that all human beings experience both non-reversible/linear and repetitive/cyclical temporality, since these two modes of time always and everywhere go together. Representations of time, on the other hand and obviously, can and do vary historically and cross-culturally. Differing levels of time-space distanciation at different levels of trans-local political organization are clearly major factors in accounting for this variation. Chapter 3 looks inside two texts of the Buddhist chronicle (*vaṃsa*) genre to show how they textualize time. Here, looking at the outside of Pali texts, I want to argue that the ordering of society and of the universe, in an objectified discourse of Tradition, are simultaneous, material and conceptual-imaginative forms of the structuration of the time-space continuum. Both exemplify the increasing time-space distanciation which characterizes the transition from hunter-gatherer to agrarian society, and the progression within the agrarian stage from small-scale community to state or empire, in the course of which arise the conditions for the construction and transmission of transcendental visions and for the clerical traditionalists – who may, as in the Buddhist case, be or include "asocial" ascetics – who do the constructing and transmitting.

The line of argument of this section seems to me analogous to one put forward by Maurice Bloch (1974, 1977), writing of contexts relatively less "civilized" (in the non-pejorative sense used here), where "dealing with traditional leaders, [ethnographers have found it] difficult to class their activities as political or religious [and to decide] whether they are to be thought of as chiefs and kings or priests" (1974: 68). He differentiates between everyday speech acts, characteristic of the pragmatic, material-historical plane of immediate realities and sensitive to its changing and novel exigencies, and the more formalized language of the liturgical-ritual, where all is formula, regularity and repetition (cp. Bloch 1989). Using Ian Hacking's (1983) terms from the philosophy of science, one might say that the latter is concerned with representing the world, the former with intervening in it. Noting that ritualized speech is characteristic of political oratory in his cases, Bloch wonders whether religion is "a special variety of the political process, an extreme form of traditional authority" (1974: 77). In the Theravāda Buddhist case, the role distinction between chiefs or kings and priests (monks) is quite clearcut (albeit that they were often members of the same elite families), and there seems no reason to make "religion" a sub-category of a higher-order "political." But it does seem useful to see both "politics" and "religion," in the senses used here, as complementary and overlapping varieties of civilizational articulation, spread in the supposedly – and in large measure actually – unchanging prestige language of Pali, structuring the time-space continuum in which human life was both lived materially and construed in authoritative traditions of representation.

I.d. The cultural logic of asceticism[35]

Gunawardana's phrase "antagonistic symbiosis" is a useful shorthand label for the manifold relationship between kings and clerisy, as a complementary opposition within the elite of agrarian societies. I have just argued that this symbiosis was not a historically contingent alliance but an intrinsic feature of the civilizational work of articulating order. It is now necessary to explore a little further both the symbiosis and the antagonism; and to do so I first return to Gellner (1988). Despite the fact, he says, that

> agrarian society is doomed to violence . . . it does not always place violence at the summit of excellence, though the Western equation of nobility with military vocation does so. Sometimes it places the scribes/legitimators above the swordsmen, though we must remember that it is the scribes who write the record and formulate the principles . . .
>
> Agraria does on occasion invert values . . . They [i.e. values] may conspicuously defy, rather than mirror, the social hierarchy. It may commend ascesis or humility rather than display conspicuous consumption and assertiveness. These inversions of values, of the utmost importance in the history of mankind, can be seen in part as devices employed by rival elements within the wider clerisy. One way the legitimators gain influence and power is by being outside the formal system, by opting out, and ascesis or humility constitutes a kind of conspicuous self-exile. The logic of the agrarian world, however, does not allow such values to be implemented consistently and universally. (pp. 154, 155–6; cp. 225)

Asceticism as a way of life, of course, cannot be implemented consistently and universally in any society, agrarian or other. So one must try to understand how asceticism can be valued in a society – as and when it is, which is by no means everywhere – given that the majority of people necessarily do not and cannot adopt it as an actual lifestyle. One is not dealing with issues of motivation here: no doubt there are as many motivations as there are ascetics, and I am happy to accept William James' suggestion, elaborated in the Buddhist case by Carrithers (1983), that there is, simply, a taste for the perceived virtues of purity, simplicity, and celibacy which certain human beings have. The question here is rather to understand the cultural logic by which collectivities privilege a minority option. It is not my purpose to attempt an answer to the question

[35] This section has profited more from Silber (1995) than is apparent from the few references to it in the text.

why certain civilizations, notably the Southern Asian, accorded celibate asceticism such pride of place where others did not. Perhaps such questions are unanswerable. I am asking, rather, given that Southern Asian civilization did privilege asceticism, what is the underlying logic of the situation?

It is, I suggest, something like this: from among the many and various responses to physicality, one first connects the body and sexual reproduction to the inevitability of aging and death. If what is brought into being by physical means is always subject to decay and death, and if it is to be possible to imagine and aspire to a kind of well-being which will not decay and die, then that state must be non-physical, or at least even if in some sense physical then asexual, because not physically reproductive.[36] And if the final state of felicity is asexual, then perhaps the highest form of human life is asexual. If, lastly, as in most Southern Asian cases, the state of salvation is not conceived as achievable only after death but also during life, then clearly celibacy is a *sine qua non.* Thus sociologically, given the constitutive role of sexual reproduction in networks of kinship, landownership and other forms of social and economic interrelationship and exchange, ascetic celibacy – what one might call the state of being professionally unmarried – is a perfect index of and marker for what Silber (1985, 1995) calls, elaborating on Victor Turner's terminology, an alternative structure.[37] This social status can be represented ideologically as an "asocial" condition, outside production and reproduction, despite its place in social hierarchies, as in Sri Lankan caste and the Siamese *sakdi na* status systems, and the inevitable political and economic relations between the Monastic Order as an institution and its social milieu.

The alternative structure of asceticism "outside society" embodies the particular form of cultural universalism/individualism proposed by the Buddhist transcendental vision: Buddhist soteriology is immediately applicable and relevant for anyone, anywhere, but in so far as the ultimate attainment, nirvana, requires a life of

[36] MacDannell and Lang (1988) show that although celibacy has been a subject of much dispute in Christianity, Christian visions of heaven before modern times have been wholly asexual, even where bodily resurrection has been envisaged.

[37] Brown (1985) offers a clear and convincing account of this aspect of the value of virginity in early Christianity. Silber (1995: 40 n. 6, 171 n. 112) cites other scholars who have seen Christian monasticism as "antithetic reflection" of wider society.

permanent celibacy, it is not, in principle as well as in practice, for everyone – that is, not everyone all at once (Collins 1994).[38] There are, one might say, at least two kinds of universalism, which claim either (i) that everyone can, and should do X, or (ii) that everyone is permitted to do X (if individually capable), but no-one is required to do X. Where X = seeking salvation in this life, the first is characteristic of Christianity and Islam (obviously, since according to them we only have this life), the second of Theravāda Buddhism. Theravāda is thus universalistic, even though virtuosos, aiming personally at nirvana here and now, have in fact in the traditional, historical world been few and far between, despite the heroic frequency of enlightenment in the world of Pali canonical texts.

Gellner's phrase "conspicuous self-exile" recalls, perhaps deliberately, Peter Brown's work on the late antique holy man, and the "rituals of disengagement" which made possible his particular, and usually very publicly visible social role(s) – as with the stylite saints on top of their pillars, dispensing practical and often political advice to all and sundry.[39] The ubiquitous ascetic rhetorical images of "leaving society," or "fleeing the world," are only in vary rare instances anything like literally true. Ascetics, like cowboys, may ride off into the sunset, but there is always another day – and they need to eat. The paradigmatic Christian solitary, St. Antony, was said by his biographer and champion Bishop Athanasius to have been provided with food by angels, which is not exactly the kind of explanatory hypothesis favored by modern scholars. In Buddhist stories, solitary sages living in mountains and/or forests regularly come down to villages for salt and citrus fruit, two obvious necessities for good health. Even in those rare cases where ascetics actually do live, for the most part, away from other human beings, nonetheless the *idea* of their doing so can be culturally central. In the vast majority of cases the "aloneness" of the monk and nun – what many dictionaries and books tell us, wrongly, is the meaning of the word "monk" – is not physical isolation but the

[38] Nonpermanent celibacy, as in the case of Buddhist communities adopting the eight Precepts on *Uposatha* days, is immaterial to this point. For the various Precepts, and a brief account of who takes them, and when, see Wijayaratna (1990: 181, Appendix 3).

[39] See Brown (1971, 1978, 1986, 1988, 1992 and 1995), in the last of which he offers reflections on the much-cited 1971 article. Fowden (1993: 3–4) makes effective use of the image of St. Daniel the Stylite in conversation with an emperor and a king. The approach is already visible in Gellner (1969: 78).

social fact of their singleness: that is, the fact that they are single, unmarried, and so in the original sense of the word celibate (see Collins 1988).

The cultural logic of Buddhist asceticism, then, places celibacy at the top of the moral hierarchy, as a reflection and embodiment of (and, ideally, a means to) disembodied, nonreproductive nirvana, and institutionalizes it in the monastic community. This cannot be a universal option, or even a majority option at any given time, as is signaled by the Monastic Rule requiring monks and nuns to eat only such food as is given to them by laity (Wijayaratna 1990: 56–75). The doctrine of rebirth allows this to be, nonetheless, a form of the cultural universalism characteristic of transcendental visions: everyone will have their chance, in the long run. Members of the Monastic Order and laity together play out a form of socio-religious theater (Collins 1994, 1997), a drama in which the minority option of celibacy is at one and the same time at the top of, and outside of any and every social hierarchy.

To speak of collectivities "privileging" a minority option runs the risk of reification and myopic methodological holism: one must acknowledge that the symbiosis of kings and clerics has involved real as well as rhetorical antagonism. If this book were concerned to give a narrative account of the use of Buddhist ideology by people in premodern Southern Asia, as opposed to a formal analysis of its place in civilizational history, it would be necessary to depict individuals and groups in co-operation and conflict as agents making history. But I want to see the antagonism and the symbiosis not as alternative moments in an ongoing relation between historical agents, but as intrinsically related ingredients in the production of agrarian-elite ideological power, viewed as a process and as the backdrop for my own historiography of concepts, images and stories in texts. With this in mind I suggest that, from the macro-sociological, *longue durée*, world-historical perspective, one can view Buddhist monks and nuns, perhaps indeed all world-renouncers, as being culturally analogous to court jesters and clowns. That is, they are structurally situated to say things to and about kings which others cannot – "You're going to die, you know!" "And soon!" "And what about the first Precept?!"[40] – but

[40] The first, that is, of the five Precepts of Buddhist ethics, against killing.

their position is such that saying them is permissible, an acceptable and accepted part of the civilizational status quo.

I have argued elsewhere (Collins 1993c and 1996), and try to show later in this book, that Pali texts do in fact contain far more humor – usually of a fairly dry and ironic kind – than they are usually credited with; but the making of overt jokes is not the point here. Shulman suggests that the standard character of the Brahmin as clown (*vidūṣaka*) in Sanskrit drama, "like so many clowns and ceremonial fools throughout the world, has the freedom both to see and to state simple, sometimes shocking truths" (1985: 161). Buddhist clerics were not and are not ceremonial fools; but if one looks from a viewpoint which emphasizes the sheer force of military and political power, the wielders of ideological power can seem relatively powerless, at least in the short term. On the other hand, the potential for discursive one-upmanship possessed by ascetic specialists in death and transcendental visions gives them, as Shulman puts it, "what may be a universal feature of clowning – the reflexive gift of the commentator, who is capable of framing experience and of switching frames almost at will" (1985: 164); that is to say, their role position, rhetorically outside the temporal world of production and reproduction, facilitates socially sanctioned reflection on, and second-order evaluation of it, from the thus constructed viewpoint of death and timelessness.[41] The symbiosis of kings and Buddhist clerics, then, did not exclude critical commentary on the former by the latter, sometimes of a severe and uncompromising sort: as in the *Mūgapakkha Jātaka* (6.2), where acting as a king is said to lead, necessarily, straight to hell. But the antagonism between them was not of the mutually exclusive sort: they were both, so to speak, employed by the same company – the agrarian state – at the elite, civilization-producing managerial level.

So far this section has used a simple dichotomy between kings and clerics. A more complex analysis of the cultural logic of asceticism requires that one subdivide the latter, looking at what Gellner calls "rival elements within the wider clerisy"; and to do so I first move out from the Buddhist tradition in particular, both to premodern

[41] One can recall here the freedom of speech (*parrēsia*) allowed to, and characteristic of "another, notoriously eccentric figure, the philosopher" in the ancient Mediterranean world (Brown 1992: 61–70).

Southern Asian civilization as a whole and back to what was said earlier about the conditions of agrarian society in general. The analytical scheme being employed here first divides agrarian society into peasant tribute-givers and elite tribute-takers. When the latter category is divided into two one has a tripartite structure of workers (production), warriors/kings (coercion) and clerics (cognition). When the category of clerics is divided into two, the ordinary (ritual functionaries) and the virtuoso (ascetic salvation-seekers), one has an elite triumvirate of kings, "priests" (using the word in a way which includes both Brahmins and Buddhist monks as ritualists) and ascetics. Burghart (1978, 1985; cf. Das 1977: 18, 56), speaking only of what he calls the "Hindu Social System," and drawing much of his data from fieldwork in Nepal, delineates three hierarchies, each with one of the triumvirate on top. "Brahmans, ascetics and the king each claimed their superiority in the particular world in which they lived," and "each person based his claim in terms of a particular hierarchy which was the exhaustive and exclusive order of social relations." The Brahmanical priestly hierarchy is expressed in terms of ritual purity and "the sacrificial body of Brahma." Ascetic hierarchy is expressed in terms of "the cycle of confused wanderings"; that is, rebirth and release from it. Kingly hierarchy, which is found most clearly in "panegyrical and epigraphic sources," is expressed in terms of a "tenurial hierarchy which was derived from [the king's] lordship over the land," a lordship construed as a divine marriage between god-king and the earth (1978: 520–1). *Mutatis mutandis* these three kinds of hierarchy are also perceivable in European Christianity, where Tellenbach (1991: 38–60) speaks of them as the royal (theocratic), the sacramental (priestly) and the ascetic (monastic). In abstract terms, these are hierarchies as seen, respectively, by kings, ordinary-ritualist and virtuoso-ascetic clerics in the conditions of Agraria.

In the Buddhist case, the ordinary-ritualist clerical hierarchy is not so much an explicitly proclaimed discursive artifact as the ensemble of attitudes and behaviors which led, for example, at the upper end of the social hierarchy, to aristocratic members of the monkhood presiding over the coronation ceremonies of kings, adding a transcendentalist gloss to the mundane display of power; and at lower levels to their being employed to chant protection verses at weddings, house buildings, and the like, and to assist in the transfer of merit to dead relatives. Relations between the three groups were such that each one could, from the top of its own hierarchy, look down on the others; but also any two could gang up on the third. Both kinds of cleric could oppose kings, for example, from the institutional position of the monkhood, which as the "field of merit" for the laity had a higher soteriological status than any king, enmeshed as he would be in "the five kinds of sense-pleasure" (Collins 1982: 169), and condemned to the use of violence. Ascetics, with the king as supporter, could oppose ordinary monks from the point of view of the radical renouncer (Silber 1981, 1995), claiming that monks should introject and live Buddhist ideology rather than merely exist as institutional emblems of it.[42] Kings and ordinary-ritualists could oppose ascetic-virtuosos, as for example in the Thai case, looking from the point of view of established social hierarchy on potentially wayward and undisciplined "wandering monks."[43] Pali texts can be found, at all periods, which reflect these three viewpoints; sometimes more than one of them at the same time.

I conclude this discussion of asceticism in the Buddhist transcendental vision as it began, with some ideas from Ernest Gellner, this time in an admittedly incomplete piece called "Notes Towards a Theory of Ideology." Religious and other ideologies, he says, can be distinguished from the wider class of systems of ideas by what he calls their "offensiveness" (using the word in a special sense, following Kierkegaard):

> Ideologies contain hypotheses, but they are not simply hypotheses. They are hypotheses full of both menace and sex-appeal. They threaten and they promise; they demand assent with menaces; they re-classify the moral identity of the believer and the sceptic; and they generate a somewhat new world. The world is different according to whether one looks at it from within or without a given ideology . . .
>
> It seems to me that this offence-generating characteristic of ideologies is *inherent* in them, that it is implied in their very intellectual content . . . [I]deologies contain contentions which are fear- and hope-inspiring, and are meant to be such to anyone, anywhere. (1979b: 118)

[42] This was an important part of royal "purifications" of the Monastic Order, when kings often acted in concert with forest monks against what Carrithers (1983) calls "domesticated" monks, as in the case of Parakkamabāhu I and the monk Kassapa (Gunawardana 1979: 315–6). It has also, for example, been an important alliance in Thailand, in the cause of modern nationalism: see Keyes (1971), Tambiah (1984), J. L. Taylor (1993).

[43] Bunnag (1973: 54), J. L. Taylor (1993: 170–1), Tiyavanich (1997); cf. Collins (1997).

To call ideologies "offensive," outside of the particularities of Kierkegaard's theology, may be misleading, although the ambiguity between its normal sense and the technical sense in which it is being used here is useful in thinking about the *Vessantara Jātaka* (section II.a below and Chapter 7). Gellner glosses the word as both "exciting" and "terrifying"; one can add "enticing," "alarming," "thrilling." In general, the fear inspired by Buddhist ideology is of rebirth in hell (and, when one is inside the system, any rebirth at all); it promises multiple felicities, including the ultimate kind, nirvana. A transcendental vision is not one of the immediate givens of everyday life; rather, it sets the everyday in a larger, and consciously critical (because not obvious) frame. I suggest that part of the point of asceticism is to affront, and in the present technical sense offend against the foundations of ordinary human community, a community which ascetics cannot replace, but must live within. That is to say they can both reject and depend on the two bases of human community: the production and storage of food (and, in all social contexts more complex than that of non-storing, immediate-return hunter-gatherers, of wealth), and the bearing of children, with all the affective concomitants of that process, from conception to upbringing. This view of asceticism is consonant with what Gellner calls the "double status" of ideology:

It is a well-known feature of ideologies that they claim to be intellectually sovereign. The truth, Spinoza said, is the touchstone both of itself and of falsehood. From the inside, ideologies are not merely true: what is far more important is that they provide the very criterion for telling truth from falsehood . . . But certain odd, and indeed most significant, consequences follow if one sees this trait in conjunction with their offensiveness . . . A claim can only give offence, in the sense intended, within the context of some *other* and wider world, of some other set of rules, which it manages to offend, and which it did not itself invent or sanction . . . Both the bait and the trap, indeed, can only have their efficacy in terms of some prior world, a world *preceding* the one to be defined and logically dominated by the ideology in question. So, in a curious way, ideologies tacitly and implicitly admit that they do not dominate or fill out the world after all. They function in a world they did not themselves make. (1979b: 122–3)

Eagleton has also commented on this:

A dominant ideology has to recognize that there are needs and desires which were never simply generated or implanted by itself . . . [This is] its Achilles heel, forcing it to recognize an "other" to itself and inscribing

> this otherness as a potentially disruptive force within its own forms . . . Any ruling power requires a degree of intelligence and initiative from its subjects, if only for its own values to be internalized; and this resourcefulness is at once essential for the smooth reproduction of the system and the permanent possibility of reading its edicts "otherwise."[44]

In the Buddhist case it is not the ability of subjects/agents to read its edicts "otherwise" in a contestatory or rebellious sense which is relevant here. (No-one could accuse Buddhist asceticism of not recognizing that there exist desires which it did not itself generate.) The important issue is the fact that the ascetic edicts of Buddhism cannot be read other than "otherwise" by the majority of those whom one can call, in varying senses, its "adherents"; and this is necessarily true of it in any civilizational, *longue durée* context. Buddhist ideology – in both its ordinary-ritualist/emblematic and virtuoso-ascetic/actual forms, in different but overlapping ways – was situated at the head of a moral hierarchy, a position which was at one and the same time at the top of and "outside" social hierarchy. Thence, as a product of the elite-civilizational work of order-making, moving seamlessly from the living/visible to the dead/invisible, it could be used simultaneously to articulate universal and social order and to offend against the virtues and assumptions of everyday social order, in both its productive/reproductive and "gentle violence" forms. As a form of (analytically autonomous) ideological power, it could be used to co-operate with and to challenge military-political and economic power within the agrarian state. Just as the world of Buddhist ascetic ideology existed – necessarily – in a preceding and continuing non-ascetic world, so too Buddhist political-religious universalism existed – contingently, historically, but in this like every other universalism – in certain specific times and places of a preceding and continuing material-historical world. This wider world it could not dominate or fill.

II. THE PALI IMAGINAIRE IN REAL WORLD HISTORY

I said at the outset that this book wants to create a kind of double vision, which can hold both the inside and the outside of texts in view together. One of the terms in the subtitle of this book can

[44] (1991: 45–6). The first and second sentences cited are in reverse order in the original.

begin to suggest what this means: the "Pali imaginaire" is a mental universe created by and within Pali texts, which remained remarkably stable in content throughout the traditional period, but which moved, as a developing whole, through various times and places within the premodern material-historical world. This second part of the Introduction starts from a general methodological discussion of the inside and outside of Pali texts in section II.a. Sections II.b, c and d consider the nature of Pali language and the place of Pali Buddhism in history; and section II.e then addresses the idea of a history of the imaginaire, and its relation to other kinds of historiography.

II.a. On the inside and outside of texts

Dominick LaCapra, although writing about the "great" books of the western literary canon in intellectual history, describes well an aspiration of this book: he wants to write

> not from the perspective of a social history that inquires into the uses of texts for the empirical reconstitution of the past but from the distinctive perspective of an intellectual history that inquires into the relationship between social processes and the interpretation of texts . . . [A] problem often elided or not emphasized in a social history of ideas is that of the relation of social to textual processes. (1983: 41)

There are many differences between the texts of which he speaks and those in the Pali tradition, but it is worth raising in relation to them the question he addresses: how to balance a documentary interest in texts – what they can tell us about their time and place – and what he calls a dialogical approach, which asks questions about the relationship between present historian and the past history he or she reconstructs, about the uses of language in both source material and historiography, and about various things to which he refers under the category of "worklike" aspects of a text, as opposed to the "documentary."

The documentary aspects of a text are those factual and literal dimensions of it which contain, or can be used to infer references to empirical reality. The worklike aspects of a text are those dimensions of it which operate on or supplement empirical reality in a critical and transformative way, involving commitment, interpretation and imagination:

We usually refer to *The Brothers Karamazov* and *The Phenomenology of Mind* as works, and to a tax roll, a will and the register of an inquisition as documents. But the work is situated in history in a way that gives it documentary dimensions, and the document has worklike aspects. In other words, both the "document" and the "work" are texts involving an interaction between documentary and worklike components that should be examined in a critical historiography. Often the dimensions of the document that make it a text of a certain sort with its own historicity and its relations to sociopolitical processes (for example, relations of power) are filtered out when it is used purely and simply as a quarry for facts in the reconstruction of the past. (A register of an inquisition, for example, is itself a textual power structure with links to relations of power in the larger society. How it functions as a text is intimately and problematically related to its use for reconstruction of life in the past.) Conversely the more documentary aspects of a work are neglected when it is read in a purely formalistic way or as an isolated source for the recovery of past meaning. (1983: 30–1)

He identifies six areas of investigation in the relations between texts and "their various pertinent contexts" (1983: 35). Among them is that of society to texts, mentioned above; another is that of culture to texts, and here he makes what is for my purposes an important distinction, which refers to different relations between historian, material and audience:

Insofar as an approach is documentary, it may validly function as a processing of "primary source material" that enables the nonexpert reader not to go to the sources or the archives themselves. But the very point of a dialogical approach is to stimulate the reader to respond critically to the interpretation it offers through his or her own reading or rereading of the primary texts. (1983: 48)

In the case of the Buddhist texts dealt with in this book, there are some obvious difficulties: very few readers will know Pali; and although there exist many translations of Pali texts, mostly canonical, they were pioneering ventures made for the most part in the first few decades of this century, with very few lexicographical or other aids. Their style – not to mention their simple mistakes – is rarely such as to give a modern nonspecialist a real sense for the original. For many, perhaps most nonspecialist readers this book will, therefore, function as a processing of primary source material. There is, however, at least one major exception to this, a text to which Chapter 7 is devoted: the great *Vessantara Jātaka*, a story which is universally agreed to be at least as important in

Southern Asian Buddhism as the biography of the Buddha, perhaps more so. There are many versions of the story throughout Asia: there are two in Pali, and many in Southern Asian vernaculars. The *Vessantara Jātaka*, the longer of the two Pali versions by far, has been very well translated by Margaret Cone (in Cone and Gombrich 1977).[45]

A full treatment of this text must wait; but I want to use it here to exemplify two contrasting but equally simplistic transitions between the inside and the outside of Buddhist texts, made in such a way as to ignore their vitality and multivalence. (Both come from books I otherwise admire, and recommend.) The crucial issue is that Prince Vessantara, in the last birth as a human being of the rebirth sequence which culminates in our Buddha Gotama, fulfils the Perfection of Generosity by giving away not only vast wealth but also, after he has been banished from his kingdom to the forest by an angry populace, his children and wife (in that order). When this is taken in a realist manner, clearly, it is difficult to accept morally in any sense, leave alone as the culminating point of the Buddha's previous career fulfilling the Perfections of Buddhahood. Gombrich (1971a: 267) found two monks in Sri Lanka who responded to his questioning on this point by saying straightforwardly that Vessantara was wrong. Swearer describes the events thus:

> As we might expect and as the logic of true *dāna* [generosity] requires, soon after Vessantara and his family are happily settled in their simple jungle hut, the prince is asked to give up his children to serve an old Brahmin, Jūjaka, and his young wife. When Indra appears in disguise and Vessantara accedes to the god's demand that he give up his wife, the prince's trials come to an end. Having successfully met this ultimate test of generosity – the sacrifice of his wife and children – Vessantara's family is restored to him and he succeeds his father as king of Sivi. (1995: 10)

The choice of wording here entirely ignores the fact that giving away one's children and wife to slavery is obviously and intensely offensive to everyday moral sensibility.[46] It is true that almost every

[45] See Chapter 7 for the division of labor in their work.

[46] Swearer (1995: 178) cites the biblical story of Abraham and Isaac in a note; this is dismissed by Gombrich (Cone and Gombrich 1977: xxii) with "to quote a parallel is not a moral argument." This is true, but given the use by Kierkegaard of the Abraham and Isaac story, and given the relevance I am assuming here of Gellner's use of Kierkegaard's notion of the offensiveness of ideology, the Vessantara story might necessitate some revision of "Buddhist morality," conceived in simple normative-universalist terms.

traditional audience for the story would have known that the protagonists would, at the end, "live happily ever after"; but it seems to me wrong to assume from this fact that the Vessantara story is simply a rather unusually extreme instance of the virtue of generosity. This is taking a fact about the outside of the text – that generosity is emphasized and valued in Buddhist ideology, and practiced under this description in cultures influenced by it – and reading (or rather ignoring) the inside because of it. As will be seen, the Pali text here goes out of its way to emphasize the pathos of these scenes, choosing deliberately strong language to intensify and highlight the emotions of both the characters and the audience.[47]

In one place Spiro (1971: 108) agrees with Swearer's approach, as – inevitably and to a degree correctly – does everyone who writes about the story: the story's "sacrificial idiom provides the charter for and reinforces the Burmese belief in the religious efficacy of giving." But he also cites some of the most dramatic passages from the earlier "standard" English translation by Rouse,[48] in a psychoanalytical account of Burmese monasticism as egocentric and narcissistic, in the Freudian sense.[49] Although "simply to abandon one's family would provoke intense social disapproval in Burma," nonetheless for Spiro the text is "an impressive historico-mythic charter" for the socially acceptable practice of abandoning one's family to enter the Monastic Order. This approach does look at the inside of the text,[50] but moves immediately to the outside, here to the supposed psychology of Burmese men, taken as being simply continuous with what appears to be the psychology of Vessantara.

In this case both the movement from outside to inside – "since we know about generosity in Buddhism, we can ignore our unfavorable reaction to Vessantara's actions in the text and cite it as evidence for the importance of that virtue" – and that from inside to outside – "Vessantara's actions are egocentric and so we can infer that narcissism is one of the unconscious 'motivational bases for recruitment' into the monastic order" (Spiro 1971:

[47] Note, however, that this is not true of all versions, so one must avoid essentialism.

[48] In Cowell et al. (1895: vol.6): this is a very inadequate rendering (cf. Cone and Gombrich 1977: v).

[49] (1971: 343–7), cited with approval by Gombrich (Cone and Gombrich 1977: xxvi–xxvii).

[50] Or rather, of the translation: Chapter 7.1 n. 16 discusses a reading by Spiro entirely dependent on Rouse's misleading choice of English terms.

337ff.) – ignore any possibility of complexity in the relation of text to context, reading the Vessantara story wholly in a reductive, documentary mode. Chapter 7 argues that if one looks at the work-like aspects of the Pali *Vessantara Jātaka*, it can be seen to confront, in a quite extraordinarily direct and open-ended way, the real human difficulties attendant on the minority option of asceticism, as well as the offensiveness – in Gellner's Kierkegaardian sense – of Buddhist ideology. It is at the same time a lyrical evocation and summation of the whole gamut of Buddhist felicities. In this way it performs both of two functions of art identified by LaCapra: "the escapist function of imaginary compensation for the defects of empirical reality and . . . the contestatory function of questioning the empirical in a manner that has broader implications for the leading of life" (1983: 45). Both of these two functions – importantly, not merely the first – also characterize two particular forms of art central to this book, sometimes as alternatives, sometimes as both present simultaneously: the composition of utopias, and the elaboration of a transcendental vision which offers salvation from all conceivable ills.

The artistry of the Vessantara story was appreciated in 1878 by Captain C. J. F. S. Forbes, "Officiating Deputy-Commissioner, British Burma," albeit not without imperialist paternalism, who tells us that "one of the characteristics of the Burmese race is their intense love of dramatic performances" (1878: 143). He describes a version of the story as "one of the most affecting and beautiful compositions in Burmese," and recounts a theatrical performance of the episode where Jūjaka, "the villain of the piece,"

> times his approach, while the mother is absent, [and] works on the charitable disposition of the Prince, who, after sundry struggles with his paternal feelings, gives his two children to the greedy Brahmin. It must be remembered that Waythandara [Vessantara] is himself conscious that he is the coming Buddha, and must practice to the very utmost the law of self-abnegation to attain that lofty position for the benefit of all human beings. With a bleeding heart he sees the Brahmin drag off the children, silencing their piteous entreaties with blows. Then the mother returns to find her little ones gone. Her agonised appeals are beautiful in their simple pathos, and I have seen men moved to tears by a good representation of this play. (1878: 150)

The remark about Vessantara's consciousness is debatable (but the audience's awareness of "his" future Buddhahood is relevant);

nonetheless his words suggest that we might read the story neither as an awkwardly excessive sales pitch for Buddhist ideology[51] nor as a guileless piece of self-revelation by narcissistic males, but as a work of art which can embody deep, if different – and perhaps theoretically incompatible – human feelings and aspirations. His account would seem also to suggest that, in our terms, the piece has elements of both tragedy and melodrama.

II.b. What is Pali?[52]

The Buddha, so far as the record permits us to say, lived and taught in northeastern India, but Pali is a form of Middle Indo-Aryan (MIA) probably based for the most part on one or more dialects from the northwest; in the form redacted to us it shows evidence of some remaining eastern forms, of later Sanskritization and of medieval grammarians' ideas of correct usage. It has been called an "artificial" language (Hinüber 1982, 1983); and an "ecclesiastical koiné" (KRN no. 84). The word *pāli*, which originally meant "(canonical) text", came to refer to the language in the early modern period through a misunderstanding of the compound *pāli-bhāsā* as "Pali language," rather than "language of the (canonical) texts."[53] Something like a Pali Buddhist school in India, perhaps more than one, must have existed; but we have no direct evidence, only the claims of later historiographers. The earliest extant written materials in India are Aśoka's inscriptions, from the third century BC, which contain variations of linguistic form and are based on related dialects of MIA. There is some evidence of Pali in India later, although it is disputed whether these cases are really Pali or a Prakrit closely related to it.[54] It may always be the case, as it certainly is some-

[51] Jones (1979: 133–4), naively realist, is embarrassed and irritated, in a rather English way: "Although the extravagance of the giving of . . . Vessantara is greatly lauded by the poet, and although this theme of totally unreserved generosity is such a popular theme of Indian poetry generally, it does nevertheless have some very disconcerting features. . . In these stories giving has become almost a self-indulgence. It is on such an extravagant scale that it bears little relation to the actualities of life, neither does it consider the possibly harmful effects of such lavish generosity on its recipients; it shows a total disregard for personal feeling and it retains a rather distasteful ulterior, contractual nature."

[52] See also Gombrich's (1994) answer to this question, with which mine is in full agreement. Overviews, with references to specialist articles, can be found in Norman (1983), and KRN Nos. 38, 61, 84.

[53] See Pruitt (1987), Hinüber (1994[1977]: 76–90), and on the need to put "canonical" in parentheses Collins (1990a).

[54] See Hinüber (1985).

times, that Pali inscriptions in India were made by (or for) monks from Sri Lanka or mainland Southeast Asia. In looking at the whole historical career of Pali, and comparing it with other forms of Old and Middle Indo-Aryan used as prestige languages in Southern Asian Buddhism, there seems to be a difference between attitudes to language use in early Indian texts such as those of the Pali Canon, and those characteristic of Pali Chronicles, commentaries and other literature in later Sri Lanka and Southeast Asia, and perhaps also of texts in differing forms of Sanskrit in later India.[55]

The attitude to language choice in early Buddhism is usually discerned in two ways: by inference from the historical fact that Indian Buddhism as a whole used different forms of Old Indo-Aryan and MIA, and/or from two short texts in Pali which seem to authorize the use of different dialects, although both of them in fact defy definitive interpretation. In the more famous (Vin II 139), two monks in a very short and entirely contextless *Vinaya* passage discuss with the Buddha which *nirutti* (Skt *nirukti*, which perhaps means dialect) may be used to preserve his Teaching. The usual interpretation is that they were asking to translate it into metrical Sanskrit, on the model of the Vedas, and that the Buddha refused, authorizing the use of whatever dialect was appropriate. It has been argued, however, that the text should be understood in exactly the opposite way: that the Buddha ordered monks to use only his (the Buddha's) own dialect.[56] I see no way to decide

[55] Extant texts from Indian Buddhism are in forms of what Edgerton called Buddhist Hybrid Sanskrit (BHS), some of them in Sanskrit. Hinüber (1989, cp. 1994[87]: 198–232) argues as follows: we know from Buddhaghosa's commentary to the Pali *Vinaya* (fourth to fifth centuries AD) and from later history (Bizot 88), that monastic ordinations in different lineages had always to be performed with exactly the same, precise pronunciation of the Pali formulas. To mispronounce an ordination liturgy rendered it invalid. If, he argues, a given school (defined in terms of monastic lineage) chose a particular kind of MIA for its ordination rituals, it was likely then to redact its entire Monastic Rule in that same form. If it redacted the Rule in that form it was likely to redact the rest of its canon in it too; and thence likely to use that form for all its texts. Bronkhorst (1993) considers the issue of Buddhist Sanskrit texts' attitude to their own language. As discussed presently, later Theravāda texts regard Pali as the naturally given, "root language" of all beings; they use terminology from the Brahmanical Sanskrit *Mīmāṃsā*, for whom Sanskrit was the eternal, basic language. Certain Jain texts also take this attitude to their form of Prakrit (cf. also Granoff 1992). No BHS text says this, but Bronkhorst adduces evidence to suggest that perhaps some Buddhists did so; and that some might have taken BHS to be identical to Sanskrit.

[56] Brough (1980), KRN nos. 38, 42. The phrase is simply *sakāya niruttiyā*, "in own dialect." Whose?

conclusively between the two, although the first does seem preferable, if one has to make a choice. The second passage (M III 234–5) is easier, although it too has been interpreted in diametrically opposed ways. Here, in a *Sutta* passage, the Buddha refers to various different words used in different regions for a pot, rather in the way modern Americans might list terms for carbonated drinks used in different regions: "pop," "soda," and the like. It seems to me (and to the commentary: Ps V 32) that the Buddha's directive here is to use whatever word is locally usual, without becoming attached to any one local usage.[57]

Early Pali texts distinguish languages and persons as *āriya* (as in "Indo-Aryan") or *aviññātara-milakkha*, "incomprehensible" or "uncomprehending barbarians." Skt *mleccha*, like Greek *barbaros* (and Skt *barbara / varvara*), "barbarian," is an onomatopoeia: such people can only make ugly, meaningless sounds. Skt *mleccha* becomes *milakkha* in Pali, with the same meaning but now without the self-evident rationale of the Skt word. A distinction was made between the Middle Regions (*majjhimā janapadā*) of northern India, where the Aryans lived (corresponding to the Brahmanical Skt *ārya-varta*; see Deshpande 1993) and Neighboring Regions (*paccantimā janapadā*), where barbarians lived (e.g. S V 466). Although the former was regarded as better – living in a Neighboring Region is given as an example of bad karma (D III 264) – speakers of both could be ordained in the monkhood: one of the Monastic Rules stipulates that anyone can leave the Order by publicly announcing the intention to do so, in either Aryan or barbarian.[58] This contrasted with a later *Vinaya* regulation, which specifies that legal transactions of the Order had to be performed in correctly pronounced Pali to be valid (Sp 1399–1400; Hinüber 1994[87]: 198–32). Commentarial texts redacted in their final form in Sri Lanka from the fourth to fifth centuries AD, but con-

[57] Cf. KRN no. 82 on *nirutti-patha* as "way of speaking." Note however that Horner's "official" Pali Text Society version (1959: 282) has the opposite. Here, as elsewhere with early uses of *nirutti* in Pali, it is not clear whether the word refers to an entire language or dialect, or simply to a lexicon of referring terms.

[58] Vin III 27–8. For such an announcement to be valid it must be understood and accepted by at least one other monk or nun: thus if monk A wants to leave, his announcement to that effect must be understood by at least one person B. A and B can speak an Ariyan or barbarian language: hence there are four possible combinations. In the two situations where A or B speaks Ariyan, the other milakkhan, and so A is not understood by B, the announcement is not considered legally valid, and so A is still subject to monastic law. If both speak either Ariyan or milakkhan, it is valid.

taining material from centuries earlier in Sri Lanka (and perhaps also from India yet earlier, though this is difficult to prove), refer to a number of specific languages as *milakkha*. They are Tamil, Telugu, Oriya, Greek, and some others not identified.[59]

Early texts, therefore, recognize a hierarchy of preferred languages or dialects, but do not privilege one absolutely. A greater emphasis on the importance of Pali, although not a completely different attitude, is seen in Pali Chronicles and commentaries, redacted in Sri Lanka from the early centuries AD and later in Southeast Asia. They called Pali Māghadan, probably to associate it with the charisma of Aśoka, whose center was in Magadha. They saw it as special, uniquely valuable, and assigned a specific status to it, which I call "naturally-given." It was the "root language (*mūla-bhāsā*) of all beings" (Mhv XXXVII 244, Vism 441 = XIV 25). Normally, one passage says (Vibh-a 387–8, cp. Moh 186), a child learns language from its parents. If its mother speaks Tamil, its father Andhaka (Telugu), it will speak Tamil if it hears the mother first, Andhaka if it hears the father first. But if a child hears neither – such as one growing up alone in a forest far from villages – it will spontaneously, through its own nature (*attano dhammatāya*), speak Pali.[60] Pali is the first language to appear at the beginning of each cosmic eon; unlike languages appearing later, it does not change (ibid.). Those who attain a level of Buddhist knowledge called "Discrimination in Language" – that is, who uncover in themselves the original, root language – find that the only obstacle to learning the Buddha's word when spoken in Pali is the physical one of the sound impinging on the ear; the moment it does so "the meaning arises in a hundred, a thousand ways." But texts in other languages have to be studied over and over again. Certain words "arise spontaneously" at the start of each eon: they are words for natural objects such as the sun and moon, and Buddhist psycho-physical technical terms, which "make their own names as they arise" (ibid., As 390–2, Paṭis-a 306–7).[61]

The Pali lexicon is thus fundamental; it is called the *sabhāva-*

[59] Sp I 225, Sv 176, Vibh-a 387–8; cp. Ps I 138, Mp I 95.

[60] Comparable stories about a "natural" language occur elsewhere, of course.

[61] The Pali for "arising spontaneously" is *opapātika*, equivalent to the Brahmanical *Mīmāṃsā* Skt *autpattika*. A passage in the Skt *Abhidharma-dīpa* (Jaini 1977: 109, 113, 393; cf. Davidson 1990) uses another *Mīmāṃsā* term to describe such words: *apauruṣeya*, "impersonal'; that is without an inventor, human or divine – the very term used by the *Mīmāṃsā* for the Vedas.

nirutti, which in one place the prolific translator Ñāṇamoli rendered "individual-essence language" (1975: 487), in another "natural language" (1991: 127). It is that which denotes things "in accordance with the way they really are" (*yathābhucca*). It was thus the quickest and most efficient language for soteriological purposes, but not a necessary one: stories are told of monks in Gotama's Dispensation in Sri Lanka, and others at times without a Buddha, attaining enlightenment after hearing songs sung by slave-girls about the inevitability of old age and death; in one case it is specified that the language used was Sinhalese (Spk I 273–4, Pj II 397).

Any text could be composed in or translated into Pali; and as can be seen from Norman (1983), Pali literature comprises many different genres. What has come to be the dominant tradition of "Theravāda" Buddhism – created and perpetuated by the Mahāvihāra monastic lineage – has chosen as a self-defining characteristic the transmission of a closed canon in Pali, and the use of Pali for it, commentaries on it and other later literature, as a prestige language to carry and embody its universalism (Collins 90a) But what kinds of text had to be in Pali, to achieve their purpose? At least two:[62] (i) *the performatively efficacious*, such as texts recited at certain monastic rituals, as when the *Pātimokkha*, the Monastic Rule, is recited, or in monastic ordinations. Successful monastic ordination required that the liturgy be pronounced correctly. Bizot (1988) has shown the importance of this for the history of lineages, and hence of Buddhism, in Southeast Asia; and (ii) *the ritually fixed*, such as *Abhidhamma* texts used at funerals and in meditation. Swearer (in Lopez 1995b: 336–42) translates a Northern Thai funeral text which correlates the Pali names of the seven books of the *Abhidhamma*,[63] letters of the Pali alphabet and syllables of the formula *namo buddhāya* (honor to the Buddha), with days of the week and their astrological significance, elements of the human body and other things. Texts concerned with the conceptual deconstruction and dissolution of the body and mind

[62] This account merely gives a few examples: a comprehensive review is impossible and unnecessary here.

[63] The third part of the Canon, mostly scholastic matters of psychology and philosophy rather than narratives and sermons, and specifically the lists of psycho-physical elements in to which human persons are analyzed.

– as are most of those in the *Abhidhamma* – are appropriate for funerals, but if the appropriateness were purely semantic, wholly vernacular texts would be better: more people would understand them. Perhaps the "naturally-given" character of Pali psycho-physical referring terms may be thought necessary to their instrumental and/or expressive functions at funerals. It is certainly relevant to their use in meditation practice, although here one can give an external functionalist explanation also. It is not often realized that Buddhist meditation is very often very discursive; the word *kammaṭṭhāna-pāli*, "text of the meditation subject", is a technical term in meditation manuals.[64] From the internal, Buddhist perspective, the meditator is better able to see the reality of the body and its parts through using the terms which most directly describe them: that is, the "naturally-given" Pali lexicon. From the external point of view, it is obvious that standardizing such meditation texts is useful: monks could move, as they often did, to any part of the (Pali) Buddhist *oikumenē*, near or far, and find the same shared world of practice. The inner world prescribed in the manuals becomes the world accurately described in, because constructed by, the imaginaire. (One might recall Bloch's characterization of political-religious language as formalized, ritualized and repetitive.)

The inner world of meditation is a long way, culturally if not geographically, from the world of Southern Asian kings and emperors; but although rulers may not have cared for meditation, they did care that correct meditation – in Pali – was being done in their realm. In the historical chronicle called *Cūlavaṃsa* in the West, an extension of the ancient *Mahāvaṃsa* into modern times, the eighteenth-century Sri Lankan king Vijayarājasiṃha, "the Lord of the Earth," is said to have

> realized that the Dispensation of the Conqueror was declining in (Sri) Lankā because a community of monks could not be found [to preach, ordain new members, etc.]. He formed the intention to invite (members

[64] In the meditation on the body, for example, the manuals list thirty-one (or thirty-two) parts into which the body is to be analyzed, and thus seen as impermanent, unsatisfactory and not-self; they are to be learnt by heart, so that they can be recited in forward and backward order, and then in more complicated subdivisions (1–5, 5–1, 6–10, 10–6). Each time the meditator is first to recite them out loud, vocally, then mentally; only after these recitations is "penetration" into them possible (*paṭivedha*, a term for Buddhist understanding). See Collins (1992b).

of) the Monastic Order [from elsewhere], and tried repeatedly to discover where the Dispensation of the Sage still existed. When he heard from the Olandas [the Dutch, now in control of parts of the southwest of the island, who were trading in and between Sri Lanka and mainland Southeast Asia] the good news that it existed in various countries, in the regions of Pegu and Rakkhaṅga [Arakan; both in Burma], and Sāminda [Siam], he had letters written in the Root-language [i.e. Pali], gave them to ministers and others and sent them here and there to discover the state of the Sage's Dispensation in different countries. When the Lord of Men heard it said that the Dispensation existed successfully and in a pure state in the region of Ayojjhā [Ayudhaya] he gave a letter along with various presents and instruments of worship to ministers and sent them to bring sons of the Conqueror [monks] back from there to Lankā. (Mhv XCVIII 87–93)

The ideological value of such an attitude to Pali is, I think, twofold. In the first place, there is the claim to have access to a language, and to states of knowledge and being expressed in it which are exempt from contingency. Brahmanical Hinduism denied contingency by removing the Veda and Vedic Sanskrit from history completely (Pollock 1989). Islam, as far as I understand it, does not deny history, but on the contrary validates a specific moment in it – the occasion on which God spoke to Muhammad through the angel Gabriel, in Arabic.[65] Pali is exempt from contingency by being naturalized or even biologized: it exists before the artificialities (*kittimā*, Skt *kṛtimā*)[66] of humanly derived culture and language are imposed, and it is what emerges after they are cleared away by the Buddhist virtuoso's Discrimination in Language. Linguistic non-contingency, whether nonhistorical, specifically located at the conjunction of eternity and history, or naturally given, is both a representation created by transcendentalist ideology, and, when successfully disseminated, part of what creates the autonomy of ideological power and the social position of the clerics who control access to it.

Secondly, Pali was a sign of trans-locality, in both space and time. The fact of a text (oral or written) being in Pali was already a "work-like" aspect of it, already said something about it and what it doc-

[65] The Buddha, according to Pali commentaries (Sv 27, Pj I 101, Pj II 135) spoke Pali, the root language, and miraculously those who did not understand it heard him speak in their own language, *sakabhāsā*.

[66] These are: general names (*sāmañña-nāma*), names (indicating) qualities (*guṇa-nāma*), artificial or made-up names (*kittima-nāma)* and spontaneously occurring names (*opapātika-nāma*). See Collins (1993a: 385–6).

umented, real or imaginary. A text in Pali had *ipso facto* trans-local and trans-temporal reference, linking the here-and-now spatially to the broader world of Buddhism as a contemporary whole, and temporally to the past of Gotama Buddha (which modern scholarship accepts as historical), and to the deeper and further temporal horizon of past and future Buddhas (which is, for scholarship, mythological). I would want to make detailed corrections and qualifications to parts of what Benedict Anderson says about Pali in his deservedly celebrated *Imagined Communities*, but he is right to say that it was, in a larger perspective, like Chinese and Arabic an example of "the sacred . . . languages [which] were the media through which the great global communities of the past were imagined," at least by the elite. Often enough, the relevant factor would not have been the actual use of such a language, but the *idea* of it, the symbolic, figurative value of its existence. These global communities and linguistic-cultural systems preceded the nation as, according to Anderson, the "taken for granted frames of reference" for human society: the religious community (which was, in modern terms, international) and the dynastic realm (1991: 14).

II.c. What is "traditional" Theravāda Buddhism?

As mentioned at the outset, any periodization of history is contestable, and is better seen as a heuristic device than an empirical hypothesis. I find it most useful to periodize Buddhist history not in relationship to presumed events, institutions or periods within it but to what can be known by modern academic observers, and how.[67] The first or *early* period lasts from the time of the Buddha (whenever that was[68]) to that of Aśoka. Some of Aśoka's inscriptions mention Greek kings, who can be dated with confidence, and so his reign, *c.* 268–239 BC, provides the first really secure historical data we have for Buddhism, and indeed for any ancient Indian history. We have some archaeological data for the northeast of India before Aśoka's time (Erdosy 1988, Chakrabarti 1995), but none of it would permit anything like a rich reconstruction of culture. For that we have to turn to texts, whose extant form is

[67] This is a development of, and I hope an improvement on Collins (1990a, b).

[68] Currently the trend of opinion is to bring the Buddha's dates forward somewhat from the usual date given in western scholarship, *c.* 543–483 BC, to some time later in the fifth to fourth centuries BC. See Bechert (1991, 1992), especially Gombrich (1992c).

universally the result of post-Aśokan redaction. It is possible that Aśoka himself, or one of his immediate Maurya predecessors, introduced writing to India (Hinüber 1990), and in the Buddhist case the consensus of scholarship has been to accept the approximate accuracy of the statement in the *Dīpavaṃsa* and *Mahāvaṃsa* (in their extant form not earlier than the fourth or fifth centuries AD) that the Pali Canon was written down for the first time in the second half of the first century BC[69] We have no reason to doubt that, in general, many of the texts later redacted in writing do afford us reliable knowledge of pre-Aśokan texts.[70] But we cannot have anything like a full picture of pre-Aśokan Buddhism – necessarily a wider reality than the merely textual – and the normative role these texts had in traditional Buddhism must adversely affect any attempt to use them as documentary witnesses for an event-history of Buddhism in the early period.

In the second, *traditional* period there is an increasing amount of textual material; we also have inscriptions (texts of a different sort), coins, paintings, sculptures and other material remains, although neither material remains nor texts are as extensive as those to which historians of the classical or medieval west apply their skills. Non-textual remains from the past can be used to balance and sometimes correct what is gleaned from texts – as Gregory Schopen has been showing to great effect in recent years[71] – but such materials are mute witnesses without help from texts to interpret what they meant, or might have meant to contemporaries.

It is impossible to date the third or *modern* period precisely, although it is quite clear that something new and fundamentally different has come into being. One might say it is the period of modernist Buddhism, in which the self-definition of the tradition has come to include, as an intrinsic component, the reaction to western colonialism and science; but it would be wrong to suggest that all Buddhists in Southern Asia have felt the impact of these forces to the same extent and in the same way. What is meant by the term will become clear, I hope. The briefest definition would be: that period in which Pali has ceased to be an obvious and

[69] These texts say that the commentaries were written down at this time; but those extant we owe to later editors such as Buddhaghosa in the fifth to sixth centuries.

[70] On "the value of the Pali tradition," from this viewpoint, see Norman's article with that title (KRN no. 56).

[71] E.g. Schopen (1979, 1987, 1988).

viable linguistic and textual medium to express contemporary Buddhism. Collins (1982: 23) cited some remarks by Coulson, in which he distinguished, on the one hand, between a living and a dead language; and between a natural and a learned language, on the other: "a language is natural when it is acquired and used instinctively; it is living when people choose to converse and formulate ideas in it" (Coulson 1976: xxi). The point was to suggest that in traditional Theravāda, like Sanskrit (in Coulson's example) for the poet Kalidāsa, for Buddhists who concerned themselves with the composition and redaction of texts, Pali was a learned but living language. An emblem of the modern period, for me, is the fact that then Pali became both a learned and a dead language: somewhere, depending on local circumstances, between the beginning of the nineteenth and the early twentieth centuries.

European traders and colonialists were active in the Buddhist countries of Southern Asia from the end of the sixteenth century, and increasingly thereafter came to influence the cultures they were conquering and reporting on. And from the nineteenth century on, when most of the scholarly data on Buddhism of all periods was collected and made available in its modern form, the various aspects of what has become known as Buddhist modernism – scripturalism, rationalism, etc. – strongly influenced the image of the tradition then being constructed, both by Buddhists and their western observers.[72]

What kind of knowledge can we have of these three periods? Of the traditional and modern periods we can have the same *kind* of knowledge we have of any other historical period: always revisable, in both fact and interpretation, but after a time usually affording a generally reliable picture, depending on the extent and trustworthiness of data. But in relation to the first and earliest period, matters are very much more difficult, and my tendency here is to skepticism. It is certainly possible to present speculative accounts of what early Buddhism was, and even to make guesses as to "what the Buddha taught."[73] Gombrich (1988) is a fine

[72] The term "Buddhist modernism" was coined by Alexandra David-Neel (1911), and has been popularized by Bechert, (e.g. 1966). See Malalgoda (1976), Bond (1988), Gombrich and Obeyesekere (1988). On the use of the term "scripturalism" here, see Collins (1990a: 115 n. 51).

[73] I allude to the title of Rahula's deservedly well-known and much-used textbook (1967).

example, offering in consciously Popperian fashion a clear, forthright and thus defensible hypothesis about "Gotama Buddha's Problem Situation" (Chapter 2), "The Buddha's Dhamma" (Chapter 3), and much else besides. I know of no other work anywhere near as useful or as interesting for pre-Aśokan Buddhism, and I certainly do not want to inhibit intellectual courage of the kind his book displays.[74] But the speculative approach tends inevitably to see the culturally instantiated Buddhism of the traditional world, if not as a degeneration, at least as an "accommodation between Buddhism and society in ancient India" (the title of Gombrich's Chapter 5) and thereafter in Sri Lanka and Southeast Asia. This inevitably leads to a divorce between "original" or true" Buddhism and the vicissitudes[75] of human nature and social life. The approach derives from Weber;[76] as he famously put it, in this view "ancient Buddhism" was only and essentially "a religious 'technology' of wandering . . . mendicant monks," whose "specifically unpolitical and anti-political status religion" was "the most radical form of salvation striving conceivable"; Buddhist teaching for the laity, on the other hand, was "an insufficiency ethic for the weak," which "only later and gradually developed" (1958: 206, 215).

I do not mean to argue that the Buddha was not a celibate ascetic who taught his monastic followers a way to final salvation, seen as a definitive and complete release from rebirth. But there is no need to assume that when he taught non-celibate householders, as the texts say, the way to heaven (and other things), he was doing something extraneous to his real message. We cannot know

[74] Recent scholarship in Europe has tried to discern not merely what the Buddha taught in general, but what was the exact chronology of his teachings, down to the order of his thoughts on the very first day (Vetter 1988); and to disentangle "authentic" from "inauthentic" parts of the texts attributed to him (Bronkhorst 1986). The results of this effort, on which a great deal of philological virtuosity has been spent, strike me as a form of orientalist fantasy. Both Wiltshire (1990) and Ray (1994) show that conspiracy theories – "early Buddhism was really X, Y, Z, but this has been suppressed by the monastic textual tradition" – are still alive and well.

[75] As in the subtitle of Spiro (1971): *Buddhism and Society: a Great Tradition and its Burmese Vicissitudes.* Spiro's book is a classic example of the approach I am trying to counter: but I should add that I find it nonetheless still very useful, and still required reading for anyone interested in (or by) the matters I have discussed in this book.

[76] Weber's view of South Asian religions was flawed in many ways, and has had some deleterious effects on subsequent scholarship, especially that of nonspecialists. But what he was able to achieve with the quantity and quality of material available to him is little short of miraculous.

how far the individual whom we know as Gotama Buddha did or did not set out to create the World Religion which we know as Buddhism, nor how much of what it became he would have accepted or rejected. But one should not use methodologically individualist speculations about the world of pre-Aśokan Buddhism, about which we can have no direct knowledge, to determine our perception of traditional Buddhism, in regard to which our knowledge, although like all historiography contestable, is based directly on historically reliable data. Speculative reconstruction of early Buddhism from textual evidence is, I believe, in the long run inevitably compromised by the fact that the texts as we have them were intended, in the traditional period, to construct an ideal in the past which could be set against a present reality, which was a priori different and defective. There are certainly historiographical methods for extracting documentary-style data from such texts, whose worklike aspect was very far from empirical history of the modern sort. But any endeavor to narrate an event-history based on early Pali texts must reproduce the long-discredited positivist approach to myth: remove the supernatural, or otherwise unbelievable, and a "kernel" of empirical history remains. For example, if the Buddha is represented as conversing with one or more gods, this approach holds that the meeting with gods did not happen – since we know they don't exist – but what he is represented as saying, nonetheless, reliably documents his real, historical teaching.

This book aims not to think in terms of the historical Buddha, what he intended, and what happened to his original message. It starts from Buddhism as a fact of premodern Southern Asian civilization in the traditional period, part of the elite-civilizational work of articulating (enunciating) order. In this view it is a phenomenon deriving not from one or more ideal individuals from mythic antiquity but from actual, historical collectivities. In regard to the subject matter of Part 1 of this book, for example, I think that it is a mistake – but one made by almost all scholarship on the issue hitherto – to infer, from the correct perception that within the discourse of Buddhism the highest kind of felicity is said to result from the individual (celibate) treading of the Path to nirvana, that academic historiography and sociology should start from that fact, or in other ways privilege it in understanding what "Buddhism" was or is. In dealing with Buddhism as a civilizational phenomenon, I suggest, one should start from the assumption that it was – to whatever extent it was – a cultural-ideological project of ongoing collectivities, in which celibacy could only be a minority option. In the earlier parts of the traditional period the relevant collectivities would have come from the elite in any given area, gradually expanding to include a greater number of peasants and others: but in any instance, anywhere, the majority of such collectivities would have been non-ascetic. One must therefore try to understand nirvana not only on the ideological surface, as the goal of a minority asceticism attainable only by individuals, but also more deeply, in the culture-producing engine-room, as it were, as part of a shared, collective imaginaire. Such an understanding is part of what this book attempts to provide.

The word imaginaire is taken from contemporary French historiography, and it might be helpful, as an analogy to what is meant here by "traditional Buddhism," to refer to LeGoff's idea of an "extended Middle Ages." He argues that "from the standpoint of culture, the [European] Middle Ages fall between the end of the schools of the ancient world and the mass education of the nineteenth century"; this latter was "the time when modernity was fully embraced" (1988: 22, 19). This whole period was (as partially quoted earlier)

> dominated by Christianity, by a Christianity that was at once a religion and an ideology and that therefore enjoyed a very complex relation to the feudal world, which it both contested and justified. By this I do not mean to suggest that Christianity today is dead or moribund, only that since 1850 it has not played the same key role that it played between the fourth and nineteenth centuries. (1988: 21)

In the Buddhist case, the traditional period runs from the earliest datable materials, the third century BC, to the time when colonialism and modernity began to introduce irrevocable changes into Buddhist culture in the nineteenth century. In thinking about the issue of historical stability or change in this period, it is vital to separate the history of the Pali imaginaire from the wider historiography of society and culture in Southern Asia. Section II.e argues that the parameters provided by the socioeconomic contexts and institutional structures of the historical societies where Pali texts played a role were indeed subject to change, but they remained sufficiently constant that the Pali imaginaire could continue to describe and prescribe a plausible world. In taking texts from such a long period to be, for my purposes in this book, homogenous, I do not mean to perpetuate an orientalist myth of a changeless East, floating dreamily and aimlessly down the sea of time with a kind of idiot mystical grin. There were any number of changes on the political, social and all other levels, as the next section demonstrates. But I think it can be shown that the Pali imaginaire remained, for the most part, a stable ideological force. The contents of this book are taken from Pali texts at all stages of the traditional period: an imagined world of very great complexity and subtlety was transmitted and added to over many centuries, with scarcely any significant change, at least in the grand issues of felicity, time and timelessness which are my concern.

The coming of modernity shattered the traditional world of Buddhism, just as it had more gradually and less violently dismantled the traditional Christian world in Europe. The texts described in Parts 1 and 2, and at least parts of the imaginaire they constructed, have continued into the modern period, but to write a cultural history of modern Theravāda would require another whole book. Although much from the traditional Pali imaginaire remains alive in the modern period, or at least did until very recently, its civilizational role has become quite different in the political, social, economic and other conditions of modernity, in the industrial, capitalist, and, for most of its history European-colonial, world system. It remains to be seen how the Pali imaginaire will cope with what Giddens (1991) calls the conditions of "High Modernity," and whether, indeed, it will survive in it at all. Nobody who is aware of contemporary realities throughout Buddhist Southern Asia can have any reason for careless optimism.

Note: on the concept of modernity in Buddhist Southern Asia

Section I.a defined the *modern* period of global history in terms of industrialism and/or capitalism. These are indeed the factors which transformed much – though not all – of human life beyond anything which could be imagined in or from the conditions of agrarian society. But not all of the globe is industrialized even now: are these places then not "in" the modern world? In an obvious sense they are, by definition, since they exist in the same time as everyone else. That this is not a trivial, definitional point is well shown by Fabian (1983), who criticizes anthropologists who set contemporary others in a time behind ours, at an "earlier" stage of history – what he calls "allochrony." Equally obvious, it seems to me, is the fact that scientific knowledge and its application in the economic and political conditions of industrial capitalism and European imperialism has utterly changed the lives of almost everyone on the planet, some for better (in material terms), some for worse. What percentage of people now alive has not been touched by some combination of: the wealth produced by modern industry and technology, the ecological damage done by them, the advances in medical science, the disruptions, cultural and otherwise, of colonial rule and of the modern capitalist world system, and so on? Not zero, perhaps, but not much more.

But rather than proceed here by definition and systematic argument, I will exemplify one of the main themes of this book – that narrative is as important a cognitive function, a mode of culture-making, and a mode of truth-claiming, as is systematic thought – by telling a story, one which will be familiar to specialists in Theravāda and/or Thai history.[77] It takes place in later eighteenth- and early nineteenth-century Siam, a place from which, under its modern name of Thailand, have come a number of modern ethnographies which have shown how much, in the day-to-day lives of peasants away from cities (especially Bangkok, a place where modernity is all too clearly visible), the aspirations and fears characteristic of traditional Buddhism remain in force. But peasants do not write books, or govern nations, and the story which suggests what is meant here by "modernity," and its importance in bringing an end to the world of traditional Buddhism, involves both.

In 1767 the Empire of Ayudhya came to an end when Burmese armies destroyed the capital city (and, alas, its extensive libraries of Pali texts). The first king thereafter, Taksin, was in some ways orthodox, in traditional terms, commissioning (unsuccessfully) a new edition of the Canon (*tipiṭaka*) and of an allegedly traditional Thai treatise on the "Three Worlds." But he was executed because, amongst other things, he tried to have the monkhood declare that

[77] My account follows the classic article by C. Reynolds (1976), as well as his unpublished (1973) thesis, Butt (1978), Kirsch (1978) and Wyatt (1982); other works are cited in the text.

he had reached a high level of Buddhist sanctity, and to be thus worthy of veneration by them. The next king was Rāma I, founder of the current royal dynasty, in what is now called the Early Bangkok Empire, who established political control over vast areas of what are now Thailand, Burma, Laos and Cambodia, once again creating a polyethnic political formation ruled from a Siamese capital city. He claimed to be restoring the glories of Ayudhya, although in fact, as is usually the case, he was innovative, in what Wyatt (1982) calls his "subtle revolution." He instituted reforms of the Buddhist monkhood, sponsored (successfully) a new edition of the Pali Canon, and had a chronicle written about the council at which this was done. His governmental style was culturally cosmopolitan: he sponsored a new Thai version of the *Rāmāyaṇa*, called the *Ramakian*, and had texts translated into Thai from Chinese, Sanskrit, and Pali. He, like Taksin, wanted an edition of the Three Worlds treatise, and commissioned one in 1783 immediately after his accession to the throne, even before he commissioned the new edition of the Canon. Not completed until the early years of the next century, this work may be taken as emblematic of Rāma's self-proclaimed restoration of traditional Thai Buddhism. The Three Worlds, albeit in Thai, is an excellent introduction to the traditional cosmology, and much else besides, of the Pali imaginaire (its author lists many Pali texts among his sources). Its hierarchical view of the social and cosmic worlds is a perfect example of the ideological enunciation of power in a premodern, "class-divided," tributary state.[78]

The influence of European cultural, religious (missionary) and scientific practices increased in the early nineteenth century. Two grandchildren of Rāma I can stand for two indigenous reactions. Rāma III (r. 1824–51), was "a vigorous defender of many traditional values," who "bequeathed a Siamese empire that was more powerful and extensive than at any previous time" (Wyatt 1984: 175, 180). Mongkut, however, who became a monk in 1824 perhaps to avoid dangerous competition with Rāma III, was much

[78] Thai *Trai Phuum*, Pali *Traibhūmi-kathā*; translated into French by Coedes and Archaimbault (1973), and into English by F. E. and M. B. Reynolds (1982). The history of the text itself, and arguments over the relative value of the editions which are extant from Taksin and Rāma I is discussed in Jackson (1993). The value of the Three Worlds as an accessible exemplification of the traditional Pali imaginaire is not affected by the arguments over the actual date of its composition, referred to in the text below.

influenced by western knowledge. This has been chronicled at length: here are two examples. As a monk he inaugurated a monastic group called *Thammayuttika,* aiming to return to the strict observance of the Buddha's time, as recorded in the Pali *Vinaya.* While reform movements have been common throughout Buddhist history, initiated by monks or kings or both, Mongkut's had a particular historicist flavor, perhaps influenced by his apparently avid discussions with Christian missionaries.[79] As a monk, and later as king (1851–68) he encouraged knowledge of western science. With his support, in 1867, the Minister of Foreign Affairs published "the first Siamese printed book issued entirely under Siamese sponsorship." It

> divided the *Traibhūmi* cosmography into two, the natural world and religion, each category of phenomena having a set of "laws" which guided its workings. The book presented examples from the *Traibhūmi* cosmography, referring to it by name, and then countered the *Traibhūmi*'s explanations with alternative ones drawn from meteorology, geology, and astronomy . . . Religion in [the book] was not so much philosophy and theology as social ethics; and Buddhist social ethics were realizable through Siamese institutions.[80]

Mongkut's modernizing moves, however, proved more corrosive of the traditional Thai world than he would have liked. As Jackson (1989: 45) puts it, "Mongkut's religious rationalism was not complete . . . while [he] criticized local and regional forms of Thai religion as superstitious, he did not radically question the legitimating ideology of the monarchy." His "incomplete rationalism" did not foresee that openness to the West (a policy continued by his son Chulalongkorn) and challenging "local supernatural or magical beliefs" were also, in the long run, challenging "the hierarchical metaphysic of the royal form of Buddhism" as well (1989: 46). Thence, in a familiar story, later developments culminated in a constitutional monarchy in 1932, the rhetoric (if not the reality) of democracy and egalitarianism, and a contemporary Thailand both booming and devastated through industrialism and capitalism. The Three Worlds treatise continues to have a great signifi-

[79] C. Reynolds (1973: 84); cp. ibid. p. 95: "Only the *Thammayuttika* examines the Pali texts directly, ignoring the encrustations of habit and commentary interjected by Buddhist clerics according to their own lights'.

[80] C. Reynolds (1976: 214–55); cp. Malalgoda (1976) on the ownership and use of printing presses in colonial Sri Lanka, and also Collins (1990a: 115 n. 51) comparing "scripturalism" in premodern and modern Theravāda.

cance in contemporary Thai political and cultural debates; but none of the contending voices, even the most conservative, has been able to give direct assent to the text's cosmography (Jackson 1993).

Some features of this story may have to be changed: Vickery has recently argued that the usual attribution of the Three Worlds to a king in the fourteenth century is wrong, and that although elements of the text are indeed traditional (in both linguistic and doctrinal senses), it may be that the extant text "as an integrated composition dates from after 1778, and is the work of the various commissions established by Taksin and Rama I" (1991: 33). If so, we have another example of an invented tradition, not in the sense that the content of the Three Worlds is new, but that its rhetorical status as the "traditional" Thai text *par excellence* is the creation of modern political and cultural agendas.[81] But the main features of the historical narrative seem secure, though they may be added to; and the interpretation of events, although debatable, will probably remain tied to a general modernization/secularization perspective, at least for the foreseeable future.

This story, I hope, demonstrates that although it is difficult to arrive at an exact definition of modernity, which might apply to anything and everything in Southern Asian Buddhism, something very definite has changed. The change in the nature and role of Buddhist ideology is, certainly, more obvious at the elite level, now identifiable as the public politics of a nation-state rather than the civilization of a premodern, often imperial political formation. It may be less evident on the surface of the everyday life of peasants; but that, on the other hand, is nothing new.

II.d. A political biography of Pali Buddhism

The previous section has outlined my view of what Pali is, or was, and of the kinds of knowledge I think we can expect to have of the three periods of Theravāda Buddhist history. But if, as claimed, the Pali imaginaire was a relatively stable mental universe in a

[81] Even more drastic rewriting of Thai history will be necessary if the so-called Ram Khamhaeng inscription – on which is based most "knowledge" of the thirteenth-century Sukhotai kingdom – turns out to be later, perhaps even a nineteenth-century "forgery." See Chamberlain (1991), especially the paper by Piriya Krairiksh, pp. 257–70.

changing material-historical world, what is the story of its spread in the specific times and places of traditional Southern Asia? Overall, one can say that in the *longue durée* of agrarian social order, the socioeconomic structures in which the Pali imaginaire was sustained as an elite mental-cultural *Lebenswelt* were remarkably constant. Erdosy, a scholar of early Indian archaeology and history, writes that by the sixth to fourth centuries BC "the technological base of the economy in this period [had] already reached a level not to be significantly exceeded until the 20th century" – that is, until the coming of industrialism (1988: 112). What follows is a lightning tour, somewhat impressionistic but detailed enough I hope to demonstrate what Lieberman calls in his study of sixteenth- to eighteenth-century Burma (1984) *Burmese Administrative Cycles: Anarchy and Conquest c. 1580–1760*, and the dynamic of localism and trans-localism in the political domain. I have twice referred to what some writers see as an "evolutionary" development of social organization: through family societies, local groups with or without leaders termed Big Men, early agrarian states, regional and trans-regional polities, kingdoms and empires, in Buddhism of "Wheel-turning Kings," *cakkavatti*-s. In Southern Asia sociopolitical formations oscillated back and forth over this continuum, although as Lieberman stresses (1987) the long-term trend is in the direction of larger-scale polities and centralization. The place of Buddhist ideology was notably different in India from what it became in Sri Lanka and Southeast Asia. The following survey aims to highlight the specific historicity of the political formations in which Pali Theravāda was, or was not, an ideological force in premodern Southern Asia.[82]

What can one say of Buddhism in India before Aśoka, who reigned in the third century BC? From my remarks in the previous section, silence might seem the better option. But I will not take it, since there is a well-known and widely accepted story to be told, albeit that it can be criticized on grounds already mentioned. It is given here *faute de mieux*. The study of early Indian history – which means, given the evidence available and present purposes, of north India before the Mauryan empire, which began in the

[82] This account draws on the works mentioned on pp. 81–2, and others mentioned in the text.

fourth century BC and reached its apogee under Aśoka in the third – continues to struggle with the problem of assessing the relative weight of textual and archaeological evidence. But a reasonably clear picture can be drawn.[83] At this time, as far as the evidence allows us to know, Brahmanism was more strongly established in the countryside of north India, more so in the west than the east, since it had been established there longer. It was suited to a rural society, since Brahmanical social hierarchy was more easily stabilized there, and social order more easily enforceable, on the basis of ritual alone. Urban centers and state formations had begun to arise, especially strikingly in the northeast, along the Ganges, where a competing plurality of ideologies was emerging. Texts of the later Vedic tradition produced by Brahmins at this time, the *dharma-sūtra*-s, show both an uneasiness about urban life and a concern with "the laying down of explicit codes of conduct . . . [The fact] that rulers are now explicitly enjoined to enforce correct behavior, signals a change in the orientation of government away from rituals and in the direction of secular administration based on force" (Erdosy 1988: 16) The connection between early Buddhism and urban government and trade, as suggested in its texts, has long been known.[84] Recently, moreover, Olivelle has argued plausibly that the appearance in Brahmanism at this time of ascetic thought and practice, as evident from the *Upaniṣad*-s, may be the result of urbanized Brahmins accommodating a trend towards asceticism within their own tradition, as against the continuing opposition of their (culturally speaking) "country cousins."[85] Although there is extensive evidence of urban centers at this time, and of a more complex social differentiation than earlier, there is no evidence of the larger kind of imperial metropolis which arose from the time of the Mauryan empire. There were a number of regional divisions, called *janapada*-s or *mahājanapada*-s, whose names are given variously in different texts but which are usually said to number sixteen. These were not at first equivalent

[83] Summary accounts are Ghosh (1973), Sharma (1983), Thapar (1984), Allchin (1995) and Erdosy (1988, 1995). Erdosy (1988) contains a judicious and helpful discussion of the problems of dating both Brahmanical and Buddhist texts, and of relating both to the archaeological data currently known. I am not concerned with precise dating: so much depends on the date of the Buddha, at present under much discussion, as mentioned earlier. [84] Gombrich (1988: 49–59) offers an elegant summary.

[85] See Olivelle (1992), Introduction section 2, and (1993), Chapter 2.2–3. Earlier van Buitenen (1981: 12) had sketched out a similar idea.

to political units, but were areas which contained powerful clans, ruled by local chiefs grouped in tribal oligarchies. They are sometimes called *gaṇa-saṅgha*-s, not unreasonably translated as "republics." But the *janapada*-s gradually came to be political units, particularly after the Kosalans conquered the Buddha's own clan, the Sākyans; and the transition to monarchical rule was in process during the Buddha's life. After the Buddha's death, the sixteen *janapada*-s were reduced to four main rivals; and eventually that of Magadha became dominant, thus laying the foundation for the Mauryan empire, centered on Magadha (Erdosy 1988: 118–50).

At least two views of sociopolitical order can be discerned in those Pali texts usually accepted to be early.[86] One is that of small-scale oligarchies, which were – according to a received opinion widespread both in scholarship and, for example, in modern Sri Lankan politics (Kemper 1991) – preferred by the Buddha (but see 6.3.a below). The other is monarchy, and in particular the figure of the Wheel-turning King (*cakkavatti*, Skt *cakravartin*), who conquers the four corners of the earth (6.5.a). The latter poses a delicate question of interpretation. We know there were no large-scale political formations in India before the Mauryan empire; should we infer that texts which speak of such a thing are later than Aśoka? If we note with Gombrich that "the representation of one's own king as a world-ruler of untrammeled power is a commonplace of the ideology informing Vedic ritual" – i.e. even earlier than the Buddha's time – we may conclude with him that "it was an institutionalized fantasy" in both Vedic and early Pali cases (1988: 82). But it is also true that in a larger perspective, as noted earlier, there has never anywhere in history been a case of a self-proclaimed "universal" or "world" empire which was anything more than an institutionalized fantasy, although there have been many which used such rhetoric.[87] The fact that for documentary purposes it is possible that references in early Buddhist texts to

[86] They are: the majority of the *Dīgha, Majjhima, Saṃyutta* and *Aṅguttara Nikāya*-s, and the *Sutta Nipāta*, with perhaps some other short texts from the *Khuddaka Nikāya*. The *Abhidhamma* has always been accepted to be late; recent evidence is tending to suggest that the version of the *Vinaya* we have is a later redaction, although it too contains no reference to imperial formations.

[87] At one time the sun may never have set on the British Empire, but it always shone on other parts of the world as well. See Pagden (1995) for an account of how the rhetorical universalism of the Roman Empire was (and in some cases was not) taken up by the early modern Spanish, French and British Empires.

oligarchies are empirically based, whereas those to Wheel-turning Kings are not, tells us nothing either way about the relative priority of one or the other. All talk of empire ("world" or otherwise), of kingdom, or indeed of social order in any form, is always in LaCapra's terms worklike as well as documentary, involving imaginative and projective supplements to empirical reality (fantasies) as well as empiricist *reportage* of it.

The rise of urban centers for the elite, and the production of a food surplus by the "peasants" under their governance in ancient India are obviously connected processes: it would seem that the two were mutually encouraging.[88] Although no doubt many factors lay behind the increase in food production, one plausible candidate is the increased growing of rice (a higher-yield crop than the earlier dominant barley), and in particular the technique of transplanting rice in wet-land cultivation. According to Sharma "although the later Vedic people grew rice, *vrīhi* [the word then used] was a rainy season crop whose yield was limited on account of its being sown in the field. Obviously the people did not know the art of paddy transplantation, or wet paddy production, which appeared later as a winter crop" (1983: 161–2). Rice grown by the latter method was known as *śāli* (1983: 96). It is thus perhaps significant that one of the best-known texts of the Pali Canon, the *Aggañña Sutta*, with its "social contract" story of the origins of society, describes the earliest rice as *śāli* (Pali *sāli*), a surplus of which was used to create the institution of kingship, by exchanging rice (tax) for the administration of justice.[89]

In India, one might say, history begins with Aśoka, whom later Buddhists writing in Sanskrit and Pali claimed as a linguistic and ideological forebear. But his inscriptions tell a different story: their Middle Indo-Aryan is not identical to that of any extant texts, and he patronized Buddhism along with other members of the clerisy, in the manner of most Indian rulers. The Kuṣānas in the northwest in the first to third centuries patronized Buddhism, mostly the Sanskritic Sarvāstivāda (which may explain the later prevalence of Sarvāstivādin

[88] See Olivelle (1993: Chapter 2.2 n. 85) who cites Ghosh (1973: 19–21) and Erdosy (1988: 126).

[89] But note that in this story clerical irony represents the first king's punishing miscreants as "evil" (*pāpaka*). See Collins (1993c), with Huxley's (1996) criticism of the idea that this is a social contract story.

Buddhism in Central Asia) but also other Indian groups; and they issued coins portraying Greek and Persian deities. The Buddhist centers of Amarāvatī and Nāgārjunīkoṇḍa were built under the Sātavāhanas and Ikṣvākus further south around the same time, but they patronized Brahmins as well. Buddhism received support from the Guptas in the fourth and fifth centuries in north and central India, from Harśa in the seventh, the Pallavas in the south during the sixth to ninth centuries, and the Pālas in the northeast during the eighth through twelfth centuries (notably at the universities of Nālandā and Vikramaśīla): but never exclusively. We need to understand better, empirically and historically, how these competing articulations of order and cultural universalism could coexist as forms of ideological power. Analytically, of course, we can simply see the clerisy – Hindu, Buddhist, Jain and other – as an internally differentiated class of legitimators; but how this differentiation and coexistence in ideology interacted with other forms of social power in these tributary systems remains unclear. Perhaps the increasingly hegemonic role of Sanskrit as the prestige language of politics and culture in general, as opposed to the restricted sphere of Brahmanical liturgy and law, is a place to start. (It may not have been, despite conventional wisdom, a widespread political or "literary" language before the first centuries AD: see Pollock 1996)

Outside what is now India, a note is necessary on ecology, territory and the political imagination. Sri Lanka is a special case. In the earliest centuries Buddhism was probably strongest in the ports and the royal city of Anurādhapura, although inscriptions in cave-dwellings occur in many other parts of the island (Paranavitana 1970). From the second century BC until the British conquest in the nineteenth the island was repeatedly fragmented into regional power-bases and reunified "under the one umbrella" of a king, but with the Portuguese and then the Dutch controlling the southwest coast from the sixteenth century. The image of royal power as an expanding circle was applied here to an island, and so a sense of territorial boundedness arose, which is both rare before modern times and analogous, at least in this respect, to nationalist views of legitimate power: it may in this respect be called a kind of proto-nationalism. Warfare with South Indian kings occasionally took place on the mainland, but the ideology of the Wheel-turning King in Sri Lanka did not usually lead to imperial ambitions beyond the island. In what are now Burma, Thailand, Laos and Cambodia the absence of such obvious natural boundaries addressed a permanent challenge to the kingly rhetoric of the universal Wheel-turning King whose power extended outward to the edges of the earth. Polyethnic empires were centered on river plains around the Irrawaddy and Chao Phraya in what are now Burma and Thailand, the Tonle Sap in Cambodia and the Mekong on the Thai-Laos border, with mountain ranges in between. The Mon linguistic and cultural area did straddle what is now southern Burma and central/south Thailand, but this was rarely converted into a single political domain with imperial power over others. Military forays such as those from Burma to Thailand in the sixteenth and eighteenth centuries did, however, occasionally bring the actual geography of mainland Southeast Asia into some relationship – at least of synecdoche – with the ideological geography of the Wheel-turning king conquering all four islands around Mt. Meru.

Buddhism arrived in Sri Lanka at the time of Aśoka, in the third century BC. From at least the first century AD various forms of Buddhism (including Mahāyāna and Sanskrit) co-existed, albeit with a strong, perhaps dominant Pali tradition. From the eighteenth century – but perhaps not before then, despite conventional histories – at the time of the monk Saranaṃkara under the Nayakkar (i.e. South Indian) king Kirti Sri Rājasiṃha, the Mahāvihārin lineage of Theravāda was retrospectively constituted as the sole preserver of pure, authentic, original Buddhism. Here as elsewhere, the rhetoric of revival may mask the creation of something new. The language of purity and reform was everywhere an important part of royal sponsorship and control of Theravādin monastic lineages. Parakkamabāhu I in the twelfth century is the best-known example (Gunawardana 1979). Amongst the many ways in which rulers could impose the spatial and temporal universalism of Buddhist ideology on the various local sources of opposition within their territory, notably among the clerics themselves, were: the moral-legal vocabulary of purity in behavior, of authenticity in monastic ordination ritual and thus of lineage precedence; the conspicuous consumption, or rather the conspicuous production of purified versions of the Pali Canon (itself an item of rhetoric rather than reality, a cultural idea, or ideal, rather than a physical, practical fact); and the repossession of land donated to monastic groups judged impure in one way or another, along with the jurisdiction of the state formerly donated with it.

In Southeast Asia in the first millennium AD polities in which Buddhism existed were on the Indic model – that is, rulers supported various schools of Buddhism, Mahāyāna and Hīnayāna, along with Hindu deities. Examples are the trade kingdom of Śri Vijaya in Sumatra (important for Buddhist education and scholarship) from the seventh century, and the agriculture-based empire of Angkor in Cambodia from the eighth. The latter turned to Pali and Theravāda from the mid-thirteenth century, although exactly how remains unclear. Pali inscriptions have been found in the Pyu area of central Burma, perhaps from the fourth century, in the Mon areas of southern Burma and Thailand from the sixth, and from the present Thai–Cambodia border in the eighth,[90] but in all three places Sanskrit language and Mahāyāna were also found. At first Pali texts and Theravāda monastic lineages were carried primarily by itinerant monks along sea trade routes, and thence inland to small-scale regional centers in agrarian *milieux*, without yet being significantly combined with other forms of social power.

In the second millennium, there was virtually no Pali presence in insular Southeast Asia. All over mainland Southeast Asia in the second millennium on the contrary, monks from the Mahāvihārin and other lineages, and indigenous monks sent to Sri Lanka for ordination, introduced what was called the "Sinhalese Order" (*sīhala-saṅgha*), with royal support. This process did not occur in historical or cultural isolation. The earliest examples of such Theravāda hegemony do predate the arrival of Islam as a political force in the late thirteenth century, but only by a century or two, a brief span in the *longue durée*. Muslim traders had been known in port cities for centuries beforehand. European Christians arrived in the sixteenth century. Historians such as Reid (1988, 1993) and Lieberman (1993), seeking patterns in Southeast Asian history as a whole, have seen Theravāda on the mainland and Islam on the

[90] Rohanadeera (1987) reports an inscription apparently datable at 761 AD which contains the opening verses of the *Telakaṭāhagāthā*, a sophisticated, Sanskritic Pali poem from Sri Lanka of unknown date, but usually thought later than the eighth century (Malalasekera 1928: 162–3, Norman 1983: 156). 761 would be surprisingly early for such a text, and Rohanadeera's arguments for a fifth-century composition date are not fully convincing.

islands from the fourteenth century onwards, as analogous forms of universal, scripture-based salvation religion, elements in a general process of political centralization,[91] monetization of the economy, and (to use a modern term) internationalization in both economic and political spheres. Of course the cultural outlook of peasants may not have been affected by these things, although they would have felt their effects; and it is dangerous to infer from an objective past situation as we now perceive it that historical agents at the time were conscious of the same thing. But the elite of different societies, the relevant agents of the Buddhism revealed in most of the written records, would have been aware of the larger world in which they lived.

Interaction between Theravāda ideology and military-political power on the Southeast Asian mainland began in the agriculture-based empire of Pagan in Burma in the eleventh century. This was seen by later Theravādins as the beginning of an instant Pali Buddhist hegemony there (a view often repeated in modern historiography), but inscriptions and iconography show that other forms of Buddhism and Indian religion continued to exist. From this time onwards, Pali Theravāda became dominant in more and more polities: e.g. in Pagan, Burma, from the eleventh to thirteenth centuries, the Mon state of Pegu in the thirteenth, the First and Restored Toungoo empires from the fifteenth through seventeenth centuries, the Konbaung empire of the eighteenth and nineteenth; in Thailand the Sukhotai and Lan Na polities in the thirteenth and fourteenth centuries, the Ayudhaya empire of the fourteenth through eighteenth (interrupted and ended by devastating defeats at the hands of Burmese armies), the early Bangkok empire of the eighteenth and nineteenth, and in Cambodia from the thirteenth century the various smaller kingdoms which arose in the territory of the old Khmer empire centered at Angkor, between periods of Siamese and Vietnamese control. Sanskrit language continued everywhere to be used occasionally for literary

[91] This is more marked on the mainland. Lieberman (1987: 182) points out that "about 1320 the political map of mainland Southeast Asia included at least twelve genuinely independent empires and major kingdoms. In 1520 there were eight. By 1810, only three: Burma, Siam and Vietnam." Of course, there were many and various reasons for this; but the ideology of the trans-local, (rhetorically) "universal" power of the Wheel-turning King, who was usually also seen as a Future Buddha (see Chapter 5), was certainly important in the indigenous discourse which accompanied these changes (see also Aung-Thwin 1985: 60–2).

and other purposes; and traces of Sanskrit Buddhism are perceivable even now (Strong 1992).

Looking back over its political history, one can focus on language to sum up the difference between Buddhism in the Indic model of clerical-ideological power, and that of Pali Theravāda elsewhere in Southern Asia. In the Indic model, the use of Sanskrit as the language of trans-localism (as witnessed in the epigraphic record from central Asia to Java) implied nothing about the content of the dominant ideologies – kings would normally support Śaivites, Vaiṣṇavites, Jains, Buddhists and others, with or without one being a favored group. When there is in this part of the premodern world an isomorphism between a single language and a unitary ideology (at least in the case of forms of Indo-Aryan: I leave aside Arabic and Islam) it is Pali and Theravāda Buddhism, in Sri Lanka from the beginning of the first millennium AD, and in mainland Southeast Asia from the beginning of the second. In this case royal elites seem to have chosen, at specific moments in history, what Andrew Huxley (1990) called "the Pali Cultural Package." This included Theravāda Buddhism, written law, and monastic institutions and lineages. In the Indic model, there seems to have been, as Sheldon Pollock (1996) puts it, a "Sanskrit cosmopolis" in most of the first millennium AD, and in parts later, stretching from Afghanistan to Cambodia, in which the language provided an "aesthetic of power," which functioned as an ideology by imposing a single medium of expression – and by excluding others – rather than by giving voice to a single belief system. To choose Pali as the prestige language for textual embodiments of ideology – it seems to have been used only sparingly in epigraphy – was to privilege Sinhalese monastic lineages, the closed canon of the Mahāvihāra, and more generally the systematic and narrative thought of the Pali imaginaire.

II.e. What this book is and is not trying to achieve as historiography

This section discusses the word "imaginaire" and the difficulties involved in assessing the place of an imaginaire in the real world, and in the civilization whose representative or expression it is taken to be, and then gives the reasons, historical and methodological, why the Pali imaginaire is treated here as a stable and cohesive ideology throughout the traditional period, in relationship to historical change in Southern Asia.

The use of "imaginaire" as a noun has become widespread in recent scholarship, due initially to the influence of historians and Marxists in France. Burke (1990: 71–3) traces a connection between "imaginaire" and "ideology" in the *Annales* historians and in political philosophers such as Althusser, who defined ideology as "the imaginary [or imagined] relation of individuals to their real conditions of existence (*le rapport imaginaire des individus à leurs conditions réelles d'existence*)." Durkheim's notion of *représentations collectives* is a forerunner of both usages. Sometimes, as in the work of Jacques LeGoff, it has the slightly more precise sense of a nonmaterial, imaginative world constituted by texts, especially works of art and literature. Such worlds are by definition not the same as the material world, but insofar as the material world is thought and experienced in part through them, they are not imaginary in the sense of being false, entirely made-up. This again, has Durkheimian ancestry: Hubert and Mauss (1898: 137) spoke of *la sphere imaginaire de la religion*, insisting that this sphere exists. "Religious ideas exist, because they are believed; they exist objectively, as social facts."[92] It seems to me preferable to retain the French, as the word cannot really be translated. Both the French *imaginaire* and English "imaginary" as adjectives mean fictive, unreal; thus in both languages Castoriadis' *L'institution imaginaire de la société*, translated as (1987) *The Imaginary Institution of Society* offers a prima facie paradox, an arresting incongruity. Used as a noun *imaginaire* can refer to objects of the imagination, the ensemble of what is imagined, without implying falsity; it can also refer to specific imagined worlds, and so can be used in this sense in the plural. English "imagination" primarily refers to a faculty or activity of the mind; while it can also refer to the objects of that faculty, the domain of the imagined, it is not usually used of specific imagined worlds, and cannot be used thus in the plural. It is not easy to translate *imaginaire* in this sense: LeGoff's *L'imaginaire médiéval* becomes (1988) *The Medieval Imagination*, and Duby's *Les trois ordres ou l'imaginaire du féodalisme* is (1980) *The Three Orders: Feudal*

[92] "*Les notions religieuses, parce qu'elle sont crues, sont; elles existent objectivement, comme faits sociaux.*"

Society Imagined, neither of which quite catches the nuance of the original. Some writers have begun to use "imaginary" as an English noun in this sense, but this is incomprehensible unless one already knows what it is translating. I prefer to use the word as an unitalicized Anglicization like "Renaissance" or "genre." Burke (1990: 71–3) uses "social imagination," which does contain a helpful implicit reference to related notions such as social memory (Fentress and Wickham 1992).

LeGoff (1988: 1–3) tries, with limited success, to delineate separate meanings for "imaginaire," "representation," "symbolism" and "ideology"; but as the opening discussion of Duby (1980: 1–9) shows (cf. Bisson's foreword, ibid. p. vii) these distinctions are difficult to retain in practice. Unambiguous terminological precision is not possible; but this is not to abandon the hope of achieving clarity in these matters. (Duby's [1985] "Ideologies in Social History" is a useful theoretical treatment.) For LeGoff, as mentioned, "literary and artistic works" are the principal primary sources for the historian of the imaginaire; and although he explicitly rejects the distinction made by LaCapra between "great" and "mediocre" art, he agrees with him that they both differ from the usual documents quarried by historians for "information relevant to the subject matter of traditional history: events, institutions, major characters, and, more recently, marking progress of a sort, *mentalités* [mental outlook as expressed in discourse and artifacts]." Such works "were not produced to serve as historical documents, but are a historical reality unto themselves" (1988: 3).

Many problems arise whether one makes or does not make a distinction between the representations, discursive and other, of an imaginaire and the world which they represent. As LaCapra puts it:

> One of the more challenging aspects of recent inquiries into textuality has been the investigation of why textual processes cannot be confined within the bindings of a book. The context or the "real world" is itself "textualized" in a variety of ways . . . [and] one is "always already" implicated in problems of language use as one attempts to gain critical perspective on these problems. (1983: 26–7)

His use of scare quotes indicates the difficulties; but these words remind one that the distinction between the inside and the outside of texts, obvious though it seems prima facie to common sense, can itself be problematic.[93] This is particularly true of historiography, where both gaining access to and describing the realities of the past are densely textualized activities. In writing a political biography of the Pali imaginaire the last section assumed for the most part an unproblematic division between the content of the Pali imaginaire, which was largely ignored, and the material-historical world across whose terrain its course was plotted, to which independent historiographical access was taken for granted. How, given a sensitivity to both the distinction and the connection between the inside and the outside of texts, does one introduce the ideas and values of such imagined worlds into civilizational history? Many writers, even one as realist as the great *Annales* historian Fernand Braudel, simply beg the question and write of them as foundational: he introduces *A History of Civilizations* to its high-school readership by describing civilizations as geographical areas, societies, economies and "ways of thought," and in relation to the last says that

> in every period, a certain view of the world, a collective mentality, dominates the whole mass of society . . . These basic values, these psychological structures, are assuredly the features that civilizations can least immediately communicate to each other . . . Here religion is the strongest feature of civilizations, at the heart of both their present and their past . . .
>
> [T]he ceaseless constraints imposed by geography, by social hierarchy, by collective psychology and by economic need – [t]hese realities are what we now call "structures" . . . These are the "foundations," the underlying *structures* of civilizations: religious beliefs, for instance, or a timeless peasantry, or attitudes to death, work, pleasure and family life. (1993: 22, 27–28)

But as regards "ways of thought" or "collective psychology", this is precisely what is denied by opponents of the Dominant Ideology Thesis, and dismissed as the Myth of Cultural Integration by Archer (1988), as discussed earlier. One can then go to the other extreme, and assume that there is no ideological domination of the peasantry by the elite in an agrarian society, only oppression by means of violence or the threat of it. In the area of Buddhist Studies, analogously, one might be tempted to dismiss Pali texts as

[93] Hanks (1989) offers a useful conceptual and bibliographical survey of "Texts and Textuality," in relation to this and other problems. Berkhofer (1995) discusses the issue at length in relation to historiography.

an elite, male celibate preserve, of no historical or ethnographic value.[94] It is certainly necessary to make a clear distinction not only between the Pali imaginaire as a specific, constructed mental universe and the material-historical world, but also between it and the wider textual-cultural world in which it is to be located. We will never have enough evidence to calibrate the significance of the content of Pali texts precisely at different times and places: we must use our own historical imagination. But whatever the difficulty of quantitative, demographic assessment, to banish Pali texts from civilizational history in Southern Asia would be in its own way unrealistic, and self-defeating.

I doubt that the lived world of any individual, leave alone any group, has ever coincided precisely, with no remainder, with the imaginaire of (some or all) Pali texts. The Pali imaginaire is not equal to the imaginaire (still less "the culture") of premodern Southern Asian Buddhism, and obviously was only one element of civilization in Southern Asia[95]. This is in part because of the emphasis laid by Pali texts – by no means exclusively – on soteriology; Cousins (1984: 279–80) speaks of this as Buddhism's "incompleteness . . . [which] is a consequence of the Founder's concentration upon the most essential." Many other parts of Southern Asian culture are neither required nor prohibited by Buddhist soteriology, notably that other kind of "religion" which I prefer to call localized supernaturalism. This kind of concern enters into Pali texts, of course, since it was an entirely natural and accepted part of the world presupposed by them. But there was no need for such things to be woven into a coherent, comprehensive and nonlocal ideological whole, as was certainly the case with soteriology. As mentioned earlier, I am struck – and hope readers will come to share this view – by the coherence and stability of the Pali imaginaire in the traditional period, whose cosmology and soteriology was preserved and developed, but never disruptively changed, over the two thousand years of the traditional period of Southern Asian Buddhism. The redaction of the Pali texts which

[94] Gregory Schopen's rhetoric at times comes close to such a view: see Schopen (1987: 193–4, 1991: 1ff.).

[95] Cp. Hodgson's sensible remarks, on Arabic and Islam, about the difficulties deriving from the fact that "it has largely been philologians who have – by default – determined our category of 'civilizations': a civilization is what is carried in the literature of a single language, or of a group of culturally related languages" (1974: 31).

have come down to us was the work of countless thousands of hands, voices and minds: the detailed precision and cohesion of the world thus collectively represented and constituted is remarkable. This world was the work of an elite, viewed from the social-historical perspective adumbrated in section I; and even within that social stratum it would have been the direct concern of only a small, educated sub-elite. Clearly to put something in Pali was to accord it a special kind of significance; and the specialness of the Pali imaginaire evidently called forth a kind of conscientiousness and care for which wider patterns of cultural creation and transmission had no need. Enough people knew enough about the Pali imaginaire to redact a very large corpus of textual materials, over two millennia, with scarcely any self-contradiction or inconsistency.[96] And this world – widely valued whether or not it was directly appropriated – was transmitted to others without knowledge of Pali by vernacular compilations from Pali texts, such as the Thai Three Worlds treatise discussed earlier, vernacular narrative and other commentaries on Pali texts (often in the form of mnemonic Pali verses fleshed out by vernacular exegesis), and vernacular translations.[97]

The Pali imaginaire, then, even within the areas which can be called Theravāda Buddhist, is only a partial and debatable witness to the underlying, foundational structures of civilization (assuming, with Braudel, that it makes sense to speak in this way at all). Why then concentrate on it? First, it seems necessary to adopt

[96] For the kind of small exception which proves the rule see Chapter 4 n. 43 concerning the *Loka-paññatti*, a text translated (or as some prefer, transposed) from Sanskrit to Pali in eleventh- to twelfth-century Burma (Denis 1977: ix). There is, as far as I can see, only one area where one might point to a significant and unintentional aporia in Pali systematic thought (there are, as Chapter 2 will argue in relation to nirvana, a number of intended aporias): this is the idea of "the Attainment of Cessation" (*nirodha-samāpatti*, discussed in 1.2.b; see also Griffiths 1981, 1986). This, however, is not a problem which developed historically, *pace* Bronkhorst (1986): it is the refraction in Pali texts of a fundamental tension in South Asian virtuoso religion, between enlightenment seen as the possession of a transformed understanding or as a state of transformed consciousness. This, in my view, a tension present in Pali texts from the very beginning.

[97] For examples of texts in the latter two categories, see R. Obeyesekere (1991) and Brereton (1995). Hallisey (1995) offers a valuable reminder that in the early days of western study of Theravāda, vernacular texts were prized as sources, but thereafter a fixation on Pali as "original" Buddhism pushed them from view, a process encouraged by a "similar 'metaphysic of origins' in the Theravāda itself" (1995: 43). Even regarding the textual history of Southern Asia the present work can only be partial, in a descriptive sense (see text below). Those with different historiographical aims than my own must attend to what Hallisey calls "the local production of meaning."

some principle of limitation over what threatens to become an impossibly large body of material (this is already a long book). Second, and more important, redacting a text in Pali was a decision with performative, worklike meanings: everything extant in Pali is therefore the result of a choice to include it in that corpus and redact it as such. The choice of a single prestige language for soteriology in texts, in contrast to the multifarious vernaculars of pragmatic communication, is one part of what Weber referred to as the intellectualist rationalization and unification of the "polytheism" of everyday life. It thus seems reasonable to investigate the imagined world of texts about which that decision was made. The Pali imaginaire constituted one potential resource, one textually externalized world of meanings on which historical agents could draw to construe their lives and aspirations, individually and collectively, at different times and in different places, to a greater or lesser extent. To what extent will always be a matter of debate, which will rarely if ever be resolved empirically.

Even where Pali texts were a significant cultural presence, we need to distinguish between the idea of "Pali texts," and especially the idea of the "Pali Canon," and what might be called the practical canon: that is, works in actual use at any given places and times;[98] unfortunately, we will almost never have any real knowledge of what such a practical canon might have been in specific locales before recent times. Still more must we distinguish between the Pali imaginaire taken, as is done here, as the content of the entire range of extant Pali texts, and the culturally salient content of the actual texts present and appropriated at given places and times. Nonetheless, I take as constitutive of the Pali imaginaire any and every Pali text from the premodern period, but only those of which there is a western edition. There are many Pali texts not edited in western editions, and so it is quite possible that the discovery and editing of other such texts in the future might add to or change what is said here. Such is the progress of knowledge. My procedure may seem artificialist – and indeed it is. But that is a methodological virtue not a vice, for two reasons. First, on a practical level, although the percentage of readers of this book who will have access to Pali texts and the ability to read them will be small, it

[98] See Keyes (1983: 272), Collins (1990a: 103–4); cp. Skilling (1992: 113).

nonetheless seems to me part of scholarly propriety to choose materials which are available to others for independent assessment: in principle, then, anything and everything said in this book about particular texts, or the Pali imaginaire as an ensemble, can be checked.

The second reason is methodological, involving an analytical and historiographical strategy which Archer (1988) calls "analytical dualism." This is a strategy of understanding which deliberately separates what Karl Popper called "World Three," the world of produced meanings – in his words the "objective content of thoughts" – from those of "World One," physical objects or states, and "World Two," "states of consciousness or mental states" (Popper 1975: 106–90). This would, of course, be wholly unrealistic for the purposes of historical and ethnographic description, and it is important to signal immediately that one of the main aims in positing such an analytical dualism is to overcome substantive dualism in history, philosophy or sociology.[99] Archer distinguishes, following Lockwood (1964), between "Cultural System Integration," which she describes, somewhat too narrowly for my purposes, as a matter of logical consistency between elements of culture, and "Socio-Cultural Integration," which is a matter of causal cohesion between cultural agents:

> The . . . distinction [between Cultural System and Socio-Cultural Integration] therefore maps onto that between culture without a knowing subject and culture with a knowing subject . . . [C]ulture as a whole is taken to refer to all intelligibilia, that is to say any item which has the dispositional capacity of being understood by someone. Within this I then distinguish the Cultural System, which is that sub-set of items to which the law of contradiction can be applied . . .
>
> Clearly the Cultural System and Socio-Cultural life do not exist or operate independently of one another; they overlap, intertwine and are mutually influential. But this is precisely the point, for I am *not* asserting dualism but rather the utility of an *analytically* dualistic approach, the main recommendation for which is the very fact that it allows this interplay to be explored. (88: xvi–xvii)

Archer has good, theoretical reasons of her own for grounding the systematic nature of a Cultural System in "propositions . . . [i.e.] statements which assert truth or falsity," while acknowledging that

[99] "Analytical, as opposed to philosophical, dualism is an artifice of convenience" (Archer 1988: 143).

"obviously we do not live by propositions alone (any more than we live logically" (ibid.; cf. pp. 136, 145–6).[100] My purposes are different: looking at nirvana as part of the wider category of the Buddhist discourse of felicity, along with ideas and narratives about other forms of imagined well-being, I attempt to understand it both in logic – what I call systematic thought – and in narrative, along with imagery as a bridging discursive form. I adopt her terminology but base the "systematic" nature of the Pali imaginaire, as a Cultural System, not on a logical system, but on two different things. First, there is the a priori unity given to the ensemble of Pali texts by the very fact of their being redacted in Pali: this is what I called earlier a shared worklike aspect of them, in LaCapra's terms.[101] Such an a priori unity, of course, might be the only thing which these texts shared: they might be full of logical contradictions, narrative disjunctions, and all manner of other chaos. But in fact they are not, and the a posteriori cohesion of the imagined world of Pali texts is the second thing on which I want to base their systematic nature, in the sense of the word relevant to Archer's analytical dualism.

The point of introducing Archer's analytical dualism is, to adapt her words, the very fact that it allows one to conceptualize the existence of interplay – that is, both difference and interconnection between the Pali imaginaire, as a Cultural System, in which integration is a matter of consistency in logic, narrative and imagery, and Socio-Cultural Integration, or lack of it, in the history of Southern Asia, which is necessarily "more disorderly" than any Cultural System (Archer 88: 197ff.). One can thus avoid reading Pali texts, naively, as if they were somehow a direct expression of Southern Asian history and culture, and also – the other extreme – avoid dismissing their content as irrelevant to "real life," in a crudely materialist fashion.[102] The phrase "Pali imaginaire," as

[100] For Popper, World Three consists in "scientific and poetic thoughts and works of art," and "problems and problem situations" (1975: 106, 107), albeit that for him also "the most important inmates of this world are *critical arguments*" (ibid.). Robertson (1991: 85–6) criticizes Archer's concentration on logic and propositions as a "bias" which "precludes her from attending to expressive meaning and to morality." For her own purposes this is not a failing.

[101] Cp. Archer: "By definition the cultural intelligibilia form a system, for all items must be expressed in a common language (or be translatable in principle), since this is a precondition of their being intelligible. . . The [Cultural System] contains constraints (like the things that can and cannot be said in a particular natural language)" (1988: 104, 107).

[102] Furthermore, severing immediate connection between Pali texts and what is taken to be their context of use enables one to avoid premature restrictions on what one takes

here defined and used, has a reasonably specific denotation, unlike "Buddhism" or "Buddhist culture," and the very specificity and artificialist separation of this textual realm allows one, or so I hope, to think through the issue of its place in Southern Asian society and history in a subtler, more nuanced and more realist manner. I suggest that the best way of exploring the interplay between imaginaire and history is not by any one author – and certainly not myself – attempting to write a comprehensive, or somehow uniquely privileged history, but for historians of different stripes to write in the knowledge, or at least in the hope that their work will be read in conjunction with other forms of historiography. Recently Berkhofer (1995) has been concerned at length and usefully with the question of authorial voice in history writing, and the problems of necessary partiality and prejudice, even in the most innocent of senses: what "Great Story" is being presumed, since there must be one in any historiography, however specific and localized? Solutions considered are collective volumes, under collective editorship, or the inclusion of different voices – say, native American as well as academic historian in writing the history of the United States' West – in a single volume.

It seems to me this problem is itself somewhat individualist in conception, and too focused on the writing side of the communication process: however strong and controlling a single authorial voice might be (as in the present work), any single book forms part of a community of works and scholars. If a reader has only one book to read on any given topic, he or she is indeed at the mercy of the single author's voice, and his or her prejudgements and choices. But when any single reader has multiple books, and therefore voices, to consult, there is necessarily a plurality of voice: and that is the reception situation envisaged in and for this book. This study is intended to complement other works on Southern Asia: there are more or less conventional political and social histories, oriented to modern nation-states, such as those of Kulke and Rothermund (1986) on India, De Silva (1981) on Sri Lanka, Lieberman (1984) on Burma, Kasetsiri (1976) and Wyatt

those texts to be capable of expressing. One example is the over-hasty passage from inside to outside, and vice-versa, in the case of the *Vessantara Jātaka*, mentioned earlier; another would be the usual reading of the *Cakkavatti-sīhanāda Sutta*, the "Lion's Roar on the Wheel-turning king," as a triumphalist "legitimation" of kingship, an interpretation whose simplistic myopia I will try to bring out in Chapter 6.

(1984) on Thailand, and Chandler (1992) on Cambodia; others, such as Aung Thwin (1985) on Pagan, and Mabbett and Chandler (1995) on *The Khmers*, attempt a greater degree of integration between cultural description and the chronological history of institutions and dynasties; yet others take on the area of Southeast Asia as a whole, either from the point of view of economic and political history, such as Hall (1985) and Lieberman (1993), or from a standpoint such as Reid's two-volume (1988, 1993) study of the period 1450–1680, which employs a Braudelian approach to focus not on the chronology of events but on a quantitatively based description of everyday life. Clearly none of these works, nor others of their kind, can be, separately or together, wholly adequate for getting at ideas, ideals and values; for these one turns, inevitably, to the kinds of "literary and artistic" texts on which LeGoff bases *l'histoire de l'imaginaire*, and which I take Pali sources to be. This book can complement other kinds of historiography, but it cannot offer an immediate picture of what was in people's heads, even when they thought about the kinds of issue, such as death and pleasure (in my terms, felicity), to which Braudel looks for "the 'foundations,' the underlying *structures* of civilizations." It can only offer what might have been in their heads, in so far as they thought in the manner available to us through its externalization in Pali texts. It is difficult to see how what was in people's heads could be available to us other than in texts, Pali and vernacular: making inferences from material remains, economic statistics, and other such things without guidance from indigenous texts seems hopelessly vulnerable to ethnocentrism and arbitrary subjectivity.

Although for these and other reasons this book concentrates on the Pali imaginaire, it would be a great mistake to see it as unique, hermetically sealed off from the rest of cultural production in Southern Asia. Many of the themes to be dealt with in this book – the soteriology which envisions a final, timeless escape from rebirth and temporality (Part 1), and central motifs such as the Wheel-turning King (Chapter 6), as well as relatively less significant themes such as the paradisial land of Uttarakuru, existing to the north of the cosmo-geographically central Mt. Meru, and the celestial palace-vehicles called *vimāna*-s (Chapter 4) – can be found throughout Southern Asian traditions, not merely in other kinds of Buddhism. These, and other things to be described here, are not simply parts of the Pali imaginaire but parts of Southern Asian culture in general; that is, they are parts of premodern high culture which have gradually permeated the cultural life of what Braudel referred to as "the great mass of society" during the second millennium AD, and especially in the nationalizing, and other, conditions of the last two centuries.

It is important to note also, and conversely, that the same general conditions of plausibility discussed here in relation to Pali texts – the production of culture in agrarian states and empires – were able to support a variety of different transcendental visions in polities of much the same kind, often simultaneously, in what was called earlier the Indic model of the relations between clerical-ideological and military-political power. My discussion of the material conditions of Pali Buddhist cultural production is, accordingly, not meant to "explain" it, or "explain it away," in a "reductionist" manner,[103] but to provide a realistic context for my own project of Southern Asian historiography, and to facilitate connections between it and other kinds, examples of which were just given.

So much for the methodological reasons for working with an analytical dualism between a circumscribed but comprehensive Pali imaginaire and its civilizational context(s). I want now to explore its concrete historicity a little further, by broaching the complex issue of the relation between change and/or stability in the ideological world of an imaginaire, and in the political, military, economic and other spheres. The orientalist view of "the East" as a place, in Wolf's (1982) words, of "people without history," is, alas, alive and well. The clichés are many, and deserve to be ignored: it lacked the forward-looking dynamism and "rational restlessness" of Europe;[104] time there is (or at least was, before modernity?!) cyclical rather than linear,[105] and so on. On the other hand, recent stress on indigenous agency in former European colonies can sometimes insist on seeing change in principle, for what I think are political rather than historiographic reasons. There are, to be sure, good, post-colonialist reasons for emphasizing the maleficence of stereotypical assumptions about

[103] The quotes here are meant to indicate that I am not sure what this charge means.
[104] Mann (1986: 398, 501, etc.). A trenchant, if at times exaggerated critique can be found in Blaut (1993).
[105] See Chapter 3 for remarks on time and historiography in Pali texts.

change and stability in "the East"; but much of the discussion on this issue could be had in relation to Europe also. It is primarily from the perspective of his knowledge of Europe that Duby speaks when he says, in an essay on "Ideologies in History," that

> Ideologies also perform a stabilizing role. This is obviously the case with systems of representation whose function is to guard the privileges of ruling groups; but it is also true of opposing systems which invert but nonetheless reflect the first set. The ideal social organization to which the most revolutionary ideologies still aspire is still perceived . . . as the establishment of something permanent; no utopia preaches permanent revolution. This tendency toward stability can be explained by the fact that ideological representations share with all systems of values a heaviness, an inertia, since their framework is made up of traditions.
>
> [Various factors] minimize change in ideological representations as they are passed from one generation to another. (1985: 153)

Similarly LeGoff asserts that

> certain fundamental structures persisted in European society from the fourth to the nineteenth centuries, bestowing a coherent character on a period of some fifteen centuries . . . The Middle Ages were shaped by a dominant ideology that was neither a reflection of a material base nor an idealist motor of history but an element essential to the operation of the feudal system. (1988: 21)

And it is presumably on Europe also, at least in the first instance given his own major field of concern as a historian, that Braudel bases his claim that a structure of the *longue durée* is both a "construct" (*assemblage*), a form of "archictecture" for the historian, and a "reality" which time "uses and abuses over long periods": such structures are "hindrances [that] stand as limits . . . which man and his experiences can scarcely go beyond. Just think of the difficulty of breaking out of certain geographical frameworks, certain biological realities, even particular spiritual constraints: mental frameworks too can be long-term prisons."[106]

[106] (1980: 31, translation emended.) The English version obscures matters somewhat: it translates the original (1965: 50–1), *ne peuvent guère s'affranchir,* "can scarcely go beyond" as "cannot go [beyond]." This is too strong, implying a greater determinism and relativism than Braudel's text admits. It also adds a definite article to the final phrase, *prisons de longue durée,* giving "prisons of the *longue durée,*" which erases his play on words – that mental frameworks are like long prison sentences – and removes the implicit suggestion that just as prisoners are free to react as they wish to the conditions imposed on them, and will or may one day go free, so those under the sway of an elite, perhaps "dominant" ideology, are free to react to it as they wish, and may one day escape its hold.

Although these remarks by Duby, LeGoff and Braudel may perhaps overstate the stability and influence of elite ideologies in premodernity, they do serve to remind one that there are differential rates of change in historical time. In Southern Asia one can find as many changes on the level of *histoire événementielle* as anywhere else; some of them – the rise and fall of dynasties and empires – were mentioned in the political biography of Pali given above. Conversely, some kinds of long-term historical structures are permanent, such as the geographical-territorial conditions of the way the relationship of sovereignty to land was conceived differently in the island of Sri Lanka and mainland Southeast Asia; this unalterable difference can give rise to the same style of meditation on the *longue durée* as is found in the famous opening section of Braudel's (1972) *The Mediterranean and the Mediterranean World in the Age of Philip II.* The question of change is an empirical one, and opinions can rationally differ on the importance and extent of historical change at different levels and in different contexts. Aung Thwin, for example, has repeatedly argued that Burmese society before the British conquest was characterized by stability rather than change at the long-term level, despite all the changes in event-history: he writes that in

> the classical Burmese state . . . in the entire pre-colonial era . . . five major institutions of Burmese society persisted to affect thought and behaviour, hence history and events. [They were] merit as a primary path to salvation within the context of Theravāda Buddhism; "redistribution" as the predominant economic system; patron-client ties and "cellular" organization as the essence of social and administrative hierarchies; hierarchy as the dominant principle of justice and law; and *kamma* as the ultimate legitimator of authority . . . [These] were as important to thirteenth century Burmese society as they were to nineteenth century Burma. (1983: 46)
>
> We cannot assume that Burmese society changed in fundamental ways just because a great deal of time had elapsed or because there had been political and dynastic upheavals. As [Stephen Jay] Gould wrote with regard to the function of time in the development of the human and other animal species, "[it] is a matrix for both change and stability". It is thus neutral and not, as often assumed by most historians trained in the west, "a motor for progress." (1991: 593; cp. 1995: 87–91)

This approach can be taken to lead to the clearly undesirable generalization that Burma was entirely static until the British conquest, as Lieberman (1987, 1991) charges, who prefers to stress the slow but continuous linear change brought about, *inter alia*, by the increasing volume and economic importance of maritime trade, and the increasing centralization of political power. Both Lieberman and Reid (1988, 1993) see the adoption of Theravāda Buddhism by kings as itself an important element in this increasing centralization.

Indeed, a story can be told of how evolution in maritime technology and trade brought about changes in the pattern of state formation throughout Southern Asia (Hall 1985), as centers of political and military power were affected by the growth in long-distance sea trade, which was added to the earlier and continuing pattern of irrigation-aided agriculture and inland riverine trade as sources of the necessary surplus wealth. One example is the gradual movement of Burmese capital cities from the inland irrigation-based polity of Pagan in Upper Burma (Aung Thwin 1990) to the Lower Burma coastal capitals of Pegu and modern Rangoon. Another is the movement of Siamese imperial capital cities south, along the Chao Phraya river to its mouth and the sea, from Sukhotai to Ayudhya to Bangkok; for the same reasons there emerged in insular Southeast Asia city-states in harbor towns and at strategic points along sea-routes (Lieberman 1993). An analogous account can be given of how political power in Sri Lanka changed as a result of developments in the technology of its resource base: for over a millennium the island was ruled from two capital cities in the northern Dry Zone, which depended on an extensive system of irrigation (Gunawardana 1971), first from Anurādhapura, between the second century BC to the tenth AD, and then from Polonnaruva in the next two centuries. But the irrigation system collapsed, thanks in part to warfare, both with South Indian forces and between contending parties in the island itself. It was replaced by weaker concentrations of power to the south and southwest, more dependent on trade, and more vulnerable both to forces from mainland India to the north, and later to European colonial powers along the western seaboard (De Silva 1981: 17–129).

How is one to decide between, or at least balance continuity and change in the Southern Asian long term? One solution would be to apply Braudel's eirenic remarks: "Movement and stability complement and explain one another. We may choose without risk either approach to the civilizations of the Mediterranean, even if we take what is at first sight their least significant aspect, that miscellany of trivia and daily happenings which rises like a cloud of dust from any living civilization" (1972: 757–8). Perhaps it might be more fruitful in the Southern Asian case, about which we have so much less information, to apply analytical dualism, and ask about change in ideology and in other spheres separately. It seems to me that the sub-section of Southern Asian civilization I am calling the Pali imaginaire was in itself for the most part an unchanging ideology, which was repeatedly adopted by kings in changing circumstances. A telling instance of the gap between ideology and practical knowledge is provided by Gunawardana (1987). He shows that in Sri Lanka, from the second century AD, there existed increasingly accurate empirical knowledge of geography, thanks to the extensive maritime and trade contacts which existed with both west (the Roman Empire and later Islamic areas) and east (Insular Southeast Asia, China); traditional cosmo-geography, however (to be discussed in 4.1.a), retained its imagined world of four continents, one in each direction, and seven concentric circular oceans, all arranged around Mt. Meru, with the hierarchy of heavens beginning on its slopes and extending up into increasingly rarefied space above.

Elsewhere in Southern Asian civilization, a powerful model of a changeless realm of discourse imperfectly transmitted in and through the changing world of humanity, the Sanskritic *śāstra* traditions, held that what exists among us as an actual text is a "direct or indirect, complete or abridged revelation" of a transcendent *śāstra,* whose transcendence (*apauruṣeyatva,* the fact of not being composed in time by any individual person, human or divine) was modeled on that of the eternal Veda (Pollock 1985: 516). In the Brahmanical tradition, this paradigm of knowledge led to a denial of history, or at least of the production of historiography as a discursive genre (Pollock 1989). As Ludden puts it:

Sanskrit texts collected under the heading of *dharmaśāstras* were composed over many centuries, during which the world of their authors and interpreters changed dramatically; yet these texts comprehend a static, closed world of morality and culture. Inscriptions, *vamcavalis* [*sic,* genealogies], epics, *bhakti* lyrics, chronicles, *prabandas* [*sic,* treatises], and other texts, in addition to visual evidence from architecture and archaeology, reflect cultural activity organized inside that closed world. (94: 19; cf. Pollock 1993)

In Theravāda Buddhism – unlike Sanskrit Buddhism, which in this respect resembles more the Brahmanical learned tradition in its attitude to history and canonical authority – there was perhaps the strongest commitment to history as a mode of knowledge and legitimation in premodern Southern Asia outside of Islam (Collins, 1994ms.). Nonetheless the epistemology and ontology of Theravāda (on which see Chapters 3 and 5) held that the changes of history are but variations on a timelessly given pattern of reality (that is, the ensemble of Existents, *dhammā*, denoted by the naturally given Pali lexicon). It is the role of Buddhas to rediscover it from time to time, and the task of the historically instantiated Teaching owed to any individual Buddha, his Dispensation (*sāsana*), to preserve it. Such a traditionalizing, conservative ideology, although never in fact immune to change, often reacts to the fact of newness and change by emphasizing traditional themes ever more firmly. This can occur even in recent times, where iconographic developments in northern Thailand have been seen as an attempt to preserve at least the cultural memory of traditional Buddhist cosmology (Ferguson and Johannsen 1976). The dissemination of the traditional cosmology of the Three Worlds treatise by Siamese kings at the turbulent end of the eighteenth century, discussed in section II.c, is an example from the late-traditional/early-modern period.

The main contents of traditional Pali texts remained constant, but not wholly so. In this book Parts 1 and 2 for the most part proceed ahistorically, since my concern there is with the content and dynamics of the Pali imaginaire, not in what historical developments can be seen in it. But developments there were, albeit that the changes are additions and increased emphases rather than unprecedented innovations. Chapter 1 shows how the concept of nirvana becomes increasingly determinate in the tradition of scholastic texts, and is exactly positioned in the categories of the *Abhidhamma* as a *dhamma*, here meaning a separately existing object of consciousness, to which access is gained through the mind, conceived as a sixth sense. Chapter 2 discusses the puzzling fact that the image of nirvana as a city, absent from the canonical texts, becomes in the commentarial period (fifth to sixth centuries AD) and thereafter a ubiquitous trope, so familiar as to be often enough a dead metaphor. Chapter 3 describes how temporal distanciation becomes increasingly evident in the genre of Pali *vaṃsa* texts, both quantitatively, in the lengths of time textualized, and qualitatively in the intensity of their textualization. Chapter 4 presents the unified cosmology which had developed by the time of the commentarial period, correlating the vertical hierarchy of heavens with horizontal spatial-material geography as well as with states of consciousness, as had been done earlier. Chapter 5 shows that whereas in the earlier texts the logical possibility of multiple Buddhas, past and future, is clearly recognized, but no individual figure is much developed beyond being given a name, the future Buddha Metteyya later becomes a very significant figure. The coincidence of two Great Men – a Wheel-turning King and a Buddha at the same time – is, one or two culturally insignificant cases aside, unique, and is part of the rationale for speaking in that regard of a Buddhist millennialism. Chapter 6 argues that the irony and moral criticism evident to a modern reader in early texts such as the *Aggañña* and *Cakkavatti-sīhanāda Sutta*-s is lost in the traditional imaginaire. Chapter 7 attests how, as Buddhist texts come to reflect wider patterns of cultural life and civilizational modes of representation, a story such as that of Vessantara, unlike what has come down to us as the earliest texts, can incorporate the difficulties as well as the heroics of nirvana-seeking.

So it would be possible, were I looking to trace historical development in the Pali imaginaire, to do so. But such developments would be minor, and irrelevant, given the main concern of this book with that imaginaire, namely what was called earlier the cultural logic of asceticism, and the discourse of felicity into whose wider world of representation the discursive analog of asceticism – nirvana – enters as a constitutive element.

III. NIRVANA AND THE DISCOURSE OF FELICITY EU-TOPIA AND OU-TOPIA

Section I outlined the perspective from which this book looks at Buddhism, in relation to stages of world history and to the study of civilizations, and in the light of an analytical account of ideology and power in agrarian states. Section II tried to set out the nature and historiographical status of the Pali imaginaire, as seen from the empirical disciplines of Indology and Southern Asian history, and in the light of certain theoretical and methodological choices in sociology and social history. Section III continues to make connections between my work and that of other scholars, but I begin now to move more directly to center stage the specific textual subject matter of this book and my own conception of how best to set about understanding it. To that end I first return, in the first two subsections, to some basic features of tributary, civilization-producing societies, and the material dimension of aspirations to felicity in them; and then turn to some conceptually fundamental, and for some readers no doubt wholly familiar matters of Buddhist doctrine.

III.a. Poverty, pipedreams and perfectibility: ideal individuals and culture-producing collectivities

Section I.a cited Berger on the irony of the concept of an agricultural "surplus," used in accounts of the development of cities, larger-scale political formations, and civilization: for peasants, the "surplus" had to be produced and given up first, before they could feed themselves. Rösener, writing of European peasantry, sounds the same note:

> After many a peasant had fulfilled his numerous obligations to the local lord and the Church, there was barely enough left for him and his family to survive . . . Exposed to the perils of the elements, famine, animal disease and warfare, a large number of Late Medieval peasants lived at the edge of an abyss . . .
> [R]ecent investigation in the fields of social and economic history has shown that mass indigence, undernourishment and starvation were basic components of social life prior to the mid-nineteenth century. (1994: 80, 143)

James Scott, citing C. H. Tawney on China and referring to various parts of Southeast Asia, generalizes the point: "Lilliputian plots, traditional techniques, the vagaries of weather and the tribute in cash, labor and kind exacted by the state brought the specter of hunger and death, and occasionally famine, to the gates of every village" (1976: 1). Harbans Mukhia, considering at some length the question "Was there feudalism in Indian history?" concludes there was not: premodern Indian agrarian history was characterized by "high fertility of land, low subsistence level and free peasant production" (1995[81]: 130). "Far less labour was required for agricultural operations [in India]. Moreover these operations could be spread over a much longer period in the course of the year ... [and so there was not] a highly concentrated demand for large amounts of labour in short periods" (ibid.: 121–2). Hence there was no "extraneous control over the peasant's process of production" as there was in Europe, and the Indian peasant's dependence on his lord was not "rooted in his very conditions of labour" as was the European's (ibid.: 113; cp. 94). But

> If the Indian peasant's control over the process of production differentiated him from his medieval European counterpart, there is little reason to believe that he also enjoyed a higher standard of living. We have noted earlier that nature in India allowed the peasant to subsist off very meagre resources; what nature permitted as the minimum level was made the maximum by social organisation. There are continual references in our sources to the heavy demand of revenue and other taxes from the peasants and the consequent miserable level of their existence (ibid.: 127–8).

It would be wrong, however, to assume that, without the rapacity of tribute-takers, all would have been well, and all manner of thing would have been well. Had all members of agrarian society been filled with the milk of human kindness, and the extraction of a surplus restricted, after rational and collective discussion, to such necessary matters as the provision of social order (and art?), a vast amount of human suffering could have been avoided. There were nonetheless objective limits to the creation of wealth, at least as seen from a standpoint after the Industrial Revolution.[107]

E. A. Wrigley contrasts premodern organic and modern industrialized societies, to explain "Why poverty was inevitable in traditional societies";[108] he examines "the constraints common to all traditional societies which meant that the ambition to achieve a general escape from poverty belonged to the realm of pipe-dreams rather than policy" (1992: 91–2). In practice it was possible for some to be wealthy, and individuals who were not could hope for changed circumstances, perhaps in a future life, on earth or in heaven, in which they would be rich while others were poor. But before the enormously increased capacity to produce wealth brought about by the Industrial Revolution, generalized

[107] This standpoint is also one of pollution, consumerism, and other joys of modern life – the point being made here is not that industrial society is better than agrarian society: just wealthier.

[108] This summarizes longer accounts he has given elsewhere: see Wrigley (1987: especially 1–17 and 1988: especially 1–33).

prosperity – as opposed to subsistence – could only be a pipe dream, not a realistic policy goal in the empirical, pragmatic world.[109] Material wealth was only a possibility for some, so any ideology which enunciated cosmic and social order had necessarily to include minority good fortune and majority (at least relative) ill-fortune in its matrix.

Wrigley identifies various reasons for agrarian society's poverty: for example, before the exploitation of mineral fuels, notably coal, to provide energy for industrial machines, the organic fuel available to supply power to human muscles (i.e. food), and to the simpler technology then possessed (wood, mostly) was, like everything else in the natural world, both limited and fluctuating. An important point emerges from an argument usually attributed to Malthus, which

> expressed in its crudest form, is that adventitious improvements in living standards among the labouring poor will always prove short-lived because they will tend to cause mortality to fall and fertility to rise, thus increasing the rate of population growth, and the resultant additional supply of labour will soon force wages back towards some conventional minimum . . . [But] the argument attributed to Malthus usually fails to do justice to the nature and subtlety of his thinking. He asked to be granted two *postulata* – that food is necessary to support existence and that "the passion between the sexes" is a constant . . . Interpreted in an extreme and mechanical way, [his] schema can lead to the assertion that populations are kept constantly close to a precipice over which some fraction will plunge from time to time because of a chance event, such as a run of poor harvests. (1992: 96)

When Malthus' idea is applied to actual societies, account has to be taken of differences in marriage practices – whether marriage was "a moveable feast responsive to economic pressures" (i.e. whether in harder times marriages were contracted at a later age) – and whether or not "celibacy was comparatively common" (1992: 97). This is not the place to attempt a study of these matters in the premodern societies through which the trajectory of Theravāda Buddhism was traced earlier; but there is, no doubt, a story to tell of the interaction between factors of this kind and Buddhist monasticism: for example as a temporary, pre-marriage *rite de passage* among young men in mainland Southeast Asia. Late

[109] I find this historical perspective a helpful way to approach the collection of essays on *Ethics, Wealth and Salvation*, edited by Sizemore and Swearer (1990).

marriages and widespread celibacy could allow food production to grow, in favorable circumstances, without an increase in population to offset the gains made, and so a universal Malthusian precipice scenario would be inappropriate. Thus

> The standard of living prevailing in a traditional society might therefore vary substantially from a "worst case" in which many people lived on the margin of bare subsistence to a situation in which even the labouring poor were reasonably well-buffered against outright starvation and most families could secure the four main necessities of life [food, clothing, shelter and fuel] and even aspire to modest comforts. (1992: 97)

This book uses the term *felicity* to refer to a wide range of things which can all be seen as forms of salvation. Perhaps one could speak of aspirations to comfort, of the modest and more ambitious kinds, and of the reassurance that the universe is such as to contain many kinds of comfort, including the possibility of one which is entirely secure from misfortune.

This kind of focus on the material conditions of elite ideologies such as that of the Pali imaginaire, its framework of plausibility, provides the crucial background to the claim made earlier that scholarship should not base its approach to premodern Buddhism on what is privileged within the ideology – the individual quest for nirvana – but on an analysis which sees that ideology as the creation and vehicle of a culture-producing collectivity. The relevant collectivity was, in the long-term historical view, first a dominant class (or at least elements of it), for whom the Pali imaginaire, when adopted, was a source of cohesiveness and morale; and second, wider numbers of people in the dominated classes, as the earlier high culture spread downwards. In either case the ascetic quest for nirvana could only ever be a matter of immediate concern for a minority;[110] it was quantitatively marginal, in the gamut of imagined felicities as in actual practice, but it was qualitatively central, through its syntactic role in the discourse of felicity as a whole. If there is, to borrow a phrase from Ernst Bloch, a principle of hope in humanity, or in part of it at least, it is only common sense to see that the illuminations it offers will be refracted through the prism of the embodied imagination, and that this imagination will be constituted in and through the lived

[110] To some extent this has changed in Buddhist modernism; see Gombrich and Obeyesekere (1988).

world. The picture of pre-industrial societies sketched here in very broad brush-strokes could and should be augmented by more detailed studies: Crone's (1989) survey of *Pre-Industrial Societies* would be a good place to start. But enough has perhaps been said to suggest what I see as the necessary, historically realist background against which we, situated on the pinnacle (or cliff-edge) of modernity, can see traditional Buddhist felicities. Studies of Buddhist hopes for salvation usually concentrate on the most ambitious of them, the transcendence of desire and death by the heroic Conqueror (*jina*), as in Horner's (75[36]) *The Early Buddhist Theory of Man Perfected.* Perfectibility may be a universal, or at least very general human ideal;[111] but I want to see nirvana not as an example of a free-floating, ahistorical ideal, but as one aspect of a congeries of Buddhist felicities imagined by flesh-and-blood human beings in the material-historical world. And the point about premodern poverty is that collective, universal material wealth, of the kind industrial society made possible (though never actual), was not a possible goal in that world.

Empathetic understanding of the past requires not only that one think oneself into another world, but also that one make an effort to think away certain aspects of one's own lived world. These reflections on poverty and the framework of plausibility should, I think, affect modern evaluations of the non-nirvanic felicities elaborated in the Pali imaginaire. When one encounters Buddhist texts which describe, as objects of religious ambition, conditions of natural abundance, unlimited food, physical beauty, forest paradises, earthly and heavenly palaces sparkling with jewels and precious metals, conditions of peace on earth and goodwill to all; and when one encounters historians or anthropologists who report that nirvana was and is the immediate goal of very few people or no-one, it is easy for a nonhistorical modern mind to conclude, as is so often done, that "all Buddhists should *really* aspire to extinction in nirvana, but the overwhelming majority prefer the more materialistic and hedonistic goals of rebirth in heaven, or as a rich person on earth." This is an anachronistic, myopic, even inhuman

[111] See Passmore (1970). This work deals in passing with Buddhist ideas, approaching them in the spirit of its time, the late sixties. Oddly, perhaps, or at least so it seems with the benefit of hindsight, Passmore wrote (p. 304 note) that the epoch was experiencing "the Buddhicization of Europe." For some remarks on the idea of perfection in Buddhism, see the Critical Discussion after Chapter 5 on the definition of millennialism.

evaluation: sitting, in conditions of affluence, in a modern armchair, or at a modern desk, and constructing a pure, "spiritual" Buddhism which soars above the trivial business of mundane, imaginable happiness. It assumes that the work of understanding consists in finding an ahistorical answer to the question "what would it be like for me – as I am, now, in the modern West – to be a Buddhist?" There are certainly many circumstances in which this would be a perfectly good, indeed necessary question, notably when Theravāda is presented confessionally by Buddhist modernists; but these are not the circumstances in which the discussion of this book is set.

Wrigley claims:

That poverty was the lot of the large majority of people in all or almost all societies before the industrial revolution is widely recognised. Poverty is a general and rather abstract concept. Its reality was bitter and particular: a hungry child, apathetic from lack of food; a shivering family unable to buy fuel in a harsh winter; the irritation of parasites in dirty clothing and the accompanying sores and stench. The extent and severity of poverty is difficult to express in quantitative terms for lack of relevant data in most cases, but that the poor were very numerous and that they suffered greatly at times is an assertion unlikely to be widely challenged. (1992: 91)

It may be that some features of this picture, based on data about European peasantry, would not apply in quite the same way to Southern Asia: winters, for example, are in most places not so harsh so regularly, although perhaps monsoons and bacterial disease might balance the account somewhat. The monk Māleyya would agree with Wrigley: visiting the Tusita heaven, he was asked by the future Buddha Metteyya about circumstances on earth, and replied succinctly, "The rich are few, the poor are many; the happy are few, the unhappy are many; the attractive are few, the unattractive are many; the long-lived are few, the short-lived are many" (Appendix 4, p. 621).

Pali texts are well aware of economic and social stratification, and the similarities and differences between rich and poor. A standard passage contrasts them:

One person is born into an inferior family: an outcaste family, of hunters, bamboo-workers, cart-makers or garbage-carriers, which is poor, with little to eat and drink, scratching a living, where food and clothing are

hard to find. He is ugly, swarthy, undersized, sickly – blind or deformed or lame or crippled; he doesn't have food, drink, clothes, a vehicle, garlands, perfumes or ointments, nowhere to lay (his head), nothing for a lamp (to see by).
Another person is born into a superior family: a wealthy kṣatriya (noble) or Brahmin family or one of the bourgeoisie[112], which is rich and powerful, with many possessions, plenty of gold and silver, with all the appurtenances of prosperity, and abounding in money and (stored) grain. He is handsome, attractive, winsome, with a beautiful complexion. (Vin IV 6, S I 93, A I 107, Pp 51; cp. Horner 1940: 173–4)

One text illustrates an argument that the karmic result of some deeds depends on the doer with a reflection on socioeconomic status: a poor man will go to jail for theft, whether the amount is small or great, whereas a rich man will not, for the same crime (A III 250–1). In one thing, of course, the lives of rich and poor are alike: they both end in death (e.g. Ja IV 127), "rich and poor alike feel the touch of death" (M II 73 with Ps III 308).

III.b. The traditional "problem" of nirvana

The traditional "problem" of nirvana refers both to a conceptual difficulty and to what has been, ever since the European discovery of Buddhism in the early nineteenth century, a prime site for cultural stereotypes. To begin with the conceptual difficulty: in common with other Indian religious traditions, Buddhism holds that all sentient creatures pass through a series of lives: variously as human beings, gods, animals and several kinds of spirit. This process, called *saṃsāra*, "the round of rebirth," is seen as the realm from which salvation, better said release or liberation (*mokṣa*), is to be sought. Different traditions understand the process differently, and have produced various notions of the "soul" or "self" which transmigrates and is released. Buddhism, however, denies the existence of any continuing self or soul, holding that the process of rebirth – a word which modern Buddhists writing in English prefer to "reincarnation" – involves an individual but ever-changing continuum of impermanent and impersonal elements (Collins 1982). Nirvana, literally "blowing out," "going out" or "quenching" (of a

[112] *Gahapati-mahāsālā*, wealthy merchants or landowners (Chakravarti 1987: 64ff.). Kṣatriyas, Brahmins and Gahapatis wielded military-political, ideological and economic power respectively.

flame: 2.1.a) refers to the cessation of this process, to the ending of all conditioned, impermanent and unsatisfactory elements of existence.

For many interpretative purposes it is vital in reading Buddhist accounts of nirvana to realize that the word can refer not only to the state of the enlightened person after death, but also to the state realized within that person's lifetime (as with the Buddha at the age of thirty-five, before he began his forty-five–year teaching career). It is conceptually easy – whether or not one believes such a condition to be possible – to understand the idea of a psychological state, and of a continuous series of such states, characterized not by greed, hatred and delusion (to use standard Buddhist technical terms) but by selflessness, equanimity and compassion, with no suffering apart from the inconvenience attendant on physical ills.[113] The traditional "problem" of nirvana concerns rather the question, "What happens after the death of an enlightened Buddhist saint?" It has often seemed that the answer can only be one of two positions: either nirvana is some kind of "super-existence," such that the denial of self, the refusal to speak of any eternal essence, must not mean what it seems to mean; or else, the doctrine does indeed mean what it seems to mean, and so nirvana must be nothingness, extinction. The Buddhist doctrinal position can be stated simply. Nirvana is indeed the ultimate religious goal, a state of release from all suffering and impermanence, but no language or concepts can properly describe it. It is *atakkāvacara*, "inaccessible to (discursive) thought" (It 37, Ud-a 391). In particular, it cannot be described as the state of a (or *the*) self. Modern Buddhist writers use the analogy of a tortoise unable to describe to a fish the experience of dry land.[114] Such an appeal to indescribability, or ineffability, is, of course, very common in religion: indeed, as is argued in the Introduction to Part 1, I think it must eventually be made in relation to any notion of final salvation, Christian, Hindu or other. The attitude is rarely, however, quite so consistent and uncompromising as in the case of the Buddhist nirvana.

The problem of final nirvana was raised in the early centuries of

[113] See Chapter 1.2.b; one might also think of Enlightenment as a skill: Collins (1994).

[114] For example, Rahula (1967: 35). The same point is made in relation to tadpoles and frogs in the well-known film "Footprint of the Buddha," in the BBC/Time-Life "Long Search" series.

Buddhism, as evidenced in a dialogue allegedly recording a conversation between the monk Nāgasena and a second-century BC Bactrian Greek king called Milinda.[115] In what is often called the "Hindu Renaissance" of the nineteenth and twentieth centuries, it was usual to say that the Buddha was only concerned to deny the small, egoistic self, not the grand Cosmic Self whose identity with the Absolute (*brahman*), was the truth of nirvana just as it was of the salvation taught in the *Upaniṣad*-s. On the other hand, many of Buddhism's opponents in premodern India claimed that nirvana must be nonexistence (Narain 1963: 312–3). Welbon (1968) provides a history of modern western scholarship on nirvana, charting the oscillation between these two interpretations, which Buddhism would call eternalism and annihilationism (2.2.a).

Although scholarly understanding of nirvana, in this oscillation between what are often called, misleadingly, "positive" and "negative" views of it, has been continuous with Southern Asian (non-Buddhist) approaches, it also developed from quite distinctive roots in nineteenth-century Europe. Nirvana was the subject of protracted and vigorous debate in popular journals and magazines, as well as in works of scholarship, as Philip Almond (1988: 104–6) has described. In 1870 the Unitarian Richard Armstrong wrote: "It is the opinion of one . . . who for a score of years has laboured amid the poorest of the London poor, that that great population ignores God altogether, and looks to death with longing, not as a better birth, but the end, deliverance, annihilation. These are our English Buddhists. *Their* hope too, is Nirvana." In 1850, the *Prospective Review*, a journal not destined for a wide readership among the London poor, thought on the contrary that the Buddha meant by nirvana "no more than what Wordsworth sings – 'Man who is from God sent forth, Must yet again to God return.'" Similarly in 1857 Francis Barham wrote that nirvana was "deification, apotheosis, absorption of the soul into God, but not its annihilation"; and earlier, in 1817, William Ward had also described it as absorption, but "since Buddhists reject the doctrine of a separate Supreme Spirit," added that "it is difficult to say what are their ideas of absorption." By the end of the century, Almond

[115] I.e. Menander, in the *Milinda-pañha*: see Norman 1983: 110–11, and for parts of their debate Chapter 1.3.

says, the annihilationists had the upper hand. In 1884–5 the Countess of Jersey devoted an article to "Buddhism and Christianity" in the *National and English Review* (motto: "What is the Tory Party, unless it represents National feeling?"). She was neither the first nor the last to hold that "Buddhism, *as he* [the Buddha] *taught it*, is not the religion of the five hundred millions who are said to reverence his shrines. It is impossible that it should be. Such minds as in the West embrace the Religion of Humanity, may in the East embrace pure Buddhism."[116] On the subject of nirvana she was interestingly inconclusive:

> The precise meaning . . . of Nirvána is still warmly debated amongst the learned, and I shall not venture to pass an opinion. I would only, with all due deference, ask the opponents of the annihilation theory two questions, i.e. What remained to be absorbed? and Into what was it absorbed? . . . I presume I shall be told in answer to my second question, that whatever did remain was absorbed into the Kosmos, but I do not know that this makes it any clearer, or that to be taken into a soulless universe is really distinguishable from annihilation. However this may be, Buddha probably held out to the Hindús the hope for the future which answers their desire. Races left to themselves have generally evolved from their own imaginations a heaven suited to their human tendencies . . . but none who have attempted to draw aside the clouds overhanging futurity seem to have fixed their hopes on so melancholy an ending as that which the Hindús regard as the acme of bliss (ibid.: 586–7).
>
> [She ends more assertively:] We must now bid him farewell. If Gautama Buddha built his house on the sand, it was no ignoble building, and we may trust that long ere this he has found a better home than Nirvána (ibid.: 591).

That the niceties of Buddhist thought should have been the subject of so much, and such heated, if sometimes bemused attention in nineteenth-century Europe may seem odd; but it helps to set the debate about nirvana in the religious context of that place and time. MacDannell and Lang (1988) show how the Christian conception of heaven changed significantly in the eighteenth and nineteenth centuries. Some writers proposed the new idea that family life, including sexual intercourse, continued in heaven, in contrast to the standard earlier view that celestial life was celibate. But what concerns me most here is a difference of opinion as to whether the heavenly life was one of rest or of activity. Whereas

[116] (1885: 588); partly cited in Almond (1988: 39).

earlier images of heaven, they say, had conceived celestial life as static and theocentric, consisting in a timeless Beatific Vision or endless singing of praises, as in a church service, the new understandings, influenced no doubt by industrialization and the idea of progress, held that the saved continued to work and to improve. For example (1988: 278–9, 279–80):

In 1857 the popular Baptist preacher Charles Spurgeon (1834–1892) cautioned that "the idea of heaven as a place of rest will just suit some indolent professors." Idleness, for Spurgeon, existed as one of humanity's worst sins, almost as evil as drunkenness . . . Heaven, as the divine summary of the goodness of earthly life, must be a place of work . . .

The Encyclopaedia of the Presbyterian Church (1884) mused that if heaven was "a state of inaction," we should as soon think that it was also "a nursery of vice." Levi Gilbert (1852–1917) argued that "enforced idleness is one of the worst forms of punishment known" and so heaven could not possibly be "celestial lubberland – a paradise of tramps."

Although these speculations about nirvana and heaven can seem painfully or amusingly naive now, according to Geoffrey Rowell these and other related

nineteenth-century debates about eternal punishment and the future life are not . . . to be dismissed as peripheral matters. They bring into sharp focus the gradual breakdown of an accepted pattern of human understanding, and provide a case-study of the ways in which Christian writers and thinkers still committed to that tradition of understanding criticized and attempted to renew that tradition, often at the cost to themselves of much agonizing doubt and questioning. (74: viii)

Thus the nineteenth-century European debate about nirvana, scholarly and nonscholarly, took place in a context of self-doubt and change within Christian culture, with a new but not entirely self-confident emphasis on salvation as a state of active, energetic self-improvement.

This context makes more comprehensible the channels into which understanding and evaluation of nirvana were directed. According to Almond (1988: 49–50):

The indolent Oriental mind was also thought of as the cause of the Buddhist doctrine of Nirvana, conceived of as a passionless, emotionless rest where the tired soul dreamlessly slumbers. Nirvana, wrote Fannie Feudge, "is the summum bonum of the Buddhist, the very *ne plus ultra* of the indolent East Indian's ideas of happiness here or hereafter." The desire for rest among Orientals was for [Graham] Sandberg the reason for Buddhists fixing upon the ideal of Nirvana. Clearly without any fear of contradiction, he felt able to declare that anyone with any experience of Oriental peoples: "will confess that the one idea of the highest happiness they possess is of rest – absolute immovable rest. Let a Hindu lie as a log and sleep, he is then deliciously, intensely, happy . . . With the natural tendency of the Hindu philosopher to imagine nothing logical unless pressed forward to the utmost extremity, even though it involves the *reductio ad absurdum*, the Sanskritic Buddhist made Nirvana his acme of absolute painlessness and rest".

Thence also, in a trope still very much alive in popular, and even some academic accounts of Buddhism, comes the idea that an earlier, "negative" construal of nirvana along these lines was replaced in Mahāyāna Buddhism by the "positive" goal of the Bodhisattva, tirelessly and self-sacrificially working for the benefit of all beings.[117] It was not noticed that Mahāyāna was almost always dealing with a quite different goal, enlightenment without any final nirvana.[118]

Part 1 tries to show that the fundamental mistake in previous discussions of nirvana in the Theravāda tradition has been the attempt to produce a quasi-Buddhist account, an account which accepts Buddhist conceptual presuppositions but not the conclusions which Buddhists have drawn from them, nor respects the silences which they have preserved. The presuppositions of Buddhist thought precisely and deliberately disallow any resolution of the eternalism/annihilationism dichotomy. In order to construct an account of nirvana which does not rely on Buddhist presuppositions I start here in the Introduction to describe the wider category of the Buddhist discourse of felicity.

III.c. The varieties of Buddhist salvation: action, imagination, discourse

The issue of a dynamic between the local and trans-local has been raised already. Section I.c described two varieties of elite-civilizational articulation in agrarian states: the trans-local and trans-temporal ordering of the universe in cosmology and soteriology, and of society in the discursive enunciation of both "political" and

[117] This is not, it must be admitted, unlike some of the attitudes in some Mahāyāna texts, such as the *Saddharma-puṇḍarīka Sūtra* and Śāntideva's *Bodhicāryāvatāra*.

[118] Mahāyāna thought about nirvana is not without its own difficulties: see Williams (1989: 52–4, 181–4).

"religious" authority. Section II.d traced trans-localism in the political sphere, in the spread of Pali Buddhism across the times and spaces of premodern Southern Asia. This section discusses trans-localism in the sphere of religion, using that word of both what I call *soteriology* and *localized supernaturalism.*

Bryan Wilson uses the idea of salvation in a very broad, sociological sense:

> Whatever may be its theological content, for the sociologist salvation has meaning only as an experience in this world. Men may seek salvation from evil conceived in many forms – from anxiety; illness; inferiority feelings; grief; fear of death; concern for the social order. What they seek may be healing; the elimination of evil agents; a sense of access to power; the enhancement of status; increase of prosperity; the promise of life hereafter, or reincarnation [or liberation from rebirth – S.C.], or resurrection from the grave, or attention from posterity; the transformation of the social order (including the restoration of a real or imagined past social order). The common core of all these specific forms of salvation is the demand for reassurance. (1973: 492)

Elsewhere (1982: 27ff.) he speaks of the concern for salvation as a manifest function of religion, as opposed to whatever latent functions may be perceived by sociologists or others; and he distinguishes between "spiritual" conceptions of salvation, such as nirvana or the kingdom of god, and "particularistic" conceptions. The content of the former is variable, but all members of the category

> are metaphysical, and the means to their attainment are insusceptible of rational justification or pragmatic test. In this they differ from particularistic conceptions of salvation, in which specific help is sought – cures; protection; temporal well-being. By promoting spiritual conceptions of salvation, to which empirical proofs are irrelevant . . . the higher religions assert their difference from the purely magical and the local. (1982: 29)

(Wilson is fully aware, of course, that ideas, words, objects, etc. connected to the "spiritual" forms of salvation are everywhere used for local instrumental-material ends.) Spiritual and particularistic forms of salvation are best thought of as two ends of a spectrum. On the one hand, there are matters of ultimate concern,[119] where

[119] This phrase, from Paul Tillich, is sometimes offered as a definition of religion; but rather than being a useful definition of all the things we can legitimately call religious, it is an indication of the restricted range – sometimes to vanishing point – which supernaturalism has come to have in modern society.

what Gellner calls a "generic, all-purpose salvation" (1988: 91), offers "an escape from an overall intolerable condition, rather than merely the rectification of a specific ailment or complaint" (1988: 80). On the other there are matters of immediate concern, concrete physical or psychological ills for which practical solutions are sought.

Mandelbaum (1966), writing mainly but not only of South Asia, refers to these two ends of the spectrum of "salvation" as "transcendental" and "pragmatic" "complexes":

> The transcendental complex . . . is concerned with the ultimate purposes of man. The pragmatic complex, by contrast, is used for local exigencies, for personal benefit, for individual welfare. While acts of the transcendental complex are directed toward such concerns as the proper fate of the soul after death and the maintenance of the social order, the pragmatic looks to the curing of a sick child, the location of a lost valuable, victory in a local tussle.

Weightman (1978) sees the "maintenance of social order" in the Hindu case as not falling wholly into the transcendental category, and so adds to Mandelbaum's dichotomy a third, mediating (or, for many Hindus, encompassing) form, the *dharmik* . Gombrich (1988), not surprisingly in the Theravāda Buddhist case where salvation is an individual matter, opposes "soteriology" to "communal" religion, arguing that the main emphasis of Buddhism is the former. David Gellner (1992), in relation to Newari Buddhism, prefers "soteriology" and "this-worldly" religion, the latter having both "communal" and (individual or collective) "instrumental" forms. The terminology of all these suggestions cannot easily be harmonized, particularly since in the Hindu case there can be genuine disagreement (between Hindus as between scholars) as to the exact relation of the transcendental concerns of individual liberation from rebirth, *mokṣa*, and the proper ordering of society. Chapter 6 here shows that this was an issue which exercised the minds of Buddhists also. Exactly how far what one can call in any specific context "Buddhism" goes in the direction of particularistic, pragmatic, communal or instrumental forms of salvation (which it always does) is in most cases a difficult and unnecessary line to draw.

What is the position of supernatural beings in all this? At the particularistic level they are ubiquitous: in Southern Asia, regardless of which elite, rationalized soteriology (if any) may be present, the world is quite naturally and ordinarily thought to contain countless different supernatural beings, of various sorts, malevolent and other. There are Hindu soteriologies which involve, at the most ultimate level, some form of relationship – often of identity – between the individual and God (personal or impersonal), howsoever either are conceived. Buddhist soteriology, however, does not require in itself interaction between humans and gods, although those on the Path might well interact with them; and it denies the existence of any God (whether conceived as personal or impersonal), outside the conditioned universe of space and time, *saṃsāra* . So one can say that – apart from very recent cases of Buddhist modernism – people who adopt Theravāda soteriology, in whatever sense and to whatever extent they do, are polytheists on the everyday level, and atheists on the level of transcendental vision. Older western definitions of religion made reference to God or gods a necessary part of the concept, and so the ethnography of Buddhist societies has caused a certain amount of definitional trouble (Spiro 1966, Southwold 1978).

An extended passage from Peter Brown's recent study *The Rise of Christendom*, is worth quoting here, for two reasons. First, its elegance nicely captures polytheism as a form of human life, not simply as a theological category. Second, because he is speaking of the Roman Empire before the imperial adoption of Christianity, the passage supports the view that polytheism is, as it were, the default mode of supernaturalism, ubiquitous in the premodern world except where Christianity or Islam (or in a more restricted sphere Judaism) succeeded to a greater or lesser extent in suppressing it. He writes:

> Diocletian's empire was an overwhelming polytheist society. It was assumed, as a matter of common sense, that there were many gods, and that these gods demanded worship through concrete, publicly visible gestures of reverence and gratitude. The gods were there. They were invisible and ageless neighbors of the human race. Knowledge of the gods and of what pleased and displeased them tended to be a matter of local, social memory, kept alive by inherited rites and gestures. *Religio*, the apposite worship of each god, stressed (even idealized) social cohesion and the passing on of tradition in families, in local communities . . . Nor were the gods airy abstractions. Vibrant beings, their lower orders shared the same physical space as human beings. They touched all aspects of the natural world and human settlement. Some gods were considerably higher than others. The *religio* that these high gods received depended, to a large

extent, on the self-image of their worshippers. Mystical philosophers yearned for the higher gods, and beyond them union with the One, the metaphysically necessary, intoxicating source of all being. Such high love lifted the soul out of the body, in a manner that made all earthly cares fall silent. But the other gods were not replaced by this experience. They were demoted, not denied. Philosophers were superior souls. They did not share the coarse concerns of the multitude. But no one denied that average gods existed also, for average persons. It was believed that such gods hovered close to earth. They "stood close by" their worshippers, ready to maximize, and to maintain, in return for due observance, the good things of life. (1996: 20–1)

With adjustments for the Theravāda Buddhist case – for "philosophers" read "ascetic monks and nuns"; alter the objects of their metaphysical yearning from "higher gods" and "union with the One" to "rebirth in the Brahma worlds" and "attaining non-theistic, non-cosmogonic nirvana"; and understand "soul" in a manner compatible with the doctrine of not-self – and this is exactly its situation throughout premodernity, and in many parts of the modern, non-secularized world. In quantitative sociological terms, clearly, philosophers, and ascetic monks and nuns will always be in a minority. Mabbett and Chandler state the case plainly: "Buddhism in Southeast Asia (or in any place where it is part of the culture of a whole society) consists of many things, and the peculiarly rational teaching with which westerners often identify it is only one. Few Southeast Asians would recognize the intellectual version of the religion as their own practice" (1995: 116–18). Modernist Buddhism in urban middle-class contexts often, though not always, denies rather than demotes the beings placated and petitioned in localized supernaturalism.

Since I wish to stress the local/nonlocal element, I refer to the particularistic end of the continuum variously described above as *localized supernaturalism*, and the other as *soteriology*. Wilson's use of the category of "salvation" across the whole spectrum is a useful device for gathering together different forms of reassurance, and – I would add – the felicities corresponding to them; but it obscures the qualitative, categorial difference at the "spiritual" end, where the salvation is *final*. At the supernaturalist end, one is dealing with a multitude of invisible, and so in our terms supernatural beings, who, like its visible inhabitants, live in the universe of space and time, and who have the power to cause and alleviate particular sufferings. For convenience, one might distinguish three kinds of supernatural being in Southern Asia: (i) village gods and goddesses, and a whole gamut of lesser spirits, ghosts and the like, whose existence is localized in a very small area; (ii) regional gods and goddesses, who are known and worshiped over a wider region; and (iii) trans-local "high" gods and goddesses, who are known and worshiped anywhere (though not everywhere). Often local gods, of both the first and still more often second kinds, are taken to be manifestations or forms of those of the third.

Village supernaturals do not usually appear in theology or soteriology, although there are often local legends and stories about them; people simply interact with them, for various purposes. Regional deities figure widely in myths, which are usually composed about events happening in particular places (see Hardy 1993); theologies are sometimes articulated involving them (such as Kālī in Bengal). Trans-local deities are widely known, although they are not always and everywhere "worshiped" in the same way or to the same degree. They are pre-eminently the deities who appear in theologies and soteriologies (where they are theistic). An interesting category of supernaturals is that of the *nat* spirits in Burma. They are "spirits associated with features of the landscape and with family lines . . . as well as homeless ghosts, demons, and so on"; but organized in the traditional group of thirty-seven, headed by Indra, they become symbols of royalty and kingdom, where the *nat*-s are to Indra as his domain is to the king: this is because "ideally a Buddhist kingdom should be organized as a microcosm . . . of the Buddhist view of the universe as a whole in order that the proportion between merit and status-power characteristic of the universe as a whole be mirrored in the political and social arrangements of a Buddhist kingdom" (Lehman 1987: 575–6; cp. Shorto 1967, 1978).

Even in this case, however, where Buddhist elite-civilizational articulation is certainly in play, the supernaturals are localized in a specific royal space. Buddhist soteriology, on the other hand, as a form of trans-local, cultural-imperial universalism, offers "an omnibus to-whom-it-may-concern guidance towards generic recovery" (Gellner 1988: 81), which is atheist and has no intrinsic relation to any particular time and place. It is, of course, subject to various forms of contingent localization: places in India associated with the Buddha's life, and elsewhere which he visited, places where relics are located, and so on. It is true, moreover, as argued earlier, that some form of localization is in this sense a ubiquitous feature of the presence-and-absence discourse generated by transcendental visions; but specific localization of this sort is quite different from the restricted localization characteristic of the particularistic, pragmatic end of the spectrum of salvation/felicity.

It is vital to notice that what Gellner calls the overall intolerable condition responded to by a spiritual conception of salvation, a soteriology, is not necessarily, indeed is not usually an ailment or form of distress (or an ensemble of them) in any immediate physical or psychological sense. As is the case with the Buddhist concept of *dukkha*, suffering or better unsatisfactoriness, the very perception that the world is a place of suffering, in the full Buddhist sense, is the result of thought and reflection, the result of looking at the world from a learned, evaluative perspective (1.1.b). Both the questions to which soteriology responds and the answers which it gives are forms of rationalization, in one of the many senses in which Weber used the word.[120] They are also intrinsically discursive, in a way in which particularistic concerns are not. Such matters of immediate concern as sickness, agricultural success or failure, and so on, are here-and-now issues where menace and resolution can be experienced in direct sensory terms. They are, of course, as is everything else, mediated by language, and particular "thick descriptions'[121] even of such physical and sensory realities will be to varying degrees culture- and language-specific. But they are, nonetheless, immediate problems which appear one by one, and which call for immediate, pragmatic solutions, each of which is fitted to the particular problem at hand. The very notion of salvation, on the other hand, and the concerns to which such "spiritual" ideas are responses, arise as general and abstract issues only when human beings, or at least some of them, subject their diverse and disorganized experience to reflective

[120] For this notoriously ambiguous concept in Weber see Brubaker (1984). Schluchter (1979: 14–15) suggests there are three most important forms of rationalization in Weber: the scientific-technological, the metaphysical-ethical and the practical. It is important to Weber's conception of world history that the second and third be seen to have led to the first in Europe, and thence to the rise of industrial society, but here it is the second which concerns me: it "refers to the systematization of meaning-patterns . . . [and] involves the intellectual elaboration . . . of ultimate ends" (ibid.) in a way not tied to particular, and controversial, historical hypotheses.

[121] The term is Geertz's (1973), who adopted it from the philosopher Gilbert Ryle.

thought. To speak of a soteriology, a "system of salvation," is to emphasize two points: it is a system of a final *salvation* (here in the traditional sense) offering final solutions to ultimate problems; it is also a *system* of salvation (here in Wilson's broader sense), in the sense that it makes it possible to organize perception of the polytheism of everyday life and its ills in the discursive perspective of a single, hierarchically ordered world view. One might say: we experience diversity, we (may) think unity.[122] The discourse of ultimate concern involves both what Weber (1948: 293) called "the kind of rationalization the systematic thinker performs on the image of the world: an increasing theoretical mastery of reality by means of increasingly precise and abstract concepts," and, I would wish to add, a master-text which narrates an account of the universe and of one's place (usually central) in it, which we may call myth, story or history.

The phrase "polytheism of everyday life" also derives from Weber. He opposed "workaday mass religion" (*Alltagsreligion*) – in which actions involving religion and/or magic alike "must not be set apart from the range of everyday purposive conduct" (1963: 1) – to the rationalized religion of elites. More than once he quoted James Mill's remark that "if one proceeds from pure experience, one arrives at polytheism." For Weber the usage was metaphorical: "polytheism" here refers to the many "value spheres in the world [which] stand in irreconcilable conflict with each other" (1948: 147, cp. 1949: 17), and he opposed any attempt on the part of intellectuals to impose a unifying ideology on it (cf. Sadri 1992). For my descriptive purposes Mill's remark simply points to literal polytheism, in the sense of accepting as entirely normal the existence of multiple supernatural beings, interacting with them, avoiding them, and the like, not in the peculiarly modern sense of "believing" in them, as if this were, like belief in the single god of monotheism, an action or a quality in itself. Judaic, Christian and Islamic monotheism, as forms of intellectually rationalized unification of the cultural field, sought to proscribe everyday polytheism. Others did not. In the Buddhist case, as in the pre-Christian Roman Empire described by Brown, unification did not mean proscribing all or most forms of supernaturalism except for a focus on one high God. It consisted in a hierarchization of the field in such

122 I owe this way of putting it to Patrick Olivelle.

a way that an atheist soteriology was placed, as an add-on transcendental vision, at the summit of what became, by this addition, a somewhat less disordered polytheistic heterogeneity.

The spectrum of concerns is also a spectrum of felicities. For the moment this term need mean no more than "forms of well-being," although the next section connects the word directly to what is there argued to be the necessarily discursive nature of soteriologies, of ultimate concerns and ends. To make clearer the relations between the different kinds of felicity on the spectrum from localized supernaturalism to soteriology, it might be useful to employ some ideas and distinctions which anthropologists have used in relation to the idea of karma. It is common knowledge that karma (the idea that experience in this and future lives is conditioned by past actions, in this or previous lives) is only one of a number of different explanations of fortune and misfortune in Southern Asia. Others include such things as astrology, various forms of magic and witchcraft, possession by spirits and medicine (traditional or modern): this variety of explanatory strategies can be found in classical texts and in contemporary ethnography.[123] These other explanations are sometimes seen as deviating from or contradicting belief in karma, but this is not necessarily, indeed it is rarely the case; rather, they are the means by which karma works. As Obeyesekere (1976: 206) has shown, for example, in Sri Lanka the various concepts employed to deal with misfortune form a hierarchy, in which karma is the most general: "none of these concepts is mutually contradictory; rather, a more limited concept is often contained within a larger one. The limited concepts generally pertain to disease, and the larger ones to a wider class of misfortunes." Keyes (1983: 17) has usefully distinguished between "ultimate explanation in terms of karmic destiny and efficient explanations in terms of other mundane forces." Ultimate and efficient explanations, I suggest, differ significantly in their connection with action: to give an efficient explanation of some phenomenon is also to begin to say what can be done about it. If one is the object of sorcery, counter-measures may be possible; if one has offended a god, propitiation may help; and so on. But to use an ultimate explanation such as karma (or

[123] See the volumes edited by O'Flaherty (1980), and Keyes and Daniel (1983).

God's will, fate, or the like) is not *ipso facto* to offer any suggestion as to how the immediate situation may be dealt with. It is simply to say that the phenomenon in question exists or has happened, it is unavoidable; but it is not meaningless or unintelligible, it does not threaten to escape the webs of meaning which a given ideology provides for dealing with life. Although the ideas of karma, God's will, fate and the like, are still employed by many people nowadays, I think Giddens (1991: 109–10) is right to suggest that their use is something particularly characteristic of premodernity, where "the world is not seen [as it is generally in modernity] as a directionless swirl of events, in which the only ordering agents are natural laws and human beings, but as having intrinsic form which relates individual life to cosmic happenings."[124]

Explanations of fortune or misfortune in terms of karma, then, are only salient in certain circumstances, and in certain ways. I want to suggest that in the Pali imaginaire the explicit and direct aspiration to ultimate felicity in nirvana is, analogously, only salient in certain circumstances, and in certain ways. This does not mean that other conceptions of felicity are opposed to nirvana, any more than limited explanatory concepts are opposed to the wider concept of karma. Nirvana offers the most all-embracing and secure resolution of suffering: it defeats suffering conceptually, in the broadest, most abstract and ultimate way. The next two sections claim, in summary fashion, as is argued throughout the book, that nirvana is implicit in the statement of any Buddhist aspiration to well-being, and is thus ever-present, just as the ultimately explanatory notion of karma is implicit in the statement of any efficient explanation, which is the practically useful identification of some particular means by which the force of karma has operated. Other kinds of felicity – heavens, earthly paradises, Metteyya's millennium, the Perfect Moral Commonwealth of a Good King – may be called efficient in a sense analogous to that used in relation to karma. Here the connection is not so much with action, although of course various forms of religious action are directed towards the attainment of them. The connection is rather with the possibilities for extended imaginative and narra-

[124] Naturally, Buddhist modernists standardly refer to karma as an example of, or at least analogous to, a "natural law" of science.

tive construal, on a cultural as well as individual level. Part 1 argues that the concept of nirvana is precise and its imagery rich, but that it cannot become the content of a narrative. Other ideas and images of felicity, on the contrary, do not defy the narrative imagination; they can become part of the work of Buddhist culture in a way that nirvana cannot, and – this is crucial – is *intended* not to be.

I have said that matters of ultimate concern are primarily matters of discourse, of thought and imagination; matters of immediate concern require present action for short-term pragmatic ends; there are also matters of intermediate concern, such as good rebirth, which involve present action for deferred imagined ends. As a rough generalization this will do; but of course it is only rough. What Pocock says about the German verb *handeln,* and what is missed by the translations "act" and "action" in English versions of Weber's work is helpful here:

> It's important to note that this word connotes rather more than action, if you think of *action* as opposed to words or thoughts. *Handeln* connotes *action-with,* "trafficking" as in Shakespeare's "the two hours traffic on our stage" in *Romeo and Juliet,* and "commerce," as in Goldsmith's "friendship is a disinterested commerce between equals." *Handeln* might, then, be better translated "dealing," because when you have "dealings" with someone these involve thought, speech, motives, feelings and actions. (1975: 23)

The cognate noun *Handlung* is particularly welcome to me, since, as is evoked by Pocock's reference to Shakespeare, it can also refer to the plot or narrative of a story or play. The full relevance of this will become clear in Chapter 3 and thereafter. Here let me simply say that while what I there call the syntactic value of nirvana as the final period (full stop) – the "sense of an ending," in Kermode's (1967) phrase – is vital to the Buddhist master-text, it is the other kinds of felicity with which more narrative "traffic" can be had. Both semantic and syntactic values in the discourse of felicity, in both its systematic and narrative modes, are together the means by which Buddhist culture "deals with" suffering and its resolution (in Pocock's Weberian sense), by explaining misfortune and by constructing an imaginaire in which concepts, images and narratives of good fortune can cohere together in a unifying and rationalizing ideology.

III.d. Textuality: Good-place(s) and No-place(s)

This section addresses some issues fundamental to the book as a whole, by what might seem an odd route: nuances in the meanings of the words *utopia* and *felicity*. The point here is more than verbal: I want to use this discussion to create, as it were, a membrane through which osmosis between the inside and the outside of Pali texts can take place; or, to revert to an earlier image, I aim to use reflection on these words to put together the spectacles which will permit double vision of both inside and outside at the same time.

The founder of the modern European genre of utopian writing, Thomas More, referred to his *Utopia* in Latin as *Nusquama*, "Nowhere," but it seems he intended the title to be a Greek pun on *eu-topia*, "Good-place," and *ou-topia*, "No-place." Thus More has Anemolius ("Wind-bag"), Poet Laureate of Utopia, write, in the voice of the island itself:

> Me Utopie cleped [called] Antiquitie,
> Voyde of haunte [habitation] and herboroughe [harbour]
>
> Wherfore not Utopie, but rather rightely
> My name is Eutopie: A place of felicitie.[125]

More did not want his text to be seen definitely as lying on one or the other side of an ambiguity which continues to exist throughout the subsequent utopian tradition: utopias as descriptions of real (actual or possible) ideal societies or as acknowledged fictions which embody a critique of the writer's actual society. Sometimes authors are aware of the distinction between the two, and are clear about which they intend (or, as was More, clear about what they wanted not to be clear about). Sometimes they are not, or it is irrelevant to them (see Manuel and Manuel 1979: *passim*).

I want to use the play on ou-topia and eu-topia in another way as well: a text by definition presents us with *a* world, which cannot,

[125] This is the best-known English version, by Ralph Robynson (printed in 1551); the Latin text, printed in 1516, reads *Utopia priscis dicta ob infrequentiam . . . Eutopia merito sum vocanda nomine*. Both versions are cited from Lupton (1895: xciii). The recent version in More's *Collected Works*, vol IV (Surtz and Hexter 1965: 20–1; cf. 279), has "The ancients called me Utopia or Nowhere because of my isolation. . . Deservedly ought I to be called by the name of Eutopia or Happy Land," which is more literal but suits my purposes much less well. For the play on words see Lupton (1895: xl), and amongst others Manuel and Manuel (1979: 1), Kumar (1991: 1).

obviously, be *the* world in which it exists as a representational artifact, written-material or oral-aural. The world of the imaginaire inside any text is necessarily ou-topia, No-place, in relation to the real places of the material-historical world in which it exists as an artifact; but this imaginary No-place nonetheless exists, in a different sense, in the historical world, as LeGoff suggests in proposing that one can write histories of it. Given that, as both Frye (1965) and Kumar (1991) suggest, utopias are a species of literature, all such representations are always and everywhere both eu- and ou-topias.[126] The last section argued that soteriology, in the sense there intended, was necessarily and intrinsically discursive: that is, both the questions addressed and the answers proposed are matters of ultimate rather than immediate concern, providing ultimate rather than efficient explanations. Pali texts refer to nirvana by a number of terms which can have spatial reference (*āyatana, pada, dhātu*: Chapters 1 and 2.3.d, with n. 49). In a standard exegesis, the epithet *sugata*, used of the Buddha and meaning something like "one who is in a (particularly) good way" (KRN no. 88), or "The Happy One," is interpreted as *su(ndaraṃ ṭhāṇaṃ)gata*, literally "he is going/has gone to a good (beautiful) place."[127] None of these terms for place can be taken literally, since nirvana is an unconditioned Existent (a *dhamma*) outside space and time (1.1.c). Thus nirvana is not only eu-topia, Good-place, metaphorically, it is also ou-topia, No-place, twice over: first, by Buddhist definition, it exists outside the spatiotemporal locations of the conditioned world of rebirth, *saṃsāra*; second, in my argument, it is part of the discursive, textual world of soteriology embodied in the Pali imaginaire, which is, one might say, No-place in history.

A double reference, to eu-topias as imagined well-being in the ou-topia of texts, is also implied in my choice of the word "felicity." In the first place, it groups together nirvana and other, more imaginatively "efficient" forms of Buddhist well-being. One might equally well use this latter term, bland though it is, or "happiness,"

[126] Kumar distinguishes usefully between utopias as story and as theory: in my terms this is to refer to utopias in narrative and systematic thought. (See further the Conclusion to Part 2.)

[127] E.g. Vism 203 = VII 33. The compound suffix *-gata* does not necessarily imply movement; it can be taken to mean no more than "is in'. It can also be taken to mean "understand': thus the phrase expounding the meaning of *sugata* could be taken to mean "who understands the good place." Such a "play on words" is called a *nirutti*, Skt *nirukti* (see Collins 1993c: 316).

although this is a somewhat shop-soiled word to use in some Buddhist contexts (see the discussion of Pali terms in 2.2.b and 4.1.b). "Flourishing," a common translation for Aristotle's *eudaimonia*, is perhaps too tightly connected to the idea of human life as actively lived to be appropriate in the Buddhist case, either for nirvana or for some of the more refined and contemplative heavens (to wit, the Brahma worlds; 4.1.a). The word felicity in itself is not intended to do any explanatory work: in this sense it is simply an abstract classificatory label distant enough from everyday usage to beg a minimal number of questions, and to put the complexity of the idea – in both problematic and polysemic senses – more into explicit relief than a word like "happiness" would. All these Buddhist notions of felicity, regardless of their manifest content, share the latent function of providing present reassurance, of offering imaginative alternatives to present unsatisfactoriness.

But there is a second area of meanings of the word "felicity," which is equally important: the idea of a felicitous phrase, or felicities of expression – that is, successes, elegances and other good qualities of discourse. Thus "Buddhist felicities" are twofold: forms of happiness or well-being in the world(s) – Good-places and the No-place – represented in the Pali imaginaire, and also qualities of that imaginaire itself, as a textual phenomenon of the historical world. Earlier I quoted LaCapra's claim that a "problem often elided or not emphasized in a social history of ideas is that of the relation of social to textual processes" (1983: 41). In the Buddhist discourse of felicity, nirvana is the closure-marker of both its systematic thought, structuring and making a *system* out of the felicities (and sufferings) present in its cosmology as a whole, and of its narrative thought, as the full stop (period) which marks closure in its master-text, as well as in numerous actual texts. This twofold syntactic value of nirvana, as the possibility of closure in the systematic and narrative discourse of felicity, is a fact within texts, a textual process; such a discourse is of crucial significance to the Buddhist project of theodicy, in the wider sense given to Weber's term in the next section. And that is a social process.

III.e. Decentering and recentering nirvana

I want to argue against a widely, indeed as far as I can see universally accepted consensus among those who have been concerned with the historiography and ethnography of Buddhism.[128] Earlier, when introducing the *Vessantara Jātaka* in section II.b, I chose two writers whose work I otherwise admire to exemplify the approaches being argued against. In the same way here I cite from the work of Charles Keyes, deservedly regarded as one of the leading contemporary anthropologists of Theravāda Buddhism. In a classic article (1977) on "Millennialism, Theravāda Buddhism and Thai Society," he says:

> A number of students of millennialism have argued that Buddhist beliefs do not lend themselves to millennial interpretations. Some have seen the belief in *nirvāṇa*, which is central to Buddhist doctrine, as inhibiting millennial aspirations. Since the quest for *nirvāṇa* has as an essential concomitant the rejection of all worldly concerns, it follows that Buddhist beliefs cannot be called upon in support of this-worldly millennial aspirations. [He then cites an example of someone holding this view – S.C.] This argument cannot be sustained, since the assumption that [the] *nirvāṇa*-quest is central to Buddhism is not tenable for the vast majority of peoples who claim adherence to Buddhism. What A. T. Kirsch [67: 122–3] has said of Thai Buddhism is confirmed by observers of Theravāda Buddhist practice in all Buddhist societies: "Seeking for nirvana or 'extinction' is primarily a religious goal of the sophisticated Buddhist, more particularly the monk [Keyes adds: and then, only a few monks]. Unsophisticated Buddhists and laymen are more likely to see their religious goal as 'paradise' or 'heaven' and/or enhanced rebirth status in future existences."

Part of the problem here is the Weberian use of the Christian-theological notion of the "worldly," which is misleading for comparative purposes. Keyes is right to reject the a priori notion that millennialism is somehow not to be expected in Buddhism. But I want to focus on two claims: first, that belief in nirvana is "central" to Buddhist doctrine, and second, that the nirvana-quest is not "central" to almost all Buddhists in practice.[129]

I want to decenter nirvana from our view of "Buddhist doctrine"

[128] The approach has deep roots. Weber's too-strong distinction between "the cultured professional monks" of "Ancient Buddhism," as virtuosos, and the "magical," "mass religion" of a peasant laity has been influential (e.g. 1948: 267–301, 1958: 204–90); but he was by no means the first: see Collins (1982: 13–14), Almond (1988).

[129] The range of felicities in the Pali imaginaire corresponds to the range of things aspired to by Buddhists "in practice," to the allegedly "unsophisticated" goals listed by Kirsch. Note that ethnographers such as Kirsch and Keyes are reporting from modern societies, where, as I have stressed, what was formerly the elite world of the Pali imaginaire has spread downwards to become part of a "popular" Buddhism.

by focusing this book as a whole not on nirvana as the manifest but ineffable goal of asceticism and meditation (albeit that this is the subject of the opening chapters), but on the discourse of imagined felicity as the central category of both description and analysis, in which nirvana has most importantly a latent, syntactic value. I aim to provide, along the lines suggested by Wilson's use of the term, a wider account of "salvation" in the Pali imaginaire, which is usually restricted to nirvana itself, as embodied in both systematic and narrative thought. The discourse of felicity, both problems and solutions, is one of concepts, images and – for most people above all – stories. The provision of such accounts of happiness (temporal or timeless), the good life, and the ideal society, is a necessary part of Buddhism's theodicy, in the extended sense of that term customary in sociology after Weber. But in this extended sense of theodicy the role of religious ideologies in coming to terms with evil and suffering should not be seen as limited to the doctrines and narratives which explain the existence of what is bad: they must also provide visions of what is or could be good. Individuals may or may not aspire directly to one or another kind of felicity: such visions can perform their function merely by existing. The underlying logic here is something like this: "if the universe is the kind of place which can contain such happiness(es), even if not for me (in the immediate or even medium-term future), then it is a place where one can live meaningfully" (again, in the Weberian sense of the word). And Buddhist felicities are not a random collection of good things, but a coherent imaginaire structured and completed by narratively unimaginable nirvana.

I want to recenter nirvana in our view of Buddhism "in practice," through exactly the same analysis. It need not be relegated to the margins of Buddhist culture, in a view which says "yes, nirvana, doctrinally, should be the aim of all Buddhists, but in practice it is irrelevant to most of them." Ascetic withdrawal from production and reproduction can never be directly, empirically, other than marginal to any continuing human society. One might say that everywhere in Buddhism nirvana is nonetheless symbolically central, but the notion of symbolism has been too widely and indiscriminately used in these matters to be useful any longer. Manifest, conscious, immediate concern with nirvana must always be a specialist matter. But the syntactic value of nirvana – as both that which structures and systematizes the cosmology of imagined felicities, and provides the sense of an ending in the Buddhist master-text – is available to all, and in fact ubiquitous. The possibility of closure, as I am scarcely the first to suggest, is vital to the kind of Grand Narrative(s) in premodernity whose imaginatively tangible felicities in the Buddhist case occupy Part 2 of this book, and whose full stop (period) I take nirvana to be, as argued in Part 1. Closure, as the sense of a completed structure and of an ending, cannot be ever-present, explicitly, in that which is structured and narrated: the horizon of thought is not what one can see, and while a story is being told, it cannot end. But closure is always implicit in a system, throughout its structure, and in traditional narrative, throughout the telling of the story (as is Gotama's final nirvana in the "Birth Story of Prince Vessantara"). It is in this sense, as the implicit culmination and unification of the entire spectrum of well-being, that nirvana is central to any and every expression of felicity in the Pali imaginaire.

PART 1

Nirvana in and out of time

Introduction to part 1

SYSTEMATIC AND NARRATIVE THOUGHT – ETERNITY AND CLOSURE IN STRUCTURE AND STORY

It is, surely, no more than common sense to recognize that people react to problems, ideas and events by telling stories about them, or by understanding them in terms of already-known stories, as well as – and sometimes at the same time as – by thinking logically or scientifically about them; and that what counts as a good story is not the same as what counts as a good argument, and vice versa. In the study of Hinduism, it would hardly be novel to insist on the fact that narratives are just as important as doctrinal or philosophical texts to our understanding of its intellectual history, as well as of its cultural and religious history more generally. Twenty years ago, for example, Wendy O'Flaherty showed clearly and convincingly that if people had thought there was no "Problem of Evil" in Hinduism, it was because they were looking in the wrong place: "in philosophy rather than in mythology" (1976: 7). In the study of Buddhism, however, this suggestion might still appear to be something new. Although in the early days of the modern academic study of Buddhism many narrative texts were made known, since that time there has been little serious work on Buddhist stories beyond the vital task, still scarcely begun, of providing editions and translations of them.

The distinction (and interrelation) between systematic and narrative thought is central to the argument of this book, but I will not rely on any special senses of the words. Jerome Bruner, who has written extensively on this issue, offers an elegant vignette of the difference: "the term *then* functions differently in the logical proposition 'if x, then y' and in the narrative *recit* 'The king died, and then the queen died.' One leads to a search for universal truth conditions, the other for likely particular connections between two events – mortal grief, suicide, foul play."[1] Items of systematic thought are related to each other logically rather than sequentially, albeit that the embodiment of them in overt speech, thought or writing will necessarily be in some order. Narrative thought on the contrary requires a specific sequential ordering of its constituent parts, not merely as a practical necessity, but as an intrinsic part of the particular way in which it produces meaning. Gethin (92a, 92b) has provided a very helpful account of the way in which Buddhist systematic thought is organized into interlocking lists (*mātikā*), the three Characteristics, four Noble Truths, five Aggregates, six (Internal or External) Sense-bases, seven Factors of Awakening, Eightfold Path, and many others.[2] Such lists facilitate both memorization and exposition, especially in an oral culture, but they do more than just that. They form the fundamental matrix of Buddhist systematic thought, as Gethin suggests, in something like the basic sense of the term *mātikā*, mother: "a *mātikā* is not so much a condensed summary, as the seed from which something grows. A *mātikā* is something creative – something out of which something further evolves. It is, as it were, pregnant with the Dhamma and able to generate it in its fullness" (1992b: 161). These lists are inter-related in three principal ways: one may subsume another, one may be substituted for another, one may suggest another by association (1992b: 155). In an oral sermon or a written text, one can begin anywhere: Gethin provides a short example by beginning with the four Noble Truths, and expanding from there to a number of other lists. Then he says:

> It is important to note that this exercise was concluded at a more or less arbitrary point. In principle the process of drawing out lists might have been continued indefinitely; certain avenues were not fully explored, while at several points we arrive back where we started, with the four noble truths, allowing us to begin the whole process again . . . We may begin with one simple list, but the structure of early Buddhist thought and literature dictates that we end up with an intricate pattern of lists

[1] (1986: 11–2): the second sentence evokes E. M. Forster's remark: "'The king died and then the queen died' is a story. 'The king died and then the queen died of grief' is a plot" (1963[27]: 93). Carrithers (1992: 92–116) offers a nicely observed ethnographic anecdote to illustrate the two kinds of thinking.

[2] A sense of how complex this form of Buddhist thought could be can be gained from Norman's (1983: 105–7) account of the last two texts of the *Abhidhamma*, *Yamaka* and *Paṭṭhāna*.

within lists, which sometimes turns back on itself and repeats itself, the parts subsuming the whole. (1992b: 153)

In Buddhist systematic thought, the beginning and end points of an exposition can differ, as can the ordering of the intervening items, without any basic change in the meaning of what is said in and through the lists thus ordered. In narrative, by contrast, differences in any of these three things must have an effect on meaning; and significant differences may lead one to say that the story has a different meaning, or even that one is dealing with a different story.[3] Narrative is necessarily sequential, in two senses beyond the fact that any discourse takes time: the specific sequencing of its constituent parts makes the story what it is, and the passage of time is intrinsic to the way it produces meaning as a story. This, I think, is part of what Hayden White means when he says that "narrative, far from being merely a form of discourse that can be filled with different contents, real or imaginary as the case may be, already possesses a content prior to any given actualization of it in speech or writing" (87: xi), and what Paul Ricoeur is pointing to when he says that "the structure of temporality" is an ultimate referent of all narratives, whether historical or fictional. I try in Chapter 3.4 to show at some length how time can be a proximate as well as an ultimate referent, in what I call the Buddhist textualization of time.

Systematic and narrative thought are forms of Buddhist soteriology, related but different modalities in its discursive rationalization of the polytheism of everyday life. In this Introduction to Part 1 I argue briefly that nirvana provides closure in both: in systematic thought, nirvana makes Buddhist cosmology (and thereby, its psychology) a *universe*, in the etymological sense of the term, a single whole. In arguing this I draw an analogy between cosmology as a discursive trope in premodern ideology, and social structure as a discursive trope in modern ethnography. In narrative thought, nirvana provides the sense of an ending, in both the Buddhist master-text and in countless actual texts and ritual sequences.

Systematic thought unifies a field, organizes it into a system, by means of a matrix of categories. In the Buddhist case this matrix centers around the concepts of *saṃkhārā*, conditioned things or events, or *saṃkhata*, (the) conditioned; these are cognitive

[3] I avoid here the difficult issue of what counts as a different story, rather than a different version of one story.

constructs which include, as their logical contradictory, the idea of *asaṃkhata*, the Unconditioned, or nirvana. This complementary opposition is what lies behind the Buddhist claim that life is suffering. But the implicit positing of nirvana as final salvation in this way is not merely an issue of logic: it is essential to the Buddhist project of theodicy. Any and every form of local, here-and-now distress, from which salvation (in the extended sense derived from Wilson in the General Introduction III.c) is sought, is understood by means of – though usually not dealt with merely by reference to – the ultimate explanatory scheme of karma, action and its effects, which operates automatically and impersonally in the universe of conditioning, *saṃsāra*, both within a particular lifetime and across a series of rebirths. In this scheme there is no injustice, no accident: all distress is in some sense merited, as a form of retribution for previous misdeeds. But the universe of conditioning and karma would itself be a pointless "mass of suffering," as Buddhist texts put it, were it not for the possibility of Release. Nirvana makes of the universe of conditioning a *system*, a conceptual structure with an outside through which the inside is ordered, and a hierarchy of values within it made possible. It is important at this point to dislodge the pervasive western assumption that discursive accounts of the universe must give it a purpose, a reason for existence; this is an ethnocentric supposition, derived from Christian narrative rationalization. The suggestion I am making here is quite different: it is that Buddhist soteriological thought requires both members of the opposition conditioned/unconditioned for its unification of everyday life to be conceptually systematic, to constitute a single *universe.* The argument is not that the universe exists *in order that* nirvana should be possible; there simply is no such teleological explanation for existence in Buddhism.[4] It is that the representation of the universe of karma, time and conditioning as a discursively constructed unity is dependent on the closure effected by the complementarily opposite idea of nirvana.

In his article "The Rhetoric of Ethnographic Holism," Robert Thornton (1988) contrasts the necessarily fragmented, partial,

[4] This is a general characteristic of South Asian religion. Even where a personal creator-God is postulated, he has no purposes in the Christian manner: rather, Kṛṣṇa creates and destroys a universe of sandcastles in play, or Śiva dances the enticing dance of creation and then the terrifying dance of death, for sheer aesthetic pleasure.

always unfinished nature of daily social life and ethnographic experience to the classifications and rhetorical tropes of the ethnographic text seen as a species of representation. Primary among these tropes is that of the social whole: "ethnography's essential fiction" (1988: 291):

> [E]thnography relies on the fact that it is an object, a text, radically removed from the initial experiences and perceptions on which it is based. The representation of reality, whether on note cards or in chapter headings is confused with reality and manipulated as objects [*sic*] in ways that culture or society cannot be. The text itself is the object of knowledge . . .
>
> A text, to be convincing as a description of reality, must convey some sense of closure. For the ethnography, this closure is achieved by the textual play of object-reference and self-reference that the classificatory imagination permits . . .
>
> The ethnographic monograph presents us with an analogy between the text itself and the "society" or "culture" that it describes. The sense of a discrete social or cultural entity that is conveyed by an ethnography is founded on the sense of closure or completeness of both the physical text and its rhetorical format. (1988: 296, 298, 299)

My point is simple: just as it is common to speak of indigenous psychologies or ethno-psychologies, and ethnohistory, so one may speak of traditional visions of society and cosmology as indigenous ethnographies.[5] As Burghart (1985: 9–10) puts it, "society" in any given time and place – in what he calls "an arena" – is an interpretation of events and processes within the arena rather than the arena itself. No-one, inside or outside the arena, can gain discursive access to it without such interpretations, emic or etic. Indigenous interpretations of the Southern Asian arena come in the form of hierarchical models, proposed by Brahmins, kings and ascetics, who in each case naturally "situated themselves at or near the zenith" of their own model. Such models are "objectifications of an arena," which "provide social scientists (who are also objectifiers of the arena) with a variety of ready-made schemes of the social universe." If, as Thornton suggests, in modern academic ethnographies social structure is a rhetorical form produced by the facts of discursive closure and of the completeness of a text *qua* artifact, so analogously the play of object-reference and self-reference in the order-enunciating discourse of indigenous ethnographies

[5] It would be accurate but inelegant to speak of "ethno-ethnographies."

permits society and the cosmos, temporally and spatially extended and complex beyond any individual's or group's possible experience, to be imagined therein as wholes, articulated as two parts of a single hierarchy. In premodern circumstances – where protocols of scientific empiricism and practices of intervention in the material-historical world weighed so much less heavily on the order of discourse and the practices of representing that world than they do now – it was possible to tolerate the kind of radical divergence between pragmatic-empirical knowledge of geography and ideological cosmo-geography described for traditional Sri Lanka by Gunawardana (1987).[6] Accordingly, the rhetorical tropes of ideology could all the more readily produce the sense of a structured whole "really out there."

The Pali imaginaire tells no cosmogonic stories, and there are no supernatural beings outside space and time to bestride the stage of its everyday polytheism-organizing enunciation of order, but narrative thinking is nonetheless pervasive and fundamental to it. In systematic thought, the idea of nirvana as the Unconditioned, timeless complement of conditioned life-in-time takes its place in a logically structured matrix of concepts produced by what Thornton calls "the classificatory imagination." In narrative thought, whose production of meaning requires the sequential ordering of its constituents, one must ask: how can timelessness, eternity, be narrated? The simple answer is that it cannot, in so far as all narrative has temporality as an ultimate referent. But timelessness can play the syntactic role of the full stop (period), bringing closure to a temporally extended narrative sequence. I offer evidence in Chapter 3 to suggest that this is the case in the Pali imaginaire. Nirvana makes possible what texts can do but life cannot: come to a satisfactory end rather than merely stop.

I want to make this claim about the role of timeless nirvana in time-structured and time-referential narrative not only as a contingent, empirical fact about Pali texts, but as a general point about the notion of "eternity." This can mean either, or both, of two things: timelessness and/or endlessness. I suggest, as a form of argument independent of the interpretative use made of it in this book, that both kinds of eternity are, despite appearances,

[6] As discussed in section II.e of the General Introduction.

unimaginable, in the sense that they are un-narratable. The classificatory imagination can certainly entertain eternity, in either sense, as a conceptual category; and images – in the Buddhist case, famously, the blowing out of a flame – can be effective mental vehicles for the incorporation of eternity into the temporal process. But no story of eternity can be told: eternity is where stories end.

Bernard Williams, in "The Makropolous Case: Reflections on the Tedium of Immortality,"[7] discusses a story – made into an opera by Janacek – in which a sixteenth-century woman, Elina Makropolous, is given an elixir of life; at the time of taking it she is forty-two, and she remains at that age for 300 years.[8] "Her unending life" says Williams (1973: 82, 91)

> has come to a state of boredom, indifference and coldness. Everything is joyless: "in the end it is the same," she says, "singing and silence." She refuses to take the elixir again; she dies; and the formula is deliberately destroyed by a young woman amid the protests of some older men . . .
>
> Her trouble was, it seems, boredom: a boredom connected with the fact that everything that could happen and make sense to one particular human being of 42 had already happened to her. Or rather, all the sorts of things that could make sense to a woman of a certain character; for [she] has a certain character, and indeed, except for her accumulating memories of earlier times . . . seems always to have been much the same sort of person.

He formulates two requirements for any future life to be considered a form of immortality for *me* – that is, for this conscious embodied person here-and-now. It must be the case that:

(i) "it should clearly be *me* who lives forever,"[9] and that

(ii) "the state in which I survive should be one which, to me looking forward, will be adequately related, in the life it presents, to those aims I now have in wanting to survive at all."

Makropolous' life satisfies the first condition, but not the second; for it is, Williams claims, a necessary consequence of being a self-conscious and self-reflective personality that such an extraordinary extension and repetition of experience should result in a state of frozen, inhuman detachment.

7 Citations are from Williams (1973).

8 Perrett (1986: 223 n. 2), who comes to conclusions close to my own, states that Williams' version differs in minor details from the original. Story (1971) makes some points close to those I make here, from the point of view of a modern Buddhist apologist.

9 This does not contradict the Buddhist view that there is no permanent self: "me" equals "this speciously-present consciousness, spatio-temporally located here."

It seems to me that, apart from the fact that 300 years might be thought a little too short a time to produce these dismaying effects, it is unfortunate that Williams chose to express his point in the psychological vocabulary of boredom; for that immediately allows Nagel (1986: 224 n. 3), for example, to retort that he cannot "at present" imagine tiring of life, and to ask of Williams "Can it be that he is more easily bored than I?" (It may seem a little frivolous to speak of boredom in heaven, but this is certainly an issue which has concerned Christians explicitly in the last two centuries.)[10] But the problem here is best seen, I think, not as a matter of whether certain emotions or reactions to experience are inevitable, but of the possibilities of, and constraints on narrative imagination: if one – anyone – tries to imagine his or her existence stretching forward not merely 300 years, but 300 thousand or 300 million or 300 billion, or whatever (in immortality, "world without end," these lengths of time are but a beginning), it will soon, I contend, become impossible to retain any sense of a recognizable structure of human emotions, reactions, intentions, aspirations, interrelations, etc. All these things take place in time, necessarily, but in a limited, narratively coherent length of time. It is possible to imagine the infinite extension of experience, at least in the sense of an infinite repetition of certain kinds of physical or psychological suffering and gratification. But such infinite repetition would take place in something one can only call a site for consciousness, not a person. Persons are developmental; they are born, grow up, grow old and die; they are stories with a beginning, a middle and an end.[11] The sheer quantity of experienced material in eternity, along with its a priori endlessness, would mean that one might be able to record a chronological sequence of experience, but that the coherence of narrative necessary for personhood would become impossible.

This point is made forcibly and well by Zygmunt Bauman, reflecting on Borges' short story "The Immortal." Borges emulates Jonathan Swift by attempting, or at least seeming to attempt a

[10] See, from a number of examples cited in MacDannell and Lang (1988: 276–358), the 1975 article in the *U.S. Catholic* entitled "Heaven: Will it be Boring?" The answer is no, for in heaven souls are called "not to eternal rest but to eternal activity – eternal social concern" (1988: 309 and n. 4).

[11] This has been discussed extensively in recent years: see, *inter alios*, Ricoeur (1992: 113–68), Cave (1995).

depiction of immortality as endlessness. In Part Three of *Gulliver's Travels* Swift's Struldbruggians never die, but Gulliver's "keen Appetite for Perpetuity of Life" soon abates, since he comes to realize that they simply continue to grow older, and so become hateful to themselves and everyone else. Swift's detailed account of their lives, however, only goes as far as ninety, by which time they have already reached a stage where senile dementia has clearly set in. Thereafter he mentions that "they are [not] able after Two Hundred Years to hold any Conversation," and adds, "I afterward saw five or six of different Ages, the youngest not above Two Hundred Years old" (1963: 204). This is clearly *not* an attempt to narrate endless life, but rather to suggest that anything worth calling human life cannot extend much beyond ninety. In Borges' story, the Immortals appear at first to the narrative voice to be troglodytes, for they are "naked, gray-skinned, scraggly-bearded men" who seem not to talk and eat snakes (1964: 108). The appearance is misleading, however, for one of the troglodytes turns out to be Homer, who at the time when the story is set can remember little of the *Odyssey*, since "it must be a thousand and one hundred years since I invented it" (1964: 113). (Again, a lifetime of eleven hundred years would still be but a drop in the ocean of endlessness.) For the Immortals nothing is precious, nothing worth striving for, since "if we postulate an infinite period of time, with infinite circumstances and changes, the impossible thing is not to compose the *Odyssey*, at least once" (1964: 114). Bauman (1992: 6) asks Elias Canetti's rhetorical question: "How many people will find it worth while living once they don't have to die?"

Bauman suggests that it is the fact that Borges' Immortals had a mortal past which produces their

> conception that if circumstances are infinite, deeds and thoughts are *worthless* – [a conception which] is itself a product of finite existence, of life injected with the known inevitability of death. It could make sense only to those who remembered that their circumstances were once finite and thereby *precious*: to those capable to grasp [*sic*] the significance of values, once born of finitude.
>
> The genuine immortals would not be aware that they are *not mortal*. For this very reason they elude our imagination . . . Their experience (that is, *if* there was an experience) could not be narrated in our language, which was itself begotten of the premonition of finitude and accommodated itself to the service of finite experience. (1992: 33)

It seems clear – to me at least – that Christian (or any other) conceptions of eternity as a final goal work only as the climax of a story, or as the centerpiece of a painting or tableau of salvation. In the European Middle Ages, for example, it is common to find a static picture of heaven, which resembles very closely a picture of a church service in a great cathedral, with the real God in place of the altar as the focus of devotion. Dante's vision of heaven is not so much a description of *life* there, but a record of his travels around the celestial realm, with occasional depictions of scenes, as on a stage, from different parts of it. Similarly in the study of utopias it is often said that such visions have great difficulty in providing their perfect society with a history; nothing can get better, no misfortunes can occur: it is hard to imagine much *happening* at all. Modern activist descriptions of heaven demonstrate quite clearly that it is impossible to narrate any convincing account of an endless human happiness. An activist heaven can involve, for example, family reunions, absorbing and enjoyable work, educational and sporting activities: in short, various images of human fulfilment transposed to the future life. To take but one example from MacDannell and Lang's panorama (1988: 297): Elizabeth Stuart Phelps, daughter of a Massachusetts seminary professor, wrote best-selling novels in the nineteenth century describing heaven. In one of them, we read, many souls "seemed to be students, thronging what we should now call below colleges, seminaries, or schools of art, or music, or sciences": that is, one might say, life at a New England college on a fine day in spring. One only has to ask, of course, what this "life" would be like when prolonged for billions and billions of years, with no prospect of change (or graduation?), to see the problem with this kind of imagined world.[12]

Perhaps the problem here is the conception of eternity as infinite extension: might not a better notion of eternal life be of a

[12] Certain Islamic texts, I believe, have their heaven populated by beautiful young girls and streams of wine; in the nineteenth century the Christian Reverend Sidney Smith described heaven as "like eating paté de foie gras to the sound of trumpets." Personally I'd prefer garlic bread and John Coltrane: but it is surely obvious that none of these visions taken literally, versions of what one might call the "Big Rock Candy Mountain" view of heaven, can make any imaginative sense when the form of pleasure in question is extended and repeated endlessly. (Perhaps one should speak of the Alka Seltzer approach to immortality.) In the history of utopian writing these sorts of physical-pleasure heaven are often grouped under the category "the Land of Cockaygne." See Graus (1967), Davis (1981), the Introduction to Part 2, and Chapter 4.2 below.

timeless bliss, a Beatific Vision without temporal duration? But this fails to satisfy either of Williams' requirements. Even if we can make sense of the idea of a timeless consciousness, such a prospect clearly will not be *me*. No action, no thought, no intentions, aspirations or memories can be possible without time. With no time to remember anything, leave alone to have new experiences, it would be impossible to have any sense of personality, any sense of "who one is." For this reason such a prospect, although certainly a possible aim for me now, cannot be said to be a form of *survival* – rather, for me now it is indistinguishable from death. In teaching Buddhism the question "What is nirvana?" always – and rightly – comes up in the earliest sessions. For the reasons given here, I have taken to replying that I used to worry that I couldn't understand nirvana until I realized that I didn't understand the Christian (or Islamic) heaven or the Hindu idea of absorption into the World Spirit (*brahman*), or indeed any other such conception of *eternal* salvation either: it is a mistake, I think, to assume that the presence in doctrine of a self or soul, whether individual, as in Christianity, or collective, as in (much of) Hinduism, makes eternity any the more comprehensible.

In seeking to establish this interpretative position from which to elucidate Buddhist ideas, I do not mean to denigrate religious aspirations to eternity. The Christian theologian Charles Davis (1994: 202–3), borrowing a distinction from Thomas Aquinas' discussion of human knowledge of God, argues plausibly that it is coherent to hope *that* a resolution of suffering and a fulfilment of human aspiration is possible, without knowing anything about *what* that is or might be. I would ask any reader who may think it possible to know *what* eternal happiness might be like: if it is timeless, how are *you* present, and if it is endless, what possible well-being could retain its attraction, indeed its meaning *as* well-being, when infinitely repeated? MacDannell and Lang report that among modern Christian theologians, agnosticism about the nature of heaven, or even straightforward denials of personal immortality, are now common. A good example of the former (not from their book) is provided by the Rev. F. H. Brabant, who returned in 1936 from "the silence of the veldt . . . on the Mission Field (in Zululand)" to deliver the Bampton Lectures from the pulpit of St. Mary's Church in Oxford, on "Time and Eternity in

Christian Thought." He first surveyed Greek, Christian and modern ideas, and then considered, in Chapter VIII, "The Problem at the End of This World Order – Eternal Life"; in particular, he addressed the issue of how the life of perfection in heaven could be related to activity, change and time. His own preference was for "the contemplative life," but he insisted that "God's eternity is the fullest activity of enjoyment and it would be very crude to believe that, whenever we are not 'doing things,' we are passive in the sense of asleep." Finally, he dismissed the subject with the following remark, appropriate perhaps for a sermon but a clear admission of defeat from an analytical point of view: "if scope is wanted for parading our philosophical theories, some other field should be found than the life of Heaven" (1937: vii, 218, 220).

If the argument given here is correct, one can say that of the two possible forms of eternal life, timelessness and infinite extension, the one would be equivalent to death and the other, eventually, because of infinite repetition, equivalent to hell. One way out of the dilemma, perhaps, would be to suggest that an infinite extension of life need not involve endless repetition and the awareness of it, for we might imagine an infinite series of lives, without the constraint of having a single personality or character to tie the experiences together, and remember them. There are problems here, of course, with Williams' first requirement, that such a series of personalities should be *me*. But even if we assume this problem solved, as Buddhism does in a particular way, we are confronted with a striking fact. It turns out – thanks to the history of early Indian ideas of the afterlife – that this is the problem, not the solution. As Williams says, "it is singular that those systems of belief that get closest to actually accepting recurrence of this sort seem, almost without exception, to look forward to the point when one will be released from it. Such systems seem less interested in continuing one's life than in earning one the right to a superior sort of death" (1973: 94).

It is not clear exactly which systems of belief he has in mind here: amongst others, surely, Buddhism and its conception of nirvana as release from rebirth. (Reverting to some language used above, one might say that the Buddhist view of rebirth involves precisely the idea of a site for consciousness – i.e. an individual series of karmic causal relations – which is not in itself a person, but a continuum in which narratively coherent persons – short stories – appear sequentially, each one beginning and ending in a limited stretch of time.) The equation of nirvana with extinction or death, as in Williams' remarks, is common: in Freud, for example, the wish or instinct for death also expressed as "the Nirvana principle."[13] But as an attempt at humanistic, empathetic understanding, rather than as a conceptual point, the suggestion that untold millions of our fellow human beings can have simply aspired to "a superior sort of death" as their highest conceivable goal seems rather unsatisfactory – at least if we want to avoid the kinds of nineteenth-century cultural imperialism cited in section III.b of the General Introduction. Although my account will presuppose the truth of the argument sketched out here, I want to use that argument as the basis for an interpretation of the role of nirvana in Buddhism which does not reduce the concept to an overt or covert death wish. It may still be "a superior sort of death"; but not in the sense Williams means: it is an imagined cessation which conquers, discursively at least, the suffering and death intrinsic to all life.

I assume in what follows that any notion of eternal bliss, whether timeless or endless, Buddhist or Christian, or of any other kind, cannot coherently become an object of imagination articulated in narrative. The problem is not one of logic: one can juxtapose in one's mind without logical contradiction the concept of eternity and any other concept (apart, of course, from that of non-eternity). One can also imagine any number of static paintings or tableaux of salvation. But no coherent narrative of persons (as opposed to a list-like record of experiences) in eternity is possible: and without such a narrative there can be no sense of living a life.[14]

[13] Freud (1984: 329, 413–14, 415). His use of this terminology underwent a complex development; he took the idea from Low (1920: 72), who wrote: "It is possible that deeper than the pleasure principle lies the nirvana principle, as one may call it – the desire of the newborn creature to return to that stage of omnipotence, where there are no unfulfilled desires, in which it existed within the mother's womb."

[14] Philosophical discussion of these matters is, of course, interminable. For recent treatments of duration or timelessness in eternity, see Stump and Kretzmann (1981) and Rogers (1994).

CHAPTER ONE

The concept of nirvana

To consider the concept of nirvana as a product of Buddhist systematic thought, this chapter depicts the taxonomy within which it occurs as a structured whole, rather than telling the story of how that whole came, historically, to be created. It does however, discuss the evolution of relevant ideas in pre-Buddhist Brahmanism in 1.1.a, and offers a few remarks in 1.2.b about some less than perfectly understood meditative attainments which seem to result from emphases within the tradition which are divergent and perhaps contradictory. In sections 1.1, 1.2 and 1.3 I organize the material in my own way, but the aim is to say nothing about the concept of nirvana which is foreign to the texts from which this account is taken. 1.4 and 1.5 revert to an external, etic viewpoint, in the former to dispose of what is prima facie a good question to ask about nirvana (can one "desire" it?), and in the latter to reflect on the relation between what is said and what is left unsaid in ideological discourse.

1.1. ACTION, TIME AND CONDITIONING

1.1.a. Time and salvation in pre-Buddhist Brahmanism

In this regard, as in many others, the thought of Buddhism is clearly continuous with that of the pre-Buddhist Brahmanical tradition.[1] Ideas of time and life after death had evolved slowly. The earliest Vedic religion had little that can be called soteriology: the extant texts stress the aspiration for good things in this life: sons, cattle, victory in war, and so on. The word normally translated

[1] I draw on Silburn (1955) and Collins (1982), Chapters 1 and 7. These two books, and those cited in the latter, p. 271 n. 1, contain textual citations from Brahmanical literature.

immortality, *amṛtam*, in its earliest occurrences meant more simply non-dying, in the sense of continuing life; thus it was no paradox for Vedic hymns to aspire to the possession of *amṛtam* as a full life (*sarvam āyus*) lasting 100 years. There was a notion of timelessness, an unborn (*aja*), which was, to use the Vedic image as adapted by T. S. Eliot, "the still point of the turning world" of time;[2] it was also its timeless structure, the whole rather than its temporal constituents taken sequentially. This whole was the recurring year, whose constituent parts (days and nights, months, seasons) formed the spokes of the invariable but incessant wheel of time,[3] whose movement was both symbolized and constituted by the daily and yearly cycle of the sun. But this notion was not, at the early period, the goal of a systematically articulated eschatology or soteriology.

The hope for life after death first appeared in imprecise and collective notions of going to the Worlds of the Fathers (of the Ancestors, *pitṛloka*) and/or the World of the Gods (*devaloka*) or Heaven (*svarga*). As the sacrificial ritual of the Brahmin priests was seen to be increasingly central to cosmogony and to the continual regeneration of time, there was increasing emphasis on the hope that for individuals *amṛtam*, non-dying, might be extended after death; but this was not a notion of immortality in the usual sense of that word in English. Just as life-in-time before death had been subject to *punarmṛtyu*, repeated dying, in the sequence of days and nights, in the repeated death and rebirth of the sun, and had needed constant renewal through sacrifice to keep going, so too life after death came to be seen as subject to the same limitations of temporality. If in this life *amṛtam*, non-dying, was the result of sacrificial action, then life after death also would need constant renewal, constant avoidance of repeated dying through sacrificial action – *karma* in the earliest sense of that word. A crucial implication of this was brought out finally in the *Upaniṣad*-s: just as the prolongation of *amṛtam* in this life ended in a final death, so too although life might be continued after death, this next life too would end in a second death. Thus, on a conceptual level, wanting more life was equivalent to wanting further subjection to death. This may make slightly more comprehensible, although it cannot

2 Eliot (1959[44]: 15), *The Four Quartets*, "Burnt Norton," l. 62. Eliot studied Sanskrit and Pali at Harvard.

3 Horsch (1957) is a good account of the wheel as a concept and an image in Vedic and Buddhist traditions.

explain, that radical cultural change whose wider sociocultural roots and rationale we still do not understand: that is, the fact that eventually, in the *Upaniṣad*-s and thereafter, action (*karma*) and its results came to be seen not as producing the desired object of religious aspiration, but rather as an inevitable but undesirable fact. The process of rebirth or reincarnation fueled (to use the Buddhist image) by action and its results was now thought to happen necessarily and automatically, unless an individual sought to escape from it.

By the time of the *Upaniṣad*-s, then, the evolution of ideas about *karma, saṃsāra,* and liberation from it had been finally, albeit again gradually completed. In this soteriology the goal of liberation was achieved through realizing – both understanding and making real as a fact of experience – that the essence of the individual, the microcosmic self, *ātman,* was identical with the essence of the universe, the macrocosmic self, *brahman.* There was a clear distinction between time and timelessness. The *Maitrī Upaniṣad* (6, 15, 17), for example, says that food is the source of the world, time the source of food, and the sun the source of time; it then distinguishes

> two forms of *brahman,* time and the timeless. That which is prior to the sun is the timeless and partless (*akāla, akala*); but that which begins with the sun is time, and has parts. The form of that which has parts is the year; from the year indeed are born these creatures . . . In the beginning this universe was *brahman,* the endless one – endless to the east, to the south, west, north, above and below, endless everywhere; for in it east and the other directions are not to be found, nor across, nor below nor above. This supreme self (*paramātman*), whose essence is space, is incomprehensible, unmeasurable, unborn, beyond reasoning, inconceivable. . . . He who knows this attains the unity of the One.

Such mysticism was often expressed in terms of the syllable *Oṃ* Thus the monistic *Māṇḍūkya Upaniṣad* (1) says that "this whole universe is this imperishable (syllable) *Oṃ.* The past, present and future – everything is just *Oṃ.* Whatever else there is beyond the three times is also *Oṃ.* For the monotheistic *Śvetāśvatara Upaniṣad* (6, 5), "He is to be seen as the beginning, the efficient cause of (all) combination(s), beyond the three times and without parts. Worship the glorious god who is the manifold (universe), the origin of all being, abiding in one's own (or: his own) mind, the primeval."

Apart from some exceptions in later devotional Hinduism, this soteriological structure has remained basic to all Indian religions. Eternal salvation, to use the Christian term, is not conceived of as world without end; we have already got that, called *saṃsāra,* the world of rebirth (and redeath). As just mentioned in the Introduction to Part 1, that is the problem, not the solution. The ultimate aim is the timeless state of *mokṣa,* or as the Buddhists seem to have been the first to call it, nirvana.

1.1.b. Action and conditioning in Buddhism

Silburn (1955: 200) states: "it is around the verb *saṃskṛ*– the activity which shapes, arranges together, consolidates, and brings to completion – that the reflections of the Buddha are concentrated, as were concentrated those of the *Brāhmaṇas* before him, for it is there that one finds the key to these two systems which posit a certain kind of action as the source of reality." In Buddhism, as tentatively in the *Upaniṣad*-s and throughout later Hinduism, the idea of karma is generalized from the particular and restricted sphere of sacrificial performance to morally relevant action in general.[4] But the fundamental idea remains the same. Karma is from the verbal root *kṛ,* to do; and forms of *saṃs-kṛ* provide the standard technical terminology in which continued life in the sequence of rebirths is described, as a process of conditioning brought about by action and its inevitable results. The term *saṃkhāra* is at the heart of Buddhist thought, but is difficult to translate: conditioned thing/event, (mental) formation, inherited force, construction, and others have been used. It can refer not only to an active, causal, and volitional force, but also to the results of such action, to that which is brought into being by conditioning. I use the phrase Conditioning Factor, intending by the capital letters to signal that this is a translation of *saṃkhāra,* used as a Buddhist technical term.[5] The corresponding past passive participle, *saṃkhata,* (something) made or brought into being, (a) conditioned (phenomenon), can be predicated of everything which exists, with the

[4] 'Morally relevant action,' however, is in many contexts in fact what we might regard as the sub-category of specifically ritual action, and especially those everyday rituals connected with social status.

[5] When the Pali for a technical term is not given, see the Index and Glossary.

exception of nirvana, which is the only Unconditioned Element (*asaṃkhata-dhātu*).[6]

Conditioning Factors are the fourth in a list of five categories, Aggregates (as they are called here) or constituents of personhood (*khandhā*); the others are body (*rūpa*), feelings (*vedanā*), perceptions/ideas (*saññā*) and consciousness (*viññāṇa*).[7] These five Aggregates describe exhaustively the interrelated psycho-physical events conventionally referred to as a person. Conditioning Factors are also the second of the twelvefold Dependent Origination (*paticca-samuppāda*) list. An elaborate treatment of this is unnecessary here: [8] the general fact of conditioning is called *idapaccayatā*, the fact of (everything's) having specific conditions (e.g. Vin I 5, S II 25–6). This is elaborated into the twelvefold list, the arising (*samudaya*) of which is the origin of suffering, and the cessation (*nirodha*) of which is its ending, nirvana (e.g. A I 177 and Mp II 283). The following gives what became a standard exegesis of the twelvefold list in terms of three consecutive lifetimes: [9]

(i) Past life:

With ignorance as condition there arise Conditioning Factors
With Conditioning Factors as condition there arises consciousness (at the moment of conception)

(ii) Present life:

With consciousness as condition there arise mind-and-body
with mind-and-body as condition . . . the six senses
with the six senses as condition . . . sense-contact
with sense-contact as condition . . . feeling
with feeling as condition . . . Craving
with craving as condition . . . grasping
with grasping as condition . . . becoming
with becoming as condition . . . birth (thus:)

(iii) Future life:

With birth as condition there arises old age and death, distress, grief, suffering, sorrow and unrest. Such is the arising of this whole mass of unsatisfactoriness.

[6] In the Theravāda there is one exception to this: the *Milinda-pañha* (268, 271) asserts that space (*akāsa*) is also unconditioned. Other schools accepted a variety of other "unconditioneds" (Lamotte 1988: 609–11). [7] See now Hamilton (1995).

[8] Any introductory work on Buddhism will deal with it; cf. Collins (1982: 107, 203–4).

[9] This division is found in the *Paṭisambhidā-magga* (p. 52), and the *Visuddhimagga* (578ff. = XVII 284ff.); and throughout Southern Asian Buddhist traditions.

Conditioning Factors and the Unconditioned together form the wider category of Existents (*dhammā*, both conditioned and unconditioned; see below). These categories can be elucidated by the three Characteristics (*tilakkhaṇa*): suffering, or unsatisfactoriness (*dukkha*), impermanence (*anicca*), not-self (*anattā*): [10]

(i) all Conditioning Factors (everything which is conditioned, *saṃkhata*) are suffering,
(ii) all Conditioning Factors (everything which is conditioned) are impermanent
(iii) all Existents are not-self.

The translation "suffering" for *dukkha* is in nonphilosophical contexts often best, but it is misleading conceptually. It is patently false, for Buddhists as for everyone except the pathologically depressed, that everything in life is suffering; Buddhist texts, accordingly, distinguish between three kinds of *dukkha* . There is ordinary suffering (*dukkha-dukkha*), suffering which arises through change (*vipariṇāma-dukkha*), and the suffering which is inherent in conditioned existence (*saṃkhāra-dukkha*).[11] Only the first, and to a limited extent the second, can sensibly be called suffering in the usual sense of the English word. This is why "unsatisfactoriness" is sometimes preferable as a translation: to predicate *dukkha* of conditioned things is not to describe a feeling-tone in the experience of them, but to prescribe an evaluation, one which makes sense only in relation to the opposite evaluation of nirvana, the Unconditioned, as satisfactory. A short phrase encapsulating the Buddha's teaching is very common in the texts, often used to suggest the content of the insight which converts someone to the Buddhist Path, or of their enlightening realization (these two moments can be simultaneous): literally, "everything which is characterized by arising is also characterized by cessation," or more simply: whatever begins, ends.[12] To be subject to arising is to be a conditioned and (in most but not all cases) a Conditioning

[10] A I 286, Dhp 277–9, Paṭis II 62–3 (the text is to be emended: Ñāṇamoli 1982: 262, 270 n. 10); cf. A I 26–7.

[11] D III 216, S IV 259, V 56, Vis 499 = XVI 34, discussed in Collins (1982: 191–2). Nett 12 says that the first two forms of suffering can be overcome to a certain extent in ordinary life, by good health and old age, but only final nirvana without remainder of attachment can get rid of the suffering inherent in conditioning. See 2.2.b.

[12] *Yaṃ kiñci samudayadhammaṃ sabbaṃ taṃ nirodhadhammaṃ.* This is said, for example, of the ascetic Kondañña at the end of the Buddha's first sermon (Vin I 11), and of Sāriputta, destined to be the Buddha's disciple "foremost in wisdom" (Vin I 40).

Factor in the process of time and rebirth. The second of the three Characteristics, impermanence, refers to the inevitable cessation of all such factors. Whatever is conditioned, it is said, is characterized by arising, decay, and change in what is present whereas the Unconditioned is not so characterized. Nirvana is permanent, constant, eternal, not subject to change. It is in this sense that nirvana is endless: [13] not that it is characterized by unending temporal duration, but that, being timeless, there are no ends in it.

If what is conditioned is unsatisfactory and impermanent, and the Unconditioned is satisfactory and permanent, the Unconditioned might seem to be characterizable by the reverse of the third Characteristic of what is conditioned, not-self (Collins 82 *passim*). But this is not the case. Both *saṃkhata* and *asaṃkhata*, conditioned and unconditioned, are subsumed in the wider category of *dhamma*, a term meaning so many different things that no single translation is possible: here, most simply, Existent.[14] The direct attribution of the Characteristic of not-self to nirvana is rare in the earliest literature (see Vin v 86; Collins 1982: 96); but that it should be is clearly implicit in the logic of Buddhist thought, as is made explicit in later texts. A passage of the late-canonical *Paṭisambhidā-magga* (II 238–41) lists characteristics of the Aggregates and of nirvana respectively. In most cases the paired attributes are antonyms: for example, the Aggregates are impermanent, unsatisfactory, a disease, whereas nirvana is permanent, Happiness, health. But when the Aggregates are described as empty and not-self,[15] nirvana is characterized not as their opposite but as their intensification: it is ultimately empty (*paramasuñña*) and that which has ultimate meaning (or: is the ultimate goal, *paramattha*, Paṭis II 240). The commentary here explains that "in the case of this pair (of terms) the method of (citing) opposites is

[13] "Arising, decay, change..." (*uppāda, vaya, ṭhitassa aññathattaṃ*, A I 152); "permanent..." (*niccaṃ dhuvaṃ sassataṃ avipariṇāma-dhammaṃ*; Kv 121 and ff.; cf. Kv 34 with Kv-a 27, As 341–2, Vism 508–9, XVI 71–2, Abhidh-av 74 v.723); "endless" (*ananta*, Vin V 214 with Sp 1389, Abhidh-av 82 v.772).

[14] In fact, as will be seen (1.4 below) the class of *dhamma*-s includes concepts, whether they refer to Existent or nonexistent things. Concepts in themselves exist merely as objects of thought; *dhamma*-s which have a real, external referent are those with Individual Nature (*sabhāva)*, a term of considerable complexity, and controversy, in all the schools of Buddhism. See n. 124 below.

[15] Not-self and emptiness (*suññatā*) are said earlier in this text to be the same in meaning, different only in the letter (Paṭis II 63 with Paṭis-a 567). Kv-a 179 says there are two senses of the term emptiness: the not-self characteristic of the Aggregates, and nirvana.

not used, because of the emptiness and the selflessness of nirvana."[16] Elsewhere in this text, nirvana is said to be the highest emptiness (*aggasuñña*, II 179); while both the ending of Defilements by the Arahant (a Worthy One, i.e. an enlightened person) and final nirvana are said to be empty in the ultimate sense (*paramattha-suñña*, II 184). The commentary to the latter passage states that "the Nirvana-Existent is empty of self because of the nonexistence of self"; and specifies that "both Conditioned Existents and the Unconditioned Existent are all empty of self because of the absence of a person to be classified as a self".[17]

The Buddha is reported to have said: "with regard to Conditioned Existents, what is called primary among them is the Noble Eightfold Path. With regard to both Conditioned and Unconditioned Existents, what is called primary among them is . . . nirvana".[18] In the *Visuddhimagga* (513 = XVI 90, cf. Vibh-a 89) each of the four Noble Truths is described in terms of its having or not having the qualities of permanence, beauty, Happiness and self, as follows:

(i) the first and second Truths, of unsatisfactoriness (*dukkha*) and its origin (in Craving), are empty of all four ("empty of self" here is *atta-suñña*);
(ii) the third Truth, of nirvana, is the deathless realm, empty (only) of self (*attasuññam amatapadaṃ*) – so it has permanence, beauty and Happiness
(iii) the fourth Truth, the Path, is without permanence, Happiness and self (*atta-virahita*) – so by implication it has beauty.

1.1.c. Time and timelessness

As has been seen, in the *Upaniṣad*-s time is divided into past, present and future, and the ultimate religious goal is described as outside or beyond the three times. The same thing is true of Buddhism, where the three times are interpreted in two ways:

[16] *Nibbānassa ca suññattā anattattā ca imasmiṃ dvaye paṭiloma-pariyāyo na vutto* (Paṭis-a 700).
[17] *Nibbāna-dhammo attass' eva abhāvato attasuñño. . . Saṃkhatāsaṃkhatā pana sabbe 'pi dhammā atta-saṃkhātassa puggalassa abhāvato atta-suññā ti*, Paṭis-a 638–9; cp. Moh 74.
[18] A II 34; cf. A III 35, It 88. This text is used in the meditation on calm, Vism 293–4 = VIII 245ff. For the translation "what is called primary" for *aggaṃ akkhāyati* see Collins (1993c: note 7.2).

(i) as referring to past, present and future lives; this interpretation is "according to the method of the *Sutta*-s" (sermons and narrative texts dealing with "conventional truth");

(ii) as referring to the three subdivisions of the infinitesimally brief moment in which any conditioned *dhamma* exists (arising, presence and cessation – or simply before, during and after); this interpretation is "according to the method of the *Abhidhamma* " (texts of "ultimate truth", that is, analysis into those Existents which are ultimately real). Of a number of ways of talking about time, only talk in terms of moments is literal; others are figurative.[19]

This distinction is made in the commentaries to two canonical texts which use the categories of past, present and future; they go on to say that "this division into past (present and future), is (a division) of Existents, not of time; in relation to Existents which are divided into past, etc., time does not exist in ultimate truth, and therefore here 'past,' etc., are only spoken of by conventional usage."[20] Elsewhere it is said that "time is defined (*paññatta*) in dependence on" various phenomena, such as the sequence of Existents, planting seeds and their sprouting, movements of the sun and moon, etc.; but "time itself, because it has no individual nature, is to be understood to be merely a concept."[21] The divisions of time into three periods, and the use of finite verbs such as "was," "is," and "will be," are elsewhere called (merely) "forms of expression, language, and conceptualization."[22]

The sequence of the three times is thus secondary, generated by and in the process by which Conditioned Existents (*saṃkhata-dhammā*), which are also Conditioning Factors (*saṃkhārā*), give rise to more of the same: from this it follows obviously that if that

[19] (Vibh-a 7–8, cf. Vism 473 = XIV 191) *nippariyāya, sapariyāya*: scholastic literature makes this distinction (expressed also in other words) between teachings which are direct and literal and those which are indirect or "figurative'; the latter need to be interpreted correctly by analyzing the concepts and terms used into those which refer to the ultimately real constituents of the universe, the Existents. See p. 150 and n. 41 below.

[20] Sv 991 on D III 216, It-a II 30–1 on It 53. I cite the version at It-a II 31, which is preferable to that of Sv, which is to be emended: *Ayaṃ hi atītādi-bhedo nāma dhammānaṃ hoti, na kālassa. Atītādi-bhede pana dhamme upādāya paramatthato avijjamāno pi kālo idha ten'eva vohārena atīto-ti ādinā vutto.* On the dichotomy between conventional and ultimate truth, see Collins (1982: 147–56).

[21] *So pan'esa sabhāvato avijjamānattā paññattimattako evā ti veditabbo* (As 58–9). This agrees with Elias (1992), who urges that the reified idea of time as a noun-thing should be replaced by a verbal notion – the human activities of timing.

[22] *Nirutti-, adhivacana-, paññatti-patha* (S III 71–2).

process is arrested, time will not exist. The Bactrian-Greek king Milinda, in the second century BC, asks the monk Nāgasena, as St. Augustine was to ask himself in North Africa some centuries later, "What is time?" Nāgasena's answer refers to the process of Conditioning Factors and Existents, and he states that time does not exist (*addhā n'atthi*) for those who attain nirvana and are no longer reborn (Mil 49–50). All Existents can be past, present and future, with the exception of nirvana, which cannot be characterized in this way;[23] nirvana is not *tekālika*, belonging to the three times, but *kāla-vimutta*, free from time.[24] A commentary explains that when a text refers to the Buddha's great wisdom as encompassing all aspects of all Existents, past, present and future, "nirvana, which is free from time, is also to be understood" (as known by him).[25] Elsewhere the Buddha is said to be omniscient, in the sense that he has seen and understood "everything conditioned in the three times and the Unconditioned, free from time."[26]

A verse-riddle on time in the *Jātaka* collection, along with its explanation by the commentary, expresses the point:

> Time (*kāla*) eats all beings, along with itself,
> But the one who eats time cooks the cooker of beings.

'Time" refers to such things as the morning and midday meals. "Beings" here means living beings; time does not (actually) consume beings by tearing off their skin and flesh, but it is said to "eat" and "consume" them by wasting away their life, beauty and strength, crushing their youth, and destroying their health . . . It leaves nothing, but eats everything, not only beings but also itself; (that is to say) the time of the morning meal does not reach the time of the midday meal, and likewise with the time of the midday meal (and what follows). "The one who eats time" is a name for the enlightened person, for he wastes away and eats the time of rebirth in the future by the Noble Path . . . "Cooks the cooker of beings" (means): he has cooked the Craving which cooks beings in hell, burnt it and reduced it to ashes. (Ja II 260, cited at Ps I 57–8)

[23] Dhs 241, no. 1416, cf. Moh 75, Mil 323.
[24] Tkn 22, Moh 333, Abhidh-s 43, VIII 37 with Abhidh-s-a 193.
[25] *Kāla-vimuttaṃ nibbānam 'pi gahitam eva hoti* (Paṭis-a 647 on Paṭis II 194).
[26] *Tīsu addhāsu kiñci saṃkhatam addhā-vimuttaṃ vā asaṃkhatam*; As 56, Spk II 9, It-a I 41. In this kind of text, I suspect that knowledge of the future is not prescience but a kind of a priori, "in principle" knowledge: that is, the Buddha knows the real nature of everything conditioned (viz. that it *is* conditioned), regardless of the time any particular conditioned thing might occur relative to his own temporal location.

The most common word for time, as in the passage just cited, is *kāla*, but it is not used in an explicit theory of time and timelessness. It has two main senses:

(i) time in the sense of a particular, perhaps fixed or appointed time, the right time, opportunity, etc., and

(ii) death, as in the common verbal phrase *kālaṃ karoti*, literally "to do/complete one's time."

The negative *akāla* is used to mean at a wrong/ improper/ unusual time. The form *akālika* is found once in this sense (Mil 114), but usually it means not taking time, immediate; this is especially common in a series of predicates applied to the Dhamma (i.e. the Buddha's Teaching): it is "to be seen here and now, immediate, (inviting one to) "come and see," leading onwards, to be realized individually by the wise."[27] The first two terms are applied to the holy life (*brahmacariya*, M II 146, Th 837, etc.), while the whole series is applied to nirvana (A II 158), and to a synonym for it, "the destruction of the Corruptions."[28]

The connection between *akālika* in this sense, and different connotations of *kāla* as time (of life), opportunity, and death, is cleverly brought out in a conversation, full of double meanings, between a handsome young monk called Samiddhi and a goddess who tries to seduce him, as he stands dressed in a single under-robe after a bath in the morning before going on his alms-round.[29] She addresses him in a verse, using the verb *bhuñj*, which can mean both to eat and to enjoy, the latter sense very often implying specifically sexual pleasure. The two halves of the first line are the same; the first can be rendered as: "you haven't eaten (i.e. yet today), monk, and (so) you are going begging (for alms)," and the second as "you go begging as a monk without having enjoyed (yourself first)." The second line is nonsense if *bhuñj* is interpreted as "eat," but clear if it has the other sense: "Enjoy yourself first, monk, and then [become a monk] and beg for alms – don't let (the) time pass you by."[30] The commentaries to both texts (Spk I 40, Ja II 57) explain that *kāla* here means "time of youth," and that she was telling him to enjoy pleasures while he

27 *Sandiṭṭhiko akāliko ehipassiko opanayiko paccattaṃ viññūhi veditabbo*, D II 93 *et freq.*

28 *Āsava-khaya* (A I 221). On the concept of *āsava* see Glossary; and Collins (1982: 127).

29 S I 8ff., Ja II 56–8. There are very slight differences in the narrative order in the two texts, which do not affect my point. I refer to the *Saṃyutta* version.

30 *Abhutvāna bhikkhasi bhikkhu, na hi bhutvāna bhikkhasi; bhutvāna bhikkhu bhikkhassu, mā taṃ kālo upaccagā ti* .

was young (in the immediate and medium-term future), and become a monk in old age. Given the situation, she is also telling him not to miss his (present) opportunity: in colloquial English, she is offering him the time of his life. But Samiddhi replies, "I do not know (when will be) the time (of my death); the time (of death) is hidden, it is not seen. Therefore I beg for alms without having enjoyed (the pleasures of youth); may the time [i.e. the opportunity to practice the religious life] not pass me by."[31] She tries again: "You are young, enjoy the pleasures of life, don't give up what is before your eyes [*sandiṭṭhikaṃ* – notably herself] and go running after what takes time" (*kālikaṃ*; another translation could be "what you have to wait for"). Samiddhi insists that he has given up what takes time, and is seeking after what is immediate (*sandiṭṭhika*). Sense-pleasures, the Buddha has taught him, are what takes time: they are unsatisfactory, full of unrest and danger. On the contrary, "the Dhamma (= the Teaching, the truth) is to be seen here and now, immediate . . ."

Nirvana is most commonly presented in secondary sources as freedom from rebirth, as are other Indian ideas of liberation; but as the pre-Buddhist history of ideas sketched earlier makes clear, the first suggestions of what was later to become a theory of rebirth (*punarjanman*) were in fact fears of redeath (*punarmṛtyu*). "Deathless," or "death-free" (*amata*), is both a predicate standardly applied to nirvana, and a substantive used as a synonym for it. It is the Pali form of the Sanskrit *amṛta*, but unlike that term in Vedic literature it does not mean continuing life or vitality as opposed to death.[32] It refers to a place (metaphorically), state or condition where there is no death, because there is also no birth,

[31] *Kālaṃ vo 'haṃ na jānāmi, channo kālo na dissati; tasmā abhutvā bhikkhāmi, mā maṃ kālo upaccagā ti.*

[32] Benveniste (1936) argues that the central Indo-European concept of eternity is that of a vital force, connected with ideas of youth and perpetual renovation: "the force which animates being and makes it live." In the earlier Vedas *amṛtam* is closely related to the term *āyus*, in just this sense; even when, in the *Brāhmaṇa*-s and *Upaniṣad*-s, the religious goal becomes the attainment of timelessness rather than further temporal extension, the idea of *brahman* nonetheless retains this sense of vitality and life – it is a cosmogonic force. In Buddhism, the deathless is not cosmogonic, and the idea of "eternity" is not that of an animating force, but of the complete cessation of animate activity. In this respect, as in many others, Buddhism – particularly in its Theravāda form – might be said to constitute something of an exception, or "minority report" in the Indo-European record.

no coming into existence, nothing made by conditioning,[33] and therefore no time. There is, to be sure, an inherent paradox in referring to an enlightened person's attaining timelessness (on Pali usage here see 2.1), a paradox comparable to that in religions which have a doctrine of creation and are forced to use finite verbs to denote the beginning of time. Finite verbs presuppose the usual continuum of past–present–future, which in both cases does not apply. In the Buddhist case, perhaps the best way of interpreting the situation is to assume that everything which happens, "all the action" as it were, is produced by Conditioned Elements. The process of conditioning, and thus of time, can self-destruct, with the result that time ceases to exist (at least for the individual: 3.2.c). From the perspective of time-bound, conditioned existence, and the temporally structured language which expresses it, it is possible to say that someone enters timelessness, "nirvanizes" (the event is usually referred to by a verbal form), etc.; but the temporal event denoted by such terms is not anything directly occurring in or to nirvana, but rather the ending-moment of the conditioned process. Unlike all other such moments, therefore, this has a relation to the past, but not to the future.

1.2. NIRVANA IN LIFE AND AFTER DEATH

1.2.a. The distinction between enlightenment[34] *and final nirvana*

One might think that the difference between an enlightened person before and after death was simple enough, given that the contrast between life and death is fairly unmistakable (leaving aside the genuine problem of the precise moment at which death occurs). But there has been some confusion here, both because writers have conflated the two, either in order to argue a particular case or inadvertently,[35] and because of the way the two words

[33] It is *ajāta*, *abhūta*, *akata*, *asaṃkhata*, Ud 80, and *asamuppanna*, It 37. On the interpretation of these epithets see Norman (1992b), and 1.2.c below.

[34] The metaphor of light is discussed in 2.3.a. Here the word refers to the Buddhist concepts of *bodhi*, literally Awakening, *Arahant*-ship (= "sainthood'), etc.

[35] A good example of the former is Johansson (1969: 60, cf. 61, 76–7, 107–8, etc.), who uses the idea that, as he puts it, "the difference between the two stages of nibbana is not very essential" to establish that the mind (*citta*) of the saint continues to exist after death, on the grounds that some texts speak of the mind as released in nirvana. These texts are

nirvāṇa and *parinirvāṇa* (Pali *nibbāna, parinibbāna*) are used. I discuss these words in detail in 2.1.a; it is enough here to say that they can both be used *both* for what happened to the Buddha at the age of thirty-five under the Bo-tree, *and* for what happened when he was eighty at Kusinārā, after a lifetime's career as a teacher (and for the corresponding events in any enlightened person's life). Two dichotomies used in this regard can be found in the commentary to a text in which the past passive participle *parinibbuta* is used as an epithet for someone (the speaker) who is obviously still alive. The monk Dabba exclaims, punning on his own name, which means "worthy": "He who was hard to tame has been tamed by the taming (of the Path); he is worthy (*dabba*), contented, with doubts overcome, victorious, without fear; Dabba has steadied himself, and has reached nirvana." The commentary to "has attained nirvana" (*parinibbuto*, Th-a I 46) reads:

> there are two nirvanas [or: forms of nirvana, *dve parinibbānāni*], that of the Defilements (*kilesa*),[36] which is the nirvana-element with a remainder of grasping (*sa-upādisesa*) and that of the Aggregates [see p. 139], which is the nirvana-element with no remainder of grasping (*anupādisesa*). Of these (two) that of the Defilements is intended here. So the meaning is (that) "(he has) attained nirvana" through the nirvana of the Defilements, because he has, by means of the Path, completely abandoned the Existents which one must abandon (in order to be enlightened).[37]

Similarly, when a queen refers to "those who live in this world liberated, having attained nirvana,"[38] the commentary explains that this refers to the quenching of the Defilements. On the other hand, the word *parinibbuta* can be used without elaboration to refer to a past ("dead") person who has attained final nirvana. Thus, for example, the *Subha Sutta* of the *Dīgha Nikāya* opens with the statement that it took place when Ānanda was living at Sāvatthi, "not long after the Blessed One had entered nirvana"; the com-

obviously referring to Enlightenment. For the latter see Gombrich (1972), who shows the problems caused to Spiro (1971) by his not attending to the distinction; and cf. Collins (1982: 83).

[36] The term refers to such things as greed, hatred, delusion, pride, etc., often in a list of ten. See BDict s.v.

[37] That is, he has stopped the process by which Conditioning Factors bring about future rebirth, and so will realize the Unconditioned Existent. See Collins (1982: 200–8) for this seen as a process of consciousness.

[38] *Ye vippamuttā . . . parinibuttā imaṃ lokaṃ caranti* (Ja IV 453).

mentary specifies that it was just a month later.[39] At M III 255 the Buddha describes giving a gift to "both Orders [i.e. of monks and nuns] with the Buddha at their head" (*Buddhapamukkhe ubhatosaṃghe*) and "to both Orders after the Tathāgata's [= the Buddha's] nirvana" (*Tathāgate parinibbute*). The commentary (Ps V 73) interprets *Buddhapamukka* in the first case as the Buddha's being physically "in front of" the two Orders (the term does not always have this specific sense), with monks on one side and nuns on the other. In the second case, it asks "But can a gift be given to both Orders, with the Buddha in front (of them) after the Tathāgata has attained (final) nirvana? It can. How? An image (of the Buddha) containing relics should be put on a seat facing the two Orders, and a stand put there, and when the offering of water [poured over the hand of the recipient, whether alive or in the form of a statue] and the rest have been made, everything is first to be offered to the Teacher, and (only then) given to the two Orders" (see also Sp 1142–3).

Although the distinction between enlightenment and final nirvana is quite clear, texts do not always make it, either because it is obvious which of the two "quenchings" is in question, or because the distinction is not relevant to the point being made. Often descriptions of final nirvana are applied to a living Arahant proleptically, as what will be true of him or her. An example is the earliest appearance of the dichotomy between nirvana with or without "a remainder of attachment," a passage which is worth quoting as a whole:

> [In prose:] There are two elements of nirvana . . . that with a remainder of attachment and that without. What is [the former]? Here a monk is an *Arahant*, with Corruptions destroyed, one who has lived (the holy life), done what was to be done, laid down the burden, attained the goal, with the fetters of existence wholly destroyed, released through right knowledge. In him the five (sense-)faculties remain, and because they are intact[40] he experiences what is pleasant and unpleasant, enjoyable or painful. The destruction of passion, hatred and delusion in him is what is called the element of nirvana with a remainder of attachment. What is

[39] *Acira-parinibbute Bhagavati* (D I 204); *parinibbānato uddhaṃ māsa-matte kāle* (Sv 384).

[40] Reading *avighatattā* with the text and one ms. of the commentary; other mss., and Woodward (1935: 143 n. 5) read *avigatattā*, "because of (their) not having gone," explained as "not having ceased in the cessation (which consists in) non-arising" (It-a I 166).

the element of nirvana without a remainder of attachment? Here a monk is an Arahant, with Corruptions destroyed . . . released through right knowledge. In him right here [i.e. at the end of this life] all feelings, no longer rejoiced in, will become cold . . .
[In verse:] These two elements of nirvana are set out by him who sees, the independent Sage. One element is to be seen here [and now], through the complete destruction of that which leads to (future) rebirth; but the element without a remainder of attachment, in which all existences utterly cease, occurs in the future (*samparāyikā*). Those who know the Unconditioned state, with minds released, through the destruction of that which leads to rebirth, have reached the core of the Teaching, and rejoicing in (that) destruction, have abandoned all births. (It 38–9)

In the first, prose part of this text, obviously, "the element of nirvana without a remainder of attachment" is applied to the (living) Arahant proleptically, as is clear in the future tense "will become cold . . .", and as the verses say explicitly. The commentary explains "will become cold" as "will cease in (that) cessation which is without [subsequent] rebirth" (*appatisandhika-nirodhena;* It-a I 167). According to the *Visuddhimagga* "cessation (*nirodha*) is singlefold because of its being the Unconditioned Element; figuratively [or, nonliterally, as a form of exposition, *pariyāyena*] it is twofold, through the division into (element) with a remainder of attachment and (that) without."[41] "Remainder of attachment" refers to the saint's mind and body processes (that is, the five Aggregates) and his or her experience of life-in-*saṃsāra*, which remain between the time of enlightenment and that of final nirvana, due to the force of past "karma" (e.g. Paṭis-a 323, Abhidh-s-a 165).[42]

For most people, such as all Buddhas, there is an interval between the two stages of attaining nirvana. A verse of the *Dhammapada* says to a monk, "When you (have) cut off passion and hatred then [*tato*, either "thereafter" or "by that means'] you will go to nirvana"; the commentary explains that this means "cut off the bonds of passion and hatred; by cutting these off you will attain

[41] Vism 514 = XVI 94 (also at Vibh-a 90); cp. Vism 509 = XVI 73. See Ñāṇamoli (1975: 588 and n. 26).

[42] There is some uncertainty about the evolution of this sense of *upādi* (the Skt equivalent is *upadhi*, a form sometimes found also in Pali). The term, as are related forms derived from the root *upa-ā-dā*, is used to refer both to attachment and to its results. This means that words from *upa-ā-dā* with the negative *an-* prefix can also be used of the first stage of nirvana, when attachment ceases, as well as of the second stage, when all karmic results of previous attachment cease. See CPD and BHSD s.v. *upadhi*, and KRN no. 87.

Arahantship, and then in the future you will go to nirvana without remainder of attachment" (Dhp-a IV 108 on Dhp 368). The elders Usabha and Saṃkicca both celebrate their enlightenment by saying "I do not long for life, I do not long for death, but I await my time." The commentary to the first verse explains that the monk had reached nirvana of the Defilements, but was awaiting that of the Aggregates; while that to the second says he was waiting for "the time of parinirvana . . . of the end" (*pariyosāna-kāla*) (Th 196, 606, with Th-a II 64, 257). For some people, however, the attainment of enlightenment is said to be simultaneous with that of final nirvana: these are *samasīsī*, literally "equal-headed," and defined as those in whom the exhaustion of the Corruptions (i.e. Arahantship) and the exhaustion of life happen at exactly the same moment.[43] This is said of a number of monks who commit suicide.[44]

To summarize, the following are the major terms used to refer to (1) nirvana in life and (2) nirvana after death: [45]

(1) (a) the nirvana of the Defilements, *kilesa-(pari)nibbāna*;
(b) the nirvana-element with a remainder of attachment, *sa-upādi-sesa-(pari)nibbāna*;
(c) enlightenment or Awakening, *bodhi* (2.3.a);
(d) *Arahant*-ship (= "sainthood");
(e) various words for knowledge and for the transformation of psychology and behavior (see next section).

(2) (a) The nirvana of the Aggregates, *khandha-(pari)nibbāna*;
(b) the nirvana-element without a remainder of attachment, *an-upadi-sesa-(pari)nibbāna*;
(c) in narratives the event of death (= attaining final nirvana) is usually expressed by a verbal form from *pari-nir-vā*.

1.2.b. Nirvana in life: wisdom, skillfulness, experience

In the *Saṃyutta Nikāya* the monk Sāriputta is asked by the ascetic Jambukhādaka to elucidate a series of terms, of which the first two

[43] *Apubbaṃ acarimaṃ āsava-pariyādānañ ca hoti jīvita-pariyādānañ ca* (A IV 13 = 146, with Mp IV 6–7, Pp 13 with Pp-a 186–7; cp. Sv 774).

[44] E.g. M III 266 and Ps V 83, S I 121 and Spk I 183; on the issue of suicide, see Wiltshire (1983).

[45] For Buddhas there is a third nirvana, later: that of their relics. See 3.2.b. There are, of course, many other synonyms and epithets for nirvana; see 2.1.b.

are nirvana and Arahantship; the reply is the same for both: the destruction of passion, hatred and delusion.[46] The attainment of Arahantship is both a cognitive and an affective transformation: to realize selflessness is both to acquire and retain knowledge – perhaps better said, wisdom or understanding – and to achieve a condition of the heart and mind in which all dispositions and traits which are harmful (in Buddhist eyes) are eliminated. A great deal has been written on this subject, and I mention here only a few things relevant to the overall theme of this book.[47] There are a number of distinctions to be made between the enlightenment of a Buddha and that of an Arahant, but for my purposes here it is possible to treat their attainment of nirvana in life as equivalent. The term *arahā* is often applied to the Buddha, and any enlightened person can be *buddha*, in its general sense of awakened or enlightened.[48] To achieve nirvana in life is to effect permanent changes in wisdom and in moral character, and to make possible certain kinds of experience, both in general terms and as the attainment of specific meditative and spiritual states.

Wisdom. The content of enlightenment is sometimes given as items of Buddhist doctrine, such as Dependent Origination (e.g. Vin I 1–2). It is also given as the Threefold Knowledge, which comprises the memory of former lives, the Divine Eye which sees the death and rebirth of other beings according to their karma, and knowledge of the destruction of the Corruptions (*āsava*).[49] These latter are sense-desires, (desire for future) existence, and ignorance, with (false) view sometimes added as a fourth. Two of these four Corruptions are thus cognitive, the other two affective. The Buddha is said to have attained the first two of the three Knowledges, and then knowledge of Dependent Origination; and then, by reviewing the latter forwards and backwards, he attained Omniscience (*sabbaññutā-ñāṇa*, Ja I 75–6). "Omniscience" is used with increasing frequency in the later literature as a designation for a Buddha's enlightenment; this is one thing which differenti-

46 S IV 251–2; repeated frequently elsewhere, e.g. Vibh 73, said of the "unconditioned element."

47 See, *inter alios*, Horner (1936), Ergardt (1977), Katz (1982), Bond (1984) and Swearer (1987).

48 Commentaries (Spk I 25, Mp I 115) list four *buddha*-s, including omniscient Buddhas (*a* or *the* Buddha in the English sense), and "four-truth" buddhas, i.e. Arahants, so-called because they realize the four Truths.

49 *Tevijjā*, e.g. Vin III 4–5, M I 21–3.

ates a Buddha from an Arahant, who does not become omniscient.[50]

How best can one understand the "knowledge" or "wisdom" of enlightenment? On an immediate level, of course, it is knowledge that certain propositions are true; it is also the cognitive or (to use William James' term) noetic events in which that knowledge is instantiated. But enlightenment is supposed to be neither simply a matter of possessing knowledge (which at times must necessarily be unconscious, or understood in dispositional terms), nor of knowledge-events which exist only for a certain length of time, as someone might enter into a meditative trance for a specific period. Rather, it is supposed to be a continuous form of awareness present throughout any and every activity, achieved by and embodied in the practice of mindfulness. The training in mindfulness which leads to enlightenment can be seen as learning a skill or skills, an education in certain capabilities. It is as much a fact or process of self-cultivation as of self-knowledge.[51] One can use here the distinction between knowing *how* and knowing *that*, which has become customary in philosophy following Gilbert Ryle (1949). The former kind of knowledge refers not only to non-propositional skills such as knowing how to swim or ride a bicycle; many features of this kind of knowledge are required for even the most abstract and formal cognitive operations. These skills are also forms of practice: they have to be learned through trial-and-error training, and they can be performed more or less successfully, more or less intelligently, more or less wisely. Pali words for enlightened knowledge[52] can thus be seen to denote various forms of knowing how, as well as the knowledge that certain propositions are true. When a monk or nun practices for Enlightenment, he or she is practicing a form of self-cultivation aimed at living selflessly, without suffering; the capacity to live and act thus, and the fact of doing so, are an essential part of what it means to be enlightened, to know that there is no self. To adapt R. R. Marett's well-known

[50] The meaning of the term changed over time: Jayatilleke (1963: 202–4, 376–81), Jaini (1974) and Griffiths (1990).

[51] It is only a superficial paradox that the summit of self-knowledge in Buddhism is to realize that there is no self; see Carrithers (1985) and Collins (1994), from which some of the wording in this paragraph is taken.

[52] Examples are: *aññā*, which is a technical term for Enlightenment, and *paññā*, both of which are usually rendered knowledge or wisdom, *vipassanā*, insight, and *yathābhūta-dassana*, seeing things as they really are.

remark about religion, Buddhist enlightenment is not only thought out, but also danced out.

Skillfulness. The transformation of consciousness and moral character effected by the attaining of nirvana in life, then, is cognitive, affective and behavioral. The destruction of the conceit (that) "I am," a synonym for enlightenment (Collins 1982: 94–5), is a matter of inward experience and outward, visible conduct. The kind of deportment and bodily style expected of a serious monk or nun, and a fortiori of an enlightened one, is set out in a number of texts; not surprisingly it emphasizes careful and controlled body-movements.[53] But here I consider rather the form of moral evaluation by which an enlightened person and his or her action are assessed. In what sense could someone who has attained nirvana be or do "good"? The answer distinguishes between two axes of moral evaluation (Premasiri 1976). On the first, the two poles are what is *puñña*, meritorious, and what is *pāpa*, demeritorious or simply bad. Both merit and demerit are phenomena of karma and rebirth, and so acquiring merit, however useful in the short term in attaining good rebirth, is in the long run inimical to attaining nirvana.[54] The other axis has as its two poles what is *kusala* and *akusala*, usually translated wholesome and unwholesome, or skillful and unskillful. These two axes overlap, but they are not the same. Everything that is meritorious is skillful, and everything which is bad is unskillful; but the reverse does not hold. There can be action which is skillful but which, because it is performed by an enlightened person without any trace of attachment or selfishness, does not accumulate merit. Such action is without Corruptions (1.4) and so has no karmic result. For the unenlightened, it is possible to say that there are unskillful acts – minor infractions of the Monastic Rule, for example – which may hinder desired forms of religious practice and experience, but which are not bad in the sense that they do not produce a bad karmic result.[55] Thus the action of an enlightened person (capable

[53] Carrithers (1983: 56–8), who uses the *Visuddhimagga* and his own ethnography in Sri Lanka; cf. Collins (1997).

[54] This is true of the systematic texts I am drawing on here. As will be seen in the Introduction to Part 2, in many narrative texts the separation between what is attainable through the acquisition of merit and the goal of nirvana diminishes to vanishing point; this is borne out by modern ethnography.

[55] See Wijayaratna (1990: 148–9) on the distinction between universal and conventional offenses.

neither of bad nor of any form of unskillfulness) is entirely *kusala,* entirely good but without karmic result.

If the enlightened person is characterized by skillfulness, what of nirvana? Is it good, or wholesome? No – in the classification scheme of the *Abhidhamma,* Existents can be *kusala, akusala,* or neither (*avyākata,* indeterminate): unconditioned nirvana is neither.[56] As Carter (1984) shows, it can be misleading to speak too summarily, as some writers have, of nirvana as "beyond good and evil" *tout court,* since the mental states and actions of a person who has attained nirvana in life are entirely good, in the sense of skillful, without Corruptions. But nonetheless it is clear that *final* nirvana (as opposed to an enlightened person before final nirvana), however much it may be the goal and rationale of all morality in Buddhism, is not itself a moral phenomenon in the Buddhist sense. And this is the sense in which one can say that nirvana is Buddhism's *summum bonum* . As Carter says (1984: 49), the word *attha* can mean goal, aim, profit, etc., and so in this sense "good," and *anattha* the reverse; and so the term *uttamattha,* "highest goal (etc.)" can be said to provide an analogy to *summum bonum.*[57] But although *attha* can indeed mean "good," and *anattha* "bad," in various senses, they do not form a paired evaluative dichotomy as commonly as do *bonus / malus* or good/bad. In relation to the two most common dichotomies, *puñña/ pāpā* and *kusala/ akusala,* nirvana is neither.

Experience. The most common thing said about nirvana in Buddhist texts is that it is the ending of suffering (*dukkha*). Clearly after the death of the enlightened person, at the quenching of the Aggregates, there can be no *dukkha* in any of its three forms: there is no feeling, no change, and nirvana is unconditioned. In what sense does an enlightened person, before this final attainment, escape from suffering? "There is no mental pain (*cetasika dukkha*) for one who is without longing . . . Truly all fears have been

[56] Paṭis I 85, Dhs 180 no. 983 (n.b. the text here should be corrected to *asaṃkhatā ca dhātu;* see C. A. F. Rhys Davids [1900: 231 n. 4], Tabata et al. [1987: 128]), 234 no. 1370. The *Kathāvatthu* (585) specifically records that some other Buddhists held that nirvana was *kusala,* on the grounds that it is "faultless" (*anavajja*), but that the Theravāda denied that the term could be so used.

[57] It is usually explained in commentaries as referring to Arahantship; e.g. Spk I 86, Dhp-a IV 142, 169, It-a I 64, Pj II 332, 368, Th-a II 240, 270. At Cp 171 it is used in relation to the Buddha, and Cp-a 131 glosses as "Buddhahood" (*buddhabhāva*). Ap-a 233 glosses simply as nirvana.

overcome by one who has annihilated his fetters."[58] Since by definition – in the four Noble Truths – suffering is caused by Desire or Craving (*taṇhā*), the saint who is without Craving cannot cause any more suffering. He or she can still experience pleasant and painful feelings, however, but since there is no attachment to them, no Craving involved in the experiential process, in this sense there can be no "mental pain." A number of stories about both Arahants and the Buddha make clear that they suffer both bodily pain[59] and certain kinds of mental discomfort. One episode, found in a number of texts, concerns the Buddha's leaving the noisy and troublesome monks at Kosambi to live in the solitude of the forest with an elephant called Pārileyya. He had told the monks a number of *Jātaka* stories by way of admonition, but

> in spite of his admonition he was unable to reunite them. Thereupon, unhappy because of the crowded conditions under which he lived, he reflected, "Under present conditions I am crowded and jostled and live a life of discomfort (*dukkhaṃ viharāmi*). Moreover, these monks pay no attention to what I say. Suppose I were to retire from the haunts of men and live a life of solitude."'[60]

So even enlightened Buddhas can sometimes find things irksome, uncomfortable.

Apart from the general change in experience resulting from the absence of mental suffering, there are two meditative attainments which might be classed under the head of "experience made possible by Enlightenment," albeit that at least one of them seems more an absence of experience than a special kind. They are:

58 Th 707, translated by Norman (EV I: 70). Mv-a I 9 says "a person endowed with the element of nirvana with a remainder of attachment" is freed from mental *dukkha*, and a "person endowed with the element of nirvana without a remainder of attachment" is freed from bodily pain. Taken alone, the latter, *anupādisesa-nibbāna-dhātu-samaṅgi-puggala* could imply that a person exists after final nirvana; but it should be interpreted as referring to a person on the point of attaining final nirvana ('dying'). Cf. Nett 12, cited on p. 140 n. 11 above.

59 One well-known case is that of the Buddha's disciple Moggallāna, who was murdered as a result of his killing his parents in a former life (see DPPN s.v.). Various episodes in the Buddha's life show him to suffer physically (Lamotte 1976: Appendix Note v). In the case of Arahants, this is said to be the result of past *karma*; but there seem to have been differing opinions as to whether this is the case with the Buddha (see Walters 90).

60 Vin I 352–3, Ud 41–2, Dhp-a I 56ff., in Burlinghame's (21, vol. 1: 178) translation of the latter. The word he renders "unhappy," *ukkanṭhita*, is used to mean "fed up," "discontent," often in connection with monks who are unhappy with the celibate life and long for their former wives. The *Udāna* version adds that he lived *na phāsu*, uncomfortably; the commentary (Ud-a 249) explains this as "not happily, in an undesirable way because of the dissatisfaction of mind" (*na sukhaṃ: anārādhita-cittatāya na iṭṭhan ti*). For the Buddha's love of quiet and solitude see the references gathered at DPPN I 806, II 305.

(i) the Attainment(s) of Fruition (*phalasamāpatti*) of the Path, the highest of which is in some texts associated with a meditative state called the Signless Liberation (or Concentration) of Mind (*animitta-ceto-vimutti*, or-*samādhi*); and

(ii) the Cessation of Perception/Ideation and Feeling (*saññāvedayita-nirodha*), also known as the Attainment of Cessation (*nirodha-samāpatti*) (referred to here as Cessation).

In the present state of scholarship neither of these attainments is understood clearly, nor is the relationship between them; for my purposes no extensive discussion of this unclarity is needed.[61] It is likely that from a historical perspective the prima facie lack of coherence in textual descriptions of these states betrays a real incoherence. It seems likely that a number of originally independent schemes of meditation have been put together, and an attempt made, unsuccessfully, to blend two differing emphases in the path to salvation: that which sees it primarily as the inculcation of nondiscursive, yogic, or (to use Eliade's term) enstatic states of consciousness; and that which sees it as primarily the acquisition of wisdom or understanding, a wisdom which is expressible in discursive form, albeit that the instantiation of that wisdom may not be discursive in itself.[62]

For my purposes, it is sufficient to follow the discussion of these states in the *Visuddhimagga*, Chapter XXIII (cf. the similar discussion at Paṭis-a 267–9, 318–22). This chapter deals with four Advantages of Developing Understanding, of which only two concern me here: (i) the Experience of the Taste of the Noble Fruit (*ariyaphala-rasānubhavana*) and (ii) the ability to attain Cessation. The Experience of the Taste of the Noble Fruit refers to each of the four Fruits attainable at the four stages of the Path.[63]

[61] More detailed, though inconclusive discussion of these issues can be found in La Vallée Poussin (36–7), Da Silva (1978), Schmithausen (1979), King (1980), Griffiths (1986) and Harvey (1986).

[62] The next section, from here to p. 161, may be omitted by nonspecialist readers.

[63] In the form in which they became standard in the later literature, they are: the stage of stream-winner (*sotāpanna*), after which the person will gain enlightenment within seven more lives; that of the once-returner (*sakadāgāmin*), who will be reborn on earth once more; that of the non-returner (*anāgāmin*), who is certain to attain nirvana in his or her next life, in one of the heavens; and that of the Arahant. Masefield (1986) shows that more research is needed to understand the development of this fourfold classification; but unfortunately his work is so wilfully idiosyncratic as to be an entirely unreliable guide to this question.

Such a Fruit can be experienced in two ways. First, it can occur as a momentary state of mind, as a form of knowledge, as a person progresses through the Path. Even at the first moment of entering the Path, called Change-of-Lineage, this knowledge "makes nirvana its object, the signless, occurrence-less, condition-less cessation."[64] Secondly, when this momentary state is converted into a continuous experience, it – at least that of the highest stage – seems to be closely similar to, if not identical with the Signless Liberation of Mind.[65] For this, two conditions (*paccayā*) are necessary: "turning one's attention from all signs, and paying attention to the signless element" (M I 296, cited in Vism here). The *Sutta* commentary (Ps II 353), like the *Visuddhimagga*, explains the latter as the nirvana-element. In order to make the state endure more than a moment, a specific "previous condition(ing)" (*pubbe abhisaṃkāra*, M I 297) is necessary, which determines the time at which the meditator will emerge from it (Vism 701 = XXIII 12). Although this experience has nirvana as its object, it is a conditioned phenomenon; this is explicitly stated at M III 108, where the Signless Concentration of Mind occurs in sequence after the usual list of eight Meditative Levels (cp. S IV 262–9). It is through seeing that even so refined a state is "conditioned, brought into being by (prior) volition," that enlightenment takes place. Elsewhere, however, the highest of the Attainments of Fruition, the Fruit of Arahantship, is called a kind of nirvana: at Pj I 157 (cf. Ud-a 179) a monk is said to "experience the nirvana which is called the Fruit of Arahantship."

The relation between this experience (as a moment of knowledge in the Path and as a continuous state of meditative absorption) and that of Cessation remains unclear. In a detailed study Schmithausen suggests that they seem to be "closely related, if not identical" (1979: 235–6 and notes 132–3). Buddhaghosa treats them separately in the *Visuddhimagga*, however; both here and elsewhere Cessation seems to be even more closely associated with nirvana, albeit that there remain differences. Whereas the Taste of the Noble Fruit is attained by individuals at all four levels of the

64 *Animittaṃ appavattaṃ, visaṃkhāraṃ nirodhaṃ nibbānam arammaṇaṃ kurumānaṃ* (Vism 672, XXII 5).

65 Harvey (1986) discusses various ways *animitta* appears in the texts. The "signless" liberation of mind is found in a group of three, together with the "empty" and "desireless" liberations: see, for example, Paṭis XX.

Path, Cessation is only attained by the those at the highest two, Non-returners and Arahants (Vism 702, XXIII 18).[66] Buddhaghosa says that Cessation is made to last by a predetermination of (the) time (for its duration) (*kāla-paricchedа*, 708 = XXIII 48); this suggests that, like the Signless Concentration of Mind, it is produced through conditions. But when the question is posed whether it is conditioned or unconditioned, the reply is: "It cannot be said to be conditioned or unconditioned (*saṃkhatā, asaṃkhatā*), mundane or supramundane. Why? Because it has no Individual Nature (*sabhāvato natthitāya;* cf. Vibh-a 78). But since it comes to be attained by one who attains it, it is therefore permissible to say that is produced, not unproduced" (*nipphanna, no anipphana*, 709, XXIII 52). Buddhaghosa asks "Why do [people] attain it?" The answer is "Tiring (*ukkaṇṭhitvā*) of the arising and breaking-up of Conditioning Factors, here and now [or: in this life, *diṭṭhe va dhamme*] they become without mind, attain the Cessation which is nirvana (*nirodhaṃ nibbānaṃ patvā*) and live happily" (Vism 705 = XXIII 29). The commentary here (1676) remarks, gnomically, "it is just like [or: as if] they attain nirvana with no remainder of clinging." The word "just like" (*viya*) is necessitated by the fact that nirvana, as a really existing Existent, has an Individual Nature (1.3).

There are texts in the *Sutta* collection which place Cessation in a position analogous to that of nirvana, as the ninth and culminating stage of meditative practice, added to the standard set of eight (itself probably the result of placing in sequence two originally separate groups of four); but ambiguity is never absent.[67] Since the eight levels are standardly correlated with different heavens, such that the meditator who attains one or another level is reborn in the corresponding heaven (4.1, Table 4.1), it might seem that Cessation, as the ninth level, should be in some way analogous as a "gateway" to nirvana, beyond the heavens. But this would seem to be expressly denied in the famous story of the Buddha's final nirvana. He is said to have gone through the meditative levels and arrived at the ninth, at which point Ānanda, his close but unenlightened attendant, exclaimed that his master had attained nirvana. The enlightened monk Anuruddha corrected

[66] It cannot be attained by beings in the Formless Worlds (see 4.1.a).
[67] This can be seen by comparing A IV 438–48 with A 449–54.

him, pointing out that the Buddha had only attained Cessation. The text then has the Buddha descend to the first Meditation Level, then back to the fourth, and only after emerging from that stage does he attain final nirvana (D II 156). The Buddha is reported to have said that as long as he had not entered into and emerged from all nine Meditation Levels he would not have attained full and complete enlightenment (A IV 438–48); but elsewhere it is held that enlightenment is attainable by Dry-visioned Arahants,[68] who do not experience meditative absorption at all, and those "freed by wisdom," who either do not attain the Meditation Levels or at least have limited experience of them (see Da Silva 1978).

There is also a more general problem concerning the relationship between Cessation and enlightening knowledge. As just mentioned, in a number of texts Cessation seems to be the culmination of Buddhist practice. The problem here is how to relate such an idea of salvation to the more general emphasis on understanding and insight in the attainment of the Buddhist goal. It would seem to follow from Buddhist psychology that since Cessation is the temporary suspension of Perception/Ideation (*saññā*), there could be no discursive awareness of the kind required for analytical understanding. Perhaps some redactors of texts felt this very problem, since in a proportion of the canonical passages which depict the attainment in this way there occurs the phrase "and in him [the one who has attained the state], (because of his) seeing with wisdom, the Corruptions are wholly destroyed."[69]

For present purposes, it is enough to say that the Taste of the Noble Fruit, the Fruit of Arahantship, and the Attainment of Cessation seem to be regarded, in some texts, to a greater or lesser extent, as analogous or even equivalent to nirvana, as a kind of experience or foretaste of it. But perhaps one is mistaken always to assume that in these contexts the word *nibbāna* is being used as a technical term, referring to the Unconditioned state. It is an action noun (2.1.a), which can be used (as can the causative form *nibbāpana*), to refer to various processes of extinguishing or quenching, in relation to both literal and religious-metaphorical

68 E.g. Spk I 253, Th-a III 209, Paṭis-a 584, Vism 666 = XXI 112; they are specifically said to be incapable of attaining Cessation at Vism 702 = XXIII 18.

69 *Paññāya c' assa disvā āsavā parikkhīnā honti.* References can be found in Schmithausen (1979), Griffiths (1986).

flames, as well as to the completed state of extinction or being quenched. Perhaps when *nibbāna* is placed in apposition to these meditative attainments, one should interpret it not as expressing a relation of identity between one or other state and nirvana (either enlightenment or final), but gloss it in something like the following manner: that particular process of experiential quenching called the Taste of the Noble Fruit (of Arahantship), or Cessation, where such experiential processes are clearly different from the facts of the moral extinguishing of passion, or the ontological extinguishing of rebirth. One can see such a usage of the word *vimokkha*, liberation, in the fifth chapter of the *Patisambhidāmagga* (Paṭis II 35–71), called the "Treatise on Liberation(s)," *Vimokkha-kathā* . *Vimokkha*, which can be used as a synonym for nirvana, is not used solely in that way but as an inclusive category term referring to many different processes of, or occasions for being liberated, which include the various levels of the Path, and all the Meditation Levels (including Cessation[70]). One can certainly find passages where nirvana is expressly said not to be a temporary, meditative state of mind: the commentary to a *Majjhima* passage mentioned already (Ps II 355 on M I 298) lists thirteen Existents which can be put in the category Signless Liberation(s) of Mind, and adds that although nirvana is signless, it is not a liberation of mind, and so is not included in the list.[71]

Whatever the final conclusion on these issues, if there ever is one, these meditative states are clearly seen as very highly advanced conditions, which come close to being identified with the state of nirvana in life, even though they could not in any circumstances be said to exhaust the meaning of that term.

1.2.c. Nirvana after death: it really exists!

In 1.1.c timeless nirvana was opposed to the three times, past, present and future. These are called subjects of discourse, or

[70] Paṭis I 40; the "liberation through cessation" is omitted in Ñāṇamoli's translation (1975), and should be inserted between nos. 24 and 25 on p. 241.

[71] Elsewhere there are said to be two "liberations" (*dve vimokkhā*): liberation of mind and nirvana (Ps I 43, It-a I 166, As 409 on Dhs 1367). Enlightenment is, of course, a liberation of mind in a general sense, but it is not a meditative state which begins and ends at specific times.

things one can talk about (*kathāvatthūni*, D III 220, A I 197); a text in the *Itivuttaka* (53–4) consists in a short piece of prose, in which the Buddha simply mentions the three times, after which he immediately breaks into verse:

> people think in terms of what is expressible (*akkheyya-saññino sattā*),
> they establish themselves on what is expressible;
> not (properly) understanding what is expressible,
> they fall under the power of death . . .
> Whoever is endowed with (understanding of) what is expressible,
> at peace, delighting in the peaceful realm,
> practicing carefully and standing (firm) in the Doctrine,
> that wise one is beyond (all) reckoning (*saṅkhaṃ nopeti*).

To be beyond reckoning here is to attain a state within life which cannot be counted among the categories of the temporal, conditioned world; the same thing is true, obviously and a fortiori, of the Arahant after death.[72] Another verse of the *Itivuttaka* (58) says that the saint has gone down (that is, has set, like the sun) and is no longer measurable (*atthaṃgato so na pamāṇaṃ eti*); the commentary (It-a II 38) explains that this can refer either to the Arahant or to final nirvana. When a questioner asks the Buddha first whether the saint after death is conscious, and then whether he exists, the replies (Sn 1074, 1076) are:

> Just as a flame put out by a gust of wind
> goes down and is beyond reckoning,
> so the sage free from name-and-form
> goes down and is beyond reckoning . . .
> There is no measuring of one who has gone down,
> there is nothing by which he might be discussed;
> when all attributes (*dhamma*) are removed
> so have all ways of speaking been removed.[73]

The extinguished flame is of course the best-known image of nirvana in the West. In another very well-known text, the ascetic Vacchagotta questions the Buddha about where the enlightened person is reborn; on receiving the reply that the verb "is reborn" is inapplicable, he asks if it is the case that such a person is not reborn. The Buddha replies that this term is also inapplicable (according to the commentary, Ps III 198, this was because

[72] The last line of the verses just cited occurs in a similar way in three *Sutta*-s at S IV 206–7 and 218, where it is used of the enlightened person after the break-up of the body.

[73] These verses are discussed also in Collins (1982, Chapter 4.1 and 4.2, especially pp. 127–31).

Vacchagotta would have interpreted this as Annihilation; that is, he would have understood nirvana as nothingness). He uses the analogy of a fire gone out: just as without fuel a fire goes out and one cannot say where it has gone to, so it is impossible to point out the enlightened person, since he is "freed from reckoning" by the five Aggregates. He continues with another image: the enlightened person is deep, immeasurable, unfathomable like the great ocean (M I 486–8). (This text is discussed in 2.2.b and c.) At the end of the *Brahmajāla Sutta*, the Buddha says that his body "remains (alive) with that which leads to rebirth cut off": "while his body remains, so long will gods and men see him; (but) after the break-up of the body, at the exhaustion of life, they will not see him" (D I 46). The commentary explains here that this is because he will then have reached a state beyond designation (or conceptualization: *appaṇṇatika-bhāva*, Sv 128). This term is often used in commentarial texts discussing the state of final nirvana.[74]

A number of epithets for nirvana suggest that although it can be an object of the conscious mind, it is nonetheless difficult of cognitive access, at least for those not on the Path: it is unseeable, unthinkable, nonmanifest, free of (conceptual) differentiation. Final nirvana is disappearance, in nominal and corresponding verbal forms.[75] *Anakkhāta*, "(the) not expressed" (Dhp 218), is said by the commentary (Dhp-a III 289) to refer to nirvana, "because [nirvana] is not describable (*avattabbatāya*) as being made by such-and-such, or as having characteristics such as (being) blue, etc."[76] Nirvana is indescribable, beyond the sphere of reason, and not characterized by discursive thought.[77] Considerations such as

[74] E.g. Sv 128, Spk II 331, III 210, Dhp-a II 163, Ud-a 175, It-a I 180; cp. Mil 73. The word can be spelled *apaññatti(ka)-bhāva*. It is used of the Arahant in this life (Ps II 115, 120, Spk II 83, Ud-a 353), of the Arahant now but referring proleptically to final nirvana (Ud-a 216, It-a II 33), and of both nirvana in life and final nirvana together (Spk II 82, Dhp-a II 163; Carter and Palihawadana [1987: 453 n. 25] cite Sinhala commentaries).

[75] Unseeable, *adassana/anidassana*: S IV 370, Dh 46 with Dhp-a I 337, Dhs 192 (no. 1088), 244– no. 1441, Ap-a 344, Bv-a 257; unthinkable, *acintiya*: Sp 89 = Mv XVII 56, XXXI 125, cp. Mv-a 383; nonmanifest, *apātubhāva*: As 214; free from conceptual differentiation, *nippapañca(pada)*: S IV 370, A III 294 with Mp III 348; disappearance (noun, *antaradhāna*): e.g. Vin III 8 with Sp 187, D III 122, Mil 217; (verbal forms, from [*sam*]*antaradhāyati*): e.g. Ja I 29 = Bv-a 129–30, 176–7, 257 (where it is glossed as *adassanabhāvaṃ upagato*, "became unseeable").

[76] The Sanskrit parallels of this text, however, either omit this verse, or use another term for *anakkhāta*; see Carter and Palihawadana (1987: 471 n. 11).

[77] Indescribable, *na vattabba*: As 418; beyond . . . reason, *atakkavacāra*: It 37, Ud-a 391; not . . . discursive thought, *avitakka-avicāra* Dhs 182 (no. 998), 236 (no. 1385), Moh 137.

these can lead one to stress the incomprehensibility and paradox of nirvana;[78] and it might seem difficult straightforwardly to use either of the English words "existence" or "nonexistence" of it. But in the lexicon of Buddhist systematic discourse nirvana is a genuine Existent, not merely a conceptual one: an element in the classificatory scheme of ultimately existing things. As Mil 270 says, it is an *atthi-dhamma*, something which (really) exists, not a *natthi-dhamma*, something which does not, as is the case with Existents which are merely concepts (i.e. objects of the mind but only that). "Nirvana exists, . . . it can be known by the mind" (that is, it can be the object of the mental sense-base).[79] The classification of nirvana as an external Existent, a possible Mental Object, is elaborated most carefully in *Abhidhamma* texts, to which I turn presently, but first I consider some *Sutta* passages widely cited in secondary literature, which assert that nirvana exists.

Udāna 80–1 contain four *Sutta*-s, in each of which the Buddha "instructs, rouses, heartens and delights" a group of monks "with a talk connected with nirvana" (*nibbāna-paṭisaṃyuttāya kathāya*), and ends with a Spirited Utterance (*udāna*, the name of the collection as a whole). The contents of the talks on nirvana are not given; the commentary suggests that they were about nirvana and the way to attain it through following the Path. (The commentary interprets all four passages in terms of nirvana's relation to the Path.) When the Buddha uttered the *Udāna*, the commentary explains, he was filled with rapture and joy (*uppanna-pīti-somanasso*) through recalling the good qualities of nirvana. In modern scholarship usually only the third of these Utterances is cited; sometimes the first is given. There are analogous passages elsewhere in the Canon, and the third occurs by itself at It 37–8. At Ud 80–1 the passages have clearly been redacted together as a group, in sequence; the commentary (Ud-a 388–97) takes them to constitute a continuous argument. This seems to me to be interesting in its own right, whether or not the materials which the redactors juxtaposed and the commentary explains were or were not previously discrete.

[78] Slater (1951) is a sympathetic and useful, albeit now rather outdated account in these terms.

[79] *Atthi nibbānaṃ . . . manoviññeyyaṃ* (ibid.). On nirvana as a mental object, classified under the headings of Mental Sense-base and Mental Data Element, see below pp. 175–6.

(*1*) *The Buddha's first Spirited Utterance* is:

That sphere (*āyatana*) exists, monks, where there is no earth, no water, no heat and no wind, where the sphere of infinite space does not exist, nor that of infinite consciousness, nor that of neither-perception-nor-non-perception; there is neither this world nor the other world, neither moon nor sun; there, I say,[80] there is no coming and going, no duration (of life, to be followed by) death and rebirth; it is not stationed,[81] it is without occurrence(s), and has no object. This, indeed, is the end of suffering.

According to the commentary, this "makes clear that nirvana is an existing state in the ultimate sense" (*nibbānassa . . . paramatthato vijjamāna-bhāva-vibhāvanaṃ*). The verb *atthi*, to be, translated here as exists, is glossed by *vijjati*, is found, and by *paramatthato upalabbhati*, "is found in the ultimate sense" (on these terms see p. 173 below). The Buddha made his utterance, so the commentary alleges, because he knew that some monks listening to him had been wondering, given that all Existents are brought about by causes, what was the cause of the Nirvana-Existent (*nibbāna-dhamma*)? There cannot be an answer to this question, of course, since what is unconditioned cannot be caused by anything. But nirvana can enter into causal relations with the conditioned world of experience, as the commentary here exemplifies: it can be the object of the knowledge which arises as the fruit of the Path, just as physical forms (and other sensory objects) are the objects of eye-consciousness, etc. The standard analysis of sense-experience in Buddhism is causal: the object, the internal sense and the contact between the two together cause the experience (Collins 82: 103, 141). The word *āyatana*, which is just as vague as English "sphere," has many different meanings. One of them is "Sense-base," of which there are twelve: that is, the six senses (the usual five plus mind, as always in Buddhism) and their objects. The commentary here is taking *āyatana* in the sense of "Mental Object Sense-base" (*dhammāyatana*, the object of the mental sense), more precisely as the object-condition of Path-knowledge (its *ārammaṇa-paccaya*, one of the twenty-four modes of relation catalogued in *Abhidhamma* texts). For this reason the word gloss for *āyatana*, is

80 Reading here *na* (or *no*) *ubho candimasuriyā tatra p'āhaṃ*, with Ud-a 391 and F. L. Woodward's list of errata in the reprinted PTS edition of the text. See also Windisch (1890: 105).

81 That is, it is not a rebirth Destiny; on such "stationing" see Collins (1982: 213–18).

kāraṇa, cause. That is to say, although unconditioned and timeless, nirvana can nonetheless come into a causal relation with a spatio-temporally located event of human consciousness.

This first Utterance, according to the commentary, contains an argument from opposition: because Conditioned Existents exist, so nirvana must exist as an unconditioned *dhamma*, since of all really-existing Existents (those with "individual nature") there exists an opposite.[82] Among the examples given, which include both contradictories and contraries, are suffering/Happiness, heat/cold, birth/non-birth. (This form of argument, and the text cited by the commentary here, will recur presently.)[83] So the text's assertion is being construed as implying an argument: the Buddha lists various objects and events of the changing, differentiated and conditioned world (any would have done), and states that their contradictory, undifferentiated nirvana, (therefore) exists.

(2) *The Buddha's second Spirited Utterance* is likewise in the text an assertion, construed by the commentary as, if not fully an argument, at least explicable by means of what it sees as a coherently interrelated set of propositions: the four Noble Truths. It is:

It is hard indeed to see the desireless[84]; it is not easy to see the truth. Craving is fully understood for one who knows; there is nothing (left) for one who sees.

This seems straightforward; although exactly what "nothing" means here is not at first sight clear. In the first line, the com-

[82] *Paṭipakkhattā sabhāva-dhammānaṃ.* Elsewhere it is said that "nirvana is one, but it has many names because it is the opposite of the names of all conditioned things" (*ekaṃ eva hi nibbānaṃ nāmāni pan' assa sabbasaṃkhatānaṃ nāma-paṭipakkhavasena anekāni honti*); for references and discussion see 2.1.b.

[83] One other point from the commentary here is worth noting: the reason why moon and sun are not found in nirvana, it is said, is because darkness can only exist where there are physical forms, and moon and sun exist in order to dispel the darkness. But there is no physical existence in nirvana, and so no need for moon and sun: "in this way he teaches that the individual nature of this same nirvana is light"; see 2.2.a.

[84] There are textual difficulties here: variants are found in mss. and the PTS edition of text and commentary. The PTS text reads *anattaṃ*, not-self, citing variants; Woodward (1935) corrects this to *anantaṃ* and translates "infinite." The PTS commentary has two readings. The first is *anataṃ*, construed as "un-bent," taking *nata* to be from *naṃ*, to bend or incline, used metaphorically for desire (*taṇhā*) since desire inclines people to sense-experience and sense-pleasure. Thus nirvana is *anata* because it is without desire. The second is *anantam*, construed as "without end" (*anta-virahitaṃ*) because nirvana's Individual Nature (*sabhāva*) is permanence. It also records the opinion that *anantaṃ* is taken by some to mean measureless (*appamāṇa*). CPD s.v. *anata* says that *anantaṃ* is unmetrical, and corrects to *anattaṃ* and *atta-virahitaṃ*, "not-self" and "without self."

mentary takes "the desireless" and "the truth" to refer to nirvana. In the second, it says, fully to understand Craving is fully to understand the first and second Noble Truths, suffering and its cause (*taṇhā* = Craving), and to experience (by means of the fourth Truth, the Path) the third Truth, the cessation of Craving and suffering (= nirvana). The last clause is taken also to refer to the absence of Craving, and hence of the "round of Defilements" (*kilesa-vaṭṭa*), that is to say of rebirth. The problem of differentiating this sense of there being nothing (= there is nothing left of Craving and suffering) from simple nothingness (= non-existence), seems to be what lies behind the commentary's remarks introducing the third Spirited Utterance, which continue immediately and seamlessly after its exegesis of the second Utterance, and before it cites the third Utterance itself. Some monks, it says, listening to the Buddha's next sermon on nirvana, wondered, as on the first occasion, how nirvana can "exist in reality and in the ultimate sense" (*sacchik'aṭṭha-paramatthena upalabbhati*), given that no condition for it has been stated by the Buddha, whereas he has clearly said that ignorance and the like are the conditions of rebirth and suffering. The Buddha knew of their doubt, and made the next Utterance in order to dispel it, and to defeat the Wrong Views held by ascetics and Brahmins for whom anyone speaking of nirvana is just telling stories,[85] and by "outsiders" such as materialists and others (*lokāyatikādiyo*) who hold that it does not exist because it has no individual nature (*sabhāva*). This utterance also "illustrates the existence [of nirvana] in the ultimate sense" (*paramatthato atthibhāva-dīpanaṃ*).

(3) *The Buddha's Third Spirited Utterance* is:

There exists, monks, that [no substantive is used] in which there is no birth, where nothing has come into existence, where nothing has been made, where there is nothing conditioned. If that in which there is no birth . . . [etc.] did not exist, no escape here from what is [or: for one who is] born, become, made, conditioned would be known. But since there is that in which there is no birth, where nothing has come into existence, where nothing has been made, where there is nothing conditioned, an escape here for what is [or: for one who is] born, become, made, conditioned is known.

[85] *Nibbānam nibbānan ti c'āha taṃ vatthumattaṃ eva.* Cp. It-a I 160–3, *tathā vuttamattaṃ eva,* "just words."

This Utterance is the one most commonly quoted, usually by itself. Unlike the others, it does appear in the text as an argument rather than simple assertion(s), although it is not easy to see exactly what the argument is, as will be seen. Before coming to that, however, I should mention that the translation here differs from that standardly given, and follows the analysis (though not the exact words) of Norman (92b).[86]

The usual translation, as in the PTS version by Woodward (1935: 98) is this: "Monks, there is a not-born, a not-become, a not-made, a not-compounded (etc.). Monks, if that unborn, not-become, not-made, not-compounded were not, there would be apparent no escape from this here that is born, become, made, compounded." A problem with this, as Norman points out, is that at least the first epithet in this version, and perhaps the others, could also apply to *saṃsāra,* the round of rebirth, since it is universally regarded as beginningless (and endless: 3.2.c). The "unbornness" and the endlessness of *saṃsāra,* however, are quite different from those of nirvana. In the case of *saṃsāra,* the passage of time – that is to say, the conditioned arising and ceasing of Existents which produces time – has always occurred and always will: temporal duration is infinite, in the sense of having no boundary point in the past or future. Nirvana, to the contrary, does not involve temporal duration at all, and so it cannot be "unborn" and unending in the same sense. Norman suggests that the past participles *-jāta, -bhūta, -kata, -saṃkhata* should be taken here as action nouns (there are many other examples of this usage), and the adjectival compounds construed not as descriptive determinative but as possessive/exocentric: that is, instead of not-born or "unborn," etc. as in the standard translation, one renders "of/in which there is no birth," etc., as in my translation here. This solves the problem in construing the epithets differently in the case of nirvana, in a way which clearly expresses nirvana's timelessness. Nirvana is that in which temporal duration does not take place, since there is no conditioning, and so the usual events of conditioned duration do not take place. There are no births, no ends,[87] nothing becomes (= changes), nothing is made, and, as universally said, there is no process of conditioning.

[86] Nonspecialists may skip the next three paragraphs.

[87] This is why I interpreted *ananta,* endless, as meaning "there are no ends in it" on p. 141 above.

An intricate but solvable problem remains with the fourth epithet, *asaṃkhata.* As has been seen, this is used elsewhere both as an adjective applied to, and as a substantive synonymous with nirvana, and I have translated it there as a descriptive determinative, "(the) Unconditioned." If one takes this to mean "not having come into existence through previous conditions," then it too applies to *saṃsāra.*[88] This problem can be solved, if one interprets the term *asaṃkhata* in two ways: as (i) "not (originally) brought into being by conditions", and (ii) "not maintained in being by conditions." Both *saṃsāra* (because temporal duration is beginningless) and nirvana (because of the nonexistence of temporal duration) would then be *asaṃkhata* in the first sense, but only nirvana could be unconditioned in the second.

Once this interpretation of the epithets used here is understood, one can make more sense of other passages also. Interpreting *ajāta* as a possessive adjective, "without birth," can distinguish the sense in which it applies to *nibbāna* from the descriptive determinative meaning "unborn" when that is used, for example, in relation to future time (as an equivalent of *anāgata:* see PTC s.v. *ajāta*). At Pj I 180, the word *amata,* deathless, is glossed by the phrase *na jāyati na jīyati na mīyati ti,* which Ñāṇamoli (1960: 195) renders "neither is born nor ages nor dies"; and at Dhp-a I 228, *amatapadaṃ* is glossed with *amataṃ vuccati nibbānaṃ taṃ hi ajātattā na jiyyati na miyyati,* which Carter and Palihawadana (1987: 110) render "Deathless means Nibbāna. Nibbāna, because of being unborn [i.e. without beginning] is not subject to old age and death." In both these cases one can now see that the verbs, which are passive in form although (in the case of the last two) translated as intransitives in English, should in fact be taken as impersonal. That is to say, at Pj I 180 one would translate "(it is deathless because) there is no being born, no growing old and no dying;"[89] and at Dhp-a I 228, "because of there being no birth (there) there is no growing old, no dying." As mentioned earlier, the passage redacted here as the Buddha's Third Spirited Utterance occurs

[88] So indeed would all others which presuppose a time before *saṃsāra,* and with it time, began; such as *akammaja,* not born from *karma,* predicated of nirvana at Mil 268, 271.

[89] This interpretation is also suggested by the phrase preceding this, which Ñāṇamoli renders, accurately, as "since in this case 'no arising is evident, [no subsidence (fall) is evident] no otherness of what is present [is evident]', therefore, taking it that . . ." The passage partly cited, and which Ñāṇamoli completes with the words in square brackets, is A I 152, cited on p. 141 above.

also at It 37–8, where two verses are added; the second refers to the escape from what is born, etc., as a "place" (*padaṃ*) which is *ajātaṃ asamuppannaṃ asokaṃ virajaṃ* – all of which can now be seen to be possessives, to be rendered "where there is no birth, nothing arisen, no sorrow, (and which is) without stain."

The third Spirited Utterance has the form of an argument, in three propositions:

(i) nirvana exists;
(ii) if it did not exist, there could be no escape from *saṃsāra*;
(iii) but since it does exist, there is therefore an escape from *saṃsāra*.

Stated abstractly, this is:

(i) X exists;
(ii) if X did not exist, Y could not exist;
(iii) but X does exist, therefore Y exists.

In symbolic form this is: $\exists x$. If $-x \supset -y$. $\exists x \supset y$, which is fallacious. The same form of argument would hold for:

(i) the Atlantic Ocean [= a mass of water, not earth, sand or rock] exists;
(ii) if the Atlantic Ocean did not exist, swimming from Europe to America could not exist;
(iii) but the Atlantic Ocean does exist, therefore swimming from Europe to America exists.

This is obviously invalid; (i) and (ii) hold, since the Atlantic Ocean exists and water is a necessary condition of swimming; but (iii) does not follow, since the existence of water is a necessary but not sufficient condition for it to be possible to swim across oceans: other factors militate against that. In the case of the third Utterance's argument, imagine, as did some Mahāyāna Buddhists, that there are beings who are intrinsically incapable of attaining nirvana; imagine further that all other beings have already attained nirvana. In this case, (i) and (ii) would hold, i.e. that nirvana exists and that if it did not there would be no escape from *saṃsāra;* but not (iii), since other factors militate against that: i.e. there must also exist beings capable of making such an escape, which in this case there are not.

One can save the Utterance from this fallacy by making either of two moves. First, in (ii) and (iii) Y may be understood not as the actual, instantiated fact of escape from *saṃsāra*, but merely the possibility of such escape (without discussing other factors). In this case the argument is valid. One can still dispute the major premise: the existence of nirvana here is not proved, or even argued for, it is merely stated. Second, the optative tenses in (ii) can be taken precisely to assert that X is a necessary but not sufficient condition for Y, and the words *yasmā . . . tasmā* (since . . . therefore) in (iii) to assert further that X is indeed not only a necessary but also a sufficient condition for Y.[90] This saves the sequence of assertions from formal fallacy, but once again, nirvana's existence has not been proved.

The Buddha is depicted as making these Utterances to an audience of monks: preaching to the converted, as it were. One might then assume that nirvana's existence is assumed by all concerned. But the commentary does not. Just as it took the assertion of the first Utterance that nirvana exists to be based on an argument from opposites, so here in the third Utterance it takes the assertion that nirvana exists to be in fact based on an argument from the existence of the Path. It restates the point of the Utterance thus (Ud-a195):

> monks, if there were no Unconditioned Element whose individual nature is to be without birth, etc., then there would no escape in this world from Form and the rest, which are called the five Aggregates, whose individual nature it is to be characterized by birth, etc., and (their) remainderless calming would not be made known, would not occur, would not come about. But since the factors of the Eightfold Path, which occur with nirvana as their object, (do) completely cut off the Defilements with no remainder, from this the nonoccurrence of, the disappearance of, and the escape from all the suffering of rebirth is made known.

It is important that the Buddha's argument here is addressed to monks. Its form is: if and only if Nirvana exists can the Path be efficacious in completely removing the Defilements; since (as all concerned, speaker and audience agree) it is thus efficacious, nirvana therefore really exists, in the ultimate sense. The logical form of this argument is:

(i) if and only if X [nirvana] exists, Y [escape from *saṃsāra*] exists;
(ii) Y exists;
(iii) therefore X exists.

[90] I owe this suggestion to Paul Griffiths.

The symbolic form of this is: Iff $x \supset y$. $\exists y \supset x$, which is valid, although it cannot prove the existence of nirvana to those who do not already accept (ii).

The commentary's exegesis could also be seen in the light of a different kind of philosophical analysis, whose argument is analogous to a Kantian transcendental deduction. One takes an existing phenomenon, Y, and asks, "What must be the case for Y to exist?"; and the answer is that the existence of X must be assumed. (This form of argument recurs in 1.4.) At the end of the commentary's remarks on this Utterance, it concludes "in these and other ways, the existence (*atthibhāva*) of the Unconditioned Element in the ultimate sense can be shown by reasoning (*yuttito . . . dīpetabbo*)."

Just as the first and third of these four passages, in the *Udāna* text, contain existential assertions about nirvana, so the second and fourth refer to the psychological and practical aspects of the way to attain it. The commentary states that some monks, listening to the Buddha's fourth sermon, thought that although the Buddha had set out the splendor of nirvana, and its many advantages, he had not yet shown a way to achieve it. How could they practice to achieve that goal? In order to dispel their uncertainty, he gave voice to

(4) *The Buddha's fourth Spirited Utterance*:

For one who is attached there is uncertainty; for the unattached there is no uncertainty. When there is no uncertainty there is tranquillity; when there is tranquillity there is no yearning; when there is no yearning there is no coming-and-going; when there is no coming-and-going there is no dying and being reborn; when there is no dying and being reborn there is no "here," "there" or in between[91]. This, indeed, is the end of suffering.

The commentary concludes: "Here also the Blessed One described to these monks the splendor of deathless great nirvana, which is the cause of the calming down of all the unsatisfactoriness of rebirth, (and is attained) through right practice."

The commentary to the four *Udāna* passages, then, takes them to be a connected sequence which does not merely assert, but also

[91] The commentary here (Ud-a 398, referring back to 92) takes this phrase to refer to this world and the next world (= any rebirth destiny).

argues for, the existence of nirvana as the goal of the Path. The conception of nirvana as the (really existing) opposite of conditioned things is also found in the well-known story of the Buddha's past life as Sumedha, when he made the aspiration to become himself a Buddha. (The commentary to the first Spirited Utterance quotes verses 4–6 of those cited below.) Before meeting the Buddha of that time, Dīpaṅkara, to whom he made his aspiration, Sumedha was a Brahmin householder who became an ascetic. This first embracing of the ascetic life had been prompted by the following reflections: [92]

I am subject to birth, decay and disease. Then do I seek that calm refuge free from decay and death.
Let me discard this putrid body filled with all things that are foul and depart hence with no yearning and desire for it.
There is and there will be such a path, for it cannot but be.[93] I will seek that path to win perfect release from becoming.
Just as where there is pain there is pleasure, so where there is becoming non-becoming is to be desired.
Just as where there is heat there is cold, so where there is the three-fold fire Nibbāna is to be expected.
Just as where there is evil there is also good, so where there is birth non-birth is also implied.
Just as when a man who has fallen into filth, having seen a lake full to the brim, does not seek it, it is not the fault of the lake;
So when there is present the lake of immortality (*amatantale*) that washes away the stain of Defilements, if one seeks it not, it is not the fault of the lake of immortality.

Does unconditioned nirvana exist in the same sense as Conditioned Existents? In general usage the verb *atthi* in Pali has all the ambiguity and imprecision of the English "to be." Ñāṇamoli (1975: 621 n. 16) has usefully distinguished between (i) *atthi* in the sense of *upalabbhati*, "is found," i.e. exists as a *dhamma* in the ultimate sense, and (ii) *atthi* in the sense of *uppanna*, "has arisen" (in the process of conditioning).[94] Nirvana exists in the first sense,

[92] Ja I 4–5 = Bv II 7–14, translated in Jayawickrama 1990: 5–6.

[93] *Na so sakkā na hetuye*, "it cannot not be." *Hetuye* is an infinitive of *bhavati/hoti;* the exact linguistic analysis is disputed (Norman EV II 154, ad Thī 418), but the meaning is not in doubt.

[94] Kapstein (1987: Chapter 4) is a helpful treatment of how passive verbal forms from *upa-labh*, (= is found), were sometimes taken ontologically (= exists), sometimes epistemologically (= is [veridically] perceived). At S II 17 (= S III 134–5) it is said that Right View avoids the two extremes of existence and non-existence (*atthitā, natthitā*), and

but not the second. The same point can be made by saying that conditioned things exist as occurrences or events, using the verb *vattati* with or without the prefix *pa* (Skt *pra-vartate*), whereas nirvana does not. This verb is from the Vedic root *vṛt*, to turn, and it preserves echoes of the old Vedic idea of time as a turning wheel. In Sanskrit, the opposed terms *pravṛtti*, action, occurrence, and *nivṛtti*, quiescence, cessation, are standardly used to express this dichotomy (Bailey 1985). In Pali, *appavatta*, non-occurring or non-occurrence, can be used as a predicate or synonym of nirvana.[95] A passage of the *Visuddhimagga* (496 = XVI 23, cp. 497 = XVI 28) collates the four Noble Truths with the occurrence and nonoccurrence of the round of rebirth:

(i) suffering = occurrence
(ii) Craving as the cause of suffering = bringing about occurrence
(iii) nirvana as the ending of Craving and suffering = non-occurrence
(iv) the Path = bringing about [or: leading to] nonoccurrence.

The opposed terms *vaṭṭa*, round (of rebirth) and *vivaṭṭa*, absence of the round, express the point also, and preserve the Vedic wheel-image. This is elaborated clearly at Vism 576–81 = XVII 273–98, which describes the twelve elements of Dependent Origination as a wheel. The "Wheel of Life" is, of course, a ubiquitous feature of Buddhist iconography. This contains the twelve elements of Dependent Origination around the circumference, the three "roots" of suffering (passion, hatred and delusion) in the center, and in between these the five possible rebirth Destinies: hell(s), the animal world, that of ghosts or spirits, the Human World and heaven(s).[96] A term for such a Destiny, or such a world,

of thinking "everything exists" (*sabbaṃ atthi*) or "nothing exists" (*sabbaṃ natthi*). This notion was to be greatly elaborated in later Buddhist literature, especially that of the *Prajñāpāramitā* texts and the Mādhyamika school, specifically in relation to their understanding of nirvana, and its relation to *saṃsāra*. In this Pali passage the point is that Right View sees that things in the world arise, and so they exist, temporarily, in dependence on conditions; but it also sees that they cease, and so they do not exist independently (which would mean, according to Buddhist thought, changelessly and permanently). The commentary (Spk II 32) glosses *atthitā* and *natthitā* as "eternality" and "annihilation," *sassatam, ucchedam*. The teaching of Dependent Origination – that things arise, cease, and leave their results – is a middle way between these two extremes.

95 Ud 80, in the first of the four passages, cited on p. 165 above, Paṭis I 11 with Paṭis-a I 93, I 59 (cf. Vism 648–9, XXI 37–42), Mil 197, 326; cp. *appavatti* used at Sv 225, Spk I 21, Vibh-a 113; Moh 74 *nivatti-lakkhaṇa*.

96 This is the case in most Theravāda texts: some other versions, as standardly in Tibet, for example, have six, adding a realm of "anti-gods," *asurā*. See Denis (1977).

is *gati*, and although nirvana is sometimes called a *gati*,[97] it is not a Destiny in the same sense. At M I 73–4 the Buddha says that he knows the five Destinies, and the way leading to them; he adds that he also knows nirvana and the way leading to it. The commentary glosses the word *gati* variously, and adds that nirvana is not exactly or wholly a *gati*, but rather the escape from all such Destinies.[98]

Although nirvana is "wholly other" than all Conditioned Existents, as an item of the Buddhist scholastic classification scheme it can be categorized like any other *dhamma*. The extensive analyses of Existents found in the Abhidhamma text *Dhammasaṅgaṇi* use the phrase *asaṃkhata-dhamma*, the Unconditioned Existent, in the main body of the text, and in the parallel parts of the "commentarial chapter" at the end use the word nirvana. The Unconditioned Element/Nirvana is:

(i) grouped with matter (*rūpa*), and some other Existents, in so far as it is not determined (*avyākata*) (that is, neither good nor bad in karmic terms), and not to be put aside either by seeing or (meditative) development.[99] It is, however

(ii) classed along with the four mental Aggregates as *nāma*, the mental.[100] But it is also

(iii) clearly distinguished from mind, in the subjective sense: it is not mind, not a concomitant of mind, and separate from mind.[101]

The apparent contradiction here, between nirvana as mental but not mind, can be explained as follows. In the classification of twelve Sense-bases (*āyatana*: as explained earlier, these are the six senses, including mind, and their objects), the mental is divided into Mind and Mental Objects or Data (*dhammā*, Existents). Nirvana is classed as a Mental Datum, part of the *dhammāyatana*,

[97] It is, for example, the highest *gati*, Vv 35, 12, Ps II 370, Spk III 246, and the *gati* of Arahants (Vin V 149, Pj II 346; cp. Dhp 418 = Sn 644, Th-a III 180–1, etc.)

[98] *Na kevalaṃ gatiṃ eva, gatinissaraṇaṃ nibbānaṃ* (Ps II 36–7). The term *agati*, "(the place) where there is no rebirth," is used as a synonym of nirvana (some mss. read *nibbana* here) at Dhp-a III 158, Ja V 489. Cp. Pj II 368 *gati-vipamokkhaṃ nibbanaṃ*, "nirvana is the release from (all) Destinies', and Vism 495, XVI 18 *sabbagati-suññattā*, "the fact of (nirvana's) being empty of all Destinies." Nett 45 states that in comparison with the worlds of men and deities hell is a bad destiny; but in comparison with nirvana all kinds of rebirth are a bad destiny (*sabba-upapattiyo duggatī*).

[99] Dhs 180, no. 983 = 234, no. 1370, and 183, no. 1008 = 237–8, no. 1393 respectively.

[100] Dhs 227, no. 1309; cf. Abh-s 43, VIII 38, Spk III 88.

[101] Not mind, *no citta*, Dhs 209, no. 1188 = 253, no. 1511; not a concomitant of mind, *acetasika*, 209, no. 1190 = 253, no. 1513; separate from mind, *citta-vippayutta*, Dhs 209–10, no. 1192 = 254, no. 1515; cp. for this, and what follows, Moh 74–5.

the Mental Data Base, but explicitly said not to be included in the Aggregates.[102] Similarly when to this list of twelve is added the six resultant sense-consciousnesses, to give eighteen Elements (*dhātu*), it is included in the *dhammadhātu*, the Mental Data Element, but not classed with the Aggregates.[103] That is to say, it is classed alongside the four mental Aggregates as "the mental" by the *Dhammasaṅgaṇi*, as in (ii) above, because it can be an object of awareness, not because it forms part of the mind of a person to whom it appears as a Mental Object. Since it is not classifiable within the Aggregates, it is external, not internal.[104] The opposition between internal and external usually marks the distinction between the Existents occurring in the Aggregates called self and in those called other (e.g. Dhs 187–8, nos.1044, 1045). But Cousins (1983–4: 101–2) is surely right to suggest that external (or as he renders it, "without") can mean either (i) the within of other people, or (ii) everything which is not within. Nirvana here (and at Vibh 115) is without or external in the latter sense.

Interpreters of Buddhism – including the *Oxford English Dictionary*[105] – have often sought to understand nirvana in terms of the ideas of other traditions: for example, as the equivalent of *ātman/brahman*, said in the *Upaniṣad*-s to be only characterizable in negative terms; or even of the god of monotheism, seen in the perspective of negative theology, the *via negativa*, in which god's real nature cannot be known directly, but only by the resolute denial that he (or she, as is possible in India) is characterized by anything known in the created world. It seems clear from the kinds of passage cited here that this cannot be justified in terms of the emic categories of Buddhism itself. It may be that, from an external, etic perspective, those whose tastes run in the direction of syncretism might be able to insist on the fact that nirvana is said to exist, but to be ineffable,[106] in order to make one or another kind of comparative assimilation. But a crucial difference between nirvana and God(dess), the Hindu

[102] Dhk 5, no. 28, with commentary p. 118; cp. Vibh 72–3, Vism 484, XV 14.

[103] Dhk 7, no. 58; cp. Vibh 89, Vism 487–8, XV 31, 34.

[104] Dhs 241, no. 1418; cp. As 424, Vibh 115, Vibh-a 288, 309, Moh 90.

[105] "Nirvana: In Buddhist theology, the extinction of individual existence and absorption into the supreme spirit, or the extinction of all desires and passions and attainment of perfect beatitude" – which is about 50 per cent correct, although even the second definition needs commentary.

[106] See the words used of it, cited on p. 163 above. "Ineffability" is easier said than understood (Scharfstein 1993).

idea of *brahman*, the Chinese Tao, etc., is that nirvana is never said to be the origin or ground of the universe;[107] to attain the ineffable, timeless state of nirvana is not to return to (union with) the source of things, but simply (!) to transcend time and suffering. There is no ultimate beginning of things in Buddhism.

1.3. THE EXISTENCE OF NIRVANA AS A SUBJECT OF DEBATE

In Buddhist texts in Sanskrit, as in Brahmanical texts, it became common to present doctrines in the form of actual or possible debates, either between Buddhists and non-Buddhists or between different schools within Buddhism. With the major exception of the *Kathā-vatthu*[108], such debates are rare in Theravāda (see Collins 1982: 24–5). There are, however, some passages of this kind in which the existence of nirvana is explicitly argued for. The discussion here draws from the *Milinda-pañha*, *Visuddhimagga* 507–9 = XVI 67–74 (and commentary), *Sammoha-vinodanī* 51–4, *Mohavicchedanī* 133–6, and Chapter 11 of the*Abhidhammāvatara*. The arguments given in these texts overlap a great deal, although they are not given in the same order. I do not go through all of them in their entirety; it is clearer and briefer to summarize what I see as the three main points:

(i) nirvana exists, the only Unconditioned Existent, the opposite of all Conditioned Existents;

(ii) it is not merely the destruction of the passions, the non-existence of the Aggregates;

(iii) it is the object of the knowledge which arises in the Path; as an object of knowledge, it is not merely a concept, but a reality with "individual nature." It is thus knowable, but not producible or causable.

[107] Tuck (1990: 35) discussing nineteenth-century philosophical idealism, shows well why so many then, and now, find nirvana so hard to interpret: "transcendental idealism, although it did shift the focus of philosophical discourse from metaphysics to epistemology, did little to eliminate the long-standing Platonic assumption that an ontological foundation was necessary – that there must actually be something casting the shadows onto the wall . . . Without at least this existential ground [i.e. in Kantian terms, the noumenal existence of the objective world and the transcendental ego, S.C.] there could be no epistemology. Without some ontology, philosophy was nonsense."

[108] This is a record of the supposed refutation of many different views held by other Buddhists, redacted in the *Abhidhamma* collection. It does not contain, however, any extended treatment of the existence of nirvana.

The opponents in these debates seem to be both non-Buddhists, as throughout the *Milinda-pañha*, and other Buddhists.

Indian philosophy acknowledges three common "means of knowledge" (*pramāṇa*):

(i) *pratyakṣa* (Pali *paccakkha*), perception or experience,
(ii) *anumāna*, inference or logical proof, and
(iii) *śabda* (Pali *sadda*) or *śruti* (Pali *suti*), verbal testimony (= scriptural authority; in Buddhism often *Buddha-vacana*, the Word of the Buddha, or some equivalent).

All three are found, separately or together, in these discussions of the existence of nirvana. The account of a debate on nirvana in *Visuddhimagga* Chapter XVI concludes by asserting that "because it can be arrived at by a special knowledge which succeeds through untiring perseverance; and because of the word of the Omniscient One, nirvana is not non-existent (*nāvijjamānaṃ*) as regards individual nature in the ultimate sense," and cites the third of the Buddha's Spirited Utterances (Ud 80–1).[109] The commentary (Vism-a 1148) explains that these two sources of knowledge refer, respectively, to the fact that nirvana's existence is proved for Noble Ones by their own experience (*ariyānaṃ paccakkha-siddhatā*), and for others through inference (*aññesaṃ anumānasiddhatā*). It continues (1148–9) by stating that the sermon recorded in the *Udāna* was not taught by the Buddha merely on his own authority (*na attano āṇamattena*) as "Lord and Master of the Dhamma," but "by reasoning, out of compassion for the (kind of) person for whom words are the highest thing" (*padaparame anukampamāno yuttito*). "The (kind of) person for whom words are the highest thing" is found elsewhere in lists of character-types, and is described there as "the person in whom, although he hears, remembers and recites much, there is no understanding of the Dhamma in this life".[110] Understanding or arguing for something *yuttito*, "through reasoning," is contrasted with doing so "through (the citation of Canonical) *Sutta*-s" (*suttato* Vism 562, XVII 202 = Vibh-a 173), or "through (traditional) hearsay" (*anussava-vasena*, Pj II 103); both of these are contrasted with "personal knowledge" (*atta-paccakkha*,

[109] Vism 509 = XVI 74; the translation is by Ñāṇamoli (1975: 581, with slight emendations). Moh 136, also citing the *Udāna* passage, has "nirvana exists in the ultimate sense, through the reasoning stated here, and through the word of the Omniscient One."

[110] Pp 41 = Mp III 131 on A II 135 = Spk I 202, II 4–5; cp. also Pp-a 223.

Ps I 196, Dhp-a III 404). In the *Milinda* (69–70) the king asks how those who have not attained nirvana know that it is Happiness (*sukha*); Nāgasena replies that just as people who have not had their hands and feet cut off know that it is suffering (*dukkha*) by hearing the cries of others who have, so one can know that nirvana is Happiness through hearing the words of those who have seen it (*yesaṃ diṭṭhaṃ nibbānaṃ tesaṃ saddaṃ sutvā*).

The arguments can be summarized thus:

(i) Nirvana exists, unlike the self postulated by non-Buddhists, the "nature" (pakatī) *posited by the Sāṃkhya system of Hinduism, or (impossible objects like) a hare's horn.*[111] This is known through the appropriate means (*upāya*), which is the practice of the Path, and through the "eye of wisdom."[112] This is also proved by the argument from opposites, already encountered in the commentary to *Udāna* 80. Vism-a 1149 is very similar to both Ud-a 396 and It-a I 162; these texts argue that full understanding of sense-desires, etc., which "have something beyond (them)" (*sa-uttara*) shows that the escape from them must exist (*nissaraṇena bhavitabbaṃ*), as that which is the opposite of, and whose individual nature is devoid of, Conditioned Existents.

In Vism 509 = XVI 72–3 and Moh 136 the (non-Buddhist) opponent asks whether the permanence (*niccatā*) of nirvana is the same as that of atoms, etc.[113] The Theravādin replies that it is not, because of the absence of a cause (*hetu*) (in the case of nirvana). Vism 509 = XVI 72–3 asserts that it cannot be said that atoms, etc., are permanent because of the absence of arising (presence and cessation), "because (the existence of) atoms, etc., is not proven." In Moh 136, the opponent asks if atoms, etc., are unconditioned. The reply is that they are not (i) because their unconditionedness has not been proven, and (ii) because there could not be a plurality of unconditioned things. "If there is to be an unconditioned, it

[111] This last is standard in Indian philosophy. As Williams (1981: 233) has remarked, the tradition has never clearly distinguished between that which could not exist because its description is self-contradictory – the usual example is "the son of a barren woman" – and that which could exist but is unexampled. "A hare's horn" is in the latter category (unless "hare" is so defined as to make having a horn impossible).

[112] Vism 507 = XVI 67, Abhidh-av 79, 81, Moh 135.

[113] Vism-a 1147 says that "etc." includes time (*kāla*) and the Nature (*pakati*) and Person/Soul (*purisa*, Skt *puruṣa*), categories of the Sāṃkhya school.

must be single" (*yadi hi asaṃkhataṃ nāma bhaveyya, eken' eva bhavitabbaṃ*). It is possible to differentiate Existents in terms of space, time and individual nature because it is possible to differentiate their causes; in relation to what is unconditioned and therefore without cause, no such divisibility of individual nature is possible. "Therefore it must be single (and) permanent" (*tasmā ekam eva niccaṃ bhavituṃ arhatī*).

(ii) Nirvana is not merely the destruction of passion, hatred and delusion, but exists separately (pāṭiyyekkaṃ). This point is made in relation to an opponent who argues that it is "mere destruction,"[114] and who cites the *Sutta* from the *Jambukhādaka Saṃyutta* (S IV 251–2) mentioned on p. 151 above, in which the ascetic of that name asks Sāriputta what nirvana is, and is told that it is the destruction of passion, hatred and delusion.[115] The Theravādin argument is made variously: since in the *Sutta* which occurs next in the same collection (S IV 252) the same answer is given to the question, what is Arahantship, it would follow that Arahantship and nirvana would be the same, which cannot be the case. Arahantship is a phenomenon which arises in, and as the best possible state of the four mental Aggregates; whereas nirvana, which does not "arise," is included in the category of Mental Data, but not in the Aggregates (see p. 175 above). The meaning of these *Sutta*-s therefore "is to be (carefully) examined" (Abhidh-av 1980); they are texts "whose meaning is to be elucidated" (*neyyattha*, Vism-a 1144–5).[116] When equated with the destruction of passion, etc., nirvana here is said to be a metaphor, or figurative usage.[117] The phrases "destruction of passion," etc., are also said to be synonyms for nirvana (Vibh-a 54, *adhivacanāni*, a term which can also be used to refer to metaphorical or figurative usage; see CPD s.v.).

If this argument does not succeed, a *reductio ad absurdum* of the opponent's position is suggested, as follows. If nirvana were merely the destruction of passion, hatred and delusion, it would be multiple: one nirvana for the destruction of passion, another for that of

114 *Khayamattaṃ*; cp. Sacc 305 (*khayamattaṃ na nibbānaṃ*), and also Vism 293 = VIII 247.

115 Vism 508 = XVI 69–70, with Vism-a 1144–5, Vibh-a 51–2, Abhidh-av 79–80, Moh 133.

116 The opposite is "whose meaning has been elucidated" (*nītattha*; cp. the sub-commentary to Vibh-a 51–2, cited in Ñāṇamoli [1987: 66 n. 28]. This opposition can be expressed variously: "of implicit or explicit meaning," "whose meaning is indirect or literal," etc. See Collins (1982: 154, and references cited at n. 12 there).

117 *Upacāra*, Vism 508, XVI 70, Vism-a 1150, Abhidh-av 80; cp. Ud-a 396–7, It-a I 163.

hatred, and so on. Since nirvana in this sense is the destruction of all Defilements, the numbers could be very large: 1500 is the biggest given, although potentially "there is no limit to these nirvanas," Vibh-a 53. (This argument is also given repeatedly in the *Kathāvatthu*, e.g. 317–30, in order to deny that anything other than nirvana could be unconditioned.) If nirvana were merely the destruction of passion, it would follow that "blind fools and animals" would attain nirvana after sexual intercourse, since their passion is thus (briefly) got rid of.

(iii) If nirvana did not exist, or were merely the destruction of passion, etc., it could not be the object of the knowledge which arises in the Path, beginning from the very first stage of the Change-of-Lineage, and so the Path would be futile.[118] This argument, like that of the third Spirited Utterance, presupposes acceptance of the Path; and the Vibh-a version has the opponent explicitly assent to (the existence of) both Change-of-Lineage and the Path. This point, as suggested earlier in relation to the commentarial exegesis of the third Spirited Utterance, is at least analogous to a "transcendental deduction" in the Kantian sense: since the Path exists, it must be the case that the goal of the Path exists.

In the Vism version the Buddhist opponent is depicted as both accepting the existence of the Path and maintaining that nirvana is not a separate reality attained by it: the Path is not rendered futile by the fact that through it nonbeing (*abhāva*) is attained, he argues. This would seem to be the position, often taken also by non-Buddhists, ancient and modern, that nirvana must be nothingness. (Vism-a 1143 suggests that what is meant here is "nonbeing" of the Aggregates as the aim of the Path.) The reply to this is that the past and future are forms of nonbeing (again, according to the commentary, of the Aggregates), but this is not equivalent to the attaining of nirvana.[119] The opponent suggests that the nonbeing in question is that of the present (Aggregates), and the Theravādin reply, naturally, is first to accuse him of self-contradiction (if there is nonbeing of the present, it

[118] Vism 507–8 = xvi 68, Vibh-a 53–4, Moh 133, Abhidh-av 80–1; cp. Spk III 88 on S IV 251.

[119] Similarly, later in the same section, it is said that if nirvana were mere absence of the Defilements, the Path would be rendered futile, since Defilements can be absent, temporarily, before entering the Path at the first "Path-moment." At Abhidh-av 80 it is said that in this case "foolish ordinary people" (*bālaputhujjana*) who attain meditative concentrations without passion, etc., could also be said to attain nirvana by that means.

could not be occurring as the present), and then to assert that nirvana is attained supported by Aggregates then present. Later the commentary (1150) argues that if nirvana were merely nonbeing (*abhāvamattaṃ*), it would be impossible to ascribe to it all the predicates which are found in both the *Sutta*-s and the *Abhidhamma*. "There is no individual nature of nonbeing, by which it could be described in such ways as 'profound, unconditioned,' etc. Nonbeing is just nonbeing."

In two of these texts (Vibh-a 53–4, Abhidh-av 80), a different but related point is made about nirvana as the object of knowledge at the moment of Change-of-Lineage (that is, at the beginning of the Path). The opponent is asked whether at that moment the Defilements have been destroyed, are being destroyed, or will be destroyed. His answer, naturally, is that they will be destroyed (i.e. at the moment of Arahantship). The Theravādin is then able to trap him in the self-contradiction of asserting that nirvana, which according to him is just the (complete) destruction of Defilements, is known at a time when the Defilements are not yet (completely) destroyed. If the opponent says that at the Path-moment they "are being destroyed," the reply is to ask which Defilements are being destroyed, and which have already been destroyed by the nirvana (as object of knowledge at this moment) which is complete destruction of them. If the Defilements are completely destroyed only at the moment of Arahantship, what could be the object of knowledge at previous moments of the Path? One should say, says the Theravādin, that it is "on coming" to nirvana (*taṃ āgamma*) that passion, etc., are destroyed.[120] It is argued that no form of insight or knowledge which has Conditioned Existents as its object would be capable of cutting off the Defilements completely; nor is meditative absorption, which can suppress the Defilements but not cut them off; thus "there must exist an object of knowledge of the Path which can effect their abandonment by (complete) cutting off. This is the Unconditioned Element."[121]

The *Abhidhammāvatara* (81–2) has the opponent assert that nirvana is "just a concept" (*paññatti-mattaṃ*). This, it is argued, is

[120] The phrase *taṃ āgamma* is used thus at Vism 507 = xvi 65; Vism-a 1141 glosses this as "reaching nirvana by virtue of its being a cause of the Mental Object [seen in Path knowledge]" (*ārammaṇakaraṇa-vasena patvā*).

[121] Vism-a 1149–50; cp. Ud-a 396, It-a I 162–3.

unsuitable (or illogical, *ayuttaṃ*), since nirvana as an object of thought is said to be indescribable and immeasurable (*na vattabba, appamāṇa*, Dhs 239 no. 1408, cf. As 412, 418), and such predicates could not be applied to what was only a concept. As a referring term, the word "nirvana" is, of course, a *paññatti*, a "concept" or designation: but it refers to something which really exists. The next chapter of this work (Abhidh-av 83–4) contains a sixfold analysis of concepts,[122] which categorizes them according to whether they refer to things which do or do not exist. They are:

(1) Concepts which refer to what exists (*vijjamāna-paññatti*), which designate a *dhamma* which exists "in the ultimate sense"; examples are form (*rūpa*), and feeling (*vedanā*), etc.

(2) Concepts which refer to what does not exist. This category is subdivided into two:

(2a) The terms "man," "woman", etc., which "are established only by worldly usage" (*lokanirutti-mattasiddha*): these are conventional terms, which can be analyzed and reduced to collections of Existents, which exist ultimately.

(2b) Terms which designate non-existent theoretical postulates, which do not exist even at the conventional level. In the texts cited on p. 143 above time was said to be "merely a concept," and the terms "past," "present" and "future" merely conventional usage; that is, they are non-existent in sense 2a. But when the word "time" is used not as a matter of everyday usage but as a theoretical postulate, as at Vism-a 1147, where it is classified with atoms, and with the "nature" and "person" of the Sāṃkhya system, it is classed with things which are non-existent in sense 2b. Abhidh-av 84 cites "nature" and "person" as examples of non-existent things "imagined by heretics" (*titthiya-parikappita*); Pp-a 172 cites these two and atoms. Another example given of such a non-existent is "the fifth (Noble) Truth."

The remaining categories blend what exists and what does not; thus:

(3) "Concepts which refer to what does not exist along with (or by means of) what does," such as "a person who possesses the

[122] Also found elsewhere: Moh 110–1, Pp-a 171–2, Abhidh-s 43–4, VIII 41–2, with Abhidh-s-a 194; cp. Ps V 50–1. See Warder (1971: 188ff.).

threefold knowledge"; here the threefold knowledge really exists, but "the person" does not (in sense 2a, as above).

(4) "Concepts which refer to what exists along with what does not," such as "a woman's voice" (voice exists, "a woman" does not).

(5) "Concepts which refer to what exists along with what exists," such as "eye-consciousness," "ear-sense-contact" (both exist ultimately).

(6) "Concepts which refer to what does not exist along with what does not," such as "a king's son" (neither exist ultimately).

The words "cessation" and "nirvana" "designate the Unconditioned," and exemplify "the concept of the Unconditioned," which is a "concept which refers to what exists."[123] Scholastic texts distinguish what exists from what does not by referring to the presence or absence in Existents of an Individual Nature (*sabhāva*): to have an Individual Nature is to exist "in the ultimate sense." The category of Existents in the widest sense includes concepts (Dhs 226, nos. 1306–8), all of which exist in the sense that they can be the objects of thought and so form part of the *dhammāyatana*, the Mental Data Sense-base, and the *dhammadhātu*, the Mental Data Element. But concepts of things which do not exist, that is, which do not exist other than as objects of thought, do not have Individual Nature, and so they do not exist in the ultimate sense.[124] The Individual Nature of nirvana is described variously: "nirvana, whose Individual Nature is eternal, the deathless, the shelter, the refuge, and so on" (Vism 215 = VII 75; on these lists of terms see 2.1.b); it is its "characteristic of peace" (*santilakkhaṇa*, Abhidh-s-a 165), the fact of being unconditioned (Vibh-a 51), and so on.

Nirvana can be seen by the knowledge which arises in the Path, but it is not merely an object of mind: it is an external, unconditioned reality. For this reason, it can be known, but it cannot be produced or caused. In the *Visuddhimagga* (508 = XVI 71), the Theravādin

[123] *Nirodho nibbānan ti ādikā asaṃkhatadhammassa paññāpanā asaṃkhatapaññatti . . . vijjamanapaññatti yeva* (Pp-a 175).

[124] *Sabhāva* (Skt *svabhāva*) was important to other Buddhist schools, notably the Sarvāstivāda, against whose scholasticism (rather than that of Theravāda) Mahāyāna thinkers usually argued (Williams 1989: 60–3, 69–72). On *sabhāva* in Theravāda scholasticism, see Ñāṇamoli (1975: 317–8 n. 68) and Warder (1982: xvii–xviii).

asserts that nirvana is without origin, because there is no first beginning. The opponent objects that it is not without origin, since it exists when the Path does; the reply to this is that nirvana is attainable by the Path, but it cannot be caused to arise by it.[125] At Abhidh-av 81, nirvana is distinguished from the mere destruction of the Defilements, on the grounds that such destruction can be brought about (literally "made," *karīyati*) and "caused to arise," whereas nirvana cannot: it can only be known; someone who does know it is a "knower of the un-made" (*akataññu*)[126]. This same point is made at length in two passages in the *Milinda* (268–70, 323–6): Nāgasena distinguishes between "the Path for experiencing nirvana" (*nibbānassa sacchikiriyāya magga*) taught by the Buddha in many ways, and "a cause for the arising of nirvana" (*nibbānassa uppādāya hetu*), which he did not teach.

This last point is not special to Buddhism; some version of it is present, probably, in all religions (one cannot "take heaven by storm"). Karl Potter (1963) has shown that this is an issue, perhaps a paradox, which underlies all Indian religion. The path to the goal cannot be said straightforwardly to cause the goal, since that would make it part of the conditioned universe from which liberation is sought; but at the same time the goal cannot be completely unrelated to the path to it, for obvious reasons.[127] Different traditions have had different levels of looseness of fit between their path and its goal; perhaps the most general formal solution has been to hold (using a western philosophical distinction) that the path is a necessary but not sufficient condition for attaining the goal. In the Theravāda case, it is not possible to realize nirvana without the Path; but the Path, the fourth Noble Truth, is a Conditioned Existent, part of the conditioned world, whereas nirvana, the third Truth, is the (only) Unconditioned Existent.[128]

[125] *Pattabbaṃ . . . maggena, na uppādetabbaṃ;* cp. Vism 696, XXII 126.

[126] This word is used in two senses in Pali: the sense found here takes it as *akata-ññu;* it can also be taken as *a-kataññu,* in which case it means "ungrateful" ('someone who does not acknowledge what has been done [for him]'). For a verse deliberately punning on these two senses of the word (and of others), see KRN no. 46.

[127] In that case no path, no one lifestyle or system of thought and action would lead to the Goal any more than any other. The whole soteriological imaginaire would be self-canceling. Arguably, something like this has happened on occasion in some of the less successful modern western adaptations of Zen Buddhism.

[128] Nett 14, Vibh 116, cf. Vism 515, XVI 102, et freq. Cf. the passage from A II 34, cited on p. 142 above.

1.4. CAN ONE DESIRE NIRVANA?

This chapter so far has endeavored to stay close to the modes of exposition used in Pali texts. Now I pose a question which no Buddhist text, to my knowledge, has ever posed. The question is – in English – important; there is an answer to it in English, but also in Pali technical terms, which will further elucidate Buddhist systematic thought.

The question "Can one desire nirvana?" is one which crops up standardly in introductory classes or discussions of Buddhism; indeed it should do, if those involved are paying attention. The point can be put a number of ways: if desire is the cause of all suffering, what about the desire for nirvana itself? This can be generalized to all action viewed under a Buddhist guise: is not the motivation of any purposive action governed by desire – if only in the formal sense that its purpose is the achievement of some goal – and so the idea of being desireless is either self-contradictory or destined, logically speaking, to end in catatonia? The first answer to this is one of English usage: it would be better to talk of the aspiration to nirvana rather than the desire for it, of purposive action as intentionally oriented towards its goal rather than as desiring it. Less blandly, one can say that nirvana is not the kind of thing towards which affective states of Desire (= Craving), in the Buddhist pejorative sense, can be directed. By way of comparison, imagine a young and excitable Christian nun exclaiming "Oh, I really *lust after* being selfless like Mother Theresa!" Leaving aside any judgments about whether this is a correct view of Mother Theresa, or about the usefulness of imitating her, it is surely obvious that in such a case one would want to say something like "Look, being like that (i.e. what you suppose her to be like) is something you can't lust after: either you are mistaken about what your affective state in this matter really is, or you have simply misused the word. Lust can only take as its object people or things viewed as means of sexual gratification." Correspondingly, what Buddhism would call Desire in the bad sense simply cannot take nirvana as its object. Of course Desire (perhaps in all but the sexual senses) can certainly be directed towards the *idea* of nirvana, to the concept or even the word. But to understand the nature of nirvana not as a concept or a word, but as the real Existent referred to by them, is necessarily to understand more clearly what affective states can and cannot take it as their intentional object.

One can put this most precisely by using Buddhist technical terms. The adjectival pair *sāsava/anāsava*, with and without Corruptions,[129] is applied to affective states, intentional actions and other things.[130] Almost all words used to denote emotions and intentions can be described as one or the other. Happiness (*sukha*), for example can be with or without Corruptions (A I 80–1); the commentary here (Mp II 153) explains that the former is "the Happiness of the round of rebirth (*vaṭṭa*), brought into being by conditions," the latter as the "Happiness of nirvana (*vivaṭṭa*), not brought into being by conditions." Happiness with Corruptions includes things not in the Buddhist Path but not in themselves (for certain agents) bad karma, as well as the results of good karma. The Desire of a married couple for each other, for example, does not break the third Precept (against "misbehavior in sexual matters");[131] and making merit to gain well-being either in this life or the next is unequivocally good action, albeit a second-best. (In the terms used above in 1.2.b, it is meritorious and so skillful; but there are modes of skillful action which are situated above merit and its results.) But there are certain states which cannot be without Corruptions, certain words to which it is not possible to add the adjective *anāsava*: the two most obvious, perhaps, are *taṇhā*, literally thirst, thus Craving, Desire (as in the second Noble Truth) and *upādāna*, attachment, clinging. To suppose that such emotions, and actions based on them, could be directed to nirvana would simply be, in Buddhist terms, a category mistake. So if the question "Can one desire nirvana?" presupposes this sense of the English word desire, the answer is No; if desire is understood in such a way that it could represent a Buddhist psychological term of which *anāsava* could be predicated, the answer is Yes, but that has nothing to do with the second Noble Truth, and so neither self-contradiction nor catatonia can be in question.

[129] They are: sense-desires, (desire for) existence, and ignorance, with (false) view often added as a fourth.

[130] See Collins (1982: 90–1) for its use with the Buddhist virtue of Right View.

[131] See, for instance, Wijayaratna (1990: 167–70), who includes the rather pleasant conversation between the Buddha and an old married couple called Father and Mother Nakula (A II 61–2; and cf. DPPN s.v. Nakulapitā).

When a person makes a resolution or expresses the aspiration to Buddhahood or nirvana, among the words used are *abhinihāra*, *panidhi*, *paṭṭhāna*, and *saṅkappa* (as in the second component of the Eightfold Path, *sammā-saṅkappa*, Right Resolve). None of these can be used for a "desire" in the pejorative sense.

1.5. SILENCE AND THE PRODUCTION OF MEANING

This chapter has tried to articulate what Buddhist systematic thought says about the concept of nirvana. It is a real, external and timeless Existent, not merely a concept; the *Abhidhamma* classification scheme places it in the categories of Mental Object Sense-base and Mental Object Element, but not in any of the Aggregates, bodily or mental. It is the ultimate goal of Buddhist soteriology, to be attained both experientially, in this life, as (i) the facts of the Destruction of the Corruptions, the possession of wisdom/skillfulness and the absence of mental suffering; and (ii) an object of consciousness for those on the Path, momentarily and for longer periods. It is also the state or condition (metaphorically, the place) which is the destiny of an Arahant or Buddha after death (but it is not a Destiny within the universe). It *is*, ontologically, but it is not the origin of things, the ground of being. For Buddhists, whether practitioners of the Path or ordinary people, the appropriate response is to accept on faith – better, with confidence or trust, *saddhā* – that nirvana exists as described, and to aspire to achieve it, in the shorter or longer term. As is often said (much more often, indeed, in books about Buddhism than in Buddhist texts), useless speculation beyond what is given in the teaching is simply a hindrance to practice.

This, as far as I can see, is all that is said about nirvana as a concept. It is, I submit, quite clear; but it is also clear that external academic scholarship cannot and should not stop at this point: it wants, rightly, to ask more questions. The issue is: how to find a way to understand nirvana from the external (etic) point of view which preserves the internal (emic) characterization of it, without simply restating what that is?

I claimed in the General Introduction that previous scholarly discussions of nirvana have often mistakenly attempted to produce a quasi-Buddhist account, an account which accepts Buddhist conceptual presuppositions but not the conclusions which Buddhists have drawn from them, nor respects the silences which they have preserved. It is possible now to begin to specify more precisely what that means, although the argument is not complete until the end of Part 1. If, as an historical scholar, one is attempting to understand what nirvana meant, as a matter of conscious reflection, to the authors, redactors and audiences of the texts which make up the Pali imaginaire, then one must both elucidate what was done with nirvana within the conceptual matrix of systematic thought, and accept what was not done, without making the imperialist attempt to place oneself in Buddhists' shoes and "do it better," by filling in the silences, vocalizing their meaning. Silence outside discourse means, of course, nothing by itself. Silences within discourse, on the other hand, are part of the way it produces meaning; and this is especially important in ideology, where silences, moves not made and paths not taken, are often best construed not as deficiencies of vision or of logical acuity, but as choices. With the exception of the meditation state of Cessation, discussed briefly in 1.2.b, where the present state of scholarship does incline me to believe there may be an historically produced inconsistency, if there are aporias in Buddhist thinking about nirvana – the next chapter discusses two – they are there on purpose: not because of inadequacy or failure, but because the silences in and around the concept of nirvana are part of the production of meaning in the discourse of felicity.

The General Introduction II.e cited Duby's "Ideologies in Social History" in connection with the stabilizing role of ideologies in history. I think he is right to say that

> once individual data have been identified, the next stage is to collate all these traces so that the system in all its formal coherence can be reconstructed. Here great attention must be paid to the silences. Interpreting silence as absence represents a much greater mistake in this kind of history than in economic history. Omissions are an essential part of ideological discourse, and their meaning must be analyzed. (1985: 157)

Such an analysis should not take the form of supplying extra semantic content beyond that which is given to the concept of nirvana in the texts. Rather, I want to see nirvana as having the syntactic value of a closure-marker, structurally and narratively. But speaking of (and leaving silences about) nirvana in terms of its position in a taxonomy of systematic thought is not, of course, the only way Buddhists have had of speaking about it, of assigning it semantic value. Before coming directly to the issue of what Chapter 3 calls "Nirvana, Time and Narrative," it is necessary to investigate the imagery of nirvana, which is another and vivid way it can become part of the imaginative work of Buddhist culture. Here too, just as Buddhist systematic thinkers are concerned with the nature and limits of what is sayable in the description of existence (= Existents), so the interpreter of Buddhism must be concerned with the nature and limits of what is sayable in interpretation.

CHAPTER TWO

The imagery of nirvana

2.1. WORDS FOR NIRVANA

2.1.a. *The words* (pari-)nirvāṇa *and* (pari-)nibbāna

Sanskrit *nirvāṇa* is *nibbāna* in Pali, just as *parvata*, mountain, is *pabbata*. (For the change *ṇ–n* see below.) Modern historical philology derives *nirvāṇa* from the verbal root *vā*, to blow, with the prefix *nis* (changed to *nir* before *v*), the most common sense of which is negative or privative. From the earliest Sanskrit texts *nir-vā* has been used intransitively: to go out, be extinguished. Causative (and so transitive) forms of the verb are common: to make go out, extinguish. The English "blow out" and "quench" are useful translations in both cases, since they can be intransitive or transitive. *Nirvāṇa* in Sanskrit can be a past participle or adjective meaning "blown out," but it is more commonly used in both Sanskrit and Pali as a noun, referring to the event or process of blowing out, quenching, and also to the resultant state. When the term is used as a soteriological metaphor in Buddhism the standard image is not of wind or some other agent actively putting out a fire, but of a fire's going out through lack of fuel:

> Just as an oil-lamp burns because of oil and wick, but when the oil and wick are exhausted, and no others are supplied, it goes out through lack of fuel (*anāhāro nibbāyati*), so the [enlightened] monk . . . knows that after the break-up of his body, when further life is exhausted, all feelings which are rejoiced in here will become cool. (M III 245; cp. S IV 213, V 319–20)

An enlightened nun recalls "then taking a lamp I entered my cell . . . [and] taking a needle I drew out the wick. The complete release of my mind was like the quenching of the lamp" (*padīpass' eva nibbānaṃ*).[1]

The verb *nir-vā* also means to be allayed, refreshed or exhilarated; and the causative form *nirvāpayati* means to cool, refresh, or delight (MW s.v.). A similar sense can be seen in the Pali term *nibbuta*, which is used as a past passive participle of *nibbāyati*, meaning blown out, quenched, but which is in fact to be derived from the root *nir-vṛ*, meaning satisfied, happy, tranquil, at ease, at rest (MW s.v.).[2] This ambiguity, or perhaps better polyvalence at the level of etymology is replicated on that of semantics, since nirvana is both the extinction of all conditioned existence and the highest happiness. An episode in the Buddha's biography plays on the two meanings of *nibbuta*: before he renounces household life, prince Gotama is riding into town. A girl sees him pass, and because of his handsomeness exclaims, "(His) mother must be happy (*nibbutā nūna sā mātā*), (so too his) father, the woman must be happy who has a husband like him." The prince, adopting the homiletic style which was to become, six years later, his *métier*, responds by reflecting to himself, "She says that the mother's heart is made happy/at rest/tranquil (*mātuhadayaṃ nibbāyati*), but what should first be happy/at rest/tranquil for the heart to be happy/at rest/tranquil?" He answers his own question: "When the fires of lust, hatred and delusion are at rest/quenched (then) it (= the heart) is happy/at rest/tranquil/quenched (*rāgaggaṃhi . . . nibbute nibbutaṃ hoti*)" (Ja I 60–1). Echoes of this meaning can still be alive when the word is used in relation to nirvana in the usual way: the monk Udāyin says "a great, blazing fire abates [or: "calms down'[3]] without fuel, and when the embers are calmed [*santesu*, which can also mean "at peace'] it is said to be extinguished (*nibbuto*). This simile has been taught by the wise to make clear the meaning [or: "the goal," *attha*]" (Th 702–3).

[1] Thī 116, translated by Norman (EV II: 15; cf. the references given by Norman on p. 86). The monk Kassapa uses this image immediately after the Buddha's final nirvana: D II 157.

[2] The nominal form *nibbuti* is also found. See Thomas (1933: 124), Norman (1992b: 10–1). PED, s.v. *nibbāna*, connects both words with the uncompounded root *vṛ*, to cover; but the idea of "covering" is not found in other uses of the verb *nir-vṛ*, nor in exegeses of *nirvāṇa/nibbāna*.

[3] Reading *upasammati:* see Norman (EV I: 223 ad v.675 and CPD s.v.). The same verses are found at A III 347, where some mss., followed by PTS, make the point even more obvious by substituting *saṃkharesu*, Conditioning Factors, for *aṅgaresu*, embers.

As was shown in Chapter 1, *parinibbāna* and *parinibbuta* can be used for both enlightenment and final nirvana. It has been claimed that there is a subtle difference of denotation between the nouns *nirvāṇa/nibbāna* and the compounded form with *pari-*, as with the corresponding verbs, but this seems to me doubtful: the difference between the two, as commonly with prefixes, seems rather to be one of slight intensification, often lost in practice. But in either case, the imagery of quenched fire is built into basic Buddhist soteriological terms; and the metaphor is by no means dead, as the examples given here, and those in 2.3.b below make clear. But traditional exegesis usually offers an alternative derivation, from the modern point of view imaginative rather than historically accurate: it takes *vāna/vāṇa* to be the same as *vana*, desire, and so construes *nirvāṇa/nibbāna* as "without desire." Since *vana* can also mean forest, and *vāna* sewing, further plays on words are possible. (More detail on the points made in this paragraph are given below.)

It is common in English to speak of attaining or entering nirvana, but verbal forms from the roots (*pari-*) *nir-vā* are by far the most common means of referring to the events, and states, of enlightenment and final nirvana. It is also common to say that the Buddha died, or to refer to the death of an enlightened person; sometimes equivalent words are used in Pali (2.2.a), but this usage can be misleading. In so far as these words simply refer to the end of life, without implying anything about what may or may not exist afterwards, there is no problem; but in modern English they can carry the assumption that afterwards the dead person is no more. The possibilities "exists," "does not exist," both and neither are all explicitly refused as inapplicable to the enlightened person after death (2.2.a); and as was shown in the previous chapter, nirvana itself certainly exists. For both these reasons, in certain contexts it seems useful to me to coin the English term *nirvanize*, inelegant though it is, as an attempt to preserve both the form and the ambiguities of the Pali.

Various verbs are used on occasion with the substantive *nibbāna* as their object: examples include forms derived from the roots *gam*, to go, and *adhi-gam*, to go to or reach. Both of these verbs can have the meaning "to understand" (i.e. reach by knowledge) so no spatial metaphor need be implied; verbs of knowing (*jan*) and seeing (*dis*) are also used. Forms derived from *pa-āp* and *ā-rādh*, both meaning to reach or attain, are found. The most common verb meaning to enter, *pa-vis*, is not found with *nibbāna* in the earlier texts (but see 2.3.e on the city of nirvana); however both *okkamāna*, from *o-kam*, to descend, and *ogadha*, traditionally taken to be from *o-gāh*, to dive into,[4] are used with a general sense of "entering." Lastly, one finds in some post-canonical texts the verb *pakkhandati;* literally this means to jump, leap or fall into, but Ñāṇamoli (1975: 766, 786; 1982: 67, 201) chose to translate it "enter." In all these cases, and others not cited, no doctrine of nor attitude to nirvana is to be inferred from the linguistic usage. One of the commonest uses of the verb *o-kam*, descend, for example, is in connection with sleep: the English "fall asleep" is a close parallel, but in neither case would it make sense to infer that going to sleep involves downward spatial movement. These metaphors are dead.

The following four numbered sections, which may be omitted by nonspecialists, give a more detailed analysis and exemplification

(1) The derivation and form of *nirvāṇa/nibbāna*. As stated above, *nirvāṇa* is from the root *nir-vā* . MW cites the transitive usage, "to blow (as wind)" from the *Rāmāyaṇa* (here *nis* is used, as is possible, as a strengthening or confirming prefix); and then gives the intransitive (passive) "to cease to blow, to be blown out or extinguished." Ñāṇamoli (1975: 319 n. 72) speculates that "the original meaning was probably "extinction" of a fire by ceasing to blow on it with a bellows (a smith's fire, for example)." Whitney (1885: 157) cites present stems for the root *vā* in both *-vāti* and *-vāyati/te*, and states that "the forms from the pres[ent] stem *vāya* have mostly the sense "be blown or exhausted," and are generally referred to a different root, 2 *vā* . The two, however, seem evidently only two sides of the same original root, nor are the forms capable of being clearly divided between them." MW gives *nirvāṇa* first as "mfn. blown out or put out," and *parinirvāṇa* similarly first as "mfn. completely extinguished or finished," which might suggest he was taking them as past passive participles. Edgerton (BHSD 325),

[4] The commentarial exegeses of this term, which are followed by most modern translators and philologists, understand it in this way. It may, however, from a historical point of view, be incorrect. See further p. 198 below.

under his entry for *parinirvāti*, cites an example of this: "in a literal sense: *dīpāḥ· parinirvāṇāḥ·* (past passive participle [the lamps] *went out*)." Whitney (1889 no. 957) lists *vā* as one of the roots taking *-na* as the suffix for the past passive participle; the suffix *-na* is also used (ibid. no. 1177) to make adjectives and nouns; examples given are *uṣṇa*, "hot," from root *uṣ*, to burn, and *praśna*, "question," from *prach*, to ask. In view of the fact that the root here can be taken as transitive or intransitive, there seems to be little point in attempting to decide between these two derivations for *nirvāṇa* . In any case, there seems to be in Pali no example yet discovered of *nibbāna* or *parinibbāna* used as a past passive participle or an adjective.

The dental *n* instead of retroflex *ṇ* is said by Norman to be an eastern form (1992a: 270 and Sn 664, where he refers back to a study by Alsdorf; cf. Norman 1992b: n. 79). As discussed in section II.b, Pali is closest to dialects of Middle Indo-Aryan from the north west of India, but there are a number of forms which are claimed to be eastern (sometimes called "Māgadhisms"; see KRN no. 72).

(2) The traditional derivation of *nibbāna* in Pali commentaries. From a historical point of view the idea of quenching/quenched fire is clearly the image underlying the word; but although *nibbāna* is often used in a literal sense (of fires, lamps, etc.) in Pali texts, the standard commentarial exegesis of the word in its applied Buddhist usage ignores this, and sees *vāna* (or *vāṇa*) as the equivalent of *vana*, desire (from the root *van*, to desire; the word *nibbana*, "without desire," is found outside this context). Thus Vibh-a 314, in explanation of *nibbāna*, states *vāṇaṃ vuccati taṇhā. Sā tattha natthi ti nibbāṇaṃ:* "Craving is called desire. Since that does not exist there, it is without-desire." Elsewhere, the prefix is explained by reference to the root *ni-kkham*, to abandon or renounce, so that *nirvāṇa* is the "state of the renunciation of desire and Craving" (or: "the desire which consists in Craving") (*nibbānan ti taṇhā*-vāna*to* ni-*kkhantabhāvena evaṃ vuttaṃ*, Mp I 55, cp. Pj I 151, 152, It-a I 164, II 107, Nidd II 185 on Sn 1094, As 409, etc.). Given that the homonym *vana*, "wood," "jungle," exists, various plays on words involving this meaning are possible: e.g. Dhp 283 with Dhp-a III 424, translated by Carter and Palihawadana (1987: 315–6), and Th 691 with Th-a III 9, dis-

cussed by Norman EV I: 224 ad loc., A III 346 with Mp III 371, Ps I 11, Pj I 111, As 364. *Vāna* can also mean "sewing" (from a root "to sew" or "weave", cited as *ve, vāyati* by MW, and as *vā, vi,* or *u* by Whitney [1885: 157]); there is already a canonical image of desire (*taṇhā*) as "the seamstress" (*sibbanī*, A III 399–401, Sn 1040–2 with Nidd II 276), and so *ni-bbāna* can be elucidated as abandoning the desire which weaves together life to life, (by means of) *karma* and its result (*Yā pan' esa taṇhā bhavena bhavaṃ phalena vā saddhiṃ kammaṃ vinati saṃsibbatī ti katvā vānan ti vuccati. Tato ni-kkhantaṃ vānato ti nibbānaṃ,* Spk I 196, cp. Sv 465, Vism 293 = VIII 247, Abh-av 79).

(3) The words *parinirvāṇa* and *parinibbuta*. It has been claimed that there is a specific grammatical distinction between these terms and *nibbāna/ nibbuta*. Thomas (1933: 121–2 n. 4), attributing the idea to E. Kuhn, stated that: "*Pari* compounded with a verb converts the verb from the expression of a state to the expression of the achievement of an action: *nirvāṇa* is the state of release; *parinirvāṇa* is the attaining of that state." In a later work (1947: 294–5) he also claimed that a person "*parinibbāyati*, attains the state, and then *nibbāyati*, is in the state expressed by *nibbāna*." The way the terms are used, however, does not support his view: the two are interchangeable, in both literal and metaphorical-religious senses. Commentaries give the terms as explanations of each other (e.g. Th-a I 46, translated and discussed in 1.2.a p. 148; cf. Norman EV I: 119 ad Th 5). At D II 340 an ascetic instructs his child servant "tend your fire, let it not go out" (*mā ca te aggi nibbāyi*), which clearly refers to the event of "quenching" rather than the state. (See also Bv 31 vv.31–2 and Khp 5 v.14 = Sn 235, cited in 2.3.b.) In relation to the past passive participles, of course, which are the most commonly employed forms of the verbs, it is almost impossible, and almost always pointless, to make any distinction between *parinibbuto* as "having attained quenching" and *nibbuto* as "being in the state of being quenched." *Pari* can be an intensifying prefix, and I prefer to see the difference between the two as simply one of slight intensification, which here as often is lost in actual usage (as both *cāga* and *pariccāga* mean simply giving up, renunciation). (This seems to be the way PED understands *parinibbāna*, etc., although in general its entries on these terms are confused and unreliable, from the linguistic point of view.) *Abhi*

can also be an intensifying prefix, and so the forms with *pari-* should, I suggest, be seen as similar to *abhinibbuto*, "completely quenched" (e.g. Ud 29 with Ud-a 195). Intensifying prefixes are standardly added to simple forms of words, and given as synonyms, throughout the *Dhammasaṅgaṇī*, the *Abhidhamma* lexicon of psychological states, which in this way resembles traditional South Asian dictionaries.

(4) Verbs used with the substantive *nibbāna:*[5] forms derived from

(a) *gam*, to go: *nibbāna-gāmin*, going or leading to nirvana, is found as an epithet of both *magga* and *patipadā*, the Path (e.g. D II 223, M I 73–4, III 4, S IV 371, Dhp 75), as are *-gama* (Th 86, S V 11) and *-gamana* (S I 186, Dhp 289, Th 1212, Ap 390), with the same meaning. The past passive participle *gata* is found, both in compounded (e.g. Nidd I 20, 160) and uncompounded (Spk III 3) forms. Pet 35 has *nibbānaṃ gacchati* (text as emended by Ñāṇamoli 64: 43 n. 112/13).

(b) *adhi-gam*, to go to or reach: e.g. M I 17, 173, S I 22, II 278, A I 162, III 214, It 104, Th 1165, Thī 113. For *adhi-gam* and *gam* as understand (= reach by knowledge) see Sp 117, Sv 893, Ja VI 287, Sadd 315.

(c) *jan*, to know; e.g. M I 4–6, 73, Ud 28, Kvu 404; from *dis*, to see: M I 510–1, A I 147, III 75 (cf. 1.2.c and 1.3 for seeing nirvana at various stages of the Path); and from *sacchi-kṛ*, to make evident to one's own eyes, to realize: e.g. D II 290, 315, M I 56, II 242–1, S V 10–1, 49, A I 8, III 423.

(d) *pa-āp*, to attain: e.g. *nibbāna* compounded with *-patta*, "having attained" (Nidd I 20, 93, 205), and *-patti*, "the attainment of" (D III 272, M I 227, S I 189; -s*ampatti* at Khp 7, J II 414); cf. also Nidd I 446 (*sampāpeti*), Ap 469 v.12 (*pāpuṇissati*), It-a I 69, II 84 (*–sampāpaka-magga*).

(e) *ā-rādh*, to attain: e.g. M III 4, A III 294, 295, Nidd I 33, Nidd 2 269, Th 990, Thī 6, Nett 158.

(f) roots comparable in meaning to "enter." *Okkamāna*, derived from *o-kam*, to descend: A IV 111, 230, and *-ogadha*, traditionally taken to be from *o-gāh*, to dive into: e.g. M I 304, S III 189,

[5] Most of the terms I cite here are also used, sometimes extensively, with synonyms for *nibbāna*, such as *amata*, deathless, *nibbuti*, tranquillity/extinction, *bodhi*, enlightenment, *santi*, peace, etc.; but I deal here only with their use in connection with the actual words (*pari-*) *nibbāna*.

V 218. Commentarial exegeses (followed by many modern translators and philologists) take the latter term as equivalent to *ogāḷha*, the past passive participle of *o-gāh*, and thus meaning "entered into" (*-anupaviṭṭhaṃ*, Ps II 370, Spk III 246), "established in" (*patiṭṭhitaṃ*, Spk II 336); cf. *nibbān-ogadha-gāminaṃ* at A II 26, glossed as "leading into" (-*antogāminaṃ*) at Mp III 42. However, it may rather be a form of *ogādha*, "a firm basis, footing": see CPD s.v. *amatogadha* and *ogadha*.

(g) *pa-khand*, to jump: Paṭis I 66, 194 (*pakkhandana;* for the latter cp. Paṭis-a 689, Ps II 299), translated by Ñāṇamoli (1982: 67, 201) as "enters into" and "entering into (launching out into)" respectively; cp. Vism 656 = XXI 64, 673 = XXII 5 (quoting Paṭis I 66), translated by Ñāṇamoli (1975: 766, 786), and Sv 1019. The commentary to the Vism 673 passage (cited by Ñāṇamoli, 1975: 786) glosses the word as *anupavisati*, enters; Paṭis-a 525 (on Paṭis I 194) as *cittassa nibbāne vissajjanaṃ*, "the sending of the mind to(wards) nirvana."

2.1.b. Other referring terms and definite descriptions

In what is traditionally regarded as the Buddha's first sermon after his enlightenment, he explains the third Noble Truth, the cessation of suffering, as: the fading away without remainder and cessation of that same Craving, giving it up, relinquishing it, letting it go, not clinging to it.[6] A repeated commentarial exegesis of this explains:

'Fading away without remainder," "cessation" and so on are all just synonyms for nirvana [*nibbāna-vevacanān' eva*]. For on coming to nirvana, Craving fades away without remainder and ceases, and so it is called "the fading away without remainder" and cessation of that same Craving. And on coming to nirvana, Craving is given up, relinquished, let go of, is not clung to, and so nirvana is called . . . "giving up, relinquishing, letting go, non-clinging."

For nirvana is one and the same. The names for it are just various synonyms, through their being the opposite of the names of all conditioned things, such as fading away without remainder and cessation, giving up,

[6] Vin I 10, S V 421: *yo tassā yeva taṇhāya asesavirāganirodho cāgo paṭinissago mutti anālayo.* The compound *asesa-virāga-nirodho* can be analyzed as a dependent determinative (*tatpuruṣa*), "complete cessation by means of dispassion" (see Ps II 309), or as a coordinative (*dvandva*). For these as alternatives, see Pj II 505, Vism 507 = XVI 64.

relinquishing, letting go, non-clinging, destruction of greed, destruction of hate, destruction of delusion, destruction of Craving, that (sphere, state, etc.) where there is no arising, no process, no sign(s), no longing, no striving, no rebirth, no (re)appearance, no (rebirth) Destiny, no birth, no aging, no disease, no death, no distress, no grief, no unrest, no defilement.[7]

Such synonyms are used ubiquitously in place of the word *nibbāna* throughout Pali literature; and strings of such terms, ending with *nibbāna*, are common. Thus at D II 36 one reads "this place (*ṭhāna*) is . . . hard to see, that is to say the calming of all formations, the relinquishing of all bases of rebirth, the destruction of Craving, dispassion, cessation, nirvana." At M I 163 the Buddha recounts that being himself subject to birth he saw the danger in birth and so sought "that which is without birth, the unsurpassed rest-from-exertion[8], nirvana," and then repeats the same thing with other terms, describing nirvana as "without aging . . . illness . . . death . . . grief . . . defilement."

In the "Collected (Sayings) on the Unconditioned" (*Asaṃkhata-saṃyutta* of the *Saṃyutta-nikāya* [S IV 359–68], a long series of *Sutta*-s is introduced by the sentence "I will teach you the Unconditioned, monks, and the way leading to the Unconditioned." The Unconditioned is said in each text to be the destruction of passion, hatred and delusion, while the way to the Unconditioned is described differently each time, as various kinds of Buddhist practice. There then follows a series of thirty-two abbreviated *Sutta*-s (S IV 368–373) which list thirty-two synonyms of "unconditioned" including *nibbāna;* in each case the opening phrase is "I will teach you . . . and the way leading to . . .", each of which is to be elaborated in the same way as was *asaṃkhata.* They are:[9]

[7] Vibh-a 113, Sv 801, Patis-a 161; cp. Moh 133, Vism 498 = XVI 3, 507 = XVI 64–5.

[8] *Yoga-kkhema;* on this term see Norman EV I: 128.

[9] This set of passages is often referred to in secondary sources, as in Kasulis' entry for nirvana in Eliade (1987), but it is badly in need of being reedited. The text of the PTS edition, and perhaps that of the manuscripts on which it was based, seems to be rather jumbled (see the critical apparatus and the editor's comments in Feer, 1894: x–xi). The first section (*vagga*) of the *Saṃyutta* (359–61) contains eleven different *Sutta*-s, in the first of which the Way leading to the Unconditioned is "mindfulness concerned with the body" (*kāyagatā sati*); the rest of the *vagga* gives a total of forty-five different kinds of practice, listed in ten *Sutta*-s under their common headings (the four foundations of Mindfulness, the five faculties, the Eightfold Path etc.). At the end of this *vagga,* here called the *Nibbāna-saṃyutta* in one recension (362), there occurs the usual summary list (*uddāna*) of the *vagga*'s contents, given here as the eleven things which were said to be

the end, (the place, state) without Corruptions, the truth, the further (shore), the subtle, very hard to see, without decay, firm, not liable to dissolution, incomparable, without differentiation, peaceful, deathless, excellent, auspicious, rest, the destruction of Craving, marvelous, without affliction, whose nature is to be free from affliction, *nibbāna*, without trouble, dispassion, purity, freedom, without attachment, the island, shelter (cave), protection, refuge, final end.

A later handbook for exegetes, the *Netti-pakaraṇa*, contains sixteen modes of conveying teachings (*hāra*)[10], one of which is by means of synonyms (*vevacana*). In the section illustrating this there is another long series of synonyms for and epithets of nirvana; it includes all those in the *Saṃyutta* passage just cited, and most of those cited above from D II 36 and M I 163, along with

the subduing of pride (or "intoxication"), elimination of thirst, destruction of attachment, cutting off of the round (of rebirth), empty, very hard to obtain, where there is no becoming, without misfortune, where there is nothing made, sorrow-free, without danger, whose nature is to be without danger, profound, hard to see, superior, unexcelled (without superior), unequaled, incomparable, foremost, best, without strife, clean, flawless, stainless, happiness, immeasurable, (a firm) standing point, possessing nothing.

"the way to the Unconditioned" in the eleven *Sutta*-s. The second *vagga* opens with the same list of forty-five different kinds of practice, excluding mindfulness concerned with the body, but giving each in a separate *Sutta* instead of under their group headings as in the ten *Sutta*-s of the first *vagga* (362–8). (The omission of *kāyagatā sati* may be because this is the same as the "mindfulness of the body" given in the foundations of mindfulness, here dealt with separately.) There then follows the list of thirty-two synonyms, at the end of which (373) the last given is *parāyaṇa*, "the final end," set out in a *sutta* with mindfulness concerned with the body as "the Way to the final end," and followed by the instruction – also given in the first of the list, *anta*, "the end" (368) – that it is to be expanded in the same manner as was *asaṃkhata*. The summary list here contains thirty-three items, being the word *asaṃkhata* and its synonyms. If we have forty-five (or forty-six) "Ways" to the Unconditioned, and thirty-two synonyms for *asaṃkhata*, we have a grand total of 1485 (or 1518) possible *Sutta*-s in the *saṃyutta* as a whole. Clearly what is being given here – as elsewhere (Gethin 92a) – is a matrix or set of matrices which could be used to generate a large number of possible sermons, each focusing on a different aspect or epithet of nirvana. It would be desirable to have this *saṃyutta* reedited on the basis of more recensions of the text than were available to the PTS editor.

In the summary list of contents (*uddāna*) given at S IV 373 the Pali titles are: *asaṃkhatam antam anāsavaṃ saccañ ca pāraṃ nipuṇaṃ sududdassaṃ ajajjarantam* [there are other readings here: the word is spelt *ajajjara* at S IV 369] *dhuvam apalokitaṃ anidassanaṃ nippapañ ca santaṃ amataṃ paṇītañ ca sivañ ca khemam taṇhākkhayo acchariyañ ca abbhūtam anītikam anītikadhammaṃ nibbānam etaṃ Sugatena desitaṃ avyāpajjho virāgo ca suddhi mutti anālayo dīpaṃ leṇañ ca tāṇañ ca saraṇañ ca parāyanan ti*.

10 This is Ñāṇamoli's (1962) rendering, followed by Norman (1983: 110).

A similar, longer list is found in the medieval grammar *Saddanīti* (p. 70); the terms are called *pariyāya-vacanāni*: "figurative or metaphorical expressions," or simply "synonyms."

Many, perhaps most of the terms given as synonyms or meanings of nirvana are negative or privative in grammatical form. A scholastic digest of *Abhidhamma*, the *Mohavicchedanī* (p. 75) says that nirvana has "infinite modes" (*ananta-ppakāraṃ*), since it can be opposed to all the categories of Conditioned Existents; it cites the examples "not mind, not associated with mind, not matter, not past, not future, not present, not the Path, not the Fruit (of the Path)." It is possible to emphasize this linguistic fact to interpret the doctrine of nirvana as a *via negativa*, an apophatic form of transcendentalism. But this is not an interpretation for which any very strong support is given in Pali texts. The *Paṭisambhidā-magga* (II 239) gives a long list of epithets for the five Aggregates, along with their opposites for nirvana: most of the former are (grammatically) positive, and their opposites negative/privative. But it also says the Aggregates are "no protection, no shelter, no refuge," and "their cessation, nirvana [is] protection, a shelter, a refuge." The same text states that one should see the Aggregates "as a disease, and their cessation as nirvana, which is health"; but it would be implausible to suggest that because the word for health is *ārogya* (from *a-roga*, non-disease), there is here a "negative" characterization of nirvana. The commentaries on Ud 80 (cited in 1.3), and on the third Noble Truth cited here, say that there are many names for nirvana because it is the opposite of all conditioned things; such terms can be positive or negative grammatically, depending on the aspect of conditioned existence to which they are opposed.

2.2. TWO APORIAS

2.2.a. *Is there consciousness in nirvana?*

Consciousness is one of the five Aggregates, and the Cessation of the Aggregates is final nirvana: it is impossible that consciousness, at least in this sense, could exist in nirvana. A person's consciousness is transformed at the moment of enlightenment, and comes to an end when he or she nirvanizes at the end of that life: to use the terminology employed in Collins (1982: 205–7), in the life of an enlightened person constructive-consciousness (= that which constructs new life through Conditioning Factors) comes to an end at enlightenment, while constructed-consciousness (= continuing experience, existing because of past Conditioning Factors) comes to an end with the last conscious moment of psycho-physical life. S II 83 and Spk II 81 use the analogy of firing a pot: when a pot has been fired in an oven it is taken out and set on a level piece of ground; it does not cool immediately, but does so after some time, and only the inanimate pieces of the pot then remain. So too the Arahant, set on the level ground of unconditioned nirvana (*asaṃkhata nibbāna-tala*) after attaining enlightenment, does not nirvanize on the same day, but lives for fifty or sixty years before he does so "after the arising of (his) last (moment of) consciousness"; thereafter only his bodily relics are left.

The process of rebirth can be described as an ever-changing series of conscious moments passing from one "station" (*ṭhiti*) to another (= conventionally speaking, from one life to another), until final nirvana is reached; when there is no further stationing of consciousness.[11] When texts (e.g. S I 122) speak of someone nirvanizing *apatiṭṭhitena viññāṇena*, two renderings are possible: either "with an unstationed consciousness" (= with consciousness, but an unstationed one), or "without a stationed consciousness" (= with no consciousness-Aggregate stationed anywhere in *saṃsāra*). The former is ruled out by the fact that nirvana is the cessation of the Aggregates; the latter cannot be equivalent to "become non-existent," since nonexistence is one of the four locutions recognized as logically possible for the state of the enlightened person after death, all of which are refused: one cannot say "is," "is not," "both is and is not," or "neither is nor is not" (Collins 1982: 131ff., and 2.3.b below). When a text (M I 140) states that a monk whose mind is released is "untraceable" (*ananuvejja*) while he is alive, the commentary (Ps II 117) makes a distinction between untraceability and nonexistence. The word *tathāgata*, it says, taking this not in the usual sense of a Buddha, but in that of any enlightened person, can mean two things. If it refers to a being (= an autonomous independent self, the existence of which is denied by teaching of not-self), then such a thing is simply non-existent (*asaṃvijjamāna*), in

[11] See Collins (1982: 213–8). Note that p. 216 l. 37 should read "and the monk is released." The original edition mistakenly added "not" here; this has been corrected in the paperback edition.

the here-and-now as much as in final nirvana. If it refers to an enlightened person, then anyone searching for that person's mind while he or she is still alive will not find it (it is unfindable, *avindeyya*, Ps II 117 ll. 15, 17, *avindiya* ibid. l. 27): how could they do so when such a person has attained final nirvana? All the words for untraceable, non-existent and unfindable here are from the root *vid*, to find, so no distinction in their meaning can be derived from their etymology.

In 2.1.a above I said that the most common word used to refer to the last event of an enlightened person's life is the verb *nir-vā*, with or without the prefix *pari-*, and commented that it can be misleading to speak of such a person's "death," in so far as that word in modern English can carry the connotation that thereafter the dead person does not exist, and in this case Buddhist texts explicitly deny that "does not exist" is a possible locution with respect to an enlightened person in final nirvana. How far do Buddhist texts use words meaning to die or death in this context? The word for time, *kāla*, is used with forms of the verb *kṛ*, to mean "make or complete (one's) time," i.e. to die (e.g. of an enlightened person at D III 122, S IV 398–400). "The death (*kālakiriyā*) of one person is to be (most) regretted by the people . . . (that is, the death) of a Tathāgata" (A I 22, glossed with *parinibbāyi* at Mp I 115). The Unanswered Questions concern the existence of the Tathāgata "after death" (*paraṃ maraṇā*). Mindfulness of death (*maraṇa-sati*), described in the *Visuddhimagga* (229–39 = VIII 1–41), involves the practice of comparing oneself with others, including enlightened monks, Pacceka-buddhas, and Buddhas themselves: in the case of a Buddha, the meditator is to reflect that "even he was suddenly quenched by the downpour of death's rain (*maraṇavuṭṭhi-nipātena ṭhānaso vūpasanto*), as a great mass of fire is quenched by the downpour of a rain of water" (Vism 234 = VIII 23, translated by Ñāṇamoli 1975: 252).

The use of these terms should be seen in a Buddhist perspective. The word death (*maraṇa*) is said to refer to different events, in different kinds of discourse (Vibh-a 101, Vism 229 = VIII 1): it can denote

(i) momentary death (*khaṇika-maraṇa*), the constant dissolution of conditioned phenomena;
(ii) conventional death (*sammuti-maraṇa*), which is when, as ordinary language has it, a person dies; in more precise

terminology – in Buddhist terms, in ultimate truth – this is "the cutting off of the life-faculty included within a single life";[12] and

(iii) "death as (complete) cutting off" (*samuccheda-maraṇa*), which is an Arahant's death, not followed by rebirth (*kālakiriyā appatisandhikā*).

Is the third sense of death the kind of not-living which Williams meant by referring to a "superior sort of death," after a series of lives[13]? An enlightened person's death is followed by "nonexistence" (*vibhava*), in one meaning of that polyvalent term. *Vibhava* is given as the first in a long list of synonyms for nirvana in the *Saddanīti* (70–1). Four other senses of *vibhava* are also given, of which two are relevant here. First, it can be a simple equivalent of words meaning "destruction"; in this use the word itself does not carry any ontological implications, any more than does the ubiquitous "cessation" (*nirodho*). Second, it can be used in the "view of annihilation." Both this view and its complementary opposite the "view of eternalism" assume that a self exists independent of the process of conditioning; but where eternalism holds that the self both exists now and will continue to exist after death, annihilationism holds that it exists now but will end at death (Collins 1982: 5, 35, 104–5, 181–2). It is in this same sense that there can be, in Buddhist terms, Craving for nonexistence: Craving has three forms, for (sensual) pleasure, for existence (in a new birth), and for nonexistence (*bhava-, vibhava-taṇhā*) (e.g. Vibh 365, Sv 800, Spk II 15). Craving for nonexistence assumes the existence of a self, but pessimistically desires its annihilation. When nirvana is said to be *vibhava* it should be understood not as absolute nonexistence – as shown in 1.3 nirvana has "existence," *atthitā*, from root *as*, to be – but as the opposite of *conditioned* existence. The latter is the sense of *bhava* when used as the tenth link in the chain of Dependent Origination (1.1.b.). The Pali–English Dictionary defines *bhava*, from the root *bhū*, be or become, as "'becoming,' (form of) rebirth, (state of) existence, a 'life'." One of the senses of the prefix *vi-* can be "apart from," "separate from"; and this sense is the one to be seen in the use of *vibhava* as an equivalent of

[12] "Conventional death" is also what is referred to by metaphorical expressions such as "dead tree" (Vibh-a 101 refers to such phrases as *vohāra-mattaṃ*, "merely ways of speaking"). For the "life-faculty" see Collins (1982: 227–30). (Cf. also Ps I 216–7 and Spk II 13.) [13] Cited and discussed in the Introduction to Part 1 above.

nirvana: it is "apart from rebirth-existence." This nonexistence of nirvana is equally well called unconditioned existence (see 1.3 on the Theravāda denial that nirvana is simply nonexistence, *abhāva*). In almost all texts, *vibhava* in this sense is used rather than *abhava* or *abhāva*, nonexistence; on rare occasions, however, one finds *abhāva* in this context[14].

Further discussion of texts relevant to this issue is postponed until 2.3.b, since to extend it requires consideration of the imagery of fire: what is left when a fire goes out? I suggest in 2.3.b and c that the imagery of fire, and that of the ocean's depth, do not provide a solution to the conceptual aporia, but rather the means to express and embody it. On the conceptual level there is an impasse, at least for systematic thought: nirvana is the cessation of the consciousness Aggregate, but that is not equivalent to becoming non-existent: nirvana is beyond designation (*apaññattika-bhāva*: 1.2.c and 2.3.b). The *Mahāvaṃsa* (XVII 56), remarking enthusiastically on the fact that the Buddha, although in nirvana (*parinibbāna-gato*, ibid. 65), can still benefit human beings by means of a miracle performed by his relics, says that "Buddhas are inconceivable (*acintiyā*), and inconceivable are the qualities of Buddhas; inconceivable (too) are the (karmic) results of (actions performed by) those who trust in the inconceivable!"[15] A nirvanized consciousness is not non-existent, in the sense in which the past does not exist (e.g. Sv 121, 506, 635, Ja V 149), nor in which entities such as a self or person independent of the process of conditioning do not exist, like a barren woman's son: it is untraceable.

One could say, in quasi-Buddhist terms, that apropos the enlightened person "in" nirvana, existence and nonexistence here are two extremes, between which Buddhism proposes the Middle Way. But for a scholar to say only that would be to do no more than reproduce a cliché, put on a Buddhist disguise and pretend to say something illuminating from a scholarly perspective. What we have here, I suggest, is an example of the way silences within discourse are themselves part of the production of meaning (1.5). For Buddhism, rebirth as an ongoing system involves human (and other) lives occurring *seriatim* in beginning-

[14] E.g. Mhv-ṭ I 139 on Mhv I 38, *so Bhagavā abhāvaṃ gato*. For *abhāva* as non-existence, see Sadd 66–7. [15] Found also at Ap 6, Sp 89, and in some mss. of Mhv XXXI 125.

lessly conditioned individual sequences of karmic causality, spatially continuous in each lifetime from the birth-moment of the body to its death-moment, and temporally continuous as consciousness-series throughout. Persons are strung along this series like pearls on a thread. What is thus *said* gives the Unsaid – unconditioned nirvanic existence and happiness – an immediate *point d'appui* in the understanding, since – as argued earlier – the idea of conditioning carries with it, as a silent companion, its own opposite: the lexical items *saṃkhārā*, Conditioning Factors, and *saṃkhata*, the conditioned, come already equipped with their own negation, *asaṃkhata*, the Unconditioned. This Unconditioned exists, semantically, in relationship to what is said, as a silent, unsayable Unsaid, a moment in the dynamics of discourse. The absence of a cosmogony in Buddhism[16] means that there is no systematic articulation, no overt *saying*, of how such sequences of conditioned consciousness came into being, originally, in a metaphysical sense: what is beginningless cannot have a beginning. (Psychologically they come into being through ignorance and Conditioning Factors: 1.1.b.) Correspondingly, what is left when conditioned consciousness goes out of being is also Unsaid: Buddhist final salvation, one might say, is open-ended. A karmic sequence of Conditioning Factors occurs until enlightenment as both constructive- and constructed-consciousness (Collins 82: 200ff.). At enlightenment, constructive-consciousness within the sequence ceases. At final nirvana constructed-consciousness is succeeded by timeless nirvana (which can be seen as a temporal event only from the conditioned, temporal point of view). That which replaces the constructed-consciousness of the sequence, temporally extended and variegated according to different lives, and that which supervenes on the destruction of "the conceit (that) 'I am'" (Collins 1982: 100–3), which has prevented all beings in the series from realizing nirvana just as it has provided them with the means of more than simply indexical self-reference, is untraceable, unsayable, beyond designation. One can say that it is not nonexistence, and it is a timeless bliss; to say more would be to rush in where Buddhas fear to tread.

[16] Using the word in its normal, ontological sense; Reynolds (1985) shows that one can speak of Buddhist cosmogony in other senses.

2.2.b. *Is nirvana a state of happiness?*

Since final nirvana is the cessation of the Aggregates, just as there can be no consciousness in that sense, so there can be no feeling (*vedanā*) and no determinate perception or ideation (*saññā*); that is, no conscious experience in terms of conceptual categories, "this is blue," for instance, or "this is happiness." At the same time, however, it is said to be a form of happiness, one of a standard list of three: that of mankind, of the gods, and of nirvana (e.g. Dhp-a III 51, Ud-a 111). Nirvana is the highest happiness;[17] this phrase is often analyzed as referring to Arahantship (e.g. Spk I 67 on S I 25, Ud-a 102 on Ud 10). The Buddha, immediately after his enlightenment, enjoys "the happiness of release" (*vimutti-sukha*); the commentary explains this as his Attainment of Fruition (1.2.b).[18] Arahants also experience the happiness of release (M II 104, S I 196 with Spk I 286, Th-a III 52). Ud 11 says that the happiness of the senses and of the gods are not worth one sixteenth part of the happiness which comes through the destruction of Craving; the commentary (Ud-a 108) states that this is the Attainment of Fruition. When Th 236 says that "by practicing the religious life this man prospers in happiness" (*sukhaṃ edhati*), the commentary explains this as "he attains, experiences the happiness of nirvana and the happiness of the Attainment of Fruition."[19] The happiness of nirvana here is probably the Attainment of Cessation; the use of "experiences" (*anubhavati*) here confirms that the happiness in question is a state of mind attainable by the enlightened person during life (1.2.b). But final nirvana is also *sukha*: the *Paṭisambhidā-magga* (I 12, 59–60, cited at Vism 648–50 = XXI 37ff.) gives a series of synonyms for final nirvana, which include "non-arising" and "nonoccurrence" (*anuppāda, appavatta;* cf. 1.3.), all of which are "safety" (*khema*) and happiness.

Clearly the word *sukha*, like "happiness," can refer to a number of different things. A passage repeated (with some variations) in a

[17] *Paramaṃ sukhaṃ*, e.g. M I 508–9, S I 25/Spk I 67, Dhp 202–4/Dhp-a III 261, 262, 267, Ud 10/Ud-a 102, Th 35/Th-a I 104, 884/III 63.

[18] *Phala-samāpatti*, Vin I 1 with Sp 953, Ud 1 with Ud-a 33–6; and cf. Ud-a 21, 208. "The happiness of release" can in fact be ascribed to all four of the stages of the Path (Paṭis I 195).

[19] Th-a II 93, taking *edhati* as transitive and *sukhaṃ* as its object, probably wrongly (see CPD s.v.).

number of commentaries[20] cites different canonical phrases to show that *sukha* can be used variously: *inter alia*, it denotes

(i) pleasurable feeling(s);
(ii) the "root of happiness," as in the phrase "happy is the arising of Buddhas" or the "cause of happiness," as in the phrase "the accumulation of merit is [i.e. brings] happiness"; and
(iii) nirvana, as in the phrase "nirvana is the highest happiness."

For these reasons, some translators have chosen different renderings for relevant words in different contexts. Ñāṇamoli (1975: 85–6 n. 6) explains his rendering of *pīti* as "happiness" (often translated, as in 4.1 below, as "rapture") and of *sukha* as "pleasure" or "bliss," when they are used in the meditation sequence of *jhāna*-s, as follows:

> In loose usage *pīti* (happiness) and *sukha* (pleasure or bliss) are almost synonyms . . . The valuable word "happiness" was chosen for *pīti* rather than the possible alternatives of "joy" (needed for *somanassa*), "interest" (which is too flat), "rapture" (which is overcharged) or "zest." For *sukha*, while "pleasure" seemed to fit admirably where ordinary pleasant feeling is intended, another, less crass, word seemed necessary for the refined pleasant feeling of *jhāna* and the "bliss" of nibbāna . . . "Ease" is sometimes used.[21]

In European-American philosophical tradition, the two dominant traditions of thought on this issue stem from Aristotle and the Utilitarians. Modern scholars prefer "flourishing" for Aristotle's *eudaimonia*, since that concept is broader than "happiness" in ordinary English; and both defenders and opponents of utilitarianism have spent much effort in analyzing the relationship between (felt) pleasure and the ("less crass") notion of happiness[22].

In the Buddhist case it is possible to mark the distinction between *sukha* as pleasant feeling and as a broader evaluative term quite precisely. Ordinary sensual happiness, and the happiness engendered by meditation, are said to be matters of feeling, but only up until the third Meditation Level (*jhāna;* there are eight such levels: 1.2.b and 4.1.b). Both happiness and suffering are absent at the fourth level. The happiness of the third level, aban-

[20] It-a I 74–5, Th-a I 27, As 40–1, Moh 76.

[21] For remarks on the translation of these terms, see Aung (1910: 277), Cousins (1973: 120–2), Gethin (1992a: 154–5), and 4.1.b below.

[22] For surveys see McGill (1967) and Den Uyl and Machan (1983); and cp. Annas (1993: especially 44–6, 329–34, 426–35, 453–4) for discussion and reference to more recent literature.

doned at the fourth, is cited by the commentarial discussions mentioned above (see n. 20) as an example of *sukha* referring to "pleasurable feeling(s)." The pleasurable feeling of the third level is said to be "exceedingly sweet, since there is no happiness higher" (Vism 163 = IV 174). The happiness involved here is the highest kind of pleasurable feeling: if there were a Buddhist version of Bentham's hedonic calculus, this would be quantitatively the highest point. In the fourth level the meditator's feeling is neither suffering nor happiness; this is not the mere absence of suffering and happiness, but a third type of feeling distinct from them (Vism 167 = IV 193). Nonetheless the fourth level is itself also said to be *sukha*, which must therefore refer to a qualitatively distinct mode of happiness. Its predominant characteristic is equanimity (*upekkhā*), said to be a form of happiness in so far as it is peaceful (Vism 404 = XII 131, Th-a I 223).

At M II 35–7 the Buddha discusses with an ascetic the idea of a completely happy world (*ekantasukho loko*) and the way to achieve it; that world is obtained through the fourth Meditation Level, and the way to it is the first three levels. In another conversation, recorded twice in the Canon,[23] the monk Udāyi and a carpenter by the name of Fivetools disagree about the Buddha's teaching: Udāyi holds that he teaches three kinds of feeling, happy, unhappy and neither, Fivetools that he teaches only two kinds, happy and unhappy, and that the third feeling is in fact included in the category of "peaceful, sublime happiness." Their disagreement is reported to the Buddha, who says that they were both right: "I have said that there are two kinds of feeling in (one) sense,[24] three in another" (and more elsewhere). He goes on to say that anyone who thinks that ordinary sensual pleasure is the highest form of happiness is wrong, since there is a happiness more excellent and sublime than this: the happiness of the first Meditation Level. He then says that the same thing is also true of the first level. It is not the highest: there is another more excellent, which is the second level. The same is true of the happinesses engendered by all the eight levels, through to the Attainment of Cessation (of Perception/Ideation and Feeling), which is the culmination of the

[23] M I 396–400, in the "Discourse on Many (Kinds of) Feeling," *Bahuvedanīya Sutta*, and S IV 223–8.

[24] Or: for (one) reason, *pariyāyena*, glossed by the commentaries Ps III 114, Spk III 80 as *karana*; both terms can be used to mean various things.

sequence (cp. A IV 414–8). But if others should object, the Buddha says, asking how the Attainment of Cessation can be included in the category of happiness, they should be told: "The Blessed One does not assign (Cessation) to (the category of) happiness with reference to happy feeling; for . . . whenever and wherever happiness exists, the Tathāgata assigns this or that to (the category of) happiness."[25] Commentaries explain:

> Here from the fourth level onwards the feeling of neither suffering nor happiness (which occurs) is also said to be happiness in the sense that it is peaceful and sublime. Cessation occurs as happiness in that it is the kind of happiness which is not a matter of feeling. For happiness which is a matter of feeling (occurs) through the five strands of sense-pleasure and through the eight (Meditation Level) attainments.[26] Cessation is (an example of) happiness which is not a matter of feeling. Whether the happiness be a matter of feeling or not, it is all happiness in that it is taken to be a state of non-suffering . . . [The phrase in the texts] "happiness exists" means that there exists either the happiness which is a matter of feeling or that which is not a matter of feeling. [The phrase] "the Tathāgata assigns this or that to (the category of) happiness" means that he assigns to happiness everything which is non-suffering.[27]

In any vocabulary terms analogous to English "happiness" will be applied to more than just experientially tangible kinds of pleasure (bodily and mental). To see how final nirvana – after the cessation of the Aggregates of Feeling and Perception as well as in their temporary absence in the Attainment of Cessation – can be designated *happy*, it might be useful to consider happiness, as non-suffering, in relation to the three types of suffering (unsatisfactoriness) discussed earlier (1.1.b): (i) ordinary suffering; (ii) suffering brought about by change, impermanence; (iii) suffering inherent in the fact of conditioning:

(i) To ordinary suffering corresponds ordinary happiness, both matters of experience, of feeling, *vedanā* in Pali.

(ii) When texts say that ordinary happiness is, from a higher perspective, suffering, commentaries explain that this is the kind of unsatisfactoriness brought about by change.[28] A monk pre-

[25] *Na khu āvuso Bhagavā sukhaṃ yeva vedanaṃ sandhāya sukhasmiṃ paññāpeti, api c' āvuso yattha yattha sukhaṃ upalabbhati yahiṃ yahiṃ tan taṃ Tathāgato sukhasmiṃ paññāpeti.*

[26] That is, as a feeling of happiness in nos. 1–3 and as the feeling of neither suffering nor happiness in nos. 4–8, which is "happy" because peaceful and sublime.

[27] Text at M I 400, S IV 228, commentary at Ps III 115, Spk III 80. This is no doubt the sense of "live happily" which made Vism-a 1676 liken the Attainment of Cessation to final nirvana (see 1.2.b).

[28] E.g. S IV 207/Spk III 76, It 47/It-a II 14, Th 986/Th-a III 100.

sents the Buddha with a dilemma: did he not say that there are the three kinds of feeling, but also that whatever is felt is (a case of) suffering? The second statement, he replies, was made in relation to the impermanence of conditioned things (S IV 216); the commentary explains that impermanence here is the fact of death; and there is no suffering greater than death (Spk III 78).

(iii) Nett 12 (cf. 1.1.b n. 9) says that the first two forms of suffering can be overcome to a certain extent in ordinary life, by good health and old age, but only final nirvana without remainder of attachment can get rid of the suffering inherent in conditioning. Gods and goddesses in heaven live for very long periods of time, enjoying ordinary happiness to a very high degree (4.1.c); and they suffer the unsatisfactoriness of change only for a brief period before their demise, when five signs of impending death appear (4.1.a). In the formula for the memory of past lives, it is said that a person remembers about each life "I experienced such-and-such happiness and suffering there"; when the Buddha says this of himself, including his penultimate birth as a god named Setaketu in the Tusita heaven, commentaries explain that he experienced divine happiness there, his only suffering being the unsatisfactoriness inherent in all conditioned things (Sp 161 on Vin III 4, Ps I 125 on M I 22). All conditioned phenomena are empty of happiness, in that they are unsatisfactory because subject to arising and decay (Vism 489 = xv 40, 628 = xx 86).

Just as the suffering of impermanence (for the most part), and the unsatisfactoriness of conditioning (wholly), are not descriptive but prescriptive, not depictions of lived experience but evaluations of it from a transcendentalist perspective, so the parallel forms of happiness in nirvana – permanence (= non-duration) and freedom from conditioning – make sense as evaluations but become aporetic when seen as characterizing a state to which conditioned, unenlightened beings may aspire. In one *Sutta* the enlightened Sāriputta announces that nirvana is happiness. A monk by the name of Foolish Udayī (Lāḷudayī) asks how there can be happiness in nirvana when there is no feeling there. Sāriputta replies by saying that precisely the absence of feeling is happiness (A IV 415).

The two aporias discussed in this section can be simply stated: nirvana is without the Aggregate of consciousness and without any *feeling* of happiness, but to attain it is not to become non-existent, and to accede to the highest bliss. These aporias seem to me to belong in this chapter with the imagery of nirvana, rather than in the first with the concept of it, as they exemplify what Griffiths called the "contradictions, which bedevil thinking on the matter of immortality . . . [but which] may be stilled by poetry though they prove an endless riddle for philosophical argument, 'stilled' in the sense of 'calmed' and also 'preserved'" (cited in the Preface). Griffiths' reflections proceed with reference to Proust and Tennyson, but the point can be made with regard to less sublime – though not necessarily any less deeply felt – representations of death and what is beyond it: epitaphs and inscriptions on gravestones. Here are some examples, culled at random from recent books on the United States.[29] The general cultural-religious framework, in so far as there is one – death, judgment, heaven or hell, perhaps with an interim stay in purgatory – is tolerably clear, and yet the language used is marvelously various, and marvelously capable of producing meaning precisely through its imprecision. The dead can be present in the grave, with or without the hope of moving elsewhere: e.g. "Here lies . . .", "Asleep in the earth," "Only sleeping"; or they can be gone from it: e.g. "Weep not, papa and mama for me, for I am waiting in Heaven for thee." "Budded on earth to bloom in heaven" is perhaps ambiguous between the two. The dead can be already "At peace" (mode unspecified), or for the moment "Asleep in Jesus, blessed sleep, from which none wakes to weep," while expectations of "eternal life" (mode again unspecified) are, of course, legion. On a recent visit to the Vietnam Veterans Memorial in Washington, always a striking experience, I saw a hat placed before the wall, with a single sheet of paper next to it: the hat, it said, had been made by a veteran in honor of his dead comrades; there followed a poem, and the message ended with "May God rest their souls." The writer, no Tennyson, seemed not to be highly literate: the hand was poor,

[29] Jordan (1982), Meyer (1989). Meyer (1989: 1) quotes the memorable remark of the New England Puritan Cotton Mather in 1693: "The stones in this wilderness are already grown so witty as to speak." No doubt he would have preferred silence in the case of a 1975 gravestone in Pennsylvania (ibid. pp. 95–6), whose epitaph gives the name of the deceased, followed by "Hi everyone! Have fun, See you later."

with various infelicities of grammar and orthography. In such a case it would be inappropriate, clearly, to suppose that understanding the closing words would require trying to work out exactly what the writer thought, aiming to achieve perfect clarity at the level of systematic thought: what kind of soul is in question? Does it move, wander about, unless God makes it rest? What does it do at rest? Is it awake? Is it happy? And so on. Not only the function, I suggest, but also the meaning of the remark is constituted through the simple image – kinesthetic as much as visual – of finding rest, and its value lies precisely in its capacity to bring satisfactory closure, obviating questions about the current existence and condition of the war dead. In the case of Buddhist ideology, analogously, I want to suggest that like the veteran's closing hope that his comrades were "at rest," the meaning of nirvana can be carried by, expressed in, constituted through images just as well as, indeed often better than through concepts. Is there consciousness and/or happiness in nirvana? Well, just as a blazing fire might go out . . . This is not an answer on the level of systematic thought: but it is a discursive moment which brings into being the Unsaid, the Unconditioned, and preserves nirvana as a contradiction-stilling enigma.

2.3. IMAGERY AND EXPRESSIBILITY

In *Selfless Persons* I discussed patterns of imagery concerning personal identity and continuity, and its cessation in nirvana. According to them, nirvana is the final "going forth from home to homelessness," no longer constructing body-houses to live in time; it is the termination of organic growth, where the planting of seeds and their maturation to fruit (i.e. sequences of cause and effect), no longer take place; and it is the place where the river of temporality ceases flowing, or where the ocean of time reaches its further shore (on this last see 2.3.d below). Here I investigate others, some well known, some not.

2.3.a. (En)light(enment)

The words enlightenment and enlightened for *bodhi* and *buddha* do not render them exactly. They are from the root *budh*, to be awake, and so more faithful to the original would be "Awakening" and "Awakened"; this would also avoid confusion with the metaphor behind the eighteenth-century European enlightenment. But these terms are so firmly entrenched in English usage for Buddhism and other Indian religions that it seems pointless to try to change matters, and I am content to use them. It seems appropriate to open discussion of the specific imagery used of nirvana by considering how, and how far, metaphors of light are found. Such imagery is, of course, very common in many religious traditions;[30] in Buddhism, with very rare exceptions it is, characteristically, found in an epistemological rather than ontological sense.

Motifs connected with the sun are earlier than Buddhism, as is evident from the title given to the Buddha's first sermon, the "Turning of the Wheel of the Doctrine" (*Dhammacakka-pavattana-Sutta*), which is a counterpart of the wheel of the Wheel-turning King (*cakka-vatti*) turning through the sky (6.5.a), and from the epithet of the Buddha as a "kinsman of the sun" (*ādicca-bandhu*). The nineteenth-century Sanskritist Senart saw Buddhism as a form of sun mythology; nowadays in this regard it only seems possible to say that while these discursive motifs might perhaps tell us something about the archaeology of the Buddhist lexicon, they tell us nothing about Buddhism as a historical phenomenon. But the imagery of light remains a living part of historical Buddhism, in a number of ways. The analogy between ignorance as darkness and wisdom as light is ubiquitous: a few examples will suffice. A praise-formula about the Buddha's preaching is put on one occasion into the mouth of king Ajātasattu: "Excellent, Lord, excellent. It is as if someone were to . . . bring an oil-lamp into a dark place, so that those who had eyes could see what was there. Just so the Buddha has expounded the Dhamma" (D I 85, translated by Walshe 1987: 108). A series of words meaning light, a lighted torch or lamp (*āloka, obhāsa, pajjota, ukkā, pabhā*) are used in this way in different texts: It 108 says that good monks are bringers or makers of light; the text and its commentary (It-a II 155) interpret the light as that of wisdom, as do the commentaries to two occurrences of the phrase "wise men are light-makers". The same words are found in a series of short texts which describe four lights: those of the

[30] According to the OED the metaphorical, religious use of the words "enlighten," etc., in English is as old as the literal use.

moon, sun, fire and wisdom (or the Buddha), the last, naturally, the best.[31]

The word nirvana, as has been seen, embodies the image that an enlightened person goes out like a fire; on occasion it is said that while alive a Buddha blazes brightly, illuminating the world, like a fire, the sun, stars, or lightning.[32] The previous Buddha Maṅgala was particularly striking in this respect:

Whereas with the other Buddhas their bodily radiance spreads around to the distance of eighty cubits, it was not so for him, for the radiance of that Blessed One remained all the time suffusing the ten thousand world-systems. Trees, the earth, mountains, oceans and the like, not excepting cooking-pots and so forth, appeared as though covered with a film of gold . . . [T]he moon, the sun and the other heavenly bodies were not able to shine by their own radiance. The distinction between night and day was not felt. The beings went about their business at all times in the light of the Buddha as they do by day in the light of the sun . . . When he passed away in Nibbāna having remained on earth for ninety thousand years all the ten thousand world spheres became a mass of darkness at one blow. There was great weeping and lamentation among the inhabitants of all the world-spheres. (Ja I 30–1, 34, translated by Jayawickrama, 1990: 39, 44)

A comparable description is given in other texts of the future Buddha Metteyya (5.1 and 5.2): it will be impossible to distinguish day from night because of his radiance. People will know it is sunset and evening from the sound of birds and from flowers closing; and they will know it is sunrise and morning from the sound of birds and from flowers opening (Dbk 120–1; cf. Dasab 301–2).

If the world is brightened by a Buddha's presence, and darkened by his nirvanizing, what of nirvana itself: is it light or dark? I have so far come across only two places where light is mentioned ontologically in relation to nirvana rather than epistemologically to the person who, or knowledge which realizes it. These are both from the *Udāna* and its commentary. At Ud 9, the monk Bāhiya is killed by a calf, and his body burned; when asked what is his destiny, the Buddha replies simply that he is nirvanized (*parinibbuto*), and describes a place "where there is no water, earth, fire nor air; no stars shine there, nor sun nor moon, and darkness is not

[31] "Light-makers," Sn 349 with Pj II 349, Th 1269 with Th-a III 200; wisdom as the best light, A II 139–40; the light of the Buddha, S I 15, 47. For further references to the light of wisdom see CPD s.v. *āloka*.

[32] E.g. Ja I 29 vv.219–21, Bv 23 vv.215ff.; cp. Bv 28 vv.34–5 with Bv-a 140–1.

found." The commentary (Ud-a 98) states that the last phrase is added in case someone should think that nirvana was permanently dark; but there is no darkness in nirvana because no matter (*rūpa*) exists there. What this means is spelled out in the commentary to the first of the four Spirited Utterances discussed in 1.3, which describes the "sphere" (*āyatana*) "where there is no earth . . . moon or sun." It explains that the reason why moon and sun are not found in nirvana is that darkness can only exist where there are physical forms, and so moon and sun exist in order to dispel the darkness. But there is no physical existence in nirvana, and so no need for moon and sun. "In this way (the Buddha) teaches that the individual nature of this same nirvana is light" (*iminā āloka-sabhāvaṃ tass'eva nibbānassa dasseti*, Ud-a 391).[33]

The imagery of light is widespread enough to make the slight mistranslation of *bodhi* and *buddha* as enlightenment and enlightened admissible. But just as the image is not found in the original words, so although the pattern of light imagery is common it is not built into the very structure of the Buddhist worldview and the terms of art used within it, as is the imagery of quenched fire in the word nirvana.

2.3.b. *The quenching of fire, the setting of the sun*

Nirvana, the quenching of fire, is an unreducible image, a fundamental semantic device without which Buddhism in its historical expression would be impossible, quite literally unthinkable. Buddhist fire-imagery has always been familiar in the West, both before and after T. S. Eliot chose "The Fire Sermon" as the title for a section of *The Waste Land*. The translation to which Eliot referred in an endnote reads: [34]

All things, O priests [better: monks] are on fire. And what, O priests, are all these things which are on fire?

The eye . . . forms [seen by the eye] . . . eye-consciousness are on fire; impressions received by the eye are on fire; and whatever sensation, pleasant, unpleasant, or indifferent originates in dependence on impressions received by the eye, that is also on fire.

[33] The *Nibbāna Sutta*, a recently edited text from Southeast Asia, however, says that nirvana is not light, or "brilliance" (*tejo*, p. 122). See p. 228 and n. 61 below.

[34] This was Warren's (1896: 351–3) version of Vin I 34–5 = S IV 19–20. Eliot (1972[40]: 39 l. 308, 48).

And with what are these on fire?
With the fire of passion, say I, with the fire of hatred, with the fire of infatuation [better: delusion]; with birth, old age, death, sorrow, lamentation, misery, grief, and despair are they on fire.

The *Sutta* then says the same thing with regard to the other five senses (including mind) and to the experiences to which they give rise. Enlightenment is attained by turning away from sense-experience, so that the three fires in all six senses go out. In *Selfless Persons* (Collins 1982: 84), I suggested that Buddhism deliberately reverses the central fire-image of Brahmanism, developed in and through reflections and elaborations on the Vedic fire sacrifice in the *Brāhmaṇa*-s, *Upaniṣad*-s and thereafter. There the fire of the inner self (*ātman*) – the warmth of life – and that of the universe (*Brahman*) – manifested as the sun and operative in the ripening of plants – are identical; according to another figure, individual selves are sparks from the fire of *brahman*. Both traditions centered their imaginaire around the imagery of fire, but in Brahmanism fire is an image for what is good and desirable, whereas in Buddhism the reverse is true. Gombrich (1990) has argued convincingly that whereas in the structure of Buddhist thought there are two basic reasons for suffering and rebirth, ignorance and desire, they were not represented as two fires, since early Buddhism wanted to parallel the three fires of the Brahmanical sacrifice; hence the choice, in Warren's renderings, of passion, hatred and infatuation.

In "The Fire Sermon," fire expresses the omnipresence of suffering. Elsewhere, as in two conversations between the Buddha and the ascetic Vacchagotta, the image is applied directly to rebirth and release. In the first (S IV 398–400) the Buddha says that he does not explain (the state of) an enlightened person who has passed away and died (*abbhatītaṃ kalaṅkataṃ*) in terms of rebirth, saying that he has been reborn in this or that place; rather, he explains it simply by saying that such a Supreme Person has made an end of suffering. "Just as a fire, Vaccha, burns with fuel but not without fuel, so I declare (that there is) a (place of) rebirth for one who is with attachment, but not for one without" (*upādāna* is used both for "fuel" and "grasping"). The fuel for rebirth, of course, is desire (*taṇhā*). In the second conversation, the "Discourse to Vacchagotta on Fire" (*Aggi-vacchagotta-Sutta*, M I 483–9), the Buddha explains that in the case of an enlightened person none of four possible alternatives applies, or is fitting (*na upeti*): one cannot say that he or she is reborn (*upapajjati*), is not reborn, both is and is not reborn, or neither is nor is not reborn. This parallels the standard Unanswered Questions about the enlightened person after death: one cannot say that he or she (i) is, (ii) is not, (iii) both is and is not, (iv) neither is nor is not (see Collins 82: 131ff.). Vacchagotta confesses himself bewildered, and the Buddha uses the fire-image in explanation:

[The Buddha:] If a fire were burning in front of you, would you know [that this was so]? [Vacchagotta says yes.] If someone were to ask you, "Depending on what is this fire in front of you burning?", how would you reply?
[Vacchagotta:] [That] this fire burning in front of me burns because of its fuel of grass and sticks.
[The Buddha:] If this fire in front of you were to go out, would you know [that this was so]? [Again he says yes.] If someone were to ask you, "This quenched fire [which was] in front of you, in which direction has it gone from here – east, west, north or south?", how would you reply?
[Vacchagotta:] (The question) is not appropriate (*na upeti*), Gotama, sir. The fire burnt because of its fuel of grass and sticks; since that (fuel) is exhausted and no other has been supplied, the fire is without fuel and so is designated "quenched."

The Buddha then applies the same reasoning to the enlightened person: it is for this reason that he or she is freed from being designated by the Aggregates.

The previous chapter, speaking of the ineffability of nirvana, cited two verses from the *Sutta-Nipāta* (1074, 1076), which said that the saint after death, like a flame put out by a gust of wind "free from name-and-form goes down and is beyond reckoning," and so cannot be described or measured. The phrase "goes down" can refer literally to the sun's setting, but it is also applied to the enlightened saint, as in Sn 1074. Thus the Buddha Maṅgala "blazing like a mass of fire, nirvanized like the setting sun".[35] A verse attributed to the Buddha says "the wise go out, like this lamp;"[36] the commentary says that a lamp which was burning next to the Buddha happened to go out, enabling the comparison. It glosses "go out" as "cease to burn" (*vijjhāyanti*), and explains that the wise are Arahants who, "at the cessation of the last moment of

[35] *Jalitvā aggikkhando va suriyo atthaṃgato va . . . nibbāyi*, Bv 31 vv.31–2.
[36] *Nibbanti dhīrā yathāyaṃ padīpo*, Khp 5 v. 14 = Sn 235. Commentary at Pj I 194–5.

consciousness . . . go beyond the reach of conceptualization" (*paññatti-patha*). The term *apaññattika-bhāva*, a state beyond conceptualization (1.2.c) is often used in conjunction with the imagery of quenched fire.[37]

Texts of this kind do lend an initial plausibility to the claim by some scholars that it is possible to read from this imagery a specific doctrinal position, via an analogy with what they take to be early Indian scientific ideas about fire. Schrader (1905: 167) was probably the first to express this idea. He asserts that "the common Indian view is, since the oldest time [*sic*], that an expiring flame does not really go out, but returns into the primitive, pure, invisible state of fire it had before its appearance as visible fire." Frauwallner's espousal of the view has been influential. He wrote that "the flaming up and extinction of fire means for the Indian of the ancient times not the origination and destruction of fire but that the already existing fire is therethrough visible and becomes again invisible."[38]

Insofar as it is an attempt to construe the aporias of nirvana, as do Buddhists, as not implying that after an enlightened person nirvanizes there is nothing, such an analysis might be commended. But it must be rejected, for two main reasons. First, the texts which Schrader and Frauwallner cite are, with one exception,[39] Brahmanical, and all are later than the earliest Buddhist texts: to argue that they represent the "ancient Indian" view in its entirety simply begs the question of whether Buddhism shared that view. It seems to me more likely that the Brahmanical texts were trying to rationalize, according to their own understanding, the dramatic and quite un-Brahmanical fire-image which the success of Buddhism had made popular. This is, perhaps, debatable; but the second reason is decisive. In the majority of uses of fire-imagery in Buddhist texts the fires which go out or go down

[37] E.g. Sv 393–4, 595, Spk II 83, III 210, Dhp-a II 163, Ud-a 175.

[38] English translation in Frauwallner (1973: 178). The suggestion appeared again recently in Harvey (1990: 66).

[39] This is Mil 326–7, cited by Schrader. King Milinda asks in what place nirvana is "stored up" (*sannihita*), arguing that if there is no such place, there will be no possibility of nirvana's arising (*utthānokāsa*), in the way that crops and flowers arise from the earth, fruit from trees, and precious stones from mines. The question is clearly absurd from the Buddhist point of view: Nāgasena explains this by using the example of fire produced from two sticks: nirvana is nowhere "stored up," but it can be realized by proper practice. This is obviously not intended to propose a view about the ontological status of quenched fire, and hence nirvana.

like the sun,[40] are – like the three fires of Greed, Hatred and Delusion – precisely what must be *wholly* eliminated for release to be possible. If these fires simply returned to their "primitive, pure, invisible" state, then according to Buddhist logic and psychology, their invisible existence and potential reappearance would make release impossible.

To concretize the fire-image into a conceptually specific doctrine as do Schrader and Frauwallner is an example of what the last chapter described as filling Buddhist silences, vocalizing their meaning. Scholars who do this often have their own account of what Buddhism must really mean, one which is divergent with the discourse of Buddhism itself. This is the case with Schrader and Frauwallner (for the latter see Collins 1982: 10). Schrader states confidently that

> without any doubt the question of the Parinibbānaṃ is, although not identical with, yet dependent on the question of the *attā* or substance, so that, if it were certain that the Buddha declined the idea of a substance in every sense, the answer concerning the Parinibbānaṃ would of course be that it was annihilation in every respect . . . I cannot explain here the reasons why, to my way of thinking, philosophy is forced to accept the metaphysical conception of the Absolute One . . . I only state that the Absolute One, in its very sense, as also, for instance, in the sense of Māṇḍūkya Upaniṣad 7.2, is something without and beyond the three Avacaras [spheres of existence] of Buddhism, and therefore not touched by the doctrine of *anattā*. (1905: 159, 60)

As so often, the exegete of Buddhism concludes from his own philosophy that Buddhism must agree with him. Thomas (1933: 130) remarks tartly, of Schrader's argument, "with such premises much can be proved." Schrader's view is not difficult to express: had the redactors of the early texts understood the fire-image in this way, they could very easily have said so. Since they did not, as interpreters we should accept that fact and ask, rather, what does this imagery achieve *as it is*? The answer, I suggest, is that it is an imaginative embodiment of the manner in which what can be said

[40] The word *atthaṃgata* is used (as are other terms meaning calmed, ceased, etc.) not only of the enlightened saint but also of the qualities and phenomena which must be eliminated for enlightenment to take place: e.g. at Vibh 195 it is used with *abhijjhā*, covetousness, and *domanassa*, mental pain, in a series of terms meaning "are destroyed, vanished, dried up," etc. Vibh-a 263 glosses *atthaṃ* as *nirodha*, cessation. Dhp-a III 453 glosses the phrase in Dhp 293, *atthaṃ gacchanti āsavā*, "the corruptions come to an end," as *parikkhayaṃ abhāvaṃ gacchanti*, "become destroyed and non-existent."

about nirvana as a concept ends in a silence. The dynamic of the quenching of a fire, or the setting of the sun, and of the associated idea of "cooling,"[41] depicts with perfect clarity a movement from activity and suffering to rest and peace, while deliberately withholding focus on the aftermath. The image does not solve the aporia, it states it.

2.3.c. *Ocean-deep, unfathomable*

One image which does apply to the aftermath is that of the ocean. In the "Discourse to Vacchagotta on Fire," immediately after the exchange cited above, the Buddha says that the enlightened person after death is "profound, immeasurable, unfathomable like the great ocean" (M I 487; also at S IV 376–9). Earlier in the conversation, it will be recalled, the four alternatives "is reborn," "is not reborn," both or neither had all been rejected as inapplicable to the nirvanized saint. The ocean image, which of course has parallels in many religious traditions, should not in Buddhism be concretized into the doctrine that the individual self is merged into universal being, like a river into the ocean (Collins 1982: 260–1). As an autonomous image, to say that an enlightened saint after death is "immeasurable, unfathomable like the great ocean" is to evoke, again with perfect clarity, the sense in which an enlightened saint nirvanizes, and thereafter cannot be described either as existing or not existing, but only as "untraceable." The clarity of such an image is not, indeed, conceptual clarity: but since the doctrine asserts that none of the available conceptual possibilities is appropriate for the situation, the image says as much as can be said.

Oceanic imagery of this kind fits into a wider pattern of water imagery in the early texts (Collins 1982: 247–61). Some examples relevant here are: just as streams move toward the ocean, so practicing the Path moves toward the ocean of nirvana.[42] The ocean and nirvana share four qualities (Mil 319): the ocean is (i) empty

[41] Forms of the verb *sīti-bhū*, to become cool, are often used in association with, or as synonyms of nirvana.

[42] See Collins (1982: 260–1, 284 n. 41), and add S V 38–41. Spk III 32–40, on S IV 179–81, states that the description there of an ocean refers to "the ocean of nirvana" (*nibbāna-sāgara*); and Moh 249 explains the term Stream-winner as someone who has attained the first stage of the Path which is called a stream because it tends towards the ocean of nirvana (*nibbānasamudda-ninnatāya sotasaṃkhātassa maggassa*).

of all corpses, (ii) not filled by all the rivers which flow into it, (iii) the abode of great beings, and (iv) "flowering" with abundant "wave-flowers"; nirvana is (i) empty of all defilements, (ii) not filled by the beings who attain it,[43] (iii) the abode of great Arahants, and (iv) flowering with the flowers of knowledge and freedom. In the compound *nibbānogadha*, if *ogadha* does mean "plunging into" as the commentarial tradition maintains (see p. 198), the image is clearly one of deep water: *amatogadha*, plunging into the deathless, is common, both by itself and placed in apposition to *nibbāna*;[44] *amatantala*, the pool or lake of the deathless, is also found.[45] In related figures, the Buddha's teaching is said to sprinkle or anoint his listeners with the deathless, or to enable them to drink it.[46] Here there are clearly deliberate echoes, as often with *amata*, "deathless," of its other sense as "nectar," the drink of the gods.

2.3.d. Land, safe from the sea of time

A nirvanized saint after death is ocean-deep; but nirvana is also, very commonly, the escape from the ocean, river or stream of rebirth, the haven of the further shore (again, of course, an image not confined to Buddhism). The image is exemplified in an extended simile from the *Saṃyutta Nikāya* (S IV 172–5): a man is in danger from four venomous snakes, five murderous enemies, and a burglar with a sword; he finds an empty village, but is told that it is about to be plundered by robbers. He sees a great stretch of water, of which "this shore is (full of) uncertainties and fears, the further shore safe and without fear," but can see no boat or bridge to take him across. He makes a raft and crosses over. The simile is explained: the four snakes are the four Great (material) Elements, earth, water, fire and air; the five enemies are the five Aggregates; the burglar is passion and lust; the empty village is a

[43] Other texts (Vin II 238, A IV 202–3, Ud 53–5) say that just as no depletion or filling of the ocean is seen, despite rivers flowing into it and rain falling from the sky into it, so no depletion or filling of nirvana is seen despite many bhikkhus attaining it. The commentaries here (Mp IV 111–2, Ud-a 303) make the thought clearer: at times when there is no Buddha in the world, sometimes not even a single person attains nirvana, but it is not empty; when a Buddha is present, innumerable beings attain it, but it is not thereby filled. [44] By itself, e.g. M II 196, S V 41, Sn 635; with nirvana, e.g. Paṭis I 22, Sv 65.

[45] Ja I 5, Ap-a 5, Bv 10 with Bv-a 70.

[46] Sprinkle, S III 2, Pj II 176; drink, Sv 858, Spk I 236, Mp II 124, Ja III 397, etc.

name for the six internal Sense-bases; the robbers are the objects of sense, the six external Sense-bases; the great stretch of water is "the four floods of pleasure, (repeated) existence, (wrong, harmful) views, and ignorance; this shore is the psycho-physical individual; the further shore, safe and without fear, is nirvana; the raft is the Path."

The *Visuddhimagga* pictures "knowledge of equanimity about Conditioning Factors," (Vism 656–7 = XXI 64–5; Ñāṇamoli 1975: 766, translation emended) thus:

When sailors board a ship, it seems, they take with them what is called a land-finding crow. When the ship gets blown off its course by gales and goes adrift with no land in sight, then they release the land-finding crow . . . If it sees land, it flies straight in the direction of it; if not, it returns and alights on the mast-head. So too, if knowledge of equanimity about Conditioning Factors sees nirvana, the state of peace, as peaceful, it rejects the occurrence of all Conditioning Factors and enters only into nirvana. If it does not see it, it occurs again and again with Conditioning Factors as its object.

Such land could also be an island. "Tell me sir," the Buddha is asked, "of an island (*dīpa*) for those who are overcome by old age and death, (like those) standing in the middle of a lake when a very fearful flood has arisen." "This island," he replies, "without possessions, without grasping, matchless, I call it "quenching" [*nibbāna*], the complete destruction of old age and death" (Sn 1092–4, translated in Norman 1992a: 123). The Buddha also is like an island: "As an island in the ocean is a support for beings who are shipwrecked in the great ocean, so [he is] like an island for beings who are sinking in the ocean of *saṃsāra*, where no support is to be had" (Bv-a 38–9). The refuge of nirvana is firm, high, dry land: "I was able to bring myself up from water to land (*thala*)," says the monk Ajjuna, and the commentary explains that the water is the great flood of *saṃsāra*, and the land nirvana.[47] The word *thala*, from the root *sthā*, to stand (firm), is often found with the image of arriving at the further shore (= nirvana).[48] The ground of nirvana is also smooth and pleasant (S II 108–9); it is "the unwavering (place),"[49] and offers "unwavering happiness"

[47] Th-a I 197 on Th 88; cp. Pj II 568 and Nidd I 430 on Sn 946.

[48] E.g. S I 48, IV 174, It 57, Ud-a 167, It-a II 171, et freq.

[49] *Acalaṃ* with or without *pada/ṭhānam*: see PTC s.v. *acala* for references. The usage is especially common in the *Apadāna*.

(Th 264); unwavering because immovable or firm (*akuppa*, Th-a II 109). "The unshakable, the immovable" is, of course, nirvana.[50] The Arahant's release is immovable because it has immovable nirvana as its object; unlike the unstable, fearful ocean of rebirth nirvana is "without fear from any quarter" (*akutobhaya*).[51]

2.3.e. The city of nirvana

In many texts, as in those on "the unwavering" just cited, words are used of nirvana which suggest that it is a place or has spatial location (*pada, āyatana, thāṇa*),[52] as in the Buddha's first Spirited Utterance about it (1.3). The epithet *sugata*, one who is in a (particularly) good way, or one who has fared well, is standardly explained as meaning *sundaraṃ thāṇaṃ gacchati*, "he goes/has gone to a good (beautiful) place" (e.g. Vism 203 = VII 33). This provides, as was mentioned in section III.c of the General Introduction, a verbal parallel to *eu-topia* in Thomas More's punning title; and Buddhists would certainly reply, if asked *where* the Good-place of nirvana really is, that it is only metaphorically a place, really it is No-place, *ou-topia* . In later texts the place occupied by nirvana in the Buddhist imaginaire is a city, a site of perfect happiness located at the end of the Path.

The image of nirvana as a city is not found explicitly in any canonical text; but it seems to be, as the commentary thinks, implicit in a *Sutta* entitled "City" in the *Saṃyutta Nikāya* (S II 105–6, with Spk II 117–8), where the Buddha gives an autobiographical account of his enlightenment. The *Sutta* is in the "Collection of Texts about Causation," and the content of his enlightenment is given as the chain of Dependent Origination. Thus, he concludes, "Vision arose, understanding arose, cognizance arose, knowledge arose, light arose"; and he adds a simile:

(It is) just as if a person, wandering through the jungle forest, were to see an ancient road, an old straight path traveled by men of former times, and were to go along it; (and) as he went along he were to see an ancient town, an old royal city inhabited by men of former times, with parks,

[50] *Asaṃhīraṃ asaṃkuppaṃ*, Sn 1149, with Pj II 607, Nidd II 99.

[51] Immovable Arahant, e.g. M I 167 with Ps II 174, et freq.; without fear from any quarter (on *akutobhaya* see Norman EV I: 176 ad Th 289; cf. S I 192 with Spk I 278, A II 24, It 122, Th 1238 with Th-a III 195).

[52] E.g. S III 143, Sn 204, 1086, Th 725, Thī 97, Nd 1 343; Dhp 255, Vv 77 v. 855, Thī 350.

groves, ponds and walls – (a) delightful (place). [The man sends news of his find to the king, suggesting that he rebuild the city.] And (then) the king or the king's minister were to rebuild the city; and after some time that city were to thrive and increase, become rich, prosperous, and crowded with people.

In the text the Buddha only gives an explanation of the old road: it is the Noble Eightfold Path, "traveled by Perfectly enlightened Ones of former times." The commentary explains: the man's wandering in the forest is the time spent by the Gotama in past lives fulfilling the Perfections after vowing to become a Buddha at the time of Dīpaṅkara Buddha, the road is the Path, and the city is the city of nirvana. Whereas the simile, it continues, speaks of an external city which one person saw but another rebuilt and made habitable, in the Buddha's case the same Teacher both saw the city and made it habitable.[53] It goes on to make more specific analogies between elements of the city and elements of Buddhist practice (it has four doors, which are the four stages of the Path, and so on).

Elsewhere commentaries explain other similes in a comparable way. Another *Sutta* in the *Saṃyutta Nikāya* (S IV 194–5) contains a simile of a king's border-town, with six doors, to which messengers come with a message for the lord of the town. In the text the border-town is said to be the body, the six doors the six senses, and the lord of the town consciousness. The commentary takes the simile further: the lord of the border-town is a dissolute son of the king of a prosperous great city, who must be reminded of his royal task. The prosperous great city is the city of nirvana, the king the Buddha, the border-town the psycho-physical individual, and the dissolute son the mind of a monk in need of training (Spk III 60–2). The "Discourse on Relays by Chariot" in the *Majjhima Nikāya* (M I 145–51) describes a sequence of purifications, and states that the religious life is not led for the sake of any of them, but for the sake of final nirvana: the sequence is likened to seven relays by chariot, which take king Pasenadi from his palace in the city of Sāvatthi to that in Sāketa. The commentary (Ps II 157) explains that king Pasenadi is the practitioner afraid of old age and

[53] One might say that by implication here there is an inner city, seen with the eye of wisdom as Mil 218 says, discussing this text; but nirvana as a real Existent is also external, not in the sense intended by the commentary here, but in that it is the object of the mind's eye rather than something in the mind itself, as was seen in 1.2.c.

death, Sāvatthi is the city of the psycho-physical individual, and Sāketa the city of nirvana. Just as on arrival at Sāketa the king enters the palace and enjoys food and drink surrounded by his family and friends, so the practitioner enters the palace of Dhamma and while seated on the couch of Cessation, surrounded by his good qualities, enjoys the supermundane happiness of the fruits of the Path. Arahants are said to enjoy the same happiness by commentaries to texts which describe the enlightened person, *inter alia*, as one who has "lifted the crossbar, filled in the moat, (and) put down the flag": it is as if there were two cities, one a city of robbers (the psycho physical individual), the other a safe city (*khema-nagara* = the city of nirvana); a great warrior (the practitioner) thinks that the safe city will never be free from fear while the city of robbers stands, and so decides to destroy it. He takes his armor (of morality) and sword (of wisdom), goes to the robber-city and attacks it; he cuts down with his sword the pillars set up at the city gate (uproots desire with the path of Arahantship), lifts the crossbar (of ignorance), fills in the moat (of rebirth), pulls down its flag (of conceit), and sets fire to it before entering the safe city of nirvana.[54]

In the late-canonical *Apadāna* one reads of "the city without fear" (*abhayaṃ puraṃ*, Ap 47 v.133), glossed by the commentary (Ap-a 291) as the city of nirvana; and at Ap 584 v.6 the Buddha's former wife Yasodharā says that she will "go to the Unconditioned city, where there is no old age and death" (*ajarāmaraṇaṃ puraṃ asaṃkhataṃ*). In another late-canonical work, the *Buddha-vaṃsa* (32, v.3) the past Buddha Sumana is said to have "built a city, the excellent, glorious city of Dhamma." The commentary elaborates: "the "city" is the city of nirvana . . . Nirvana is said to be a city because it is the sphere and dwelling-place of Noble Persons, (both) learners and adepts, who are established (there) and have penetrated the essential nature of Dhamma" (Bv-a 155).[55] But the first explicit mention of the city of nirvana comes from the *Milinda Pañha* (276, 332–3, 354), in parts of that text which, though not among the earliest, are pre-commentarial (see Norman 1983: 110–12).

[54] M I 139/Ps II 116–7, A III 84/Mp 264–5, Nidd I 21/Nidd-a 85–6.

[55] Cf. Ap 44 vv.94ff., where the commentary (Ap-a 285–6) does not equate the city of *dhamma* with the city of nirvana. An account of the city of *dhamma* can be found also at Mil 329–47, especially 341.

The image of the city of nirvana is only suggested in the early texts, but elements of the later elaboration, in commentaries and other texts, can be found in early sources. The Buddha is said to have opened "the door of the deathless" (*amata-dvāra*); commentaries explain that this door is the Noble Eightfold Path.[56] The canonical image does not specify what the door leads into, but once (Vv 97 v. 27), when the phrase is used of the previous Buddha Kassapa, the commentary (Vv-a 284) explains that he opened "the door, [that is] the Noble Path to the great city of nirvana, which had been closed since the disappearance of the Dispensation of the Blessed Koṇāgamana" (i.e. the Buddha before Kassapa). There is no consistency over the details of the image. Elsewhere morality (*sīla*) is said to be either the way to the city of nirvana, or its door.[57] The Noble Eightfold Path can also be its door; this is the case also when the city has four doors, from the east, south, west and north: these are the four Foundations of Mindfulness.[58]

It might seem as if the imagery of arriving at the city of nirvana conflicts, in terms of connotation if not denotation, with the image of nirvana as the final, and highest form of "leaving home for homelessness" (Collins 1982: 167–76); but a remarkable simile in the commentary to the Buddha's final nirvana suggests otherwise. Before he nirvanizes, the Buddha attains all the meditative attainments (D II 156). He goes from the first Meditation Level up to the ninth, the Cessation of Perception and Feeling (1.2.b). His attendant, the as yet unenlightened Ānanda, thinks he has nirvanized, and exclaims that this is so, but he is corrected by the Arahant Anuruddha. The Buddha then comes back from the ninth to the first (where discursive thought is possible: 4.1.b), then goes back up to the fourth (which is a state of happiness in the sense explained in 2.2.b), and nirvanizes after emerging from that level. The commentary (Sv 594) compares this to a man going to a foreign country first embracing all his relatives before he leaves; so the Buddha experienced every form of meditative felicity before entering the city of nirvana.[59] The sub-commentary (Sv-pṭ

[56] E.g. Vin I 7/Sp 963, D II 39/Sv 471, M I 168–9/Ps II 178, 181, S I 137–8/Spk I 199, 203, It 80/It-a II 87.

[57] As the way at Cp-a 293, Abhidh-av 89 v.796; the door itself at Bv-a 11, 121, Vism 10 = I 24.

[58] The Path as the door at Sv 881, Spk III 212, cp. Sp 962; the four doors at S v 755, Ps I 240, Vibh-a 216.

[59] *Nibbāna-puraṃ pavisanto . . . videsa-gacchanto ñāti-janaṃ ālingitiā* [*sic*] *viya sabbaṃ samāpatti-sukhaṃ anubhavitvā paviṭṭho.*

II 239) explains that the Buddha experienced all the meditative attainments every day.

The city of nirvana becomes a commonplace in the later literature, with or without detailed elaboration.[60] The last examples cited show that no consistency was sought over the details. In later texts such as the *Tuṇḍilovāda* and *Nibbāna Sutta*-s (= TS and NS below), two "allegedly noncanonical" texts probably composed in recent centuries,[61] one finds long lists of correspondences between parts of the city and Buddhist practice, many of which seem purely formal; the comparison with a city may here be no more than an efficacious device for grouping and memorizing a list of doctrinal items. Hallisey writes that although the first of these two texts is not included in the Canon

> this is not to say that its contents are markedly different from other discourses in the Pali Canon. On the contrary, the *Tuṇḍilovāda Sutta* provides a concise illustration . . . of the logic and structure of traditional Theravāda Buddhist practice . . .
> The basic idea of the city of *nibbāna* is quite common in the Buddhist literature of medieval Sri Lanka,[62] but the term also seems to be a conventional form of reference rather than a live metaphor. (1990: 155, 163)

There is some variety in which aspects of Buddhist practice correspond to which parts of the city. For example, in TS the wall is the Perfection of Patience (193), in NS morality (122); in TS the door is in one place generosity (174, also 193), in another morality (177), while in NS it is knowledge (122). In TS there seems to be an image within an image, when the city's water tank is itself said to be "like nirvana."[63] Hallisey says that this variety

[60] E.g. at Sv 571, 594, Spk I 224, when speaking of the Buddha's final nirvana; cp. also Ja I 5, Bv-a 70, 72, Spk II 82–3, Vibh-a 113–4, Abhidh-av 119 v.1261.

[61] Hallisey (1990, 1993), who edited both texts, suggests the eighteenth century as a possible date for the first; it seems impossible at the moment to date the second. Hallisey prefers the term "allegedly non-canonical," taken from K. D. Somadasa (1990: 156 and n. 2), to the word "apocryphal," "since it is less likely to prejudge the whole issue of the status of such texts" (1992: 97 n. 2). References to the texts are by page number of Hallisey's editions.

[62] (This can now be seen in R. Obeyesekere [89]; S.C.)

[63] According to Hallisey (personal communication), the phrase *kiṃ taṃ jīvaṃjīvakādisakuṇaganehi sevitaṃ* on p. 194 should be taken in the sense "What is (the tank which is) frequented by flocks of birds such as parrots?', and the answer emended to *nibbānam taḷākasadisam*, "nirvana is like the tank."

suggests that the serial simile might be derivative from and secondary to a more fundamental conventional metaphor of the city of Nibbāna, which itself is linked to the conventional metaphor of Nibbāna as a "place" . . . On the basis of what can be seen in the *Nibbānasutta* we may be able to avoid the temptation to dismiss a common image of this sort as an over-used "literary ornament" or "figure of speech" . . . Rather, we can see that such common images are probably better understood as "conventional metaphors", part of the normal ways that Buddhists talk about, conceive and even experience their own situations. (1993: 108–9)

Section II.e of the General Introduction said that it is not the aim of this book to trace a history of ideas in the chronologically sequential sense; hence I need only note the fact that the image of the city of nirvana is absent in the earlier texts, if implicit in some, but so frequent as to be a commonplace, a conventional metaphor in later literature, from the time of the earliest extant commentaries, in the fourth to fifth centuries AD. No doubt the change has to do with the involvement of Buddhist ideology with the larger-scale, wealthier cities, strongholds of kings and merchants, which had developed by that time, and which were often, in intention at least, the safe well-ordered central capitals of the order-enunciating kings and "emperors" in whose train the Pali imaginaire marched across Southern Asia.

2.3.f. Other images: health, freedom; and image-lists

Etymology is not necessarily a trustworthy guide to the meaning of words, but at least it can give some idea of the archaeology of their use: the English concept of salvation, from Latin *salus/salvus*, is thus, at least in its origins, connected with ideas of safety, freedom from harm, and health. The Buddhist concept of *dukkha* refers to all sorts of ills, and nirvana is of course freedom from all of them. Words like *roga* and *agha*, which can mean disease in the literal sense (not just dis-ease in the general sense of *dukkha* as unsatisfactoriness), appear in descriptions of the suffering of rebirth: the arising of the Aggregates is the arising of *dukkha*, of diseases (*rogānaṃ*), and of old age and death (S III 31–2); "I teach disease and the root of disease (*agha, aghamūla*) . . . [The Aggregates are] disease . . . The root of disease is desire" (S III 32). Two verses which say that an enlightened saint "know[s] health (*ārogya*) properly because of the destruction of the [corruptions]," and that someone claims "I see what is . . . diseaseless" (*aroga*), are said by the commentary to refer to nirvana.[64] The four Noble Truths have often been said to be based on a medical model: the disease, its etiology, prognosis for recovery and medicine, but Wezler has shown that this was not the case: there is no evidence for such a scheme at the time of the Buddha (Wezler 1984 and Halbfass 1991: 245; cf. Zysk 1991: 38, 144–5). But the analogy of medicine is common. There are two kinds of disease, the Buddha says, physical and mental; some people can be free from physical disease for up to fifty years, but apart from the enlightened, rare are those who are free from mental disease even for a moment (A II 142–3). Nakulapitā, an old man physically ill, constantly ailing, comes to the Buddha to ask for some words of comfort; the Buddha tells him to train himself in the thought that although his body may be sick, his mind need not be. Sāriputta sees Nakulapitā a little later, looking well and serene; on being told what the Buddha had said, he elaborates it into a discourse on not-self. The commentary concludes by remarking that people in the world can be sick in both body and mind; Arahants may be sick in body but not in mind (S III 1–5, with Spk II 256). The Buddha is like a doctor (M II 256–60, Mil 172); in the city of Dhamma he has a medicine stall and a pharmacy, where his medicines are the four Noble Truths, the four Foundations of Mindfulness, etc. (Mil 334–5). Nirvana has three qualities of medicine: it is a refuge (or help) for those who are afflicted with the poison of the Defilements, it brings an end to all (forms of) *dukkha* (as medicine to disease, *roga*), and it is nectar (= the deathless, *amata*) (Mil 319).

To reach nirvana is to become free from rebirth, so terms such as *mokkha, vimokkha,* from the root *muñc,* to be free(d) or release(d), are ubiquitous, as are synonyms. Sometimes the idea is elaborated into an image. To get rid of the five Hindrances[65] (temporarily at the first Meditation Level, and wholly with enlightenment) is like being out of debt, regaining one's health, being freed from prison or slavery, and reaching safety after a journey through the wilderness (D I 73, M I 275–6). Nirvana affords release from the prison of conditioned existence (*bhavacāraka,* Bv-a 69). Playing on the word *nirodha,* cessation, in the third Noble Truth, it

[64] Sn 749, 788, translated by Norman (1992: 86, 92); commentaries at Pj II 507, Nidd I 84.
[65] Desire for sense-pleasure, ill-will, sloth and torpor, restlessness and worry, doubt.

is said that "*ni* signifies absence, and *rodha* means a prison (*cāraka*); therefore because it is empty of all (rebirth) Destinies, there is (in nirvana) no confinement by suffering, which is called the prison of *saṃsāra*" (Vism 495 = XVI 18, Vibh-a 84, Moh 131).

Some texts juxtapose different images, as in the "Discourse to Vacchagotta on Fire," discussed in 2.3.b and c above. 2.3.a cited a text where a Buddha blazes brightly before "going out": Bv 72 v.26 says this also of the Buddha Tissa, and the next verse adds that he went out (*nibbuto*) like a cloud dispersed by the wind, frost by the sun or darkness by a lamp. The *Visuddhimagga*, described by Ñāṇamoli (1975: xxx) as "a detailed manual for meditation masters and a work of reference," occasionally offers lists of similes (presumably for the use of teachers and exegetes). At 478–9 = XIV 220–1 (translation by Ñāṇamoli, with excerpts from the commentary, 1975: 544–5), three similes for the Aggregates are juxtaposed, from which one can draw inferences about nirvana in two cases:

the body is:	a sick room	a prison
feeling is:	the sickness	punishment
perception/ideation is:	the cause of sickness	the offense
Conditioning Factors are:	bad food, which provoked the sickness	the punisher
consciousness is:	the sick man	the offender

Nirvana, accordingly, is like regaining health and escaping from prison.

At 512 = XVI 11 it is said that the four Noble Truths can be illustrated in different ways, which are given in Table 2.1.

At 665–6 = XXI 90–108 (translated by Ñāṇamoli 1975: 777–8), in a section describing different kinds of knowledge, a list of twelve similes is given, of which the last six are relevant here:

Just as a man faint with hunger and famished longs for delicious-tasting food, so too the meditator famished with the hunger of the round of rebirths longs for the food consisting of mindfulness occupied with the body, which tastes of the deathless [or "nectar," *amata*].

Just as a thirsty man whose throat and mouth are parched longs for a drink with many ingredients, so too the meditator who is parched with the thirst of the round of rebirth longs for the noble drink of the Eightfold Path.

Table 2.1

Dukkha	Origin of *dukkha*	Cessation (nirvana)	The Path
a burden	taking up the burden	putting down the burden	means to put down the burden
disease	cause of disease	curing the disease	medicine
famine	drought	abundance of food	adequate rain
enmity	cause of enmity	removal of enmity	means to remove enmity
a poison tree	the tree's root	cutting the root	means to cut the root
fear	cause of fear	freedom from fear	means to attain freedom from fear
this shore	the great flood	the further shore	effort to reach the further shore

Just as a man frozen by cold longs for heat, so too this meditator frozen by the cold of Craving and (selfish) affection in the round of rebirths longs for the fire of the path that burns up the Defilements.
Just as a man faint with heat longs for cold, so too this meditator scorched by the burning of the eleven fires[66] longs for nibbāna [the calming of the eleven fires].
Just as a man smothered in darkness longs for light, so too this meditator wrapped and enveloped in the darkness of ignorance longs for the light of knowledge consisting in path development.
Just as a man sick with poison longs for an antidote [to get rid of the poison], so too this meditator sick with the poison of defilement longs for nibbāna, the deathless [or: ambrosial] medicine that destroys the poison of defilement.

The *Milinda-pañha* also contains a large variety of images, sometimes organized into lists. King Milinda asks if there is an quality or attribute (*guṇa*) of nirvana found in other things, something which might merely illustrate (nirvana) by means of a simile[67]. Nāgasena replies that in regard to its true or essential nature

[66] These are the fires of passion, hatred . . . despair, given at the end of the Fire Sermon, cited in 2.3.b p. 221 above.
[67] *Kiñci opammanidassanamattam*; I take the force of *-matta*, "merely," here to refer back to the statement, repeated by the king in the previous sentence, and reiterated by Nagasena's reply, that no simile can in fact render evident the true nature of nirvana.

(*sarūpato* [68]) there is not, but there is in regard to its qualities or attributes. He then lists one attribute of a lotus, two of water, three of a medicine (given above on p. 230), four of the great ocean (given on p. 221), five of food, ten of space, three of a precious jewel, three of red sandalwood, three of cream of ghee, and five of a mountain peak (Mil 317–18: see Horner, 1964: 154–60).

The Conclusion to Part 1 returns to the importance of imagery in the Pali imaginaire, and its relation to both systematic and narrative thought. For that discussion, it will be necessary to retain from the present discussion only the two most important images: quenched fire, and the city of nirvana. In the closing pages of this chapter, where multiple images have tumbled thick and fast on top of each other, the reader may well feel exasperated: do all these images make it easier to think nirvana, or more difficult? But that too might be an aporia which Buddhist texts would be content to leave unsolved.

[68] Taking *sa* here in the sense of *sva-* (cf. Vism 508 = XVI 70).

CHAPTER THREE

Nirvana, time and narrative

In the first two chapters, describing nirvana as a concept in systematic thought, and as embodied in and/or illustrated by imagery, I have quoted from many texts, and referred to still more, but with the partial exception of those from the *Udāna* and its commentary discussed in 1.2.c no attempt was made to deal with extended passages, whose literariness would demand its own attention and interpretative care. In this chapter I begin to attempt that, and continue to do so throughout the rest of the book. My concern here is with the way the Pali imaginaire textualizes time, and with nirvana as a narrative closure-marker, both in narrated time and in the time of narration. The texts discussed are the *Buddhavaṃsa* and *Mahāvaṃsa*; section 3.4. a looks briefly at the *vaṃsa* genre in general, and these two texts in particular, while sections 3.4.b and c offer interpretations of them based on a close reading of the relevant selections, which are translated in Appendices 1 and 2. But before coming to that, it is necessary to criticize and dismiss what I propose to call "the myth of The Myth of the Eternal Return," which makes a wholly misleading and completely mistaken dichotomy between "the West and the rest," claiming that "western" time is linear, and aligned with a propensity towards history, while elsewhere – notably in "the East" – time is cyclical, and aligned with a propensity to myth. My own argument is only complete by the end of this chapter, when the two *vaṃsa* texts have been examined; but I first mention some encouraging signs in very recent literature on time which suggest that the Myth of the Eternal Return has, at last, had its day.

3.1. THE MYTH OF "THE MYTH OF THE ETERNAL RETURN"

The last two decades have seen an explosion of scholarly interest in narrative, as a mode of discourse in fiction, historiography and elsewhere, and of self-perception in psychoanalysis, autobiography, and experience in general. Narrative is a textual/cultural form, and a cognitive process.[1] Part of this interest has focused on time, which is obviously and intimately involved in the special form of representation constituted by narrative. It seems to me, unfortunately, that when writing about time, calendars, and so forth, cross-culturally, few scholars seem able to avoid some version of the Myth of the Eternal Return. Much, though not all of the responsibility for this must lie with Mircea Eliade, who in his influential book of that title, and elsewhere, lumped together pagans, primitives, Archaic Man (*sic*, for both words), the civilizations of "the East," notably Indian Brahmanical religion, and more besides, into the single category of "the traditional," opposed to modern, that is western Historical Man.[2] The fact that this was more often than not to praise the former and criticize the latter is irrelevant to the point that this dichotomy makes serious culturally and historically differentiated thought about these issues well-nigh impossible, in Europe as much as anywhere else.[3] As Trautmann puts it, thanks to Christianity (notably Augustine, on whom see below), and thence to Hegel, Marx, and James Mill in the nineteenth century, as well as to Eliade in the twentieth, "in the master narrative of modernity, India finds a place alongside other non-European civilizations as the embodiment of the premodern . . . [But] in respect of Indian time the master narrative is [now] cracked beyond repair" (1995: 167, 186).

The widespread emphasis recently within the academy on the notion that knowledge is historically and culturally located has led many writers to use the qualifying adjective "western" in relation to what they are writing about. This usage, when it is well

[1] See, e.g., Berkhofer (1995), Bruner (1986, 1987, 1990, 1991), Chatman (1978), Martin (1986), Mink (1987), Mitchell (1981), Polkinghorne (1988), Ricoeur (1984–88). Cf. Prince (1987) for definitions and bibliography.

[2] See, for example, Eliade (1954) and (1957). Useful criticism can be found in J. Z. Smith (1991). In general Eliade's grasp of Buddhism is weak: see Gombrich (1974).

[3] For example, Gould's excellent *Time's Arrow, Time's Cycle* begins by reproducing the conventional Eliade-derived picture (1987: 10–16), complete with references to "Judaeo-Christian" and western particularity, then spends the book showing that both metaphors were present throughout the European discovery of geological "Deep Time" in the eighteenth and nineteenth centuries. Conversely, Hillis Miller states that certain assumptions, including "origin and end" and "linearity," are fundamental to "western ideas of history and western ideas of fiction" (1974: 460), then spends the article arguing that Nietzsche, George Eliot and Walter Benjamin did not make them.

intentioned, may seem harmless, but there is a crucial slippage of meaning inherent in it, from the sense of the qualifier as simply descriptive of European-American tradition in some domain, without prejudice as to what may be true of other traditions, to the exclusivist sense of "western and not other." The ambiguity can be seen in a textbook on *Narrative Fiction: Contemporary Poetics* by Rimmon-Kenan. In the chapter on time, she states on the first page – as is surely true – that "time is one of the most basic categories of human experience" (1983: 43); but on the next page we are told that "our civilization tends to think of time as a unidirectional and irreversible flow, a sort of one-way street. Such a conception was given metaphoric shape by Heraclitus early in western history: 'You cannot step twice into the same river, for other waters and yet other waters go ever flowing on.'" (3.4.b below cites an exactly parallel metaphor in the *Buddhavaṃsa*.) It is not clear whether Rimmon-Kenan restricts her remarks to "our (western) civilization" because she does not know whether or not they apply anywhere else, which is perfectly reasonable, or whether the implication is that the non-west has some other way of thinking about time than as unidirectional and irreversible. If so, this would be difficult to harmonize with the generalizing remark on the first page – for now we would have time as basic to (all) human experience but differentiated between West and Rest – and contrary to another general remark she makes a few sentences after the last passage cited, and which also seems to me surely true, that time is "repetition within irreversible sequence."[4]

It is important to state clearly here that the argument is not against the use of the dichotomy between linear and cyclical time as a means of analysis: on the contrary, in the form non-repetitive/repetitive it informs the whole account of nirvana, time and narrative to be given in this chapter. The argument is against the use of it as a form of cultural description and differentiation. Barbara Adam (1995: 19–42) offers an excellent and thorough critique of those who identify time with "historical, chronological dating" and so see non-modern (i.e. non-western) societies as having a "cyclical" view of it. As she puts it,

[4] She thinks this paradoxical, which I do not. Toolan's version is perhaps better: "time is perceived repetition within perceived irreversible change" (1988: 48). The two phrases about perceived time could be reversed.

it is essential to appreciate that all social processes display aspects of linearity and cyclicality, [and] that we recognize a cyclical structure when we focus on events that repeat themselves and unidirectional linearity when our attention is on the process of the repeating action. (1995: 38)

Our idea of time must consequently always entail both rhythmic recurrence and beginnings and ends, perimeters and horizons. It is therefore important that we never lose sight of one whilst our focus is on the other. Rhythms and irreversible processes must be understood *together* since, on their own, neither could account for that which is expressed by the idea of time. (1990: 33)

This is true for any society or individuals, at any time. In the General Introduction I.c, I referred to an article by Bloch (1977), "The Past and the Present in the Present," in connection with soteriology and the state (his "religion" and "politics"). Here, on the other hand, it is worth citing a criticism of what Bloch says about time there made by Howe (1981). Bloch takes Geertz to task for claiming that the Balinese have only a nondurational, static, cyclical concept of time.[5] This is not because Bloch thinks there is not such a kind of time (for him it is the "religio-political") but because he wants to contrast to it (pragmatic) "notions of durational time [used in contexts of] practical activities, especially agriculture and un-institutionalized power," which the Balinese, like all peoples, also have (1977: 284–5). Bloch is right to criticize Geertz for attributing only one kind of time to the Balinese; Howe is right to criticize Bloch for seeing the two kinds of time as a mutally exclusive dichotomy:

The evidence, in my opinion, makes it appropriate to designate Balinese representations of duration as exhibiting properties of both cyclicity and linearity . . . [T]he Balinese possess only one notion of time and . . . this incorporates both cyclical and linear features . . . [F]rom the evidence adduced concerning Balinese culture I would claim that repetition (cyclicality) and irreversibility (linearity) are both integral features of Balinese notions of duration. Duration, and the succession of events, is something the members of all societies experience though they represent it differently. (1981: 231)

All human experience of time – including, quite evidently, the agricultural activities Bloch wants to class as durational/linear – always involves both repetition and non-repetition. However much any particular tradition of representation may privilege, or seem

[5] "Person, Time and Conduct in Bali," in Geertz (1973). See also Gell (1992: 78–93).

to privilege, one or the other, in fact they imply one another, such that both will always and everywhere co-exist, to varying degrees (Elchardus 1988: 45–7; Alheit 1994). Brown (1991: 94–4, 133; cf. Nowotny 1994: 54) is right to suggest that this is a human universal based, in part, on biological facts about human bodies: circadian and other rhythms establish repetitiveness and cyclicality, while the process of growth, maturation, aging and death establishes non-repetitiveness and linearity. Young (1988) shows, in an extensive review of the subject, that both cyclicality and linearity are ubiquitous and obvious features of societies also.

A particularly strong version of the dichotomy is found in an influential article by Edmund Leach, "Two Essays Concerning the Symbolic Representation of Time." He thinks that "our modern English notion of time embraces at least two different kinds of experience that are logically distinct and even contradictory" (1977: 125). These two "kinds of experience" are of repetition – metronomes, clocks, pulses, seasons – and non-repetition: the process of living, growing old and dying. Religions, he says, "purport to repudiate the reality of death" by subsuming non-repetition into repetition, such that death becomes a process of new birth: indeed, he says, were it not for "religious prejudice" the two aspects of time would not be embraced under one category at all. The first point about religions seems to me well taken, but the second completely wrong: the perception of repetition and of non-repetition logically imply one another. It is only through the continuous and connected experience of a single, irreversible trajectory through time that it is possible to recognize events as *repetitions* at all: for example by setting the recurrence of the seasons against the non-repetitive course of one's own life. And it is the constant repetition of objective phenomena set against subjective change that makes the irreversibility of aging the vivid individual experience that it is. In moving through an irreversible sequence of life-experiences one can both perceive that sequence as the repetition or recurrence of roles and patterns of interrelationship – son/daughter–parent–grandparent, child–youth–adult, student–teacher, and so on – and recognize that one's own instantiation of them, in the empirical perspective of one lifetime, is once-and-for-all. As a general matter of conceptualization and cognition it seems to me obvious and natural to class together both what happens for the first time, uniquely, and what happens repeatedly, in the overall category of *event*. Time is that in which events occur; or, one might say, in order to avoid unnecessary reification, the human activity of timing is a way to systematize event-changes, and the question of whether it is more salient to represent a given instance as unique (as all events necessarily are, from the non-repetitive perspective) or as the instantiation of a pattern is an issue logically secondary to the fundamental activity of timing.[6]

"Other cultures" do not have another, deeply "other" way of existing in time. The language used to express time-relations will no doubt often be very different from that of the Indo-European syntax common to Pali and English. But however much particular representations of time in language may be irreducibly thick descriptions, and however much the meaning of time in particular lexicons may be constructed by the work of culture, at a minimalist level perception of the non-repetitive physical processes of growth, aging and death, and of the repetitive occurrence of seasons, generational roles, etc., is universal. Every day, every week, every year moves everyone closer, irreversibly, to death; each day, week and year is a recurrence of the same circadian, calendrical and/or seasonal patterns; and every individual's unrepeatable accession to a new stage of life is but one more example of the genre. Representations of time will obviously vary from place to place, from time to time, across different social strata at one and the same place and time, and indeed in one individual for different purposes (subatomic physicists, astronomers, and farmers can all celebrate anniversaries, enjoy sunsets, and feel grief at funerals). The truth – indeed the truism – that the repetitive and non-repetitive modes of time exist simultaneously, always and everywhere, seems to me so monumentally obvious that it becomes difficult to see how the mystifications of theologians like Augustine and Eliade could ever have succeeded in obscuring it. How can one put this? To borrow from Samuel Beckett: when everyday the sun shines, having no alternative, on the nothing new, the pace at which all that fall fall, never slows, nor does it ever quicken.[7] In Buddhism, the power of impermanence over human life – a power to which even Buddhas must

[6] The choice of wording here is influenced here by Elias (1992); see 1.1.c, n. 21. For a recent review of anthropological writing on time see Munn (1992).

[7] With thanks to Christopher Ricks (1993: 29ff., 62–3, and *passim*).

one day succumb[8] – is the shared, always repeated experience of Everyman and Everywoman, and it is the Truth taught, as is periodically necessary, by Everybuddha.

As has been mentioned, an *éminence grise* of the *longue durée* in producing the false sense of Christian, and thence western uniqueness is Augustine, who was quite happy to confess himself incapable of saying what time is, and at the same time to berate "pagans," notably Greeks, for having a mistaken cyclical view of it, a characterization of Greek thought shown clearly to be wrong, in historiography (Momigliano 1977: 107–26, 179–204), and in a wide range of philosophical, literary, scientific and other works (Lloyd 1975, Sorabji 1983: 184–5). In the case of Eliade, even if one restricts his grand claims to Southern Asia, they are still hopelessly over-generalized. His descriptions of "Indian" thought rely for the most part on the liturgical texts of early Brahmanical sacrificial ritual, in the description of which his vocabulary can be useful. This is hardly surprising: all liturgies are for the most part invariant; and the ideology of such Brahmanical ritual was cosmogonic, claiming to regenerate the universe by revivifying the creative energy of the primordial sacrifice (through macro- and micro-cosmic parallels).

Given the absence in Buddhism of any myth or metaphysics of cosmogony (and a corresponding absence of any end to collective time, on which see below), the notion of a special time-outside-time, *illud tempus*, as the beginning and ending condition of the cosmos, periodically recaptured in the "sacred time" of ritual, is at best irrelevant. The Pali imaginaire is permeated with concern for temporality, and it textualizes time in concentrated and subtle ways, as I aim to show in 3.4.b and c below. If one approaches this concern, and these texts, with the minimalist universalism about non-repetitive and repetitive time as possible forms of experience suggested here, one can then see that both modes of time are the object of representation, but that differing texts foreground one or the other aspect of time according to their different aims.

[8] Cf. 2.2.a on the Mindfulness of Death, 3.4.b below on Atthadassī Buddha, and the note to Mhv II 33, translated in Appendix 2.

3.2. ENDINGS WITHIN NARRATED TIME

It is now usual in studies of narrative to distinguish between the time covered by the events and situations represented, and the time taken by the representation: this is story time versus discourse time, *erzählte Zeit* versus *Erzählzeit* (see Prince 1987); endings in the two times, of course can and often do coincide. I want to argue that in the Pali imaginaire nirvana provides "the sense of an ending"[9] in both:

(i) in narrated time, coherence and resolution in one lifetime are derived in part from connectedness with previous and subsequent lives: the problem of evil and injustice is understood as part of the cosmic scheme of *karma*, cause and effect, a scheme in which, ultimately, there is no injustice, for all get their just deserts. But the sequence of lives as a whole, the very fact of conditioning and *karma*, finds its own resolution, its own avoidance of meaningless chronology, in the possibility of Release. Nirvana can offer satisfactory closure, where the mere breaking-off of life occasioned by death cannot;

(ii) in the time of narration, mention of nirvana can be seen to signal closure in the actual performance-time of texts (reading, reciting, and in other contexts).

There is a clear and persuasive consensus among scholars about the function of endings: Barbara Hernnstein Smith describes poetic closure as "a modification of structure that makes *stasis*, or the absence of further continuation, the most probable succeeding event. Closure allows the reader to be satisfied by the failure of continuation or, put another way, it creates in the reader the expectation of nothing" (1968: 34). Prince's *Dictionary of Narratology* defines "end" as follows (1987: 26):

> The final incident in a Plot or Action. The end follows but is not followed by other incidents and ushers in a state of (relative) stability. Students of Narrative have pointed out that the end occupies a determinative position because of the light it sheds (or might shed) on the meaning of events leading up to it. The end functions as the (partial) condition, the magnetizing force, the organizing principle of narrative: reading

[9] This is the title of Kermode (1967), a deservedly well-known and influential work. For my purposes, however, it must be said that this work is wholly dominated by Christian forms of thought, and its rare moments of cross-cultural hypothesizing are limited by his acceptance of the linear/cyclical dichotomy (e.g. 1967: 35–6).

(processing) a narrative is, amongst other things, waiting for the end, and the nature of the waiting is related to the nature of the narrative.

Finally, Ricoeur adds an important rider: "it is in the act of retelling rather than in that of telling that this structural function of closure can be discerned." In any telling, "the configuration of the plot imposes the 'sense of an ending' . . . on the indefinite succession of incidents," but when a story is already known, to follow it is "to apprehend the episodes which are themselves well-known as leading to this end" (1984: 60).

3.2.a. Ending(s) in non-repetitive time

Part of the work of culture in regard to death, it seems safe to say, is to transform it from a mute biological event, an arbitrary cessation, to a comprehensible life-cycle transition within an articulated narrative, and so provide an acceptable closure to the material, embodied saga we (can thereby) call a biography. Without such an ending individual lives are, just as much as collective history, just one damn thing after another, coming to a stop wherever they happen to, for whatever reason (or none). A major function of religious ideologies in premodern civilizations was to provide a discursive representation in which individual and/or collective endings could make sense, to offer a resolution to mere chronology, an ordering of the chaos of moments, by narrating individual lives as parts of a master-text.[10] Texts and textualization – the civilizationally enunciative work of clerics, constructing and maintaining a socially prestigious, or at least elite Tradition – are not therefore simply decorative, elaborating a "high" culture for aesthetes; but construing inevitabilities of life and death which concern everyone.

I am using the words "text" and "textualize" in two ways. First, there is what I am calling the Buddhist master-text. The word "text" here refers not to an individual sequence of words, embodied in some oral or written artifact, but to an overall narrative of the universe, rebirth, and salvation; this is an abstraction, an ideal object implicit in, or presupposed by particular texts. Second,

[10] This recalls a common perception of modernity: we can no longer tell satisfactory stories of our lives, for there is no satisfactory ending. The constant preoccupation with the necessity and impossibility of ending in Samuel Beckett's later writings may be taken as the paradigm of such a view.

there are just such actual texts, oral or written; one might, on occasion, include iconographic objects or ritual sequences in this second category. No such text, clearly, could ever be coterminous with the master-text, but can only instantiate some part(s) of it.

I argued in the Introduction to Part 1 that eternity as either endlessness or timelessness cannot be narratively figured; and as has been shown in the first two chapters, both the concept and the imagery of nirvana eventuate, by design, in aporetic silence. Nirvana is the full stop (period) in the Buddhist story, the point at which narrative imagination must cease. But this cessation provides the sense of an ending rather than a mere breaking-off.[11] Nirvana is a moment within a discursive or practical dynamic, a formal element of closure in the structure of Buddhist imagination, texts and rituals. This is the sense in which I want to say that nirvana has a syntactic as well as a semantic value: it is the moment of ending which gives structure to the whole. The fact of narrative structure and closure provides a meaningful and satisfying resolution, although in itself nirvana has merely the formal value of a closure-marker.

The ending of unsatisfactoriness, the closure of the Buddhist story, can be taken in relation to any individual, to any single sequence of lives, albeit that the paradigmatic story of such an ending is, of course, the story of Gotama the Buddha. There seem to have been very few complete biographies of the Buddha, as separate, individual texts, in early Buddhist history,[12] but the whole iconographic record shows that the main features of the Buddha-legend must have been widely known: if not, obviously, the sometimes complex depictions of particular scenes, by both iconic and aniconic means, could not have made sense to those for whom they were intended (Dehejia 1990). For any individual, the denouement of the story of spiritual liberation – *Bildungsroman* on a cosmic scale, and the completion of a Sentimental Education, of

[11] The term *pariyosāṇaṭṭhena*, literally "in the sense of an ending," is used in relation to nirvana frequently in the *Paṭisambhidhā-magga* (e.g. I 22, 23, 34, 75, 76, II 85, 125); and the compounds *nibbāna-pariyosāna* and *-parāyaṇa* (M I 304, S III 189, V 11, 218, etc.) both mean "with nirvana as an end."

[12] See Lamotte (1988: 648ff.) I share Lamotte's skepticism (ibid.: 176–9), although for different reasons, about the attempt by Frauwallner (1956) to show that there was a comprehensive biography of the Buddha incorporated into a text, "the Old Skandhaka," which also dealt with Monastic Rules, the early Councils, etc.

a special kind – is both the discovery of Truth and a change in being. Buddhist thought about rebirth and release blends what might otherwise be distinguished as epistemology and ontology. When the saint realizes the Truth, it is not that he or she has simply acquired some new knowledge, but rather that such knowledge instantiates a new existential state or condition.[13]

3.2.b. Ending(s) in repetitive time

Famously, perhaps notoriously, four alternatives are all said to be inapplicable to the state of an enlightened person after death: it is wrong to say that he or she exists, does not exist, both exists and does not exist, or neither exists nor does not exist (cf. 2.3.c). While naturally most attention has been paid to the logic of this fourfold denial, it is also important in relation to Buddhist attitudes to relics and images, as has been pointed out by Obeyesekere (1966: 8) and Smart (1973: 74–9). In this sense it can be misleading to say that the Buddha "died," or is now "dead" (2.1.a). This is the case for precise linguistic and philosophical reasons (Collins 1982: 131–2); but equally as a part of religious culture it connects with the widespread and varied senses in which the Buddha is still – somehow – present, or at least powerfully represented.[14] In fact, the continuing status of the Buddha, through his teaching, images of him and relics (of differing kinds) is incorporated by the Pali imaginaire into a scheme which expresses marvelously the view of time as "perceived repetition with perceived irreversible change" mentioned earlier. On a number of occasions I have spoken of Buddhas in the plural: although it is still natural and comprehensible from a modern historical perspective to speak of "the" Buddha, referring to the historical figure of Siddhattha Gotama,

[13] It is not surprising, then, to find nirvana characterized in epistemological terms: what is transient has the nature of falsehood, but nirvana does not (Sn 757–8). When a verse declares "there is only one truth, there is no second," the commentaries say that this can refer either to nirvana or to the Path; and when another text says "the highest noble wisdom [is] the knowledge of the destruction of all suffering. This release, based on Truth, is unshakable. For that which has the nature of falsehood is a lie; that truth which does not have the nature of falsehood is nirvana," the commentary glosses the words lie and falsehood (*musā, mosa*) as both what is not true, incorrect (*vitatha*) and what is liable to decay (*nassana-dhamma*): Sn 884 with Pj II 555, Nidd I 292; cp. Vism 497 = XVI 26; and Ps V 59 on M III 245; cf. Pj II 509 on Sn 758.

[14] As mentioned in the General Introduction I.b, I have reservations about the vocabulary of "presence" here.

for the traditional Pali imaginaire (which does not have the definite or indefinite article) he was referred to by name, or by the phrase "our Buddha" (*amhākaṃ Buddho*), as one of a logically infinite number of Buddhas. I return to this issue in 5.1, as an introduction to the discussion there of Buddhist millennialism, and the future Buddha Metteyya (Skt Maitreya). Whereas in other forms of Buddhism the coexistence of multiple Buddhas at the same time was accepted, in Theravāda they exist in a (linear) sequence, and a wholly new form of nirvana was constructed to help express the idea: the nirvana of (a Buddha's) relics, *dhātu-parinibbāna* . I first set out three ways in which a Buddha may be said – loosely – to continue to exist, or to be a presence, in his teaching, in images, and in relics, and then return to the sequencing of Buddhas in time.

The Buddha as his Teaching. As Hallisey puts it (1992: 10; cf. Kermode 1967: 73) although for all conditioned events, animate and inanimate, "existence in time brings decay," it is also true that for the historical embodiment of the Buddha's teaching, the *sāsana*, "existence through time brings authority." On a number of occasions in the canonical texts, the Buddha identifies himself with his teaching, as in the remark that "He who sees the Dhamma sees me, he who sees me sees the Dhamma" (S III 120). Some later texts develop the idea by saying that the Teaching is his Dhamma-body (*dhamma-kāya*, or-*sarīra*), in contrast with his form- or material body (*rūpa-kāya*), which came to an end with his "death": Sv 34 says that when the monk Ānanda begins each *Sutta* with "Thus I have heard," he "makes present (or perceptible, *paccakkhaṃ*) the Blessed One's Dhamma-body"; then, by means of the immediately following phrase "at one time the Blessed One (was living at . . .)," "he shows the Blessed One's (present) nonexistence (*avijjamāna-bhāva*) and reminds (the audience) of the nirvana of (his) form-body." Similarly the monk Nāgasena explains that the Buddha exists, although he cannot be said to be in any given place, in that he can be shown (*nidassetuṃ*) by his Dhamma-body, that is to say, his teaching (Mil 1973). At Mil 1971, he uses similar language, and refers to the S III 120 passage, in saying that it is possible to know that the Buddha is pre-eminent in the same way that one can know a dead writing teacher by his (extant) writings. The word *dhammakāya* is used once in the Canon (D III 84), in a text attacking Brahmanical pride in birth, where the Buddha explains that monks are his sons in the sense that they are born from his mouth, born from Dhamma; thus "having Dhamma for a body" is said to be a synonym for the Tathāgata. The commentary here (Sv 865) interprets the word in terms of the canonical "Word of the Buddha."[15]

The Buddha as his Image. Although a number of uncertainties beset our understanding of the earlier history of images and image veneration in Buddhism,[16] there is no doubt that they came to play an important role in mediating the Buddha's presence. This is amply attested in modern ethnography;[17] and the following examples from traditional texts suffice to express the point. At M III 255 the Buddha describes giving a gift to "both Orders (i.e. of monks and nuns) with the Buddha at their head" (*Buddha-pamukha*, and "to both Orders after the Tathāgata's nirvana." The commentary (Ps V 73) interprets *Buddhapamukha* in the first case as the Buddha's being physically in front of the two Orders (the term does not always have this specific sense), with monks on one side and nuns on the other. In the second case, it asks "But can a gift be given to both Orders, with the Buddha in front (of them) after the Tathāgata has attained (final) nirvana? It can. How? An image (of the Buddha) containing relics should be put on a seat facing the two Orders, and a stand put there, and when the offering of water [poured over the hand of the recipient, whether alive or in the form of a statue] and the rest have been made, everything is first to be offered to the Teacher, and (only then) given to the two Orders" (cp. also Sp 1142–3). Jinak (1986–7) describes the seventh century AD origin in Ceylon of the Buddha-statue called the *Sīhalapatimā*, destined to have a remarkable career later in

[15] For the context, see Appendix 5 section 9, and Collins (1993c ad loc.). *Dhamma-kāya* is used often elsewhere, again in contrast to *rūpakāya*, but not in this precise sense. See Reynolds (1977: 374–89); and add to his references Ud-a 87–8, 310, It-a 103, 115–6, Vism 211 = VII 60.

[16] For example, there has been some debate recently over the significance of the distinction in early Indian Buddhism between aniconic and iconic representations: see, *inter alia*, the usual position as depicted in Snellgrove (1978), and the challenge to it by Huntington (1990). Rahula (1956: 121ff.) discusses the surprisingly rare mention of images in the Pali commentarial literature, despite their relative frequency in the historical Chronicles. (Note, however, that he is incorrect to state [1956.: 125] that no *patimāghara*, image-house, is mentioned in the commentaries: see Sp 358 and Moh 199, and add to his other references Ja IV 95, VI 125, 541, Spk III 50, Mp I 116, IV 202, Ud-a 415, Cp-a 282, Asl 334.)

[17] See Gombrich (1971a: 103ff.) for Sri Lanka, Griswold (1968) and Tambiah (1984 Part 3,) for Thailand.

Southeast Asia: a king wants to see a likeness (*rūpa*) of the Buddha; a (mythical and long-lived) nāga-king who had seen the Buddha when he made one of his visits to the island arrives, and creates an appearance (*vesa*) of the Buddha. The king venerates the *Buddharūpa* for a week, and then has the image made exactly like it.[18]

The Buddha as his relics. Statues of the Buddha, although allowing him to be "seen" in a rather obvious way, in fact are usually thought only to mediate his presence in a stronger sense if they contain relics, as is shown in the passage from Ps V 73 just cited.[19] In an often-quoted passage of the *Mahāvaṃsa* (XVII 2–3), the monk Mahinda, who has but recently arrived in Ceylon to establish Buddhism there, tells the king that he has not seen the Buddha for a long time; the king responds "Did you not say that the Buddha has attained nirvana?" Mahinda replies, "Seeing the relics is seeing the Buddha" (*dhātūsu diṭṭhesu diṭṭho hoti jino*). A similar phrase is used elsewhere in a standard commentarial passage, one which allows me to bring together the three forms of "continuing existence" I am here – loosely – speaking of. The phrase is found in a number of texts (Sv 898, Ps IV 115, Mp II 10, Vibh-a 431): "when (their) relics are extant, so are the Buddhas" (*dhātūsu hi ṭhitāsu Buddhā ṭhitā va honti*). The context is that of the gradual disappearance of Buddhism: [20] as a historical phenomenon, a Buddha's Teaching, his *sāsana*, will come to an end like all conditioned phenomena (but unlike the truth of his teaching, the Dhamma, which is timeless: cf. 5.1.a). At the time of the nirvana of a Buddha's relics, they all come together and perform miracles like those of the Buddha during his lifetime. These miracles are

[18] The term *Buddha-rūpa* can often refer to a statue; but in this case, given the mythical nature of the narrative, it is not clear whether an actual statue is made by the nāga-king, or whether the "likeness" is made in some other way. The story here is modeled on one told earlier of emperor Aśoka (Sp 43–4, Mhv V 87–94; on this passage see 3.4.c below). Discussing this, Geiger (1912: 34 n. 2) and Gombrich (1966: p. 26) interpret *Buddha-rūpa* as a statue, and the *akkhi-pūjā*, "eye-worship" made by Aśoka as equivalent to the modern practice of "consecrating" an image by painting in the eyes (attested from at least the sixteenth century). The term may, however, refer to Aśoka's gazing uninterruptedly at the "appearance" with his own eyes: this is the way the commentary to the Mhv passage takes it (Mhv-t I 210), and cp. Jayawickrama (1962: 39 and n. 3).

[19] For discussion of this point see Rahula (1956: 125) and, for relic veneration more generally, Trainor (1997).

[20] To the texts cited here add Mil 133–4, Spk II 202, Moh 201–3; they speak of three or five disappearances, in different orders, covering practice, learning, realization, the marks of monastic life, and relics.

variously described: the accounts at Mp I 91 and Anāg 36 specify that the relics will take the form (*rūpa*) of the Buddha, and the latter adds that they/he will preach a sermon. When the relics disappear, however, the gods will all exclaim that "our" Buddha is (*finally*!) attaining nirvana (forms of the verb *parinibbāti* are used), and that this will be the "last sight" of him. Thereafter there is no hindrance to another Buddha's arising.

Each Buddha is connected with others, in a complex and interwoven pattern of predictions and recollections; each one, like our Buddha Gotama in a previous life as the ascetic Sumedha in the presence of the former Buddha Dīpaṅkara, takes a vow not to become an enlightened saint there and then, but rather to become himself a perfected Buddha in the future and save others (translated in Appendix 1). The Buddha in whose presence and under whose Dispensation the vow is made then makes a prediction of the future Buddhahood of the vow-taker; and the prediction is reconfirmed by other Buddhas in the enormously long interval before that end is realized. Events in the lives of particular Buddhas, as well as the careers of their relics, are similarly predicted. Although details in the lives of the Buddhas are differentiated in various ways, both the overall form and many particular events in their life stories are identical. The Truth they discover is the same, of course, as are the texts in which the Truth is embodied, at least in their general form: the teaching of previous Buddhas is also redacted in "the Three Piṭakas" (Ja I 30, Thī-a 199).

In repetitive time, therefore, the attainment – in non-repetitive time – of final nirvana by individuals (Buddhas and others), the continuing presence of Buddhas in their Teaching, images and relics, and the eventual nirvana of the relics, all instantiate a general and continually repeated pattern. The master-text which narrates this beginningless and endless sequence transcribes eternity, in two senses: its cosmology extends time backwards and forwards endlessly, in the universe of conditioning, *saṃsāra*; and it is this which provides the discursive Said through which the Unsaid – eternity as timeless nirvana – is possible as an object of thought. Earlier I called nirvana the full stop (period) in the Buddhist story; now I can add that it is a full stop in an eternal story; a full stop which brings closure to individual lives in a master-text which itself can have no final ending. The language of "cyclical" time can be unhelpful: it is not time which is cyclical, but the structure of it, the processes which occur in it: just as we think of time as a sequence of repeated days, weeks, months and years, so developed Indian thought sees these smaller-scale repetitions as parts of the much larger-scale repetitive sequence of eons. Whether or not the internal structure of each eon is seen as degenerative, such that we live in the last, evil and pain-filled *Kali-yuga*, the overall process in both Hinduism and Buddhism is one of repeated beginnings and endings, creative explosions and destructive implosions.

3.2.c. Individual versus collective time: can history end?

The Buddhist master-text has no ultimate "once upon a time": each cosmic eon begins, although there was no beginning to the sequence of eons. But in nirvana it does have its "and so they lived happily ever after." The suffering or unsatisfactoriness (*dukkha*) inherent in an impermanent and conditioned world receives no *explanation* in Buddhism, in the sense that there is no etiological myth of its ultimate origin. *Saṃsāra* is beginningless, with no earliest point (*pubbakoṭi, purimā koṭi*).[21] The *Visuddhimagga* argues that in the chain of Dependent Origination (1.1.b), ignorance and Craving are made the starting point(s) (*sīsaṃ katvā*, literally "put at the head") not because they constitute a causeless root-cause (*akāraṇaṃ mūlakāraṇaṃ*) of the world, like the original Nature (*prakṛti*) of the Hindu Sāṃkhya system, but because each represents a special(ly important) cause (*visesa-hetu*) of karma (Vism 252 = XVII 36ff.). But despite this, the beginningless round of rebirth is nonetheless resolved, understood and transcended in thought, by being placed in a master-text in which it can be brought to an end, for the individual, in nirvana.[22] One might well ask whether all sentient creatures could one day attain nirvana, and if so would the universe as a whole end? Such questions, although on a few occasions addressed in other parts of the

[21] S II 178ff., A V 113, 116, Asl 10–1, Mil 50–2, Asl 10–1, etc.

[22] The beginningless of *saṃsāra* is to be distinguished from the fact of nirvana's being the "place" without birth: in the latter case, nirvana is without birth because in it there is no process, no occurrence in time at all, whereas in the former the process of time and occurrence(s) is said not to have begun at a certain point. It – and therefore time – has always existed (cf. 1.2.c).

Buddhist tradition,[23] are said in Pali texts to be unanswered (*avyākata*) and to be set aside (*thāpaṇīya*).[24] Some readers may find surprising the absence of any notion of a collective end, any account of the ending of all humanity in non-repetitive time. But this is simply a fact of cultural difference: thanks no doubt to Judaic and Christian collectivism (amongst other things), it is a usual western assumption that dramas of time and salvation (or, indeed, damnation) must involve humankind as a whole moving from a unique beginning through non-repetitive time to its end. But Buddhist thought, like much Indian world-renunciatory religion, is individualist;[25] this can be argued in many ways, but here I refer to the fact that non-repetitive time can only end for individuals. Buddhist dramas of humankind as a whole are never-ending: only privatized, individual time can end, not public. There can be no end to history.

3.3. ENDING AS AN EVENT IN THE TIME OF NARRATION

Actual texts are of course recited in actual time; the internal durational form of a text is embodied in non-repetitive time every time it is read, or heard. Equally, when such texts are recited on recurrent ritual or festival occasions, the running through of a text's internal linear duration becomes itself a form of repetition. It is, I think, particularly important to remember in this context that throughout history, until very recent times in some (particularly urban) areas, Buddhist texts have been predominantly oral phenomena. They are said to have been preserved and "read" orally

23 See Ruegg (1969: 205–17). The Pali word *anamatagga* (Buddhist Sanskrit *anavarāgra*), applied to *saṃsāra*, is sometimes rendered as "without beginning and end." The linguistic analysis of the term is difficult: most of the contexts in which it appears suggest that it means simply "without beginning," and refer to the absence of a "first point" (*pubbakoti*); Pj II 597 and Nidd 2 273–4, however, also refer to there being no "last point" (*pacchimakoṭi*) of *saṃsāra*. A play on the syllables of the word *avijjā*, "ignorance," found in a number of texts (Ud-a 41, Vism 526 = XVII 43, Vibh-a 134) has it that "ignorance makes beings hurry on in endless *saṃsāra*" (A*nta*- VI*rahite saṃsāre . . . satte* JA*vāpeti*).

24 The questions as to whether the world is eternal or not (*a/sassata*) are the first and second of the traditional list of Unanswered Questions (see Collins 1982: 131ff.). The third and fourth ask whether it has an end or not (*an/antavā*), but this is interpreted to mean a limit in space. These questions are given at Mil 1 44–5 (cp. Mp II 308–9) as examples of the kind of question "to be set aside." There are four ways to answer questions (D III 229, A I 197, II 46, etc.): definitely, with an analysis, with a counter-question, and setting the question aside.

25 This has been argued by Louis Dumont; for an overview of his work, with bibliography, see Collins (1989).

(that is, recited and listened to) for some three hundred years before being committed to writing in the first century BC; and even after that a wealth of evidence shows that manuscripts have existed largely as *aides-mémoire* for monks, who would then recite the texts publicly (see Collins 1990a, 1992b). The modern sense of "reading" a text, here as often, leaves out of account so much of the actual experiential features of Buddhist literature in social and historical context.[26] Public recitation of a text, like a sermon, resembles a dramaturgical performance as much as (perhaps more than) it resembles the static lines-of-text model of "reading a book." The dynamics of closure, in this perspective, are more than just a general point about texts providing the sense of an ending which life (or death) cannot. They are quite literally moments in a (ritual) performance.[27]

The nirvanic ending-moment occurs in the time of narration in a variety of ways:

(i) As the end of a sermon. Commentaries note the value of ending a discourse, *desānaṃ niṭṭhāpeti*, bringing it to a climax, *(ni)kūṭaṃ* (or *-ena*) *gaṇhati*, with a reference to final *nirvana* or to enlightenment, Arahantship.[28] (Some texts of this kind are given on pp. 253–4.)

(ii) As the climax of various series of epithets and synonyms within texts. Examples of this are numerous: in the first Sermon, the Middle Way is said to "make for vision, wisdom, leading to calming, higher knowledge, enlightenment, nirvana" (Vin I 10); at A II 34 the Buddha says "With regard to both conditioned and unconditioned *dhamma*-s, the best of them (all) is dispassion . . . the crushing of pride, the removal of thirst, the uprooting of attachment, the termination of the round (of rebirth), the destruction of Craving, dispassion, cessation, nirvana." (This sequence, with variants, is found elsewhere; cp. Nett 55 which appends another

[26] Graham (1987) writes evocatively of what he calls "the sensual dimension" of religious literature, in ways which are readily applicable to the Buddhist tradition.

[27] As in the premodern West, even private reading of manuscripts was done aloud, and recitation of texts (both aloud and, when they had been learnt by heart, silently) could form part of meditation practice (see Collins 1992b), so individual learning and reciting of texts can also be seen as having a performative dimension.

[28] Final nirvana: e.g. Sv 128, Spk I 21, Ud-a 216, It-a I 180, II 33, 38, Vv-a 243, Ja I 393; Enlightenment, Arahantship e.g. Sv 227, 549, Ps I 206, II 333, III 115, Spk I 275, III 80, Pj II 596, Ja I 114, 275, 278.

long list.) At S IV 368–73 a sequence of short *Sutta*-s is made up of a long list of such synonyms (literal and metaphorical), in relation to each of which the Buddha claims to teach the Path; the sequence culminates with *parāyanaṃ*, "the end," and the concluding recapitulation of the terms themselves ends with nirvana. Nidd I 339–41 has a list of questions (*pucchā*), and 472–3 one of "subjects for discussion" (*katthāvatthūni*), both of which end with nirvana. At Paṭis I 10–15 a list of fifteen characteristics of *saṃsāra* is given, and the "first recitation-section of the text is brought to a close" (*pathama-bhāṇavāraṃ niṭṭhitaṃ*) with a catalogue of their antonyms as characteristics of nirvana.

(iv) As the climax to a list of meditational states (e.g. M II 254–6). Frequently elsewhere (e.g. A IV 414–8) the sequence of Meditational Levels (*jhāna*-s) culminates with the Cessation of Perception and Feeling. As discussed in 1.2.b, the precise relationship between the Attainment of Cessation and nirvana is unclear, but for my point here the use of it as the culmination of a sequence of salvific attainments is the significant thing.

(v) As an aspiration for the audience added at the end of recitations: the medieval text *Saddhamma-saṅgaha*, for example, which was intended for public recitation (Collins 1992b), ends most of its chapters with the verse "Thus knowing that impermanence is wretched and hard to overcome, let the wise (person) quickly strive for the eternal deathless state" (*niccaṃ amataṃ padaṃ*).

(vi) As an aspiration for the audience at the end of sermons. This can be attested by anyone who has heard Buddhist monks preaching: the monk will end with a wish that all present will one day attain nirvana, which is greeted with cries of "*sādhu, sādhu*," literally "good" or "yes," but with the same practical function as the Christian "amen."[29]

(vii) As an aspiration by authors/redactors in the epilogue (*nigamana*) of their texts, or by the scribe in the colophon of manuscripts.[30] Very often the reference or aspiration to nirvana in these contexts will be joined with a wish to be

[29] For textual references to this use of *sādhu* see Spk I 177, 320, 335, Dhp-a III 385.

[30] See Ja VI 594–6, Vism 711–2, Asl 430–1, Mhv-t 687–9, Ext Mhv 357–8, Jināl 247–50, Thūp 254, Jina-c 458–68, Saddhamma-s pp. 72–3 vv. 1–6.

reborn at the time of the next Buddha Metteya as the means to that end.[31]

In these various ways, then, nirvana gives the Buddhist sense of an ending. I conclude this section by translating some relevant texts to illustrate (i) above. The collection of brief texts called the *Udāna* (from which four consecutive sermons were discussed in 1.2.c) ends with two passages concerning the nirvana of the monk Dabba Mallaputta (Ud 92–3 with commentary at Ud-a 430–5). The prose story is almost identical in both, followed by different concluding Spirited Utterances in verse. The first goes like this (omitting some repetitions):

"Thus I have heard. At one time the Blessed One was living at Rājagaha, in the (place called the) Squirrels' Feeding-ground in the Bamboo Grove. The venerable Dabba Mallaputta approached him, greeted him and sat down on one side. As he sat there he said to the Blessed One, 'Now is the time for my final nirvana, Happy One.' 'As you wish' (replied the Buddha). Then Dabba got up from his seat, saluted the Blessed One, walked around him (ceremonially) keeping him to his right, rose into the air, and sitting cross-legged in the sky attained a level of meditation based on the contemplation of fire.[32] Emerging from that attainment he attained final nirvana: his body caught fire and burnt, leaving no ashes or soot to be seen, in the same way as when ghee or oil burns they leave no trace of ashes or soot. The Blessed One saw what happened, and at that time made this Spirited Utterance [concerning the five Aggregates which were the continuing temporal entity called, in its last phase, the monk and Arahant Dabba]:

The body disintegrated, (perceptual and cognitive) awareness (*saññā*) ceased, all feelings went cold; Conditioning Factors were calmed, consciousness set (like the sun)."

The second passage happens later at another location, where the Buddha recounts the story of Dabba's nirvana, this time concluding with "Just as it is not possible to know the whereabouts[33] of a

[31] For references see Saddhatissa (1975: 32–45), Somadasa (1987: ix), and Hundius (1990: 102, 104, 125, 153).

[32] The text has *tejodhatuṃ samāpajjitvā*, understood by the commentary as referring to the fourth Meditation Level, based on contemplation of the fire-device (*kasiṇa*); this is one of a number of *kasiṇa*-s (others are colors, air, water, etc.) used as objects for meditative absorption; see Vism 110 = III 105, 171–2 = V 5–8.

[33] *Gati*, the standard word for one's destiny in the next life. For this, and nirvana as a destiny, see 1.2.c.

burning fire gradually put out by blows from an iron hammer, so it is impossible to know the whereabouts of those who are rightly released [i.e. by means of the Path], who have crossed over the floods and bonds of passion and attained (the) immovable happiness (of nirvana)."

The very first sermon in the canonical list, the *Brahmajāla Sutta* of the *Dīgha Nikāya*, consists mostly of a long list of wrong practices and views, and assertions of the Buddha's superiority to them. But this too, as the commentary points out (Sv 128 on D I 46) is brought to a climactic conclusion by the mention of final nirvana, referring forward to the Buddha's own future: "Monks, the Tathāgata's body remains (alive) with that which (would otherwise) lead it to rebirth [i.e. Craving] cut off. While that body remains (alive) gods and men will see him, but after the break-up of the body, when life will have been completely used up, they will not."

3.4. TEXTUALIZING TIME: TWO EXAMPLES FROM THE *VAṂSA* LITERATURE

3.4.a. Vaṃsa *as a genre*

One textual genre is especially important in the representation of both non-repetitive and repetitive time in the Pali imaginaire: that of *vaṃsa*, the historical chronicles. Although many of these texts have been edited and translated for some time, they have received scarcely any study by modern scholars aside from being used by historians as a source of data for their own historiography. Serious and sympathetic investigation of them in and for themselves as a textual genre is more or less non-existent. The term *vaṃsa* (Skt *vaṃśa*) was used in India for a variety of forms of historical writing from the time of the Brāhmaṇas. In origin, probably, *vaṃsa* texts were genealogical lists; but they came to be expanded into and incorporated in narratives.[34] The original meaning of *vaṃśa* was "bamboo," and there may be some significance in this: bamboo grows by sending out one shoot, and one only; unlike our concept

[34] See the chapters by Majumdar, Perera, Warder and Godakumbara in Philips (1961); and Pathak (1966), Bechert (1969, 1978), and Warder (1972, Chapters 3–5). On *vaṃśa* and *vaṃśānucarita* as (normatively) essential features of any Hindu *Purāṇa*, see Rocher (1986: 26ff.)

of a genealogical tree, therefore, a *vaṃśa* genealogy allows only one legitimate successor at a time. Thus the term not only describes a line of transmission, a lineage, but at the same time ascribes to the members of the *vaṃsa* a specific status and authority as legitimate heirs of that transmission. In the tradition of *purāṇa* writing, two of the traditional five Characteristics (*pañcalakṣaṇa*) alleged to be present in any such text are *vaṃśa* and *vaṃśānucarita;* the former refers to a genealogy of gods, patriarchs, kings and great families, the latter to the deeds of such a *vaṃsa.* (Whether and how far these five Characteristics actually do apply to the extant *purāṇa*-s is a complex issue.) The texts in question here are not only the great compendia of mythology, theology, etc., concerning various gods such as Viṣṇu and Śiva they include also, amongst others, a little-studied genre of regional, caste *purāṇa*-s, about which Rocher says:

> Even though this type of texts relates to single castes in limited areas of the subcontinent, they are again not fundamentally different from purāṇic literature generally . . . [then, quoting another writer:] The caste-purāṇas may be considered to be the extension of *Vaṃśānucarita,* in the sense that they devote themselves to the history of some *Vaṃśa,* in the broad sense. (1986: 72)

The Pali Chronicles in this perspective are part of the literary genre of the *purāṇa,* listing the genealogy and deeds of the lineage of the Buddha and his heritage. The *vaṃsa*-s narrate stories and histories of Buddhism and of kings in Southern Asia, of various relics, images and texts, and of both past and future Buddhas. This history is, to be sure, "Sacred History," *Heilsgeschichte,* but it expresses and preserves an explicit sense of mundane historical continuity, both within the countries we now call Sri Lanka, Burma, Thailand, Cambodia and Laos, and in connecting these areas with the Buddha and Buddhism in India.

In the study of western historiography, three kinds of historical representation are often distinguished: Annals, Chronicles and History proper. It is helpful to use these categories in a preliminary way to get a sense of the texts transmitted as *vaṃsa*-s:

(i) *Annals* merely list events in chronological sequence, without narrative structure;

(ii) *Chronicles* are narratives, but they simply catalog events, continuing until the chronicler's own time, when they stop, having run out of material;

(iii) *History* is distinguished from Chronicles by its being a structured narrative organized around a guiding theme or topic, and specifically, so it is said, by the presence of narrative closure.[35] Pali *vaṃsa* texts, although often called "Chronicles" in the secondary literature, contain examples of both Chronicle and History forms of representation, as here defined.

Most of the *vaṃsa* texts begin either from an episode in the life of Gotama Buddha (such as his visits to various places), or from the former life as Sumedha, when he made the aspiration to Buddhahood. They recount the history of their specific subjects, with prophecies, predictions and temporal parallels. Texts concerning relics usually end with their being enshrined in a particular place, albeit often after a number of adventures and travels, thus qualifying as History in the sense just defined.[36] Some of the *vaṃsa*-s which do, in Chronicle-style, simply stop at a certain time (either known or presumed to be shortly before they were composed), nonetheless contain accounts of particular kings, which in themselves would qualify as History.[37] The claims I have made about nirvana providing the sense of an ending in both non-repetitive and repetitive time are, I think, true of the whole range of Buddhist literature and ritual; but it is particularly fascinating to see how this appears in the *vaṃsa* texts, in which time is concentratedly textualized. The *vaṃsa* texts – every time they are recited and retold – recount a linear historical narrative; but in doing so they both express and embody the repetitive interweaving of timeless nirvanized Buddhahood with the texture of all time, past, present and future.[38]

In *Time and Narrative* (1984–90) Paul Ricoeur argues at length and persuasively that while fictional and historical narratives are

[35] See the critical discussion by White (1987: 4ff.) referring to Barnes (1963).

[36] E.g. in European editions the *Mahābodhi-, Thūpa-, Dāṭha-, Chakesadhātu-vaṃsa*-s; and also the *Dhātuvaṃsa* (a roman-script edition and translation of which is currently being edited for the Pali Text Society; I have used a transcription kindly made available to me by Kevin Trainor).

[37] The *Mahāvaṃsa* differs from the *Dīpavaṃsa*, for example, with which it is otherwise closely parallel, in that it contains a full account of king Duṭṭhagāmaṇī; the *Hatthavanagallavihāra-vaṃsa* is mostly taken up with the story of king Sirisaṅghabodhi, but ends with two chapters about the Attagalla monastery, and closes with a verse hoping that future writers will continue to add to the text the names and deeds of its benefactors.

[38] For public recitation of *vaṃsa* and other texts, see Collins (1992b: 122 and n. 11).

indeed different in many ways, both kinds have what he calls the structure of temporality as an ultimate referent. To discuss this theme in fiction he chooses Virginia Woolf's *Mrs. Dalloway*, Thomas Mann's *Magic Mountain*, and Proust's *Remembrance of Things Past*. Borrowing a distinction from A. A. Mendilow, he states that

> these three works illustrate the distinction . . . between "tales of time" and "tales about time." All fictional narratives are "tales of time" inasmuch as the structural transformations that affect the situations and characters take time. However only a few are "tales about time" inasmuch as in them it is the very experience of time that is at stake in these structural transformations. (1985: 101)

(One can readily think of others: a recent example of the genre is Graham Swift's novel *Waterland*; in drama there is Samuel Beckett's play *Waiting for Godot*.) Clark (1990: 171) rightly points out that in Ricoeur's argument "the odds appear somewhat stacked by the selection of tales so explicitly 'about time' rather than showing the temporality of narrative to be a factor in a less conspicuous manner." For my purposes here, however, Ricoeur's selection of texts and his remarks can be used to bring out an important but unremarked aspect of the *Buddhavaṃsa* and *Mahāvaṃsa*: they too are "tales about time." To extend Ricoeur's vocabulary, in such cases time is not merely an *ultimate* referent, as it is of necessity in all narratives, but also a *proximate* one. In these Buddhist texts the passage of both non-repetitive and repetitive time is not merely, so to speak, a canvas on which the (hi)stories are painted, a ground against which events occur as figure, or the stage on which the dramas unfold, but rather is itself an important part of what is portrayed, a figure brought forward for attention and reflection, a character which should be acknowledged in a list of *dramatis personae*.

In the next two sections I look in depth at some parts of the *Buddhavaṃsa*, one of the latest additions to the Pali Canon, dating perhaps from the second century BC, and of the *Mahāvaṃsa*, one of the earliest post-canonical *vaṃsa*-s, usually dated in the early sixth century AD[39] The *Buddhavaṃsa* is both a "Chronicle of

[39] I am unconvinced by the evidence for this date, but it cannot be wrong by more than a century either way.

Buddhas" and a "Lineage of Buddhas": it narrates a sequence of enlightened Ones preceding our Buddha Gotama, starting from the story of his original vow to become a Buddha in his life as the ascetic Sumedha, and the prophecies of Sumedha's future Buddhahood made by the Buddha of that time, Dīpaṅkara, and repeated by all the intervening Buddhas. The medieval commentary to the *Mahāvaṃsa*, "the Great Chronicle," suggests that it has that name both because it describes a *vaṃsa* of great people, and because of its own greatness as a text.[40] The great people whose lineage(s) it describes are the monks who preserved the Buddha's Teaching in India and Sri Lanka, and kings in the two places. The history it recounts is both that of Buddhism from the time of Gotama to that of the Sri Lankan king Mahāsena (fourth century AD), and also of the privileged position of the Mahāvihāra monastic fraternity in the city of Anurādhapura as legitimate heirs and guardians of the Buddha's message.

3.4.b. Voice and temporal perspective in the Buddhavaṃsa*: repetitive and non-repetitive time interwoven*

(i) The structure and dynamics of the text as a whole

Table 3.1 gives an outline of the Buddhavaṃsa as a whole. Translations of the passages to be discussed in this section are given in Appendix 1. The text seems only gradually to have attained its present form. Vv.1–18 of Chapter XXVII, which list twenty-seven Buddhas before Gotama, are spoken in the third person singular; given that the commentary at the end of the previous chapter states that these eighteen verses, "(were) established by the Recensionists (and) are to be understood as Envoi verses" (*saṅgīti-kārakehi thapitā nigamanagathā veditabbā*, Bv-a 259), it has been thought that the *Buddhavaṃsa* originally ended here. Vv.19–20 of Chapter XXVII are spoken in the first person singular by Gotama, who says "I am the Buddha of the present time and Metteyya will be (Buddha)" (*aham etarahi sambuddho Metteyyo cāpi hessati*). The commentary does not mention these verses, nor the whole of the last chapter XXVIII concerning the distribution of

40 *Ayaṃ gantho nāmavasena mahantānaṃ vaṃsaparidīpakattā, sayam eva mahantattā pi Mahāvaṃso nāma* (Mhv-ṭ 12).

Table 3.1 *The* Buddhavaṃsa *as a whole*

1. Chapter on the Jewelled Walkway	
2. Vaṃsa of Buddha Dīpaṅkara (includes story of Sumedha)	
3. Vaṃsa of Buddha Kondañña	
4. Vaṃsa of Buddha Maṅgala	
5. Vaṃsa of Buddha Sumana	
6. Vaṃsa of Buddha Revata	
7. Vaṃsa of Buddha Sobhita	Each of Chapters 2 (vv.188–219) through 25 has:
8. Vaṃsa of Buddha Anomadassi	
9. Vaṃsa of Buddha Paduma	
10. Vaṃsa of Buddha Nārada	(i) a third-person account of its Buddha;
11. Vaṃsa of Buddha Padumuttara	
12. Vaṃsa of Buddha Sumedha	
13. Vaṃsa of Buddha Sujāta	(ii) a first-person account of Gotama's identity at that time (with prediction of Gotama's future Buddhahood);
14. Vaṃsa of Buddha Piyadassi	
15. Vaṃsa of Buddha Atthadassi	
16. Vaṃsa of Buddha Dhammadassi	
17. Vaṃsa of Buddha Siddhattha	
18. Vaṃsa of Buddha Tissa	(iii) a third person account, in list form, of its Buddha, his city, the names of his family, disciples, etc.
19. Vaṃsa of Buddha Phussa	
20. Vaṃsa of Buddha Vipassi	
21. Vaṃsa of Buddha Sikhī	
22. Vaṃsa of Buddha Vessabhū	
23. Vaṃsa of Buddha Kakusandha	
24. Vaṃsa of Buddha Koṇāgamana	
25. Vaṃsa of Buddha Kassapa	
26. Vaṃsa of Buddha Gotama (his formulaic autobiography)	
27. Chapter on miscellaneous things (previous Buddhas listed, Metteyya mentioned in v. 19)	
28. Chapter on the distribution of (Gotama's) Relics	

Gotama's relics, but concludes instead with a systematic account of the similarities and differences between Buddhas, and also includes verses closely resembling some given at the end of the *Mahāparinibbāna Sutta* (D II 167–8). The commentary on the latter text (Sv 615) says that these were added by the monks of Sri Lanka. The last verse states that "the ancients (*porāṇikā*) say that the dispersal of the relics . . . was (done) out of compassion for living beings" (Bv XXVIII 13); "the ancients" are commonly referred to in commentarial texts, and are usually taken to have been earlier teachers in Sri Lanka (and perhaps India). Clearly there have been changes and additions to the text. For my purposes, it seems a reasonable assumption that whatever has happened, some narrative redactorial voice ended the text; but nothing essential in my reading depends on assumptions about this.

The text as we have it begins and ends with an anonymous voice, which may here simply be called that of the Redactor.[41] The first two chapters include verses in direct speech, put in the mouths of various characters, human and divine. Vv. 80–81 of Chapter I, in the first person singular, are spoken by the Buddha, as are Chapters II-XXVII, in both third and first persons singular: according to I 79 his account is derived from his recollection of former lives. In the last chapter, XXVIII, the voice of the anonymous Redactor returns.

The text as a whole tells a story clearly situated in non-repetitive time. The account of Sumedha and Dīpaṅkara in Chapter II is situated "a hundred thousand eons and four incalculable eons ago'[42] (Bv II 1); the first nine Buddhas only predict that Gotama will become Buddha "innumerable eons from now," but from Padumuttara, the tenth, specific decreasing lengths of time are given (Bv XI 12, "a hundred thousand eons from now . . ."; Bv XII 13, "after thirty thousand eons . . .", etc.). Such lengths of time are, of course, unacceptable for modern historiography, but I am not concerned with that issue: however incredible such time-specifications may be for modern historians, they nonetheless establish for the text a single and internally coherent enumeration of a non-repetitive temporal sequence. Set in this enumerated sequence of non-repetitive time are accounts of the twenty-four Buddhas preceding Gotama, in Chapters II–XXV. Apart from Chapter II, the long account of Sumedha and Dīpaṅkara, the chapters are all of roughly the same length, or rather brevity, being between twenty-four and thirty-eight verses long.[43] Each chapter deals with a different Buddha and is entitled the *vaṃsa* of that Buddha; but both the form and content of each chapter is exactly parallel, with many

[41] See n. 1 to Appendix 1.

[42] This word should not be taken to mean that the number is infinite: just that it is so large as to be in practice uncountable; as Charles Hallisey (personal communication 1993) puts it, it is like children in English referring to "gazillions."

[43] Chapter XXV is an apparent exception to this, but this is because certain verses are omitted in other chapters but written out in full here; see next note.

passages repeated word-for-word. Each chapter has three sections (see the translation of Chapters III and XX given in Appendix 1):

(i) approximately ten verses giving a third-person account of the Buddha whose *vaṃsa* is being described;

(ii) a first-person account of the person at that time who would eventually be reborn as Gotama. This section includes a standard passage, always in almost identical wording, in which there is a prediction by the contemporary Buddha of the future Buddhahood of Gotama, an outline sketch of his biography, the names of his family and chief monks, etc. (see Chapter III 9–24); it concludes with "when I had heard his words," and is followed by

(iii) a third person account (more or less in the form of a list) of the city of the Buddha at that time, the names of his family, chief monks, nuns, male and female lay followers, the species of tree under which he gained enlightenment, the names of his chief male and female attendants, his height and life span.

All these chapters end with similar verses referring to the particular Buddha's final nirvana, and then with a mention of the shrine (*cetiya* or *stūpa*) built as a memorial to that Buddha.

Chapter XXVI, spoken in the first person by Gotama about himself, is of necessity different; the first and second sections are coalesced, while the third is exactly parallel. This autobiographical account ends with a reference to his future nirvana; in the version of the text now extant the reference to his relics (and by implication their being installed in *stūpa*-s) is separated out to form the concluding Chapter XXVIII. In Chapter XXVII, in the text as we now have it, Gotama refers forward to the next Buddha, Metteyya.

Ignoring for the moment the Buddhas, and chapters, between Dīpaṅkara and Gotama, some of the relevant temporal relationships can be set out as in Table 3.2.

The formulaic biography of Gotama given in the narrated future by Dīpaṅkara in II 60–9 and by each of the Buddhas between Kondañña in III 11–16 and Kassapa in XXV 16–25 is almost exactly identical in each case. Moreover, the biographies of the twenty-four Buddhas given by Gotama in the narrated past are very similar, both to the biography of Gotama they each recount in a narrated future, and to each other. Finally, the autobiography given by Gotama in the narrated present of XXV (especially vv. 13–20) has a closely similar form. Thus, taking a sequence of

Table 3.2

	----- time ----->				
	Time of Buddhas and Bodhisattas before Dīpaṅkara	Time of Sumedha and Dīpaṅkara	Time of Gotama Buddha	Time of Redactor (and any recitation); time of narration	Time of Metteyya
Buddha as narrator	pre-narrative past	narrated past	narrated present		narrated future
For Sumedha and Dīpaṅkara	past referred to as exemplar	narrated present	narrated future		
For gods, etc. in II 81–107, 178–186[a]	past referred to as exemplar	narrated present	narrated future		
Redactor and Reciter(s) of extant Bv	<---------	---narrated---	– pasts ----->	implied present of narration	narrated future

Note:
[a] this is explained in the next section (ii), on Sumedha and Gotama across time

Table 3.3

	----- time ----->				
narrator	narrated –>				
	Buddha 1	Buddha 2	Buddha 3	Buddha 4	Buddha 5
Buddha 2	past	present	future	future	future
Buddha 3	past	past	present	future	future
Buddha 4	past	past	past	present	future

any five Buddhas, one can set out the temporal relationships between possible narratives as in Table 3.3.

This table could be extended in either direction, such that what appears here for Buddha 3 would be true of all of them: his formulaic (auto)biography, regardless of whether it is set in the narrated past, present, or future, will be identical.

It might seem from what has been said so far that repetitive time is dominant in the Buddhavaṃsa, but this is not the case. In the next section I try to show this by close attention to the story of Sumedha, as told by Gotama. But non-repetitive time is emphasized throughout in a variety of ways, notably by a striking simile which appears first in the story of Sumedha and is repeated in every subsequent chapter concerning a past Buddha.[44] When each Buddha has predicted the future Buddhahood of the contemporary predecessor of Gotama, men and gods exclaim:

72. "If we fail (to profit from) the Teaching of this Lord of the World [i.e. the contemporary Buddha: in the first case Dīpaṅkara], then at some time in the future may we come face to face with this one [i.e. the contemporary predecessor of Gotama, in the first case Sumedha].

73. Just as when people who (are trying to) cross a river (but) fail

[44] They are not printed in Chapters IV through XXIV of the PTS edition, although Jayawickrama's (1974) textual apparatus shows that they were written out in full in at least one (Thai) manuscript. They were, nonetheless, clearly meant to be recited in full in each chapter: the commentary to the relevant parts of Chapters IV–VI (Bv-a 150, 158, 164) instructs the reciter to "expand in eight verses," as in Chapter III. This is not repeated, but the principle has by now been clearly established.

to reach the opposite bank (at that place, may) reach it further down and so cross the great stream,
74. In just the same way if we all let slip (the opportunity offered by) this Conqueror, then at some time in the future may we come face to face with this one."

While this river image fits in with the ubiquitous Buddhist pattern of the river or ocean of rebirth, contrasted with the further shore of nirvana (Collins 1982: 247–61), in this context it is not merely a general "river of time" which is contrasted with timeless eternity, but one of non-repetitive time, like Heraclitus' river, here positioning Buddhas and the opportunities for salvation they provide in a linear, irreversible sequence. It is in this non-repetitive river of time that the sequence of lives from Sumedha to Gotama – which we might call an elongated "biography" – takes place. Just as any single lifetime, as lived and as narrated in (auto)biography traverses annual seasons, days/months of the year, etc., which recur, and proceeds on an individual course through a fixed, pre-given set of stages of life (such as child–parent–grandparent), so the sequence of lives Sumedha → Gotama traverses chapters which have the same form and in which similar content recurs, and proceeds through similarly progressive stages in the sequence from aspiration to fulfilment: that is, the ten Perfections, the meeting with each Buddha, his prediction of future Buddhahood, etc. So Buddhas, as events in time, repeat the same pattern; but the river of time flows on.

(ii) Sumedha and Gotama across time

In these ways then, both non-repetitive and repetitive time are textualized and foregrounded in the *Buddhavaṃsa* as a whole. Now I turn to Chapter II 1–187 in greater detail, to show both how the temporal perspective of the narrative moves back and forth along non-repetitive time, across the multi-lifetime sequence from aspiration to fulfilment; and also how the "I" of the Buddha, speaking in the narrated present, overlaps and coalesces with the "I" of Sumedha, speaking, thinking and acting in the narrated past. These, I contend, are not merely techniques within a given temporal horizon, but means by which temporality itself is made a proximate referent of the text. The coalescing of Sumedha and Gotama is not intended to cancel out time and difference, but is a device to create what I have called the elongated (auto)biography of Sumedha → Gotama, and to show – textually, one might say, to embody – the fact of its passing through a matrix of repetition within non-repetitive, irreversible time. What follows is an analysis of this section of the text in terms of voice and temporal perspective, with added remarks on particular verses:

1–5 are spoken by Gotama in the narrated present; Sumedha is introduced by Gotama in the narrated past, in the first person; this use of the first person to describe Sumedha's actions, words and thoughts continues throughout the text (see nn. 7, 9 and 39 in Appendix 1).

6–26 are reflections of Sumedha before becoming an ascetic, in the narrated past, referring to his immediate intentions and longer-term aspirations for the future, which are to be fulfilled in the narrated present of the text as a whole.

27–58 narrate Sumedha's actions, thoughts and words, starting with his becoming an ascetic and then with regard to the Buddha Dīpaṅkara; also included are words of others in direct speech. Sumedha makes the aspiration to become a future Buddha rather than an enlightened Arahant in the then-present.

59–69 give Dīpaṅkara's prediction of Sumedha's future Buddhahood as Gotama [i.e. a voice in the narrated past refers to the text's narrated present as its own narrated future].

70–4 report actions and words of "gods and men." They introduce the image of the "river of time": by means of this image their voice, in the text's narrated past, both connects the then-present to their narrated future, the text's narrated present, and keeps them separate.

75–80 tell of the departure of Dīpaṅkara and his monks, and then give Sumedha's thoughts.

81–107 are spoken by gods and men. They delineate a series of portents which happened in the past – that is to say the pre-narrative past of the text as a whole (the commentary explains that they had seen previous Buddhas and Bodhisattas, Bv-a 99) – which they see happening "today" (*ajja*, i.e. their present, the text's narrated past), and on the basis of which they predict future Buddhahood for Sumedha (as Gotama, in the text's narrated present).

108–14 recount thoughts of Sumedha, referring to his future, in the narrated present of Gotama. The verb used in 109–14 in connection with Sumedha-Gotama's Buddhahood is grammatically the present tense: the commentary (Bv-a 103) states that is used because what is asserted is "certain, inevitable": thus I translate "I am (to be) a Buddha!" Note that the examples used to show both that the word of Buddhas [in this case, the Buddha Dīpaṅkara] is "always certain" (*dhuvasassataṃ*, which could also be rendered "assured and eternal"), and that "assuredly (*dhuvaṃ*) I am (to be) a Buddha" are constancies of nature such as gravity and the sequence of night and day: v. 111 is remarkable, and bears repeating:

> As death is always certain for all beings, so too what is said by (the) excellent Buddhas is always certain – assuredly I am (to be) a Buddha!

So the utter finality of death for each individual in non-repetitive time becomes here one of the eternally repeated phenomena which exemplify the certainty and eternality of what is said by Buddhas. This single verse may perhaps stand as an emblem of the way non-repetitive and repetitive time are interwoven, and balance each other, in this text.

115–65 give the thoughts of Sumedha, in Gotama's first person, as he/they run(s) through the list of Perfections in formulaic manner, adding a simile to each self-exhortation. In v.115 Sumedha speaks in the first-person present tense (for future) "I (will) contemplate" (*vicināmi*), while in subsequent verses the future form *vicinissāmi* is used. In all cases Gotama then gives the reflection in the past tense ("examining, I saw then," *vicinanto tadā dakkhiṃ*, present participle and aorist). The practice and fulfilling of these Perfections, of course, is precisely what fills the time between Sumedha and Gotama.

166–71 give portents which occurred during Sumedha's contemplation of the Perfections.

172–74 recount Dīpaṅkara saying that the future Buddha Sumedha/Gotama is reflecting on "the Dhamma that was followed by former Conquerors"; the commentary (Bv-a 116) reminds us that the Perfections were fulfilled by them in what I am calling the text's pre-narrative past, "at the time they were future Buddhas" (*bodhisattakāle*), as Sumedha is now resolving to do (in his future).

175–86 recount how gods and men encouraged Sumedha to attain Buddhahood and teach the Dhamma, in the same way as (*yathā . . . tathā*) previous Buddhas.

187 has Gotama conclude the narrated past concerning Sumedha, in what is almost certainly the third person aorist (see n. 39 to the translation).

The *Buddhavaṃsa*, then, interweaves non-repetitive and repetitive time constantly, throughout the text. One of the most obvious events of non-repetitive time is the closure brought to each Buddha's story by his nirvanizing. Every chapter ends with this, often with the remark "Are not all conditioned things worthless?" (*nanu rittā sabba-saṅkhārā*),[45] and with some kind of reflection on impermanence. Thus at Koṇḍañña's nirvanizing in III 37, the text reminds us that "that Conqueror's supernatural attainment was unequaled, and his (attainment of) meditation was fostered by wisdom: it has all disappeared"; similar sentiments are expressed at the end of almost every Buddha's life. All of them, like Atthadassi at XV 25 "came to (an end, because of) impermanence" (*aniccataṃ patto*), "like a fire at the waning of its fuel."[46] The river of time flows endlessly on,[47] never turning back, but providing the temporal location for the individual disappearances of Buddhas and other enlightened beings into timelessness.

3.4.c. Calendar time, the succession of generations, documents and traces in the Mahāvaṃsa*:* [48] *non-repetitive time dominating repetitive time*

(i) The structure and dynamics of the text as a whole

In passing from the *Buddhavaṃsa* to the *Mahāvaṃsa*, one would normally be said, not without justification, to be passing from the realm of legend to that of history. Be that as it may, I wish here to read the latter text also as a tale about time. Here the authorial voice is plain and consistent: in the opening stanzas, the author (in later texts identified as the monk Mahānāma) or reciter speaks to his audience in the first person, instructing them to listen to what

[45] *Rittā* (Skt *rikta*) is most easily translated by "empty," but that word is standardly used for *suñña*, in what is usually a metaphysical sense (= "empty of self"). Perhaps "vacuous" or "hollow" would serve here.

[46] Cf. 2.2.a. pp. 203–4 for the practice of meditation on the inevitable death of Buddhas.

[47] Cp. Collins (1982: 260–1) on the fact that river imagery is not used for what has seemed in the West since Edwin Arnold ("the dewdrop slips into the shining sea") an obvious application of it: the river of (individual) time flowing into the ocean of nirvana.

[48] The phrases used here and in the subheadings of this section are intended to recall the subheadings in a chapter of Ricoeur (1988: 104–26), called "Between Lived Time and Universal Time: Historical Time."

he says; at the end of each chapter a penultimate verse in ornate meter sums up its moral, while the last verse gives the chapter title, setting it "in the *Mahāvaṃsa,* composed to bring serene confidence and (religious) animation[49] to good people." There are a number of uses of indexical markers for place, "here," referring to the island of Sri Lanka as a whole, and to the city of Anurādhapura and/or the Mahāvihāra monastery, and in at least one place there is a reference to the authorial present, "even today" (*ajjāpi*).[50] This temporal distance (and connection) between the present authorial voice and the past it narrates remains strong throughout, constructed and maintained by elaborate and constant references to precise dates and times after the Buddha's nirvana. This temporal referencing is, in part, what makes me call the text a "tale about time," but there is more to it than that.

The overall structure of the text is given in Table 3.4 below. Translations of the passages to be discussed in this section are given in Appendix 2. The numbers of verses taken to cover varying numbers of years show clearly that the text is not a "chronicle," in the sense of a diary-like record of events in passing time, but is organized and focused on a series of interrelated topics. The narrated times of what I have called the first and second motifs within the first theme overlap; most of Chapters V and XI 7 to XX 28 take place within the space of the forty years of king Devānaṃpiyatissa's reign. The *Mahāvaṃsa* is often presented (wrongly, in my opinion) as a "court chronicle" expressing a Buddhist ideology of church–state relations. This is not the place to argue against that view in general, but it is relevant to call attention to the continuous parade of kings, good, bad and indifferent, brought before the eye (or rather, ear): all of them die, like Uttiya in the third century BC, showing that "this impermanence destroys everyone in the world" (*aniccatā esā sabba-lokavināsinī* XX 57). (Compare the laments in the *Buddhavaṃsa* at the final nirvana of a Buddha, mentioned in the last section.) This elegiac tone pervades the *Mahāvaṃsa;* in my view, not only should such a tone forestall the unidimensional interpretation of the work as a triumphalist "legitimation of Buddhist kingship," but also (and more importantly here) it serves

[49] For the words *pasāda* and *saṃvega* see Appendix 2 n. 2.
[50] "Here" at I 30, 57, 67, X 77, XXIII 26, XXIII 19, 28, 95, XXXIV 39, XXXVI 82, 113; "today" at XXV 74.

Table 3.4 *The* Mahāvaṃsa*: structure and content*

Prelude: The Buddha visits Sri Lanka (I, 84 verses cover 8 years)
I – The Tathāgata's Visits (to Sri Lanka)

First theme: Buddhism comes to Sri Lanka (II–XX, 1398 verses cover 382 years, of which 235 are parallel in first and second motifs)

First motif: Buddhism in India (II–V, 423 verses cover 235 years)
II – Mahāsammata's *Vaṃsa*
III – The First Council
IV – The Second Council
V – The Third Council

Second motif: Sri Lanka before Buddhism (VI–XI, 326 verses cover 310 years)
VI – Vijaya's Arrival
VII – The Coronation of Vijaya
VIII – The Coronation of Paṇḍuvāsudeva
IX – The Coronation of Abhaya
X – The Coronation of Paṇḍukābhaya (Anurādhapura)
XI – The Coronation of Devānaṃpiyatissa

First and second motifs combined: from Aśoka's missions to (one year after) the deaths of Mahinda and Saṃghamittā (XII–XX, 649 verses cover 69 years)
XII – Buddhism Goes to Different Countries
XIII – Mahinda Arrives
XIV – (His) Entry into the City (of Anurādhapura)
XV – The Acceptance of the Mahāvihāra
XVI – The Acceptance of the Cetiyapabbata-vihāra
XVII – The (Buddha's) Relics Arrive
XVIII – Receiving the Great Bodhi-tree
XIX – The Coming of the Bodhi-tree
XX – The Monk (Mahinda) Attains Nirvana

Interlude: The Five Kings (XXI, 34 verses cover 96 years)

Second Theme: The Dutthagāmaṇī Epic (XXII–XXXII, 863 verses cover 50 years)
XXII – The Birth of Prince Gāmaṇī
XXIII – Acquiring Warriors
XXIV – War between the Two Brothers
XXV – Dutthagāmaṇī's Victory
XXVI – The Consecration of the Maricavatti-vihāra
XXVII – The Consecration of the Lohapasāda
XXVIII – Acquiring the Resources to build the Great Stūpa
XXIX – Beginning the Great Stūpa
XXX – Making the Relic Chamber
XXXI – Enshrining the Relics
XXXII – (Duṭṭhagāmaṇī's) Entry into the Tusita-heaven

Table 3.4 *(cont.)*

Coda: A Chronicle of Kings; Mahāsena (XXXIII–XXXVII, 507 verses cover 429 years)
XXXIII – Ten Kings
XXXIV – Eleven Kings
XXXV – Twelve Kings
XXXVI – Thirteen Kings
XXXVII – King Mahāsena

to reinforce one's sense of the inexorable march of non-repetitive time. I turn next from these general considerations to a detailed analysis of the first two chapters, translated in Appendix 2.

(ii) Calendar time

The opening section (Vv. 1–5) of the first chapter introduces the work; vv. 6–11 recount the list of Buddhas from Dīpaṅkara to Gotama. In translation this may seem to be simply a versified list; in the Pali, rhyme and assonance lend it the quality of a chant, and no doubt a gifted reciter would make this evident.[51] After this hymnodic reminder of the enormous lengths of time preceding Gotama's enlightenment, the narrative switches straight to – one might say, cinematically, focuses down on – the most iconographically famous scene in Buddhist culture, the Buddha sitting at the foot of the Bodhi-tree. The event is dated and set in Uruvelā; we are told he spent seven weeks there, then went for the Rains Retreat to Benares before returning to Uruvelā for the winter. Vv. 17–20 state the place and precise time (length of time after his Buddhahood, month, date and time of day) of the immediately subsequent event, his setting out on a first visit to Sri Lanka. In v. 24 he visits, for the first but not the last time in the chapter, the site of a future *stūpa;* vv. 37–42, in a kind of "flash-forward" technique, give a brief later history of it. His second visit occupies vv. 44–70; the place and precise time of his departure is again specified:

[51] Jonathan Walters (personal communication 1993) tells me that a similar list is found in a modern book of Pirit (Pali *paritta)* chants (that is, verses recited for "Protection" from various ills). If this or some similar list of Buddhas was used for this purpose at the time of the *Mahāvaṃsa,* then this section would also serve in this text as an opening aspiration for success and the prevention of ills, such as regularly occurs in ritual (and other) performances.

"in the Jetavana (park) for the fifth Rainy Season after his Enlightenment... on the morning of the Uposatha day in the dark half of Citta month" (44, 46–7). At 48–57 there are two stories of the past; to continue the cinematic metaphor one might call them flashbacks, or, following Richman's usage, branch-stories.[52] The description of the Buddha's third visit (time and place of departure specified as before, 71–3) contains repeated "flashes-forward" to future shrines, as he goes to the sites on which they will stand, at vv. 75, 77, 78–9, 80, 81 (twice) and 82. The first three sites are in the south and east of the island, the fourth is close to, and the last three are in Anurādhapura. To an audience familiar with contemporary geography, this would have been like an imaginary guided tour of significant places on the island – again, cinematically, giving a bird's-eye view of them – ending at the place of the future city the *Mahāvaṃsa* celebrates as the home of the Mahāvihāra.

Whereas the section of the *Buddhavaṃsa* discussed above depicted a sequence of non-repetitive time, and then used changes in narrative voice and temporal reference to move back and forth along it between narrated past and narrated present, this first chapter of the *Mahāvaṃsa* uses calendrical marking to plot out non-repetitive time precisely, and then moves between the narrated past and narrator's present by sending the Buddha to places which in the future (the narrator's present) would be famous and religiously significant. Scholars have read the *Mahāvaṃsa* almost exclusively in search of data to write their own histories; for this purpose the account of the first months after the enlightenment given in vv. 12–16 is dismissible as a very condensed version of what is found earlier and at greater length in the *Vinaya*, while the rest of the chapter is dismissible as legend, interesting only, if at all, for its bearing witness to what is alleged to be premodern nationalist sentiment in Sri Lanka. But if one tries to discern the text's own concerns, then it becomes apparent that – with the exception of the introductory vv. 1–5, and the list of Buddhas at 6–11 (to which I will return) – the narrative of the whole chapter is organized by

[52] See Richman (1988). This narrative technique – breaking off from the main story to recount the past of some character(s) – is a standard feature in Buddhist literature, both *vaṃsa* histories and stories: see for example Dhp-a I 83–113, translated by Burlinghame (1921, vol. 1: 193–217); and a corresponding Sinhala version in Obeyesekere (1989: 148–72).

means of temporal markers, mostly those of calendar time, which create for the audience historical depth and thereby both connection to and separation from the time of the Buddha. Later in the work, in Chapter VII, the arrival in Sri Lanka of Vijaya, the first Sinhala king, is made contemporary with the Buddha's nirvana: the ideological significance of this has often been noted; but more important, from the present perspective, is the fact that this simultaneity, along with the calendrical marking of the Buddha's three visits and the ubiquitous dating of events from the time of his final nirvana, constitute within the text a common temporal matrix within which the history of the Buddha and Buddhism in India can be narratively situated alongside the local history of the island. These are not Eliadean origin myths set in a time-outside-time, *in illo tempore* .

(iii) The succession of generations

The second chapter of the *Mahāvaṃsa* is one of the shortest but in some ways the most extraordinary of the work as a whole. I would guess that for almost all modern readers, on first reading, it skims past the eye like a kind of obligatory but hurried list, as if the author felt it necessary to "begin at the beginning," but raced through to the time of the Buddha as quickly as possible. But here perhaps more than anywhere else in the work, a second look – one which allows the text's own concerns to appear – reveals an unusual but effective narrative technique. It starts by connecting the Buddha to the first king of the eon, a trope well known in other places in Southern Asian Buddhism (Collins and Huxley 1996). Vv. 2–6 list names of his descendants; again, in translation the rhyme and assonance of the Pali are lost: vv. 2, 4b and 5a, for example, all end with *duve*, "two" (doubled in 5a). From 5b/6a the kings and their "sons and grandsons" begin to be numbered; indeed vv. 7–11 consist solely of numbers, with the exception of connectives and the three names given in 10 and 11. Vv. 10–22, ending with *no jino*, "our Conqueror," consist exclusively, apart from connectives, of names, numbers, and words for king, sons and grandsons. These, we are told, reigned "one after the other, in sequence." Here indeed is a densely packed parade, expounding to the audience a series of kings in non-repetitive time. Some are worthy of mention by name, many hundreds of thousand of others are, literally, nothing but numbers; only a few of them would have been well known, like Vessantara and his son Jāli, famous from the *Vessantara-jātaka* (4.3.a, 5.2.c, and Chapter 7). Also likely to be familiar to an audience conversant with Buddhist stories is Makhādeva, given (in 10) after the series of verses containing only numbers. He (a former life of Gotama) told his barber to inform him when gray hairs appeared on his head; the latter did so, calling them "death's messengers;"[53] Makhādeva immediately renounced kingship and became an ascetic.

Vv. 25–32 contain a more conventionally discursive narrative, but they too might seem almost a game with numbers, had we not by now been alerted to the serious functions of enumeration. They treat the relationship between Siddhattha (Gotama) and king Bimbisāra, who were friends, like their fathers before them; the course of their interrelated lives is expressed by intertwining the ages they had reached at certain points in each other's career. Bimbisāra died before the Buddha, murdered by his own son, "the great traitor Ajātasattu" (1931). The Buddha, in his turn, died before Ajātasattu; we are told that this was in the eighth year of the latter's reign, and that he continued on the throne for twenty-four more years. The whole extraordinary series of enumerated persons and events in non-repetitive time is brought to a climax with verse 33, where a play on words contrasts the Buddha's power with his lack of power to avoid death (cp. the meditation on death, Vism 234 = VIII 23, cited in 2.2.a).

Skillful recitation could draw from the Pali verses of Chapter II something like a chant, cataloguing names and numbers of kings, all of whom progressed relentlessly toward death; even the Buddha, who was in a religious sense more powerful than any king, succumbed to "the power of impermanence." The legitimation of royal power some would see in the first line's assertion that the Buddha was "born in the lineage" (*vaṃsa-ja*) of the first king Mahāsammata, and in the listing of generations of kingly families, has to be set against the end, where the biographies of two kings and the Buddha are intertwined. The first, Bimbisāra, was indeed a good Buddhist; the second, his son Ajātasattu, was a parricide, guilty of one of the most heinous crimes in Buddhism (or anywhere else). This chapter is entitled "the *vaṃsa* of Mahāsammata,"

[53] *Deva-duta*, the first term glossed always as *maccudeva*, the god of Death (e.g. M II 75 with Ps III 310, Ja I 138–9; cf. DPPN s.v. Makhādeva).

recalling the *Buddhavaṃsa*, all but three of whose twenty-eight chapters have *vaṃsa* in their title; but unlike that text this chapter of the *Mahāvaṃsa* does not emphasize repetitive time to the same extent as non-repetitive; the succession of generations, the *vaṃsa*, is a lineage emphatically in non-repetitive time. This is the focus of most of the *Mahāvaṃsa*: the placing of two time-drenched chapters at the start of the work shows, I think, that time itself is one of the themes of the work, and the second chapter especially establishes for it what I have called the elegiac tone.

It would have been possible, in the second chapter, for the author to have mentioned at least the three Buddhas before Gotama – Kakusandha, Koṇāgamana and Kassapa – since they lived in this eon, after king Mahāsammata. Had the text been concerned with comprehensive, universal history, they might have been included: after all, the Buddha Gotama is in their *vaṃsa* as well as in that of Mahāsammata. But the aspect of time textualized so expertly here is not that which mentioning previous Buddhas most often constitutes. Even the list of Buddhas given in the first chapter, although it might connote something of the repetitive aspect of time the *Buddhavaṃsa* is so concerned with, in this context seems mainly to conjure up a sense of profound temporal depth before a more limited and precisely dated temporal matrix is provided for the Buddha's visits to Sri Lanka. But there are parts of the *Mahāvaṃsa* which introduce previous Buddhas into its account of events dated by the number of years after the Buddha's nirvana, and/or regnal years. At Chapter v 87ff., a serpent-king who has lived for the whole of the present eon, and so has seen its four Buddhas, is asked by Aśoka to make a likeness of a "Wheel-turning King of the Good Dhamma" (*saddhamma-cakkavatti*). He does so, giving it the thirty-two major and eighty minor marks of a Buddha. Geiger's translation (1912: 33) speaks here of "a beauteous figure of the (*sic*) Buddha," as if it were a portrait of Gotama; but nothing in the text (or commentary, Mhv-ṭ 208–9) supports the use of the definite article. It would seem more likely that the idea is of a generic likeness of *a* Buddha, or all Buddhas, synthesized from the four whom the serpent-king has seen.

In a longer passage, Chapter xv 34–5 and 57–165, the monk Mahinda first locates the (future) site of the Bodhi-tree of "our Tathāgata" in the same place as that of the three previous Buddhas; then, in one of the rare long speeches the *Mahāvaṃsa* puts into the mouth of a character, he gives in succession four structurally similar accounts of visits by each of the four Buddhas of the eon to the same place in Sri Lanka, the site of the (future) Great Stūpa at Anurādhapura. This passage is comparable to the visits by Gotama to future *stūpa* and *cetiya* sites in Chapter I, and similar to *Buddhavaṃsa* II 176–187, where "gods and men" encourage Sumedha to (future) Buddhahood, drawing on the examples of previous Buddhas. Here Mahinda predicts to king Devānampiyatissa the future prowess of Anurādhapura, drawing on stories of previous Buddhas. So the *Mahāvaṃsa* does know of repetitive time, but subordinates it to the non-repetitive time of this eon, and more specifically to the non-repetitive time enumerated from the death of Gotama Buddha.

(iv) Documents and traces

In some places in the *Mahāvaṃsa*, as in the *Buddhavaṃsa*, the device of past voices predicting the future (either the narrated past or the narrator's present) is used to move back and forth along the linear sequence of time. This can be seen in the case of the monks at the Second Council foreseeing the Third Council (Chapter IV), and repeatedly in the Buddha's foreseeing the future of his Teaching in Sri Lanka and the installation of his relics at Anurādhapura. Prophecies are usually made in thought or speech, but in one case writing is added as a medium of connection between past and present. In Chapter XV 68ff., Mahinda has just told king Devānaṃpiyatissa (third century BC) the stories of former Buddhas, and predicted the building of a *stūpa* with a relic-chamber. The king announces that he will build it, but Mahinda tells him not to, and foretells that his descendant Duṭṭhagāmaṇī (second century BC) will do so. The king then has the prediction inscribed in stone. Later, in Chapter XXVII, the prediction is recovered, first verbally: Duṭṭhagāmaṇī "called to mind the well-known oral tradition" (*vicintesi vissutaṃ sussutaṃ sutaṃ*) of Mahinda's prediction. He then searches the palace, and finds a gold plate kept in a chest with the prediction written on it.[54] He has it read aloud: "In the future, after one hundred and thirty-six years, king Duṭṭhagāmaṇī son of Kākavaṇṇa will cause this and that to be

[54] The discrepancy between its having been written on stone and found on gold-plate is probably only apparent; significant writings seem to have been made on different materials simultaneously, and the story thus has verisimilitude, if not – for us – historical accuracy.

built."[55] Here, as elsewhere, a written document may be seen as an icon of persistence through time, in Peirce's sense of the word: an icon is a sign which "exhibits or exemplifies its object," and which is in some way "similar to its object."[56] The motif of the (intended) longevity of written materials, whether inscribed on palm-leaf or some other material, is as common in South Asia as in the classical west: *scripta manent*, "what is written endures" (Collins 92b).

Rather than go further into the obscurities of Peircean distinctions and definitions, I will explore the Ricoeurian terminology I have used in the headings of this section. He writes: "if archives can be said to be instituted, and their documents are collected and conserved, this is so on the basis of the presupposition that the past has left a trace, which has become the monuments and documents that bear witness to the past. But what does it mean 'to leave a trace'?" (1990: 119). His answer takes up two senses of the word "trace" found in Littré's (French) Dictionary: the more general sense of "any mark left by a thing," and the more specific "vestige that a human being or animal has left on the place where it passed" (ibid.). Playing on the French homonymy between "passed" (*être passé*) in the sense of having passed by or through somewhere, and "past" (*être passé*) in the sense of having happened, he continues, after referring to Augustine's *Confessions*,

> the past falls behind. It passed this way. And we say that time itself passes. Where then is the paradox? In the fact that the passage is no longer but the trace remains . . .
>
> People pass, their works remain. But they remain as things among other things. This "thing-like" character is important for our investigation. It introduces a relationship of cause and effect between the marking thing and the marked thing. So the trace combines a relation of significance, best discerned in the idea of a vestige, and a relationship of causality, included in the thing-likeness of the mark. The trace is a sign-effect. (1990: 119, 120)

Ricoeur's definitions – or wordplays – apply well to an inscription bearing a prediction from the past, whether on stone or gold plate: it is "a documentary trace" in his sense, and so comparable in this sense to other kinds of trace: relics and shrines (*cetiya*).[57]

[55] The abbreviation is in the text: *idam c' idam ca . . . karessati*, XXVII 7.
[56] Peirce's phrases, cited in Burks (1949: 675).
[57] It may be of interest here to note that the word "shrine," according to the OED, is derived from Latin *scrinium*, meaning "a case or chest for books or papers."

The analogy between books and relics in Buddhism has received considerable attention recently, inspired by Schopen's deservedly celebrated (1975) article on "the cult of the book." More work needs to be done on the issue, notably on how far, and in what ways, the physical artifacts we call books (Skt *pustaka*) are necessary to the cult in question: often the texts cited as evidence in this regard can be interpreted as referring rather to a "cult of the text" (Skt *grantha*, Pali *gantha*; Collins 1992b), oral and/or written. But there is no doubt that this is an important connection of ideas, and a promising avenue for research.[58] In pursuing it, one should avoid the assumption that the veneration or worship (*pūjā*) of books is necessarily "magical" or otherwise irrational, or that such action is somehow contrary or irrelevant to appreciating what is written inside them. It was argued in sections I.a-c of the General Introduction that the existence of a consciously objectified tradition of transmittable, prestige discourse (of which literacy and books are a subcategory) was an achievement of civilization, not a universal human phenomenon (unlike "culture" in a broader sense); and in section III.c that soteriology, in both its questions and its answers, is necessarily discursive. In this light, to pay honor to and revere books, or other texts, is to celebrate at least two things (neither of which need be apparent, in this form, to agents; indeed this form of vocabulary is highly unlikely to be available other than in scholarly hindsight): first, that in a general sense, human achievements and aspirations have attained the level of trans-locality and universality where soteriology is possible; and second, that the tradition in question – here, obviously, Pali Buddhism – is not only capable of asking such questions in a heritage-conscious manner, but that the books being venerated contain the answers. To assume that book veneration is necessarily irrational would be like assuming that a benefactor of a modern university is only acting rationally if he or she also enrols in one of its courses.

To return to relics as a wider category: translating the word *dhātu*[59] as "relic" is in a sense misleading, since "relic," from Latin *reliquiae*,

[58] For references in Pali texts see Chapter 6 n. 86 below, Geiger (1929: 334, 343, 1960: 67), Collins (1990ms.). Gomez (1987) reviews the issue broadly; and Kinnard (1966) deals with Indian Buddhism of the Pāla period.

[59] The word *sarīra*, literally "body', is also used to refer to relics, often but not always in the plural; this may be considered a short form of *sarīra-dhatu*, "bodily relic" (e.g. Vv verse 1006, with Vv-a 269).

"(things) left behind", carries, as it were, its temporality on its face, which *dhātu* does not.[60] This is a polyvalent term in both Pali and Sanskrit: a selection of meanings from dictionaries is: layer, stratum, constituent part, ingredient, primary element, natural condition, property, factor, item, principle, (verbal) root. The relevant sense here is that of a part of the Buddha's body – bones, teeth or hair – which is usually preserved in a religious monument, usually a hemispherical mound of earth covered with bricks, and called either a *thūpa* (Skt *stūpa*) or a *cetiya* (Skt *caitya*). The concept *cetiya* is wider than that of *stūpa*.[61] Any Buddha-shrine is a *cetiya*, whereas a *stūpa* must contain a relic; and relics can also be kept in other containers. Both *thūpa* (*stūpa*) and *cetiya* (*caitya*) are from verbs meaning "to pile up,"[62] and seem originally to have referred to burial mounds. As has been seen, a major theme of the first chapter of the *Mahāvaṃsa* is the Buddha's going to various sites in Sri Lanka which will be in the future places of worship, as *stūpa*-s or *cetiya*-s. In one place he plants a tree, as "a shrine, which (contains objects) I have used." This renders *paribhoga-cetiya*, which is part of a standard classification of shrines: the second is *sarīra-* or *sārīrika-cetiya*, one "connected with a bodily relic" (Mil 341), and the third *uddesika-* or *uddissaka-cetiya*, one "indicating," or "pointing to" (the Buddha): the last refers most obviously to images (Ja IV 228, Pj I 221–2, Dhp-a III 251, Sadd 928). The tree becomes a shrine since the Buddha made use of it (cf. Mhv-ṭ 110). In his tour of the island at the end of the chapter, he "went up to (the top of M.) Sumanakūta and placed his footprint (there)" (i.e. M. Sumanta, or Adam's Peak, I 77). This renders *padaṃ dassesi*, literally "he made his foot manifest (there)" (the verb is the causative from to see, thus "show"). The commentary explains (Mhv-ṭ 114) that by making a footprint he made a foot-shrine (*padavalañjaṃ padacetiyaṃ akāsi*).[63]

In later chapters of the text, relics and monuments to house

[60] In Latin, the word *memoria* could be used both for tombs of dead saints and relics (LeGoff 1992: 71).

[61] I use the Sanskrit form of the latter as it has become common in English, at least among Indologists.

[62] Respectively, from *stup*, said to have been invented to account for *stūpa*, and *ci*, *cinoti*; in Pali commentarial exegesis the latter is regularly connected with *cittikaroti*, "to honor."

[63] Footprints are common in Southern Asian texts as signs of a departed religious figure, notably of Kṛṣṇa; they were one of the aniconic means by which Buddhas were represented in the earliest Buddhist iconography.

them become a major theme, occupying much of Chapter XV and all of Chapters XVII, XVIII, XXVIII–XXX. Successful transmission of Buddhism to Sri Lanka (or anywhere else) requires that the Message/Dispensation (*sāsana*) and the Monastic Order (*vinaya*) should be established there; but the material, "thing-like" marks of its transmission as a historical event include also relics and shrines, both those produced by the Buddha's visits and those built later when his bodily relics are brought. As mentioned earlier, in Chapter XV Mahinda tells Devānaṃpiyatissa that three former Buddhas left things they had used in the same place on the island as relics, *dhātu*-s,[64] and that Gotama meditated on that very same spot – which is itself the place where the Great Stūpa is to be built in the future (vv. 160–7). Later he tells the king that it is a long time since he has seen the Buddha; when the king is puzzled, since the Buddha is long dead (*nibbuta*), Mahinda replies, "When one sees relics one sees the Buddha" (XVII 3; cf. 3.2.b). Relics are then brought to the island; they arise from their case and perform a miracle identical to one performed by the Buddha (XVII 44). In the immediately following verses, the narrative moves back to the Buddha on his deathbed, where he makes five resolutions (*adhiṭṭhāna*) concerning a branch of the Bodhi-tree and relics, and their performance of miracles at the time of Devānaṃpiyatissa and of Duṭṭhagāmaṇī. Later, in Chapter XXXI 97ff., relics perform the same miracle at the time of Duṭṭhagāmaṇī, this time taking on the appearance of the Buddha, as he had predicted.

This kind of language – especially when combined with that of Chapter XXXIV 61, which uses the word *buddhupaṭṭhāna*, "service to the Buddha," of a king honoring the Great Stūpa – might lead one to think that relics are being simply identified with the Buddha, such that they make him present in an immediate way. But just as the coalescing of the "I" of Gotama and Sumedha in the *Buddhavaṃsa* did not cancel the temporal difference between them, so here Chapter XVII ends (v. 65) with a clear reminder that there is a difference between relics and the historical Buddha: "In this way the Lord of the World, even though in nirvana (*parinibbānagato*) truly brought great benefit and happiness to people by means of his bodily relics: how could one describe (the benefits and happiness obtained) when the

64 Vv. 88, 122, 157: Mhv-t 358 explains that they are *paribhogadhātu*-s, "relics of use."

Conqueror was alive?" Relics and shrines are traces of the past, in Ricoeur's sense both signs and effects of the Buddha. In the text of the *Mahāvaṃsa*, the non-repetitive time so carefully constructed and maintained throughout makes the relationship between the Buddha and relics/shrines one of coalescence, in the sense used earlier, rather than identity; the Buddha is a past mediated through temporal connection-and-separation rather than im-mediate presence.

The General Introduction I.b argued that all transcendentalist ideologies involve a dialectic between a postulated locus of value outside the here-and-now and the places, events, material objects, etc., among which human life is lived. Theravāda Buddhist transcendentalism is particularly severe; as has been seen, nirvana is radically atemporal and immaterial, and neither the concept of existence nor that of nonexistence (nor both nor neither) can grasp the nature of an enlightened person after his or her death. The Buddha is thus not capable of being imagined in as direct a relationship with the here-and-now as, say, the Christian Eucharist, the incarnation of Hindu deities in statues, or Mahāyāna Buddhist multiple Buddhas and Bodhisattvas currently existing in other Buddha-fields, who can be reached by visualization (or other means). In Theravāda, and to a greater or lesser extent in that of all Buddhism, the act of signifying the Buddha-in-atemporal-nirvana is intertwined with the act of signifying a past figure in a temporal field. Relics are particularly good signifiers for this latter purpose. In Buddhist terms, the historical Gotama was a series of interconnected mental and physical events (*dhamma*-s) in space and time; at his final nirvana the series of mental events came to an end (albeit that this is not equivalent to his becoming nothing), as did most of the physical events, with the exception of his bones, teeth and hair. These continue to exist as relics, quite literally parts of the Buddha's physical being in the same way that they were during his life, but now disconnected from the other physical and mental events which then occurred. The surviving Mahāvihārin version of Theravāda has a particularly historicist perspective (Collins 94ms.), evident for example in its conception of the authority of its scriptural tradition as the Word of the (historical) Buddha (Collins 90a). It is not surprising, then, that it should enact the dialectic between transcendental and mundane in part through temporal connection-and-separation;

nor that, parallel to its use of relics for this purpose, it should produce a rich genre of *vaṃsa* texts, some at least of which are not only tales of time but "tales about time": tales about endless *saṃsāra* in which nirvana provides (repeatedly) the sense of an (individual) ending.

Conclusion to part 1

MODES OF THOUGHT, MODES OF TRADITION

The last proposition in Wittgenstein's *Tractatus Logico-philosophicus*, "whereof one cannot speak, thereof one must be silent," is not without a certain pomposity, and so Ernest Gellner's somewhat uncharitable observation that the original sentence in German can be sung to the tune of Good King Wenceslas is not inappropriate, albeit philosophically irrelevant.[1] More directly pertinent is an observation made by a contemporary of the early Wittgenstein, the mathematician and philosopher Frank Ramsey: "What you can't say you can't say, and you can't whistle it either."[2] What you can't say about nirvana you can't say, and you can't picture it by means of imagery either. In both the *Tractatus* and Buddhism, the ineffable is brought into being as an aspect of the effable.[3] Inexpressible, timeless nirvana is a moment in the Buddhist textualization of time, the explicit or implicit closure-marker in its discourse of felicity. It is the motionless and ungraspable horizon, the limit-condition which makes of the Pali imaginaire a coherent whole. From within Buddhist ideology, one would need to add the proviso that nirvana exists beyond any historically specific imaginaire – the Dispensation (*sāsana*) of any Buddha – which points toward it;[4] it is the object of Path-consciousness, a reality which can be attained by the Path. But an external interpreter cannot, or at least for the

[1] (1979a: 8): *wovon man nicht sprechen kann, darüber muss man schweigen.* The translation given is Ogden's (1922), the one in which the *Tractatus* was first known to English speakers; Pears and McGuinness's (1961) rendering is less portentous: "what we cannot speak about we must pass over in silence." [2] Cited in ibid. p. 9.

[3] Gellner (1979a: 7–8) compares the *Tractatus* to Eliot's *The Waste Land*, in compositional style and *Zeitgeist*. The use of the last proposition to effect closure can be added to his list of Wittgenstein's poetic devices.

[4] Cf. Collins (1982: 83) on Buddhist doctrine as a direction arrow.

purposes of interpretation need not make this assumption. From such a perspective one needs only to discern how nirvana exists in the dynamics of Buddhist ideology, as that which circumscribes the felicitous imaginaire as good to think, good to imagine, and good to narrate. Part 1 has shown that Pali texts do indeed speak of nirvana, up to a point, but also that the process of speaking about it leads up to silence, a silence within discourse which creates meaning as such. External analysis of the meaning of nirvana should not, I have argued, proceed vicariously, by speaking on the Buddha's behalf, filling in the silences (in the spirit of Ramsey, one might say: whistling to keep one's spirits up). Etic understanding should preserve and respect the emic silence, while being able itself to continue speaking.

The Pali imaginaire is the central artifact, mode and sign of tradition-making and transmitting in the Theravāda Buddhist civilizational enunciation of order. Its discourse of felicity provides a coherently organized cornucopia of happinesses, a rich and variegated textual field which defeats suffering and death, insofar as texts can. In this book so far the analysis of Buddhist felicities within that discourse has shown nirvana in a somewhat austere light: the satisfactions it offers in systematic thought are those of conceptual clarity and circumspection; in imagery those of elegance and embodied aporia; in narrative those of a mute sense of an ending, the expectation of nothing. I have suggested that nirvana has semantic value in concepts and imagery, and syntactic value in its role as the concluding period (full stop) in an eternal, beginningless and endless story. Since the sense of an ending is produced not merely in the abstract, in the ethereality of thought, but also practically, in the dramaturgical-ritual performances of Buddhists (notably the public recitation of texts), nirvana plays its role of closure on the level of pragmatics also. In the General Introduction III.c I cited the sociological vocabulary of manifest and latent functions; the analysis proposed here sees the semantics of nirvana as manifest, its syntax and pragmatics as latent.

If scholarly understanding proceeds in part by making distinctions and clarifying differences, it does so also by making connections and illuminating similarities. In Part 1 I have been concerned to distinguish between systematic and narrative thought; in this brief conclusion to it I will trace their affinity, by arguing that imagery is the bridge, the mediating link between them. The two most common images of nirvana in the developed tradition are the quenching of fire and the city. Buddhist systematic thought presents a static arrangement of ideas, which are connected by logical not temporal relations; its narratives, whether the overall master-text or the stories told in actual texts, are by necessity temporally structured. The imagery of fire is built into the vocabulary of the systematic thought in which the concept of nirvana exists; but it also has a temporal dimension, embodied in the verbs or verbal notions within the image: it is of fire *going out* or *quenched* . This temporal dimension is, in microcosm, the same as that of the larger-scale stories and histories in which narrative thought textualizes both time and timeless nirvana. So not only is the image intrinsic to the vocabulary of Buddhism (attachment-fuel, nirvana-quenching); it also contains – in a nutshell, or, to use a South Asian metaphor, in seed form – the narrative movement from suffering to resolution and closure in which nirvana's syntactic value is to be found. The city of nirvana can be a static object of textual vision; but in the notion of the city as the destination point of a journey, the terminus of the Path, which is again intrinsic to Buddhist systematic thought, there is also a microcosmic version of the entire Buddhist master-narrative. The Path to salvation is thus, in the image as in the master-narrative, a journey through time from the city of the transient body to the city of timeless and deathless nirvana: the city without fear, as one of the earliest texts to use the image calls it. The images set the logic of the concept in motion: once there is motion, there is temporal extension, and once there is temporal extension there is narrative.

Part 1 has discussed systematic and narrative thought for the most part merely *as* modes of thought. I am, however, not so much interested in discovering a hypothetical individual psychology or phenomenology in Pali Buddhism (though of course what I have said would not be irrelevant to such an aim), as in trying to bring alive and into currency a different way of writing the history of its ideas: in relation to this latter goal systematic and narrative thought, interconnected through patterns of imagery, are better taken as modes of tradition, forms of collective memory. Transmittable, textual traditions – though by no means the only, or even the most important mode of traditionality in general[5] – have nonetheless a specific importance in the civilizations of premodern agrarian states, as was stressed in the General Introduction I.b and c. They both construct an ideology and exclude potential others (this is the sense in which one can speak of dominant ideologies). As Ludden (1994: 3) puts it, such civilizations were "the projects of state [male] elites." In the words of Halbwachs cited in the General Introduction I.b, part of the social status of an elite, especially but not only in premodern societies, lies in its claim to preserve an ancestral heritage which has value for the society as a whole. So Chapters 1–3 have not only been exploring the inside of Pali texts, seeking the logical, imaginative and narrative meaning of nirvana; they have also been concerned to delineate the modes of traditionality and textuality which were the vehicle of the wider Buddhist discourse of felicity. It is seeing this wider discourse – in which minority asceticism has its special cultural logic – which makes it possible, looking at the outside of the texts, to get a clearer picture of their place in civilizational history.

In the terms used in the General Introduction III.c, the Pali discourse of felicity includes not only the *ultimate* well-being of nirvana, but also a range of imaginatively *efficient* conceptions of non-nirvanic happiness. Part 2 will be concerned with these efficient conceptions.

[5] See Shils (1981), Nyíri (1988, 91), Connerton (1989), Fentress and Wickham (1992), Ingold (1993), Rowlands (1993). Turner (1994) shows how very difficult it can be to specify what a "tradition" actually is, and what might be the causal and other processes by which "it" is learned and transmitted. Fortunately I do not have to address those problems here.

PART 2

Paradise in heaven and on earth

Introduction to part 2

UTOPIA AND THE IDEAL SOCIETY

This Introduction does two things: first, two qualifications are made to what has been said previously about Buddhist thought and imagery, both of which bring the ultimate felicity of nirvana closer to other kinds of imaginatively efficient felicity than would seem to be possible given the logically discrete categories of the conditioned and the Unconditioned; second, it briefly introduces the categories of ideal society in the work of the historian J. C. Davis, which I use to organize these imaginatively efficient utopias.

Chapter 1.2.b, apropos the skillfulness of the enlightened person, made a clear distinction between the evaluation of action in terms of merit (*puñña*) and in terms of what is skillful or wholesome (*kusala*), arguing (after Premasiri 1976) that whereas the acquisition of merit through good action by an unenlightened person, done necessarily with some degree of attachment, entails (good) rebirth, the skillful action of an enlightened person, done without attachment, does not. Thus an enlightened person can be said to do "good" in the latter sense, but not in the former. But as was remarked there (pp. 154 n. 54), this distinction, while clearly discernible in texts of systematic thought, tends to diminish to vanishing point in others, particularly narratives. The relevant point for the present discussion is not, obviously, that enlightened persons might – absurdly – come to be thought capable of acquiring *puñña* by means of meritorious behaviour with attachment, and so obtaining good rebirth, but rather that nirvana comes to be seen as the apex of what can be acquired by merit rather than a goal qualitatively different from it, as the pinnacle of what can be attained by good *karma* rather than something beyond *karma*. It is not that the distinction between *puñña* and *kusala* is consciously abandoned: it is simply disregarded. Although it is true that the assimilation of the two categories is found more commonly in the later literature, it does occur in two relatively early texts, the "Treasure-Store Discourse" (*Nidhikaṇḍa Sutta*, Khp 7), redacted in the *Khuddaka Nikāya* of the *Sutta Piṭaka*, and the "Questions of King Milinda" (*Milinda Pañha*), which includes material from different periods but as a whole is earlier than the time of Buddhaghosa, fourth to fifth centuries AD (Norman 1983: 111–2). In both, nirvana occurs as the culmination – unsurprisingly – of a list of good things. In the former, laying up a store (of merit, according to the commentary, Pj I 221) by means of almsgiving, etc. is said to lead to every human excellence – *inter alia* beauty of appearance and voice, local kingship or Wheel-turning Kingship (6.5.a) – as well as to the pleasure of the divine worlds and the attainment of nirvana (*nibbāna-sampatti*, v. 13). In the latter (Mil 341) an extended image describes the Buddha's General Store (*sabbāpaṇa*), which contains many things for sale, to be bought by the currency of *karma*:[1] they include good birth, wealth, long life, beauty, divine bliss and nirvana (referred to also in a verse as the Unconditioned and the Deathless).

Such an assimilation can be seen frequently in narrative texts,[2] where Buddhahood is standardly referred to as Omniscience, and the giving of gifts is taken to the extreme of physical self-sacrifice.[3] While it is not impossible to construe such sentiments as the latter in terms of Buddhist systematic thought – along the lines that extreme giving becomes identical with selfless, detached renunciation (both are meanings of the word *cāga*, for instance) – it is clear that in practice such fine distinctions as that between merit and what is skillful are often ignored, as modern ethnography abundantly attests. Here is one example from the medieval collection called *Dasavatthu-ppakaraṇa*, which develops themes already present in earlier stories about former lives of the enlightened nun Uppalavaṇṇā.[4] In the first life recounted she is a poor girl who

[1] *Kamma-mūla* – other senses of *mūla* are in play here also: root, basis, foundation, etc.
[2] For examples in translation see n. 29 in 4.1.c.
[3] This is particularly evident in the *Paññāsa Jātaka* collection: see Horner and Jaini (1985), Jaini (1986a).
[4] Dasav no. 13; cf. Thī 224–35, Thī-a 182–99, Ja no. 527; and DPPN s.v. Uppalavaṇṇā. On this text and others of its genre, see Norman (1983: 153–4).

works long and hard to get a garment dyed with safflowers. She then meets a disciple of the Buddha Kassapa who has lost his robes, and gives the garment to him. Thanks to this gift she is reborn in heaven, and then as a human woman of divine beauty; after another life in heaven she is reborn at the time of our Buddha Gotama. She is so beautiful every king and rich man in India wants to marry her; unable to choose between them her father asks her if she would become a nun. She does so, and attains enlightenment. The story ends with verses extolling the value of giving (Dasav 58 vv. 5–7): those who give garments to the virtuous (i.e. monks and nuns) are (thereafter) always beautiful and attractive; those who give, whatever the gift, obtain the threefold happiness – human, divine, and the happiness of nirvana (*nibbāna-sukhaṃ*).

A second way in which nirvana is assimilated to other Buddhist utopias is through the image of it as a city. There are two aspects to this. First, just as the city of nirvana becomes standard in the later literature (2.3.e), so the heavens are ubiquitously referred to as cities. As Hallisey says, "the image of the city of Nibbāna could suggest a continuum between *nibbāna* and the possible forms of rebirth found in saṃsāra. The same conventional metaphor that 'defines' existential conditions as 'places' (*thāṇa*) which [occurs in the earliest texts] with reference to Nibbāna, was also used with respect to [the heavens]."[5] Thus nirvana and the heavens, while clearly opposites according to some criteria – the one Unconditioned, the other conditioned, the one ultimate bliss (*sukha*), the other always unsatisfactory (*dukkha*), however pleasant temporarily – can also be regarded through this image as differing in degree rather than in kind. The second aspect concerns kings. Just as Islamic kings often patterned their palaces on the garden of paradise,[6] so too kings are said in Buddhist texts to live in palaces and cities like those in heaven. (Not for nothing, of course, is it the case that the same word *deva* can mean both god and king.) The parallel is found in the earliest texts, as in the *Mahāsudassana Sutta*, where the eponymous king's city is compared to a city of the gods.[7] *Jātaka* story no. 415 tells of a king Brahmadatta of Benares who on the day of his consecration decorates his city like a city of the gods, with 16,000 dancing girls looking like celestial nymphs. Later he

5 (1993: 113); he cites a number of representative texts.

6 See references given in n. 9 below, and for examples Moynihan (1979), Lehrman (1980) and Brookes (1987).

7 D II 169, cf. II 146–7; this text is discussed in 6.5.b.

builds a jeweled pavilion in front of his palace, and sits on a jeweled throne there surrounded by his ministers, the 16,000 girls, and others, looking like Sakka, king of the gods, surrounded by his divine retinue (Ja III 407–10). This trope is found not only in story texts, but also in the historical Chronicles, and it was used by actual, historical kings[8]. Earthly kings could not, of course, be thought to be literally "in nirvana," but some forms of hyperbole, both textual and historical, which describe them as future Buddhas, and sometimes "as if" they were Buddhas now (6.5.a), put the two together, at least on an impressionistic level. Both aspects of the image of nirvana, heaven, and (royal) capitals/palaces as cities suggest that the radical otherness characteristic of nirvana as a concept in Buddhist systematic thought is lessened in narratives, in which the sharp distinction between the conditioned universe and the Unconditioned is not always so strongly stressed, and where royal, celestial and nirvanic felicity can often seem, by association of ideas and images rather than by direct assertion, to be homogenous rather than heterogenous.

The word *utopias* appears in the subtitle of this book, and *paradise* in the title of Part 2; Chapters 4, 5, and 6, and subsections of them, use words and phrases taken from a five-part classification of ideal societies developed by J. C. Davis, the title of whose (1981) book I have used for this Introduction to Part 2. My reason for doing all this is to facilitate connections – for those who wish to make them – between the Pali imaginaire and utopianism in European and American tradition, and modern scholarship on it. Those who do not wish to make these connections may ignore the words and classification system entirely: nothing I have to say substantively about Buddhism is dependent on these avenues for comparative understanding, save for the points about textuality, eu-topia and ou-topia already made in the General Introduction (III.c). In using Davis' typology I want his terms to sit lightly, as it were, on the Buddhist material. The Conclusion to Part 2 returns to some questions arising from this invitation to comparative reflection on utopianism cross-culturally. Readers who are not interested in these matters may ignore what is said both there and in the remainder of this Introduction.

[8] Duncan (1990), and Aung Thwin (1985).

First, a few words on terminological generality and specificity. In the title given to Part 2, "Paradise in Heaven and on Earth," the word *paradise* is intended in a very general sense, as in the OED: "a place like or compared to Paradise [earlier defined as the terrestrial Garden of Eden, or Heaven], a region of surpassing beauty or delight, or of supreme bliss," or even more widely "a state of supreme bliss or felicity." In the Buddhist case this definition is in one sense inappropriate, because of the word "supreme": only the felicity of nirvana is, ultimately, supreme above all others. The word "paradise" derives from an old Persian word meaning a garden or walled enclosure, a specific meaning which has remained central to Islamic eschatology.[9] As will be seen, each Buddhist heaven has its own garden, and Buddhist kings, like Islamic ones, liked to make their palatial residences isomorphic to such heavenly realms. But the particular features of paradise as a garden – lush greenery, water and the like – although to be found in some Buddhist paradises, are not standard features as in the Islamic case (no doubt for the obvious reason of difference in climate and ecology).

Similarly, in the book's subtitle the word "utopia" is intended in a general, everyday sense, to point in an overall manner to Buddhist versions of what the OED (s.v. utopia 2) calls "a place, state or condition ideally perfect in respect of politics, laws, customs and conditions" (taking the last four terms disjunctively). Part 2, however, uses Davis' more narrowly defined typology, in which "utopia" has a quite specific meaning, as one among five different types of ideal society: the Land of Cockaygne, Arcadia, the Perfect Moral Commonwealth, the Millennium and Utopia proper. It may seem perverse to do this, since, as will become clear, there is no Buddhist utopia in Davis' sense; but I hope the reasons for doing so will become evident. When a writer proposes a restrictive definition of a term which has wider meanings in everyday language, he or she can do so only for purposes specific to their own project. Davis has his own, good reasons for using a restrictive definition of utopia, and I find his typology also useful for Buddhism. It helps to give one form of coherence and order to what might otherwise seem to be a heterogenous collection of

[9] MacDonald (1966: 341–52), Smith and Haddad (1981), Partin (1987: 184), Blair and Bloom (1991).

material; and the absence of a utopia in Davis' restrictive sense tells us something important about Buddhist ideology and the genre of intellectual activity we call social theory (see the Conclusion to Part 2; and Collins 1988).[10]

Davis presents his terms, in Weberian fashion, as ideal types: that is, they do not delineate mutually exclusive empirical groups but conceptual categories, which will almost always be mixed in differing ways in particular, actual cases. The two problems to which they respond are those of material and sociological scarcity: the limited amount of satisfactions available, and the differential distribution of them in any given population. Together these constitute "the collective problem . . . [which is] the reconciliation of limited satisfactions and unlimited human desires within a social context . . . We can distinguish utopia and four alternative types of ideal society by the way in which they deal with this issue" (1981: 19, 36). The types are:

(i) *The Land of Cockaygne*, the name of a medieval peasant fantasy (see Morton 1952 and Graus 1967) in which the paucity of satisfactions is solved by imagining a superabundance of them: it is "a world of instant gratification, of wishing trees, fountains of youth, rivers of wine, self-roasting birds, sexually promiscuous and ever-available partners."[11]

(ii) *Arcadia*, in which nature is bountiful, but the collective problem is solved more significantly by the moderation of desires, and people live in a state of peaceable and calm harmony with nature and each other, usually in a rural setting.

(iii) *The Perfect Moral Commonwealth*, where natural resources are at a normal level, but society is made harmonious (if nonetheless hierarchical in many cases) by the behavior of individuals, who attain by moral effort a greater or lesser degree of perfection.

(iv) *The Millennium*, which is not so much a type of ideal society as a manner of attaining it: not by human effort but by some kind of supernatural intervention, "independent of the wills

[10] The only discussion of Theravāda Buddhist ideas which I have seen in the literature on utopianism is contained in a few pages by Chesneaux (1968: 89–93). He is dependent on Sarkisyanz (1965), who can be an unreliable source (see 5.2.d). Kollmar-Paulenz (1993) is a useful source for Tibetan Buddhist utopianism.

[11] This phrase, and the next three cited, are from the summary account in Davis (1984: 8–9).

of individual men and women." (Of course, people's fate after the millennium can obviously be affected by their behavior, and in the Buddhist case being present at the time of the future Buddha Metteyya will be the result of volitional action, *karma*, in previous lives.)

(v) *Utopia* proper. Here human beings and nature are taken as they are, wicked and inadequate, and the solution to the collective problem is found in the imposition of order: systems of social organization and control. "Such systems are inevitably bureaucratic, institutional, legal and educational, artificial and organizational . . . The utopian's prior value is not happiness but order, and while he may go on to consider the happiness that might be built on that order, this is not necessary." And of course it is just these qualities which have led many, especially in the twentieth century, to see such a society as exactly the opposite of ideal, as a *dystopia.*

With these introductory remarks, I now turn to Buddhist felicities other than nirvana. Perhaps the simplest way of introducing them would be to say that they provide answers to the question "What is it like, in the Pali imaginaire, to be happy?" (or at least: to live in conditions of happiness).

CHAPTER FOUR

Heaven, the Land of Cockaygne and Arcadia

4.1. LIFE IN THE HEAVENS

4.1.a. Buddhist Cosmology

It is easy to overlook the Buddhist heavens. Textbook depictions of Buddhism often reduce them to an incidental diversion, something like a pleasant vacation separate from the hard work of the Path to nirvana. From a certain kind of abstract, doctrinal point of view this is understandable, and it is certainly characteristic of Buddhist modernism; but it seriously distorts the place of the heavens in the premodern Pali imaginaire. In fact a great deal of attention is paid to them in numerous texts, and the spectrum of felicities they offer is depicted at length and with care. Their place in the Buddhist universe of evaluative discourse is determined by the conceptual opposition between desire (*kāma*) and its gradual renunciation, which is constitutive both of the temporally extended dynamic of the individual path from *saṃsāra* to nirvana, and also of the spatially extended hierarchy of the cosmos. Buddhist cosmology postulates three Spheres (*avacara*) or Levels (*bhūmi*), each of which contain thirty or thirty-one worlds (*lokā*), ordered hierarchically. In Table 4.1 these are numbered 1, 2, and 3. They are:

(1) the Formless Sphere (*arūpāvacara*): 16 worlds = Meditation Levels 5–8;
(2) the Sphere of (refined) Form (*rūpāvacara*): 16 worlds in 4 groups = Meditation Levels 1–4, and
(3) the Sphere of Desire (*kāmāvacara*): 10 or 11 worlds (see n. 4 on the *asura*-s), which are the six heavens of the gods (*devā*), the Human World, and 3 or 4 Subhuman Worlds. *Rūpa* can be translated "matter" or "body," so the heavens of spheres 1 and 2 – which are all Brahma-worlds to which access is gained only

Table 4.1 *Buddhist cosmology, with maximum length of life in each world*

Brahma-worlds (*brahma-lokā*):

1. The Formless Sphere (*arūpāvacara*): 4 worlds

8th. *jhāna* Neither perception nor nonperception (84,000 eons)
7th. *jhāna* Nothingness (60,000 eons)
6th. *jhāna* Infinite consciousness (40,000 eons)
5th. *jhāna* Infinite space (20,000 eons)

2. The Sphere of (refined) Form (*rūpāvacara*): 16 worlds

4th. *jhāna* 7 worlds:
Akaniṭṭha Devas (16,000 eons)
Sudassī Devas (8,000 eons)
Sudassa Devas (4,000 eons)
Atappa Devas (2,000 eons)
Aviha Devas (1,000 eons)
Asañña-satta Devas (500 eons)
Vehapphala Devas (500 eons)

3rd. *jhāna* 3 worlds:
Subhakiṇha Devas (64 eons)
Appamānasubha Devas (32 eons)
Parittasubha Devas (16 eons)

2nd. *jhāna* 3 worlds:
Ābhassara Devas (8 eons)
Appamāṇābhā Devas (4 eons)
Parittābhā Devas (2 eons)

1st. *jhāna* 3 worlds:
Mahābrahma Devas (1 eon)
Brahmapurohita Devas (half an eon)
Brahmapārisajja Devas (third of an eon)

3. The Sphere of Desire (*kāmāvacara*): 10/11 worlds

Good Destinies (sugati)

Deva-Worlds (*deva-loka*):

Paranimmitta Vasavatti Devas (9,219,000,000 human years)
Nimmānarati Devas (2,304,000,000 human years)
Tusita Devas (576,000,000 human years)
Yāma Devas (144,000,000 human years; the god of Death, Māra, lives here)
Tāvatiṃsa Devas (36,000,000 human years)
Cātummahārājika Devas (9,000 human years)

The Human World (*manussa-loka*) (lived on four separate island-continents; apart from Uttarakuru [4.2.a] no fixed length of life)

Bad Destinies (duggati):

Table 4.1 *(cont.)*

Subhuman worlds (no fixed length of life):
[Realm of asuras (anti-gods, demons); sometimes omitted; see n. 4]
Realm of ghosts (*peta*-s)
Realm of animals
Hell(s) (*Niraya*)

through meditation – could be termed respectively those of the Immaterial Level, where the Brahmas[1] are disembodied, and those of the Level of (Refined) Matter, where the Brahmas have purified bodies. Just as the first Meditation Level is free from pleasures deriving from desire (2.1.b), so these Brahma-worlds which parallel the Meditation Levels are above the Sphere of Desire.

Table 4.1 gives an outline of Buddhist cosmology; it emphasizes within this tripartite scheme a fourfold categorization of worlds, since there are significant differences in the kinds of felicity (or its absence) to be enjoyed in them. From the bottom up these are: the Subhuman Worlds, which are Bad Destinies, the Good Destinies of the Human World and the Deva-heavens, and the Brahma-worlds. The terminology is a little inconsistent, but this need not be misleading:

(1) The word *sagga*, heaven, can be used of all twenty-six worlds above the human, or of a lesser number of them, most commonly the six heavens of the Deva-loka.[2]

(2) Similarly the word *deva*, god (from root *div*, to shine), can refer to different classes of being (or subsets of them). From the most general to the most specific these are:

   (a) all beings above the human level, Devas of both genders and ungendered Brahmas (on gender see below). Beings in the Brahma-world can be called *brahmāno*, Brahmas and so differentiated from *deva*-s;

[1] The proper name of the Indian god Brahma is here used as a class term.

[2] For *sagga* as all twenty-six, e.g. It-a II 139. Pj I 170 defines it as the Worlds of Desire and (Refined) Form only. A standard Graduated Talk proceeds from almsgiving (*dāna*) and morality (*sīla*) to heaven (*sagga*) and finally to Renunciation (*nekkhamma*); commentaries usually gloss *sagga* as the Cātummahārājika and Tāvatiṃsa heavens. For references see CPD s.v. *anupubbikathā*.

(b) gods and goddesses collectively, in the Deva-worlds
(c) male gods in the Deva-worlds.

(3) Female beings in the Deva-worlds can be differentiated from male gods by being called *devī*, goddess, *devadhītā* (corresponding to the masculine *devaputta*), literally daughter (or son) of a god, but better as junior or young goddess (god); other words are found, such as *accharā*, divine maiden, nymph, and *devakaññā*, divine girl.

(4) The unmarked term *devatā* (feminine), deity or divinity, can be used in all cases.

In the whole range of Pali texts, not surprisingly, there are certain complexities and ambiguities in matters of detail,[3] but the account of Buddhist cosmology presented here is clear enough for my purposes. It can be taken as the view of things presupposed by almost all texts.[4] The cosmological hierarchy is related to geography, again not without minor ambiguities and variations in different texts.[5] Mt. Sineru (Skt Meru) is at the center of the world; it is surrounded by seven concentric rings of mountains separated by rings of sea. In the outermost sea are the four continents, arranged at the four cardinal points; ours is Jambudīpa, to the south. (See 4.2.a on the others, especially the paradisial Uttarakuru to the north.) The hells are below the earth; ghosts and animals inhabit the earth along with humans and some earth deities (such as those

[3] Gombrich (1975) shows this to be true of Indian cosmology generally; cf. Kloetzli (1983, 1987). Le Goff (1984) describes an analogous variety in early and medieval Christian ideas of the afterlife.

[4] I have drawn from the "Heart of Dhamma" chapter of the canonical *Vibhaṅga* (Vibh 401–36) and Part 5 of the medieval digest *Abhidhammattha-saṅgaha* (pp. 22–8 in Saddhatissa [89]); translations in Thittila (1969: 514–59) and Nārada (1975: 233–77). Cp. *Loka-paññatti* Chapter 10, in Denis (1977). I have not translated the names for the different worlds, although they are not without their own interest: see Vibh-a 519–21, translated by Ñāṇamoli (1991: 291–3). An accessible account of the Three Worlds, from the later Thai treatise *Traibhumikathā*, can be found in Reynolds (1982). Some lists omit the *asura*-s, as does the normal Theravāda version of the Wheel of Life, which thus depicts five realms: of the gods, humans, animals, ghosts and hell-beings. See Khantipalo (1970) for a modern version; for the issue of whether there are five or six realms see Mus (1939), the Introduction to Denis (1977) and Hazlewood (1987). The Tibetan versions, which are probably more familiar in the modern West, do have it, and thus depict six realms. Snake(-like) beings called nāga-s can be an exception to the generalization that the realm of animals is a bad destiny, since they can live luxuriously, in a kind of "paradise" (see text below; and cf. Vism 427 = XIII 93). They are sometimes classed as *bhumma-devatā*, earth deities.

[5] See the summaries in Gombrich (1975) and Ñāṇamoli (1975: 218–19); Pj II 442–3, As 297–8.

inhabiting trees). Starting on the slopes of Mt. Sineru is the world of the Cātummahārājika gods, each of whom presides over a class of earth deities: Dhaṭaratha is king of Gandhabbas, Virūḷha of Kumbhaṇḍas, Virūpaka of nāgas, and Kuvera Vessavana of Spirits (*yakkha*-s). The other heavens extend above Sineru, vertically. If a rock as large as the gable of a house were dropped from the lowest of the Brahma-worlds, it would take a year to reach the earth; each Brahma-world thereafter is twice as high as what is below it.[6] By far the most common of the worlds above the human to appear in narratives are the Tāvatiṃsa and Tusita heavens of the Deva-loka. Sakka (Skt Śakra, i.e. Indra), king of the gods, lives in Tāvatiṃsa, but visits Tusita regularly; Buddhas in their penultimate life live in Tusita, as does the next Buddha Metteyya (Skt. Maitreya) currently. The outermost ring of mountains (sometimes of iron) constitutes the wall around the world, whereon are written the originals of Pali law-texts.

This cosmo-geography is related to soteriology, by the parallel between the higher heavens of the Brahma-world and the levels of meditation (see next section). Both of them are free from desire, albeit temporarily: for a brief time to human consciousness in meditation, for eons as a Brahma deity. The parallel between levels of cosmology and levels of meditation adds a further note to the discussion in 1.2.b concerning the ambiguous status of the Cessation of Perception and Feeling. As mentioned there, this is often added as a ninth and final level of meditation, but it does not appear in the cosmology; one might infer that it is a state outside the cosmos, and thus equivalent (or parallel) to nirvana. But Cessation lasts for a specific length of time, as do all Meditation Levels; and so while it is not in space it is (at least from the external perspective) in time, and so in that sense within the universe. Brahmas in the immaterial, Formless Worlds cannot attain it (Vism 705 = XXIII 29): if such a Brahma's mental processes were to cease, then since such a being has no body it would be "beyond designation," just like those who have attained final nirvana, which is clearly an unacceptable suggestion.[7] The numerical values assigned to the maximum length of life in each heaven, very large but precise, serve to underscore the conceptual difference between them and timeless nirvana.

[6] Thus Loka-p X: text in Denis (1977) vol. 1, p. 66. DPPN s.v. *brahma-loka* gives the figure of four months.

[7] Vism-a 1273: *apaññattiko va bhaveyya anupādisesaya nibbānadhatuyā parinibbutasādiso.*

The gods of the Deva-worlds are of different sizes when they are born: those in the highest heaven, the Paranimmittavasavatti gods, are like an eleven-year-old on earth. But they all grow to maturity in a week. Brahmas in the Worlds of Refined Form remain the same size throughout their lives (Loka-p 68–9). Unlike humans, gods do not become old and wrinkled, and their divine beauty and enjoyment grow greater day by day (Ja IV 109). When the time comes for the gods of the Deva-worlds to die, five signs appear: their flowers fade, their clothes become dirty, their armpits sweat, their bodies discolor, and they no longer take pleasure in their celestial home (It 76, Ja V 278, Sv 427, etc.). They then go to the Nandana pleasure park (of which there is one in each such heaven, Ja I 49), where their demise is like snow dissolved by heat, or a flame blown out by the wind (Spk I 39–40). Dying in the Brahma-world is as painless as ending a meditative trance.

The distinction between the heavens of Desire and the Brahma-worlds is important for a number of reasons. For my purposes the most significant difference between the two spheres is in the mode by which they are imagined, and in the possibilities for narrative in either case. This distinction in imaginative mode can be called one between an *external-sensory* perspective on the one hand, and an *internal-mental* one on the other:

(i) In the first case, heavenly happiness in the Deva-worlds is depicted in terms of visual, aural, olfactory and other sensory experience, situated in a world shared by more than one person; it provides a scenario in which events happen, characters interact, and so on. Accordingly, there are many stories of these worlds, whether in the first person by a character, or in the third person by a named character or invisible authorial voice.

(ii) In the second case, given that the bliss of the Brahma-worlds is organized in parallel to, indeed as identical to, the individual and internal states of body and mind achieved through the sequence of Meditative Levels, narratives of events taking place within any of these worlds are much more difficult, indeed for the most part impossible. (This is different from the case of beings leaving the Brahma-world and going either to the Deva-world or to the Human World, where they interact with gods and/or human beings, of which some examples are given in 4.1.c.) Although the forms of happiness possible in the Brahma-worlds are taken to be more refined than those of the Deva-worlds, the imagery used to depict the parallel kinds of meditation happiness can be very striking, as 4.1.b shows.

A useful insight into the nature of Buddhist heavens can be gained by juxtaposing two distinctions, which emphasize different ways of dividing the cosmological hierarchy:

(i) The Brahma-and Deva-worlds together can be opposed to those below them. Here, in both Brahma- and Deva-worlds there is only spontaneous birth (*opapātika*), which is, *inter alia*, without sex. "Womb-birth," involving sexual reproduction,[8] is found only among humans, animals, ghosts and earth deities[9].

(ii) The Brahma-worlds can be opposed to the Deva-worlds, of which only the second is in the World of Desire. Beings in the Brahma-worlds have no gender, whereas those of the Deva-worlds do, as do all other beings in the Worlds of Desire.[10]

Brahmas in the lowest two or three groups of Brahma worlds, corresponding to the first, second and third Meditation Level, do experience kinds of physical pleasure, in the form of rapture (*pīti*), which can be very intense (see below). This pleasure, however, is what I am calling internal-mental, accessible through the individual introspection of meditational experience. Gods and goddesses in the Deva-worlds experience heightened and gendered sensuality of the external-sensory kind, but not genital, reproductive sexuality (unlike the earth deities living alongside

[8] There are a few exceptions which do not affect this point; e.g. Jātaka no. 540 cited in 4.1.c, where two human ascetics have a child without intercourse.

[9] There are various forms of birth, but the details are not relevant here. (See the texts cited in the next note.) The reason for the *asura*-s not having sex is probably that in pre-Buddhist Brahmanism, whence they were taken, they were classed along with the gods, as equal rivals. Hell-beings are without sex, I assume, both because that would be a form of pleasure inappropriate to hell, and because they spend all their time being physically tortured in various ways, and so don't have the time or opportunity.

[10] Vism 551ff. = 148ff., Vibh-a 160ff. The general picture is not without ambiguous exceptions. (Cf. n. 43 below for a comparable inconsistency in one text on the issue of sex in heaven.) At Vibh-a 52 women are said to be able to attain "companionship with the Brahma-parisajja gods" in the very lowest Brahma-world, but not with the Mahābrahmas; and it claims that although neither male nor female gender (*linga*) is present in the higher Brahma-worlds, it is possible to say that "a man is reborn" there, since Brahmas have the shape (*santhāna*) of men. Elsewhere, however, in such contexts (e.g. As 321) *liṅga* and *santhāna* are synonyms; and in the case of the Formless Worlds, there is no physicality at all, and so there could be no "shape." This is another case, all-too-familiar, where something unmarked for gender is assimilated to maleness.

humans.[11]) (The next section returns to the distinction between sensuality and sexuality in the Deva-worlds.) The sensual happiness of the Deva-worlds is inferior to the bliss acquired through monastic celibacy and meditation, both on earth and in the Brahma-heavens; but as beings outside the process of sexual reproduction they are higher in the cosmological-soteriological hierarchy than those in the (lay) Human and Subhuman Worlds. Their happiness is of the same kind as that enjoyed by (gendered and sexual) humans in fortunate circumstances, notably kings, but it is purer and more refined, inclining towards the less physical happinesses of the spiritual life.

4.1.b. Celestial pleasures in meditation

As has been said, and as set out in Table 4.1, the higher heavens of the Brahma-world are aligned with, and attained by means of the eight Meditation Levels (*jhāna*).[12] Rebirth in one of these worlds, as with rebirth in general, occurs because the content of the last moment of consciousness before death is something like an epitome of one's life, and gives rise to rebirth in a corresponding destiny (in one of three ways: see Collins 1982: 244–5). Thanks to this connection of consciousness, it is possible to imagine what the happiness of the Brahma-worlds is like by looking at accounts of what is experienced in the *jhāna*-s, since "there is no rebirth in the Brahmā world without *jhāna*".[13] The description of the sequence of *jhāna*-experience is standard, found in many texts.[14] The two most important words in the present context, whose meaning cannot be captured in translation are *pīti*, Rapture, and *sukha*, Happiness. Chapter 2.2.b cited Ñāṇamoli's (1975: 85–6) discussion of *pīti*, which he renders as "happiness"; in a valuable analysis, Cousins (1973: 120–2) chooses "joy" but concludes that *pīti* "must surely take its place in the list of terms best left untranslated" (see also

[11] For an example of an earth deity clearly intent on sexual pleasure, see the story of the monk Samiddhi and the goddess in 1.1.c.

[12] See Collins (1982: 215–18), the texts cited in the next note, and Vism I 99–200 = VII 18–9, 415–6 = XIII 33–5.

[13] Vism 415 = XIII 33, translated by Ñāṇamoli (1975: 456). For rebirth in the Brahma heavens through meditation (especially, but not only through the *Brahma-vihārā*, "Divine Abidings") see D I 251–2, Vibh 424–6 with Vibh-a 520–2, Vism 199–200 = VII 18, 372 = XI 123, et freq.

[14] Details given here are from D I 75ff. with Sv 217ff. and Sv-pṭ 340ff., M I 276–8 with Ps II 321–3, As I 15–8, and Vism 139ff. = IV 79ff.

Table 4.2 *Meditation Levels 1–4*

Level	Characterized by:
1	Applied and Sustained Thought, Rapture, Happiness
2	Rapture, Happiness
3	Happiness (of the body)
4	"Happiness" (in a specific sense)

Gunaratna 1985: 59–66.) Pali treatments of *pīti* are cited and discussed below. The rest of this section is a composite picture, made up from the texts cited in note 3. Some sentences are direct translations, others summaries or paraphrases. Table 4.2 schematizes the experiences of the first four Meditation Levels.

When a person in the preparatory stages of meditation realizes that the five Hindrances are destroyed in him,[15] delight (*pāmujja*) arises, (and) a gentle kind of Rapture (*taruṇa-pīti*, Sv-pṭ I 340) makes his whole body tremble with thrills of pleasure. As his mind is enraptured, his body is soothed; as his body is soothed he experiences Happiness; and as he experiences Happiness his mind becomes concentrated. Then, detached from (pleasures based on) desires and from unwholesome states of mind,[16] he enters into and remains on the first Meditation Level (= any one of the three lowest Brahma-worlds), which is characterized by Applied and Sustained Thought,[17] by Rapture and Happiness. Just as a skilled bathman or his apprentice might gradually sprinkle water on bath-powder in a metal dish and knead it, so that the powder, in a lump, becomes completely filled with moisture within and without, but no moisture drips out, so in just the same way the meditator drenches, saturates, fills and pervades his body with the Rapture and Happiness arising from detachment, and there is no part of his body whatsoever which is not pervaded with this Rapture and Happiness. Rapture here can be of five kinds: the minor, which is

[15] The unmarked masculine is used, which I follow, but the description applies to women meditators also.

[16] But not from all sensuality (see below): the terms are *kāma* and *akusala dhamma*, which are here associated with *rāga*, passion, and *lobha*, greed (Vism I 40 = IV 83; see Ñāṇamoli 1975: 145–6). The terms here refer to what are for Buddhism the baser pleasures, notably sex.

[17] *Vitakka, vicāra:* see Cousins (1992).

merely capable of making the hairs on one's body stand on end; the momentary, like flashes of lightning at different moments; the streaming, which breaks (into streams) whenever it streams down the body, in the same way as a wave breaks on a beach;[18] the exciting or uplifting, which can literally lift the body up into the air; and the suffusing or pervading, which fills the body like a bag filled by blowing (air into it)[19] or a rock-cave inundated with water.

On the second Meditation Level, he attains a unity of mind without applied and sustained thought, but Rapture and Happiness remain. The feeling of Rapture and Happiness over the whole body is of the same kind as that of the first Level, but here it is compared to an enclosed lake pervaded by the cool waters of an underground spring. According to a modern Burmese practitioner of meditation:

> There is a tingling sensation in every part of the body, much more pleasurable than any sexual experience, including orgasm. In orgasm, the pleasure is restricted to one organ, whereas this meditation pleasure suffuses the entire body; it is felt in all of one's organs.

Spiro (1971: 56), who cites this report, also quotes similar remarks from a psychoanalytic paper on Buddhist meditation by Alexander (1931), who draws on the canonical accounts of the *jhāna*-s as summarized by Heiler (1922) to speak of "a pleasure completely freed from the genitals, an orgasm diffused through the whole body" (1931: 134). I mention the comparison not because I find the psychoanalytic approach useful for explanatory purposes, but because a distinction made by Freud helps bring out the nature of the Rapture experienced in meditation. To take up again the discussion at the end of the previous section, there are three modes of physical pleasure possible in the Buddhist universe: those of

(i) gendered and sexual humans, animals, ghosts and earth deities;
(ii) gendered but nonsexually reproductive Deva-worlds, and
(iii) the ungendered and nonsexually reproductive Brahma-worlds corresponding to the first, second and third Meditation Levels.

[18] So CPD, s.v. *okkantika;* Ñāṇamoli (1975: 149) has "breaks over the body again and again like waves on the sea shore."

[19] *Dhamitvā pūrita-vatthi*; *vatthi* means bladder, but the reference to blowing suggests that the image here is blowing into a bladder removed from an animal's body and used as a bag.

The second and third modes here involve a heightened sensuality increasingly distant from genital sexuality,[20] which might be elucidated by analogy with Freud's concept of children's sensuality, which he labeled (somewhat perversely) "polymorphous perversity"; that is, the child's alleged capacity to experience sensual pleasure on every part of its body, which precedes the localization of pleasure onto the genitals and the reproductive sexual act. Such pleasure appears in a significant episode in the Buddha's biography. After renouncing the lay life, and practicing extreme self-mortificatory asceticism without finding what he was seeking, he remembered a time when, as a child under a tree while his father was plowing, he attained the first Meditation Level. The memory stirred in him the reflection that "I am not afraid of that Happiness which is free from (pleasure based on) desires and unwholesome states of mind" (M I 246–7). He decided to eat moderately, and so evolved the Middle Way between asceticism and sense-pleasure, which led to his enlightenment.

On the third Meditation Level, "because of the lack of attachment to (or, passion for) Rapture" (*pītiyā ca virāgā*), the meditator no longer experiences it, but only Happiness of the body, along with equanimity and mindfulness.[21] The body's being pervaded with this Happiness is like lotus flowers growing in water and drawing nourishment from it, with its moisture suffusing them from root to tip. Were the meditator not to remain vigilant, however, this Happiness of the third *jhāna* would revert to Rapture and become again associated with it (i.e. he would fall back to the second *jhāna*), just as an unguarded suckling calf taken away from its mother will always return to her. "Beings are [normally] passionate about [are attached to, *sārajjanti*; have *rāga* for] Happiness, and this Happiness [of the third level] is exceedingly sweet; there is no Happiness higher than this. But here [that is, when the meditator successfully remains at the third level] there is no passion for Happiness, thanks to the power of mindfulness and full-awareness" (Vism 163 = IV 174, As 174). According to the commentary here (Vism-a 145) Rapture, unlike Happiness, is characterized by cheerfulness (a word which elsewhere denotes

[20] There are almost no exceptions to this: see n. 43 on p. 323 below.

[21] There are some complications here which I pass over. This "body" is interpreted as "the mental body" during meditation, and as "matter born from consciousness" thereafter (see Ñāṇamoli 1975: 169 and 715–17).

smiling or laughing) and gladness (*pahāsa-odagya*), terms which are also among those used to define Rapture in the *Dhammasaṅgaṇi* (10 no. 9, etc.). A mind in a state of such Rapture on the second level is called gross, in so far as it is characterized by elation (*uppilāvitatta*, cp.CPD s.v.), and so the meditator passes to the third level, wishing to avoid such grossness. In the Happiness of the third level the only such element of grossness is the fact that one pays attention to one's Happiness; so the meditator abandons this and passes on to the fourth level (D I 37).

The relationship between Rapture and Happiness on the first three levels is quite precisely defined, at least in terms of lexical categories. (For what follows see Vism 145 = IV 100, As 117–8.) "Where there is Rapture there is Happiness, but where there is Happiness there is not necessarily Rapture." The presence of Rapture requires that a person feel passion for Happiness; in the absence of passion, as here in the third level, Happiness remains alone. Because of the active presence in Rapture of passion, it is included in the Aggregate of Mental Formations, whereas Happiness is classed in that of Feeling. Rapture can be compared to a man in a desert wilderness seeing or hearing water at the edge of a forest, and going towards it in a state of eagerness and delight (*hattha-pahattha*); Happiness is like his drinking the water and enjoying the forest shade.

In passing to the fourth level, the meditator first abandons joy and sorrow (*somanassa, domanassa*), then (explicit) Happiness and suffering (*sukha, dukkha*) – the two pairs are classed as mental and physical, respectively – and attains a state of equanimity, mindfulness and purity. The feeling here is called "without Happiness or suffering" not simply because these qualities are absent but as a third, independent category (Vism 167 = IV 193). The meditator suffuses his whole body with mental purity and cleanliness, like someone sitting down in a clean white robe with the robe touching every part of his body. As mentioned in 2.2.b, although (explicit) Happiness is absent at the fourth level, Happiness of a different sort (based on equanimity) is present. Sv 219 (cf. Ps II 323) and Sv-pṭ I 343–4 (citing Vibh-a 180), commenting on the simile, say that the Happiness of Equanimity here consists in "being suffused with (a sense of) refreshment" (*utu-pharaṇa*). The experience of this level cannot be called "happiness" in an ordinary sense; but since it is less gross, more subtle than the lower levels, it can be evaluated as a kind of happiness. The same thing is true of Happiness in the four higher Levels, numbers 5–8.

4.1.c. The Brahma-heavens in stories

The experience of Rapture and/or Happiness in the Meditation Levels and Brahma-worlds is intense and internal; not surprisingly, there are few depictions of these worlds from a visual or other sensory perspective, other than mention of beauty and brightness without a narrative context (e.g. Vibh-a 520). The Brahma-world which appears most in stories is that of the Ābhassara gods, parallel to the second Meditation Level, with both Rapture and (passion for) Happiness: the gods there are said to "feed on Rapture," and to be completely pervaded by Happiness. They cry *aho sukhaṃ*, "Oh (what) Happiness!" (D III 218); the commentary remarks laconically, "it seems that a great greed for existence arises in them."[22] Light flows from their bodies like (sparks from) the flame of a torch (e.g. Vibh-a 520, Mp IV 27). One text depicts human ascetics with no possessions and so nothing to worry about, saying that they are as happy as Ābhassara gods, since they spend their time in the Happiness of meditation (Ja VI 55). When the universe contracts at the end of an eon beings are reborn in that world; when it starts again to evolve, some beings in that world die and are reborn on earth (as in the *Aggañña Sutta*, translated in Appendix 5), and some are reborn in the world immediately below it. In one version where the latter is the case, the rebirth world is called "an empty Brahma-vimāna."[23] In a satire on Brahmanical cosmogonies, the story has it the first being to be reborn there, thanks to his karma, is for a while alone. He becomes lonely, and wishes for company; at that very moment other beings are reborn there also (due to their own karma). All of them, including the first, foolishly conclude that the first being is the Creator-God Brahmā, bringing beings into existence merely by his wish (D I 17ff., III 28ff.).

Although stories taking place within the Brahma-worlds are

[22] *Tesaṃ kira bhavalobho mahā uppajjati* (Sv 1001).

[23] See 4.1.d below on *vimāna*-s, which are heavenly dwellings and/or vehicles; the commentary (Sv 110) explains this as the level of the *Brahma-kāyika* gods, a term which usually refers to gods in the three Brahma-worlds corresponding to the 1st *jhāna*. See Vism 414ff = XIII 32ff., translated by Ñāṇamoli (1975: 456ff.).

almost non-existent, the ungendered immaterial or refined-sensual happiness of the Brahma-worlds can be relevant to other kinds of narrative. For example, two Jātaka tales (no. 263, Ja II 328ff. and no. 507, Ja IV 468ff.), the Lesser and Greater Birth Stories about Seduction (*Culla-*, *Mahā-palobhana-jātaka*) both describe the rebirth on earth of the future Buddha from the Brahma-world, as a prince surrounded by luxury. There being no desire in the world he has just left, he remains disgusted with it, and refuses any contact with women. He is called Anitthigandha, literally "he for whom there is no smell of women." As a baby he allows himself to be handled only by male servants, and drinks milk only from the breasts of women hidden behind a curtain or disguised as men, or which has been pressed out from a nurse. He passes his childhood in a meditation room. When he is grown his father wants him to marry, and has a young dancing girl successfully tempt him into desire with music and song. After the prince "learns the taste of desire" (*kāma-rasa*), he is driven by possessiveness to run amok, sword in hand, declaring that the girl is to be his alone. The king banishes them both, and they live in the forest. An ascetic flies in, is seduced by the girl and loses his supernatural powers. The prince realizes the dangers of desire, and thereafter lives a life of meditation, and becomes bound for the Brahma-world once more.

In another tale (Ja V 72–4, no. 540) two beings die from a Brahma-world and are reborn as boy and girl in two families of hunters; they are handsome and look like gold, and refuse to harm any living thing. Later, their parents want them to marry; but they both refuse, saying "What need have I for the household life?" Their parents celebrate a marriage nonetheless; but the two live together in celibacy, "individually, like Great Brahmas" (*mahābrahmāno viya ekato*). The king of the gods makes them a forest hermitage, and they both live there "developing the lovingkindness of the Sphere of Desire" (*ubho kāmāvacara-mettaṃ bhāventā*); thanks to this the animals and birds in the region live together in friendship and nonviolence. Later when Sakka discovers that they are going blind, he suggests that they conceive a child; when they refuse he provides one for them by having the future Buddha descend from heaven into the woman's womb, when the man merely touches the woman's navel with his hand (cp. Ja IV 377–8).

4.1.d. Stories of the Deva-heavens

The absence of stories taking place within the Brahma-worlds is due to the fact that experience there is internal and mental. Rapture and Happiness are in part located in the body in the lower Brahma-worlds and Meditation Levels; this is an internally experienced physicality which has no need of external, sensory input. The pleasures of the Deva-worlds, on the other hand, being external and sensory, presuppose a shared external world; and so it is possible to tell stories of events taking place in them. The Pali imaginaire has not missed its opportunity. A certain god, reborn in the Tāvatiṃsa heaven in the Sphere of Desire, is said to have wandered about in the Nandana park with a group of divine maidens, "enjoying divine sense-pleasures,"[24] and to have exclaimed (mistakenly, as the text goes on to point out) "Those who don't see Nandana don't know (what) happiness (is)!" The commentary (Spk I 30, on S I 5) explains that he had only recently been reborn in that world, with a body five miles high, the color of burnished gold; he made this declaration "wearing divine clothes, bedecked with divine ornaments, wearing divine garlands and perfumes, well sprinkled with sandalwood powder, (being thus) covered, inhibited and enveloped by the five kinds of divine sense-pleasure, overwhelmed by greed (*lobha*) not seeing that nirvana is the escape from greed." Unlike the Brahma-worlds, where the only greed is the "greed for existence," the Deva-worlds offer more immediately recognizable pleasures. Commentaries to the "Graduated Talk" (p. 299 n. 2 above) standardly describe the "Talk on Heaven" as a form of seduction.[25] Rebirth in Deva-loka heavens as well as in the worlds of humans, ghosts, animals and hell(s) is a product of the "corruptions" (*āsava*-s) of desire, (Craving for) continued existence and ignorance (A III 141).

In many stories which focus on the material rewards of merit-making rather than the value of celibacy, the heavenly Worlds of

[24] The adjective "divine" (*dibba*) here qualifies "the five kinds of sense-pleasure" (*pañca-kāma-guṇa*), a standard term for the pleasures of lay life; see Collins (1982: 269–70).

[25] E.g. Sv 472, Mp IV 101, Ud-a 283; cf. Bv-a 121–2. The verb is *palobheti*, a causative related to *lobha*, greed; it is used in the usual sense of English "seduce" of a man at Thī 387 and of women in general at Sn 703 (see Norman 1971: 39/143 and 1992a: 80/283 respectively). Horner (1978: 173) renders it "tempt."

Desire are depicted in enthusiastically sensual terms, without the need to compare them negatively either with the Brahma-worlds or with nirvana. The good deeds in question are often seemingly insignificant acts of generosity and morality, rather than grand and lavish displays. A few examples must suffice, showing the range of experience imagined; the most common motif in such contexts is that of brightness and visual splendor, produced most commonly by jewels and precious metals. (Recall that the root meaning of the word *deva* is to shine.) The *Vimāna-vatthu* and its commentary contain numerous stories of lay men and women making some religious gesture, usually giving alms on a small or more lavish scale, and thereby being reborn in a heaven, with a *vimāna.* As elsewhere in South Asian literature, this refers to something described both as a palace and a vehicle capable of flying through the air; the term is used here untranslated.[26] Thus at Vv VII 4 and Vv-a 302–3 a layman builds a "fragrant hut" (*gandhakuṭi*) for the Buddha on a mountain. He dies and is reborn as a *devaputta* in Tāvatiṃsa. "On top of a golden mountain a *vimāna* arose, indicating plainly the power of his karma: radiating a network of rays from various jewels, (it was) encircled with decorated railings, shining with many and various adornments; (it had) evenly proportioned walls, pillars and stairways, and a delightful pleasure park." The monk Moggallāna, on a tour of the heavens,[27] sees it and exclaims on its wonders to the young god: "On a mountain made of gold, shining on every side, the *vimāna* is covered with a network of gold and fitted with nets of tinkling bells. (Its) well-built eight-sided pillars are all made of beryl, each side fashioned with the seven precious things: beryl, gold, crystal, silver, cat's eyes [emerald and crystal], pearls and rubies.[28] Its painted floor is delightful – no dust flies up there! Many (golden-)yellow roof-beams have been fashioned to support the peaked roof. Four staircases have been made in the four directions; with rooms (made) of various precious things it shines like the sun. (Its) four railings are evenly proportioned and (well) laid-out in (every) part; they blaze out brilliantly

[26] See the entries for the word in PED and MW. A tree can be the *vimāna* of the earth deity living in it (e.g. Ja I 328, 442, IV 154).

[27] The theme of the traveler's tale, found often in this context in Buddhist stories, is a frequent motif in both medieval and modern European literature depicting the other world (heaven, hell, purgatory), and utopias.

[28] This list differs slightly from the usual, which is: gold, silver, pearl, gems, beryl, diamonds and coral.

in all four directions. (Even) in (such an) excellent *vimāna*, glorious *devaputta*, you stand out (clearly) with your luster, like the rising sun." Descriptions of this kind can be found throughout Buddhist story-literature; it can be taken as the standard image of heaven.[29]

Vimāna-s can be surrounded by gardens, trees, lakes, etc., in a mode of imagination clearly patterned on architecture and landscape, but they can also be moving vehicles such as a boat with a wish-fulfilling tree (Vv I 6–8) or a chariot (V 13–4). In the story of Sesavatī's *vimāna* (Vv III 7, Vv-a 156ff.), the monk Sāriputta returns to his mother's house, recompenses her for his upbringing by setting her on the Path, and then attains final nirvana in the very room in which he was born. Crowds come to do reverence to him, including Sesavatī, who brings perfume and flowers. One of the king's elephants runs wild, the crowd scatters in fear, and Sesavatī is crushed to death. She is reborn in Tāvatiṃsa as a goddess, but then comes back to earth to worship the Buddha: "accompanied by a thousand divine maidens, her body adorned with sixty cartloads of ornaments, illuminating the ten directions with her great divine supernatural power like the sun and moon, she went in her *vimāna* to salute the Teacher with her mind calm and trusting in the three Jewels. She got down from her *vimāna*, saluted the Blessed One and then stood with hands together." The monk Vaṅgīsa sees her, and describes her *vimāna*: it is "beautiful, a delightful well-fashioned dwelling, covered with nets of crystal, silver and gold, its surface painted in various colors, provided with arched gateways and strewn with gold. And as the sun in the autumn sky lights up the ten directions, dispelling the darkness with its thousand rays, so does your *vimāna* here blaze high in the sky, glowing like smoke-crested (fire) at night. Set pleasantly in the sky, it dazzles the eye like lightning. Resounding with *vīṇā*-s, drums, cymbals and gongs, it is as opulent as Sakka's city (in heaven). There are red, white and blue lotuses, blue waterlilies, Jasmine-trees, (red) Bandhukas and Anojakas, blooming Sal-trees and

[29] Such stories are found in many places: apart from the canonical texts, see, *inter alia*, the commentaries to the *Peta-* and *Vimāna-vatthu*, translated by Kyaw (1980) and Masefield (1989) respectively (the latter is made up almost wholly of such stories), the *Jātaka*-s (e.g. no. 541, Ja 116ff.), translated by Cowell et al. (1895–), the story sections from the *Dhammapada* commentary, translated by Burlingame (1921), the *Dasavatthuppakaraṇa and Sīhalavatthuppakaraṇa*, translated by Ver Eecke (1976) and (1980), and *Paññāsa-jataka*, translated by Horner and Jaini (1985) and Jaini (1986a). See also Appendix 4.

flowering Asoka-trees; it is filled with the fragrance of various excellent trees. A glorious, beautiful lotus-pond like a network of gems is near at hand for you, which has Salaḷa-, Breadfruit- and Bhujaka-trees, along with creepers in full blossom overhanging palm trees. Whatever flowers grow in water and whatever trees grow on land, in the human, nonhuman and heavenly (worlds), all these are found in your dwelling."

Other *vimāna*-stories depict music, song and dance. One, the "Great Chariot Vimāna" (Vv v 14, Vv-a 270ff.), borrows conventional descriptions from other South Asian poetic literature to emphasize the physical beauty of heavenly women. Moggallāna, touring the heavens, first exclaims to the god inhabiting a particular *vimāna* on its beauties and on those of the horses which pull it (e.g. the sound of their hooves and neighing is like music). He goes on to describe the retinue of women: "They stand in your chariot with gentle doe-like eyes, curved eyelashes, smiling and softly spoken, with networks of beryl over their exquisite skin, perpetually honored by gandhabbas [celestial musicians] and great deities. Clad attractively[30] in red and yellow garments, with wide eyes and red make-up, born in good families, elegant with white(-toothed) smiles, they stand ready in the chariot with hands together. (Wearing) golden bracelets and beautifully dressed, they are good looking, with slender waists, (perfect) thighs and breasts, well-formed fingers and fair faces, and stand ready in the chariot with hands together. Others, their hair well braided and cleverly interwoven with shining and well-arranged (garlands), stand ready in the chariot with hands together . . . Blown by the wind, the garlands and ornaments on their arms give out a charming sound, pure and beautiful, fit to be heard by all those who know (music) . . . [Music is also made by *vīṇā*-s, and divine maidens dance on lotuses.] When what is danced, played and sung comes together as one[31], the divine maidens dance here and fine women (standing) on both sides illuminate them. You are happy here, (with joy) awakened by the many musical instruments, honored as if you were [the king of the gods, Sakka]."

[30] The word is *ratta*; Horner (1974: 123) has "clad in red," Masefield (1989: 414) "impassioned"; the commentary (Vv-a 280) glosses as *rajanīya-rupa*, "with enticing appearance."

[31] *Sāmenti ekato*: Horner (1974: 124) has "seem all the same," which doesn't quite fit the mood; Masefield (1989: 415) has "mingle as one." The commentary (Vv-a 282) says this means when all three have the same "flavor" (*rasa*), referring to the Indian aesthetic theory of discrete artistic flavors or moods.

In other contexts, such descriptions of women might be connected with the idea of sexual enjoyment; but here, if this text is working with the usual understanding of gods in the Deva-worlds as sensual but not sexual, their physical attractiveness, one might say, is of an aesthetic rather than erotic kind. One must, I assume, interpret similarly a divine marriage in the forty-seventh story of the *Sīhalavatthu* collection, where three junior gods quarrel over a divine maiden (*accharā*) whom they all want; each one vies to prove his devotion to Sakka, but Sakka ends their quarrel by declaring his own love (*pema*) for her; she then follows him "to be his wife" (Sīh: 120). The word for "wife" here, *bhariyā*, means literally "one who is to be supported"; their relationship is, perhaps, a Platonic if sensually charged special friendship. At Ja VI 279 one reads of "divine girls seducing junior gods" (*devakaññāyo devaputta-palobhinī*); but it is not said what they entice them to do. In general, the enjoyments of the heavens are of a delicate kind; a partial exception is the mention in one *Jātaka* of the Āsāvatī creeper in the Cittalatā grove of the Tāvatiṃsa heaven. Its name means "full of hope," and it is so called because it bears fruit but once every thousand years; a "divine drink" comes from this fruit, which causes those who imbibe it to lie drunk on a couch for four months. Those junior gods who are addicted to drink have to endure their thirst for it for the thousand years, during which they return to the grove constantly to ask after the creeper's health (Ja III 250–1).

The "Discourse on Fools and Wise Men" (*Bālapaṇḍita-sutta*) of the *Majjhima Nikāya* (no. 129, M III 163ff.) depicts the bad consequences here and now of bad action, and those in the future such as life in hell and as an animal. The rewards of good action, likewise, occur both immediately (one has a good reputation and avoids punishment from the king) and in the future, through rebirth in heaven. When asked to give an analogy for divine happiness, the Buddha offers a standard description of the good fortune of a Wheel-turning King, who has Seven Jewels and four powers (6.5.a). The latter are physical beauty, long life, health and popularity; among the former is the "Jewel of a Woman." She is described as beautiful, "surpassing human appearance but not attaining the look of a goddess": the touch of her body is like that of cotton or silk, her limbs are warm when her husband is cold, cool when he is hot, her body has the fragrance of sandalwood and her mouth that of lotuses. But compared with the physical and mental happiness of the gods, this is like a tiny stone compared to the Himalayas.

4.1.e. Heaven and hell together, on earth and below: nāgas *and* petas

Heavenly pleasures can also be enjoyed at or below the human level by two kinds of being: nāgas, who are both snakes and a kind of "earth deity" (they can also take human form), and ghosts (*peta*-s, who are superior to nāgas on the scale of materiality, Vibh-a 12). They experience celestial happiness of the external-sensory kind, interspersed with hellish suffering. Nāgas can behave like ordinary snakes, often living in or around anthills, but they often live in palaces under water. In the "Birth Story about Campeyya" (Ja IV 454ff., no. 506), the future Buddha is reborn as a nāga-king, "with a large body like a wreath of jasmine." Seeing his animal body he feels remorse (for having previously desired to be reborn thus), and considers suicide. But a female nāga, thinking him to be Sakka, the king of the gods, leads a group of others in paying reverence to him, with music. "Then the nāga-dwelling became like Sakka's dwelling, and his thoughts of death abated. Discarding his snake-body he sat on a couch wearing all kinds of beautiful ornaments. From then on he had great glory as the ruler of the nāga-realm." He lives like this for a while, by turns acting religiously in the hope of leaving the animal world, but then being seduced back by the female nāgas. Later, when observing a Buddhist fast-day in the Human World, he is captured by a snake-charmer; later still, he is shown to the king, who learns that he is a nāga-king and asks to see his palace. The nāga-king builds in his palace a wall and watch-towers made of the Seven Jewels, and adorns the road leading to it; the palace is full of flowers, gold, various perfumes and trees, divine music and young nāga-girls dancing. When the human king arrives, he is given divine food and drink, which he and his entourage enjoy for seven days, "taking delight in divine sense-pleasures." Thereafter he asks the nāga-king why he wished to leave all this luxury, detailing the heavenly delights of the palace in familiar terms: it is a *vimāna* shining bright like the sun, there are beautiful girls, ponds with all manner of fine birds, trees, perfumes, etc. The nāga-king's answer is that purification and moral restraint are only possible in the Human World: "When I attain a human birth, I shall make an end of suffering." The human king is impressed, and leaves with many hundreds of cartloads of gold, silver and jewels.[32]

In this story happiness as a nāga is mixed with the misfortune that the Path to nirvana is not available to such a being. Other stories tell of male and female ghosts who despite living in a Bad Destiny have a *vimāna*, in which they experience divine happiness either for short periods alternating with periods of suffering, or simultaneously with it. Many of these stories have the *vimāna* out to sea, which is visited by human voyagers. In one story (Ja IV 2–3, no. 439, and cp. Ja I 239–40), Mittavindaka is an impious merchant, who goes to sea. Because of his misdeeds the ship is becalmed, and the sailors draw lots; Mittavindaka loses and is set adrift on a raft, after which the ship sails away. He comes to an island where he sees four female ghosts living in a crystal *vimāna*. They experience happiness for seven days and then suffering for seven. Mittavindaka enjoys seven days of happiness with them, after which they depart and he puts to sea again. He repeats the experience with eight female ghosts in a silver *vimāna*, and again with sixteen in one made of jewels, then with thirty-two in one made of gold. Thereafter he visits a hell, and learns of the harsh truth of karma. In another story (Ja V 2–3) a Brahmin judge accepts bribes and gives false judgments; but he does one good deed and is reborn, "like someone awakened from sleep," on an ornamented couch in a golden *vimāna* in the Himālayas, bejeweled and handsome, surrounded by sixteen thousand divine girls. He enjoys himself thus every night; but being a "ghost with a *vimāna*" (*vemānikapeta*) during the day his divine body disappears, to be replaced by one as big as a palm tree, constantly on fire. On both hands he has but one finger, with a nail like a big spade; with these he tears flesh from his own back and eats it, all the time screaming with pain.

In these stories, happiness and suffering alternate. In the next, this theme occurs along with that of a continuous blend of both. At Pv II 12 and Pv-a 151ff., a normally moral woman is enticed into adultery, but denies it when charged. Likewise five hundred other women are asked about her but deny her adultery. The adulteress is reborn as a female ghost with a *vimāna* in a mango grove on the

[32] Other Birth Stories with heavenly nāga-palaces are nos. 524, 543, 545.

shores of a lake in the Himālayas, with a lotus-pond. She experiences divine enjoyment during the day, but at night she is attacked and eaten alive by a ferocious black dog the size of an elephant; when he throws her body, now like a skeleton, into the lotus-pond she is restored and goes back to her couch in the *vimāna*. The five hundred women are reborn as her slaves; this is their only suffering, but after five hundred years of divine enjoyment without men they become dissatisfied. They float heavenly mango fruits down the Ganges, hoping that they will entice men to come in search of the fruit, with whom they can then enjoy pleasure. One fruit finds its way to the king's palace; he gives a piece of it to a condemned criminal to test, who exclaims at its divine taste. Eating a second piece his gray hair and wrinkles disappear and he becomes extremely handsome, like a young man. The king sends a forest-dweller in search of the fruit; at dawn he enters the mango grove, which is described in the usual paradisial terms – trees laden with fruit, birds singing, the grove shining with the radiance of various jewels. The women try to entice him, but he thinks he has not made enough merit to deserve such divine enjoyment and so returns to the king. The king goes there himself, and the women perceive him as a *devaputta* newly reborn. They bathe him, give him divine clothes, food, etc., and wait on him "according to his wishes." He spends 150 years in this manner; then one night gets up at midnight and sees the female ghost devoured by the dog. He kills the dog, and then questions the female ghost about her past, giving another elaborate description of the heavenly scene. She tells him her story and invites him to enjoy "nonhuman" pleasures with her. He does so, but comes to weary of it; he makes the female ghost take him back to his home; she does so unwillingly, because of her attachment to him, but gives him many valuable jewels. The king, inspired (*sañjātasaṃvega*), makes merit and becomes bound for heaven.

In this story the adulteress before the dog is killed resembles the female ghosts and the Brahmin judge in the stories just recounted, who oscillate between suffering and happiness at different times; later, when the king announces he will leave, the heavenly enjoyment cannot make up for her sense of loss. The other women suffer only in that they are her slaves; and after five hundred years they feel dissatisfaction. Thus they too combine suffering with heavenly enjoyment. Other stories show a similar blend: at Pv IV 1 vv.18–21 and Pv-a 215–16, for example, a trader is usually well behaved but on one occasion hides the clothes of some friends for fun. When he dies he is reborn as a ghost among the earth deities. Because of his acts of virtue he receives a divine white horse as swift as thought, his appearance shines in every direction, and his divine smell wafts everywhere, but because of his trick with the clothes, he is naked. In another, king Pāyāsi is converted to Buddhism and gives alms, but carelessly and of inferior quality. He is reborn as a spirit *(yakkha)* in the world of the Cātummahārājika gods, in an empty *vimāna*; however, thanks to the merit of a former inhabitant it has a grove of acacia trees outside the door, whose attractive and sweet-smelling flowers make it shine continuously.[33]

4.2. THE LAND OF COCKAYGNE

4.2.a. Continuous

One of the regular appurtenances of the heavens and heavenly *vimāna*-s is a wishing-tree (*kappa-rukkha*); like other celestial things and beings, wishing-trees shine (Pv-a 176). Modern ethnography reports that small images of wishing-trees are used in ritual (e.g. Bunnag 1973: 118). The Arahant Kapparukkhiya Thera declares that "(in the past) I made a wishing-tree of various (fine) cloths, and placed it at the excellent stūpa of the [former] Blessed One Siddhattha: in whatever birth (I have had since then), whether divine or human, a wishing-tree has stood shining at my door" (Ap 90; no. 40, 1–2). Food can be taken from such trees, but more usually it is garments and jewels, as in the story of Jotika (see below); at Vv-a 12 a goddess in the Tāvatiṃsa heaven wears jewel-like garlands coming from a wishing-tree and divine clothes from a wishing-creeper. One earthly place which has a wishing-tree is Uttarakuru, the northern continent of the Human World. Each continent has its special tree, which lasts for the whole eon: Jambudīpa (our world) has the Rose-apple tree (whence its name), Aparagoyāna to the West the Kadambara, and Pubbavideha to the East the Sirīsa (Mp IV 34). Uttarakuru is inferior to Jambudīpa in one crucial way: only in the latter is the

[33] Story at Vv VII 10 and Vv-a 331–52; cp D II 354–7, Vv VI 10 and Vv-a 297–9.

religious life of celibacy, *brahmacariya*, possible,[34] as is the appearance of Buddhas, and Wheel-turning Kings (Vv-a 18). But the people of Uttarakuru, taken as a whole, excel both other humans and the gods in unselfishness and lack of possessiveness (A IV 396, and see below). Their virtue, which comes naturally to them (Vism 15 = I 41, Vism-t 50), is displayed in a setting of abundance, especially of food; on occasion, such as during times of famine and hardship in Jambudīpa, non-Buddhist ascetics (e.g. Ja V 316) as well as the Buddha and his monks (e.g. Vin I 27–8, III 7) visit Uttarakuru to beg for alms: it represents a permanent possibility of sustenance. It is the standard of comparison for wealthy cities everywhere (e.g. Mil 1–2).

Uttarakuru is described in the *Āṭānāṭiya Sutta* of the *Dīgha Nikāya* (no. 32, D III 194ff.) by Vessavana, one of the four great kings (*cātummaharāja*-s), who lives there with a retinue of spirits (*yakkhā*). (He is also called Kuvera, as the text translated shows; this is the name, in Pali and Sanskrit, where it appears as Kubera, of the god of wealth. The legend of Uttarakuru as a land of perpetual abundance is found in other South Asian traditions.) He admits that not all spirits are well disposed towards the Buddha and his monks (indeed, in many stories they appear as ferocious, red-eyed, man-eating demons), and teaches the Buddha some protective verses to keep him and his followers safe from harm.[35] In them, it is asserted that beings in all four quarters revere the present and former Buddhas; in the case of Uttarakuru there is a detailed description: "In the region where pleasant Uttarakuru and lovely (Mt.) Neru[36] are found, human beings are born who are unselfish and not possessive.[37] They do not sow seeds or use plows, these people, (but) eat rice which ripens without cultivation. They cook (this rice), which is without powder, (already) husked, pure, sweet-smelling and ready for cooking,[38] on self-heating crystal

[34] A IV 396, Mp IV 188: but see below n. 43.

[35] The term is *rakkhā*; later the more usual *paritta* is used of them. (On this kind of text see Skilling 1992.) The verses describe the spirits as peaceful and friendly, and so one may regard these protection verses as euphemistic, in the original sense of the word.

[36] I.e. Sineru (Skt Meru). The commentary (Sv 964–5) says that the eastern side of the mountain is made of silver, the southern of gems, the western of crystal and the northern of gold; thus here *sudassano*, lovely or good to look at, means "of gold."

[37] The commentary, Sv 965, specifies that this means possessiveness about women. There is no selfishness such that a man says "This is my wife." When they see their mother or sister, no desire arises in them. See further on this below.

[38] *Akaṇo, athuso . . . taṇḍula-phalo. Kaṇa* is a fine red powder under the husk; *thusa* is the

stones,[39] then they eat it as their (only) food [i.e. they do not need to add curries or condiments to it: cp. Vism 418 = XIII 50]. They go everywhere on (vehicles pulled by) cows and other solid-hoofed animals. They make vehicles for women, men, young girls and boys,[40] who go everywhere (on them); mounting their vehicles they travel around, as the servants of their king. Their glorious king has a carriage pulled by elephants, one pulled by horses, a celestial carriage, a palace and a palanquin. They have built cities (which reach) up into the sky, Ātānātā, etc. [a euphonious list of names is given]; but the royal seat of the great king Kuvera, sir, is called Visāṇa, and so the king is named Vessavana. The ministers who proclaim his orders are Tatolā, Tattalā [another euphonious list of names is given]. Lake Dharaṇī is there, from which clouds (take water to) rain, from where the rains spread. There is the Bhagalavatī Hall, where the spirits do reverence (to the king). There are trees continuously bearing fruit, in which various flocks of birds swarm; (the trees) resound with the cries of peacocks and herons, along with pleasant-sounding cuckoos and the like.[41] There are birds which cry "Jīva" ("[long] life!"), and some which sing a five-note scale, [and other kinds of bird]."

The *Lokapaññatti*, a cosmological text probably translated from Sanskrit in fourteenth-century Burma, gives further details. In its tenth chapter there are a series of comparisons between the four continents and worlds of the gods. Some relevant remarks on Uttarakuru are, in the order given in the text, (Loka-p, pp. 68ff.) as follows: a newborn baby in Uttarakuru is like one of six months in Jambudīpa. Men in Aparagoyāna are one-and-a-half-times the height of those in Jambudīpa, those in Pubbavideha that much taller again, and those of Uttarakuru that much taller again. (Thus if an average height for adult males in our world were 5′9″, in Uttarakuru it would be over 19′.) People in the other three continents can be of various different skin-colors, but those in Uttarakuru are always white. Those in Jambudīpa trade in all

husk or chaff which grows around rice and corn; *taṇḍula* refers to husked rice (PED "ready for boiling'), so a cumbersomely literal rendering of *taṇḍula-phala* would be "having a fruit which consists in husked rice."

39 The commentary explains *tuṇḍi-kīra* as *joti-pāsāṇa*; at Dhp-a IV 209, in the story of Jotika's wife from Uttarakuru (see text below), the mode of cooking of these stones is described.

40 The commentary, followed by modern translators, takes the compounds here as meaning they make women, etc., into their vehicles, i.e. ride on their backs. This is bizarre and unnecessary.

41 Reading *kokilādīhi vagguhi.*

manner of things, both in goods and in animals, those in Aparagoyāna trade only in cows, those in Pubbavideha only in grain, but those in Uttarakuru do not trade at all. People in Jambudīpa and Aparagoyāna kill animals and eat their flesh, those in Pubbavideha do not kill animals but eat their flesh when they die naturally, people in Uttarakuru neither kill nor eat animals at all. In the other three continents corpses are taken out by people and either burned or abandoned, but in Uttarakuru none of this happens; there are birds to take away the dead, who carry them beyond the mountain and eat them there. People in the other three continents live in houses made from various materials, but those in Uttarakuru live in large trees called Mañjūsakas[42], which are shaped like houses. People in the other three continents take and give women in marriage, buying and selling them, but those in Uttarakuru do neither: when a man or woman desires someone, he or she looks at the other intently; if the latter does not see this, someone else tells her or him "He/she is looking at you"; then the two go off to be alone together. Denis (77: Tome II p. 82 n. 55) quotes from other texts which go into this further. The Pali *Chagati-dīpanī* says that they go to the foot of a Mañjūsaka tree: if they are an appropriate couple to make love, the tree hides them (by bending its branches and leaves down); if not, it remains motionless. In this case they conclude that they are not suitable for each other, and leave. (A related Chinese text [ibid.] specifies that they should not be relatives, either in the mother's or father's line.) Women in the other three continents conceive and give birth to children, and also nurse them; in Uttarakuru women conceive and give birth to children, but do not nurse them. When a child is born he or she is set out at a crossroads, and both the mother and other people then put their little finger into the child's mouth, and a nutritive juice comes out from it. Men and women live separately: when a child is seven days old it is taken to live with the appropriate gender group. (The similarity to the life of the Guardians in Plato's *Republic* is obvious and striking.) Finally, although in all four continents some people remain celibate all their lives, the number of times the others have intercourse varies: people in Jambudīpa do it innumerable times, in Aparagoyāna ten

[42] From *mañjusā*, treasure-chest; this is a very large tree, bearing all flowers that grow in land or water, and giving off celestial perfumes. See DPPN s.v.

times, in Pubbavideha six or seven, and in Uttarakuru four or five.[43]

Although in Uttarakuru itself women are not given and taken in marriage, women from there can marry humans on other continents. The "woman-jewel" of a Wheel-turning King, cited above as an analogy for the happiness of heaven, is either taken from the Madda clan in Jambudīpa, or comes to him of her own accord from Uttarakuru, because of the power of his merit (Sv 626, Pj I 173). A wealthy banker at Rājagaha, Jotika, who later becomes an Arahant, is also fortunate in this respect; and his story is worth telling at length, for the number of motifs it contains relevant to this discussion (Dhp-a 207ff.). On the day of his birth, all the weapons and jewels in the city shine, so that the city is a single blaze of light. When he reaches marriageable age, Sakka smooths out a great plot of land for him, and then commands that a seven-storey palace arise from the ground, built entirely of the seven precious

[43] In this list of comparisons between the continents and the heavens, the *Lokapaññatti* refers to marriage, sex and childbirth in the six heavens of the Deva-world, in three passages which are difficult to interpret together with absolute precision. I shall call them passages A, B and C; they occur, in the order A, C, B, at Loka-p 74–5. Passage A says that in all the heavens of the Deva-loka there is taking and giving of *accharā*-s in marriage; and that from Jambudīpa up to the Tāvatiṃsa heaven there is *duve indriya-samāpatti*, which Denis takes as "l'union des sexes". It goes on to add that in the four heavens above Tāvatiṃsa (see Table on p. 298) instead of *indriya-samāpatti* other things happen: in the Yāma heavens gods and goddesses merely embrace (*aliṅganti*), in the Tusita world they hold hands, in the Nimmāṇarati heaven they laugh (*hasanti;* or simply "are happy'), and in the Paranimmitavasavatti heaven they look deeply into each other's eyes (*cakkhunā cakkhum abhinijjhāyanti passanti*). If *indriya-samapatti* here does refer to sexual intercourse rather than some less specific "enjoyment of the senses" (a possible translation), then this passage contradicts what I claimed earlier is the usual view, that no gods apart from the earth deities have sex. (Note also that it is said here that celibacy is possible in Uttarakuru, a view denied elsewhere, as has been shown.) But this is a difficult question to resolve. In passage B, a little further on, it is said that the gods of all the heavens of the World of Desire, and not just those in the lowest two, *methunaṃ dhammaṃ patisevanti* innumerable times (like humans on Jambudīpa). This phrase usually refers to the act of intercourse, but since passage A has just specifically denied that this is true of the gods of the upper four heavens, in their case the phrase must here be metaphorical, or unspecified (*methuna* literally means just "pairing"). Passage C says that goddesses in all these heavens do not menstruate or give birth: babies simply appear on their laps, and they accept them as their children and look after them (for the week before they become adults). Thus if gods of the lowest two heavens are indeed being said in passage A to have sexual intercourse, passage C shows that this is entirely separable from childbirth (paradisial enough, I suppose, in the premodern world). Whether passage A is or is not saying that gods in the two lowest heavens have intercourse, in either case this account as a whole, passages A, B and C taken together, nonetheless delicately preserves the idea of sensual pleasure becoming more restrained as one goes up, literally, from the earth into the higher worlds of the World of Desire.

things (see p. 312). He then encircles the house with seven walls, with wishing-trees all around; he puts huge pots of treasure at the four corners of the house, along with stems of sugar cane made of gold, as thick as the trunk of a young palm tree, with leaves made of gems. A woman is brought to Jotika by deities from Uttarakuru, bringing with her a single small measure of rice and three crystal-stones. This feeds her, Jotika and their family for the whole time before he becomes a monk: whenever they want to eat, they put rice in a cooking pot on the stones, the stones burst into flame immediately, and then go out again when the rice is cooked. Whereas in Uttarakuru itself the rice is so good that it can be eaten without curries and sauces, here they do cook such things, but by the same method. They also use the crystal-stones for light, and never need fires or lamps. When people hear of Jotika's wealth, they come from all over Jambudīpa to see; he uses the rice from Uttarakuru to feed them, lets them take clothes and jewelry from the wishing-trees, and opens his pots of treasure for them to take what they need. They all do so, but the amount of treasure in the pots does not diminish even by a finger's breadth. Later, during a visit by king Bimbisāra, Jotika's wife stands near the king fanning him, and tears come to her eyes; Jotika explains that this is caused by the king's clothes, which have taken on the smell of the lamps he has sat by, whereas his wife has never seen the light of a flame or a lamp. Later, Bimbisāra is killed by his son Ajātasattu, who tries to take Jotika's wealth, but cannot do so. Jotika, roused (*uppanna-saṃvega*) by Ajātasattu's behavior, becomes a monk and attains enlightenment. The moment he does so, all his wealth disappears and deities take his wife back to Uttarakuru.

One aspect of the medieval Land of Cockaygne tradition in Europe, according to Morton (1952: 17), "infuriated the moralist" and earned it a bad reputation: the absence of work there. It was Lubberland, *Schlaraffenland*. But as he says (ibid.), "in a world where endless and almost unrewarded labour was the lot of the overwhelming majority, a Utopia which did not promise rest and idleness would be sadly imperfect." Absence of work is implicit in Buddhist stories of the heavens and Uttarakuru, although it is not normally emphasized. In one Jātaka story, however, the theme is explicitly recognized, and although there certainly is a moral to the tale, it is not that hard work is necessary, rather prudence. In the rather oddly titled "Birth Story of the Sea-merchants" (no. 466, Ja IV 159ff.), a thousand families of carpenters who take money advances for work which they can't do are forced to run away to sea. They come upon an island, in which there grow, spontaneously, rice, sugar cane, bananas, mangoes, rose-apples, breadfruit, coconuts, and other things. A shipwrecked sailor lives there; through eating the rice, sugar cane, etc., he has a large body; he is naked, with long hair and beard. The carpenters send some men to reconnoiter the island, and as they come ashore the man, who has just breakfasted and drunk sugar-cane juice, is happily lying on his back in the cool of the shade in a lovely spot where the sand is like silver plate. "Those who live in Jambudīpa plowing and sowing aren't as happy as this; my island is better than Jambudīpa!" he thinks, and sings joyfully a verse to that effect. The men hear him and go to see him. After assuring them that he is human, he declares that their arrival on his excellent island must be a result of their merit; he invites them to live contentedly there, where there is no need to work with one's hands, and one can simply live on the rice, sugar cane, etc. There is only one thing to fear: there are supernatural beings living there also, who are disgusted at the sight of human urine and excrement; they must always be careful to dig a hole in the sand and hide it. The families are in two groups, one led by an elder who is a foolish and greedy man, the other by one who is wise and not greedy. They all live there happily for a while, becoming big-bodied like the first inhabitant, but one day, because they haven't had any liquor for a long time they make some from sugar cane and get drunk. They dance, sing and play around, but in their forgetfulness urinate and defecate wherever they like, not hiding it. In so doing they make the island "disgusting and loathsome," and the deities get angry. They resolve to flood the island with sea water to clean it in two weeks' time, and in so doing kill all the carpenters. A moral (*dhammika*) deity decides to warn them. One evening, after their meal, as they are sitting talking happily at their doors, the deity appears in full regalia, and makes the whole island a single blaze of light; he tells them of the deities' plan, and advises them to leave. When he has gone, another deity, this time a cruel one, appears in the same way, but tries to persuade them that the first deity was lying, and just wanted to make them leave. The foolish and greedy carpenter and his followers believe him; the wise one suggests they build a ship, in case what the first deity said was true. The others ridicule the idea; so when the flood comes the wise carpenter and his followers escape, and the others are drowned.

4.1.b. Occasional

Such abundance as is permanent in Uttarakuru or on the desert island of the last story, or which is held for a long time as by Jotika, can also occur for short periods, on special occasions. The commentary to the *Buddhavaṃsa* (Bv-a 79ff.) says that certain miracles always occur on four occasions: at the moments of conception and birth of a future Buddha, and at those of his enlightenment and Preaching of his First Sermon. The following are among the events which took place at the birth of the former Buddha Dīpaṅkara: the entire universe trembled and quaked, drums and *vīṇā*-s played sweet music by themselves, fetters everywhere were broken, all illnesses went away spontaneously, the blind could see, the deaf could hear, the dumb talk and the lame walk. Ships traveling abroad quickly reached their destination, all precious things (jewels and metals) in the sky and on earth shone, the fire in the Niraya hell went out, the water in rivers flowed (smoothly) and a glorious light shone in the space between worlds. The surface of the ocean was extremely calm and its waters sweet, no heavy winds blew, and trees were covered in bloom. The moon and stars shone more brightly than usual, and the sun was not too hot. Birds came down from mountains and trees to share in life on the ground below, and a cloud covering all four great continents rained gently. Gods and goddesses in their heavenly homes danced, sang and played music, crying out with joy and making merry, while ordinary people on earth suffered neither hunger nor thirst. Animals who were usually enemies felt great love for each other: crows joined with owls, dogs played with wild boars, snakes with mongooses, and mice took hold of cats' heads with confidence. All living things spoke to each other in a kindly way, and the entire universe was filled with divine perfumes and garlanded with delightful flags.[44]

[44] See Appendix 4 for comparable events which will occur just before the birth of the next Buddha Metteyya. Ja I 51, translated in Jayawickrama (1990: 68), and Jina-c vv.92ff., text and translations in Rouse (1904–5) and Duroiselle (1982), tell of similar events at the birth of Gotama.

Almost as important an occasion as the birth of a Buddha, in world-historical terms, is the consecration of a Wheel-turning King, and especially emperor Aśoka in the third century BC The *Mahāvaṃsa* (Mhv V 24ff.)[45] says that when Aśoka was consecrated king some of the gods brought water from lake Anotatta, a lake in the Himālayas whose water is always clean and cool, along with thousands of teeth-cleaning sticks from the nāga-creeper which is found there, and medicinal myrobalan and gallnuts, and ripe mangos of excellent color, smell and taste; others brought clothes of different colors and a divine drink from lake Chaddanta (also in the Himālayas). Moribund deer, pigs and birds in the city came of their own will into kitchens (either everyone's or perhaps just the king's) and died there; tigers herded cattle and brought them to their pens, and people's fields, farms, reservoirs, etc. were guarded by wild deer and boars.[46] Nāgas brought from their *vimāna* fine cloth, perfumes, unguents, and flowers; and parrots brought ninety thousand cartloads of rice from lake Chaddanta: mice removed the husk and powder without damaging the rice. Bees made honey, and bears worked as blacksmiths, swinging hammers in forges, while delightful honey-voiced cuckoos sang sweetly.

The struggle for food and comfort can be suspended on less *welt-geschichtliche* occasions. In the sixty-seventh story of the *Sīhalavatthu* an Arahant who has lived thirty years in a great forest, supported by just one family from a village, attains nirvana. Sakka has a five-sided peaked pavilion made for him out of the seven precious things; for the seven days of his funeral ceremony and then for three days more, divine sandalwood and leaves from various celestial trees rain down; every tree which is big enough carries a flag of divine cloth, and celestial instruments play. Gods and men can see each other (gods are usually invisible); people are not afflicted

[45] The introduction to the commentary on the *Vinaya*, written at the same time and drawing on the same materials, has a closely similar version (Sp 42ff.); see Jayawickrama (1962: 37–8).

[46] These two verses are found only in some mss., and are not found in the commentary, written probably around the tenth century; Geiger (1908: 31) printed them only in the critical apparatus and labeled them "spurious." For my purposes, although it is likely that they were not written by Mahānāma, it is enough that somewhere in the tradition they were seen as an appropriate addition. The first verse provides a striking parallel with the European Land of Cockaygne – where *inter alia* geese fly roasted on spits and larks fly into people's mouths dressed in a tasty stew (Morton 1952: 16, 220).

with hunger or thirst, excrement or urine (Sīh 144–5). In this tale, abundant sensory delights are complemented by the absence of hunger and thirst, rather than the provision of unlimited food; in other stories, nature (stimulated by supernatural forces) unleashes abundance. At the beginning of the story of Aṅkura and the ghost (Pv-a 112ff.), for instance, a man is reborn as a spirit (*yakkha*) in a tree, with a right hand which grants all objects of desire (*kāmadada*): it is "all golden, dripping with honey, bearing five (fingers which give what one desires), with various tastes flowing from it" (v.11). Aṅkura is a merchant who travels with five hundred carts of goods, along with a Brahmin also with five hundred carts. They get lost in a wilderness without water, and exhaust their supplies, but then come on the spirit's tree. It is very tall, with dense foliage, and so affords much shade; they pitch camp underneath it, and the spirit stretches out his right hand and gives them first water, and then whatever food and drink they desire.

Finally, whereas in Aṅkura's story the spirit's generosity is motivated by a previous good turn Aṅkura had done him, in the story of Niggardly Kosiya[47] (Dhp-a I 367ff., Ja I 345ff.), the supernatural power of Moggallāna and the Buddha teach Kosiya a lesson. Kosiya is a mean banker in Sugartown (*sakkharaṃ nāma nigama*), who has millions but neither gives anything away nor enjoys anything himself. His wealth is useless, "like a lotus-pond surrounded by demons." Coming home from the king's palace one day, he sees a hungry man in the countryside eating a cake, and starts to feel hungry himself. Reaching home, he is afraid to ask openly for a cake since he thinks that will bring many others asking for food, which he will have to pay for; he stays silent, becomes pale and emaciated, and is forced to retire to bed. His wife asks what is wrong, and finally elicits from him the acknowledgment that he wants to eat a cake like the one he had seen the hungry man eat. She exclaims that with their wealth they could feed all Sugartown, but is told "What of them? Let them work for their own food." She offers to make food (and is refused) for fewer and fewer people, finishing with just the two of them and then at last just Kosiya himself. He makes her hide with him in a room on the seventh

[47] This is Burlingame's (1921: vol. 2, pp. 49ff.) rendering of *Macchariyakosiya*. Cowell et al. (1895: 145ff.) have "Millionaire Miser."

floor while she cooks a cake for him from broken grains of rice, with a little milk, ghee, honey and molasses. The Buddha is aware of all this, and sends Moggallāna to bring Kosiya, his wife and the food she has cooked, back to him. Moggallāna goes there, and uses magic to force Kosiya to agree to give him one small cake; but each time a small piece of cake mixture is put in the pot, it becomes huge and overflows. Finally Kosiya tells his wife to give the monk one cake, even if it has to be a big one, to get rid of him; but she finds all the cakes are stuck together. When Kosiya in despair tells her to give him all the cakes, Mogallāna preaches to them both and converts them. They return to Rājagaha magically, where the cakes feed the Buddha, five hundred monks, Kosiya and his wife; when all the monks in the monastery and even the scavengers who eat scraps have eaten their fill, there is still much left over. The remains are thrown onto a hill by the city gate, which is then known as "Cake Hill."

4.3. ARCADIA

In the stories recounted in 4.1.d and 4.2, the problems of scarcity and competition are overcome by sheer abundance, with some exceptions such as the unselfish people of Uttarakuru, or those stories where hunger and thirst are absent rather than satisfied. I group together the materials in this section under the general label Arcadia: they portray an idyllic situation in which scarcity and competition are resolved by people, usually ascetics or Buddhist monks, reducing their desires and living in peace, in natural settings which are fruitful but not exuberantly abundant.

4.3.a. Paradise in the forest

The association of religious life with the forest is ancient and ubiquitous in South Asia. Forests are seen both as difficult places where a harsh ascetic life must be endured, but also as places of natural beauty enabling a life of simplicity and ease. Frequently it is the very practice of asceticism which transforms the forest from the first to the second.

In the verses of the nun Subhā (Thī 366ff.), she recounts the story of an attempted seduction by a man "on the way to Jīvakamba wood," which she repels by rather drastic means. The man praises the beauty of her eyes so much that she takes one out of its socket and gives it to him; "His passion ceased immediately," she recalls (v.397). At the outset of their conversation the man simultaneously evokes the beauty of the forest and its dangers (if she goes there alone): "You are young and pretty – what can asceticism do for you? Throw away your yellow robe: come, let's enjoy the wood (while it is) in blossom. The towering trees waft a sweet (scent) everywhere; the first (days of) spring are a happy season: come, let's enjoy the wood in blossom. When the wind rustles the flowering peaks of the trees it's as if they cry out with joy: what pleasure will there be for you if you go down to the wood alone? Do you want to go (there) without a companion, to that lonely and frightening great wood, where there are hordes of beasts of prey, and which is disturbed by she-elephants excited by their bulls? [If you come with me] you will be like a shining (golden) statue, like a divine maiden (an *accharā*) strolling in the Cittaratha park (in the Tāvatiṃsa heaven)" (vv. 370–4). The same combination of the forest as simultaneously dangerous and comfortable is found elsewhere, notably in the *Vessantara Jātaka* (see below), where the hardships endured in the forest by Vessantara, his wife and children oscillate as the narrative progresses with evocations of the forest as a natural paradise providing the perfect setting for Vessantara's virtue. In the *Mūgapakkha Jātaka,* when prince Temīya enters the forest with almost all the population of his father's kingdom, it is specifically said that they build a hermitage where the huts for women are in the centre, protected by the men's all around (6.2; cf. the "Birth Story about Hatthipāla" below).

The motif of the pleasant forest hermitage occurs in innumerable stories in the *Jātaka* collection. Often the notion is introduced simply in a formulaic phrase: a pleasant spot (*manorama bhūmibhāga*), an attractive forest grove (*rāmanīya vanasaṇḍa*) or an attractive region of the Himālayas (*rāmanīya Himavanta-padesa,* e.g. Ja III 31, 64, 110). On occasion longer descriptions of sylvan beauty are offered. In the *Kuṇāla Jātaka* (no. 536, Ja 412ff.)[48] the Story of the Past is introduced by the following

[48] This *Jātaka* is unusual in that it has a commentary on the prose section, including this description, which is written in a poetic style, with long compounds, unusual for the *Jātaka*-s. The translated section is at Ja V 419–20, Bollée (1970: 13–5); the translation is Bollée's (ibid. pp. 126–7).

words: "On the eastern side of this very Himavat, king of mountains, there are (rivers) that have their origin on slight and gentle mountain-slopes, in a place (covered) with blue, white and red lotuses and [many other flowers and trees: a long list is given, elaborated in the commentary], adorned with flowering runners of the *atimuttaka* creeper. This is a region resounding with the cries of geese, *pilava* ducks, *kādamba* geese and *kāraṇḍava* ducks, inhabited by a great number of *vijjādhāras* [sorcerers] and *siddhas* [magicians], recluses and ascetics, haunted by the best of deities, spirits (*yakkha*-s), [other semi- or super-natural beings], and big snakes – now then in such a delightful jungle thicket there lived a spotted cuckoo named Puṇṇamukha who was very sweet-voiced and whose eyes moved to and fro in a lively way."

The heightened but delicate sensuality of such places, which are often compared to the celestial worlds, is on occasion infused with sexuality. In Story no. 30 of the *Sīhalavatthu* (Sīh 68ff.), a woodsman at the time of Aśoka gets lost in a region of the Himalayas where there are many flowers, fruits, animals and nonhuman beings, and comes across the forest dwelling of an ascetic who lives on roots, leaves and fruits. One day, despite the ascetic's warning not to go to a certain pond, he does so. He finds an excellent pool, four-sided, with staircases and without mud, surrounded by sweet-smelling flowers, whose water is pure and cool, etc. (That is, it is both hypernatural and the result of artifice, like a swimming pool.) He sees a group of *kinnarī*-s bathing and playing there,[49] looking just like young goddesses. Smitten with passion, he returns to the ascetic's hut and mopes in the fire-room. The ascetic returns, and discovers the problem; he gives an elaborate and detailed description of their bodies, and tells the woodsman that such divinely beautiful creatures are not to be seen by someone with an unsteady mind. (The implication, of course, is that the ascetic can look at them without fear since his mind is steady.) Although he contrasts the touch of their bodies, which is delightful like cotton wool, with that of the woodsman's, rough like a pig's hide, he tells him how to catch one. The woodsman does so, and she becomes his wife, bearing him two children.

[49] *Kinnara*-s and *kinnarī*-s are semidivine bird-men and -women, just as nāgas are "snake-people."

The "divine" nature of forest hermitages is often a result of the fact that they are made by Sakka's workman (the king of the gods), Vissakamma.[50] As a god, Vissakamma is invisible, and so from the human point of view his ready-made hermitages spring from nothing. In the "Birth Story of Hatthipāla" (Ja IV 489–90, no. 509) Sakka tells Vissakamma to go and build a large hermitage, since the young prince is renouncing the world, along with most of the inhabitants of Benares. He makes one "by his divine power . . . in a pleasant spot on the banks of the Ganges," with seats and beds strewn with twigs and leaves, and provided with all the requisites for a renouncer. At the door of each leaf-hut he puts a meditation walkway, with a coating of cement and a flat board to rest against. Here and there are blossoming bushes covered with fragrant flowers of various colors, and at the end of each walkway there is a water tank with a fruit tree next to it: each tree bears all manner of fruits. As is usual in such cases, Vissakamma writes a message on the wall: "Anyone who wishes to renounce may take these requisites." He banishes from the area all frightening noises, and all fierce birds and beasts, and all nonhuman beings. The prince finds the hermitage and the message, and settles down there, putting a hut for women with young children in the middle, one for older women next to it, one for childless women next to that, and all around them huts for men.

On more than one occasion, a visitor to a forest hermitage greets the one who dwells there with the polite inquiries, "I hope you are well, sir; I hope you are in health, sir; I hope you can live by gathering food and that there are roots and fruits in plenty. I hope that there are few gadflies and mosquitoes and creepy-crawlies. I hope that you meet with no harm in this forest thronged with wild beasts."[51] The reply is always in the positive: and this can scarcely be thought to be by good luck. A recurring motif in these contexts is that of animals being calmed and aggression pacified by the virtue of an ascetic. This theme has already been exemplified, in the stories of the two beings from the Brahma-world who marry but live in celibacy, and of the conditions obtaining at the time of a Buddha's birth (4.2.b above). In the earliest canonical texts one finds the idea that protection from snakes can be got by

[50] This character goes back to the Brahmanical Vedas, where he appears as Skt *Viśvakarma*, "the All-maker."

[51] Ja V 323, VI 532, 542; translation from Cone and Gombrich (1977: 50, 55).

practicing the meditation on lovingkindness, or friendship (*mettā*) towards them, and by reciting protective verses to them.[52]

This motif, and many others of paradise in the forest (which is one of the most common themes in the Jātaka stories), can be exemplified by the *Vessantara Jātaka*, which is, as mentioned in the General Introduction, perhaps better known in Buddhist cultures than even the story of Gotama Buddha's own life (see Chapter 7 p. 497). Often known simply as *Mahājātaka*, the "Great Birth Story," it tells of events in the penultimate human birth in the sequence which was to become Gotama Buddha, when he brought to perfection the virtue of giving; thereafter he was reborn as a god in the Tusita heaven, before his last and final birth as Siddhattha Gotama. The overall story, parts of which were mentioned in the General Introduction, is this: Vessantara, crown prince of the Sivis, practices almsgiving on a lavish scale. One day he gives away the state elephant, and the people angrily demand that he be banished from the kingdom. His father, Sañjaya, accedes to their wish and after discussions between the family members, who include Vessantara's wife Maddī and his mother Phusatī, Vessantara goes with Maddī and their two children to the Himalayan forest. Living there as an ascetic, he gives away his children to a Brahmin, and then his wife, to Sakka disguised as a brahmin. Sakka gives her back, and the children are ransomed by Sañjaya. The Sivis have a change of heart towards Vessantara, and his parents go to the mountain forest with a huge retinue to recall him. After a scene of reconciliation he reenters the city as the newly crowned king. Chapters 5 and 7 have a great deal more to say about this story, but here I concentrate on attitudes to the forest, and events in it, showing the regular oscillation between what one might call, for brevity, the bad forest and the good forest, with the latter predominant.

When Vessantara first tells his wife of his banishment, the forest is bad: he says, "I go to the terrible forest, infested with fierce wild beasts. My life is at risk alone in the great forest" (495/18)[53]. Maddī insists she will go with him, and in a long series of verses,

[52] Vin II 108–9, A II 72–3, cp. Ja I 144ff. For further references to ascetics living with animals, in a comparative context, see Collins (1988: 110–11 and n. 46).

[53] In what follows I give two references, one to the page number of the Pali text and one to that in Cone and Gombrich (1977), from where all translations are taken (see Chapter 7 n. 5).

tries to persuade him that their life will be good (496–7/19–20). Some examples: "Seeing the children, sweetly chattering with their dear voices, playing in the lovely hermitage, you will forget kingship . . . When you hear the murmur of the river as it flows, and the singing of the fauns, you will forget kingship . . . When you see the peacock with its tail-feathers dancing on the heights surrounded by the peahens, you will forget kingship . . . When you see the trees blossoming in the winter, spreading their fragrance, you will forget kingship." He agrees to her accompanying him, and they go to ask permission of his parents, who accept that Vessantara should "endure this misfortune in the forest," but are disinclined to let Maddī go. The king lists "the unbearable things there are in the forest": they include mosquitoes, snakes, bears and other fierce animals. "Even at midday when the birds are settled down together, the great jungle is full of noise. Why do you wish to go there?" (506–7/28). Maddī insists, saying that the life of a widow is even worse. Sañjaya then tries to keep the children, but Maddī says "They will bring pleasure into our sorrowful life in the jungle" (509/30). Despite the king's detailing all the fine things the children are used to and will lack in the forest, it is agreed that they will go too. On the journey, the children see fruit trees and cry to have the fruit. The trees, hearing them, bend down of their own accord, "by the power [*tejas*] of Vessantara"; moreover, "out of pity for the children spirits [*yakkha*-s] shortened the road" (513–4/34). They stay briefly in the kingdom of the Cetans, who describe the journey they still have before them, and the destination. "And then, most honored sir, you will see lovely Mount Vipula with its cool shade, densely covered by clumps of trees of many kinds . . . [Later] you will see, most honored sir, a lovely banyan tree, with fruit sweet as honey, growing on a pleasant crest and giving cool shade . . . When you have passed the difficult terrain of the mountain, and the sources of the rivers, you will see a lotus-pond surrounded by karañja and kakudha trees, its copious waters between accessible banks thronged with fish like the finny carp. It is regular and square, sweet and fragrant. Build a leaf-hut to the northwest of that, and when you have built it, busy yourselves with gathering food." When they reach the lotus-pond, Sakka asks Vissakamma to go and build them a hermitage; he does so, with two leaf-huts, covered walks, flowering shrubs here and there, etc., writes his usual message and drives away all spirits, wild animals and birds whose cries are frightening. Vessantara and his family settle down there, and "because of the power of the Great Being's friendly sympathy, even the animals for three leagues in every direction began to live in harmony with one another" (519–20/39–40).

The narrative now switches to Jūjaka, the henpecked and ugly Brahmin who is to be given the children. On the journey, "urged on by his wife, greedy for his pleasures, the Brahmin endured hardship in the forest, the home of fierce wild beasts, the haunt of the rhinoceros and the leopard" (525/45). Chased up a tree by dogs, he describes Vessantara himself as a kind of paradise: "He is like the earth, for he is a refuge for those in need . . . like the ocean, for those in need go to him, as rivers flow to the sea . . . like a lovely lake, with cool water that is good to drink, and beautiful fords, its surface dotted with lotuses and sprinkled with pollen from their filaments," and like various trees which ease the fatigue of the weary with their shade (526/45–6). Jūjaka meets a Cetan hunter, who describes the life of Vessantara as an ascetic in the forest, in an extended passage called in the text the "Short Description of the Forest." It is full of the now familiar motifs: trees in bloom and fragrant, "cuckoos intoxicated with the liquor of the blooms [who] make the mountainside resound to their sweet singing," fragrant breezes and trees looking as if they were hung with bright banners; and amidst all this Vessantara, "looking like a Brahmin with his matted hair and garment of animal skin, with his hook and sacrificial ladle, sleeping on the ground and reverencing the sacred fire" (528–32/47–50). Jūjaka next meets a real Brahmin ascetic, Accuta, who gives another description of Vessantara's life in the forest. This is similar to the previous one, full of paradisial motifs, but very much extended: it occupies eight pages of the Pali text (532–40). A few examples: "Thronging among the branches and foliage [najjuha birds and cuckoos] call out to the passer-by, delighting the newcomer, giving pleasure to those who live there . . . There glides flowing water, pure and fragrant, the color of lapis lazuli, thronged with schools of fish. Not far from there in a spot as entrancing as the gods' Nandana Grove is a lotus-pond with a covering of white and blue lotuses . . . Here is a narrow footpath which leads straight to the hermitage. Reaching there a man knows no hunger, no thirst, no discontent, there where the king Vessantara lives in peace with his children" (534, 539/52–3). The botanical and zoological detail here, in what the text calls the "Long Description of the Forest," is mind-boggling; I think deliberately so. Cone and Gombrich omit forty-two verses, which are made up largely of the names of plants, trees and birds, relegating them to an appendix. They suggest (77: v) that "this tedious botanical catalog, inserted before the story's climax, may well have built up suspense in an audience already familiar with the plot, but can only dishearten the solitary reader." Their editorial decision was correct, and I agree that building up suspense is one function of the list. But from the present perspective this "catalog" can also be seen to build up a sense of encyclopedic profusion, emphasizing and intensifying the sense of miraculous fertility and abundance surrounding the virtuous Great Being in his forest paradise.

After the children have been given to Jūjaka, Maddī returns, her way home having been barred by gods disguised as wild animals. She laments their absence, contrasting the pain of that with the beauties of the forest and the hermitage where they used to play: "Always before this hermitage has looked to me like a fairground, but today, when I cannot see my children, the hermitage seems to be spinning round" (559/69). In the remaining parts of the story, other paradisial and utopian motifs are found (7.5). Here it suffices to mention three more scenes. First, when Sañjaya and the children go with the army to the mountain forest to recall Vessantara, Maddī sees the children for the first time. Already, in the scene where she discovers the children are gone, she says "My breasts are full, my heart bursts" (559/68); now, some time later, "When Maddī saw the children in the distance, and knew they were safe, quivering like the goddess of drink, she sprinkled them with streams of milk from her breasts. She trembled, and with a loud cry fell senseless, and lay stretched on the ground. The children rushed up to her, and they too fell senseless on top of their mother. At that moment two streams of milk flowed from her breasts into their mouths, and if they had not received so much relief, the two children must have perished, their hearts parched" (586/90). Vessantara also falls senseless, as does everyone else. To revive them, Sakka sends down a shower of rain. It is as if nature itself (with some aid from the divine world) is responding to the depth of emotion in the scene with its own life-giving strengths. Second, when Maddī has recovered, and has been bathed and clothed in jeweled finery, "that best of princesses shone with the radiance of a goddess in Nandana" (590/94). Finally, before they return to the city Sañjaya organizes a month-long festival of forest sports. While these are going on "no wild animal or bird in the great jungle harassed anyone" (591/94); they all came to witness Vessantara's departure, in peace and silence.

4.3.b. Monastic simplicity

In stories of life in the forest ascetics are commonly said to live on roots and fruit. Practical considerations obviously play a part in this, but on occasion other reasons are given. In some accounts of Sumedha's life as an ascetic he is said first to receive ordinary food as alms from people, but then to give it up: in the *Jātaka-nidāna* version (Ja I 10), this is because, he says, "This greasy food gives rise to intoxicating feelings of pride and virility. There is no end to the suffering arising from food. I should give up all food derived from grain which is sown and cultivated, and subsist on fruits that come my way." The commentary to the *Buddhavaṃsa* (Bv-a 78) adds another reason: Sumedha goes to live at the foot of a tree – which is good for one who is solitary (*pavivitta*) since it curbs envy in regard to dwelling place, and the fallen leaves dispel the perception of permanence – and gives up food derived from grains, eating only fruit that has fallen naturally from trees; "content (*santuṭṭha*) with wild fruits, living independent of others, without greed for food, (such a person) is a sage of the four quarters."

The qualities of being solitary and being content (with little) are standardly combined with others, such as "having few wants" (*appiccha*) and "not being gregarious" (*asaṃsagga*), in descriptions of the lifestyle of ideal monks in the here-and-now, not only in stories of long ago and far away.[54] I have tried to show elsewhere (Collins 1988), in a comparison with early Christian monasticism, that these qualities of self-sufficiency (to use the Greek idea,

[54] For references, see especially PTC and CPD s.v. *appiccha*, *asaṃsagga*, and PED s.v. *santuṭṭhi*. The last, "contentment," is often used of a monk's accepting happily the simple life of monasticism (e.g. Spk I 122, Mp I 78–80; cf. Collins 1988: 111–12); but he can be discontented even with such good (*kusala*) states, in the sense of wanting to progress further (Dhs 234 no. 1367): the commentary here (As 407) spells out the ideal advance in contentment, from pious laymen to ordained monk to Arahant, and says that it is only from the time of attaining Arahantship (that) he is said to be greatly or completely content (*mahā-santuṭṭho*).

autarkeia) combine with the virtue of friendship[55] to provide the ethical and psychological basis of the ideal monastic life. Thus the monk who has these qualities is as free as a bird: "He is content with sufficient robes to protect his body, and sufficient alms-food to sustain his stomach. Wherever he goes, he takes (these qualities) with him as he goes – just as a bird on the wing takes its wings with it wherever it flies. Thus is a monk content" (e.g. D I 71). Monks who possess these virtues live harmoniously. Earlier I cited a common form of greeting to ascetics in the forest, asking about mosquitoes, etc. There is an analogous form of greeting for monks living in communities, whether in the forest (as is the case in the example given next) or not. Three monks were living together in a wood not far from the town of Nādika, where the Buddha was staying at one time. He went out to the wood after evening meditation to converse with them. At the entrance to the forest the "forest-keeper" (*dāyapāla*) stopped him: "Don't enter the wood, ascetic, three [monks] are living there seeking their own (highest) good." But one of the monks, Anuruddha, heard him and told him to let the Buddha come in. The Buddha greeted him:

"I hope that you are all keeping well, Anuruddha, that you all are comfortable, and that you have no trouble on account of alms-food?"

"We are keeping well, Blessed One, we are comfortable, and we have no trouble on account of alms-food."

"I hope that you all live in concord and agreement, Anuruddha, as undisputing as milk with water, viewing each other with kindly eyes."

Surely we do, venerable sir."

"But Anuruddha, how do you live thus?"

"Venerable sir, as to that, I think thus: 'It is a gain for me, it is a great gain for me that I am living with such companions in the life divine [*brahmacariya*].' I maintain bodily, verbal and mental acts of lovingkindness [*mettā*] towards these venerable ones in public and in private. [I think] 'Why should I not set aside what I am minded to do and do only what they are minded to do?' And I act accordingly. We are different in body, venerable sir, but only one in mind, I think" (M I 206, translation in Ñāṇamoli [n.d.: 218–19]).

[55] Pali *mittatā, mettā* (on which see Collins 1987a), Greek *philia*.

This ideal of kindly non-disputation is also found in the (ideal) procedures for monastic self-government, to be discussed in Chapter 6. These have often been called democratic, and indeed there are procedures for voting and majority decisions. But it is more properly described as a form of gerontocracy where wise elders preside over a profoundly conservative – ideally, changeless – way of life (6.3).

As has been seen, the epitome of the lay person in happy circumstances is the king. But royal happiness is inferior to that made possible by the monastic life. The Arahant Bhaddiya, who came from a royal family, frequented forests and lonely places, and was heard from time to time to exclaim "O the happiness, the happiness!" Some other monks heard him, and thought that he was discontented with the monkhood and was remembering his previous life as a king. He explained that this was not the case: his exclamation had to do with the happiness he now enjoyed, living without fear in forests, compared to his life as a king, always surrounded by guards and ever fearful (Vin II 183–4, Ud 18–20, Ja I 140, Th-a III 52). In the "Discourse on the Advantages of the Monastic Life" (*Sāmaññaphala Sutta*, D I 47–86) the parricide king Ajātasattu goes one evening to see the Buddha, who is staying in a nearby forest with twelve hundred and fifty monks. As Ajātasattu approaches he panics, fearing an ambush, since the whole group is completely quiet. He is reassured, and asks the Buddha what are the advantages of the monastic life, compared to those of other vocations, through which men bring happiness to themselves and their family. The Buddha's reply moves from the ease and simplicity of the monk's life, where morality and the practice of guarding the doors of the senses bring faultless and unsullied happiness (D II 70), to the pleasures of meditation, as discussed in 4.1.b, and finally to enlightenment.

4.3.c. The Kaṇha-jātaka *(no. 440, Ja IV 6–14)*

I end the chapter with a translation of a short Birth Story in its entirety, which exemplifies in vignette many of the topics discussed in this section. *Jātaka* stories all have the same structure: first, a Story of the Present (*Paccuppanna-vatthu*) gives some incident in the Buddha's life, which leads him to tell a Story of the Past

(*Atīta-vatthu*); at the end of the story, in a section called *Samodhāna*, the Buddha identifies characters in the Story of the Past with various contemporaries, in the "Buddha's retinue" (*Buddha-parisā*).

The Teacher told this story in the Nigrodha Park at Kapilavatthu, apropos a smile. At that time, it is said, while he was walking around the Nigrodha Park in the evening with a company of monks, he smiled at a particular place. The elder Ānanda (thought) "I wonder why the Blessed One smiled? Tathāgatas don't smile without a reason: I'll ask him"; and with his hands together politely he did so. The Teacher said "In the past, Ānanda, there was a sage by the name of Kaṇha (Black): he enjoyed a life of meditation in this place, and through the splendor of his virtue Sakka's dwelling trembled." But since this (short) sketch was not clear, at the elder's request he told a (longer) Story of the Past:

"Once upon a time, when Brahmadatta was king of Benares, there was a childless Brahmin; he undertook (the vows of) morality in the hope of getting a child, and the future Buddha was reborn in his wife's womb. At his name-giving ceremony they gave him the name Kaṇhakumāra because of the black color (of his skin). By the time he was sixteen he was as handsome as a jeweled image, and his father sent him to Takkasilā to be educated. When he had completed his education he came home, and his father found him a suitable wife; in due course he inherited all his parents' property and position.

One day he was inspecting his treasuries, and sitting there on a fine couch he picked up a golden plate and read what had been written on it by members of his family in the past: 'So-and-so acquired this amount of wealth, so-and-so that much.' He reflected, 'One can still see the wealth acquired by these people, but not them: not one of them took it with him. No-one can tie his wealth up in a bundle and take it to the other world. Wealth is held in common with the five fears,[56] and so it's worthless – its (only

[56] Reading *pañcannaṃ verāṇaṃ sādharaṇabhāvena*, with the Burmese recension. These five fears, which are variously interpreted, are the fear due to (or concerning) livelihood, fear of disapproval, fear of (embarrassment in) assemblies, fear of death and fear of bad rebirth. See A IV 364, Vibh 379, Vibh-a 505–6, etc. (references in CPD s.v. *ajīvikabhaya*). My translation attempts to keep the play on words between something's being worthless, *asāra*, in one sense but in having a (true) worth, *sāra*, in another.

true) worth is in (being given away as) a gift. The body is held in common with many diseases, and so it's worthless – its only true worth is in making greetings [e.g. with hands together], etc., to the virtuous. Life is under the sway of impermanence, and so it's worthless – its only true worth is in (making possible) the practice of Insight Meditation in terms of impermanence, etc. So if I'm to get the true worth of (these) possessions, I must give them away, as gifts.' He got up from his seat, went to see the king, and obtained his permission to start a great gift-giving (ceremony). But even after seven days he saw no diminution of his wealth, and thought 'What's the use of wealth? I will renounce the world while I'm still young, obtain the (supernormal) knowledges and the (meditative) attainments, and be destined for (rebirth in) the Brahma-world.' He threw open all his doors with the words 'Take it, it's yours!', getting rid of his material wealth as if it was some impure thing he detested, and with the crowd weeping and wailing left the city and went to the Himalayas, where he renounced (the world) in the Sage-renunciation.[57]

Looking for a pleasant place to live he came upon a spot and thought, 'This is where I'll live'; making a gourd tree the (equivalent of a) village where he got his food, he resolved to live at the foot of this very tree. He did not live near a village but was a forest-dweller; he didn't make a leaf-hut but lived at the foot of the tree in the open air,[58] in a single position. If he wanted to lie on the ground he did so; using his teeth as a pestle he ate only uncooked food, once a day at a single sitting. He patiently endured earth, water, fire and air alike: these were the Special Ascetic Practices he undertook to live by.[59] [It seems that in this Birth Story the future Buddha was outstanding in having few wants (*parama-appiccha*).][60]

[57] *Isipabbajjā*, a term standard in the *Jātaka* stories for renunciation at a time when there is no Buddhist Dispensation (*sāsana*) in existence. Such a renunciation may (as in this case) or may not be in accordance with Buddhist values. See CPD s.v.

[58] That even a leaf-hut could become a form of "household life" is expressed in the story of Gotama's forebear Sumedha (cf. 3.3.b). He also renounced the world as a Sage, and first built a leaf-hut and meditation walkway; later he got rid of his hut, because it had "all the comforts of a house" and "eight disadvantages" (Ja I 6, 8–9). See the translation in Jayawickrama (1990: 8, 12–3).

[59] The *dhutaṅga*-s, or as here *dhutaguṇa*-s, are a list of thirteen supererogatory ascetic practices; see the second chapter of the *Visuddhimagga*, translated by Ñāṇamoli (1975: 59ff.). Kaṇha here undertakes five of them: eating in one sitting, living in the forest, in the open air, at the foot of a tree and in one position.

[60] This is obviously a remark inserted by a redactor. Note that the Buddha as narrator says, in the text below, that Kaṇha was "outstanding in being content (with little)."

Soon he acquired the (supernormal) knowledges and (meditative) attainments, and lived enjoying the sport of meditation.[61] He did not go elsewhere looking for different kinds of fruit, but when it was the season for his tree to bear fruit, he ate that; when it had flowers he ate them, when it had leaves he ate them, and when it had no leaves he ate the bark. In this way, outstanding in being content (with little), he lived for a long time in this place. Every day in the morning he collected what was ripe from that tree, never getting up (from there) out of greed to collect (food) in another place. Sitting in his place he stretched out his hand, gathered the fruit which was within range of his hand, and ate whatever was there without distinguishing between what was pleasant and what was not.

In this way he was outstanding in contentment (*parama-santuttha*), and through the splendor of his virtue Sakka's yellowstone seat appeared (to him) to be hot. [It seems that it becomes hot when Sakka's life is at an end, or when his merit is at an end, or when some other being of great power wishes (to occupy) that place, or through the splendor of great and powerful ascetics or Brahmins who do what is right[62]]. Sakka wondered, 'Who is this who wants to make me fall (from here)?' and saw the Sage Kaṇha living in this place gathering fruit from the tree. He thought, 'This sage practices fierce austerities, he mortifies his senses. I will make him roar a lion's roar in giving a talk on Dhamma, and when I have heard that which makes for bliss I will do him a favor by making his tree bear fruit permanently; and then I'll come back (here).' With his great supernatural power he came down swiftly and stood behind (Kaṇha) at the foot of the tree. In order to test him, to see if he would get angry when someone spoke ill of him, he spoke the first verse:[63]

1. 'This man is black and eats black food in this black place: how I dislike him!'

Kaṇha heard this, sought with his Divine Eye to find who it was who was speaking with him, and discovered that it was Sakka.

[61] *Jhāna-kīḷitaṃ kīḷanto*, a striking but common phrase in these contexts. See 5.2.b.

[62] This is another redactor's remark. "Do what is right" renders *dhammika*, "according to *dhamma*."

[63] Birth Stories are – in theory, though in my view not historically – freestanding verses around which were then added explanatory prose, along with a word-commentary. So the verses in each story are numbered.

Without turning round and without looking at him, he spoke the second verse:
2. 'A person is not black because of his skin; a (true) Brahmin's worth is within. The person who does bad deeds is black, Sakka.'

He elaborated on this with an account of the seven bad deeds which bring on (such) blackness, with their divisions such as being singlefold, etc.; castigating them and praising good qualities such as morality, he taught Dhamma to Sakka as if he were making the moon rise in the sky. Sakka was delighted at the talk on Dhamma, and full of joy he invited the Great Being to choose a favor, in the third verse:
3. 'This was well said, Brahmin, nicely spoken and to the point; I will grant you a favor – whatever you want.'

At this the Great Being thought 'This fellow was testing me, wondering if I would get angry when I was spoken ill of, when he criticized the color of my skin, my food and the place where I live. Now he knows I am not angry he is pleased and offers me a favor. He must think I practice the religious life in order to gain the power (which one gets from becoming) Sakka or Brahmā. To make him certain (that this is not the case) I must choose these four favors: "May no anger or hatred for anyone arise in me, nor any greed when someone else is successful; may no (improper) affection for others arise in me; may I have balance of mind."' Thus for the sake of making Sakka certain he chose four favors in uttering the fourth verse:
4. 'If Sakka, who is lord of all beings, is granting me a favor I hope that I can live[64] wholly without anger, hatred, greed and (the attachment which comes with) affection: these are the four favors (I choose).'

Then Sakka thought, 'The sage Kaṇha chooses the most irreproachable favors; I will ask him what are the faults in those qualities (of anger, etc.).' He asked him (that question) in the fifth verse:
5. 'What danger do you see in anger, hatred, greed and affection, Brahmin? Answer me that question.'

The Great Being said 'Just listen,' and spoke these four verses:
6. 'I do not approve of anger, because anger, arising from impatience, grows from little to much, it hangs on and brings a lot of trouble.

[64] Reading *vuttiṃ*, "mode of behavior, livelihood."

7. I do not approve of hatred, because when a man is angry he starts with words, then there is physical contact, then fist (-fighting), then the stick, and he ends up with the sword; and hatred has its origin in anger.
8. I do not approve of greed, because where there is greed there is aggression and violence, fraud and cheating.
9. I do not approve of (improper) affection, because numerous fetters abide in the mind, tied together by affection, causing distress.'

When Sakka heard the answer to his question he said, 'Wise Kaṇha, you have answered these questions well, with the grace of a Buddha: choose another favor'; and he spoke the tenth verse:

10. 'This was well said, Brahmin, nicely spoken and to the point; I will grant you a favor – whatever you want.'

Then the future Buddha spoke the next verse:

11. 'If Sakka, who is lord of all beings, is granting me a favor, may no great afflictions occur to me, as I live here alone in the forest, to cause hindrance (to my asceticism).'

On hearing this Sakka thought, 'Wise Kaṇha chooses a favor which is connected with nothing material, but (rather) which is connected to his practice of asceticism.' He was even more pleased, and to grant him yet another favor he spoke another verse:

'This was well said, Brahmin, nicely spoken and to the point; I will grant you a favor – whatever you want.'

To express which favor he chose, the future Buddha taught him Dhamma in speaking the final verse:

12. 'If Sakka, who is lord of all beings, is granting me a favor, let there be no mental or physical harm to anyone anywhere because of me: this is the favor I choose.'

Thus six times the Great Being chose a favor based on the value of renunciation, for he knew that the body is subject to decay, and that Sakka could not make it otherwise. Although the purification of beings in the three Doors [sc. in actions of body, speech and mind] does not lie in Sakka's hands, still he [Kaṇha] chose these favors as a way of teaching him the Dhamma. Sakka made the tree bear fruit permanently, and honored the Great Being by putting his hands together at his head; with the words 'May you live in good health' he went back to his own dwelling.

The future Buddha maintained his (life of) meditation, and was destined for the Brahma-world."

When the Teacher had given this teaching, he said to Ānanda, "I used to live in this place," and connected the Birth Story (with the present): "at that time, Ānanda, (the monk) Anuruddha was Sakka, and I was the sage Kaṇha."

CHAPTER FIVE

Millennialism

The concept of millennialism (millenarism, millenarianism) is not easy to define and use comparatively. It is standard in scholarship on modern events and movements in Southern Asia, and on the motifs in traditional Buddhism which are often said to lie behind them, or which, it is alleged, have to be grasped in order to understand them. At the end of this chapter a Critical Discussion considers the concept and its application in the modern world. For the moment, in continuing to concentrate on the imaginaire of premodern Pali texts, my use of the term does not presuppose a definition or ideal type. Its purpose is to group together Buddhist conceptions of felicity in which two motifs are foregrounded: first, prospective temporal distance or futurity – the ideal is always situated at a remove from the present, in future time; second, the felicity is imagined either to be brought about by or in some other way to be connected with a specific person or persons – here, of course, most commonly the future Buddha Metteyya (Skt Maitreya), but also other future Buddhas. I hope that this chapter and the Critical Discussion will achieve some clarity both about the sense of the word "millennialism" in connection with Buddhism, and about the variety of ideas and events so named. But such clarity can be arrived at only inductively, not a priori.

The first section of this chapter returns for a moment to the issue, broached in Chapter 3.2.b, of a plurality of Buddhas. That section viewed multiple Buddhas from a perspective concerned with the textualization of time, as an instance of repetition through non-repetitive, irreversible temporality. Now I want to distinguish between two issues: on the one hand, the possibility of multiple Buddhas as a matter of logic, as an implication of the most basic Buddhist doctrines; on the other hand, the growth of stories about them, the development of narratives in which they are not abstract possibilities, mere numbers and names, but characters with individual biographies. In order to do this, I return to the distinction between systematic and narrative thought, introduced and discussed in Part 1.

5.1. PAST AND FUTURE BUDDHAS IN EARLY PALI TEXTS

5.1.a. On the very idea of a plurality of Buddhas

V. S. Naipaul relates a story somewhere, described (if I remember correctly) as an old Indian tale, about a king who offered a prize to anyone who could give him something which would make him happy when he was sad, and sad when he was happy. It was won by someone who gave him a bracelet on which was engraved "all things must pass." Contrast this with the Buddhist statement that "all conditioned things are impermanent." Naipaul's story is comprehensible immediately, by anyone, without the need to embed it further into a particular ideological context (whether or not there was one, and whether or not that context might imbue the engraved sentence with more specific connotations). In the Buddhist case, on the other hand, further exegesis is required to make sense of the statement itself.[1] Although historical and other kinds of information are likely to help in elucidating the statement, one obvious way of setting about understanding it is to adumbrate for it a systematic, theoretical context, by coming to see what it presupposes and implies. And one way to do that is to ask questions. Here is one: does the truth of impermanence apply to itself? Will or might it one day become false that "all things are impermanent"?[2] The answer is: no. Impermanence is a characteristic of the conditioned universe of space and time (but not of the timeless Unconditioned) which obtains universally, eternally, and so the proposition which asserts it is always and everywhere true, whether anyone knows it or not. To use a simple example: "2 + 2 = 4" is always true, whether or not anyone utters the equation. It

[1] This is even more obviously the case with the later version, "all conditioned *dhamma*-s are momentary." For the historical progression from the one to the other see Collins (1982, Chapter 8).

[2] There is an analogy here with the Cretan Liar paradox: Epimenides the Cretan said that "all Cretans are liars." If the statement is true, it implies its own falsity.

might become the case that after a nuclear catastrophe, for example, there could be no-one left to know, or say that "2 + 2 = 4"; but that will not stop it being true. Similarly, the eternal truths of Buddhism – such as impermanence, conditioning, not-self – constitute the *dhammatā*, the way things truly, timelessly are. In the terminology of Buddhist systematic thought, the category-matrix of existing things (Existents, *dhamma*-s) never changes. (In the developed view of what the General Introduction called the traditional period, the ahistorical Pali lexicon which best names this category-matrix never changes.) Actual instances of Existents, however, are impermanent. Types, one might say, are eternal, tokens of them are not.[3]

"Seeing (things) as they really are," *yathābhūta-dassana*, is a standard synonym for enlightenment. Any particular utterance about the way things really are, of course, as an event or sequence of events in the spatio-temporal universe, is contingent, conditioned and impermanent. Knowledge and utterances of the truth about things constitute the *sāsana*, the Dispensation of the Buddha: as an historically instantiated and institutionalized body of knowledge, it is itself subject to the truth of impermanence. One day it too will disappear. This fact is recognized in the earliest texts. For example, a series of short texts called "Dangers in the Future" (*anāgata-bhayāni*) includes the prediction that monks lax in discipline and in transmitting the Buddha's word will bring harm to the dhamma (A III 100ff., especially 106–7). In the "Elders' Verses" (Th 920–48 and 949–80), the monks Pārāpariya and Phussa lament the future degeneration of the tradition. And famously, if uncomfortably for modern sensibilities, when the Buddha reluctantly admits women to the Monastic Order, he predicts that it will now last for only 500 years, instead of the 1,000 it would have without them.[4]

Another question: how many times has the truth been discovered, and what will happen after Gotama's Dispensation has succumbed to the law of impermanence? A number of answers are possible, in the sense that they are not logically self-contradictory: he could be the only Buddha, there could be a specific number, or there could be an infinite number of truth-discoverers. And the choice here is, in part, related to the question of whether the uni-

[3] Contrast this with modern historicism, which holds that types can also change.

[4] Vin II 256, A IV 278 (the number was later revised to 5,000). Cf. *Anāgatavaṃsa* vv.134ff. (5.2.b).

verse is infinite, whether it has a beginning or end; as discussed in Chapter 3.2.c, traditional Theravāda assumes a beginningless and endless universe. Individual series of lives in non-repetitive time can come to an end in nirvana, but, as said there, Buddhist dramas of humankind as a whole are never-ending. History passes (linearly) through repeated cycles of time, in the sense that the larger-scale sequence of eons, just like our shorter sequences of days and months, constantly repeats the same pattern. In such a worldview, it strikes me as difficult (though not self-contradictory) to imagine Gotama Buddha as a unique "prophet," like Christ, or as a final and definitive one, like Muhammad – at least if one considers whether a culturally viable religion could be based on the idea that knowledge of the truth, and thus the possibility of salvation, had been recently discovered and would be soon forgotten, just once, or for the last time, in a universe without beginning or end. But one need not speculate on what is or is not culturally viable, since the earliest texts provide an answer to the question: they say that there is a plurality of Buddhas. This answer is taken up and developed to its logical conclusion by the later tradition: as 5.2.d below shows, later texts state explicitly that past and future Buddhas are infinite.

It is easy to find examples in the earliest texts of the assumption that there have been and will be multiple Buddhas. "Whether Tathāgatas arise or do not arise, this fact remains (true) [or "this state of affairs obtains"]: (there is) the (conditioned) existence of Existents (*dhamma*-s), the regularity of [the way in which] Existents [are conditioned], the fact that things have specific conditions" (S II 25).[5] A number of texts recount how, after Gotama's enlightenment, the Brahmā Sahampati persuaded him to teach, despite his initial hesitation. In one short version (S I 140) Sahampati declares, "Those Blessed Ones, who in the past were Arahants, Perfectly enlightened Ones, (all) lived honoring the Truth [i.e. by teaching it], respecting it, adhering to it. [So too will] those Blessed Ones who in the future will be Arahants, Perfectly enlightened Ones . . . May he who is now the Blessed One, an Arahant,

[5] A I 286 adds to this "(that) all conditioned things are impermanent": *uppādā vā Tathāgatānaṃ anuppādā vā Tathāgatānaṃ ṭhitā va sā dhātu, dhammaṭṭhitatā, dhammaniyāmatā, idappaccayatā* (*sabbe saṅkhara aniccā*). My rendering of *dhammaṭṭhitatā* and *dhammaniyāmatā* is guided by Spk II 40.

the Perfectly enlightened One . . . [do the same]." A curious episode related a number of times in the Canon (D II 81–3, III 99ff., S V 159–61) tells of how Sāriputta "roared a lion's roar," declaring that there is no ascetic, Brahmin or Blessed One (i.e. Buddha) past, present or future who is greater or wiser than Gotama. The Buddha, in a tone somewhere in the areas of mockery, reproach and serious interrogation, asks him whether he has had direct, telepathic knowledge of all past and future Buddhas, and of himself (Gotama). Forced to concede that he has not, Sāriputta then explains that he based his lion's roar on an "inference from (the) dhamma" (*dhammanvāya*; D III 100, cf. Sv 880, Vibh 329, Vibh-a 417), which tells him that all Buddhas, past, present and future must be, with respect to their enlightening knowledge, the same. In the canonical text to which the later image of the city of nirvana may be traced (S II 105–6, discussed in 2.3.e), Gotama says that he has rediscovered "the ancient road, the old straight path traveled by Perfectly enlightened Ones of former times." Buddhas nirvanize once and for all, but Buddhahood recurs.

The fact that multiple Buddhas are implied by the logic of Buddhist thought does not mean, of course, that a fully worked-out system of named past and future Buddhas was present from the very start. And this, indeed, seems not to have been the case: with the exception of the *Buddhavaṃsa*, past and future Buddhas as named characters are conspicuously rare in the canonical texts, and still more so are stories about them. In the *Mahāpadāna Sutta* six former Buddhas are named and described. They are also mentioned briefly, usually just by name, in some other texts.[6] The *Buddhavaṃsa*, as discussed in Chapter 3.4.b, tells the stories of twenty-four former Buddhas, and names three more previous to Dīpaṅkara at Bv XXVII 1. Of future Buddhas, only one, Metteyya, is mentioned: once in the *Cakkavatti-sīhanāda Sutta*, translated in Appendix 3, and once, apparently as a later addition, in the *Buddhavaṃsa*. The point here, then, is that the idea of multiple Buddhas is implied by the most basic statements of Buddhist systematic thought; and that this is acknowledged by the earliest texts. The issue of narratives about them is another matter.

[6] For references, see the articles by Gombrich discussed in the next section, and EB s.v. "Buddha."

5.1.b. Who were they, and who will they be?

Many writers speak of the idea of a plurality of Buddhas as a "development" in Buddhist thought, and indeed most previous scholarly work on the issue has been devoted to the question of where belief in the Buddha Metteyya (Maitreya) originated from, and whether it was a matter of outside influence, for instance from the Persian "saviour" god Mithra Invictus (= Ajita Maitreya?)[7] An obsession with origins, of course, has been characteristic of much previous scholarship, in Indology as elsewhere. In my view, whether the particular name Metteyya/Maitreya was borrowed from outside the Buddhist tradition is an unanswerable and uninteresting question. The name might have been borrowed, but the idea of future (and past) Buddhas is intrinsic to the logic of Buddhism.

The one early text in which past Buddhas are mentioned as more than a bare list of names is the *Mahāpadāna* of the *Dīgha Nikāya* (no. 14, D II 1ff.). This discourse is exceptional in more than one way – it is the longest *Sutta* in the Canon, and for that reason the commentary says that it should be known as "the King of Discourses" (*suttānta-rājā*, Sv 480). First the Buddha recounts, in list-like repetitive form, facts about six previous Buddhas (their social class, length of life, the names of their parents, and the like), by the names of Vipassī, Sikhi, Vessabhu, Kakusandha, Konāgamana, and Kassapa.[8] Then he tells part of the life story of Vipassī, the first of the seven, noting that many of the events which occur in it are "(in) the nature of things" (*dhammatā*) for all Buddhas.[9] It is interesting to note that here the famous episode of the Buddha's seeing, allegedly for the first time in his life, "the four Sights" – a sick man, an old man, a corpse and a renouncer – and his subsequent departure from home as an ascetic, is told of Vipassī: it is not told at length of Gotama in any extant text before the commentarial period,

[7] Kloppenborg (1982) reviews this work, with bibliography. On Maitreya/Metteyya generally, see Lamotte (1988: 699ff.), and Sponberg and Hardacre (1988), especially the essays by Nattier and Jaini.

[8] The most widely used English version of this, Rhys Davids (1910: 6–7) rather obscures the style of the text here by putting the information in a table; Walshe (1987: 199–201) is better in this respect.

[9] This is a trope repeated in the *Buddhavaṃsa* commentary, which describes at length (but not including Metteyya) eight differences between Buddhas, four obligatory places, and thirty events which are "(in) the nature of things" for them all (Bv-a 296–9).

although there is a short autobiographical text at A I 145–6 which seems to presuppose the story. The story is told in a grand, "mythical" way, but also with a striking and sober realism (5.3.b).

The one early mention of the future Buddha Metteyya can be read in Appendix 3, sections 25–6. As stated in 3.4.b, in the *Buddhavaṃsa* Metteyya is named but once, in a verse which seems not to have been in the version known to the extant commentary, attributed to a Buddhadatta centuries later.[10] The figure of Metteyya was certainly known by the time of the commentaries, and perhaps some version of his story was then available (5.2.a); but it would seem undeniable that – with the luminous exception of the *Cakkavatti-sīhanāda Sutta* – narratives dealing with Metteyya were not among the earliest Buddhist stories. They are, however, more numerous in texts of the traditional period (Collins 93ms.).

The only scholar to have addressed the issue of multiple Buddhas as a theoretical and historical problem – aside from speculations on the origins of Metteyya/Maitreya and his name – is Richard Gombrich, in three articles (1980), (1992b) and (1993). In the last (p. 152) he states that in the first he had

> suggested that Buddhism may have adopted the idea of former Buddhas in order to cope with the problem of the Buddha's originality. Unlike the Brahmin teachers, he had no lineage of gurus behind him but had on the contrary made clear that he had found his teachers inadequate. This raised a problem for the authority of his claims and I suggested that that authority was bolstered by claiming, as the Jains did and had probably done first, that the Buddha's teaching stood in the tradition of a great line of teachers stretching back to time immemorial.[11]

The hypothesis about Jains arises from the fact that the number of previous Buddhas dealt with in the *Buddhavaṃsa*, twenty-four, is precisely the number of "ford-makers" (*tīrthaṃkara*-s) or Conquerors described in Jainism.[12] In the (1992b) piece, he further

[10] See Norman (1983: 93); for the identity and date of the commentator, who may have been a younger contemporary of Buddhaghosa in the fifth century AD, see Norman (1983: 146–7), Horner (1978: xxx–xxxi).

[11] In the next sentence he laments "so far as I am aware, no one has either approved or criticized my suggestion (so lively is intellectual debate in Buddhist studies)." The complaint is, alas, fair, but it means that my reflections here must mark an advance in at least one way.

[12] One could point to a disanalogy: the twenty-four Jain teachers include the present one, Mahāvīra; if one includes the present Buddha Gotama in the Buddhist list, the number becomes twenty-five.

suggested that the fact that six former Buddhas are mentioned in the *Mahāpadāna* may be the result of an ambiguity in the compound *isi-sattama*, used several times of Gotama elsewhere in the Canon: this can mean both "the best of seers" and "seventh of the seers." Gombrich thinks the former was probably the original sense, and the latter added either by misunderstanding or as a deliberate pun – since (as already noted in PED s.v. *buddha*) a list of "seven seers" is very common in Brahmanism, from the time of the Vedas. He says (1992b: 330):

> I believe that it is not absurd to think that the doctrine of former Buddhas [and future ones – S.C.] may not have been part of the teaching of Gotama, but added by his followers – possibly even as early as during his own lifetime. I doubt whether it will ever be possible to prove this conjecture; but at least the evidence here adduced may be taken to point in that direction.

This speculation is not absurd, indeed what it posits is almost certainly true, if by "doctrine of former Buddhas" is meant a narratively elaborated account, such as one finds in later texts. And of course the Buddha cannot have said everything at once. But it would be wrong, I think, to postulate that given the evidence we have, the existence of former (and future) Buddhas could have been something the Buddha would at any point have denied. It is implied by what we know of his teaching, from any and every provenance. I agree that past and future Buddhas are important with respect to authority; indeed I would argue that they are necessary for any plausible Buddhist epistemology, whether or not that was acknowledged immediately by the Buddha. But what is necessary is acknowledgment of their existence, not stories about them.

I would put the whole issue differently. The very earliest nontextual materials available for Buddhism contain evidence of belief in multiple Buddhas (Vogel 1954). One of Aśoka's inscriptions, in the third century BC,[13] records repairs made to a *stūpa* of the former Buddha Konāgamana (spelt Konākamana); the archaeological sites at Bharhut and Sāñchi (first and second centuries BC respectively) contain representations of the seven trees of the seven Buddhas ending with Gotama. Benisti (1971) made

[13] The so-called Minor Pillar Edict 6, found at Nigali Sagar in Nepal. See Allchin and Norman (1985).

the suggestion (accepted by Gombrich 1980: 67) that groups of five pillars found at Amarāvatī and Nāgārjunakoṇḍa (in the first centuries AD) represent the five Buddhas of our eon, i.e. Kakusandha, Konāgamana, Kassapa, Gotama and Metteyya. As argued in the General Introduction, any picture we draw of pre-Aśokan Buddhism must be speculative, since the earliest Buddhist texts were, in the form we have them, redacted after Aśoka; that is, at the same time as the building of the monuments just mentioned. Given this, and the fact that multiple Buddhas are implied by any basic statement of Buddhist systematic thought, the problem becomes why the redactors of the Pali Canon, apart from the *Mahāpadāna-sutta* and *Buddhavaṃsa*, were so little interested in narratives of other Buddhas, unlike contemporary iconographers and later textualists. This is not a problem I can or need solve.[14] The focus of this book is the imaginative world of post-Aśokan, premodern Pali texts; and in this world past and future Buddhas are very much alive. But it must be admitted that there are some historical issues to discuss here, and Gombrich is right to draw attention to them.

In the later literature where narratives of past and future Buddhas do occur,[15] most of them remain without real individuality, being described in brief and formulaic terms, often in what are little more than lists. This textual form is not merely an absence of detail; it has, as argued in 3.4.b, a significance of its own. The most fully described Buddhas are two: the past Buddha Dīpaṅkara, usually found in conjunction with an account of the aspiration to Buddhahood made in his presence by the ascetic Sumedha, who later became Gotama; and the next Buddha Metteyya. It is not surprising to find in other Buddhist traditions that Dīpaṅkara, Gotama and Maitreya (Metteyya) are sometimes worshiped together as a group, as are Gotama and Metteyya.[16] I am not aware of any signif-

[14] Gombrich, I think, would say that the texts have this form because the post-Aśokan redactors were simply transmitting faithfully what previous, pre-Aśokan generations had bequeathed to them. I take a less optimistic view, but there can be no certainty on these matters.

[15] For past Buddhas, see the *Buddhavaṃsa* and its commentary in Horner (1975) and (1978), and the introduction to the *Jātaka* collection in Jayawickrama (1990). For future Buddhas see the translations of the *Anāgatavaṃsa* in 5.2.b, and of the *Māleyyadevatthera-vatthu* in Appendix 4, F. Martini (1936) and Saddhatissa (1975).

[16] For the three Buddhas in Nepal, see Vergati (1982), Gellner (1992: 186); for Śākyamuni and Maitreya together on coins from king Kaniṣka of the Kuṣāna dynasty, in the first or second centuries AD, see Cribb (1980).

icant examples of this triad in Pali texts. The five Buddhas of the current epoch, as has been mentioned, may have already formed an iconographic group in the first centuries AD; and there is evidence of this also from Southeast Asia in more recent times. Two illustrations, from Thailand and Cambodia, are given by G. Martini (1969) with an edition and translation of the *Pañcabuddha-byākaraṇa;* this is an odd little tale, apparently originating along with other *Jātaka*-style tales in Thailand. Its opening section has the five Buddhas, born together in the past as five animals, all declare their intention to become Buddhas in the future.

5.2. THE HISTORY OF THE FUTURE

5.2.a. *The development of stories about Metteyya*

In early post-canonical texts Metteyya is mentioned only once, in the *Milinda-pañha* p. 159, citing the *Cakkavatti-sīhanāda Sutta.* In the next layer of Pali literature, the period of the early commentaries and the early Chronicles (*vaṃsa*-s), from about the end of the fourth to the sixth centuries AD, there is again little evidence of concern with him. Spk II 390 repeats some names from the *Cakkavatti-sīhanāda Sutta,* "in the future Metteyya will be Buddha, Saṅkha the king, Ketumatī the royal city, etc.", as if a longer list of narrative detail were known and could be alluded to thus in shorthand.[17] In the commentary to the *Cakkavatti-sīhanāda Sutta* there occurs a version of the story of Mahāpanāda's palace (the text here refers to the *Jātaka* collection: see Ja II 334, IV 325). Buddhaghosa mentions Metteyya a few times, and gives the names of his parents, Subrahmā and Brahmavatī.[18] In the *Mahāvaṃsa* (XXXII 73ff.) king Dutthagāmaṇī, on his deathbed, asks a monk which of the heavens is (most) pleasant (*ramma*); the answer is Tusita, since Metteyya is now living there. The king closes his eyes, dies and is reborn there, thanks to the notion, mentioned in 4.1.b, that one's thoughts at death condition the place of rebirth; it is said that he will be Metteyya's chief disciple when the latter becomes Buddha. But despite the comparative rarity of stories about Metteyya at this time, the conclusions and colophons of texts from this period and

[17] The "etc." is in the text . . . *ti ādi-vasena.*

[18] As 361, Pp-a 247, Vism 47 = I 135; his parents at As 415, Vis 434 = XIII 127.

later frequently include a wish by the redactor or scribe either to be enlightened at the time of Metteyya, or to meet him and receive from him the prediction of future Buddhahood.[19] The Chinese traveler Fa-Hien in the early fifth century AD tells of meeting an Indian monk in Sri Lanka, who told him a story about Metteyya which resembles that in the *Cakkavatti-sīhanāda Sutta,* with some additional details. Fa-Hien wanted to write it down, but the monk said, "This is taken from no sūtra, it is only the utterance of my own mind" (Legge 1886: 110).

Stories of Metteyya become more frequent in later literature. The most important texts edited so far are four, which are discussed in the next three sections:

(1) The *Anāgatavaṃsa* (= Anāg) translated in 5.2.b, where notes on editions are also found. As Bechert et al. (1979: 118) say, "there exist a number of versions of the *Anāgatavaṃsa* in Pali," most of them without western editions (see Collins 1993 ms.)
(2) Two texts concerning ten future Buddhas:
  (a) the *Dasabodhisattuddesa* (= Dasab), edited and translated by Martini (1936), and
  (b) the *Dasabodhisattuppattikathā* (= Dbk), edited and translated by Saddhatissa (1975); and
(3) The *Māleyyadevattheravatthu* (= Mth-v), edited and translated into French by Denis (1963), translated into English by Collins (1993b) (Selections in Appendix 4.)

Dasavatthu-pakaraṇa no. 33 mentions Mahāpanāda's palace, as in the *Cakkavatti-sīhanāda Sutta* section 26, and then gives a short version of Metteyya's story, in the form of a prediction by Gotama Buddha of the future Buddhahood of an unnamed monk.[20] This is an expanded version of the *Cakkavatti-sīhanāda* version; Metteyya's mother is called Pajāpatī, and it is said that his chief disciple will be the future king Saṅkha, who as a monk will be called Asoka.[21] The text here (Dasav 126) says that Metteyya will have

[19] See 3.3, p. 252 (vii); and Saddhatissa (1975: 36ff.)
[20] See n. 28 on v.4 of the *Anāgatavaṃsa.*
[21] This is compatible with, but expands on, what was said above about Duṭṭhagāmaṇī in the *Mahāvaṃsa.* At Mhv XXXII 81, where the prediction about him is made, Duṭṭhagāmaṇī is said to be *rājanāmāraho,* "worthy of the name of king." If one takes this as applying to his future life with Metteyya it could be an oblique reference to his being king Saṇkha before he becomes the Arahant-monk Asoka; the *Mahāvaṃsa* commentary (Mhv-ṭ 602), however, does not interpret it thus.

practiced the Perfections for sixteen uncountable eons and 100,000 (ordinary) eons, which seems to refer to the third of a tripartite division of future Buddhas found in other texts (Cp-a 329, Sv-pṭ I 128). Three "grades" of bodhisatta are recognized, according to how strong in wisdom (*paññā*) they are: those who excel in wisdom, being sluggish in faith (*saddhā*) but sharp in wisdom, take four uncountable eons plus 100,000 (ordinary) eons; those who excel in faith but are middling in wisdom take eight uncountables plus 100,000; those who excel in energy (*viriya*) but are sluggish in wisdom take sixteen uncountables plus 100,000. Metteyya is also said to be in the third category in one ms. of Mth-v.[22] The story of the meeting between Metteyya and the monk Māleyya also begins to be told at this time: story no. 3 of the *Sīhalavatthu* collection contains most of the elements elaborated in the Mth-v (Collins 1993a), although it does not mention the importance of listening to the *Vessantara-jātaka* (5.2.c).

A theme found in various non-Pali texts and in ethnographic reports,[23] but which is documented so far in only one Pali text, not yet published in a modern edition, is that of the Arahant Mahākassapa, and sometimes others, who lived at the time of Gotama Buddha, either waiting in a state of meditative trance under a mountain (which is set in India or Burma) for Metteyya to appear, or resolving that his undecaying body (or merely skeleton) should stay there until his/its final nirvana at that time.[24] When Metteyya appears, either Kassapa arises from his meditation to offer Metteyya a set of robes which he acquired from Gotama Buddha, or Metteyya takes them from his dead body.

5.2.b. The Anāgata-vaṃsa*: unprecedented well-being*

More scholarly work on what should be called the *Anāgatavaṃsa* family of texts will be necessary before any definitive conclusions about this "History of the Future" can be arrived at. Here there is need to make only a few points about it relative to the aims of this

[22] Both Cp-a and Sv-pṭ originate from Sri Lanka, and so the remark in Collins (1993a: 82 note 1) must be corrected. Another ms. of Mth-v (see ibid.) has him as excelling in faith.

[23] See Ferguson (1977, 1989), Lamotte (1988: 701), and Strong (1992: 61–4, 242–5).

[24] For the Pali text and translation, see Saddhatissa (1975: 43–4); and for Pali manuscripts with similar titles, and apparently with some connection to the Māleyya story, see the references in Collins (1993: 7 n. 1).

book. It ends, naturally, with a reference to final nirvana, to be attained notably by those who listen to a recitation of the poem, and form the intention to do the things recommended in vv. 138–42 in order to see Metteyya. The imagination of felicity from an external-sensory perspective – physical beauty, flowers, scents, precious things, etc. – is maintained throughout the poem (note that it is gods from the Sphere of Desire who build columns around the enlightened Metteyya in vv. 112–13). This kind of felicity is continued and intensified by the internal-mental happiness which can be attained both through rebirth in the Brahma-heavens and in religious practice now – what the poem calls, as do other texts (4.3.c, p. 342), enjoying "the sport of meditation," *jhāna-kīḷita*, v. 82). Both of them lead up to the bliss of nirvana. It would be wrong to suggest that the goal of nirvana is here being coalesced with the idea of (a sensory and mental) paradise, or that the poem's vision is of an undifferentiated "utopia."[25] There is a deliberately sudden and stark conceptual contrast between the sensual, indeed (however delicately suggested) sexual happiness of Saṅkha, prince Ajita (if that is his name here), and everyone alive at that time, and the enlightening realization of the future Buddha in vv.51ff. In v.51, he sees "the danger in sense-desires" (*kāmesu ādīnava*) by seeing the four Sights of the sick man, old man, corpse and renouncer, which "destroy desire and pleasure" (*kāma-rati-vināsana*), and which make him, in v.52, "dissatisfied with desire and pleasure" (*nibbindo kāma-ratiyā*). Both *kāma* and *rati* can and here do denote any kind of pleasure, but they both, especially *rati*, strongly connote the sexual form of it. In v.49, it was just said that before his renunciation "he will take his pleasure, (and be) abounding in pleasure" (*ramissati, rati-sampanno*), both terms derived from the root *ram*, to enjoy (sexually). Even in going to the park in v.50 he was "seeking pleasure" (*rati-m-atthāya*, literally "for the sake of *rati*"). Audiences capable of understanding Pali would not fail to notice the emphasis on these key-words in these crucial transitional verses. But the conceptual-lexical opposition is not immediately reproduced in the narrative imaginaire; on the contrary, this kind of text enables the various kinds of felicity, including that of nirvana, to be imagined as on a continuum, in which the narrative transition from sensual happiness to the bliss

[25] See further the remarks on the *Vessantara Jātaka* in 7.5.

of nirvana is a smooth passage from one to the other rather than the radical, categorical change it is on the conceptual level.

The Russian Indologist Minayeff published an article in JPTS 1886, republished recently as JPTS vol. II, 1886, pp. 33–53, containing various texts under the heading *Anāgatavaṃsa.* Scholars have usually referred to this as "the" *Anāgatavaṃsa,* as if there were only one such text. But although reference to Minayeff's pagination and verse numbering will no doubt continue, for lexicographical and other purposes, in our present state of knowledge it might be better to refer to the *Anāgatavaṃsa* family of texts, since various different Histories of the Future seem to have used *Anāgatavaṃsa* as their titles. In some texts the title is expanded to *Anāgata-Buddha-vaṃsa* "Lineage/History of future Buddhas" (Metteyya and others), such that the canonical *Buddhavaṃsa* can be interpreted correspondingly as *Atīta-buddha-vaṃsa,* "Lineage/History of past Buddhas." Catalogs and descriptions of manuscripts show that texts of the *Anāgata-vaṃsa* family were far more widespread than the examples in modern western editions indicate, and that they often circulated in the same manuscripts as the *Buddhavaṃsa,* as did vernacular versions of them (Collins 93 ms.). (The next two paragraphs are for interested specialists.)

Minayeff described four manuscripts from Burma. The first, A, formed the basis for his edition of a poem in 142 verses, printed on pp. 41–53 with variant readings from mss. B and C. This is the text translated here. Leumann (1919), who did not use any further mss., reedited this version (with occasional differences in the numbering of verses), along with notes in German; Leumann's text was again published, with two essays by Saya U Chit Tin and an English translation by William Pruitt, in Tin (1988)[26]. Of ms. B, a mixed prose and verse version, Minayeff printed only certain parts of the prose, with an English summary of what was omitted. These selections, containing a prediction of the gradual decline of Buddhism (various versions of which are found elsewhere[27]), were

[26] Reissued in 1992, on both occasions in a form probably difficult for most readers of this book to obtain (for details see bibliography). The translation given here differs from Pruitt's substantially only on a few occasions, although the styles of the two are quite different.

[27] For references see Collins (1992a: 238 and n. 51), and CPD s.v. *antaradhāna.*

translated by Warren (1896), and again by I. B. Horner (in Conze 1954), who omitted the final paragraph, which deals with the kinds of action which will either prevent or enable rebirth at the time of Metteyya. From ms. C, a commentary on B with the title *Samantabhaddikā*, Minayeff printed only a few pieces of information (on pp. 37–9), and occasional exegetical remarks on words in the verses as footnotes to them. The fourth ms., D, was "a quite different work"; he printed the first sentence from a ms. from Burma (hereafter Burmese D), along with its list of ten future Buddhas, starting with Metteyya. He also made reference to what he called an "incomplete copy of the same work" in Cambodian script (hereafter Cambodian D), in the Bibliothèque Nationale in Paris; unfortunately Filliozat (1993) reports that no ms. corresponding exactly to Minayeff's description can now be found there. The first sentence from Cambodian D, which gives details of where and when the Buddha gave the discourse, differs in minor details from the first sentence in Burmese D. Burmese B may have been the same as the *Dasabodhisattuppattikathā* (Saddhatissa 1975, text also in Martini 1936). Cambodian B may have been the same as the *Dasabodhisatta-uddesa* (Martini 1936).

In the (perhaps seventeenth-century) bibliographical work *Gandhavaṃsa*, an *Anāgata-vaṃsa* is attributed to a Kassapa, taken to have lived in South India in the twelfth to thirteenth centuries (Norman 1983: 161). But the verse-text purports to record a conversation between the Buddha Gotama and Sāriputta; and a version of the story in mixed prose and verse (Minayeff's manuscript B) starts with the standard opening phrase of the canonical *Sutta*-s, "Thus I have heard." On these grounds, Hugh Nevill, who collected a large number of manuscripts in Ceylon in the second half of the nineteenth century, stated that the *Anāgata vaṃsa* "certainly has equal claim with *Buddhavaṃsa* to be considered canonical" (cited in Somadasa 1989: 79). Few scholars today would argue that this text is as early as the *Buddhavaṃsa;* but in the present state of knowledge it is impossible to say when it was composed.

As discussed in 3.4.a, the term *vaṃsa* is used to mean both a lineage (a family or pupillary succession) and a textual account of such a lineage, or of places, relics, and historical events. This double meaning is analogous to that in English of the word "history," which can mean both what happened and a textual account of what happened. For this reason I render *Anāgata-vaṃsa* (hereafter Anāg) as "History of the Future," intending to keep both senses of the words: the "history" is both what is to happen and the account of it. In the translation given here, verse numbers are those of Minayeff's edition in JPTS 1886. Text-critical remarks are added in footnotes only where something significant is at issue. I have tried to make the translation readable, but I have not attempted to produce an English version which is itself, autonomously, an elegant piece of literature: my purpose here is to give the reader a reasonably accurate sense of the content of the poem.

1. The very wise Sāriputta, (also called) Upatissa the leader, the resolute Captain of the Teaching, went to the Lord of the World
2. and told him of his uncertainty on the matter of the future Conqueror; "The next wise Buddha – what is he going to be like?
3. You have eyes (to see): tell me, I want to hear (the story) in full!" The Blessed One listened to what the elder said, and replied:
4. "No one can recount completely the full (story) of Ajita's[28] great and widely-renowned mass of merit. Listen while I recount just a part (of it), Sāriputta.
5. In this Auspicious Eon, millions of years in the future,[29] there will indeed arise a Perfectly enlightened One called Metteyya, the best of (all) two-footed beings,
6. with great merit, great wisdom, great knowledge, great renown, great strength, great vigor, with eyes (to see the truth).
7. That Conqueror will arise, with a great destiny,[30] mindful,

[28] One cannot tell whether this name refers to a monk contemporary with Gotama, as it does in some versions, to Metteyya in the Tusita heaven at the time of speaking, or proleptically to the person in the last life of the series, who will become Metteyya Buddha. Minayeff's text B gives Ajita as the name of a monk contemporary with Gotama. For details and discussion of names for Maitreya, see Levi (1932) and Jaini (1988). Verse 43 here is similarly ambiguous; although v.46 and especially v.56 make it likely this is a name of Metteyya in his last birth, v.57 refers to two people by the names they have in Gotama's (narrated) present. See 5.3.a.

[29] This eon is auspicious because five Buddhas appear in it. "Millions" translates *koṭi*, usually calculated at ten million. In most cases in the text where very large numbers are given, one or more *koṭi*-s, I translate "millions and millions," since an exact numerical figure is not usually necessary. In vv.78–80, however, it does seem that numerical specificity has some significance. See vv.78–82 and n. 46 below.

[30] I assume *mahāgati* here refers to his future destiny in nirvana (see 1.2.c, n. 00 on nirvana as a *gati*). It could mean that this last rebirth is "great." This verse bristles with textual problems. Leumann (1919: 192–4) may be right to suggest that some or all of the terms here (all nominatives in *-o*) should be taken as agent nouns (usually *-ā*); see Geiger (1994: 82–3, 90).

steadfast, of profound knowledge: he will examine all things, know them, see them, thoroughly touch [i.e. experience] them, enter deeply into them and grasp them.
8. At that time the royal city will be called Ketumatī, twelve leagues long and seven wide,
9. crowded with men and women, resplendent with palaces, frequented by pure beings [i.e. *religieux*], invincible and rightly protected.
10. (There will be)[31] a king called Saṅkha: with a limitless army, he will be a mighty Wheel-turning King provided with the seven precious things;
11. with magic powers, famous, possessing all objects of desire, he will rule (his kingdom) righteously, in peace, all enemies destroyed.
12. A well-built palace will arise there through his meritorious deeds, like a celestial *vimāna*, decorated with various precious things,
13. encircled by railings, well laid out, delightful, excellent, tall and shining (so brightly that it will be) hard to look at, dazzling the eyes;
14. King Saṅkha will raise up this palace, which belonged to king Mahāpanāda, and live in it.
15. At that time there will be various streets in this city, here and there, (leading to) delightful, well-constructed and easily accessible lotus-ponds
16. whose clear pellucid water will be pleasantly cool and fragrant, with sand strewn on their even banks and filled to the brim[32]
17. covered with red and blue lotuses, open (to everyone) all year round. There will be seven rows of palm trees, and seven-colored walls
18. made of precious things surrounding the city on all sides. The royal city (now called) Kusāvatī is going to be Ketumatī then;
19. there will be a set of four glistening wishing-trees at the (four) city gates, blue, yellow, red and white.

[31] The verb, *asi*, is aorist, "he was"; if this is not a mistake, it might be the result of a confusion here with another version, which, like those of the *Dasabodhisattuddesa* and the *Dasabodhisattuppattikathā* discussed in 5.2.d, had a story of Metteyya (who is called Ajita at the time of Gotama) in a previous birth, when he was a Wheel-turning king called Saṅkha. If this were so, something would have dropped out between this verse and 14, which clearly refers to the *future* Saṅkha.

[32] *Kākapeyya*, literally "drinkable by crows" (standing on the banks).

20. Divine clothes and ornaments will arise, all (kinds of) wealth and possessions will hang there.
21. Then, in the city center there will be a square with four halls, facing the four directions, and a wishing-tree, arising through meritorious deeds[33].
22. Cotton, silk, linen and fine Kodumbara cloth will hang from these wishing-trees,
23. (as will)[34] musical instruments, tambourines, hand drums and (deep-sounding) drums
24. (and also) bracelets, arm-rings and necklaces made of precious things
25. (and also) tiaras, jewels for the brow, bracelets and jeweled girdles[35]
26. (and also) all manner of other jewelry and ornaments.
27. Through (the) people's meritorious action, they will eat pure, fragrant rice, which will grow through self-generation not cultivation, without powder, (already) husked and ready to eat.[36]
28. Two thousand two hundred and seventy cartloads will be (for them as easily had as) a sixteenth of an *ambaṇa* (is now).
29. And then, what is called (now) two *tumba*-measures of husked rice will grow from a single seed, through the people's meritorious action.
30. The people who live in Ketumatī, in Saṇkha's realm, will then wear (golden) armor and arm-rings,
31. their (every) wish will be fulfilled, they will have happy faces, heavy earrings, their bodies will be anointed with yellow sandalwood and they will wear Benares' finest (cloth).
32. They will have many possessions, (be) wealthy, awaken to (the sound of) *vīṇā*-s and gongs; they will be continuously and extremely happy (both) physically and mentally.

[33] Done in the past by the king, and perhaps by Metteyya and/or by everyone living there: cf. vv.27 and 29.

[34] The second line of vv.21–6 is the same, "will hang from these wishing-trees through meritorious deeds," lending this section a song-like aspect.

[35] Many of these names for jewels, etc. recur at Ja VI 590, in the *Vessantara Jātaka;* I have been guided by the commentary there and Cone and Gombrich's (1977: 93) translation.

[36] See 4.2.a., p. 320, and Collins (1993c: 364, 15.1), translating the same terms in the *Aggañña Sutta* (= Appendix 5). The occurrence of this motif in the story of the beginning of the eon in the *Aggañña Sutta*, and in this text about Metteyya, has led some to see the former as a Buddhist Golden Age, to be recaptured in Metteyya's millennium. I think this is overstating the case: see the Conclusion to Part 2, n. 5.

33. Jambudīpa, over (all) its ten-thousand league length, will be without thorns, unentangled, with grass in abundance[37].
34. There will be (only) three diseases: desire, hunger and old age. Women will marry at the age of 500.[38]
35. (People then) will live in harmony and friendship, always without quarrels; creepers, bushes and trees will be covered in fruit and flowers.
36. There will be a kind of grass, as soft as cotton, (that grows only) four inches high, and a gentle breeze bringing regular rainfall, neither too cold nor too hot.
37. There will be always be good weather, the reservoirs and rivers will be full, and in (various) places here and there smooth, pure sand will be strewn around, like pearls the size of peas and beans.
38. The crowded villages and cities here and there will be as pleasant[39] as an ornamented garden, so close (to each other that),
39. like a thicket of reeds or bamboo, they will be (just) a cock's flight (apart), (they will be) as full of people, I think, as the Avīci hell.[40]
40. (There will be) cities densely packed with people, rich, prosperous and safe, free from disease and distress.
41. There will be constant pleasure and amusement; and people will wander around delightedly (as if) in a (constant) festival[41], experiencing perpetual happiness.
42. Jambudīpa will be as pleasant as the broad royal city of the Kurus[42] or Ālakamandā, (the city) of the gods, which have much food and drink, much feasting, much meat and liquor.
43. He who is named Ajita will be named Metteyya, best of (all)

[37] Minayeff reads *samoharita-saddalo*; if *samoharita* (from *sam-ava-hṛ)* is the correct reading, I assume it has the same sense here as Skt *samavahāra*, "abundance'; Leumann (1919: 85) reads *samo harita-saddalo*, which means "even, with green grass."

[38] Although this text does not say so until v.130, the length of life at this time – as in the *Cakkavatti-sīhanāda Sutta* cited above – will be 80,000 years. The motif of women in paradisial-utopian conditions of extremely long life marrying (relatively) "young" at 500, is found also at D III 75 and A IV 138.

[39] Assuming *ramanīyā bhavissanti.*

[40] This rather unexpected comparison with the Avīci hell (spelt thus, not *avicī* as in Minayeff's text) is also found in the corresponding passage of the *Cakkavatti-sīhanāda Sutta.* There may be a pun with *avīci* meaning "uninterrupted"; and it is characteristic of such passages to have an ironic remark of this kind set in the middle of an enthusiastic encomium. See 6.5.c.

[41] The word is *nakkhatta,* literally a constellation (of stars); but here it refers to the festivals which take place at various astrologically auspicious times; it can be taken as short for *nakkhatta-kīḷana* or *-kīḷā*, "enjoyment at an auspicious time."

[42] I assume this is short for Uttarakuru (4.2.a). Kuru was the name of an area of Northeast India at the time of the Buddha, but it was not famed for wealth and prosperity.

two-footed beings, endowed with the thirty-two (Major) Characteristics, as well as the (eighty) Minor Marks,
44. with a golden complexion, without stain, very splendid, shining with the utmost splendor, beautiful, handsome, good to look at,
45. mighty, unequaled – he will be born in a Brahmin family, extremely wealthy and rich, from one of the best families. Unreproachable with respect to birth, he will be born into a Brahmin family,
46. There will be four palaces made of precious things for Ajita to use, (called) Sirivaḍḍha, Vaḍḍhamāna, Siddhattha and Candaka.
47. Ajita will have female attendants with perfect bodies, adorned with all kinds of ornaments, large, medium and small –
48. no less than 100,000 bejeweled women. His (chief) wife will be Candamukhī, and his son Brahmavaddhana.
49. He will take his pleasure, (and be) abounding in pleasure, rejoicing in great happiness; enjoying all (kinds of) splendor like Sakka in the Nandana Grove,
50. he will live in a house for eight thousand years. Then one day, going out amuse himself in a garden, seeking pleasure,
51. he will be wise and see the danger in sense-desires – (as is in) the nature of future Buddhas – when he sees the four signs which destroy desire and pleasure:
52. an old person, a sick person, a corpse bereft of life, and a renouncer (looking) happy. Feeling compassion for all beings,
53. dissatisfied with desire and pleasure, no (longer) expecting great happiness (therein), he will go forth [i.e. become a renouncer] seeking the supreme place of peace.
54. This unsurpassed man will undertake religious practice[43] for

[43] *Padhānacaraṃ caritvā*, literally "having practiced the practice(s) of exertion." *Padhāna* is fourfold (D III 225, etc.): self-restraint, putting away (harmful thoughts), developing one's mind (= meditating) and watching over oneself (interpreted as a kind of meditation). The tenses of verbs here make the precise sequence of events unclear. In 53 the verb is aorist, which must be just a mistake. In the first line of v.54, the indeclinable participle of the verb is to be taken as a future tense, as is the main verb: "he will make an effort (and) renounce." Participles of this kind usually, but not always, depict action undertaken before the main verb, so this verse might seem to be saying that he made his exertion(s) before he renounced; but since vv.66–7 say that he will go to the Tree of Enlightenment on the same day as he renounces, and as practicing *padhāna* for a week at the Tree is one of the thirty things common to all Buddhas (see n. 9 above), I assume that he makes his week-long effort then, so that the seven days occur in the interval between the two verbs in 67b. Thus the actions in v.54 of "going forth" and "(beginning to) make an effort," are simultaneous.

seven days, the Conqueror will go forth, jumping up (into the air) with a (*vimāna*-)palace.
55–6. Ajita will go forth, at the head of a great body of people: friends, colleagues, companions, relatives, the four parts of the army, four assemblies of the four classes, and 84,000 princesses.
57. When Metteyya goes forth, then 84,000 Brahmins, experts in the Veda, will (also) go forth.
58. Both the brothers Isidatta and Purāṇa, and 84,000 (others), will go forth then.
59. From (among that) 84,000, Jātimitta and Vijaya, a pair of boundless intelligence, will serve the Perfectly enlightened One;
60. (as likewise) will the head of household Suddhika and the laywoman Sudhanā,
61. (and also) the layman Saṅgha and laywomen Saṇghā,
62. and the head of household Suddhika and he who is renowned as Sudatta.
63. The woman Yasavatī and she who is renowned as Visākhā, at the front of 84,000 men and women,
64. will go forth as renouncers in Metteyya's Dispensation. Other townspeople and many people from the countryside, more than a few kṣatriyas, Brahmins, vaiśyas and śūdras,
65. many people from various castes, turned towards renunciation, will then adopt the homeless life in emulation of Metteyya.
66. On the day when, resolute, he makes his renunciation, on that very renunciation-day he will go to the Seat of Enlightenment,
67. very splendid, he will sit down cross-legged on the supreme enlightenment seat, the place of the invincible (One)[44], and he will attain enlightenment.
68. The Conqueror will go to the fine garden (called) Nāgavana and set in motion the supreme Wheel of the Dhamma:
69. suffering, the arising of suffering, the overcoming of suffering, and the Noble Eighfold Path which leads to the allaying of suffering.
70. Then, when the Lord of the World has set in motion the Wheel of the Dhamma, there will be people for a hundred leagues on every side (as his) assembly.
71. Many gods, in even greater numbers, will come to the

[44] Reading *aparājita-ṭṭhānamhi*, after Jayawickrama's (1974) edition of the *Buddhavaṃsa* (xxv 20); cp. CPD s.v., and Leumann (1919: 210–11).

Conqueror there, and at that time he will release millions upon millions of them from their bonds.

72. Then king Saṇkha will offer his precious palace to the Community of Monks headed by the Conqueror, and moreover
73. will give many gifts to the poor, to travelers and to beggars, (and) will hurry to the Buddha, together with his queen;
74. having a limitless army, through the power of his great royal merit, he will go to the Conqueror along with millions upon millions of people.
75. Then the Perfectly enlightened One will beat the excellent Dhamma-drum, sounding the drum of the Deathless, expounding the Four Truths.
76. The millions upon millions of people accompanying the king will all, every one of them, become monks with the formula "Come, monk."[45]
77. Then gods and men will go to the Leader of the World and will ask the Conqueror a question about the excellent state of Arahantship.
78. The Conqueror will explain (it) to them, and through the attainment of the excellent state of Arahantship by 80,000 *koṭi*-s (of people) there will be the third penetration[46] (of the Truth).
79. The first assembly will be of 100,000 *koṭi*-s of excellent people, whose Corruptions are destroyed, without taint and calmed in mind.
80. After the Blessed One has proclaimed the Pavāraṇā ceremony at the end of the Rains Retreat, that Conqueror will celebrate it with 90,000 *koṭi*-s (of people).
81. The sage, in seclusion on the gold and silver slope of Mt. Gandhamādana in the Himālayas,
82. will enjoy the sport of meditation with 80,000 *koṭi*-s of excellent

[45] As with Gotama at Vin I 12, before the institution of the Monastic Order has been founded, with established procedures for the ordination of new members by those already monks, the only way to become a monk is for the Buddha himself to use the performative phrase "Come, monk."

[46] The text does not specify what were the first and second. Bv II 196–7 (cf. Bv-a 124) says that in three consecutive sermons (referred to as the first and second "penetrations'), the Buddha Dīpaṅkara enlightened 100 *koṭi*-s of people, then 90 in the second and 90,000 in the third. Here in v.71 the figure of 100,000 *koṭi*-s is mentioned; v.74 mentions 90,000. Bv II 197–9 (cf. Bv-a 125) says that Dīpaṅkara had three assemblies of 100,000 *koṭi*-s, then again 100,000, and a third of 90,000, vv.79, 80, 82 have 100,000, then 90, then 80,000.

people, whose corruptions are destroyed, without taint and calmed in mind.
83. 100,000 people who have attained the six superknowledges and have great magical powers will constantly surround Metteyya, the Lord of the World.
84. Skilled in the Discriminations, adept with words and (their) explanations, of great learning and expert in the Dhamma, distinguished and adding luster to the Community,
85. well-trained, humble (but) resolute, they will surround the Conqueror. That nāga [i.e. Metteyya] will be at the head of these monks, themselves excellent nāgas;[47] having crossed over and arrived at peace, he will be with those who have crossed over and are peaceful;
86. when the Great Sage has celebrated the Pavāraṇā ceremony with the community of his disciples, Metteyya the best of (all) two-footed beings, full of pity and compassion
87 will rescue many beings and bring them, along with gods, to nirvana. The Conqueror will live a wandering life, in villages, towns and royal cities,
88. beating the drum of the Dhamma, sounding the conch-shell of the Dhamma, proclaiming the sacrifice of the Dhamma, raising the flag of the Dhamma.
89. Roaring a lion's roar and turning the supreme wheel, he will make men and women drink the supremely tasteful drink of Truth.
90. For the benefit of all beings capable of enlightenment, the Conqueror will live a wandering life enlightening people, both rich and poor:
91. The Seeing One[48] will establish one person[49] in the Going for Refuge; another in the five Moral Rules, another in the ten Skillful Actions;
92. to one person he will give the practice of asceticism and the four supreme Fruits [i.e. the four stages of the Path], to another analytical insight into the unequaled Dhamma;

[47] Cp. Appendix 1, *Buddhavaṃsa* III 36 n. 47.
[48] *Cakkhumā*, translated in v.3 above as "(you) have eyes to see."
[49] *Kassaci*, "someone," in the singular, repeated seven times in each of the next six lines; each one obviously exemplifies a *kind* of salvific activity Metteyya will undertake rather than referring to one individual. The syntax of the Pali is a little clumsy here; I have smoothed this out in translation.

93. to one person the Seeing One will give the eight excellent attainments, to another he will offer the three knowledges (or all of) the six super-knowledges.
94. This is the way the Conqueror will teach people; then the Dispensation of Conqueror Metteyya will be extensive.
95. When that sage sees people capable of enlightenment, he will travel 100,000 leagues in a moment to enlighten them.
96. His mother then will be called Brahmavatī and his father, who will be king Saṇkha's (Brahmin) priest, will be called Subrahmā.
97. Asoka and Brahmadeva will be his two chief disciples. Sīha will act as his attendant,
98. Padumā and Sumanā will be his two chief female disciples, Sumana and Saṅgha his two chief (male) personal attendants,
99. Yasavatī and Saṅghā his two chief female personal attendants. The enlightenment tree of that Blessed One will be the nāga-tree.
100. Its trunk will be two thousand feet[50] (thick), and it will have two thousand branches whose ends will sway gently (in the wind); it will look splendid, like a peacock's tailfan.
101. The tips (of its branches) will be continuously in bloom, with a divinely fragrant scent; (each of) its blossoms, the size of wheels, will have (enough) pollen to fill a nāśi-measure.
102. Its scent will waft for ten leagues in every direction, with and against the wind; it will scatter its flowers all around the Seat of Enlightenment.
103. People from the countryside will smell its supreme scent and come together (to visit it) exclaiming in delight at its scent:
104. 'Fortunate is the result of merit for the excellent outstanding Buddha, because of whose glory (this) unimaginable (*acinteyya*) (scent)[51] wafts forth.'
105 That Conqueror will be eighty-eight feet tall; the teacher's chest will be twenty-five feet in diameter.
106. The sage's wide, curved eyes will not blink, by day or night,[52] and he will be able to see with his eyes of flesh (any) small and large (object)
107. for twelve leagues unobstructed on every side. His radiance will pour out as far as twenty-five (leagues).

[50] The word is *hattha*, on which see Appendix 2 n. 9.
[51] As Leumann (1919: 220) suggests, the missing noun here is almost certainly *gandho*, "scent." [52] Not blinking is also a characteristic of the gods.

108. That Conqueror will be bright like a streak of lightning or a flaming torch, he will shine like the sun, just like a string of jewels.
109. The Major and Minor Marks will seem like continuous rays, countless hundreds of thousands of multicolored rays cascading (down).
110. Every time he lifts his foot (in walking), a blooming lotus will grow (to receive it), whose (larger, outside) leaves will be uniform(ly) thirty feet and whose smaller (inside) leaves twenty-five,
111. its filaments twenty feet and pericarps sixteen. The lotus flowers will be full of fine red pollen.
112. Gods from the Sphere of Desire will construct columns (of honor), then nāga kings and Garuḍa birds will decorate them.[53]
113. (There will be) eight (such) columns of gold, eight made of silver, eight made of jewels and eight made of coral.
114. Many flags, several hundred, will hang there playing (in the breeze), adorned with various precious things and decorated with garlands (like) flags.
115. (There will be) awnings decorated with strings of pearls and (other) jewels, resembling the moon, surrounded by networks of little bells and garlands of jewels.
116. Scattered around will be various kinds of flowers, fragrant and sweet-smelling, different kinds of (aromatic) powders, divine and human,
117. and various dyed cloths, beautiful with the five colors. With faith in the Buddha, they (i.e. the gods, nagas and Garuḍas) will sport all around (him).
118. Expensive jeweled gateways will be (set up) there, a thousand (feet) high, good to look at, delightful, unobstructed and firmly-set;
119. They will appear glorious, shining on every side[54]. The Buddha, at the head of the Community of Monks, will be in the middle of them,
120. like Brahmā or Indra in a *vimāna* in the middle of the members of their assemblies. They [i.e. the monks] will move

[53] Garuḍas and nāgas are paradigmatic examples of mutual enmity, so this verse is another instance of the paradisial suspension of nature's animosities (cp. 4.2.b and Appendix 4 p. 623).

[54] *Sabbatopabha:* on this epithet, variously understood by the tradition, see KRN no. 68.

about when the Buddha moves about; remain motionless when he does;
121. when the Teacher lies down or sits, along with his assembly, they will always and everywhere adopt (whichever is appropriate of) the four positions.
122. There will be these and other (forms of) worship (*pūjā*), both divine and human, and various miracles all the time,
123. in order to worship Metteyya, thanks to the glory of his infinite merit. Many people, from various castes, will see the miracles and go for refuge to the Teacher, along with their wives and children,[55]
124. (whereas) those who will listen to the Sage's words and lead the (celibate) religious life will cross over the round of rebirth, (which is) subject to death and so difficult to cross.
125. Many householders will purify then their Dhamma-eye, by means of the ten Meritorious Deeds and the three types of good action [= of body, speech and mind];
126 many will purify (themselves) through (knowledge of) the texts and experience (of what they teach)[56], piously following the Dhamma, and will be destined for heaven.
127. It is not possible to describe completely their glory, saying "It is just this much": in this rebirth, a fortunate time, (one of) perpetual, constant happiness,
128. with great glory, happiness, length of life, good complexion and strength, these human beings will (enjoy) god-like good fortune.
129. After experiencing the happiness (brought by the fulfilment)

[55] This line is a puzzle, and my translation offers what I think its significance is, given the context. Minayeff's Pali is *saputtadārā-pāṇehi saraṇaṃ hessanti satthuno;* Leumann (1919: 190) prints the first word as two, *sa-putta-dārā panehi*, and translates (ibid. 223) as *samt Weib und Kinder werden sie (erst) mit dem Leben [d.h. erst mit dem Tode] den Schutz des Meisters verlassen.* Pruitt, in Tin (1988: 49) has: "men with their families will only abandon the Teacher as their refuge at the cost of their lives." *Hessanti* can be taken as third. plural future from *bhu*, to be; Leumann and Pruitt are taking it as an alternative spelling (or mis-spelling) for *hassanti*, from *jahati*, to abandon. This is possible, as other instances of this are found. But *pāṇehi* is the instrumental/ablative plural of *pāṇa*, "living being," and I very much doubt that this can be construed as "with their lives." I assume some verb of going was originally here, and that *pāṇehi* is a scribal error for something else. The point of vv.123–4 is, I think, a contrast between those who only go for refuge, out of admiration for miracles, remaining with their families – as PED s.v. *putta* states, the phrase "with wife and children" standardly refers to a hindrance to the religious life – as opposed to those who (really) listen to what the Buddha teaches, and embrace the celibate life. Further text-critical work is obviously needed.

[56] On *agamādhigama*, see Collins (1992b: 127 and n. 39).

of desire for as long as they wish, afterwards, at the end of their lives, these happy people will enter [heaven].[57]
130. 80,000 years will be the length of life then; for as long as he lives, (the Buddha) will cause many people to cross over [into nirvana];
131. he will completely enlighten those beings whose minds are ripe (for it), and explain what is the Path and what is not to the remainder, who cannot see the Truth(s).
132. The future Conqueror will carefully set up for beings the torch [or: crucible] of the Dhamma, the Dhamma-ship, the Dhamma-mirror and the (Dhamma-)medicine,
133. along with the excellent Community of Disciples, who will have done what is to be done[58]; the Conqueror will blaze like a mass of fire, and then go out.[59]
134. When the Fully enlightened One is wholly extinguished (*parinibbute*), his Dispensation will endure for 101,000 years,[60] and after that the disappearance[61] will be hard for the world (to endure).
135. Thus is the existence of conditioned things impermanent, unstable, temporary, transitory, (subject to) breaking-up, decaying, empty.
136. Conditioned things are like a hollow fist, empty, a tale told by an idiot;[62] no-one can control them, not even someone with magical powers.
137. One should understand this as it really is and turn away from everything constructed. A thoroughbred among men [i.e. a Buddha] is hard to find, he is not born everywhere:
138. therefore, in order to see Metteyya Buddha here, do good energetically, steadfastly, anxiously (*ubbigga-manasā*).

[57] Vv.127–9 are not without their difficulties, but the point seems clear enough. Householders (v.125) who do not attain enlightenment, but become destined for rebirth in heaven (v.126), will enjoy celestial happiness in the current life, on earth with Metteyya (vv.127–8), and then will continue to enjoy it after death, in the heaven where they are reborn (v.129). Once again, as in vv.123–4, the text juxtaposes but does not confuse the felicity of the Worlds of Desire with that of "crossing over" (vv.130b–131a); v.131 itself again contrasts those who are capable of enlightenment with those who are not. [58] This phrase usually denotes the attainment of Enlightenment.
[59] *Nibbāyissati*, "he will nirvanize." For the image see 2.3.b.
[60] Assuming *c'eva sahassako* means "plus one (more) thousand."
[61] This is the gradual disappearance of his Dispensation and relics, culminating in the third nirvana, "the nirvana of the relics': see 3.2.b.
[62] Literally "the babbling of fools," *bālalāpana*.

139. All those who have acted rightly, living diligently, (whether) monks, nuns, male or female lay followers,
140. doing great honor to the Buddha [or: Buddhas, *buddhasakkāra*] and worshiping him [them] greatly – they will (all) see [Metteyya's] auspicious assembly at that time, along with the gods.
141. Lead the religious [celibate] life, give gifts properly, keep the Uposatha day (vows) and cultivate lovingkindness assiduously.
142. Concentrate on being diligent in meritorious deeds at all times: by doing good here (and now), you will make an end of suffering."

One might say that this poem depicts a continuous carnival (see v.41 and n. 41): in the first fifty verses, those alive at this time enjoy throughout their lives the "unalloyed happiness" of a festival (v.41). After Metteyya is enlightened and begins to enlighten others, the carnival continues, but now the *tableau vivant* of felicity has an enlightened Buddha at center stage. But not simply *a* Buddha: for the intensity and extent of felicity at the time of Metteyya surpasses that of previous Buddhas, including our Gotama. Not only are conditions for everyone almost perfect (see the Critical Discussion, p. 412, on the idea of perfection here), but Metteyya's own "practice of exertion" in vv.54, 66–7 (see also n. 43) is brief and apparently easy, in contrast to the many depictions, both textual and iconographic, of Gotama's hard struggle (5.3.b).[63] This is something new, something not predictable simply from the logic of Buddhist thought. It was argued earlier that reflection on the simplest truths of Buddhist systematic discourse leads to the possibility of future Buddhas: but this is in itself only the possibility of repeated and homogenous salvific moments dotted throughout non-repetitive time. One cannot deduce any specific narratives from the idea of multiple Buddhas, still less the *Anāgata-vaṃsa*'s extraordinary depiction of multidimensional and in some ways unprecedented happiness at the time of Metteyya.

It seems not to have been noticed, or at least not properly appreciated in previous scholarship, that the joint appearance of a Wheel-turning King and a Buddha, in the persons of Saṅkha and

[63] He will also be much taller than human beings are now (v.105), like the gods (4.1.a, p. 302) and the inhabitants of Uttarakuru (4.2.a).

Metteyya, is very unusual in Southern Asian Buddhism, and in the Pali imaginaire for all practical purposes unique. Other examples of the pairing can be found; it becomes a standard story motif in the *Mahāvastu*, a Buddhist Sanskrit text.[64] There are certain technical problems with the coincidence of these two "Great Men": the same amount of merit is required to become either; and when Buddhas are born, they are standardly said to have either career open to them (6.5.a). When both a Wheel-turning King and a Buddha are born at the same time, logically speaking – were the "choice" between the two careers a real choice, and not a rhetorical trope – they could both opt for the same career, which would produce the coincidence of two Buddhas (or two Wheel-turning Kings) in the same place, a possibility rarely, if ever admitted anywhere in non-Mahāyāna Buddhist traditions,[65] and impossible in Theravāda doctrine (Vbh 336 with Vibh-a 430ff.). Some Pali texts do admit of the possibility of the two Great Men together, apart from the Saṅkha/Metteyya pair. In the *Buddhavaṃsa* the Buddha Kondañña coexists with a Wheel-turning King called Vijitāvin (Bv III; Appendix 1), and the Buddha Maṅgala with one called Sunanda (Bv IV);[66] and a previous birth of our Buddha Gotama occurs as a Wheel-turning King at the time of the Buddha Sujāta (Bv XIII). The *Dasabodhisattuppattikathā* (paras. 6ff.) describes a previous life of Metteyya as a Wheel-turning King named Saṅkha at the time of Sirimata Buddha (see further 5.3.a below on names). It also describes (paras.87ff.) a former life of the elephant Pārileyya, a companion of Gotama Buddha when he took refuge from the quarreling monks of Kosambi(1.2.b), who will become the tenth future Buddha Sumaṅgala, in which he was a Wheel-turning King called Panāda or Mahāpanāda with the Buddha Kakusandha. There may also be an implicit reference to an unnamed Wheel-turning King at the time of Dīpaṅkara, depending on the interpretation of Bv II 5 (Appendix 1 n. 6). But these are obscure references in mostly formulaic stories, with nothing like the elaboration of the Metteyya/Saṅkha pair. And so this gives one more reason to apply the comparative notion of millennialism

[64] E.g. I 1, 49–54, 67–8, etc. At I 57ff. the pairing is said to happen countless times. See also Jaini (1988). [65] Cf. Armelin (1975: 22–3, 30).

[66] When the Buddha Maṅgala appears, Sunanda's "wheel-treasure" slips from its place in the sky, something which usually happens when a Wheel-turning King is about to die; see Appendix 3 and 6.5.a.

to this Buddhist case. The more or less unique coexistence of the two Great Men allows the coexistence of more than one kind of felicity: in fact, an (almost) unprecedented well-being.

An older type of scholarship might have immediately looked for the "origin" of such a "new development"; and it might, as said above, have found it in the Persian Saviour God Mithra. I would rather say that any ideological system, and any lived culture, must perforce emphasize some human aspirations, some imaginative possibilities, to the exclusion or (better) de-emphasis of others. In Buddhism generally, one does not find, ubiquitously and centrally, the millennial hope of a salvation and unprecedented "perfection" located in the future. But the History of the Future shows that it can be found; it is argued in 5.3 that this future is, as an intentional object of consciousness, both immensely distant and, in so far as it is the focus of anticipation, immediately present. In this poem at least – thanks to the fact that Saṅkha and Metteya coexist, and to the quality of felicity that coexistence makes available – there is something special about Metteyya, something which is not in principle unique in the perspective of Buddhist systematic thought, but which is qualitatively distinct in the landscape of Buddhist narrative.

5.2.c. Listening to the Vessantara Jātaka

In the prose and verse version of the *Anāgata-vaṃsa*, from which Minayeff printed excerpts as text B, are found two lists of people who, because of certain actions, will and will not see Metteyya.[67] Some of the relevant deeds are entirely predictable: those who create a schism in the Monastic Order, like the Buddha's cousin Devadatta, will not see him, whereas those who give alms, keep the Uposatha-day vows, etc. will. The hope to see Metteyya is attested in texts and inscriptions, as well as modern ethnographic reports.[68] One also finds, though less often, the assertion that if guilty of certain crimes, some people will not see Metteyya; it was made, for example, by the historical king Kyanzittha of Burma (1084–1102) in an inscription (EB I 47–52), and appears in the

[67] Minayeff (1886: 37), translated in Warren (1896: 485–6).

[68] *Inter alia*, Saddhatissa (1975: 27ff.), Gombrich (1971a: 79, 92–3, 218, etc.), Ferguson and Johanssen (1976), Aung-Thwin (1985: 38–9), Wijayaratna (1987: 86ff., 559–60), McGill (1997).

story of the Elder Māleyya (Appendix 4). One item in *Anāgata-vaṃsa* B's list of good deeds which can result in seeing Metteyya comes as a surprise: among them are "those who listen to the *Vessantara Jātaka*." Minayeff's manuscripts came from Burma, and there is other evidence of the connection between the *Vessantara Jātaka* and Metteyya there, which would show, if accepted, that it goes back to the thirteenth century.[69] There seems no evidence that this connection was made in Sri Lanka, although lists of those who will and will not see Metteyya occur in texts found there (Godakumbara 1980: 93–4; Saddhatissa 1975: 32–3). It is in Thailand that the connection became very important, through the story of the elder Māleyya, where Metteyya expressly tells Māleyya to tell people to "listen to a complete recitation in one day of the Great Vessantara Birth Story" if they wish to see him in the future (Appendix 4, p. 621). The story of Māleyya (variously spelt in Pali and Thai, where it is most often *Phra Malai*), in various versions, became one of the most important aspects of traditional Thai Buddhist culture. Manuscripts often contained the Māleyya story and the *Vessantara Jātaka* together (Brereton 1995: 61).

Modern ethnographic reports show the significance of the recitation of the *Vessantara Jātaka* in ritual contexts.[70] According to Anuman Rajadhon it can be read on "any special occasions such as the raising of funds for the wat [Buddhist temple]" (1961: 97; 1968: 168); but as he and others show, it is commonest in October, after the Rainy Season. Tambiah (1968a: 77ff., 70: 160ff.) reports that in Northeast Thailand a reading occurs during the dry season in February–March, as both a thanksgiving for the recent harvest and as a way of looking forward to the rains. Water is an important theme in the rituals during which the *Vessantara Jātaka* is read, and part of their function is to facilitate plentiful rainfall. Gerini (1892: 21–2), who speaks more generally of Siam as a whole, reports that the reading took place at the beginning, middle or end of the rainy season, during which monks were required to keep a Rains Retreat.[71] At the end of that time, he says, "the rivers

[69] See Collins (1993a: 11 and n. 2).

[70] Brereton (1995: 61–7) gives further information, from her research and from publications unavailable to me.

[71] Kinsghill (1965: 115, 1991: 228–32) says that it takes place on the full moon day of the second month (= November), following the rains. Kaufman (1960: 190–6) places it at the end of the Rainy Season.

run full and overflowing their banks, flood the country and deposit their yearly tribute of fecundating slime over the fields. All nature seems endowed with fresh impulse and the lotus flowers, symbolical of creation and the new spirit of life, may be seen in full bloom floating on the waters." In a flawed but still useful Ph.D. thesis entitled "The Vessantara Jātaka: paradigm for a Buddhist utopian ideal," McClung has stressed this ritual context for the *Vessantara Jātaka*, seeing it, through a somewhat freewheeling association of ideas, as reconciling the aspiration to nirvana with what he calls "the hedonistic desire for pleasurable rebirths" (1975: 232–3). More is said about this in 7.5, and so I postpone extended discussion till then; but it is worth recording here that the traditional millennial hope for rebirth at the time of Metteyya is connected with the story of Vessantara, in Thailand and (less certainly) Burma, in texts and their contexts, and that an important theme of the ritual contexts in which their association is enacted involves fecundating rainfall, as the object of celebration or hope. It seems clearly significant that the stories of Vessantara and Māleyya are associated, and that the association takes place most often in the performance context of fertility rituals; and it is only a superficial paradox that the values of renunciation and Buddhahood should thus be combined with fecundity and the prolongation of life: the spectrum of felicities easily encompasses and affirms both. Both are sources of happiness; both are forms of salvation from suffering.[72]

The previous section suggested that the story of Metteyya in Anāg depicts a continuous carnival within which felicity develops from the external-sensory through the internal-mental to that of nirvana. Chapter 7 argues that the reason the *Vessantara Jātaka* is one of the most popular stories in Buddhist cultures is that it provides the most comprehensive vision of Buddhist felicities: not comprehensive explicitly, since nirvana is not depicted in the text, but implicitly, since it remains in the background (teleologically)

[72] The connection is not merely textual: in the eleventh century Theravāda was imported from southern Burma into the "core agricultural zones" around Pagan by king Anawrahta; monasteries "were established at critical locations throughout these zones, and upon receiving allocations of rights to land and labor assumed a leadership role in the development of irrigation works and wet-rice agriculture in each new population centre" (Hall 1992: 241). For a comparable example in early Christianity, see Brown (1988: 437).

as the final aim of the story, in the nirvana of Gotama prefigured by Vessantara's "Perfect Generosity." The growth and interrelations of both Pali and vernacular versions of the Vessantara and Māleyya stories, and the *Anāgata-vaṃsa* family of texts, clearly represent a significant development within the Pali imaginaire: not a change, but an intensification of earlier, future-oriented and thus "millennial" aspirations.

5.2.d. Other future Buddhas, and a mistake about kings

I have argued that Buddhist systematic thought, of whatever form and at any period, must presume that Gotama is not unique. Indeed, in an infinite – beginningless and endless – universe, there must be an infinite number of Buddhas, even if the narratives about them cannot be infinite: and the tradition comes to say exactly that. The *Jinakālamālī*, a text from sixteenth-century Thailand, adds to the usual list two more names of Buddhas, Former Dīpaṅkara and Former Sakyamuni, who are thus distinguished from the later Buddhas known by those names; it also names Taṇhaṅkara, Medhaṅkara and Saraṇaṅkara as Buddhas preceding Dīpaṅkara in the same eon, as at Bv XXXVII 1 (see Jayawickrama 78: 12ff.). The *Jinakālamalī* then goes on to say that the future Buddha Gotama, previous to his aspiration to Buddhahood at the time of Dīpaṅkara, when he received his "official" prediction, as it were, had already in previous eons aspired to Buddhahood in the presence of 387,000 former Buddhas. Two texts mentioned earlier, of uncertain provenance but probably from the twelfth to fourteenth centuries, tell short stories about ten future Buddhas: the *Dasabodhisattuddesa* (Dasab) and the *Dasabodhisattuppattikathā* (Dbk). Sāriputta asks the Buddha "Surely there will be numerous other Buddhas in future eons?", as well as Metteyya in the present eon. The Buddha replies "There will be endless, uncountable (*anantāparimāṇa*) beings who, after experiencing success (*sampatti*) in the Worlds of Desire and the Brahma-worlds, will attain Buddhahood, perform the duty of a Buddha (*Buddha-kicca*), and (finally) nirvanize." "But," he goes on, "there will be ten Arahants, Fully enlightened Ones, who will arise in succession," and then falls silent (Dbk paras. 1–2, Dasab 1). This is obviously not a simple arithmetical inconsistency: the second statement clearly means there will be ten future Buddhas about whom, on this occasion, stories will be told, who can thus be more than mere names or numbers. It seems possible that the number ten was originally chosen because of the list of ten Perfections:[73] at the beginning of each of the ten sections it is said that the Buddha described therein excels in one Perfection, and then a story is told of a past life, apparently to exemplify it. However, in the texts as we now have them, the stories in fact seem to illustrate only the Perfection of Generosity, and some clearly borrow from the story of Vessantara.

In all but one of the sections, it is either said explicitly or can be inferred that at the time of the future Buddhas there will be no need for trade or agriculture.[74] At the time of Metteyya, according to the *Dasabodhisattuppattikathā*, this will be the case, and "people will live happily on meals of rice produced through the power of the Buddha." The account of Metteyya in the *Dasabodhisattuppattikathā* is longer, with a more extended paradisial account resembling that of the *Anāgatavaṃsa*, and where likewise Saṅkha's city has a wishing-tree at each of its four gates. In the cases of the Buddhas Rāma (no.2), Dhammarāja (3), and Sumaṅgala (10) there will be a wishing-tree to provide for everyone's needs; in those of Devadeva (7) and Narasīha (8) there will be a wishing-tree and fragrant rice; in that of Dhammasāmi (4) there will be a store of treasure which people will use; in that of Nārada (5) people will eat an "earth-essence"[75]; in that of Tissa (9) "pots of clarified butter, curds, oil and also all kinds of hard and soft food will appear". In the story of Raṃsimuni (6), the *Dasabodhisattuppattikathā* says, to the contrary, that everyone then will make their living by trade (alone); this is perhaps influenced by the Story of the Past, when Raṃsimuni was a merchant called Magha, who suffered repeated business failures and finally had all his wealth taken by the king. In his distress he argues with his wife and leaves home, borrowing a blanket and a large amount of gold

[73] The list of ten Perfections is used to organize other texts, such as the last ten *Jātaka* stories, which often appeared in manuscripts and iconography as a separate group of "Great Jātakas"; and the *Cariyā-piṭaka*, which recounts in verse brief stories of Gotama's past lives. See also n. 87 below: these may be (the) ten about whom Gotama makes a prediction of future Buddhahood.

[74] Anāg v.40 has the word *phuṭa-bhedanā*, which was translated above simply as "cities"; it is elsewhere taken to refer to trading and market centers.

[75] *Paṭhavi-rasa*. For this see the *Aggañña Sutta* section 11, translated in Appendix 5, and Collins (1993c: 357–8).

in order to go to Kosambī to begin trading again. There he meets a Chief Disciple of the Buddha Kakusandha, and joyfully offers the blanket and gold to him, declaring that "now I will trade for nirvana" (*idāni nibbāna-vāṇijaṃ karissāmi*). There is a wishing-tree in this section, but it is in the Story of the Past: after Magha has made his gift, aspired to nirvana and had his aspiration confirmed by the Chief Disciple, the latter leaves and a wishing-tree springs up on the spot. In Dasab the story of the past is the same, but that text says that at the time of Raṃsimuni people will live by both trade and agriculture.

These two closely related works are the only currently available textual evidence for stories of future Buddhas other than Metteyya, but in view of the many texts which seem to exist called (as is the *Dasabodhisattuddesa* in some mss.) *Anāgata-Buddha-vaṃsa*, it is not possible in the present state of knowledge to decide how widespread such stories were. Saddhatissa (1975: 20–1) cites epigraphic and iconographic evidence, from Thailand and Sri Lanka, for "the ten Bodhisattas, beginning with Metteyya"; as do Luce and Maung Tin (1923: 160) for Burma. Each section of the *Dasabodhisattuddesa* and the *Dasabodhisattuppattikathā* ends with the wish that whoever is not enlightened under the Buddhas before him will gain enlightenment there and then.

There is some evidence of historical agents hoping to become future Buddhas themselves: as mentioned earlier (p. 252 and n. 30 above), this aspiration is found in the colophons of manuscripts. It is also found, for example, in a Burmese inscription written in good Pali verse, set up by King Alaungsithu in 1141 AD[76] This offers praise to Gotama Buddha, and recounts some of the king's own good deeds; then, in the longer part of the poem, the king expresses his wish to become a Buddha himself, following the model of Gotama.[77] He hopes to meet Metteyya and receive the

[76] Luce and Pe Maung Tin (1920).

[77] Note that v.30 of this inscription has the phrase *Buddhabhāvāya āsatto*, "attached to" or "intent on the state of (being a) Buddha." The verb *sañj* (here with prefix *ā-*) is one of the two probable derivations for the word *bodhi-satta*, which I translate nonliterally as "future Buddha." The more familiar Skt form *bodhi-sattva*, usually construed, inelegantly and implausibly, as "Enlightenment-being," seems to be the result of a mistaken Sanskritization, confusing the Pali (or related MIA dialect) noun *satta* (Skt *sattva*), "being" with the past participle *satta*, which can be derived either from *sañj* (= Skt *sakta*) with the meaning "attached to" or "intent on'; or from *śak* (Skt *śakta*), meaning "capable of," "fit for." For the former of these two senses of the participle *satta* (and probably also the latter) see Spk II 21, Mp II 365; cf. Bollée (1974: 36 n. 27), KRN no. 83 p. 87).

prediction of Buddhahood from him; and thus, at the end of the poem (vv.99–100), he hopes one day to "perform all the duties of a Buddha, and reach the supreme, safe city of nirvana, without birth or death, which gives unalloyed happiness" (*accanta-sukhadāyaka*). The claim by kings to be future Buddhas is well known (e.g. Luce 1969 I: 99, Aung Thwin 1985: 46): an inscription from tenth-century Sri Lanka, saying that only future Buddhas could become kings of the island, is often quoted (e.g. Rahula 1956: 62). Unfortunately, in the literature on this issue a mistake is very often made about what that claim means. It is important to correct this mistake, not merely for its own sake, but because it has contributed to the considerable confusion in the scholarly literature on the modern "millennial" movements, to be dealt with in the Critical Discussion. In that context, it is habitually said – usually without citing any evidence – that their leaders claimed to be Metteyya; and then this claim is seen as continuous with the allegedly traditional identification of kings with Metteyya. The mistake can be traced to Paul Mus, but it appears perhaps most clearly in Sarkisyanz (65: *passim*, especially Chapter 10), in this as in other ways Mus' disciple. In Chapter 7, called "Emergence of the Bodhisattva Ideal of Kingship in Theravāda Buddhism," he states:

> Though Theravāda tenets could not promise to each believer, not even each member of the [royal] dynasty, to become a Buddha, its traditions *by implication* opened for Ceylon's kings the possibility of becoming the only future Buddha that the Theravāda admits within this World Age: there evolved in Ceylon first a cult of Mettaya [*sic*, throughout] and then ideals of the king's association with this future Buddha. Eventually this culminated in the royal ideal of aspiring to become the Bodhisattva Mettaya[78].

This is clearly wrong. There is no justification for the assumption that when a king claimed to be *a* future Buddha, he was claiming to be *the* future Buddha of this eon. (Pali and other forms of

[78] (1965: 45) in part translating Mus's words from *Barabadur*, for which he gives the reference BEFEO 1933 (33) p. 728; in the reprint, Mus (1935), the passage appears on p. 324. (Cp. also Mus's introduction to Sarkisyanz 1965: XVIII.) Sarkisyanz (1965: 62–3) even quotes a passage from the translation of the inscription of Alaungsithu I have just mentioned, in which the king states that he wishes to meet Metteyya and then "informed by such a teacher" become a Buddha himself, later. But he goes on to say immediately after the quotation that in the "transformation of royalty into future Buddhahood," "the future Buddha of Theravada Buddhism is Mettaya (Maitreya)," and continues in the same vein. Such is the tenacity of *idées fixes*. I should add that apart from this and some other imprecisions, I find Sarkisyanz's book admirable and helpful.

Indo-Aryan have neither direct or indirect articles, although other words, adjectives and pronouns, can be used if the semantic effect of either is required.) On the contrary, everyone knew that Metteyya is currently in the Tusita heaven,[79] awaiting the time when, with Gotama's Dispensation gone and forgotten, he will be reborn on earth: how could he be "identified with" or "associated with" a human king now, when Gotama's Dispensation is still, relatively speaking, alive and well? It is true, as discussed in the next chapter, that some kings (and on one occasion the scholar monk Buddhaghosa) are depicted, both verbally and in ritual settings, as analogous to Metteyya: but the texts are always clear that this is an analogy, signaled explicitly by the word *viya*, "just like" or "as if," or implicitly (but nonetheless clearly) by the context. There is an infinity of Buddhas as much in Theravāda as in the variegated collection of things known as Mahāyāna Buddhism: the only difference, obviously significant, is that in the former they happen one at a time, in a single universe, whereas in the latter they occur simultaneously, in multiple universes.[80] But one infinity can be no bigger than another. When a king, in a Theravāda setting, declared himself to be a future Buddha, especially if he also acted out the role, of course all manner of rhetorical hyperbole was going on in the here-and-now; but this is in itself no reason to think that the king was being "associated" with Metteyya, in any other than an analogizing sense, and still less being "identified" with him, by himself or anyone else.

It is now possible to make a preliminary summary of "millennialism" in traditional Buddhism. If the expectation of imminent salvation is made a defining characteristic, as it sometimes is, there was none. But if not, one can see millennialism as present in two ways:

(i) In the widespread stories about Metteyya, the next Buddha of this eon, which enabled people to aspire to be reborn on earth and meet him. Textual depictions of the conditions

[79] There may be exceptions, although this is not yet certain: kings Alaungpaya and/or Bodawpaya in late eighteenth- and early nineteenth-century Burma, and some leaders of peasant revolts in Thailand. See the Critical Discussion.

[80] The Buddhāpadāna (Ap 1ff.), an exceptional text in this and other ways, has Gotama Buddha mentally visualizing both past and present Buddhas (the latter in the plural) (*ye . . . etarahi . . . Buddhā*) coming together to talk; but no future Buddhas are included.

which will obtain at that time subtly and clearheadedly blend motifs depicting the different kinds of felicity which will be possible then, in a continuous carnival, from external-sensory well-being through internal-mental happiness to the bliss of nirvana.

(ii) In the fact that the possibility of infinite future Buddhas, and the relatively infrequent but not unexampled stories and pictures of ten future Buddhas, Metteyya and nine others, enabled some people – almost always kings – to be recognized explicitly as future Buddhas themselves, to be in the lineage of Buddhas[81]. Here it is important to remember the distinction drawn earlier between the implicit logic of multiple Buddhas in early texts and the explicit recognition, in narrative or otherwise, of individuals as storied Buddhas of the past and future. Despite the rarity of narratives about individual future Buddhas, it must be the case that if there are, logically, an infinite number of them, each of whom must practice the Perfections during immensely long periods of time, it follows that even now we must be surrounded by a very large number of them. Like Gotama in the *Jātaka* stories, they can be human beings (often kings), animals or gods. As Gombrich put it (1980: 71), concluding the first of his articles on multiple Buddhas: "the world is now teeming with Bodhisattvas . . . the supply of Buddhas [will never] run dry. Grounds for a little cheerfulness."

5.3. ANTICIPATIONS OF BUDDHAHOOD

5.3.a. Proper names, and ambiguities of reference

A topic which may not be grounds for cheerfulness in all readers is that of the names used to refer to Metteyya at different stages of what Jaini (1988) calls his "Bodhisattva career," and specifically what the name "Metteyya" currently refers to. This is an intricate and difficult issue, but one from which, I hope, a valuable insight may arise: not about the issue of Metteyya's names in itself, but about the nature of present belief in future Buddhas.

[81] *Buddhavaṃsika* (Dbk para.36), *Buddhavaṃsa* (Dasab 16). For a clear separation in Pali texts between *Buddha-vaṃsa* and *rāja-vaṃsa* see Collins and Huxley (1997).

Chapter 3.4.b described how the first person narrative voice in the *Buddhavaṃsa* coalesces Gotama Buddha with Sumedha, the ascetic in a previous life at the time of Dīpaṅkara Buddha who made the aspiration to Buddhahood which came to fruition in the life of Gotama. The first person pronoun, both when used explicitly and as implicit in first person singular verbs, could straddle the two lives. This might seem difficult to reconcile with the doctrine of not-self, but there is no real theoretical confusion here. According to Buddhist systematic thought, the process of rebirth involves, at the level of ultimate truth, no continuing person or self, whatever exigencies the linguistic use of referring terms might impose.[82] In a series of lives, what appear to be stable and unitary persons are in fact collections of impersonal and impermanent events, arising and disappearing in a beginningless process of conditioning, a process which includes both physical causation and the spiritual causation of karma. Connectedness across a series of lives occurs through the continuity of consciousness, seen as a constantly changing series of momentary events, in which both memory and temporary coherence of personality can be found, but no enduring self. Within this ever-changing continuity of consciousness the pronoun "I" functions at any given moment as an indexical, just like (indeed closely similar to) "here" and "now." On the conventional level the spatiotemporally individuated person[83] of each life can be picked out by this pronoun, and by proper names or definite descriptions. Thus one sequence of events at the time of Dīpaṅkara is known, for conventional purposes, as "Sumedha"; a later series of events in the same series, connected to the former through karma, is known for the first part of the lifetime as "Siddhattha Gotama," and after the event of enlightenment as "Gotama Buddha," "Sakyamuni", "the fourth Buddha of the present Fortunate Epoch," and so on. Strictly speaking, no such name or description should be used to refer both to events in a continuum which occur between one pair of birth- and death-moments, and also to events which occur between another such pair earlier or later in the continuum (unless the names are, in philosophical usage, two tokens of the same type). The pronominal and verbal use of the first person to refer to events within

[82] This is dealt with at length in Collins (1982).
[83] The Pali terms are *puggala* or *purisa*, person, and *attabhāva*, individuality (Collins 1982: Chapter 5).

two different birth-moment/death-moment pairs is a prime example of what the Buddha called "worldly forms of speech and expression," by which one should not be "led astray" (Collins 1982: 130).

In the case of the rebirth series which culminated in Gotama Buddha, the *Jātaka* stories provide hundreds of names for events in discrete birth–death sections (= "lives") of the series. In all cases, as in the antepenultimate life, the last as a human being before Siddhattha Gotama, when the events were known as Vessantara, the Buddha as narrative voice concludes "I was at that time Vessantara" (Collins 1982: 151–2). In the penultimate life, as a god in the Tusita heaven, two names are given in different texts, Setaketu (Sp 161, Ps I 125) and Santusita (Bv I 66, Bv-a 53).[84] So, schematically, the situation can be represented as follows:

Table 5.1

Aspiration life	Antepenultimate (last human) life	Penultimate life, in Tusita Heaven	Last, enlightenment life
Sumedha	Vessantara	(i) Setaketu (ii) Santusita	Siddhattha Gotama becomes Sakyamuni

In the case of Metteyya, things are not so simple. The name Ajita is sometimes given for the human birth at the time of Gotama, referring to a monk about whom Gotama made a prediction of Buddhahood; sometimes, confusingly, the same name is given for the young prince in the last life of the series, who becomes Metteyya. Some texts, such as the *Dasabodhisattuppattikathā* and the *Dasabodhisattuddesa*, discussed in the last section, say that the aspiration to Buddhahood was made in a life long ago, at the time of the Buddha Sirimata (Dasab Sirimatta), otherwise unknown. At that time, events in the Metteyya-series were known as Saṅkha (again confusingly, since this is also the name of the Wheel-turning king at the time of future-Metteyya). If this were not bad enough, the confusion becomes deeper when one turns to names used for

[84] The name Santusita is also used for one of the gods in the Tusita heaven at the time of future-Gotama's descent from there to become Siddhattha (Ja I 48, Bv-a 10, 272, 291).

the penultimate life – as far as we are concerned, the current one – in the Tusita heaven.

In almost all texts, this character is simply referred to as Metteyya. Once again, strictly speaking, this can only be proleptic, a shorthand form of the definite description "the continuum of events (= present 'life') which will in the future (= the next 'life') be referred to as 'Metteyya.'" It is rare for the penultimate life of the series Saṅkha/Ajita → Metteyya to be given its own proper name. In the *Dictionary of Pali Proper Names* (s.v. Metteyya), Malalasekera states "there is a tradition that Nātha is the name of the future Buddha in the deva-world."[85] This no doubt derives from the fact that in Sri Lanka, a deity known as Nātha is frequently said to be the same as Metteyya,[86] but I know no Pali text where this is unambiguously stated. The *Cūlavaṃsa* (52,47) uses the term *lokanātha* of Metteyya, probably as a (proleptic) epithet, "Lord of the World"; just as the *Anāgatavaṃsa*, translated above, uses many terms such as "Conqueror" (v.7), and "Lord of the World" (v.70) with verbs in the future tense to refer to future facts. A verse in one story of the *Sīhalavatthu-pakaraṇa* (Sīh 106, v.48) uses the word *ajita* of Metteyya currently in Tusita, but again this should probably be taken as an epithet, "unconquered", "victorious", rather than a proper name we would write with a capital letter. The *Dasabodhisattuppattikathā* says that after the past life on earth as Saṅkha, when the aspiration to Buddhahood was made, the next rebirth was in Tusita as a junior god called – yet again – Saṅkha (the *Dasabodhisattuddesa* gives no name). But, as Jaini (88: 81. n. 13) says, this "need not necessarily refer to Maitreya's present (and final birth) in that heaven, because one can be born any number of times in the world of the gods." Indeed, it would be quite abnormal if it did, such that the aspiration to Buddhahood in this case would be followed by only two rebirths before its attainment. As seen earlier, future Buddhas must practice the Perfections for millions of years; and the usual assumption is that these years are counted from the time of the initial aspiration. So schematically we have

[85] Cp. Gombrich and Obeyesekere (1988: 53), Deraniyagala (1954–5: 100).
[86] This figure is also connected, by historians, with the Bodhisattva Avalokiteśvara: see Holt (1991a).

Table 5.2

Aspiration/Prediction lives	Penultimate life (current) in heaven	Last, Enlightenment life
(i) Ajita, with Gotama Buddha	(i) Nātha (in Sri Lanka)	Ajita (in some texts) becomes Metteyya
(ii) Saṅkha, with Sirimata Buddha	(ii) Saṅkha (unlikely)	
	(iii) Metteyya	

The positive point to be taken from all this is that by far the most common way of referring, in narratives, to future-Metteyya now is the name Metteyya itself. This can be seen also in a list of names found in several texts dealing with the ten future Buddhas. The list begins with Metteyya, but all of the others (with some minor variations) are the names by which they were known at the time of Gotama Buddha.[87] (This is the case at Dasab 38 and Dbk no. 99, whose earlier story of Metteyya says that at the time of Gotama future-Metteyya was the monk Ajita.)[88] There is, of course, a Buddhist systematic analysis which can explain how and why such naming practices must be taken as both conventional and proleptic: they are the names conventionally designating the "persons" between a given pair of birth–death moments, in the series ending with [e.g.] "the Buddha 'Metteyya.'" But it seems hardly likely that in most cultural practice people would speak so strictly, and so such fine points will almost never be salient. From the point of view described in the General Introduction III.c, where salvation is, in Wilson's words, the present "experience in this world" of reassurance, the god in Tusita now referred to by

[87] Minayeff's Anāg B says that they were the Buddhas who received predictions of Buddhahood from Gotama – this would explain what I called on p. 378 the arithmetical inconsistency between the Buddha's stating that there will be infinite future Buddhas and then that there will be ten: these would be the ten whose future Buddhahood he had personally predicted.

[88] See Martini (1936: 288, 334, 413), Saddhatissa (1975: 92, 162), Bechert et al. (1979: 117–18), Tin (1988: 1 and n. 1). In the case of the second Buddha, Rāma, the same name is used for the person living at the time of Gotama in the story, but here it is not the case that the future Buddha's name is used to refer to this past life; rather two (connected) people happen to be referred to by the same name. Saddhatissa (1975: 4–5) cites and translates from an unpublished Pali text called the *Dasabodhisatta Vidhiya* (see also Somadasa 1987 I: 143) a list of four names of future Buddhas said to be currently in Tusita (Metteyya, Rāma, Pasena and Vibhūti), along with three others currently in Tavatiṃsa heaven and four "now ordained as bhikkhus upon the earth." (It is not clear who is speaking, and so to what time the "now" refers).

Buddhists as Metteyya *is* – better, functions *as* – Metteyya Buddha. And so the present aspiration for future rebirth when Metteyya becomes (or perhaps better, moves gently from potential to actual) Buddha, while not equivalent to salvation in Buddhist terms, can be seen to offer a millennial anticipation of it, from the external-analytic point of view. As was said earlier, the future time of Metteyya is an intentional object of consciousness which is both immensely distant and, in so far as it is the focus of anticipation, immediately present.[89]

The relationship between present and future here is analogous to that between a past Buddha and present relics (General Introduction I.b and Chapter 3.4.c).[90] The absence of a locus of transcendental value from the actual, material world, which is given in the very nature of transcendentalist visions, coexists with a simultaneous need for it to be in one way or another immanent in that world. For traditional Theravāda, whatever may have been true of "Buddhism" at the time of the Buddha Gotama (assuming there was one), Buddhas of the past – most importantly, Gotama – and those of the future – most importantly, Metteyya – were absent from the here-and-now. Past and future Buddhas, the former through relics, etc. (3.2.b), the latter through millennial anticipation, afforded ways in which the dialectic between transcendental and mundane could be articulated by means of temporal connection-and-separation. As mentioned earlier, there were far more texts of the *Anāgata-vaṃsa* family than the few in modern western editions, and they often circulated in the same manuscripts as the *Buddhavaṃsa.* This underscores how important in the Pali imaginaire's textualization of time is the blending of its non-repetitive and repetitive modes, and how central that form of discursive, soteriological rationalization was (along with such things as the veneration of relics) to Theravāda Buddhism's whole civilizational project.

5.3.b. Discovering the truth: realistic narrative or ritual reenactment?

An analogous way in which future Buddhas, Bodhisattas "intent on" or "capable of" enlightenment, can be said to be in a certain

[89] Holt (1991a: 220–3) reports that modernists in Sri Lanka, who prefer a rationalized, demythologized Buddhism, disapprove of the aspiration to rebirth with Metteyya.

[90] This paragraph was prompted by some remarks of Sid Kelly, for which I am grateful.

sense already enlightened, and thus sources of present reassurance, is brought out by contrasting two styles in which the famous story of a Buddha's (or: the Buddha Gotama's) enlightenment is narrated. The first is realistic narrative, in the sense that, given appropriate suspensions of disbelief, the story can be read by anyone, traditional or modern, Buddhist or non-Buddhist, as the discovery of some truths about life by a pampered and secluded young man. The second may be called ritual reenactment, in the sense that the narrative voice, many characters in the story, and even at times the Bodhisatta himself, are all aware of the preset sequence of events, and characters within the story play their roles consciously to bring about the predicted denouement.[91] This latter style, in which the leading character is *a* Buddha exemplifying the general pattern, resembles the script of a drama to be repeated in each performance rather than the reality-recording sentences of a novelist, historian or journalist.

The two styles can be blended, as is the case with the *Mahāpadāna Sutta* (D II 1ff.). Here the story of the four Sights, usually told in modern works about Gotama, is told of the past Buddha Vipassī. In the first section of the discourse, the narrator, Gotama, having listed parallel biographical details of seven Buddhas, ending with himself, then tells the life story of Vipassī, in the course of which he lists a large number of things which are "(in) the nature of things" (*dhammatā*) for future Buddhas (5.1.b). These include: the fact that he is conscious and aware as he dies from the Tusita heaven and is reborn in his mother's womb; the appearance of four gods to catch him as he is born, so that he does not touch the earth; and the fact that as soon as he is born a future Buddha takes seven steps to the north and exclaims, "I am the best in the world . . . This is (my) last birth, now there is no more rebirth!" Next, soothsayers predict that the child will grow to be either a Wheel-turning king or a Buddha and identify the thirty-two marks of a Great Man on his body. His father then brings him up in three palaces, one for each season, surrounded by only

91 A modern example of this style is Thomas Mann's *Joseph and His Brothers*, where, as Reed (1974: 341) says, there is a "conscious reliving of myth in a world of 'open identities,' where people do not distinguish clearly between themselves and the predecessors they resemble." Indeed, Joseph is not only aware of the motif – which he is currently living out – of the sacrificed and resurrected young god in past ages, but at times seems clearly to foresee, as does the narrative voice, its future use in the case of Christ.

female attendants. So far, Vipassī's story seems obviously and emphatically to be a particular exemplification of the norm. But in the next section (D II 21ff.), things change. One must suspend one's disbelief, not only in the case of the enormously extended length of life ascribed to people at that time, but also in the possibility that a young man could grow up and quite literally never encounter certain facts (his age is not specified here, and he is not said to marry and have a son, as Gotama is). If one does this, the narrative style in which his experiences are recounted is very effectively succinct and realistic. One day he goes out on a drive to a pleasure-park with his charioteer. They encounter a gray-haired old man, bent double and leaning on a stick. Vipassī asks the charioteer:[92]

"What is the matter with this man? His hair is not like other men's, his body is not like other men's."

"Prince," is the reply, "this is what is called an old man."

"But why is he called an old man?"

"He is called old, Prince, because he has not long to live."

"But am I liable to become old, and [am I] not exempt from old age?"

"Both you and I, Prince, are liable to become old, are not exempt from old age."

"Well then, charioteer, that will do for today with the pleasure-park. Return now to the palace."

After his return, "Prince Vipassī was overcome with grief and dejection, crying "Shame on this thing birth, since to him who is born old age must manifest itself!"'

On two further excursions, the prince encounters, similarly for the first time, a sick man and a corpse. The exchanges with the charioteer are similar, and each time he returns to the palace in grief and dejection: "Shame on this thing birth, since to him who is born sickness [and] death must manifest [themselves]!" It is important to see here that the prince's distress is as much cognitive as it is affective: he is rather like a child discovering death for the first time, and finding (as children do) that the difficulty it poses is as much conceptual as it is emotional.[93] How can one

[92] The translation is Walshe's (1987: 207ff.). For another example of a narratively realist telling of this part of the story, see Johnston's (1936) translation of Aśvaghosa's Skt masterpiece, the *Buddhacarita*.

[93] This point is very clearly brought out in Aśvaghosa's telling.

make sense of a life which inevitably involves sickness, old age and death? The prince is not himself suffering from any of these problems; indeed, his father redoubles his efforts to surround the prince with "the fivefold sense-pleasures," so that he will not become a renouncer and forego kingship. But when the prince goes out for the fourth and last time his cognitive distress is alleviated, by seeing a renouncer who is, the charioteer explains, "one who truly follows Dhamma, who truly lives in serenity, does good actions, performs meritorious deeds, is harmless and truly has compassion for living beings." The threat to coherence posed by old age, sickness and death is avoided by setting human life and its defects in a universe where salvation from them is possible. The figure of the renouncer clearly shifts the perspective of the story from the immediate here-and-now of a confused young man to that of the reflective, transcendentalist perspective which sets what is visible – old people, the sick, corpses – in the context of an unseen beyond which shows the incoherent visible world to be part of a larger, coherent whole. Vipassī decides to renounce on the spot (unlike Gotama, in most versions). The rest of his story is told (again, assuming appropriate suspensions of disbelief) in a historically realist way, ending with three aphoristic summary versions of "the teaching of the Buddhas." The Discourse itself ends with a brief coda in which Gotama repeats some facts about the seven Buddhas from the opening section.

Compare this with the following version of Gotama's life, found in the *Jātaka-nidāna*, which starts from his previous birth as Sumedha.[94] The story begins with Sumedha's aspiration to Buddhahood and the prediction of its future fulfilment made by the Buddha Dīpaṅkara. Sumedha then sits down and mentally contemplates the ten Perfections, to the accompaniment of various portents and marvels of the kind cited in 4.2.b. With each one he issues a command to himself, "Practice the Perfection of [e.g.] Giving"; but the atmosphere of the text, with the earth quaking and deities applauding, seems to suggest that the future fulfilment of the Perfections is not only prefigured but – since it has been predicted by Dīpaṅkara – actualized already, at least imaginatively. The text then mentions each of the intervening

[94] For a full translation see Jayawickrama (1990). Translations in the text are my own.

Buddhas, identifying who our Bodhisatta was each time, and telling brief stories along the way. Next it goes again through the Perfections, where the narrative voice in the prose speaks of them in the third person but quotes verses in which Gotama Buddha (as he is when speaking the lines) recalls in the first person an example of each as "this was my Perfection of (e.g.) Giving."

This ends the first section of the text, called the Distant Epoch. The second section, the Intermediate Epoch, begins with our Bodhisatta in his penultimate life in Tusita. The gods come to him and say "Now is the time for your Buddhahood." He makes the five Considerations, concerning the time, country, and family in which he will be born, along with the mother and mother's lifespan (she must only live one week after the birth). He goes to the Nandana grove, dies from there, and is reborn in the womb of his mother Mahāmāyā, who at this time has undertaken the Uposatha-vows during a festival. (These include temporary celibacy, so we have an immaculate conception.) Soothsayers predict a male child who will be either a Wheel-turning king or a Buddha. The birth is attended by portents and marvels; the ascetic Kāḷadevala laments that he will die before the child attains Buddhahood. After other anticipations of his future Buddhahood, his father asks what will make his son become a renouncer, and is told of the four Sights. He sets up guards specifically to prevent his son from seeing them, but is foiled by the gods, who assign four among themselves to play the role of the men in the four Sights: "now is the time for Prince Siddhattha's enlightenment," they say. The text here explicitly refers to the *Mahāpadāna Sutta* version, told of Vipassī, so that at this point in the story/drama, despite the constant reference to his future Buddhahood by the narrator, his father, and other characters, Siddhattha is presented as being (or acting as if he were?) unaware of his future, as are all Buddhas in realist tellings of their tale. But in the immediately following scene, when he bathes and dresses in preparation for the Great Renunciation (so termed, *mahābhinikkhamana*), Sakka, king of the gods, sends Vissakamma to adorn him with divine adornments; as he does so, the Great Being (*mahāsatta*, a synonym for *bodhisatta* in these contexts) is aware that a deity is involved.

Next is the scene involving a play on two senses of the word *nibbuta* (2.1.a), where a woman cries out that the parents of such an attractive man must be happy, but Siddhattha takes it as a sign of his seeking nirvana. On the next day, he announces to his charioteer that the Great Renunciation is to take place. He goes to where his wife and son Rāhula are asleep (earlier at Rāhula's birth the future Buddha made a pun on his name, saying that a bond [*rāhula*] had come into being); but he decides not to pick his son up, since he might wake up the mother and "that will hinder my going. When I am (a) Buddha [or, more simply: when I am enlightened, *buddho hutvā*] I will come and see (him)" (Ja I 62). No motive is here given for Siddhattha's wanting to pick his son up, but one can contrast the "foregone conclusion" atmosphere of this version with a brief summary of the story told in the *Atthasālinī* (As 33–4, cp. Upās 127). There when Rāhula is born, Siddhattha not only makes the remark about a "bond," but decides to renounce there and then, saying "I know the strength of affection for a son [or: I acknowledge the strength of (my) affection for (my) son, *putta-sineha*]; I will cut this bond immediately before it grows bigger." Psychological realism of this kind does not fit the *Jātaka-nidāna* style. After this point in the *Jātaka-nidāna* version it becomes the norm for Siddhattha and others to acknowledge openly his future Buddhahood; in one scene the text refers to a poem in the *Sutta Nipāta* (Sn 405–42) called the "Discourse on (the) Renunciation" (*Pabbajjā Sutta*). That text (v.408) anachronistically uses the word *Buddha* to refer to Siddhattha before his enlightenment. None of the texts mentioned here emphasize, as do others,[95] his long six-year struggle, involving supreme efforts of asceticism and near self-starvation.

Neither Metteyya, in Anāg and in the "Story of the Elder Māleyya," nor other future Buddhas in the *Dasabodhisattuddesa* and *Dasabodhisattuppattikathā*, seem to have much difficulty, in their last life, in completing their path to Buddhahood. In Anāg, the complete conceptual reversal from the enjoyment of "desire and pleasure" to their definitive abandonment by Metteyya Buddha is accomplished by a narrative which flows unbrokenly from the one to the other, and which says only that he "will undertake religious practice for a week" (v.54 n. 43 above). In the "Story of the Elder

[95] The famous statues of the Buddha as an emaciated ascetic are clearly also meant to embody the sense of struggle (see Bechert and Gombrich 1984: 42 for one example). Textual sources for Gotama's "Struggle for Enlightenment," many of which are, unusually, autobiographical, can be found in Ñāṇamoli (1972: Chapter 2), which has this phrase for its title.

Māleyya" (Appendix 4), Metteyya recounts both the history of his past fulfilment of the Perfections and that of his future Buddhahood as equally – once again, at least imaginatively – *faits accomplis.* In these settings, the historical and psychological realism of shock, difficult renunciation and struggle for understanding so carefully represented in Vipassī's and Gotama's cases in some texts and images is not apropos. Perhaps one might say that, from this perspective, in the future Buddhahood they describe, as in that of future-Gotama in texts such as the *Jātaka-nidāna,* it is the Buddhahood as much as the futurity which is salient. The underlying salvific logic goes something like this: yes, the truth of impermanence applies to everything, even to Buddhism as a historical fact: but just as one can be sure that knowledge of the truth will fade so one can (now, in the present) be reassured that some day – even if theoretically very far distant – there will be Buddhas to rediscover it.[96]

Premodern Pali texts, from this perspective, can be seen to regard future Buddhas as simultaneously distant and near. The Buddhahood of Metteyya, and the chance to meet him, in the non-repetitive time sequence in which living persons grow old and die, is a very long way away in the remote future. But as a present imaginative possibility, as a feature of the imaginaire which envisions a universe in which Buddhas repeatedly arise to bring ultimate salvation – that is, the sense of an ending into complete and absolute felicity – Buddhahood is immediately available, good to think and good to imagine here and now, again and again.

96 It should also be mentioned here that the rarity of actually seeing a Buddha is also a theme often stressed, in contexts where encouragement to religious practice rather than reassurance is the overriding concern.

Critical discussion: what is "millennialism"? Premodern ideas and modern movements

Section 5.2.d discussed briefly the senses in which one might use the word "millennial" in relation to the traditional Pali imaginaire and to premodern kings. This critical discussion first refers to the events, mostly from the twentieth century, which have been reported by historians and ethnographers as examples of Buddhist millennialism; and then returns to the question of the definition of the word. In doing so it moves from the inside to the outside of the Pali imaginaire, for two reasons. First, I think that much of the existing scholarship on modern Theravāda "millennialism" needs rethinking. The mistake referred to in 5. 2.d – confusing the aspiration to future Buddhahood with self-identification as Metteyya – is found frequently; and in fact very little evidence is presented to support the habitual claim that in modern instances of royal pretension or peasant revolt, leaders (whether king, member of a local elite, or rebellious peasant) either claimed to be or were perceived to be the Buddha Metteyya now, rather than as destined to become one of the other future Buddhas. Indeed, in many cases reported under the rubric of millennialism, there seems to have been no reference to future Buddhas at all. Readers interested in comparative studies in this area will, I hope, be able to derive greater profit from the studies referred to if they bear these points in mind. Second, this discussion illustrates the relation between the kind of textual history of the Pali imaginaire attempted in this book and the historiography of Buddhism in a wider sense. It is obvious both a priori and from countless empirical studies that the world of Pali texts is never the only system of belief or source of narratives in the societies of Southern Asia where Theravāda Buddhism is found. It always coexists, to a greater or lesser degree, with others, which may be non-Buddhist, or Buddhist but with sources of inspiration other than, or more than Pali texts. Historical agents in these societies may always draw on other sources of motivation and ideology. I am not making the obviously ludicrous argument that if something is not found in Pali texts it cannot have happened. I do want to counter the tendency to imprecise and ahistorical syncretism in these matters,[1] and to assess how far modern events and movements are or are not congruent with what might be seen as millennial belief in Pali texts. Overall, those who seek to *explain* these events and movements, looking for social, political, economic and other *causes,* should see them primarily as phenomena of modernization, of modern nation-building and in particular of the direct or indirect experience of colonialism and imperial capitalism. Modern millennialism is better seen in this light, and compared to specifically modern movements elsewhere such as cargo cults, than simply as a "Buddhist possibility" available in all sociohistorical conditions.[2]

I. HISTORICAL AND ETHNOGRAPHIC REPORTS

Sri Lanka

The only work dealing with Sri Lanka in this regard is an article by Malalgoda (1970). He begins with a brief review of some traditional motifs; and then gives a summary account of some nineteenth-century movements, whose leaders claimed to be descended from the king deposed by the British in 1815, and thus rightful heirs to the throne, which they hoped to reclaim by rebellion. He cites premodern Sinhala texts which anticipated a Buddhist king in the 2,500th year of Gotama's Dispensation; and coming forward to that time (calculated to be 1956), reports that "a definite sense of expectancy became manifest" (p. 439). In no case, however, either in the nineteenth or twentieth centuries does he cite any evidence to suggest that any claim was made that such a "king" was a future Buddha, or that anyone claimed to be

[1] This is found even in primary historical or ethnographic sources, as well in work by others (e.g. Sarkisyanz 1965a and Tambiah 1984, who – like myself here – offer second-order reflections on the primary sources).

[2] This point was first suggested to me by Todd Gibson, in a graduate essay written at Indiana University in 1988. Spiro (1970: 183–4 and n. 24) makes the comparison with cargo cults, and the Thai data are discussed usefully in relation to their political and economic context in the essays by Turton, Tanabe and Chatthip in Turton and Tanabe (1984), a volume devoted to "History and Peasant Consciousness in Southeast Asia."

Metteyya, or indeed that any mention of Metteyya was made at all. He connects traditional millennialism with his nineteenth-century data by an intervening discussion of the idea of the Sinhalese as a "chosen people": chosen to be the favored vehicle of the Buddha's Teaching, in a manner analogous to the claims made by the ancient Jewish community to be the people chosen by their god. "It would be true to say that, by and large, Buddhist millennial *movements* (as against mere *ideas*) have had their origin in this notion rather than in the belief in the advent of Metteyya" (p. 431).[3]

It is hardly surprising that after suffering conquest and the imposition of a foreign colonial regime, the victims should retaliate with attempts to drive the invaders out and restore an indigenous monarchical system, however inevitably hopeless those attempts appear now.[4] But in the Sri Lankan case there would seem to be no connection whatsoever between the uprisings and millennialism. I would guess that Malalgoda used the term since at the time of writing he was working on a thesis (which became Malalgoda 1976) at Oxford under Bryan Wilson, who was himself then writing *Magic and the Millennium* (1973). In this book Wilson argues that many of the movements he discusses can be seen as reactions against colonialism which used new forms of institutional and/or group organization, themselves modeled on the organization of the colonial powers against whom they were directed. In the thesis/book Malalgoda took up and helped popularize Obeyesekere's coinage "Protestant Buddhism," a term with almost exactly the same sense: it was intended to designate a form of modernist Buddhism which protested against the imposition of Christianity (and other things) by the British Empire, but which mimicked many of the characteristics of Protestant Christianity (in the Weberian view Obeyesekere took of it).[5]

Burma

There are three main areas in modern Burma where there is evidence that the anticipation of imminent millennial salvation has

[3] To express this view he alludes to the allegedly traditional concept of Sri Lanka as *dhamma-dīpa*, "the island of the Dhamma": see Appendix 2 n. 17.

[4] A similar analysis would apply to the revolt led by Saya San in Burma, despite Sarkisyanz (1965: 160–5); see Cady (1958: 309–21), Solomon (1969), Scott (1975), and Herbert (1982).

[5] See Obeyesekere (1972); and for recent criticism, Holt (1991b).

become an ideology in practical historical use. These are (i) kings Alaungpaya and Bodawpaya in the eighteenth to nineteenth centuries (ii) groups (*gaing*) connected with wizards (*weikza*), investigated in the 1950s and 60s by Mendelson and Spiro, but alleged to go back to the eighteenth century, and (iii) movements among the non-Burmese Karen people, in the nineteenth and twentieth centuries.

King Alaungpaya, or Alaung-hpàya (1752–60), starting as "a northern village hero" (Ferguson 1975: 183), conquered and reunited large areas of what we now call Burma (or Myanmar), which had for some time been split into smaller concentrations of power, and founded the last line of Burmese kings, the Konbaung dynasty.[6] Given his military success, it is not surprising that he claimed the title *cakkavatti*, or that he styled himself future Buddha (*alaung* means future Buddha, as in Alaungsithu, whose inscription was cited in 5.2.d). Some writers simply make in Alaungpaya's case the mistake that any future Buddha is Metteyya, but there is some evidence on the basis of which it has been proposed that he did make just that claim. In 1759, having conquered so much within Burma, he turned his attention to neighbors, including the city of Ayudhya in Siam, to which he laid siege in 1760. During the siege, Lieberman says:

As was their custom, Alaung-hpàya and his generals issued proclamations explaining that Alaung-hpàya was an Embryo Buddha and a *cakkavatti*, ordained by prophecy, who was touring the world with the sole objective of making more radiant the Buddha's religion. To Alaung-hpàya's great distress, the Faith had recently become rather dim in Siam. The Burmese urged the king of Siam to offer homage suitable to a man of such obvious religious merit.[7] Explicitly or implicitly they may have claimed that Alaung-hpàya was destined to be reborn as Metteyya, for the Siamese replied that if Alaung-hpàya's claims were valid, he should be in Tusita heaven rather than outside the gates of Ayudhya. [He then adds in a note:] In truth, the Siamese retort only made sense if Alaung-hpàya specifically claimed to be Metteyya, for no Buddhist would deny that

[6] I have used, *inter alia*, Htin Aung (1967), Ferguson (1975), Leiberman (1984) and Koenig (1990; but see Aung Thwin 1992). Much of the time, later historians simply refer to earlier ones, many of whom do not cite their sources.

[7] [Note by S.C.] This is exactly what the Wheel-turning King is said to do in the *Cakkavatti-sīhanāda Sutta*, where the kings to whom this message is delivered – along with sermons on the five Moral Rules – all rush to offer homage. Lieberman's tone here captures very nicely just how utopian (= ou-topian) such texts are.

Alaung-hpàya could be an incarnation of any of the countless future Buddhas who will *succeed* Metteyya (1984: 268–9 and n. 158).

He cites Mendelson's evidence, from a later period, to the effect that "embryo forms of Metteyya can dwell on earth even now in the person of the coming *cakkavatti*," and suggests that "possibly it was on these traditions that Alaung-hpàya drew." This can be contrasted with the account in Htin Aung (1967). He offers a less footnoted, more story-like narrative, which takes Alaungpaya's side in a rather obviously partisan way. His version includes a translation (or paraphrase) of the Siamese reply:

> Alaungpaya sent envoys into Ayuthia [*sic*], calling upon the king to surrender because he was a man destined to be a Buddha and desired to avoid bloodshed if possible. The king of Siam sent back the insulting reply: "In the lifetime of this present universe, there will appear only five Buddhas. Four have already appeared, and the one who would appear as the Fifth Buddha is now living in the abode of the gods. Surely, there cannot be a sixth Buddha." (1967: 169)

In this account, part of the "insult" would seem to be a deliberate caricature of Alaungpaya's claim to be *a* future Buddha, pretending that he professed to be the sixth Buddha in the present eon (which is something like a fifth wheel). Unless and until the original Burmese-language documents are consulted (Lieberman cites four texts[8]), with this specific issue in mind, it seems to me that we cannot decide exactly what Alaungpaya claimed, nor exactly what was the relation of that claim to the traditional idea of the king as future Buddha.

The same thing is true of Alaungpaya's son Bodawpaya (1782–1819), although here one of the original documents is available in an English translation, from the Italian text of Vincent Sangermano, a Catholic missionary who lived in Burma from 1783 to 1806. The good Father seems to have taken a rather dim view of the king, whom he calls Badonsachen. In W. W. Tandy's fine rendering,[9] he says, confusing enlightenment and Buddhahood with becoming a God:

[8] He has kindly provided me with a translation of one of these in a letter (May 1995), the text referred to in the book (269 n. 158) as KBZ p. 311; this describes the situation in much the same way as does Htin Aung.

[9] In the original edition, Sangermano (1833), these passages are on pp. 59–60; in the edition republished later (1893) with an introduction by Jardine, they occur on pp. 74–5. The most recent edition available to me is (1966), cited in the Bibliography.

Although despotism in its worst form constitute [*sic*], as it were, the very essence of the Burmese monarchy, so that to be called its king is equivalent to being called a tyrant; still has Badonsachen . . . so far outstripped his predecessors in barbarity and pride, that whoso hears it must shudder with horror. His very countenance is the index of a mind ferocious and inhuman, in the highest degree . . . and it would not be an exaggeration to assert that, during his reign, more victims have fallen by the hand of the executioner than by the sword of the common enemy. To this atrocious cruelty he has united a pride at once intolerable and impious. The good fortune which has attended him in discovering and defeating the numerous conspiracies which have been formed against him, has inspired him with the idea that he is something more than mortal, and that this privilege has been granted him on account of his numerous good works. Hence he has for some years laid aside the title of king and assumed that of Pondoghi, which signifies great and exalted virtue; nor was he content with this, for but a few years since he thought to make himself a God. With this view, and in imitation of Godama, who, before being advanced to the rank of a divinity, had abandoned the royal palace, together with all his wives and concubines, and had retired into solitude, Badonsachen withdrew himself from the palace to Menton, where for many years he had been employed in constructing a pagoda, the largest in the empire. Here he held various conferences with the most considerable and learned Talapoins [monks], in which he endeavoured to persuade them that the 5000 years assigned for the observance of the law of Godama had elapsed, and that he himself was the God who was to appear after that period, to abolish the ancient law in substituting his own. But to his great mortification many of the Talapoins undertook to demonstrate the contrary; and this, combined with his love of power and his impatience under the denial of the luxuries of the seraglio, quickly disabused him of his Godhead, and drove him back to his palace.

I find it impossible not to enjoy the vivacity of the prose, and equally impossible to trust such an account, despite the apparent precision of the reference to 5,000 years.[10] Apart from the Italian priest's evident readiness to believe anything bad of the seraglio-addicted Burmese tyrant, all historians agree that Bodawpaya was involved in frequent conflicts with different groups within the monkhood, and so Sangermano's informants may have had their own reasons for inventing such a caricature. Ferguson (75: 200ff.) does cite Burmese sources during his account of Bodawpaya's

[10] A number of scholars write as if the traditional notion was that Gotama's Dispensation would last 5000 years, and then Metteyya would come soon afterwards. But from the time of the *Cakkavatti-sīhanāda Sutta* it had been assumed that many thousands of years would elapse before Metteyya's appearance (Appendix 3).

"attempted fusion of World Emperor and Ariya Maitreya," but for what he calls Bodawpaya's "quest for divinity" gives only English-language sources, all of which seem to go back to Sangermano.[11]

In the present state of knowledge, it seems to me prudent to suspend judgment on exactly what was claimed by Alaungpaya and Bodawpaya. They might, of course, have wanted to be seen as Metteyya; and if so, I would take such an innovation to be, at least in part, a sign of the radical novelty at that time being introduced into the traditional Theravāda world – that is to say, the threatening and ultimately world-shattering military might of the European imperial powers. As Wilson (1973: 216) says, speaking of what he calls "the millennial response" in New Guinea, "conquest and domination [by colonial regimes] as such are not prerequisites . . . Cultural shock and anticipation . . . appear to be sufficient" (cp. Worsley 1968: 333). Ferguson's (1975: 180) description of Burma immediately preceding Alaungpaya's consecration as the first king of the Konbaung dynasty is apt:

> The tension within the Sangha parallels tensions within the country as a whole during this period. The Hinduized Manipuri were devastating the Chindwin area in a holy war; the first Christian missionaries entered Lower Burma; the British had a trading post at Syriam; the French were negotiating about trade and courting the Mons; the Mon–Burmese military rivalry was reaching its final peak; and the fount of orthodoxy in Ceylon only a few years before (1697) had to receive an injection of Burmese Buddhism because the ravages of colonialism had left only one monk on the whole island who could speak Pali.[12]

The second phenomenon in Burma where millennial themes are said to be found is that of the religious figures called *weikza-s* (pronounced way-za, a Burmese version of Pali *vijjā*, magic), investigated by Mendelson and Spiro in the 1950s and 60s.[13] Ferguson and Mendelson (1981: 63) call these figures "masters of the Buddhist Occult": "a weikza is conceived as a human who has

[11] Fytche (1878 I: 78) also cites Sangermano in his account, and adds an odd and unevidenced footnote suggesting that Bodawpaya's courtiers (*sic*) tried to dissuade him from claiming Buddhahood and be content with being a Pacceka-buddha (normally said only to be possible when Buddhas or their Dispensations are absent: see Collins 1992c): "but he would hear nothing less than the whole animal." This is, from a traditional point of view, even more bizarre.

[12] He cites Gombrich (1971a: 34).

[13] See the works by Mendelson listed in the Bibliography, and relevant sections of Spiro (1971). The best place to start, as I do in the text here, is Ferguson and Mendelson's (1981) overview, which contains some interesting examples of Weikza iconography. See also Ferguson (1975).

acquired supranormal powers through the mastery of alchemy, astrology, spells, signs, meditation, or other occult arts." The ancestry of such figures includes much that is not found in, or was excluded from, Pali Buddhism. Both before and after the introduction of Theravāda to Burma, traditionally said to have been by king Anawrahta in the eleventh century, there have existed forms of Mahāyāna and Vajrayāna Buddhism, as in the Tantric Buddhism of Bengal and elsewhere in northern India, and of Hinduism, as well as various forms of Indian and Chinese alchemy, and of localized supernaturalism.[14] Monks recognized as in some sense Buddhist, to whom one or more such phenomena are attributed, are often called in Burmese texts the Ari; and there has been considerable discussion as to who exactly they were. That debate does not concern me; suffice it to say that the imaginaire of Pali literature was only one part of the heritage of Weikzas, who in the modern world are usually laymen, albeit ones who claim to practice a disciplined lifestyle analogous to and overlapping that of the monastic code, the *Vinaya.* This lay aspect of the movements is part of what makes Ferguson and Mendelson (1981: 74) say that Weikza cults "can be conceived as a symbolic reaction to the shock of colonialism."

Pali texts ubiquitously attribute what we would call magical powers to advanced meditators and Arahants. The most important difference, for my present purposes, between such figures and a Weikza is that the latter "hopes to schedule his rebirth or extend his present life so that he is here on earth at the same time as the next Buddha arrives" (ibid. p. 64). Rebirth at the time of Metteyya, as has been seen, was a common aspiration in traditional Buddhism; the Weikza differs in that he takes control of the process by alchemy, so that by means of a series of controlled rebirths, or by alchemically prolonging the present life until the time of Metteyya, he can escape the arduous and uncertain path of merit-making and achieve present assurance of salvation immediately. The ability to remain (in some sense) alive until Metteyya comes, here achieved through alchemy, was claimed for certain Arahants in Burma: and this idea made its way into at least one Pali

[14] Ferguson (1975) emphasizes the persistence of all forms of Buddhism throughout Burmese history, regardless of which form happened to be sponsored by particular kings, and regardless of the frequent "purifications" of the monkhood carried out in the name of Pali Theravāda "orthodoxy."

text, as has also been seen, (5.2.a, p. 357, nn. 23–4). In addition to this, Weikzas seem to conceive of identity and rebirth in slightly different ways from Pali orthodoxy: for example, it seems to be thought possible that one person can be a partial or full manifestation of another, while the other in some sense remains in existence elsewhere. Given this, as well as the identification of any future Buddha with Metteyya in scholarly writings (including the sources for our knowledge of Weikzas), and – last but not least – the overly syncretic and simplistic way some scholars speak of the Wheel-turning King and future Buddha/Metteyya as being "associated," it is extremely difficult to articulate in any precise way what Weikzas claim, or are perceived, to be. I leave the interested reader to study the ethnographic reports for him or herself: for present purposes it is enough to say that there does seem to be in certain instances of Weikza-hood a genuinely millennial foreshortening of the time between now and the time of the future Wheel-turning King who will reign when Metteyya is born, and some kind of amalgamation of these two figures with present or past Weikzas.

Weikzas are connected with Alaungpaya and Bodawpaya.[15] After his rise to fame as a Wheel-turning King and future Buddha, Alaungpaya chose a monk called Atula as leader of the monkhood. At that time one Bo Bo Aung was a schoolmate of Alaungpaya's son, Bodawpaya; when the latter became king he disrobed Atula and tried to kill Bo Bo Aung, who had become a powerful Weikza. When Bagyidaw, Bodawpaya's son, became king in 1819, he attempted to unite the monkhood, by now badly split. The British conquered Lower Burma, and Burmese hopes were pinned on Bagyidaw's son, thought to be a future *cakkavatti*, who would conquer and reannex Lower Burma as Alaungpaya had done. But these hopes were not fulfilled because Tharrawaddy, Bagyidaw's brother, overthrew the king and drowned the young prince.[16] Stories began to circulate that Bo Bo Aung had used his Weikza powers to rescue the prince and take him to a heaven, to await the time of his descent to play the role of *cakkavatti*. According to Mendelson (1961a) and (1961b), the heavenly prince was now seen as both future emperor and future Buddha, and Bo Bo Aung has either remained alive and is manifested in certain

[15] This account is taken mainly from Ferguson and Mendelson (1981).

[16] At least this is the reason given in Burmese belief: modern historians might take a different view of the possibility of a successful Burmese rebellion against the British.

contemporary *weikza*-s, or died and been reborn as a living Weikza. To complete the confusion, Bo Bo Aung seems sometimes to be identified with the future emperor/Buddha waiting in heaven.

It is at present impossible to know – and I imagine we will never know – whether all these confusions are in the data, or in the ethnographies. The third case discussed as a form of millennialism in Burma is easier to deal with, but here also I question the analysis given by the scholar to whom we owe the descriptive material. Stern (1968) writes of two series of movements among the Karen, a people living on the Thai–Burmese border. They were not Buddhist, although they had been affected by the Buddhism of their two powerful neighbors. He cites a certain amount of the data concerning future Buddhas, Metteyya, and the figure of the Wheel-turning King, and claims that "in the light of these associations, the appearance of a millenarian cult among the Karen seems most probably the consequence of Buddhist influences upon an indigenous faith." I disagree.

The first cases described concern a Karen myth – related by Baptist missionaries in the mid-nineteenth century – that as the result of an oversight by the ancestors at the time of creation, a "White Brother" had taken a "Golden Book" overseas; one day he would return with it, bringing prosperity and, above all, political independence from their neighbors. When the European and American missionaries arrived with their bibles, they were naturally not slow to exploit the myth, and the Karen were much encouraged by the victories of the armies of white men and their book over the Burmese kingdom. The ideology of a series of Karen rebellions, first against the Burmese and later against the British, seems to have been influenced more by recently imported Christian ideas than by Buddhist millennial motifs. The one exception is the use of the name Ariya Metteyya for the coming leader: but Stern is surely wrong to introduce a Karen song, "The Lord his messengers doth send / And he himself must surely come / The priests of Boodh whose reign is short / Must leave the place to make them room," with the comment that this is "at least compatible with a corresponding expectation of the era of Ariyametteyya." To me this song seems to contain, rather than the Buddhist notion that Gotama's Dispensation must disappear before Metteyya can arise, the suggestion that Buddhism as a whole will soon disappear in the face of the appearance of missionaries (the "messengers" of the song) and the "Lord" (presumably the White Brother). I suggest, from the evidence Stern adduces, that the content of the Karen rebels' ideology was a mixture of indigenous and Christian elements, using only the Buddhist name Ariya Metteyya. Hinton (1979: 92) argues plausibly that the Buddhist ideology of the Wheel-turning King affected the Karens' aspiration to political independence; but adds "this notion is so prevalent in Southeast Asia that it would have been worthy of note if the Karen leaders had *not* tried to adapt it to their purposes." This notion is not, in itself, millennial: it is a political model of autonomy and political authority.

The second case is a series of revolts by the Telakhon sect, which survives until the present day. Here there is a very little more about Ariya: the previous four Buddhas of this eon are said to be "incarnations" of Ariya (Stern 1968: 316). But this is in the context of a broadened religious syncretism, which blends names from Hinduism, Buddhism and Christianity; when Metteyya comes, "all religions will fuse into one" (ibid.). Stern himself says that Karen anticipation of "the wealth and consequence so long denied them," which takes the form both of occasional active revolt and of passively maintaining themselves in moral and ritual purity while waiting their "Messiah," is "reminiscent of cargo cults" (1968: 318). This is, indeed, a more fruitful place to look for comparative perspective on modern Buddhist millennial movements than traditional Buddhist millennialism. In the case of the Karen, only the name of Ariya Metteyya seems to have been taken from the latter source.

Thailand (Siam)

Chatthip (1984) lists eight "Holy Men Revolts" in Thailand, the first in 1699 and the last in 1959. The term Holy Man in this context is a rendering of the Thai phrase *phu mi bun*. This means literally "one who has merit," and can apply to anyone thought to have a special amount of merit, and thus the powers and opportunities which result from it. All future Buddhas and kings are *phu mi bun*, but not all *phu mi bun* are future Buddhas or kings. Once again here, a kind of associationist logic (rather, illogic) seems to operate, such that any rebellion connected with such Holy Men is assimilated to traditional millennialism, and to the figure of Metteyya. But again, a detailed review of the evidence provides very little actual proof that such Holy Men were explicitly thought to be Metteyya. Here also the interested reader must study the ethnographic reports for him or herself. But I offer a few comments of my own.

Of Chatthip's eight revolts, only the most recent four are alleged to have involved beliefs about Metteyya. The first took place in Northeast Thailand in 1900–2, and has also been commented on by Murdoch (1974), Ishii (1975), (1986: 171–87), and Keyes (1977). Here there were prophecies of an imminent "apocalypse," involving storms and ogres, after which those who had properly prepared themselves would live in plenty, with pebbles turned into gold by the coming "righteous king." This is indeed worthy to be called millennialism, but what is the connection with traditional Buddhism? Although all four authors juxtapose discussion of Metteyya – again, wrongly seen as the only possible future Buddha – with description of the revolts, none of them cite written evidence that their leader, one Ong Keo, was seen as Metteyya. Chatthip (1984: 117 nn. 6–7) cites oral interviews in 1979 with people who were five, ten and twenty years old at the time of the revolt, but it is not clear whether they made any reference to Metteyya. Murdoch cites the statement of a French author, J. J. Dauplay (1929: 61), that many pictures in temples displayed Ong Keo "as a *Thevada* (god) [i.e. Pali *devatā*] enjoying the blessings of a Buddhist paradise." Dauplay was an agent of the French colonial government in Laos, and said that he destroyed over fifty such pictures in 1906–7, some years before Ong Keo's death. The pictures might have made or implied the claim that Ong Keo had been Metteyya in Tusita and was now reborn on earth; but they may have meant simply that he had been, or would in the next life be a god in heaven, which is a standard Buddhist notion. Dauplay's account of the revolt does not mention Metteyya, although he does call all *phu mi bun* "des sortes de Messies" (1929: 55). His colonialist disdain for "the natives" – who have "le goût du fricotage et la rage d'abuser l'autorité . . . innées dans toutes les races asiatiques" (1929: 54) – no doubt prevented him from bothering too much about what, in indigenous discourse, such "Messiahs" actually were.

Chatthip also cites oral interviews for the assertion that in revolts in 1924 (cp. Ishii 75: 123; 1986: 179) and 1936 Metteyya was expected imminently. In the case of a revolt of 1959, he reports that according to the majority of informants the leader, Sila Wongsin, claimed to be Metteyya, but adds that one person disagreed, saying that he only claimed to be someone who would be reborn in his next birth as Metteyya. Ishii (1986: 179) refers to what seems to be the same event, but says that Sila "claimed to be a reincarnation of king Chulalongkorn." Murdoch (1974) writes of a contemporary Buddhist "socialist" and "peasant leader" called Bun Khamwong. He gives a typically imprecise review of the traditional Pali materials, and says that Bun used the idea of Metteyya's coming in speeches about land reform and "the age of freedom." But he then quotes "the chairman of the local farmers' group [explaining] that Bun did not mean that the coming of the Ariya Mettaya [*sic*] in person was imminent but simply that the age of freedom was at hand" (1984: 206–7).

Thus the evidence available in English is difficult to assess, and at most tends to support the suggestion that the motif of Metteyya was involved in some of these movements, but only in a few specific contexts and in different ways. Oddly, the most straightforward evidence in this matter comes in a footnote from Keyes (77: 290 n. 29), where he refers to various tracts and pamphlets of 1968, 1973 and 1976, which explicitly refer either to the imminent arrival of Metteyya or to a person "accepted . . . as being an incarnation of the Maitreya Buddha." (The latter, again, is imprecise and difficult to interpret in terms of the usual Pali Buddhist understanding of identity and rebirth.) Most of these movements have taken place in Northeast Thailand and Laos; and all authors recognize the importance of Southern Thai (Bangkok) centralizing nationalism, and the French colonial presence in Laos. Some writers stress the fact that many supporters of the movements were peasants, and so see these cases as similar to other "revolts of the oppressed"; others that some leaders of the movements were from the local elite, deprived of power and authority by the Thai national and French colonial governments. Keyes (1977: 301–2) argues carefully and plausibly that such movements "emerge during a crisis centering around conceptions of power." Jackson (1988) accepts these analyses of the Northeastern data, and adds a report on what he calls a recent and atypical millennial movement, among the Thai political elite in Bangkok in the 1960s, 70s and 80s. Here, as with the Telakhon sect among the Karen, there were elements of modern religious ecumenism, and the movement seems to have been popular among certain groups recently deprived of power.

I will not try to come to a definitive conclusion. We need, clearly, more data; and I repeat that in my view causal, explanatory accounts of such events and movements should refer to the specific (and various) conditions of modernity, albeit that some of the motifs present are found in premodernity. The traditional Buddhist millennialism of the Pali imaginaire is indeed part of what Keyes (1977: 302) refers to when he says, correctly, that "such movements represent an ideological response formulated in cultural terms with which [the] population is most familiar." But Pali textual motifs are only one such source; there are others, such as the "magical" heritage of the Weikzas in Burma; and in Burma, Thailand and elsewhere, widespread and not specifically Buddhist ideas about invulnerability, as argued by Turton (1991), who speaks of them usefully as a form of "local knowledge." The word "millennialism" can be used constructively in these contexts, but more care than is usually shown in these matters about the exact meaning of the term is necessary if understanding is genuinely to be advanced by using it. To such a discussion I now turn.

II. A USEFUL TYPOLOGY, AND CRITERIA FOR THE TERM "MILLENNIALISM"

The remaining parts of this Critical Discussion summarize what has been said in Chapter 5 and here, and thus try to regain a sense of the wood constituted by all these trees. The simple but elegant typology suggested by Nattier (1988) is helpful. She makes two distinctions: first, as to *where* the encounter with Maitreya will take place, whether on earth or in the Tusita heaven; and second, as to *when* the meeting will occur, whether now, during the present lifetime, or later, after the present lifetime. This then generates four logical possibilities for the place and time of the meeting. It can be:

(i) Here/now – on earth, in the present lifetime.
(ii) Here/later – on earth, in a future rebirth.
(iii) There/now – in the Tusita heaven, in the present lifetime.
(iv) There/later – in Tusita, in a future lifetime.

Nattier presents this typological, ideal-typical exercise purely as a clarificatory device: most actual Maitreya beliefs and movements will blend one or more of the possibilities, and may well escape the rigid confines of this framework in some way. She uses the typology to bring together in one perspective Maitreya-motifs from all traditions of Asian Buddhism. Here I use it to look more closely at the Southern Asian Theravāda data (and so henceforth use the Pali form of the name, Metteyya):

(i) Here/now. As with the wider range of data discussed by Nattier (1988: 30), this is "a distinct minority" in the Theravāda case. No beliefs of this kind are found in traditional Pali texts. If the Burmese kings Alaungpaya and Bodawpaya really did try to be accepted as Metteyya, their attempt will have been what Nattier calls a "pro-establishment" version of this category. The other Burmese and Thai movements discussed above, again if and when it was the case that the idea of Metteyya was involved, would be for the most part anti-establishment (anti-nationalist, anti-colonialist) rebellions; and so more like the majority of movements historians and sociologists have tended to call "millennial." Some of the Thai cases, including some where Metteyya is not involved, do seem to have envisaged an imminent and sudden change for the better.

(ii) Here/later. This, by contrast, is found in the overwhelming majority of Theravāda cases. It is the central motif in the stories of Metteyya, from the canonical *Cakkavatti-sīhanāda Sutta* to the *Anāgatavaṃsa* and the story of the elder Māleyya, and also the goal set for those listening to the *Vessantara-jātaka;* and it is the case in stories about other future Buddhas (5.2.d). Inscriptions and colophons of manuscripts show that this became a standard aspiration in the Theravāda world. Whether or not this belief constitutes "millennialism" depends on whether the criterion of imminence is included in the definition of the term (see below). In the cases of Burmese Weikzas who prolong their present lives until Metteyya comes, and of the Arahants who await Metteyya's coming (in various conditions), the distinction between now and later is a little blurred.

(iii) There/now. Nattier calls this a visionary or mystical possibility. Both in Pali texts and in historical and ethnographic accounts of Theravāda countries it is even more rare than the here/now category: indeed, for individual Buddhists it may be said to be almost nonexistent, at least as a manifest content of religious practice. If the argument in 5.3.a concerning the present use of the name "Metteyya" to refer to future-Metteyya is accepted, then at the level of latent function an outside analyst may put in this category present intentional attitudes towards Metteyya, in that they are a kind of salvation in the sociological sense of being a present experience of reassurance. But I know of only one significant case either in texts or elsewhere of anyone explicitly aspiring to or having direct contact of any sort with Metteyya in Tusita now: the elder Māleyya. For Buddhists listening to that text the encounter between the elder and Metteyya is something that took place in the past.

(iv) There/later. Here we may classify the aspiration to or statement of rebirth in the Tusita heaven, as in the case of king Duṭṭhagāmaṇī in the *Mahāvaṃsa.* Here too one might put the aspiration to meet Metteyya on the way to becoming a Buddha oneself – although the encounter with him in these cases is usually said to take place on earth, at the time of Metteyya's Buddhahood.

Finally, I turn to five criteria for "millennialism" as a comparative category put forward by Cohn in a well-known and useful paper.[17] He defines millennial movements in terms of five criteria: they have the "phantasy of a salvation" which is collective, terrestrial, imminent, total and to be accomplished by supernatural agencies. It seems at first odd that on the very next page he refers to what he calls "millenarian belief" in medieval Judaism, in which "usually the coming of the messiah was relegated to some vague and distant future," which thus fails to meet the third of his criteria. The *prima facie* appearance of self-contradiction can be avoided, however, if one reads him as intending to distinguish, as did Malalgoda in relation to Sri Lanka (1970: 431), between medieval Jewish millennial *beliefs* (Malalgoda has "ideas") and *movements*[18]. It surely makes

[17] (1962: 32–3), adopted by Davis (1981: 32).

[18] Note that although Cohn's title refers to both "millenarism" and "millenarian movements," his criteria are given as applying to "movements" not "beliefs'; and the volume in which it is found is devoted to "Millennial Dreams *in Action*" (my emphasis).

sense to think that beliefs about saviors to come in the far distant future can be held happily enough for centuries; but a movement, mobilizing people for action in the here-and-now, will need stronger stuff – and so in such cases the salvation aspired to is likely to be thought of as imminent. The only ambiguity remaining, then, lies in the fact that the nouns "millennialism" and "millenarianism" most naturally refer to both beliefs and movements.

Leaving aside such verbal problems, real though they are, I now look at Cohn's five criteria in more detail, to see how far traditional Buddhist beliefs and modern movements fit them (quotations are from Cohn 1962: 31). Thus millennial salvation is seen as:

(i) *Collective*: "it is to be enjoyed by the group." This is the case when those who will see Metteyya are distinguished, as a group, from those who will not. This is the closest one comes, in the Buddhist materials, to an aspect of millennialism on which some scholars have placed emphasis. Talmon, for instance, states that one of the "major characteristics" of millennial movements is a "basic dualism": "a fundamental division separates the followers from non-followers," and "millenarism involves both *inclusion* and *exclusion:* there are always God's people within and the ungodly without" (1966: 168, 175–6). Her discussion, unfortunately, has a slipperiness characteristic of many definitional, ideal-typical exercises. The reference to "basic dualism" suggests that the division is always present, but the latter quote comes from one entry in a list of "Dimensions of differentiation – types of millenarian movements," viz. "Particular versus Universal Millenarianism." Here Talmon accepts that some movements are more universalistic: "the main emphasis may be either exclusive or inclusive." As her reference to "God's people" shows, the analysis here stays close to the specific nature of Judaic and Christian millennialism. A collectivist aspect is also found in the followers of a Weikza in Burma, collected in *gaing*-s, a word derived from Pali and Skt *gaṇa*, group. The carnival of the *Anāgata-vaṃsa*, moreover, is a collective one, although among people alive at that time those who practice the celibate life and attain nirvana are distinguished from those who merely become lay followers. But individuals could and did aspire to rebirth with Metteyya outside of any group identification; kings certainly did, as also when they aspired to meet Metteyya on their way to Buddhahood themselves. But again, in this latter case, the aspiration to Buddhahood is precisely something undertaken simultaneously for oneself and for others.

(ii) *Terrestrial*: "it is to be realized on this earth and not in some otherworldly heaven." This applies to almost all the Buddhist data; only in the few entries under Nattier's "there" categories is there any other possibility.

(iii) *Imminent*: "it is to come both soon and suddenly." As discussed already (5.2.d and earlier in this Critical Discussion), this is entirely absent from the traditional textual and inscriptional data, but possibly present in some modern cases.

(iv) *Total*: "it is utterly to transform life, so that the new dispensation will be no mere improvement on earth but perfection itself." The issue here is the word "perfect," from Latin *perficio,* to carry through to the end, to complete; in philosophical contexts the Greek equivalent would be *teleios,* complete, having attained its (proper) end (*telos*). This would be an appropriate thing to say of Metteyya, who by the time of his final nirvana will have performed all "the duties of a Buddha" (*buddha-kicca*). It would also be true, in a different sense, of those who attain nirvana then as Arahants. The general depiction of human life in the *Anāgatavaṃsa* is, perhaps, attractive to some: in Davis' terms, it contains elements of the Land of Cockaygne, Arcadia, and the Perfect Moral Commonwealth. One can imagine someone saying then, in the idiom of current American English, "This is as good as it gets!" But of course Buddhist values rule out the possibility of any form of embodied human life as an ultimate end, as humankind's best *telos.* Only nirvana can be that.

(v) "*Accomplished by agencies which are consciously regarded as supernatural*": It is odd that Cohn should still phrase the matter in this way in 1960 (the date of the conference on which the book was based), since many years earlier Durkheim had famously shown the fallacy of defining things "religious" in terms of an explicit perception of the supernatural, this being only a recent conceptual category:

To be able to call certain facts supernatural, one must already have an awareness that there is a *natural order of things,* in other words, that the phenomena of the universe are internally linked according to necessary relationships called laws . . . Now, the idea of universal determinism is of recent origin . . . [It] is territory won by the empirical sciences. (1995: 24. [1979: 36])

> So, leaving aside the requirement that it be a matter of conscious perception, are millennial agencies in Buddhism supernatural? From a modern academic perspective, the notion that a god should die in a heaven and be reborn as a human being is certainly supernatural (not to mention his or her then attaining a state beyond birth and death); but for Buddhists this is part of the perfectly natural order of things, the *dhammatā*. And the magnificence of the *Anāgatavaṃsa* "carnival," including its miracles, is, as the text itself says, a (natural) result of the merit acquired by Metteyya, king Saṅkha, and all the people reborn at that time. But then again, for modern science karmic merit operative across lifetimes is a supernatural notion. So for Buddhism this criterion seems pointless, since everything depends on which perspective one adopts. The case of the Burmese Weikzas involves supernaturalism, in the use of magic and alchemy, as there is in the predicted transformation of pebbles into gold, and the like, in the 1900–2 revolts in Thailand.

This discussion has looked at the Buddhist data through Nattier's typology, both because of its intrinsic usefulness, and because it will enable further comparisons to be made between Theravāda and other Buddhist ideas. It has also looked at them in terms of Cohn's criteria, both because the latter are commonly referred to in comparative discussions of millennialism, and because they are accepted by Davis (1981), whose categories of ideal society are used to organize Part 2 of this book.[19] I leave to others, if they wish, the task of finding some other list of criteria to define "millennialism" as a comparative category, in such a way that the Buddhist data can be accommodated without ambiguity or the need for further commentary. For this book I am happy to use the term as an overall category for Buddhist ideas of future felicity associated with Metteyya and other future Buddhas; the specific detail of the ideas and aspirations I have discussed is what is important here.

[19] Spiro (1971: 173 n. 14) accepts them in the Buddhist case.

CHAPTER SIX

The perfect moral commonwealth? Kingship and its discontents

It is scarcely controversial to observe, given the material conditions of premodern agrarian states, that social utopias of a perfect moral community flourishing under a benevolent king were more than a little distant from everyday realities. Kautsky offers a general picture of *The Politics of Aristocratic Empires* (1982: 343–4), in which

> Government is instituted in order to tax, its function is to take from the peasants rather than to give anything to them, and it can hence be understood as an extractive enterprise . . . In order to tax peasants aristocrats must control them. They do not have to direct their labor or interfere in village politics, but they must be able to deprive them of their surplus and – which requires far greater effort – keep other aristocrats from doing so. Because peasants and the land they work are the principal source of wealth in agrarian economies, aristocrats ceaselessly compete for control of the land and peasants. Warfare, both offensive and defensive, then, is required to conquer, expand, or maintain a tax base which is, in turn, required to permit warfare. Closely related to taxation, it is the only other essential function of government in aristocratic empires.

Mabbett and Chandler, writing a chapter on "Ruler and State" in their survey of the history of *The Khmers*, remind their readers that:

> Only a few generations of people living in modern western countries have ever been able to regard peace as a natural condition with its own equilibrium. Throughout Cambodia's recorded history, the Khmers have had to regard war as a normal state of society and as a factor which conditioned it . . .
>
> In South-East Asia, war was a fact of political life, and the character of kingship was moulded by preparations for armed conflict . . . Enemies were not only to be found beyond a country's borders. They lurked within each kingdom, within the capital, even within the court where rival members of the royal family and all their supporters occupied the hot days with games of intrigue . . . [They exemplify this with a story told in Burma and Cambodia; it has a] pitiless logic. He who kills the king

becomes king. This principle is grounded in the politics of succession disputes in so many kingdoms, where intriguers struggle for power and feel little compunction in murdering anyone in the way in order to take the throne for themselves. They, in their turn, are murdered by the next successful contestant. (1995: 158–60)

This can be exemplified from any period and place in Southern Asia, across which Pali texts spread as the Theravāda form of Buddhism was adopted by monarchs, many of them would-be Wheel-turning Kings (*cakkavatti*-s) seeking what they hoped would be a universal empire, emblazoned with the universal truths of Buddhism. How exactly did Buddhist ideology coexist with kingship, given the realities of such a world? The General Introduction I.a–d gave the general form of their relationship – Gunawardana's antagonistic symbiosis, LeGoff's contestation/justification – and suggested that the civilizational enunciation of social and cosmic order was the overarching project which tied them together. Furthermore, the apparent contradiction between the celibate Path and social life was resolved by seeing the particular form taken by Buddhist universalism. But were the two sides of the relation mutually-exclusive opposites, like two sides of a coin: heads we contest, tails we justify? This chapter aims to explore this issue, focusing on violence.

It is easy to see how the Buddhist ethic of non-violence could contest the premodern world (and the modern), and how the Monastic Order – whose leading members were usually taken from just the same aristocratic families who competed for kingship and empire – thereby profited from the ever-present possibility of ideological one-upmanship. The relations between king and leaders of the monkhood can thus be seen as co-operation and/or feud between rival factions of the elite. But if it is easy, given the values of Buddhist asceticism, to see how monks could criticize kings, one might ask: how could Buddhist ideology attempt to justify king(s)? Was this a matter of dishonesty, insincerity, a forced and self-contradictory accommodation of spiritual aspirations to brute facts?

One example, perhaps the high (or low) point in monastic symbiosis with royalty, is found in the account of the second to first-century BC Sri Lankan king Duṭṭhagāmaṇi given in the *Mahāvaṃsa*. Geiger (1908: 20–2, 1912: 146) was probably right in seeing the "Duṭṭhagāmaṇi Epic" as a central focus of that text, perhaps a separate composition inserted into the larger chronicle.[1] The story is important to modern Sinhalese nationalism, but in fact its treatment of the issues is far removed from the simplicities of modern pro-Sinhala, anti-Tamil sentiment. It does, however, contain some strikingly violent ideas, of which two may be cited here. When Queen Vihāradevī, wife of a ruler in the southeast part of the island, Rohaṇa, is pregnant with the future Duṭṭhagāmaṇi, she is described as having a pregnancy-craving to drink the water used to clean blood from the first sword which cut off the head of a soldier in the army of the then-king, the "Damiḷa" Eḷāra. Her craving (which is soon satisfied) is taken to be a sign that "the queen's son will kill the Damiḷas, make (the island) a single kingdom, and glorify the (Buddha's) dispensation (*sāsana*)" (Mhv XXII 47). When Duṭṭhagāmaṇi has later conquered the whole island, like Aśoka before him he is stricken with remorse at the number of people he has killed. Sitting in luxury in his palace, he "considered the great extent of his success, but remembering that he had slaughtered a whole army [the commentary, exaggerating, says that this means millions of elephants, horses, archers and soldiers], he could not be happy." Some Arahants – i.e. allegedly enlightened people – elsewhere in the island know of his condition, and eight of them fly through the air to the city of Anurādhapura to console him: when he asks how he can be consoled after such slaughter, they tell him that he has only killed one and a half human beings. The fully human had taken the three Refuges of Buddhism – the Buddha, his Doctrine, and the Monastic Order – and the other, semi-human, had taken the five Precepts; the rest of them, who "hold Wrong Views and are without morality [*sīla*, also the term for the Precepts], are to be thought no better than animals" (Mhv XXV 103–10). At the end of his "Epic," Duṭṭhagāmaṇi is taken to the Tusita heaven by gods, where he now lives with Metteyya, the next Buddha, whose first disciple he will be when Metteyya comes to earth. It is an understatement to say that such an idea, attributed to Arahants, is not easy to reconcile with the understanding of Buddhist morality usually found in Pali texts. It exists, however, as perhaps the most extreme example of what two influential collections of articles

[1] Cf 3.4.b; and see the outline of chapters given in 3.4.c, p. 269: the story occupies Chapters XXII–XXXII, 863 verses covering fifty years.

called "Buddhism and [the] Legitimation of Power" (Smith 1978a and b).

Whatever one's view of this extreme case, it is not possible to recoil from it as a unique aberration. It is unique, perhaps, in the shamelessness of its casuistry; but it stands at the violent extreme of a continuum in Pali texts, in which middling positions are found as frequently as are cases of the other extreme, complete non-violence. Violence, unstable or stable, is one of the material conditions of civilization. This may or may not be a universal, inevitable truth: it was certainly a very general truth of premodernity. On the one hand, there was the violence, actual or threatened, necessary for the extraction of a surplus and for warfare between aristocrats competing for the "right" to it; and on the other – and this, I think, is an inevitable truth of civilization – what Brown called "the more predictable, but no less overbearing 'gentle violence' of a stable social order," which made possible the existence of clerics. The idea of a secure social world was not a status quo, as it has been for the few modern western generations – in a very few parts of the world, indeed – which Mabbett and Chandler claim have been able to regard peace as a natural condition, but the object of easily comprehensible aspiration. The promise of peace offered by the holders of political and military power, however temporary and flawed its actual realization, could never be simply rejected by the holders of ideological power, however much their ideology was able, when necessary, to condemn all violence, however "gentle." They were partners, willy-nilly, in the discursive enunciation of order. In constructing and maintaining an objectified, routinized, heritage-conscious tradition, it was part of their task to celebrate the aspiration to, and when fortunate the achievement of, peaceful, civilized social existence.

In previous scholarship the question "is there a Buddhist ideal of society and politics?" has usually been taken to be an empirical one. Some writers, focusing on the life of ascetic practice as "the Path," answer in the negative; others, finding texts in the Canon which deal with society and politics (the most important of which are discussed in this chapter), answer positively.[2] Much of this

[2] One of the first to do this was B. G. Gokhale: see now his papers collected in Gokhale (1994).

debate has seemed to assume that the issue is to find out the truth about "original Buddhism," "what the Buddha taught" (and hence, often enough, what Buddhism "teaches," essentially and ahistorically). This is a quest I have explicitly disavowed.[3] From the perspective of this book, in which the Pali imaginaire constitutes an aspect of Buddhist ideology in the civilizational history of Southern Asia, the articulation of order to be found in Pali texts is necessarily both cosmological/soteriological and social. But looking at the matter this way does not mean that all one has to do is search, empirically, for views of society and politics in Pali texts and then assemble them in some coherently organized form. This would be, again, to treat the texts, or (as is more often the case) passages within them conceived separately as "proof-texts," simply in a documentary fashion, and to forget that texts also have work-like aspects, which supplement material realities imaginatively in a critical or reflective, sometimes deliberately inconclusive and open-ended way. Irony, *inter alia*, escapes the essentialist.

Pali texts which portray an ideal, and a society, can put these two objects of representation together, in an ideal society – as in the cases of the Good and/or Wheel-turning King, discussed in 6.4 and 6.5.a – or contrast them, as in the texts discussed in 6.2, where the ideal conflicts with life in society. Even when there is a portrait of an ideal society, such a utopia can have, as throughout the European tradition inaugurated by Thomas More, different kinds of relationship to the status quo in which it exists as a representational artifact. The ideal it offers, in theory or in story, can be imagined, for example, either directly as a possible (past or future) version of the actual, or obliquely as an impossible world whose meaning lies in its admonitory stance towards the actual; or sometimes both at the same time. The irony More built into his *Utopia* – eu-topia and/or ou-topia – is not an idiosyncrasy: it reflects, I suggest, something central to any relation between the textual ideal and the actual, between the ideal and the real.

Clerical ideological power and royal military-political power in premodernity are analytically separable forms or aspects of elite sociocultural dominance, whose symbiosis was always moving between the unified, the complementary, and the antagonistic.

[3] Thus, on the one hand Gombrich: "I do not think the Buddha took a serious interest in politics or intended his teaching to have political consequences" (1988: 81); and on the other Ling (1973: 173): "He may justly be described as a social and political theorist."

The reasons for this variation differed across time and place: one important variable was the extent of monastic landholding, usually extensive in Sri Lanka, variable in Burma, and less significant in Thailand and Cambodia.[4] This chapter brings together a number of relevant texts: some of them, such as the Discourses from the *Dīgha Nikāya* discussed in sections 6.3, 6.4.a, 6.5.b–c, are well known, albeit rarely interpreted, in my opinion, with the care and attention to nuance which they deserve. Others, however, are not usually consulted in these matters but are equally important. Two kinds of literature are especially valuable: *nīti* texts, collections of aphoristic verses of practical wisdom, and the *Jātaka* collection, Birth Stories of the Buddha, which together constitute the largest and most widespread fund of practical advice and *exempla* in Buddhism. *Nīti* texts were a central part of traditional monastic education (Bechert and Braun 81: xxxvii–lxvii). What Bode (1909: 82) said of the Birth Stories in Burma can be generalized to premodern Theravāda Buddhism as a whole: "to understand the literature, 'serious' or popular, of Burma, we cannot know the Pali *Jātaka* too well." But the intention here is not to amass a confusingly large collection of heterogeneous and incompatible texts; I also suggest some strategies of interpretation which I hope might help show how Buddhist clerics could draw on this fund of narrative and aphoristic *exempla* in complex and subtle ways, at different times and for different reasons, both to contest and to justify military and political power, in which the passage from antagonism to symbiosis was not a simple oscillation between opposed extremes. Sometimes it is possible to see how one and the same text – most notably the celebrated *Cakkavatti-sīhanāda Sutta*, with which the chapter concludes – could be used for both.

6.1. TWO MODES OF DHAMMA

One such strategy of interpretation is to divide the protean category of *dhamma* into two, according to the attitude taken towards violence. I call these Modes 1 and 2;[5] in both cases Dhamma is best rendered neutrally, as "what is right." The *Mahāvaṃsa* passage

[4] For Sri Lanka see Gunawardana (1979), for Burma the debate between Aung Thwin (1979, 1980) and Lieberman (1980), for Thailand Ishii (1986), and Cambodia, Mabbett and Chandler (1995: 102, 176).

[5] I owe this elegantly simple way of making the distinction to Jeff Shirkey.

discussed above shows that Buddhist ideology could be used, directly and unblinkingly, to legitimate wars of aggression;[6] but more usually the violence in question is, in theory at least, self-defense, against both external and internal aggression. I am most concerned here with the latter, the internal aggression of crime and the self-defense of society against it through punishment.

Mode 1 Dhamma is an ethics of reciprocity, in which the assessment of violence is context-dependent and negotiable. Buddhist advice to kings in Mode 1 tells them to not to pass judgment in haste or anger, but appropriately, such that the punishment fits the crime. To follow such advice is to be a Good King, to fulfill what the philosopher F. H. Bradley would have called the duties of the royal station.

Mode 2 Dhamma is an ethic of absolute values, in which the assessment of violence is context-independent and non-negotiable, and punishment, as a species of violence, is itself a crime. The only advice possible for kings in Mode 2 might seem to be "Don't be one!", "Renounce the world!", "Leave everything to the law of karma!" Many stories recommend just this. Others, however, envisage the utopia of a nonviolent king.

The word reciprocity is used in many different ways; I intend it here in only one specific sense. The reciprocity of "what is right" in Dhamma Mode 1 is constituted by the principle that good is to be returned for good and bad for bad, by human agents in the here and now. As may be universally the case, the normal expectation (the default mode) of social life is that "one good turn deserves another" and that bad is properly returned for bad.[7] In regard to the latter, the familiar idea (the *lex Talionis*) is "an eye for an eye, a tooth for a tooth," or at least "if you harm someone don't be surprised if that person harms you back (and don't complain)."

[6] Here the often slippery concept of "legitimation" has a precise meaning: the monks made Duṭṭhagāmaṇi's actions, in relation to the Buddhist Precepts, legitimate in the sense (OED, s.v.) of "conformable to law or rule; lawful; proper."

[7] This approach was suggested to me by John Gould (personal communication), apropos ancient Greece (see Gould 1989: 42ff., 60–1, etc.). His idea is that the kind of absolute ethics (in my sense Mode 2, context-independent, non-negotiable Dhamma) proposed by Plato and other philosophers owed much of its value and meaning precisely to the fact that popular values were founded on the context-dependent, negotiable reciprocity of good for good and bad for bad. For reciprocity in the everyday values of ancient Greece see Dover (1974: 180–7, and *passim).*

Reciprocity of both good and bad is expressed in the phrase "it's only fair." This is the case both privately, interpersonally, and through the public institutions of law and legal redress. Thus one instance of violence, to property or persons, may be adjudged a crime, whereas another, occurring in return for a received injury or by legal decree, is right and proper. Royal jurisprudence, and specifically the punishment of criminals, can thus best be seen as an institutionalized form of Mode 1 reciprocity.

In the Mode 2, virtuoso-ascetic sense of "what is right," any act of violence, in any circumstances, is wrong, in the sense that it will bring about its own retribution according to the law of karma. Thus, with ruthless logic, there cannot be a "Good King," because of the necessity for violence in the kingly function. Royal jurisprudence is as bad as are the ills it seeks to redress.[8] The most straightforward example of this in Pali texts is the *Mūgapakkha Jātaka*, the "Birth Story of the Dumb Cripple" (Ja VI 1ff., no. 538, discussed in 6.2), also known by the name of its protagonist, prince Temīya, who spends his first sixteen years feigning these incapacities, and others, in order to avoid succession to the throne, because he remembers having been a king in a former life and having suffered for a long time in hell because of it. It would not be impossible to see karma in Mode 2 as in a sense reciprocal, in that good and bad actions lead to good and bad results: a *Nīti* verse says that there is "suffering for bad (actions), happiness for merit(orious actions), mixed (results) for mixed (good and bad actions): every (action) attains what corresponds to it – you should be aware of the result(s) of action."[9] But this is a descriptive "reciprocity," involving a retribution which is long-term and impersonal, whereas reciprocity in Mode 1 is normative, stipulating immediate action by one person acting on another.

Practically, in the here and now, using the law of karma in a strict and literal sense as a directive for action (or rather, inaction)

[8] This is not so far from the real world as it might seem: Anderson, describing Siam before 1855 – cp. Mabbett and Chandler on the Khmers (above), and Dirks (1987) and Tilly (1985) on Indian kingship and European war and state-making (General Introduction I.c) – says that: "The state was still so archaic and so personalized in the ruler himself that there was no sharp conceptual line between execution and murder, between 'state' and 'private' killing" (1990: 35). Precisely this point is made in the *Cakkavatti-sīhanāda Sutta* (6.5.c).

[9] *Dukkhaṃ pāpassa puññassa sukhaṃ missassa missakaṃ / sabbaṃ sadisakaṃ yāti ñātabbaṃ kammuno phalaṃ* (Dhn 398).

would be a recipe for social chaos, since it removes from human agents all responsibility and capacity for social order. It is impossible that a king (or any other ruler) should leave retribution for crime to the long-term, multi-lifetime process of karma. Consequently, if Pali texts were to speak to actual rulers in the real world, something more flexible than the absolute demands of Mode 2 non-negotiable Dhamma was necessary: and that was provided by Mode 1 negotiable Dhamma, in ideas of, stories about, and recipes for the Good King. However, the construal of kingship by Mode 2 Dhamma was not only negative, such that the absolute prohibition of violence set them impossibly high standards. There was another textual mode open to ideologists, in which kingship was compatible with Dhamma in Mode 2: the utopian paradox of the nonviolent king. In external relations a Wheel-turning King transcends violence by conquering – nonviolently![10] – the whole world, all four islands of traditional cosmo-geography, and so has no enemies; internally he does so by making his Perfect Moral Commonwealth such that no-one does wrong, and so the law courts stand empty and unused. In systematic thought, the contradiction between violence and nonviolence is logically unavoidable, and so the conflict between Mode 2's "all kings are bad" and Mode 1's "there can be a good king" is insoluble. But the stories and aphorisms to be discussed in this chapter can deal with this issue, in the sense Pocock gives to Weber's *handeln* (General Introduction III.b). Some texts follow the Mode 2 contradiction to its furthest reaches, as in the *Mūgapakkha Jātaka* (6.2). Others (6.4) explore the possibilities of Mode 1 Dhamma: one *Jātaka* story, for instance, sees Dhamma as capable of harming the person who harms it (Ja no. 422, p. 454 below), while others refer to the royal executioner's block as the "Dhamma-block" or "block of justice" (Ja no. 468, p. 459 below). The "Birth Story of Advice to Kings" (*Rājovāda Jātaka*, no. 151, pp. 456–8 below) depicts two kings, one of whom follows Mode 1 Dhamma and the other Mode 2: both are commended, but the latter takes precedence (liter-

[10] As in the *Mahāsudassana* and *Cakkavatti-sīhanāda Sutta*-s, translated in Appendix 3 and discussed in 6.5.b and c below. A variant of this in the case of historical kings depicts them – the prime example being Aśoka – as having been at first violent, but later repenting it and thereafter ruling *dhammena*, "in accordance with what is right." Even an Aśoka, of course, cannot avoid the "gentle violence" of social order: for the allegedly historical example of a king who tried, see the story of Siri Saṅgha Bodhi, recounted on p. 459 below.

ally). Yet others – including some well-known *Sutta* texts – give voice to the utopianism of the Wheel-turning King (6.5.a and b): but here, as in the "Discourse on What is Primary" (6.4.a), which recounts an etiological myth concerning the origins and rationale of kingship, we must be alive to the possibility of oblique relationships between the textual and the real: hyperbole, irony, and parable.

6.2. WHY ALL KINGS ARE BAD: THE *MŪGAPAKKHA* (*TEMĪYA*) *JĀTAKA*

It is easy to find texts from all periods which take a critical view of kingship. Kings are paired with thieves, along with natural forces such as fire and water, as phenomena which can bring danger and ruin.[11] "These four will never be filled . . .: the sea, Brahmins, a king and a woman . . . A king, even if he has conquered the whole earth with seas and mountains full of unlimited riches and now rules over it, wishes to possess the land which lies beyond the sea; because all this is not enough for him, he will not be filled." This is because of the immensity of his desires, the commentary explains.[12] Other aphoristic verses express similar ideas: one, for instance, puts together "a king, the ocean, fire, a woman, an artist and a greedy man" as people or things which "have great desire(s)": "their great desire is (itself) not (to be) desired."[13] At Vibh-a 472, in explication of the monastic virtue of "having few wants" (*appicchatā*), its opposite is exemplified by fire, the ocean and a monk who desires many monastic requisites: fire will never be filled by fuel, the ocean by water, or the monk by requisites.[14] "Having few wants" standardly goes with being "content (with

[11] E.g. M I 86, A III 45–6, Vin I 112–13, et freq. The lists are not all the same; see Gokhale (1966: 16) and Gombrich (1988: 78, 81), and cf. Sarkisyanz (1965: 78–9). Heesterman (1985: 109 n. 10) cites similar examples from Sanskrit texts; there is a large area of shared Southern Asian attitudes to kingship, which need not be labeled "Hindu" or "Buddhist" (see 6.4.d).

[12] *Taṇhā-mahantatāya* (Ja V 450; translation from Bollée (1970: 162).

[13] Dhn 357, Mhn 91, reading *etesaṃ pi mahicchānaṃ mahicchatā anicchitā* (the text is uncertain). Translation cannot preserve the alliteration. There is probably also an intended pun with the word *aniccatā* (which appears in the PTS text), impermanence, to which, of course, all desire, great or small, is subject.

[14] Ja V 450 explains that the ocean is never filled by water, a Brahmin by learning (this also explains, I assume, the artist in Dhn 357), and a woman by sexual partners. The "greedy man" is presumably akin to the monk who desires many requisites: he can never get enough of whatever he wants.

little)" (*santuṭṭha*) as a virtue of the monastic life; thus, in another such verse, whereas "an ascetic is destroyed if he is not content, a king is destroyed if he is" (that is, I assume, the extent of his desires is such that he would acquire bad karma if he satisfied them).[15]

The benefits of asceticism are often contrasted with those of kingship. In one *Jātaka* story, a king has two leafy trees in his garden; one is without fruit, the other laden with fruit. Passing them on his way out one day, he tastes a fruit from the latter tree, enjoys its "divine flavor" and plans to eat more when he returns. But other people see him eat, and do likewise; such is their greed that they eat all the fruit on the tree, strip it of its leaves and break its branches. On his return the king sees the two trees, the one now bent and broken, the other still with its leaves, "shining like a mountain of jewels." He reflects that kingship is like the tree with fruit, asceticism like the one without; it is those who have something to lose who have something to fear, not those who don't (Ja VI 44–5). In another story, a wealthy Brahmin widower renounces life in the kingdom of Brahmadatta in Benares to live a life of asceticism in the forest with his baby son. When the boy is grown a girl comes to the hermitage and tempts him to desire and pleasure (*kāma-rati*). She then abandons him, and the result is that he sits doing nothing, as his father says later, "brooding like an idiot." The boy says he wants to return to the kingdom, and asks to be taught how to behave there. His father replies with a riddle: if you want to abandon the forest for life in a kingdom, beware of poison, (dangerous) cliffs, mud and snakes. The boy, naturally, does not understand, so his father explains: intoxicating drinks are poison, women are (dangerous) cliffs, possessions and honors are mud, and kings are snakes. The commentary says this is because kings get angry and ruin or kill you at a moment's notice (Ja IV 222–3). Kings' quickness to anger is a standard motif (e.g. Ja VI 294), as will be seen.

Although a Great Man with the thirty-two auspicious marks can equally well become a Wheel-turning king as a Buddha (6.5.a), Buddhas firmly reject royalty: on the day of Gotama's renunciation, Māra tempts him to give up his quest for enlightenment, saying that the Wheel-gem of such an Emperor will appear for him in seven days' time. "I know that the Wheel-gem is to appear,"

[15] Dhn 356: *asantuṭṭho yati naṭṭho santuṭṭho pi mahīpati.*

Gotama replies, "(but) I have no need for kingship" (Ja I 63). In a short text entitled "kingship," the Buddha, after his enlightenment, sits in the Himālayas asking himself "Is it possible to be a king without killing or causing (others) to kill, without conquering [or: plundering] or causing (others) to conquer [plunder], without grieving or bringing grief (to others), according to what is right (*dhammena*)?" No answer is given, but immediately after this Māra, the god of death and desire, comes and urges him to become a king; the Buddha asks why he does so, and Māra replies that the Buddha has enough supernatural power to turn the Himālayas into pure gold if he wants to. The Buddha refuses,[16] and speaks some verses, not directly about kingship but indirectly, through the idea of the insatiability of desire, which is the cause of suffering (S I 116). The text here gives no indication as to what answers to the Buddha's initial question are possible. Is it a priori no, in Mode 2 Dhamma style, as both the pragmatics of the situation and the implication of the Buddha's verses suggest? Or is a yes answer possible? The commentary (Spk I 180–1), opting for Dhamma Mode 1, thinks it is. It explains that the Buddha was thinking in that way because of his compassion for people suffering punishment in countries ruled by unjust (*adhammika*) kings; and that Māra tried to make the Buddha become a king in the hope that if he did, he (Māra) might get an opportunity (to overpower him), since "kingship is a condition (conducive to) negligence (*pamāda-ṭṭhāna*)."

A number of *Jātaka* stories tell of kings renouncing the world with many or all of their subjects (e.g. no. 70, Ja I 314; no. 509, Ja IV 473–491). As has been mentioned, the best example, and one which was very well-known, is the "Birth Story of the Dumb Cripple" (*Mūgapakkha Jātaka*, Ja VI 1ff., no. 538), also known by the name of its protagonist, Temīya. As the first of the group of ten Great Birth Stories, grouped together at the end of the *Jātaka* collection, this text circulated widely, in manuscripts, inscriptions and iconography.[17] What follows is a translation of some relevant

[16] Cp. 6.5.a below on the Buddha "vomiting" and "spitting out" the possibility of Wheel-turning kingship.

[17] See, for example, EB vol. II Part 1 (with Duroiselle's Introduction) for the circulation of the group of ten, the *Mahānipāta*, in manuscript form in Burma, and also for iconographic versions of them made in the Ānanda temple at Pagan in the eleventh century. Carrithers (1983: Chapters 4 and 5) shows the continuing popularity of Temīya's story in the modern world.

sections, with a summary in square brackets of what is not translated directly.

Once upon a time there was a king of Benares who ruled justly (*dhammena*). He had sixteen thousand women, but did not obtain a son or daughter from any of them. [His subjects complained at the lack of an heir; the chief queen Candādevī made an Act of Truth on an Observance (*uposatha*) day, in the hope of getting a child, declaring that she had lived a life of morality.] Through the splendor of her virtue the dwelling-place of Sakka (the king of the gods, Indra) seemed (to him) to be hot. Considering (the matter) Sakka realized what was going on: "Candādevī has made a wish for a child – I will give her one." He looked around for someone suitable to be her child and saw the future Buddha (Gotama), who had (previously) been king in Benares for twenty years; when (at the end of that life) he died he had been reborn in the Ussada hell, where he cooked for eighty thousand years.[18] Next he had been reborn in the Tāvatiṃsa heaven [with Sakka], and (there, now) wanted to go to a higher Deva-world at the end of that life. [Sakka persuaded him to be reborn as Candādevī's son, on the grounds that on earth he could practice the Perfections and that his birth there would benefit people; the future Buddha was then reborn in Candādevī's womb, as were five hundred other gods in the wombs of the king's ministers' wives.] At the moment (of his birth) the king was sitting on the roof of the palace surrounded by his ministers. When it was announced to him that a son had been born, he felt affection for his son – it was as if it cut through his outer skin, through the inner skin, through his flesh, his tendons, his bones, till it reached the marrow of his bones, where it lodged.[19] Rapture (*pīti*) arose in him, and his heart was at peace. The king asked his ministers if they were happy that he had a son. "What are you saying?" (they replied), "before we were without a (future) lord, now we have got a master.[20]

[18] The guardians of this hell, *inter alia*, pierce their victims' tongues with huge red-hot iron hooks and drag them around, then spread them out like ox-hides on a red-hot copper floor and attack them with stakes; the hell-beings thrash around like fish on dry land, unable to endure their suffering, howling and foaming at the mouth (J VI 112–3). See also DPPN s.v. Ussada.

[19] The text here has only *chavi-ādīni chinditvā*, "outer skin, etc."; I give the full standardized list, as at Vin I 82–3 etc. (for references see PED s.v. *naharu*).

[20] This is a sentiment found in the aphorisms of political (and other) wisdom, the *nīti* texts: thus Ln 115 and 135, "a kingdom is empty without a king," and "one should bear in mind the saying 'the king is not my friend, my partner, he is my master' (*sāmika*)."

[The king granted a favor to queen Candādevī, which she accepted but did not use, and arranged a luxurious upbringing for his son. On the name-giving day Brahmin soothsayers came, looked at the child's auspicious marks, and said] "Great King, the boy has the marks of wealth and merit; he will be able to rule all four great island(-continent)s, not just one. There is no misfortune to be seen for him." The king was satisfied (with their prediction), and when it came to the boy's name-giving day chose the name prince Temīya, because when he was born it had been raining all over Benares and he had got wet (*temīyamāno*). When he was a month old, he was dressed up and brought to his father, who looked at his dear son and hugged him, then put him on his lap and sat down delighted. At that moment four criminals were brought in; (the king) ordered that one of them receive a thousand lashes with spiked whips, one be sent to prison in chains, one be struck on the body a thousand times with swords, and the last be impaled on a stake. When the Great Being (i.e. the future Buddha) heard his father's orders he became terrified and fearful: "Alas, because he is a king my father is doing terrible things, which will take him to hell". On the next day, lying on an adorned royal bed under a white umbrella (the future Buddha) slept a little, then woke up and opened his eyes; he looked at the white umbrella, saw all the trappings of royalty, and became even more afraid than usual: "From where did I come to (be in) this royal palace?" he wondered. Remembering his past lives he understood that he had come from the world of the gods; looking further back he knew that he had been in hell, looking still further back he knew that he had been a king in this very city. He reflected, "I was king (here) for twenty years, and (as a result) cooked for eighty thousand years in hell; now I have been reborn again in this criminal-house[21]. When the four criminals were brought (before him) yesterday, my father spoke harsh words which will lead him to hell. If I become king I will again endure great suffering in hell." He was terribly afraid and the golden color of his skin faded, like a lotus crushed

[21] *Imasmiṃ coragehe. Cora* can mean specifically "thief," but I render it as the more general "criminal," both here and of the four people whom the king judges. Although it is not immediately obvious whether the future Buddha is here referring to the palace as a house where criminals are judged, or using the word to refer to his father and others who live there, since they too are doing karmically bad deeds. I think both are intended. Cp. p. 432 n. 29 and pp. 434–5.

in somebody's hand, as he lay there thinking how he could escape from that criminal-house.

Then the deity who lived in the umbrella, who had been his mother in a former life, comforted him, saying "Dear Temīya, don't be afraid. If you want to escape from here, act as if you can't walk properly, even though you can; act as if you are deaf and dumb, even though you're not. Take on these three Characteristics so as not to show your intelligence." Thus she spoke the first verse:[22]

Don't disclose your intelligence, let everyone think you an idiot; let everyone despise you, that way you'll achieve your aim.

These words comforted him, and he said: "I will do as you say, deity, you (obviously) have my interests at heart and want me to achieve my goal."

He took on the three Characteristics. The king had the five hundred young children (who had been born on the same day) brought to him, to encourage him; these children cried for (their nurses') milk, but the Great Being, terrified by the fear of hell, did not cry, thinking "Dying of thirst is better for me than to become king."

[Over the next sixteen years, as he grew up, they tried various means to make him show that he was not really handicapped, since they perceived that there was nothing physically amiss with his limbs, mouth and ears. They left him hungry, but he did not cry for food; they offered him playthings, but he was not interested; they tried to frighten him, by putting him in a house and setting fire to it, by getting an elephant to pretend to attack him, and by letting snakes loose near him which had their teeth removed and mouths tied up, but in no case did he move; they had dances performed in front of him and the other children, but though the others laughed and enjoyed themselves, he said and did nothing, reflecting that there would be no laughing and being happy for him in hell; they had someone pretend to attack him with a sword, to no avail; they had conch-shells blown suddenly and loudly near him, but he did not react; likewise they tried drums, and suddenly lighting lamps in the dark; they smeared molasses all over him and let flies bite him, they left him unwashed for a year, they heated water under his bed, all to no avail; they had him bathed and ornamented like a god, and brought beautiful women to dance and

[22] For the prose and verse structure of *Jātaka* stories, see 4.3.c, n. 63.

sing for him, but he restrained his breathing so that his body became rigid, and the women were afraid to touch him, thinking him a nonhuman spirit (*yakkha*). Finally the king consulted the soothsaying Brahmins again, who admitted that they had known the child would be unlucky, but had not told the king to spare him unhappiness; now, they advised, since the boy would bring ill-luck to the royal house, he should be taken to the charnel-ground and killed. At this his mother Candādevī reminded the king of the favor he had promised, and asked that Temīya should be made king. The king refused, so she asked that he be king for seven years only; this also was refused, and so she asked that he be king for ever shorter lengths of time, till she reached one week. The king granted this, and so Temīya was led around the city on an elephant under a white umbrella. On his return he was laid on the royal bed and his mother implored him:]

"Dear young Temīya, because of you I have not slept for sixteen years, my eyes are shriveled up from weeping, (I feel) as if my heart were breaking with grief. I know that you are not crippled, deaf and dumb: do not make me (live) without a lord." [She implored him like this for five days; on the sixth the king told the chariot-driver Sunanda to get an inauspicious chariot and horses ready to take Temīya out and kill him on the next day.] During the last night the queen beseeched the boy: "My dear, the king of Benares has ordered that you be (killed and) buried in the charnel-ground tomorrow; tomorrow you are to die, my son!" When the Great Being heard this, joy arose in him, as he thought, "Temīya, the efforts you have made for sixteen years have come to an end" – but his mother's heart was fit to break. Even so he would not speak to her, lest his desire should not be fulfiled. [The next morning, Sunanda prepared the chariot and came to the royal bedroom to get Temīya. Pushing the queen away with the back of his hand he lifted the prince up and went out.] Candādevī beat her breast and fell to the ground weeping loudly. The Great Being looked at her and thought, "If I do not speak she will die of a broken heart." He wanted to speak but acquiesced in the thought that if he spoke, sixteen years' effort would be in vain, but if he did not speak he would become a source (of good fortune)[23] for his parents.

[23] The word is *paccaya*, cause, ground, requisite, etc. I assume that the point here is that if he succeeds in his plan, then the king and queen might also renounce – as they in fact do – and so they would gain the good karma of asceticism and avoid the bad karma of royalty.

[Sunanda took him away; meaning to go out by the western gate he in fact departed to the east,[24] and through the power of the gods they went three leagues (*yojana*-s) and came to a part of the forest made to look like a charnel-ground by the gods. Then the future Buddha rubbed his hands together, rubbed his feet, got down from the chariot and walked backwards and forwards a few times, feeling strong enough to walk a hundred leagues in one day. Wondering if the chariot-driver would be able to overpower him physically, he took hold of the chariot and lifted it up as if it were a toy.[25] At this Sakka's dwelling became hot; realizing that Temīya's goal had been reached he sent Vissakamma to fit him out with divine clothes and ornaments. Temīya then revealed to the chariot-driver who he was, and preached a sermon to him, consisting mostly of verses in the aphoristic *nīti* style on the value of friendship. The chariot-driver recognized him and offered to take him home, so that he could become king. But Temīya refused:] "(I've) done with kingship, and with family and wealth! Chariot-driver, I could obtain kingship (only) through wrongdoing (*adhamma-cariyāya*)." [The chariot-driver tried again to persuade him to return, to no avail. Temīya announced his intention to become an ascetic, and explained that he had feigned being crippled, deaf and dumb because of his previous experience as a king, which was followed by suffering in hell. The chariot-driver, seeing that Temīya had cast kingship aside "as if it were a dead body," wanted to become an ascetic also; but Temīya refused, since in that case his parents would not come to the forest after him. He told the chariot-driver to go and tell the king and queen, promising to await their arrival. The driver did so, and explained to the royal couple what had happened. Meanwhile, Temīya became an ascetic. Sakka had known of his desire to do so and on his orders Vissakamma had built a leaf-hut for Temīya, equipping it with a day- and night-room, and all the necessary requisites of an ascetic. Temīya came to the hut, knew that it was Sakka's work, and took possession of it, at one point walking backwards and forwards outside it exclaiming

[24] This, presumably, like the speeding-up of their journey, is the work of the gods. Going east is more auspicious than going west, and this way they would go to a place in the forest far away from the charnel-ground, so the next part of the story can follow smoothly.

[25] This is a well-known motif in the mythology of Kṛṣṇa; perhaps the text is alluding to it here: "our Buddha was as good as your god."

repeatedly "Oh, what bliss!" (*aho sukhaṃ*).[26] He lived on boiled leaves without salt.

When the king heard what the chariot-driver said, he made elaborate preparations to visit Temīya, and then did so accompanied by a large crowd and his whole army. The king and queen arrived at Temīya's hut, exchanged greetings, and expressed their surprise that he could live on such bad food but still look healthy. Hoping to consecrate Temīya king there and then, and return home, the king spoke these five verses:]

I will give you (everything), my son, the (whole) array of elephants, the (whole) array of chariots, horses, foot-soldiers in armor, and pleasant places to live.
I will give you the women's house, beautifully ornamented; take possession of (the women), my son, you will be our king.
Clever, trained women skilled in song and dance will give you pleasure in (the fulfilment of) your desires – what will you do in the forest?
I will bring the daughters of enemy kings to you: have children by them and then you can renounce.
You are (just) a young lad, my first-born child; rule as the king, it will be good for you – what will you do in the forest?"

[But sixteen-year-old Temīya replied:]

Let a young man live the holy life, let a young man live a celibate life; renunciation by a youth – this is praised by the sages.
Let a young man live the holy life, let a young man live a celibate life; I will live that life, I have no need of kingship.
(In my mind's eye) I see (first) a little boy saying "Mummy, daddy," (and I see him later) troubling himself to obtain a beloved son, or else grown old and (then) dead without getting one.
I see a young girl, beautiful to look at, like a young bamboo shoot, (then) broken up by the wasting away of life[27].
For even the young die, both male and female; in these circumstances, what man could put his trust in life, just because he is young?
What use is it being a young man when he, like fish in shallow water, has less life (to look forward to) at the end of every night?

[26] Cp. the story of the monk Bhaddiya, formerly a member of a royal family, who made the same exclamation in a forest, and was wrongly thought by other monks to have been remembering the happiness of kingship (*rajja-sukha*), Ud 18–20, Ud-a 161ff.; cf. Vin II 183, Thī 842ff., Th-a III 52, Ja I 140.

[27] *Paluggam jīvitakkhaye*; the commentary (Ja VI 26) explains the first word by *maccunā luñcitvā gahitaṃ*, "pulled up and seized by death." I assume the idea here is that a young girl's beauty is fresh and alive like a young (green) bamboo shoot; but old age and death make her brittle and breakable like a bamboo shoot uprooted and dried out.

The world is [or: "people are"] constantly smitten, constantly surrounded; as they pass by unfailingly, why consecrate me as king?

[The king asked for the meaning of the last, riddling verse:]

By what is the world smitten, by what is it surrounded? Who (or: what) passes by unfailingly? I am asking you: explain (it) to me

[Temīya said:]

The world is smitten by death, and surrounded by old age, the (days and) nights pass by unfailingly; understand this, warrior.
Just as when a loom is stretched and (cotton) is woven, what is (left) to weave (grows) less (and less)[28], so too (does) the life of mortals.
Just as a full river runs on, never turning back, so the life of men runs on, never turning back.
Just as a full river might carry away trees growing on its banks, so beings are carried away by old age and death.

The king, at the end of the Great Being's talk on what is right (*dhammakathā*), became dissatisfied with household life and wanted to renounce: "I will not go back to the city, but will renounce here and now. But if my son were to go to the city I would give him the white umbrella (of kingship)." So in order to test him he addressed [Temīya in the same verses as before, with a few extra temptations (wealth, slaves, etc.). But he refused, giving much the same reasons as before, in seven verses. The last is:]

Criminals aspire to wealth;[29] king, I am free from (such) ties. Go away, king, begone! I have no need for kingship.

Thus ended the Great Being's lesson. When they heard it the king, the queen and the sixteen thousand harem-women wanted to renounce. The king had (this message) proclaimed by drumbeat in the city: "Let all those who wish to renounce in the presence of my son do so." He had the doors of all his treasuries opened, those of gold and the rest, and had (this message) written on a golden plate: "There are great treasure-pots at this and that place – take them!", and had (it) fixed on a pillar on the roof of his palace[30]. The citizens abandoned their homes with the doors open, as if they were shops open for business, and went to the king.

[28] Reading *yaṃ yad ev'ūpavīyati*, with CPD s.v. *upavīyati*.

[29] In this verse plainly, as earlier, Temīya seems to place kings and criminals together in the world which he is renouncing.

[30] Reading *mahātale*. This was a place where the king received visitors and advisors, and so a suitable place for such a public message.

The king renounced in the presence of the Great Being, along with a great crowd of people. Sakka provided a three-league long hermitage; the Great Being examined the leaf-huts, and assigned those in the middle to the women, because of their natural apprehensiveness, and those outside to the men[31]. Vissakamma [the craftsman-factotum of Sakka, king of the gods] created fruit-bearing trees, and everyone lived the life of asceticism, on Uposatha days either standing on the ground (and eating the fruit which had fallen) or picking fruit to eat. The Great Being knew what was going on in everyone's mind, and when anyone had thoughts of desire, of malevolence or of violence, he rose into the air and preached sermons to them. Listening to him, they quickly attained the Supernatural Knowledges and Attainments.

A certain neighboring king, hearing that the king of Benares had renounced, entered the city to seize the kingship of Benares; he saw that the city was decorated, went up to the palace and saw seven kinds of costly jewels (abandoned there). Thinking that there must be something dangerous about this wealth he sent for some drunks (who had remained in the city) and asked them which gate the king had gone out through. They told him it was the eastern; and so he went out through that gate and proceeded along the riverbank. The Great Being knew he was coming, went out to meet him and preached a sermon; the king renounced there and then, along with his entourage. Another king (did the same): so three kingdoms were cast aside. Elephants and horses reverted to living wild in the forest, chariots disintegrated right there in the forest, coins from the (royal) treasuries were scattered about the hermitage like sand. Everyone acquired the eight attainments, and became destined, at the end of their lives, for the Brahma-world. Even the animals, the elephants and horses, their minds calmed (and inspired) by the company of sages, were reborn in the six heavens of desire.

[The Buddha ended the story by identifying various characters with contemporary people, including himself as] wise (*paṇḍita*) Mūgapakkha.

It is difficult to imagine a more explicit condemnation of kingship: despite the narrative voice's assertion in the first sentence that

[31] This suggests that they are to be taken as leading a life of chastity; cf. the remarks about "thoughts of desire" made in the next sentence but one.

Temīya's father ruled justly, or "in accordance with what is right" (*dhammena*, clearly in the Mode 1 sense), Temīya (equally clearly using the Mode 2 sense) declares kingship to be "wrongdoing" (*adhamma-cariya*, Ja VI 15, p. 430 above) and twice refers to royal activity as criminal[32]. But his eu-topia – Paradise in the Forest, an Arcadia of fruit-bearing trees where even thoughts of desire, malevolence or violence bring forth sermons from the Leader, where coins lie worthless on the ground and work-animals revert from the domesticated (cultured) to the natural state – is plainly also a ou-topia: a great story, but how to apply it to real life?

In gauging the kind of relation there can be here between textual and actual, ideal and real, it may help to remember that Buddhist morality can be applied on a number of different levels of stringency. From the point of view of behavior, the five basic rules – against (unlawful) killing, stealing, sexual misconduct, lying and taking intoxicants – are, at least in the case of the first four, nothing more than requirements, at different levels of necessity, perhaps, for any form of social life. Transgressions of such basic rules must be held in check somehow, by kings or others, and by self-control, if any society is to exist and endure at all. But they can also become, when interpreted in a strict sense, rules so severe as to inhibit a great amount of normal human experience and interaction, and to constitute in themselves a form of ascetic or ascetically oriented moral heroism. Thus in Temīya's forest-dwelling Perfect Moral Commonwealth, it is merely *thoughts* of desire, rather than actions, which require admonition. The first Precept, against killing, can become a general prohibition on violence, physical and mental, such that even an aggressive thought is precluded. The second, against theft, can become a directive against any covetous thoughts. The third, which for laity is the avoidance of improper sexual behavior, for the ascetic prohibits not only all sexual behavior but also all sexual thoughts (on this see Collins 1994, 1997). The fourth prohibits not only outright falsehood but any speech whatever which is not both true and connected with the Path: that is to say, it militates against most human conversation. The fifth, against drinking alcohol, becomes an exhortation to maintain as a continuous psychic state what alcohol

[32] See p. 427 n. 21 above on the king's "criminal house" and p. 432 n. 29 on the acquisition of wealth.

is taken to inhibit: diligence (*appamāda*) and self-aware mindfulness (*sati*). From this point of view, ascetics who, according to the ideal, do indeed live a life in which a great amount of normal human experience and interaction is absent, are enabled thus not only to criticize kings for the obvious acts of carnage and oppression involved in, say, wars of conquest and predatory taxation, but also to retain the right to look askance, from a position of moral superiority, on the very maintenance of social order on which everyone relies, they as much as anyone else. No matter how far kings or other non-ascetics comply with Buddhist Precepts in actual life, there is always a more exacting version of the ideal to set before them.

In the karmic long term, every act in each individual consciousness-sequence will produce its appropriate result; so one might think, a priori, that there should be no need for human kings or anyone else to interfere with the process, still less for themselves to commit, in punishing wrongdoing, the same evils of violence and killing which karmic law will itself punish in both cases. But to imagine that any king, or indeed anyone in ordinary human society,[33] could or should have been able to live by such rules would be as preposterous as to suggest that in medieval Europe there should have been no need for human law since God, in the Christian imaginaire, eventually punishes all sinners. This point is sometimes made in all seriousness in discussions of Buddhism, and it is a good example of how orientalist scholarship, in the recent and pejorative sense of the word, de-realizes and infantilizes its object. In the European-Christian case, everyone is intimately aware, as a matter of day-by-day experience, of the continuous and changing way ideals and the *Lebenswelt* coexist, of their sometimes stark, sometimes subtle and nuanced relations of contradiction, complementary opposition, or agreement; and so it is easy to see immediately that such an abstract and simplistic deduction from universal and ideal premises – God will punish, therefore there should be no need for law – is quite inappropriate for historical understanding, however admirable the ideals may (or may not) be. The Buddhist case is just the same. From this point of view, the

[33] For isolated individuals and members of extraordinary "formal organizations" such as Monastic Orders (see p. 447 and n. 48 below), reliance on *karma* or "God's will" alone may be possible; but it requires an extremely ascetic, and/or extremely protected lifestyle.

function of stories such as that of Temīya is clearly not to describe or advocate a possible world but to make a comment on the real one.

If ascetics are construed as living, or attempting to live, in strict accordance with the dictates of karma and Buddhist morality, in what sense can their lifestyle be an example for others, an ideal society itself? Does greater stringency in the application of the Precepts dictate a special, distinctive, celibate lifestyle and the particular social role of monks and nuns, or is there a generalizable ideal of human society to be derived from the organization of the Buddhist monastic community, as prescribed in the *Vinaya* rules?

6.3. IS THE MONASTIC COMMUNITY AN IDEAL (DEMOCRATIC) SOCIETY?

A number of academic writers have alleged that despite the numerous texts in which the Buddha is depicted as accepting the existence of kings, either agreeing to their wishes or preaching to them (or both), he in fact historically both came from and continued to prefer a republican political system to monarchy. This is also an idea important to contemporary politics in Southern Asia.[34] The Buddha's recommendations for republican societies are seen as both a model of and a model for the organization of the monastic community.[35] This suggestion is based almost wholly on three pieces of evidence: first, there is the alleged historical fact that the Buddha's own clan, the Sākyans, seem themselves to have been governed in an oligarchic-republican manner (the consensus view of the historical situation at that time was sketched in the General Introduction II.d); second, there is one textual passage, which appears twice in the Pali Canon in almost exactly the same form, at A IV 16ff., and in the opening section of the "Great Discourse on the (Buddha's) Final Nirvana" (*Mahāparinibbāna Sutta*, D II 72ff.), from where it is normally quoted; and third there is the ideal model of decision-making within the monastic community given in the *Vinaya*. The next two sections discuss the latter two points.

[34] See p. 447 n. 46 below.

[35] Among many others, see Basham (1954: 97), Jayaswal (1967: 40–8) and Sarkisyanz (1965: 17–25).

6.3.a. The beginning of the Mahāparinibbāna sutta*: the* Vajjīs' *exemplary community*

I first translate the section from *Mahāparinibbāna Sutta*, the "Great Discourse on the (Buddha's) Final Nirvana," and then comment on it, both in the light of the *Sutta* as a whole, and in relation to the course of history subsequent to the conversation depicted here, as seen by the commentary. The section numbers are those of the PTS edition; I have enumerated the two groups of seven "things which lead to prosperity" among the Vajjīs and the Monastic Order as 1A, 1B, etc., in bold face, to bring out more clearly the correspondences between them.

1. Thus have I heard. At one time the Blessed One was living at Rājagaha, on Vulture Peak hill. At that time Ajātasattu Vedehiputta, the Māgadhan king, wanted to attack the Vajjīs. He said, "I will annihilate these splendid and powerful Vajjīs, destroy them, bring them to utter ruin."
2. Then king Ajātasattu addressed the Brahmin Vassakāra, the Chief Minister of the Māgadhans: "Come, Brahmin, go to the Blessed One and in my name greet him with your head at his feet, and ask him if he is well and free from illness, in good health and strong, living comfortably, saying 'Sir, Ajātasattu Vedehiputta, the Māgadhan king, greets you with his head at your feet, and asks if you are well and free from illness, in good health and strong, living comfortably.' Then say to him, 'King Ajātasattu wants to attack the Vajjīs. He said, "I will annihilate these splendid and powerful Vajjīs, destroy them, bring them to utter ruin."' Memorize carefully what the Blessed One says and report it to me. Tathāgatas do not speak falsely."
3. "Yes sir," said Vassakāra. He had fine vehicles prepared, and rode in one out from Rājagaha to Vulture's Peak hill. He went as far as vehicles could travel, then got down and approached the Blessed One on foot. When he reached the Blessed One he exchanged friendly greetings with him, and sat down to one side. Sitting there he said, "Sir, Ajātasattu Vedehiputta, the Māgadhan king, greets you with his head at your feet, and asks if you are well and free from illness, in good health and strong, living comfortably. King Ajātasattu wants to attack the Vajjīs. He said, 'I will annihilate these splendid and powerful Vajjīs, destroy them, bring them to utter ruin.'"

4. At that time the venerable Ānanda was standing behind the Blessed One, fanning him. The Blessed One spoke to Ānanda:

[1A] "Ānanda, have you heard that the Vajjīs meet together in assembly regularly?"

"Yes, sir, I have heard that they do assemble regularly."

"Ānanda, as long as the Vajjīs continue to meet together in assembly frequently, one can expect them to prosper, not to decline.

[2A] And Ānanda, have you heard that the Vajjīs come together to their assembly harmoniously, work[36] (together) there harmoniously, and (so) conduct the affairs of the Vajjīs harmoniously?"

"Yes, sir, I have heard that they do come together to their assembly harmoniously, work (together) there harmoniously, and (so) conduct the affairs of the Vajjīs harmoniously."

"Ānanda, as long as the Vajjīs continue to come together in their assembly harmoniously, to work (together) there harmoniously, and conduct the affairs of the Vajjīs harmoniously, one can expect them to prosper, not to decline.

[3A] And Ānanda, have you heard that the Vajjīs do not establish (any laws) which are not already established, and do not rescind any established (law), such that they proceed in accordance with the traditional way of the Vajjīs?"

"Yes, sir, I have heard [that they do]."

"Ānanda, as long as the Vajjīs continue not to establish (any laws) which are not already established, and not to rescind any established (law), such that they proceed in accordance with the traditional way of the Vajjīs, one can expect them to prosper, not to decline.

[4A] And Ānanda, have you heard that the Vajjīs honor their Vajjīan elders, respect them, revere them and venerate them, and pay attention to what they say?"

"Yes, sir, I have heard [that they do]."

"Ānanda, as long as the Vajjīs continue to honor their Vajjīan elders, respect them, revere them and venerate

[36] The verb here, *vuṭṭhahanti*, can also mean to rise, and has been taken by translators to mean "rise up (and depart) from their assembly." This is possible, but I prefer the sense "work," "make an effort': it is often contrasted with verbs meaning to be slack, careless, etc. (see CPD s.v.).

them, and take their advice, one can expect them to prosper, not to decline.

[5A] And Ānanda, have you heard that the Vajjīs do not forcibly carry off (married) women and young girls of good family, to have as their wives?"[37]

"Yes, sir, I have heard [that they do not]."

"Ānanda, as long as the Vajjīs continue not to carry off forcibly women and girls of good family to have as their wives, one can expect them to prosper, not to decline.

[6A] And Ānanda, have you heard that the Vajjīs honor their Vajjīan shrines, respect them, revere them and venerate them, both those inside (the city) and outside, and do not allow what was previously given to them and done for them to decrease?

"Yes, sir, I have heard [that they do]."

"Ānanda, as long as the Vajjīs continue to honor their Vajjīan shrines, respect them, revere them and venerate them, both those inside (the city) and outside, and do not allow what was previously given to them and done for them to decrease, one can expect them to prosper, not to decline.

[7A] And Ānanda, have you heard that the Vajjīs provide proper guard, shelter and protection for their Arahants, thinking 'May Arahants come to this territory in the future, and may those who are here now live comfortably'"?[38]

"Yes, sir, I have heard [that they do]."

"Ānanda, as long as the Vajjīs continue to provide proper guard, shelter and protection for their Arahants, thinking 'May Arahants come to this territory in the future, and may those who are here now live comfortably,' one can expect them to prosper, not to decline."

5. Then the Blessed One addressed Vassakāra, the Chief Minister of the Māgadhans: "At one time (when) I was living at the Sārandada shrine in Vesāli I taught the Vajjīs these seven things which lead to prosperity. Brahmin, as long as these seven things which lead to prosperity are established among the Vajjīs, as long

[37] *Vāseti*, literally "make them live (with them)"; I take the verb to have the same senses, literal and euphemistic, as the English "cohabit."

[38] There is a play on words here: "future" translates *anāgatā*, which also means "(not yet) come'; "(those who) are here now" translates *āgatā*, literally "(those who) have come."

as they live in accordance with them, the Vajjīs can be expected to prosper, Brahmin, not to decline."

At these words the Brahmin Vassakāra, Chief Minister of the Māgadhans, spoke to the Blessed One: "If the Vajjīs possess even one of these things which lead to prosperity, they can be expected to prosper, not to decline: what can one say if they possess all seven? King Ajātasattu will not be able to conquer the Vajjīs, at least not (simply) in warfare without deceit and (fomenting) internal dissension.[39] Well, I must be going now, Gotama sir, I have a lot to do."

"(Go and do) whatever you now think appropriate, Brahmin."

The Brahmin Vassakāra, Chief Minister of the Māgadhans, happily accepted what the Blessed One had said, got up from his seat and left.

6. Not long after Vassakāra had left, the Blessed One told Ānanda to go and gather all the bhikkhus who were dwelling in Rājagaha together in the assembly hall. [Ānanda did so, and informed the Buddha when they were all gathered together in the hall.] Then the Blessed One got up from his seat, went to the assembly hall and sat down on his appointed seat. Sitting there he addressed the monks: "Monks, I will teach you seven things which lead to prosperity; listen, and pay attention as I speak." "Yes, sir," they said. The Blessed One said:

[1B] "As long as monks continue to meet together in assembly frequently, one can expect them to prosper, not to decline.

[2B] As long as monks continue to come together to their assemblies harmoniously, work (together) there harmoniously, and conduct the business of the Order harmoniously, one can expect them to prosper, not to decline.

[3B] As long as monks continue not to establish (any Monastic Rules) which are not already established, and not to rescind any which are (already) established, such that they proceed in accordance with the Training Rules as they have been established, one can expect them to prosper, not to decline.

[4B] As long as monks continue to honor those monks who are elders, who are experienced, with years behind

[39] On *upalāpana* and *mithu-bheda* see Johnston (1931: 572–5), CPD s.v. I render *upalāpana* "deceit" following the commentarial story (on which see below).

them, the fathers and leaders of the community, [as long as they] respect them, revere them and venerate them, and take their advice, one can expect them to prosper, not to decline.

[5B] As long as monks do not fall under the sway of the (kind of) desire which leads to rebirth, when it arises, one can expect them to prosper, not to decline.

[6B] As long as monks look to (secluded) forest-dwellings, one can expect them to prosper, not to decline.

[7B] As long as monks – each one individually – continue to establish mindfulness, so that congenial companions in the celibate life might come [to their monastery] in the future and those congenial companions who are already there might live comfortably, one can expect them to prosper, not to decline."

First, note the place of this episode in the text as a whole: it is in the "First Portion for Recitation" of this Discourse (according to the traditional form of textual subdivision; D II 72–89), enumerated as Chapter 1 nos. 1–34 in the PTS edition, which starts from these words of the Buddha to Vassakāra and to the monks at Rājagaha, and continues as follows.

(i) In sections 7–10 the Buddha, still at Rājagaha, gives four more lists of seven things "which lead to prosperity" for monks;

(ii) in section 11 he offers a further list of six Things Leading to Prosperity;

(iii) in section 12, a narrative ellipsis which recurs throughout the first half of the Discourse, the narrative voice states, in summary form, that the Buddha preached to the monks there successively on Morality, Meditation, Wisdom and Release.

(iv) Section 13 then has him moving on to Ambalaṭṭhikā, where only the summary version of his preaching is given, before

(v) section 15 takes him to Nālandā, for a scene with the monk Sāriputta. And so on, through sections 16–25.

(vi) The penultimate scene of the first Recitation Portion, sections 26–32, depicts the Buddha in Pāṭaligāma in Magadha, where Vassakāra and another Brahmin minister are engaged in fortifying the city for their war with the Vajjīs. The Buddha accepts a meal from them – thus showing that in practice he has no quarrel with monarchy as a system – and predicts the future prosperity of the city as Pāṭaliputta (Emperor Aśoka's capital; modern Patna). As in a later section of the text,[40] where he describes the past glory of the currently second-rate place where he is to die, Kusinārā, this temporal landscaping serves both to highlight and to view from a superior, trans-local and trans-historical perspective the rise and fall of temporal power and well-being.

(vii) In the final scene, sections 33–4, the Buddha magically crosses a river by disappearing from one side and appearing on the other, after which feat he utters a verse which uses the metaphor of crossing the river (of rebirth) in a soteriological sense.

The "Discourse on the Final Nirvana" is well known to be a compilation of various passages, many of which are found elsewhere in the Pali Canon. Scholarly analysis of this *Sutta* often discounts the fact that the Discourse has been redacted as a whole, and attempts to trace the various passages found elsewhere to their individual origins, in the quixotic hope of reaching an original Ur-text. Even where this is not done, most scholarship assumes that one can treat passages such as the Buddha's remarks on the seven Things Leading to Prosperity for the Vajjīs as autonomous units, each of which can then be used as documentary evidence for our own historiography, both of society at the time of the Buddha and of his own, "original" teaching. I would rather ask: given that the *Sutta* was compiled long after the Buddha's death, what made the redactors of the Pali version choose these particular incidents, in this particular order? The Discourse is best seen, in my opinion, as a kind of travelogue of the Buddha's life and last days, "Scenes from the Life of a Traveling Preacher." Before reaching its climax in his final nirvana and the distribution of his relics, the text recounts events on his journey from Rājagaha to Kusinārā, inserting repeatedly into the early part of the narrative a formulaic, summary version

[40] Sections v 17–18, which are expanded into an entire *Sutta*, the *Mahāsudassana*, redacted separately in Pali (D II 169–98) but incorporated into the Sanskrit version of the *Mahāparinibbāna*. See section 6.5.b below on the story.

of a standard sermon on Morality, Meditation, Wisdom and Release, along with more or less detailed examples of his preaching on specific topics, meetings and conversations with various people, and an account of a continuing conversation between the Buddha and his companion Ānanda in which the climactic Final Nirvana is anticipated.

The opening scene, with Vassakāra and then all the monks at Rājagaha, depicts short-lived political and military affairs – *histoire événementielle*: in Braudel's metaphor (1980: 27), a series of explosions on the surface of time, impressive but brief – and sets them against the ageless soteriological concerns of the monastic life (focused on the *longue durée* of saṃsāric time, and timelessness). The comparison and contrast between political/military power and the values of monasticism are heightened by the further lists of Things Leading to Prosperity for monks given in sections 7–11; and the underlying sense is that although the Buddha is willing to concern himself with passing issues of power and war, his real concern is with ultimate matters of truth and salvation. The two lists recommend:

1A/1B – frequent meetings
2A/2B – harmonious conduct of business
3A/3B – conservatism, lack of innovation
4A/4B – respect for elders, gerontocracy
5A/5B – proper ("civilized") marriage practices for the Vajjīs; celibacy for monks
6A/6B – maintenance of public piety for the Vajjīs, inside and outside the city; secluded living for monks (in the forest)
7A/7B – the provision of congenial circumstances for *religieux*.

The virtues are analogous in their surface-level prescriptions for action but radically different in their respective goals.

Readers can come to their own conclusions about the possibility that, historically, a king like the parricide Ajātasattu would have sent his Chief Minister to ask a wandering holy man, publicly, how to set about attacking and conquering a neighboring territory. I find it unlikely. As in a *Sutta* where a Brahmin is said to have approached the Buddha for advice on how to perform a Brahmanical sacrifice,[41] an historically improbable event is used here narratively to establish the Buddha's

[41] The *Kūṭadanta Sutta*, discussed by Gombrich (1988: 82–4) and in 6.5.b below.

superiority over his interlocutor. The tension of the scene here is noteworthy. First we hear Ajātasattu announce his intentions, or hopes, to his minister Vassakāra in strong, even violent language (the commentary, Sv 516, glosses "destroy them" as "reduce them to invisibility"). He then tells Vassakāra to go to the Buddha, greet him politely and then simply announce his plans, in the very same violent words, without an explicit question, indeed without any explanation of why the statement is being made. He is just to note "what the Blessed One says." Vassakāra goes, greets the Buddha and exchanges opening conversational pleasantries with him, reported by the narrative voice in standard formulae. He then repeats Ajātasattu's violent and threatening words. The Buddha – here a skilled reciter could make effective use of timing – declines to answer him directly, but instead casually addresses Ānanda, who is standing behind him with a fan, and engages him in a conversation about the conditions of welfare among the intended victims of Ajātasattu's violence. Every item is laboriously repeated three times, first as a question by the Buddha, then in Ānanda's answer, and lastly in the Buddha's prediction that if the Vajjīs continue to practice it, they will prosper and not decline. The Buddha is not seldom represented as taking a markedly *de haut en bas* attitude to laity, especially kings, ministers and Brahmins. His treatment of Vassakāra here seems to be intended, if not to be openly offensive, at least to put him firmly in his place.

All the while Vassakāra cools his heels, but evidently taking note of "what the Blessed One says"; for when the Buddha finishes his catalog and deigns to address him directly his reaction is surprising, and not immediately comprehensible. What is the intended tone of his remarks? When he first speaks, he seems to be depicted as accepting, with reluctant admiration, the force of the Buddha's words: "If they do any one of these things we can't beat them, leave alone seven!" But then either an idea occurs to him, or else he adds a sardonic rider about doubt and dissension which one might imagine to have been growing in his mind all along, to the effect: "OK, maybe we can't beat them in battle, but there are other means . . ." That something is afoot here can be inferred from the fact that he goes away, having "happily accepted" what the Buddha said. Why should he be happy, when he has just heard a catalog of the Vajjīs' virtues and strengths? Because, it would seem, the Buddha's remarks have pinpointed just what he needs to do to bring about what his king Ajātasattu's violent words envisaged: he must break down the Vajjīs formidable unity by deceit and causing dissension. The commentary (Sv 522–4) has him reporting to Ajātasattu as the Buddha's own words the phrase "at least not (simply) in warfare without deceit and (fomenting) internal dissension"; and it then recounts that in fact this is just what Vassakāra went on to do, and so Ajātasattu successfully conquered the Vajjīs and incorporated them into his kingdom. If it is possible to assume that traditional audiences listening to the recitation of this *Sutta* were aware of this, Vassakāra's next words are rather pregnant with meaning: indeed he did have a lot to do. His parting remark, the Buddha's reply, and the narrative voice's final sentence in section no. 5 are all, if the course of history outside the text may be used to understand what is in it, dripping with dramatic irony. The Buddha's words, and the final sentence, are common elsewhere as narrative formulas; but their position in this section of the story gives them a special significance.

It would appear that there is a striking, Janus-faced ambiguity intended here. On the one hand, the triviality and ephemerality of temporal goods are contrasted with the seriousness of the monastic life: nirvana is an achievement "for all time." But on the other hand the virtues which characterize the monastic life, or some of them at least, prove incapable of defending a lay community which adopts them, against both Ajātasattu's crudely material force and the force of history: the "republics" (*gaṇa-saṅgha*-s), however virtuous, were, as an educated audience would have known, at the Buddha's time soon to be a thing of the past.[42] Rather than expressing the Buddha's political philosophy, this whole passage seems to me to be a subtle, by turns rueful and triumphalist acceptance (on both sides) of the disparities between temporal power, in every sense of the word, and the ascetic quest for the timeless.

[42] The commentary (Sv 522) goes so far as to say that the Buddha spoke as he did to Vassakāra out of compassion for the Vajjīs (cf. Sv-pṭ II 162). He knew that Vassakāra would interpret his words the way he did, but he also knew that in a straight fight, Ajātasattu would conquer the Vajjīs in a week, whereas if he persuaded Vassakāra to use deceit and dissension, the Vajjīs would last another three years. "It seems he (the Buddha) thought like this: so much (extra) life is a good (*vara*), since living that long they will make merit, as a foundation (*patiṭṭhā-bhūta*, i.e. of future well-being)."

6.3.b. Decision-making in the Monastic Order

Looking from a wider perspective, and leaving aside the story about Ajātasattu and the Vajjīs, it is true that the Buddha is alleged explicitly to have rejected a monarchical structure for the monastic community, albeit that (centuries) later kings took to recognizing or appointing a *Saṃgharāja*, a "King of the Community." Further on in the "Discourse of the Final Nirvana" the Buddha says that after his death the Dhamma and *Vinaya* should be the Teacher of the community (D II 154). In a *Sutta* from the *Majjhima Nikāya*, the "Discourse to Gopaka-Moggallāna" (M no. 108, III 7ff.), the same Brahmin Vassakāra, Chief Minister of Magadha, talks with Ānanda after the Buddha's nirvana. This time king Ajātasattu is having Rājagaha rebuilt, in anticipation of a conflict with king Pajjota of Avanti. Vassakāra asks Ānanda who is designated to be the Buddha's successor, and is told that no-one is: the Dhamma is their refuge, that to which they have recourse. It is also true that texts from the *Vinaya* provide much evidence to suggest that it is appropriate to speak of the monastic community as in some sense a "democracy," although this issue still needs to be looked at in detail, in light of legal history and legal anthropology, and the political (or non-political) organization of societies.[43] The *Vinaya* rules contain provisions for deciding a disputed matter by majority vote (*yebhuyyasikā*: votes were cast and counted by means of small pieces of wood called *salākā*), and by referral to a subcommittee composed of one or more monks (*ubbāhikā*).[44] Such procedural rules, along with the specific directive by the Buddha that there should be no individual as his successor, no Buddhist "Pope," do perhaps justify using the term democracy. But the overriding value here is not that such procedures are important in themselves – as, say, a way of guaranteeing individual freedoms – but rather that they are a means, resorted to only when necessary, of achieving the goal of harmony and unanimity between monks. It is suggestive of the values involved in these procedures that commentaries to texts dealing with resolving disputes by majority decision specify that the majority must be *dhamma-vādino*, "people who

[43] For old-fashioned and partial treatments, see De (1955) and Hazra (1988, Chapter 4).

[44] See the relevant entries in CPD, PED. Horner, e.g. (1952: 128ff.) would seem to be wrong in translating *ubbāhika* as "referendum" (oddly, she translates the term as "committee" in a footnote).

say what is right" (Sp 1192 on Vin II 84, Sv 1041 on D III 284). The ideal form of decision-making in the Order is for an elder to propose a resolution three times, and for the members of the community present to indicate agreement by silence. Any such proposal should be clearly in accordance with established rules, and in conformity with the Dhamma, and so able to be approved without discussion, unanimously.[45]

A community organizing its affairs by uncoerced vote rather than authoritarian *fiat*, and achieving (in aspiration, at least) a state of unanimous harmony, represents a powerful ideal, particularly in modern times; and so it is not surprising to find it so used by modern Buddhists.[46] And indeed it may well be, as Andrew Huxley argues, that a number of elements from the Monastic Rule (*vinaya*) affected non-monastic law in Southern Asia.[47] But how far could the monastic community be taken, theoretically, to be an ideal society in the traditional period? There is a glaringly obvious problem: the Monastic Order is celibate – what would happen if everyone became a monk or nun? This is impossible, in theory as well as in imagined practice: monks and nuns are dependent on laity for their food. I have argued elsewhere (1994) that the Monastic Order is best seen, in sociological terminology, as a formal organization; that is, it is not a naturally evolving human community but a particular association "established for the explicit purpose of achieving certain [specific] goals."[48] As such a formal organization, it can exist alongside of, or more accurately within any kind of natural society.

For these reasons, *inter alia*, it is not surprising that there is little

45 For an overview of decision-making in the *Saṅgha*, see Wijayaratna (1990: 122–54). That unanimity was an ideal can be demonstrated in a linguistically precise way: unanimity, from Latin *una anima*, "(having) one soul/mind," was a constant motif in Christian monastic ideals. In the text quoted in 4.3.b, the "Shorter Discourse at Gosiṅga" (M I 205ff.; cf. Vin I 350), depicting what I called an Arcadian idyll of harmonious communal life, a monk says to the Buddha that although the monks there have different bodies, they have but one mind (*ekam . . . cittam*). Cp. Collins (1988).

46 For example, Putuwar (1991), writing from a point of view concerned with contemporary Nepal, and those cited from Sri Lanka in Kemper (1991: 217–18).

47 "In terms of detailed rules, of legal hermeneutics, and even, possibly, of legal specialization and professionalism. In Burma one constantly trips over suggestions that the laity should model their behavior on the saṅgha" (personal communication 1995).

48 This phrase is from Ishii (1986: 5–6). Ishii's discussion of the monkhood is marred by his acceptance of the modern myth (invented by Sukumar Dutt) of the evolution of the Order from a primitive wandering band of ascetics, living away from human society, to a "cenobitic Saṅgha" involved with it (ibid.); see Collins (1990b).

evidence in premodern Buddhism to suggest that monastic community life was taken, *tout court*, to be a paradigm for human productive and reproductive society *as a whole*, now or in the future. Non-celibate human community was a matter of local convention (caste, patron–client relations, etc.: see Collins 1994), ordered monarchically. And so it is to the always-ambiguous ideals of kingship that I must return.

6.4. THE GOOD KING

6.4.a. Why kings are necessary, and how they began: the "Discourse on What is Primary" (Aggañña Sutta)

One of the most famous of all early Pali texts tells an etiological myth about the origins of kingship. The *Aggañña Sutta* of the *Dīgha Nikāya*, (no. 27, D III8off., the "Discourse on What is Primary," translated in full here in Appendix 5) tells a story of the beginning of this cosmic era, where genderless and immaterial beings gradually fall from that state into embodied, gendered humanity; this Fall is also an Evolution of Mankind, for it involves the gradual growth of society through the arising of agriculture and food storage, sexuality and private property. It is when theft begins that the people get together and appoint one of their number to be king; he is to keep order in return for a share of the food produced by the others. The relevant sections follows.

Then, monks, a certain being, greedy by nature, while keeping his own portion (of rice), took another portion without its being given, and ate it. (Other beings) grabbed him and said "You have done something bad, being, in that you kept your own portion but took another portion without its being given, and ate it. Don't do such a thing again!" "Alright," he agreed. [But he breaks his promise, and the same thing happens a second and third time, after which] they hit him, some with their hands, some with clods of earth, some with sticks. From this time on, monks, stealing, accusation, lying and punishment (*daṇḍādāna*) became known.

Then, monks, those beings came together and lamented, "Bad (*pāpaka*) things have appeared for us beings, in that stealing, accusation, lying and punishment have become known; what if we were to appoint one being to criticize whoever should be criticized, accuse whoever should be accused, and banish whoever should be banished? We will (each) hand over to him a portion of rice." Then, monks, those beings went to the one among them who was most handsome and good looking, most charismatic and with greatest authority and said, "Come, being, (you) criticize whoever should be criticized, accuse whoever should be accused, and banish whoever should be banished; we will (each) hand over to you a portion of rice. He agreed [and did as they asked]; they (each) gave him a portion of rice . . .

[Three etymologies are then given for *Mahāsammata*, the title of the first king, then for *khattiya* (Skt *kṣatriya*), "warrior" and *rāja*, "king."] This was the birth of the kṣatriya-group, along with the original, primary term(s); . . . [this happened] properly and not improperly" (*dhammen' eva no adhammena;* "according to what is right, not according to what is wrong") . . .

Then some beings, monks, [Brahmins who became ascetics] thought, "Bad things have appeared for us beings, in that stealing, accusation, lying, punishment and banishment have become known; let us keep away from (these) bad, unwholesome (*akusala*) things" . . .

There came a time, monks, when a kṣatriya disapproved of his own tasks, and left home for homelessness, in order to become an ascetic. A Brahmin, too, disapproved of his own tasks and left home for homelessness, in order to become an ascetic. So too did a vaiśya . . . and a śūdra . . . in order to become an ascetic. This was the birth of the ascetic group, monks, . . .

I have given a detailed analysis of this text elsewhere (Collins 1993c), where I argue, as have others (O'Flaherty 1976: 32–3, Gombrich 1988: 85; 1992a), that the original story of the Fall/Evolution of Mankind is best seen as an ironic, often richly humorous parable rather than a straightfaced "myth of origins" (although it became that in later tradition). The earliest human community is described in the (sometimes grammatically unusual) language of the Buddhist Monastic Rule: every single stage in the Fall recalls a specific *Vinaya* rule. Part of the humor of this text lies in the fact that the parable has an originally immaterial and celibate community gradually lapse into embodied society by a series of transgressions of the Monastic Rule. There are also allusions to Vedic literature (Gombrich 1992a), jokes and puns throughout the story. The title of the first king, Mahāsammata, "the Great Appointee," is chosen because his "appointment" is being seen as like the appointment of a monk within the Monastic Order. Later tradition, however, seems to have lost sight of the humor, and Mahāsammata became, for all manner of intents and purposes, the etiologically fundamental First King (Collins and Huxley 1996). Opinions may legitimately differ on the importance of humor in this text, and it is certainly true that the fundamental attitude of the story – that kingship is a response to perceived evil – is found in many other Pali texts where there is clearly no humorous intent. It is clearly no accident – on the contrary it is an acute and accurate historical perception – that the text chooses the moment when one of the beings stores food as a crucial moment in the evolution of society (Appendix 5 section 17). The society whose existence is here being accounted for is an agrarian state: the General Introduction I.a cited Gellner's remarks on the connection between agricultural storage and the necessity for violence in protecting it. The incident is precise: the *Vinaya* prohibits monks from storing food beyond seven days, and the parable has the fact of storage produce its bad effects only when one of the beings stores food for eight days.

For present purposes, it is vital to stress that in this story the legitimate punishment of wrongdoing is, at first, called bad and unwholesome,[49] as are all the other actions in the Fall, such as greed, sexuality, theft, and violence. Thus the "Social Contract"[50] between the people and the king is part and parcel of a regrettable degeneration, not a simplistically legitimatory success story. But although the events of the story constitute a Fall, nonetheless the arising of kings, along with that of the other three social classes, is said to happen *dhammen' eva no adhammena*, "according to what is right (and proper), not according to what is wrong" (D III 93, etc.). How can this be the case, when kingship is seen as essentially connected with the need to punish crime, and itself, like crime, said to be bad and unwholesome? The solution lies in the differing meanings of Dhamma, "what is right": when punishment is seen as an evil, and classed along with the crime which provokes

[49] *Pāpaka, akusala.* See Collins (1993c n. 22.1); and here Appendix 5 sections 19, 22.
[50] See Huxley (1996a) and Collins (1996) for an exchange about the usefulness of this term in the *Aggañña Sutta.*

it, we are in Dhamma Mode 2; when a king is appointed "in accordance with what is right," *dhammena*, we are in Mode 1.

6.4.b. Reciprocity and the problem of punishment; some Jātaka *(and other) stories*

Section 6.1 argued that royal jurisprudence was best seen as an institutionalized form of reciprocity in Dhamma Mode 1. The value of reciprocity can be seen in many contexts, so that the specific nature of reciprocity in jurisprudence rests on a wide and solid base. The virtue of good friendship, of gratitude and mutuality, is one of the most common motifs in the entire *Jātaka* collection (Collins 1987; Jones 1979: 105–15). Such relations can exist not only between human beings, but between animals (e.g. no. 26, an elephant and a dog; no. 157, a jackal and a lion) and between animals and humans (e.g. no. 156, elephants and men; no. 164, a vulture and a merchant). A couplet found in *nīti* texts (Dhn 206–7, Mhn 253–4) and in *Jātaka*-s nos. 223 (Ja II 205) and no. 333 (Ja III 108) advises:

> respect someone who respects (you), share with someone who shares with you; do a favor for someone who returns it; don't do anything for someone who won't do anything for you; don't (try to) be a companion of someone who won't be one to you. Abandon someone who abandons you, don't have affection (for him or her); don't co-operate with someone who has no love for you. Like a bird who knows that a tree has lost its fruit, (the wise man)[51] will look elsewhere – it's a wide world.

The "Birth Story of the Blue-green Frog" (Ja II 237–9, no. 239) was told during a war between Kings Pasenadi of Kosala and Ajātasattu of Magadha; neither could achieve final victory. The apropos of the story here is that Ajātasattu is happy when he is winning, unhappy when he is not.

"Once upon a time, when Brahmadatta was king of Benares, the future Buddha was reborn as a blue-green frog.[52] At that time people used to put nets here and there in rivers and ditches to catch fish. One day, a lot of fish went into a net, as did a fish-eating water snake; many fish came together as one and bit him, making

[51] The verse here puns on *dija*, meaning twice-born: used for birds (born from their mother and also from the egg), and for Brahmins (born naturally and through initiation). In the latter meaning the sense is "wise man," "true Brahmin," as standardly in Pali texts.

[52] In the prose *nīla* (blue) is used, in the verse and title *harita* (yellow-green).

him one mass of blood. Seeing nowhere to hide, in fear for his life he escaped from the net and lay down at the water's edge, swooning in pain. At that moment the blue-green frog jumped onto the top of the net and sat there. The snake, unable to get to a law court (*vinicchaya-ṭṭhānaṃ alabhanto*) saw the frog perched there and asked him, 'Good frog, is what these fish have done acceptable to you?' [The question is repeated in a verse.] The blue-green frog said to him, 'Yes, my good fellow, it is, and here's why: if you eat fish when they come into your territory, then the fish (will) eat you when you enter theirs. Everyone is strong in their own feeding-ground, in their own territory.' And he spoke the second verse:

A person does harm (*vilumpati*) (to others) as long as it serves his purposes. And when others harm him (back), harmed he does (yet more) harm (in turn).

When the snake's case was (thus) decided (*aṭṭe vinicchite*) by the future Buddha, the shoal of fish realized how weak he (the snake) was, came out from the net, did him to death, and departed." The teacher delivered this sermon on what is right (*dhammadesanā*), and connected the Birth Story (with the present): 'At that time Ajātasattu was the water-snake, and I was the blue-green frog.'"[53]

In this story the frog is depicted, imaginatively, as a judge in court. Among human beings jurisprudence is conducted by a king's ministers or the king himself. A king who does not punish is as contemptible as an elephant without his mate, a snake without poison, a sword without a sheath and a cave without a lion (Rn 85). In giving judgment he should not consider whether someone is a friend or an enemy (Rn 79), but should make the punishment fit the crime (Rn 25; cf. Ja V 118[54]). Just as death comes to those who are dear and those who are not, so a king should punish impartially (Rn 42). A king should punish the bad and honor the good (Rn

[53] In this story there is perhaps an implicit criticism of the whole ugly mess of harming and being harmed; the verse here is found elsewhere (S I 85), in the same narrative context of fighting between Pasenadi and Ajātasattu, where the point is that only a fool behaves in this way (and so from this perspective all kings are fools, unless they are pacifists). But in the Birth Story there is no suggestion that on the Mode 1 level, when harm has been done it is improper to harm the aggressor in return.

[54] The commentary to the passage about the Vajjīs translated above exemplifies what it understands by the phrase "traditional way of the Vajjīs" by having a king, as the highest court of justice to which a criminal might be brought, consult a written record of his predecessors' judgments to ascertain "a punishment suitable to [the crime]" (*tad-anucchavika daṇḍa*, Sv 519).

87), giving judgment carefully, in accordance with what is right (*dhammena*), not in anger but from compassion. In one story, the future Buddha is a king who encounters a former wife who had tried to kill him. In anger he decrees that her ears and nose be cut off; but he masters his anger and relents, and only has the woman and her accomplice thrown out of his kingdom (Ja II 120–1, no. 193). In the *Somanassa-jātaka* (Ja IV 444ff., no. 505), the future Buddha is born as a prince called Happiness (*somanassa*). When he is seven years old he is wrongly accused by a sham ascetic of having harmed him; the ascetic tells the king, who angrily and immediately orders the prince's execution. The prince persuades the king of his innocence, and then declares his intention to renounce. The king tries to dissuade him, and the prince replies by giving a lesson, *inter alia*, on the need for kings to act carefully: "A king who acts without due care is not good . . . A warrior-king should act carefully, not without due care; a king who acts carefully gains a good reputation. Let a lord mete out punishment (*daṇḍa*) carefully, (for) he who protects the earth regrets things done in haste." In another story, the *Sumaṅgala-jātaka*, (Ja III 439–44) a king who does not act hastily explains the right practice of kingship to a park-keeper called Lucky (*sumaṅgala*) in six verses of self-praise: "A lord should not mete out punishment when he knows he is very angry; he would cause great suffering to others, unsuitably and unworthily. He should fit the punishment to the case, (only) when he knows he is calm; when he knows what is at issue he should establish a suitable punishment. He will bring ruin neither to himself nor to others if he can soberly distinguish right from wrong judgments; a lord here who, when he wields the rod of punishment pays attention to his reputation, preserves his good name. Those warriors who act without due care and mete out punishment heedlessly throw their life away in ill repute, and when released from this life they go to a bad destiny. Those who delight in the Dhamma taught by noble ones, excellent in thought, word and deed, are well established in peace, meekness and concentration: such (kings) travel through both worlds [i.e. of gods and men, but not in hell]. I am a king, a lord of men and women; if I get angry I stop myself; exercising restraint on the people in this (same) way, I mete out punishment purposefully, out of compassion" (Ja III 441–2). The commentary to this story explains that the king practiced the ten Virtues of a (Good) King, to be discussed in the next section.

In the *Cetiya-jātaka* (Ja III 455ff., no. 422), the first king Mahāsammata is said to have lived for an incalculable length of time; then, in contrast with the *Aggañña Sutta*, where lying is one of the evils which precede and necessitate kingship, lying occurs for the first time nine generations later.[55] Before that, it is said, people did not know what the word meant. A king is the perpetrator of the misdeed (he wants to fulfill a promise made to a childhood friend, which force of circumstances has now made otherwise impossible). An ascetic appears before the king, and warns him that "When what is right (*dhamma*) is harmed, it harms (in return); unharmed it harms no-one. So let no-one harm what is right, lest what is right, when harmed, should harm him."[56] The king, however, refuses to recant, and so sinks gradually into the earth. The verb translated as "harm" here is *han*, to injure or kill; the standard Sanskrit and Pali word for nonviolence, *a-hiṃsā*, is derived from the desiderative of *han*, "to desire to injure/kill." So here one finds the idea, impossible from the Mode 2 perspective but intrinsic to the Mode 1 principle of reciprocity, that Dhamma itself can be an agent of violence.

The "Birth Story of the Owl," the *Ulūka-jātaka* (Ja II 351ff., no. 270) blends the etiology of a natural enmity with a view of kings' *raison d'être*. At the beginning of the era, human beings gather together and choose a man to be their king: he is "handsome, had good fortune, was endowed with authority, and omni-competent. The quadrupeds gathered and made a lion their king, and the fish in the great ocean made a fish called Ānanda theirs. All the birds in the Himālayas gathered together on the top of a rock, saying 'among men a king has been designated, as also among quadrupeds and fish. But we have no king in our midst; we should not live in anarchy[57], let's choose a king.'" They choose an owl; but a crow disagrees, on the grounds that the owl's face makes him look angry – if he looks like this now, when he is about to be con-

[55] Elsewhere, a verse has it that "Right appeared first, afterwards Wrong arose in the world. (Right is) the oldest, the best, the primordial (*sanantana*)" (Ja IV 101, first sentence also at Ja III 29).

[56] *Dhammo have hato hanti, nāhato hanti kañcinaṃ / tasmā hi dhammaṃ na hane, mā taṃ dhammo hato hanti* (Ja III 456).

[57] *Appaṭissava-vasa*; my translation follows CPD, which follows Cowell et al. (1895– II 242). The word *paṭissava* is derived from Skt *prati-śru*, and can mean obedience: elsewhere "disobedience" instead of "living in anarchy" is a more appropriate translation (see refs. in PTC s.v.). The combination of these two senses in relation to kings is obviously significant.

secrated king, what will he do later when he really is angry? The crow flies away and the birds choose a golden swan to be king. And ever since then owls and crows have been enemies.

It is always assumed that a king will have enemies, inside and outside his kingdom, and knowing how to destroy them is a kingly virtue (Rn 32); strength in arms is one of five powers a king needs (Ja V 120), and a fourfold army (elephants, chariots, cavalry and infantry) is a standard part of a king's entourage (PTC s.v. *caturaṅgiṇī*). In the opening verse of the "Collection of Maxims on/for Kings' (*Rājanīti*) that text is said to be "intended to increase his skill in conquering the kingdoms of others"; and later an army is one of the seven things necessary for a king (Rn 26). "Let him carry his enemy on his shoulder(s) until the (right) time has come: then he should smash (him) like a pot on a piece of rock" (said of people in general at Dhn 215 = Ln 86 = Mhn 232, and of kings at Rn 101).[58]

I have quoted a large, perhaps repetitious number of stories, to give a sense of how ubiquitous is the Dhamma Mode 1 form, and so counterbalance the tendency to over-emphasize the soteriological sense of Dhamma Mode 2. In various stories one can trace a gradual movement away from the reciprocities of good and evil to absolute values. Some texts, while not condemning kings' violence and remaining in Mode 1, nonetheless show an ironical distance from royal jurisprudence. In the *Dabbhapuppha-jātaka* (Ja III 332–6, no. 400), a clever jackal procures a fish for his wife by arbitrating in a dispute between two otters; they catch a large fish but quarrel over who should have which part. They ask the jackal to act as judge in their case; he decides that one should have the head, another the tail, while he takes the middle. Returning to his wife he explains what happened, how the otters lost what they had – one phrase used is "their wealth was diminished" – because of their quarrel. The Buddha, narrating the tale, adds his own conclusion: "in the same way, when a dispute arises between men, they have recourse to a judge,[59] since he is their guide. And so their wealth diminishes, while the king's (store of) treasure grows."

[58] Geiger (1960: 132–6, 149–63) quotes extensively from the *Mahāvaṃsa* on the history and ideals of kingship with regard to war.

[59] The word for "judge" here, also used in the Story of the Past for the jackal, is *dhammaṭṭha*, literally "one established in what is right."

The "Birth Story on Advice to Kings," *Rājovāda-jātaka* (Ja II 1ff., no. 151), does not condemn reciprocity as a principle for kings, but adds on to it as superior the virtue of doing good regardless of its position in a relation of reciprocity. The Story of the Present, giving the apropos of the Story of the Past, starts with a conversation between the king of Kosala and the Buddha.

The King of Kosala had one day been sitting in judgement on a difficult case, which had (finally) been completed.[60] [He ate his meal, washed, and came to the Buddha, who greeted him and asked where he had come from. The king explained that he had been involved in passing judgement, and so had not had an opportunity to come earlier.] The Teacher said "Great king, judging cases justly and equitably (*dhammena samena*) is a good thing; it is a way to heaven. It is not surprising that you should judge cases justly and equitably (now), when you have the opportunity to take advice from an omniscient one like myself; but it is surprising that kings in the past, when they listened to sages who were not omniscient, (were able to) judge cases justly and equitably, avoiding the four Wrong Courses and not displacing the ten Virtues of a (Good) King [on these two lists see the next section], (and so) ruling justly, (at the end of their lives) they went to swell the ranks of heaven." Then at the king's request, he told a Story of the Past:

"Once upon a time [the future Buddha became prince Brahmadatta of Benares]. After his father's death he became king, and ruled justly and equitably. He administered justice without zeal (hate, delusion and fear). He ruled justly and equitably, and his ministers also decided lawsuits justly. Because cases at law were decided justly no-one brought fraudulent lawsuits; and as there were none of these, the noise of people in the king's courtyard (coming) to bring lawsuits came to an end. The ministers would sit all day in the law court and see no-one coming to bring a suit; so they went away. The law court became superfluous." [The king saw this and decided to find out if he had any faults at all. First he asked people inside the palace; then outside the palace but inside the city; then all the villagers who lived outside the city at the four gateways. But no-one would find fault with him. Finally, entrusting

[60] Reading *gatigataṃ*; see Vin II 85, Smp 1192.

government to his ministers he left the city in disguise to search in the countryside. He went everywhere, as far as the border; still he found no-one who would find fault with him. So he turned back towards the city. At that time Mallika, the king of neighboring Kosala, who is also said to rule justly, had left his city likewise searching for anyone who could find fault with him. He found no-one and came to the same place as Brahmadatta. At the place where they met the road was only wide enough for one carriage. Mallika's driver shouted to Brahmadatta's to get out of the way but he refused. They informed each other that their respective kings were in the carriages, and tried to find a way to decide which of the two should take precedence; but they found them to be equal in age, in power, in the extent of kingdom, in wealth, indeed in every way. Then Brahmadatta's driver decided to compare them in morality (*sīla*), and asked the other about Mallika's moral behavior (*sīlācāra*). He replied with the first verse:]

Mallika matches [literally "throws"] the strong with strength [for the commentary this is by means of physical and verbal violence], the mild with mildness; he wins over the good by good, and defeats the bad with bad. Of such a kind is this king: get out of the way, driver!

[Brahmadatta's driver replies with the following verse describing his king, which is also redacted in the *Dhammapada* collection of aphorisms (no. 223):] "One should conquer an angry man by kindness, a bad man by good, a miser with generosity and a liar by the truth. This king is like that: (*you*) get out of the way, driver!"

[King Mallika and his driver get down from their carriage and make way for Brahmadatta. Brahmadatta instructs Mallika on how to behave, and returns to his city. Mallika continues on his search looking for someone to find fault with him. Finding no-one he returns to his city. Both kings give gifts and make merit, and at death go to heaven.]

Two points are worth emphasizing. First, in king Brahmadatta's Perfect Moral Commonwealth, since cases at law are judged justly no-one brings any fraudulent suits, which in fact means that there are no lawsuits; the assumption clearly is that when a king is (ideally) just his subjects will behave properly and have nothing to litigate about. Second, *neither* of the kings can discover anyone to find fault with them: although Mallika's principle of reciprocity is inferior to Brahmadatta's virtuous conduct, it is not in itself a fault. The text says that they both ruled justly (*dhammena*). That is, the nonreciprocal, absolute values of Brahmadatta are supererogatory: a Mode 2 bonus, as it were, not an essential requirement for Mode 1 social order.

Texts recommending that evil should not be reciprocated are, of course, legion. The *Dhammapada* (vv.3–5) famously asserts that "The enmity of those who bear a grudge (such as) 'He abused me, he struck me, he has got the better of me, he [or she] has abandoned[61] me' is not appeased. [But the reverse is true.] Enmities are never appeased by enmity here [i.e. in this world], but they are appeased by non-enmity; this is an eternal law (*dhammo sanantano*)."[62] In the "Discourse on the Analogy of the Saw," in the *Majjhima Nikāya* (*Kakacūpama sutta*, M I 122–9) the Buddha teaches that "even if criminals or thieves were to cut (someone) up limb by limb with a double-edged saw, if (the victim) feels anger he is not following my teaching." Such heroic virtues, obviously, cannot be shown by kings (apart from idealized ones like Siri Saṅgha Bodhi, on whom see below); but the existence of such flights of the imagination could always serve to remind kings that monastic aspirations reach higher than theirs. For kings, if nonreciprocity of evil is pushed to its logical conclusion, it ends in not punishing miscreants, as in the Temīya story, and/or pardoning those who are imprisoned; and other stories are not lacking where this is indeed the case. The problem of not punishing miscreants is often avoided by the assumption (or implication) that in the realm of a just king no-one commits crimes; elsewhere pardoning those already judged is a merciful action which just kings perform. In the "Birth Story of Janasandha (Ja IV 176–9, no. 468; cf. Ja VI 327, no. 545) the Buddha reproves a king who neglects his duties, and teaches him Dhamma by recounting the story of Prince Janasandha, on whose accession to the throne all

[61] I prefer to derive *ahāsi* from root *hā*, to leave, as at Sn 469ff., since it gives a more interesting psychological inflection to the verse; the commentary and most translators derive it from *har*, to take: thus "he robbed me," which is equally possible.

[62] Thus in Buddhism this kind of Mode 2 requirement can be contrasted with the particular version of Mode 1 reciprocity practiced by kings in punishing criminals. There is thus an exact correspondence with the Brahmanical tension and opposition between the eternal *sanātana dharma* of nonviolence and the particularist *sva-dharma* of kings; see 6.4.d below.

prisoners were released. Thereafter as king he gave alms incessantly, kept the prisons permanently open, and destroyed the block on which prisoners had formerly either been executed or had limbs cut off. The fact that the word for "executioner's block" here is *dhamma-gaṇḍikā*[63], "the block of justice," is a striking example of how different are the meanings of the word Dhamma in Mode 1 and in Mode 2.

The theme of releasing prisoners occurs twice in the Birth Story of Vessantara; I return to it in the next chapter. Here mention may be made of one king, Siri Saṅgha Bodhi (whose name, at least, is accepted to be that of a historical king in fourth-century Sri Lanka), and the ingenious way he is said to have avoided punishing miscreants without inviting anarchy. The account of him in the *Mahāvaṃsa* says briefly that he had criminals brought before him, and pretended to imprison or execute them: secretly he released them and had corpses impaled and burnt in their stead. In this way he "eliminated the danger from criminals" (Mhv XXXVI 80–1; cf. Mhv-ṭ 668). In the more elaborate version in the thirteenth century, *Hatthavanagallavihāra-vaṃsa*, the value of non-violence is contrasted starkly with *Realpolitik*. When offered the throne, Siri Saṅgha Bodhi, a future Buddha, refuses it, referring to the story of prince Temīya. Begged by the whole population, he gives a long sermon on "the many faults" (*dosa*) of kingship (Att 10), and again refuses. Finally he is prevailed upon by ministers who argue that he can first "protect the world justly and equitably" (Att 11) and then in later life renounce and live the religious life. He rules "without punishing (people) and without (using) the sword" (*adaṇḍena asatthena*, Att 20), secretly releasing prisoners after giving them money, and having corpses burnt publicly in their place. His treasurer Gothābhaya, however, assembles the released criminals into an army and threatens Siri Saṅgha Bodhi, who not only renounces the throne in his favor to avoid war, but also, when later Gothābhaya has put a price on his head, decapitates himself in front of a poor man so that he can take his head and obtain the reward. (A slightly simpler version of this part of the story occurs also in the *Mahāvaṃsa*.) The text has him do this specifically "for the sake of attaining Omniscience (i.e. Buddhahood)" (Att 23).

[63] Also spelt *-gaṇṭhika*; for references, see PED s.v.

6.4.c. Recipes for a Good King: ten virtues, four wrong courses, four forms of kindliness, five Precepts

In the Pali imaginaire, both narratively and structurally, the king is the epitome of the householder, householder and king being the complementary opposites of monk and Buddha, respectively. The king possesses what householders aspire to – enjoyment of the "five kinds of sense pleasure" (*pañca-kāma-guṇa*) – in the highest degree (Collins 1982: 170). This is reflected in the "Birth Story of Citta and Saṃbhūta" (Ja IV 390–401 no. 498), which begins with two people of this name born as outcasts (*caṇḍālā*) and friends. After a series of animal lives in which they are born together as siblings they are reborn as the son of a king's family priest and the king's son, respectively. On growing up the former Citta (the future Buddha) becomes an ascetic; the former Saṃbhūta assumes the throne. In old age the ascetic returns to try to persuade the king to renounce, without success; the king admits that his desires (*kāmā*) are too strong. The ascetic replies "if you are unable to renounce these human desires, king, establish a just (level of) taxation; and let no-one in your kingdom do wrong" (Ja IV 399). The commentary takes the first recommendation as "gather a reasonable[64] (amount of) tax, justly and equitably."

The phrase "ruling justly and equitably," as has been seen, is commonly used to refer to the proper way for a good king to rule; commentarial exegeses of it often cite the ten Virtues of a (Good) King (*dasa rājadhammā*). They can be mentioned by their title only (e.g. Ja I 260, 399, II 400, V 510), or given in full. One such passage is a conversation between a virtuous golden goose and a human king (Ja V 377–8). The human king says that his kingdom is prosperous and ruled justly; he has faultless and self-sacrificing ministers, and an obedient, sweetly-spoken, beautiful wife who has borne him children; he rules without violence, justly and equitably, without oppressing (the people) and without danger; he honors the good and avoids the bad, conforms to what is right and repudiates what is wrong; he knows the future is short, is not drunk (with sense-pleasures, says the commentary), and does not fear the other world since he stands firm in the ten things: Almsgiving, Morality (keeping the Precepts), Liberality, Honesty, Mildness,

[64] *Anatiritta*, "non-excessive," here equivalent to *an-atireka* (both from root *ric*).

Religious practice, Non-anger, Nonviolence, Patience and Non-offensiveness.[65] A king who lives according to these virtues finds his law court "as if" empty (*suñño viya*, Ja IV 370).

The ten Virtues are often seen along with the four Wrong Courses (*agati*): "doing what ought not to be done and not doing what ought to be done, out of zeal, hate, delusion and fear" (Vism 683 = XXI 55, translated by Ñāṇamoli 1975: 799). Another list of royal virtues (virtues also for others) is the four Forms of Kindliness: generosity, (a) friendly (manner of) speaking, usefulness (or helpfulness) and impartiality (or equanimity)[66]. All three lists are sufficiently well known that they can be referred to en bloc by their title (e.g. for the last mentioned Ja IV 110, V 352) – one must assume either that the audience of a recited text would know them or that the reciter could fill them in from memory.

Elsewhere the ten Virtues are mentioned alongside the five Virtues of the Kurus (*Kuru-dhammā*), which consist in keeping the five Precepts, as for example at Dhp-a IV 88, a summary version of the *Kurudhamma Jātaka* (Ja II 365–81, no. 276). In the *Jātaka* version, the future Buddha becomes king Dhanañjaya ("successful in [acquiring] wealth") of the Kurus. Not only does he practice the Kuru-virtues, but so do his queen, their family, the priests and ministers: everyone, indeed, down to the doorkeepers and prostitutes. The city's wealth is legendary, as is king Dhanañjaya's generosity. In the neighboring kingdom of Kaliṅga, however, there is a famine, and the people live in fear of disease and starvation. Taking their children in their hands they come to the king to complain and to ask him to make rain. He asks how, and is told that the kings of old used to give alms, observe morality on Uposatha days, and sleep for a week on a bed of grass. The king tries this, to no avail. Asking what else to do, he is told that the great state elephant of King Dhanañjaya can bring rain. He sends Brahmin envoys to ask for it; he is given it, but again to no avail. He is told that king Dhanañjaya practices the Kuru-virtues, and it is through the power of his virtue that it rains there every fortnight. He tells the envoys

65 *Dāna, sīla, pariccāga, ajjava, maddava, tapas, akkodha avihiṃsā, khanti, avirodhana.* For other references see PED s.v. *rāja.* The list appears shorn of any narrative context at Dhn 266.

66 *Saṅgaha-vatthuni*, see PED s.v. and BHSD s.v. *saṃgraha-vastu*; the word *sangaha* can also be construed as "support," so the compound could mean "means of support': *dāna, peyyavajja, atthacariya, samānattatā.* The precise sense of the last item is disputed: see PED, BHSD s.v.

to return the elephant, find out what are the Kuru-virtues and write them down on a golden plate.

The envoys go to the Kuru kingdom and ask the king, but he says that he cannot tell them about the virtues, since he he might have broken the first Precept, against killing. One day, he explains, he shot four arrows in different directions at a royal festival; he saw where three of them went, but the fourth went over a lake, and might perhaps have killed a fish. The envoys say this would not be wrong, since it was inadvertent, and the king agrees to dictate the Precepts: against (i) killing, (ii) stealing, (iii) misconduct in sexual matters, (iv) lying and (v) drunkenness. He then sends the envoys on to his mother, whom he says keeps the Precepts properly, but she too suspects she might have failed in one way, and sends them on to her daughter-in-law, the queen. In this way the envoys ask everyone in the city, down to the prostitutes: each of them have a measure of self-doubt about their virtue. Some examples are: the queen felt attracted to her husband's brother, and mentally entertained the idea that the king might die and she would become his brother's wife; on these grounds she thinks she has offended against the third Precept. The king's younger brother misled some people inadvertently, and fears that he has offended against the fourth Precept. The family priest had once mentally desired the king's chariot; when offered it he had refused, as he feared contravening the second Precept. Finally, a prostitute had accepted money from someone (actually Sakka, king of the gods, in disguise) for a night; but he went away and did not return. She thereafter refused to accept money from any other man, and after three years was reduced to penury. Still she would not accept anything from another man, until the king's Chief Ministers of justice told her that after three years she was entitled to earn her wages again. She was about to accept money from another man when Sakka reappeared in his former guise. The prostitute withdrew her hand from the second man and did not accept his money. Even though Sakka made himself known, told her it had been a test, and filled her house with precious things, she still reproaches herself for holding out her hand for wages from another man. (She is presumably worried about offending against the second or fourth Precept rather than the third.) The envoys from Kaliṅga returned home with the Precepts in writing; they tell the king of their experiences; he practices the Kuru-virtues and rain falls in his kingdom, averting famine.

The "Birth Story of the Three Birds" (Ja V 109–25, no. 521) has an owl, a mynah bird and a parrot, raised by the childless king Brahmadatta as if they were his children. When they are grown they offer him advice on kingship in answer to his question "What should be done, what is the main duty of someone who wants to be king?" Among other things, they advise him as follows. The owl, named Vessantara, tells him that when performing his kingly duties he should avoid falsehood, anger and laughter; to be diligent, etc.: "This will enable you to bring happiness to (your) friends and suffering to (your) enemies." The mynah bird, Kuṇḍalinī, says that a king's duty can be summed up in two phrases: "getting what you haven't got and keeping what you've got" (*aladdhassa ca yo lābho laddhassa anurakkhanā*). He should appoint ministers who are wise and sober, but nonetheless "know for yourself what your income and expenditure is, what has and has not been done. Punish those who merit punishment and favor those who merit favor" (a verse found also at Dhn 186, Ln 123, Mhn 251). The parrot, Jambuka, who is the future Buddha, gives him a lesson on what is right (*dhammadesanam ārabhi*) "like someone putting a purse with a thousand coins into an outstretched hand." There are, he says, five royal powers, in ascending order of importance: power of (i) arms, (ii) possessions, (iii) (wise) ministers, (iv) noble birth, and (v) wisdom. Finally he counsels the king in ten verses called the ten Verses on Doing What is Right:[67]

(i) Number 1 is "do what is right (*dhammañ cara*) with regard to your mother and father; if you do what is right in this world, king, you will go to heaven."

(ii) Numbers 2–8 are identical to (i) except for the insertion of a different word or phrase for "mother and father": the king must do what is right with regard to: his wife and children, his friends and ministers, the army and war-animals (horses, elephants, etc.), the villages and towns, the capital city and the countryside (of his kingdom), ascetics and Brahmins, birds and beasts.

(iii) Numbers 9–10 say that when what is right is accomplished in this way it brings happiness, as it did to Sakka the king of the gods, the other gods and those in the Brahma-heavens, who all attained their divinity in this way.

[67] *Dasa-dhammacariyagāthā*; found elsewhere (Ja I 177, IV 421–2, VI 94).

The parrot's giving of this instruction is compared to bringing the celestial Ganges down to earth, "with the grace (charm) of a Buddha" (*Buddha līḷhā*). He is made commander-in-chief, and when Brahmadatta dies he is told that the king wanted him to be crowned king. He declines, tells the ministers to administer justice, writes down the principles of justice (*vinicchaya-dhamma*) on a gold plate, and flies off to the forest (Ja V 123–5).

A number of stories, as in the *Kuru-dhamma-jātaka* summarized above, introduce a theme which appears (to modern minds) to blend magic with morality: virtuous royal behavior brings forth rain, and general prosperity. The idea is ubiquitous in Southern Asia, and found already in a canonical text (A II 74–6): if a king does what is right (which according to the commentary, Mp III 105, includes making punishments fit the crime), his ministers and all his people do so also, the moon, sun and stars stay evenly on course, rain falls and produces crops, and so "the whole kingdom is happy if the king does what is right." In the "Birth Story of the Jewel Thief" (Ja II 121–5, no. 194), a king falls in love with the beautiful wife of the future Buddha. He has a jewel secretly placed in the latter's carriage, pretends that he has stolen it, and takes him to the place of execution, where his head is placed on the "block of justice." Sakka becomes aware of what is going on, descends to earth and switches the king's and the future Buddha's bodies. The king is executed in his place, and Sakka consecrates the future Buddha king. The people cry out that their unjust king is dead, and they have a new, just one from Sakka. Sakka announces, standing in midair, "From now on this will be your king; he will rule justly. If a king is unjust, it rains out of season and does not rain in season; and three fears arise – the fear of hunger, of disease, and of riots." In a different "Birth Story on Advice to Kings" from that discussed earlier (Ja III 110–12, no. 334), an ascetic explains to a king that in the realm of an unjust king figs, oil, honey, molasses and the roots and fruit of the forest taste bitter, whereas in one where the king rules justly and equitably, they are sweet. "If he who is considered the best[68] among men

[68] *Seṭṭha-sammata*; on *seṭṭha* and compounds with-*sammata*, in relation to kings and the first king *Mahāsammata*, see Collins (1993c: 331–2 and Appendix 1).

behaves unjustly, how much more so will other people? . . . When a king is unjust the whole kingdom suffers. When a king does what is right, the whole kingdom is happy" (Ja III 111 vv.2, 4).

Once there was a careless king called Pañcāla, who ruled his kingdom unjustly, being set in the (four) Wrong Courses (Ja V 98–108, the *Gaṇḍatindu-jātaka*, no. 520). All his ministers were likewise unjust; so the people, oppressed by taxation, took their children and lived in the forest like wild animals. The villages stood empty during the day, as people were afraid of the king's men; they covered their houses with thorn-branches and went to the forest each morning. In this way they were oppressed by the king's men during the day, and by criminals at night. The future Buddha was reborn as a tree-spirit, and resolved to teach the king a lesson. He warned the king of the dangers of his unjust rule, in this life and the next; the king, along with his priest, set out in disguise to investigate conditions in his realm. They encountered various examples of the chaos and suffering he had caused, in both human and animal worlds: for example, people had to try to milk wild cows, who kicked them and overturned the milk pail. Everyone blamed the situation on the king. Finally he came to a dry water tank in which crows were attacking frogs with their beaks and eating them. Through the power of the future Buddha a frog was able to speak and rebuked the king, saying that he hoped the king and his family would be devoured in battle, as he himself was then being devoured by crows. The priest responded, "(But) frog, kings cannot extend protection to every living thing in the Human World; there is no king so unjust (*adhammacarī*) (as to be responsible for the fact) that crows eat living things like yourself!" The frog begged to differ: "If this kingdom were to have a good king, and to be prosperous, happy and content, crows would be offered excellent food to eat, and wouldn't eat living things like me!" In fact, as a woman explains to a king in the Story 50 of the *Sīhala-vatthu* (Sīh 123–6, especially vv.24ff.), conditions in the human, animal and vegetable worlds depend on the king: if the king is just, rain falls when necessary, and crops are successful; vegetables are flavorful and medicinal plants plentiful and efficacious; vices such as fraud, legal chicanery, theft and adultery are absent; cows and other milk-giving animals give milk in abundance; trees are covered in leaves and fruit; and *religieux* are virtuous and practice properly. Other texts say that when an especially meritorious king is consecrated, wishing-trees can spring up in all directions (Mp I 172, Pv-a 75).

6.4.d. Relative and universal moral codes

It will have occurred to many, perhaps all readers that the virtues and vices ascribed to kings in these lists, such as the ten Virtues or four Wrong Courses, as well as the general problematic of violence and social order, are not specifically Buddhist, in the doctrinal sense. Of course it is possible to Buddhicize virtues, for example by decreeing that the best recipients of alms are Buddhist monks and nuns, or by presenting honesty, patience and so on, in narratives whose overall sense and conclusions are Buddhist. But in themselves these virtues (if one deems them to be such) are qualities possible for all human beings. The morality of the five precepts, the *Kuru-dhamma*-s prescribed for kings, similarly, is not in itself Buddhist: one can avoid killing, theft, sexual misconduct, lying and taking intoxicants without knowing anything about Buddhism. Such action becomes Buddhist by being classified, in conceptual and behavioral terms, as a prolegomenon to or context for more distinctively Buddhist ideas and behaviors. On the other hand, to say that these virtues are not distinctively Buddhist is not to say that they are un-Buddhist. It is only to recognize that other traditions can espouse them, as indeed they have: for almost every one of the ideas about the Good King, and the virtues and vices ascribed to him discussed in the last three sections, there are parallels in the Sanskrit texts of Brahmanical Hinduism.[69] In contexts such as these it is more sensible to speak of shared South Asian (in some cases, simply, human) values and value conflicts, than to draw contrasts between essentialized entities such as "Buddhism" and "Hinduism."[70]

It is certainly true that many Brahmanical texts espouse the relativist morality of *svadharma*, against which one can set Buddhist universalism (General Introduction I.d). The morality of *svadharma* means, as Gombrich has put it, that

[69] See Bechert and Braun (1981); for surveys of what Sternbach has called "*subhāṣita* ('Elegant Sayings'), gnomic and didactic literature" in India and other areas of South and Southeast Asia see Sternbach (1969, 1974, 1981).

[70] Such a contrast mars most of the discussion in the opening chapters of Tambiah (1976).

everything is in a category which has its own nature, and its duty is to conform to that ideal nature. It is the peculiar nature/duty (*sva-dharma*) of fire to burn, of rocks to be hard, of grass to grow, of cows to eat that grass and give milk. In exactly the same way, it is the duty of a potter to pot and of a Brahmin to study and teach the Veda. (1988: 46)

In this view it is the nature and duty of a king, *inter alia*, to use violence in maintaining social order and in war. Perhaps the best-known case is in the *Bhagavad Gītā*, where Krishna persuades Arjuna, temporarily pacifist, that the particular duty of *kṣatriya* warrior-kings is to fight: he should do what it is his real nature to do. Buddhist universalism, on the other hand, as expressed for instance in the *Aggañña Sutta* (Appendix 5 sections 5–7, 27–31), holds that social categories are unimportant to morality, and that moral rules, including the Precept against murder and the more general prohibitions on violence, are the same for everyone. But in some cases, of which kingship is one, to oppose a "Hinduism" to a "Buddhism" in this way is to occlude important aspects of the matter, in relation both to the internal complexity of the two traditions and to what similarities and contrasts there are between them. As the aphorisms and stories recounted here have shown, in Pali texts the particular social role – Bradley's "station" – of kings, and what is right for them in Mode 1 as administrators of justice and punishment, can conflict with Mode 2 Dhamma and the universally applicable first Precept, against killing. Just the same conflict is visible, for example, in the dilemmas of Rāma in the *Rāmayaṇa* (see Pollock 1986: 64–73). The next chapter shows how one of the Buddhist counterparts to Rāma, Prince Vessantara (the other being the Buddha himself), struggles with the issue.

In similar ways both "Hindu" relative and Buddhist universal moral codes can lead to unexpected and paradoxical conclusions. For both, the class of morally relevant agents includes animals, gods and demons; as O'Flaherty (1976: 94) says, citing the *Mahābhārata*, in the Brahmanical *svadharma* view "it is the nature of snakes to bite, [and] of demons to deceive." From this derives what she calls the paradox of the good demon: if demons are true to their own nature, and thus good in the relativist *svadharma* sense, they are, from the human/universal point of view, evil; but if they attempt to conform to the human/universal code of morality, they violate their own true nature. So what is it to be a good demon? She shows (1976: 94–138 and *passim*) that Brahmanical narratives deal with this and other related problems in a number of different ways: there is no one, single "Brahmanical theory."

In the Brahmanical case ambiguity and paradox can arise about the nature of what is good for different classes of agent with different particular duties. In Buddhism, despite the heavy emphasis on universal moral rules, the very same difficulty arises. Is a lion to stop being a predatory carnivore? Is a king to renounce all violence? Is it morally wrong for a poisonous snake to bite the victims on whom it relies for food? The answer in many stories is simply: yes. Snakes which do not bite are "moral" (*sīlavanto,* Ja I 370–1). The *Jātaka*-s contain innumerable examples of animals acting in morally heroic ways, many of them very well known in Buddhist tradition: the hare who jumps into a fire to give food to a hungry Brahmin (no. 316, Ja III 51ff.), the stag who saves a king from a deep water-filled hole, and then preaches to him on the five Precepts (no. 483, Ja IV 263ff.), the goat about to be slaughtered who feels compassion for its killers, since they will suffer the karmic consequences of their deed (no. 18, Ja I 166ff.). The principle of reciprocity appears in both friendships and enmities between animal species: whereas Mode 1 Dhamma accepts this, Mode 2 requires that all enmity be abandoned: and narratives can be found which say this. The "Birth Story of the Mongoose" (no. 165, Ja II 52–4), for example, makes the usual assumption that mongooses and snakes are implacable enemies. But here the future Buddha, an ascetic in the Himalayas, persuades a mongoose and a snake to trust each other, and live in harmony. Some verses from this story are repeated in the "Birth Story of Paṇḍara" (Ja V 75–88, no. 518), where a snake-king of that name learns to live in harmony with a garuḍa bird, another legendary enemy of snakes. A feature of a number of utopian scenes in Buddhist texts is that natural rivals in the animal world renounce their enmity: in the "Story of the Elder Māleyya," for example, when Metteyya comes not only will "all human beings be loving and pleasant to each other," but "crows will become friendly with owls, cats with mice, mongooses with snakes, lion with deer, and so on; in this way animals which are [usually] enemies will be friendly to each other" (Appendix 3 p. 623).

I have been arguing that analogous problems of the good demon, the non-biting snake, and the non-violent king arise in both

Brahmanical and Buddhist codes of morality, in the one from its particularism, in the other from its universalism. Indeed, it is useful to ask, on an abstract level, just how universal Buddhist morality can in fact be. Any and every morality must accommodate some particularizing and context-sensitive modes of evaluation, since moral agency must in many cases be ascribed to individuals under specific descriptions, as occupying specific roles, permanently or temporarily, rather than simply to human beings as such. It is no more than common sense to recognize that parents/teachers/creditors/judges/kings, etc., will in some ways be in the same moral position as children/pupils/debtors/defendants/subjects, etc., and in some ways in a different (complementarily opposite) position. One moral code may choose to emphasize the general and perforce unspecific rules shared by all, rules which provide an overall orientation in decision-making but not action-directives as to what, precisely, is to be done and by whom (and wearing which hat). Another may emphasize action-guiding directives applicable to different individuals in different roles. One might put this in ancient Greek terms: on the one hand, the virtue of each role, or each class of persons, can be said to consist in cultivating its own particular excellence;[71] on the other hand there may be certain excellences common to all human beings (particular to them as a species), or even, as in the South Asian case, common to all sentient beings, and the issue is whether particular excellences can ever conflict with those common to all.

It might help at this point to summarize and recapitulate the argument of this chapter so far, by considering three Buddhist answers to two questions:

(i) Can there be a moral commonwealth under a king?
(ii) If so, can it be perfect?

The answers are:

(i) No to question (i), and therefore to (ii). This is, of course, Temīya's answer, because Dhamma in Mode 2 is incompatible with the necessary violence of kingship.

[71] See MacIntyre (1967: 7–8), on "the noun *aretē* [in Homer], usually and perhaps misleadingly translated *virtue.* A man who performs his socially allotted function possesses *aretē.* The *aretē* of one function or role is quite different from that of another. The *aretē* of a king lies in [his] ability to command, of a warrior in courage, of a wife in fidelity, and so on."

(ii) Yes to question (i), but the answer to (ii) must be "not quite," in the sense that social order is grounded on the mode 1 Dhamma values of reciprocity, fairness and legitimate violence.

(iii) Yes to both questions, at least in theory (or better said, as a species of representation), through the imagining of a king who is moral in the Mode 2 Dhamma sense.

Given the facts of the real world of premodernity as described earlier, it is easy to see both answers (i) and (ii) as realistic, albeit that (ii) is an aspiration for a possible world, rarely and briefly (if ever) fulfilled, rather than a matter-of-fact, practical goal in the real one. What to say of answer (iii)? This is a utopia which goes as much against the grain of the ordinary world as does the demand that snakes stop biting: this kind of king rules *adaṇḍena*, "without the stick (of punishment)" and conquers *asatthena*, "without the sword." There are, obviously, various relationships possible between such a eu-/ou-topia and the actual world, and the work-like aspects of texts expressing answer (iii) are, accordingly, manifold. Just as ambiguity and discretion were useful to More in creating his *Utopia*, so too the ambiguities involved in the variable relationship between the two modes of Dhamma and kingship were useful to the holders of ideological power when they, as historical agents in the real world, composed and redacted the Pali imaginaire. The next section, exploring answer (iii) above, first presents the Wheel-turning king as a counterpart to the Buddha, and then analyzes some texts concerning him. I perceive in them irony, even comedy: others may not: but this very possibility of different readings, I suggest, is part of their point.

6.5. THE RHETORIC OF EXAGGERATION: HYPERBOLE AND IRONY

6.5.a. *Two Big Men*

The *cakkavatti* (Skt *cakravartin* = CV), the Wheel-turning king, often translated "Emperor," is found in pre-Buddhist Brahmanical and in Jain literature. Much has been written on the CV, who has already been introduced (5.2.b); I can be brief.[72] Extensive paral-

[72] See DPPN, ERE, EB, and Eliade (1987) s.v.; Kane (1973[1946]: 66–7), Armelin (1975), Chutintaranond (1988).

lels exist between a Buddha and a CV, who are both *mahāpurisā*: this means literally either "Big Man" or "Great Man," anthropological terms for related but differing categories of leader in pre-kingship societies (General Introduction I.a).[73] Big Men are those whose power is mainly economic and political, whereas the category of Great Men includes those whose power is ideological: "warrior, shaman and ritual expert" can all be "Great Men."[74] From this point of view, one would have to call Buddhas "Great." On the other hand, since the power and prestige of Big Men is not readily transferable from one generation to the next – each has to earn it individually (Godelier 1986: 163) – it would be better to use "Big," since as the *Cakkavatti-sīhanada Sutta* (6.5.c) shows, being a CV is something which is precisely not an "ancestral heritage"; and the definition of a Buddha (*Sammā-sambuddha* or *Pacceka-buddha*) as opposed to an enlightened person (*Arahant*) is that the former are men who discover the truth for themselves, while the latter can be a man or a woman who hears the salvific truth from someone else (so they are also called *Sāvaka*-s, "hearers").

In either case, the parallel is inexact, since Big/Great Man systems are, ideal-typically, at a less complex level of social organization than kingship, whereas in the Buddhist case a CV is much bigger than an ordinary king, and of course a Buddha is much "bigger," in a different sense, than anyone else. The same amount of merit must be accumulated in previous lives by both, the same miracles occur at the birth of both, and both have the thirty-two major and eighty minor bodily marks of a *mahāpurisa*.[75] The splendor of a Buddha is compared to the splendor of a CV (Ud-a 57, 412). At the birth of such a Big Man soothsayers declare that if he remains in the household life, he will become a CV, but if he renounces household life he will become a Buddha. The former option is standardly depicted as follows: "If he inhabits a house, he will become a king, a Wheel-turning monarch, righteous, a king of righteousness (*dhammiko dhammarāja*), a conqueror of the whole world, who has obtained stability in his country, a possessor of the Seven Jewels. These Seven Jewels [or: "precious things", *ratana*] of his are as follows: the wheel-jewel, the elephant-jewel, the horse-jewel, the gem-jewel, the woman-jewel, the householder-jewel, and

[73] See Sahlins (1963), Godelier (1986: 162–88), Godelier and Strathern (1991).

[74] J. Riep, in Godelier and Strathern (1991: 29–30). [75] See DPPN s.v. *Mahāpurisa*.

seventhly the adviser-jewel. He will have more than a thousand sons, valiant, of heroic form, crushing enemy armies. He will dwell conquering this sea-girt land without violence, without a sword, (but) by righteousness [*dhammena*]."[76]

As was discussed in the General Introduction, the conceit that there might be a single ruler over the entire world goes back to pre-Buddhist times in India, when no very large political formations of any sort were known. The real world of empirical geography and power was reconciled with the rhetorical cosmo-geography outlined in Chapter 4 above by means of a classification of two or three kinds of king and CV: (i) a *padesa-rājā*, ruling over a region (extent unspecified), (ii) a CV who rules the whole of one of the four island-continents of cosmo-geography and (iii) a CV who rules all four.[77]

Despite the similarities between a Buddha and a CV, it is easy to oversimplify and overemphasize the parallel between them, especially if one makes the mistake about kings discussed in Chapter 5.2.d, and rests content with a generalizing "is-associated-with" logic of interpretation. Both a Buddha and a CV can be "kings of *dhamma*", *dhamma-rājā*,[78] and the Buddha can be "a Wheel-turning King of the (excellent) Good Dhamma:"[79] but commentaries specify that the CV's Dhamma is the ten Paths of Good Action, while a Buddha's is the nine Transcendental Attainments (Mp II 178–80 on A I 179–10). The range of a CV's power, even those who conquer all four islands, is limited, but a Buddha's power reaches from the highest heaven to the Avīci hell (Ps III 403, Pj II 453–4, Th-a III 48). The Buddha's "power" can refer either, as in the references just given, to the area over which his teaching extends (the same verb, *anusāsati*, and the related noun *sāsana*, are used for both a king's orders and a Buddha's teaching), or to the area over which the protection verses (*paritta*) he teaches are effective: this is his Field of Command.[80]

[76] This is Norman's translation (1992a: 63) of Sn p. 106 (cp. Pj II 449–50); the same passage is found elsewhere, and the commentaries all resemble that of the Sutta Nipāta passage: e.g. D I 88–9 with Sv 249–50, D II 16 with Sv 442–5. For the Seven Jewels see also, e.g., M III 172ff., translated by Horner (1959: 217ff.), Pj I 170–9, translated by Ñāṇamoli (1960: 185ff.). On the woman-jewel, see 4.1.d p. 315.

[77] *Padesa-rājāno* and CVs at Mil 267; the three CVs at Pj I 227; it is not clear from the wording of Vism 301 = IX 23 whether two or three are intended. DPPN and EB s.v. *cakkavatti* refer to Sv 249, but that text refers only to the last of the three, with no mention of other kinds.

[78] The Buddha at S I 33, 55; for the CV cf. PTC s.v. *dhammarāja*.

[79] *Saddhamma(vara)cakkavatti* Mhv V 90, Ud-a 24.

[80] *Āṇā-khetta* Vibh-a 430, Vism 414 = XIII 31.

In the last twenty-five years a phrase encapsulating the idea of a parallel between the two Big Men, or Dhamma-kings, has been widely used: the "Two Wheels of Dhamma." There is some doubt as to what the term *cakra/cakka* in the compound *cakka-vatti* originally meant (Norman EV I 241–2 on Th 822), but it is standardly taken in later Pali and Skt texts to mean a wheel. The CV's wheel is a counterpart to the Wheel of Dhamma, which the Buddha set going in his first sermon, the *Dhammacakka-pavattana Sutta* (S V 420–4). In the cultural background to both lie Vedic ideas and images of the sun, time, and the entire cosmic and social process (Eliot's "turning world" as opposed to its "still point"). The phrase has been made popular by the deserved success of the essays by Smith and Reynolds in Smith (1972), who use it to point to what Pali texts call the Buddha's Wheel of Dhamma and the CV's Wheel of Command. They cite no texts but refer back to Gokhale,[81] who cites Sv 10, where king Ajātasattu, before the First Council, juxtaposes his own *āṇā-cakka*, the Wheel of Command, with the Buddha's *Dhamma-cakka*, his teachings to be recited at that gathering.[82] A number of commentaries to texts which do not mention the *Dhamma-cakka* gloss the CV's "turning the wheel" – a metaphor never explained in the canonical texts themselves – as his turning the *āṇā-cakka*.[83] The idea of the two parallel wheels certainly points to something widespread and significant; but there are problems with adopting it uncritically. In the first place, there is a perhaps minor but still troubling logical problem: the idea that a class (the Wheels of Dhamma) has two members, itself (the Wheel of Dhamma) and something else (the Wheel of Command). More important, the explicit juxtaposition of the two wheels is not in fact very common in Pali texts, nor, when it occurs, does it always express what "the Two Wheels of Dhamma" does. The texts referred to above for the idea that the Buddha's power extends further than a CV's also say the Buddha has the two wheels: his *āṇā-cakka*, Wheel of Command, refers to his injunctions to religious practice (using verbal imperatives); his *dhamma-cakka* is the first sermon, or other occasions on which he preached the Noble Truth

[81] (1953: 164–5) (1966: 22), the latter reprinted in Gokhale (1994: 118).

[82] The same passage occurs at Pj I 95; at Ps II 278 Sakka, king of the gods, juxtaposes his Wheel of Command to the Buddha's Wheel of Dhamma.

[83] E.g. S I 191 with Spk I 278, A I 109 with Mp II 179, A III 147–51 with Mp III 283, Sv-pṭ I 381.

concerning Suffering. The word *āṇā* is commonly used of the Buddha's Monastic Rule, the *Vinaya*: thus a monk who claims that sex is not against the Rule is said to "strike a blow at the Conqueror's Wheel of Command" (Sp 870, Ps II 103). The Vinaya texts are called the Buddha's "Teaching by Command(s)" (*āṇā-desanā*), "because it has been taught with (an) extensive (panoply of) commands by the Blessed One, who is (indeed) worthy to issue commands."[84]

These textual details suggest something more important: if one simply takes the wheels of the Buddha and the CV to be parallel, without going further, one misses much of the tension and competition between the ideological power specific to members of the Monastic Order, with their ethic and/or aesthetic of asceticism, and the political-military power of kings. For although the idea of the two Big Men and their Wheels does represent the symbiosis between clerics and kings, the dissimilarity and hierarchy between them represents their antagonism. And it is easy to find texts which state that the CV is a second best, in no uncertain terms: an imaginative etymology for the word *bhagavā*, "Blessed One" tells us that "He is *bhaga-vā* because he vomited (*vamī*) and spat out the sovereignty and fame which are (usually) reckoned to be good fortune (*bhaga*); thinking as little of them as a ball of spit he cast them aside. Thus the Tathāgata gave no thought to the glory of a Wheel-turning king . . . [or to] sovereignty over the four islands . . . [thinking it] a piece of straw, though he had it within his grasp; he gave it up, left home and reached Perfect enlightenment" (Ud-a 24, cp. Bv 283). A CV is not freed from the possibility of rebirth in one of the destinies lower than the human – as an animal, spirit or in hell – as is a person who attains even the lowest of the four stages of the Path (S V 342–3, Dhp-a III 191, Ud-a 108–9); the radiant light emanating from the Buddha's body is brighter than that of thirty-two CVs (Ud-a 413). Thus one text can say "monks, two people . . . two wonderful men arise in the world, for the benefit and happiness of people, for the profit, benefit and happiness of many people. Which two? The Tathāgata, the Arahant, the Perfectly enlightened Buddha and the Wheel-turning king" (A I 76–7). But another can put the same question

84 *Vinaya-piṭakaṃ āṇārahena bhagavatā āṇābahullato desitattā āṇādesanā*, Sp 21, As 21; for more examples of the term *āṇā* used in relation to the Monastic Rule see Sp vol. VIII s.v.

in the singular, and answer that the Buddha is that one person (A I 22). Pj I 170–9 (translated by Ñāṇamoli 1960: 185ff.) gives a long and elaborate account of why a "Buddha-jewel" (*Buddha-ratana*) is better than any other, whether a CV's wheel-jewel or gem-jewel, or even the CV himself, seen as "the best among householder jewels," since even he bows down to "the homeless jewel" (defined as any monk; Pj II 178). Hence the panegyrics of the CV always come with a caveat: "a form of felicity, yes: but not the best." The happiness (*sukha*) of a CV is recognized in the lists of forms of Happiness, but it is clearly lower than the happiness of heaven (M III 172–8, cited in 4.1.d above); naturally any form of household happiness is lesser than the happiness of the monastic life.[85] From the point of view of doctrine and ascetic rhetoric, "Sovereignty among human beings, whose highest point is the state of a CV, is (a form of) happiness in so far as it comes about as was wished, through the power of *karma*, but because of the suffering (inherent in) change [1.1.b and 2.2.b] it is (a form of) suffering" (Ud-a 159).

This two-tier relation of king to Buddha, equal but inferior, can be carried by the small but significant word *viya*, "as if," or "just like". Thus at Mhv XXXVII 176–7 it is said of king Buddhadāsa of fourth to fifth-century Sri Lanka that "he had eighty good-looking and valiant sons, built like heroes, who bore the names of the eighty disciples (of the Buddha). Surrounded by his sons called Sāriputta and the like, he shone as if he were a Perfect Buddha-King (*sambuddha-rājā viya*)." In the same text at LII 47–9 it is said that Kassapa V in the tenth century sat in a monastery and "recited the *Abhidhamma* with the grace of a Buddha, as if he were making manifest (*dassento viya*) Metteyya the Lord of the World, teaching *dhamma* in the delightful Tusita (heaven) in front of a crowd of gods." In these cases, and others like them, the use of *viya* both marks the analogy and underscores, for those who wish to attend to that interpretative possibility, that it is only an analogy.[86] As

[85] A I 80, et freq.; cp. Ud-a 108 on the happiness of a CV in this respect.

[86] Even where an explicit marker like *viya* is not used, the context will usually make clear the sense intended. At Mhv XXXVII 242, when the scholar-monk Buddhaghosa has written the *Visuddhimagga* a third time in exactly the same words, after gods have stolen the first two versions but then returned them for comparison, the elders of the Mahāvihāra then exclaim "Without doubt he is Metteyya!": it is quite evident that this is meant as a comparison. In the case of Kassapa V, another way the comparison with Metteyya is kept in proportion is by adducing another, incompatible one immediately

mentioned in Chapter 5.2.d, it became common for kings in Theravāda Southern Asia to claim the status of a future Buddha (but not as Metteyya); given the fact that future Buddhahood was a present imaginative possibility, as discussed in relation to Metteyya in Chapter 5.3.a, in these cases royal political-military power tried, no doubt often with practical success, to usurp or encompass the ideological power of the ascetic world-renouncer. But such victories would only ever be tactical ones: clerical one-upmanship always lay in wait.

Thus the exaggerations of royalist rhetoric which used motifs from the Pali imaginaire ran the risk of being undermined from within: and there is no better place to see the danger lurking than in some of the very texts which have been taken, both within the tradition and by modern scholars, to express the acme of CV–Buddha parallelism. Here one might remember Shulman's words on the King and the Clown, cited in the General Introduction I.d, and their importance in understanding the cultural logic of asceticism: he refers to "what may be a universal feature of clowning – the reflexive gift of the commentator, who is capable of framing experience and of switching frames almost at will" (1985: 164). The frame in which a CV strides mightily across the imaginaire as one of two equivalent Big Men can be switched to another, by subtle means: sudden juxtapositions of temporal perspective can bring out the insufficiency, even absurdity, of temporal felicity; touches of reality in eu-topian fantasies can fracture them into ou-topias; moments of incongruous delicacy or farce proceeding from more-or-less good intentions can serve to signal – at least to those in the audience who are inclined to take the hint – that flattering exaggeration is becoming ironic overexaggeration.

6.5.b. The discourses on King Good Looks (Mahāsudassana Sutta), *and (Brahmin) Bigteeth* (Kūṭadanta Sutta)

T. W. Rhys Davids' introductions and notes to the translations of the *Dīgha Nikāya* (e.g. 1899: 160ff.) often pointed out what he saw as the mixture of humor and "ethical earnestness" in the stories.

thereafter. "Every year he would have the city decorated like a city of the gods; he would take [a written version of the *Abhidhamma* text *Dhammasaṅgaṇi*] and travel around the city streets with it in a great procession, sitting on the back of an elephant and looking as splendid as the king of the gods, together with his army in full dress" (Mhv LII 53ff.).

Gombrich (1988: 81–6; 1992) has recently brought this issue to the fore again. One of the texts Gombrich considers, the *Aggañña Sutta*, has been discussed above (6.4.a); this section looks at two more, the *Mahāsudassana* and *Kūṭadanta Sutta*-s.

The "Great Discourse on (King) Good Looks" (*Mahāsudassana Sutta*, D II 169–98, no. 17) elaborates a scene depicted briefly in the "Great Discourse on the (Buddha's) Final Nirvana" (*Mahāparinibbāna Sutta*), where Ānanda says that the unimpressive town of Kusinārā is not a fitting place for the Buddha to die.[87] The Buddha counters by telling at great length the story of Kusinārā in its glory days. The extraordinary number of scenes of wealth and enjoyment repeated throughout the story – there are any number of lists of 84,000 good things (palaces, elephants, wives, cows), all of them repeated more than once as the story unfolds – seem clearly meant to prepare for the Buddha's closing statement: "Ānanda, see how all these conditioned things are past, ceased, changed (into something else)." The Buddha declares that he was king Sudassana, and had lived and died in that place six times previous to that rebirth. The whole of the *Mahāsudassana* is incorporated into the Sanskrit *Mahāparinirvāṇa Sūtra*, as if to emphasize the contextual point. 6.3.a, dealing with a much briefer passage of the *Mahāparinibbāna Sutta* where the Buddha predicts the future celebrity of Pāṭaliputta, described this narrative technique as temporal landscaping; here likewise, impermanence and the inevitability of death, and the irrelevance of passing glory or decay viewed in that light, are underscored precisely by the elaborate emphasis on Kusinārā's past splendor in juxtaposition with its present impoverishment. The Buddha's description of the past opens with the statement that king Sudassana was a Wheel-turning king, and that his city was like a city of the gods. "Kūsināra was always full, day and night, of ten sounds: that is, of elephants, horses, chariots, large drums, small drums, *vīṇā*-s, songs, (two kinds of) cymbal, and cries of 'enjoy yourselves.'"[88] He then

[87] In the PTS edition (D II 146) the phrase is *imasmiṃ kuḍḍa-nagarake*, which Rhys Davids (1910: 161 and n. 1) rendered "in this wattle-and-daub town" (see PED s.v. *kuḍḍa*). Sv 586 glosses *nagara-paṭirūpake sambādhe khuddaka-nagarake* (cf. Ja I 391 where the remark is quoted), "in (what is only) the semblance of a town, a constricted, nasty little town" ("nasty" renders the pejorative *ka* suffix). One might emend the compound in the text to *kūṭa-nagara*, "false town" (cp. the v.l. here and for *kuḍḍa-rāja* at J V 102, 105, 106).

[88] Literally "eat (enjoy), drink, eat" (*asnātha, pivatha, khādatha*); the commentary at Sv 587 glosses all three as *bhuñjatha*, "consume, enjoy."

describes the city in the same way and with many of the same details as the descriptions of heavens and *vimāna*-s cited in Chapter 4. There were, for example, rows of palm trees made of precious metals and jewels, through which the wind played gently, giving rise to a sound which was "pleasing, arousing, intoxicating" (D II 170), as lovely a sound as that made by experienced virtuoso musicians playing five kinds of instrument (various drums and cymbals, and a wind instrument). But the sublimity of the scene is rudely interrupted: "and all the dissolutes, drunks and dipsomaniacs in the city used to enjoy themselves (dancing in time) with the music" (D II 172, with Sv 617). A comic moment such as this, drunks dancing to "the Aeolian Harps,"[89] is a signal to the audience that what Walshe calls "fairy-tale splendour" (1987: 576 n. 465) is just that: the incongruity of the scene marks the represented world as belonging only to the world of representation.

A similar note is struck in the "Birth Story of the Dumb Cripple" (6.2). At the climax of the story (p. 433 above), after Temīya has convinced his father the king to renounce, the latter orders that the doors of his treasuries back in the city be thrown open, with notices saying that their contents are there for the taking. Then, after Temīya has constructed his forest hermitage, the narrative switches to the city. A neighboring king who has heard that the king of Benares has renounced comes to take over the kingdom, but finds the open treasuries suspicious: "There must be something dangerous about this wealth," he says. He sends for some drunks (whom we only now learn are left in the city) and asks them where the king has gone. So while Arcadian celibate unanimity reigns supreme in a nearby forest the riches of the mundane world are left to the rapacious consumption of nervous thugs and alcoholics. Back to reality, as it were.

In the story of King Good Looks, the text next tells us of his seven jewels and four attainments, and his nonviolent conquest of neighboring territories by means of sermons (I return to this in some detail in the next section). Then, the story continues, he decides to build lotus-ponds between the musical palm trees, out of precious metals and jewels; he adds flowers and bathing attendants, and arranges for gifts to be given out on the banks of the

[89] This is the heading given by Rhys Davids and Carpenter (D II 183) to a later section of the text which repeats the scene, this time in the "*dhamma* Palace" built for Sudassana.

ponds, so that those who are hungry, thirsty, in need of clothing, vehicles, furniture, a wife, gold or other money can have whatever they wanted. The text earlier said that the city was rich and prosperous, and now Brahmins and householders come to the king with enormous wealth and offer it to him. He politely declines, saying that he is already enormously wealthy from "legitimate taxation" (*dhammikena balinā*): "You keep (what you have brought)," he says, "and take some more (home with you) from here" (D II 180). The Brahmins and householders feel that it would be wrong to take the money home again, so with the help of Vissakamma, the gods' master-builder, they make the king a palace called the Dhamma Palace. Audiences listening to this story, or at least parts of them, familiar with the realities of tax gathering, might well have allowed themselves, to put it mildly, a wry smile at this little scene.

In the *Kūṭadanta Sutta* (D I 127–49, no. 5), the eponymous Brahmin's name probably means "he who has big (prominent) teeth." Rhys Davids (1899: 163), taking *kūṭa* to derive from a root meaning to cut, suggested that the spirit of the character might be caught by rendering it as "the Very Reverend Sir Sharpstick Goldtooth."[90] In the story he is made to look a fool, since despite being a rich Brahmin he wants to perform an animal sacrifice but doesn't know how: to the understandable chagrin of his fellow Brahmins he has the bright idea of asking the Buddha how to do it. In reply the Buddha tells him the story of a former king Mahāvijita. The name means literally "by whom much has been conquered"; Rhys Davids translated it in the text as King Wide-Realm, and suggested in a note (1899: 175) that "we might say Lord Broadacres." If one were to adopt the pidgin English used in New Guinea and elsewhere for Big Men (van Bakel et al. 1986: 2) one could have Bigfella Winalot. Although, in the manner of Wheel-turning kings, he had "conquered the whole wide circle of the earth," he had not, it would seem, "obtained stability in his [own] country," as they do. For like Bigteeth the Brahmin he wanted to perform a lavish animal sacrifice, but was persuaded out of it by his priest, who explained that the kingdom was full of lawlessness and disorder. The way to deal with the situation, the priest said, was not through taxation or

[90] See PED s.v. *kūṭa*, which also suggests "ox-tooth."

punishment, but by giving seed and feed to farmers, capital to merchants, and food and wages to those in the king's service. Then, in Gombrich's (1988: 83) nice translation, he predicted that "those people will be keen on their jobs, and will not harass the countryside. The king will acquire a great pile. The country will be secure, free from public enemies. People will be happy, and dancing their children in their laps they will live, I think, with open doors." The king did what the priest advised, with the predicted benefits. The Buddha's parable ends with the king performing a bloodless sacrifice; Bigteeth the Brahmin does likewise at the end of the Discourse, setting free the hundreds of animals he had gathered to be killed in it.

Lord Broadacres' conversion to a kind of enlightened-despotic market-socialism paints a pretty picture: but its notion of what a monarch might do is clearly a fairy tale: as Gombrich remarks (ibid.), "we know of no Indian monarch who supplied capital to businessmen – not even Asoka claimed to have done that." There is, indeed, a serious, "ethically earnest" point here, one which is highlighted by the delicacy of the final scene with parents and children. The text can easily be read, or rather heard, by its audience (which might contain kings and/or Brahmins) as a critique of actual kingship and animal sacrifice, and a reminder of the extent to which reality falls short of the standards possible under Dhamma Mode 2. The discursive conventions of realism, as in the modern novel, are not the only means by which reality can be referred to in texts.

6.5.c. The "Discourse of the Lion's Roar on the Wheel-turning King" (Cakkavatti-sīhanāda Sutta)

The *Cakkavatti-sīhanāda Sutta* (hereafter CSS), translated in Appendix 3 – like the *Aggañña Sutta*, translated in Appendix 5 (discussed in 6.4.a) – is one of the best-known texts from the Pali Canon: but, again like the latter text, it has rarely been seriously studied as a piece of literature. Gombrich, the only scholar to have raised the issue of the textual form of the *Sutta*, thinks that "either the whole text is apocryphal or at least it has been tampered with" (1988: 84). I disagree, as also with his suggestion that "the myth is set in an inappropriate frame" (1988: 83; cf. Walshe 1987: 600–1, 603). Story-motifs, especially in an oral culture, may often be found in other combinations in other contexts; but one must still analyze particular motifs in particular texts, and attempt to understand those particular texts in their given, as-redacted-to-us form. At some point during the traditional period, it was thought appropriate to put the text together in its present form. The opening and closing sections, to be sure, seem quite separate from the intervening narrative, on the surface: in para. 1 the Buddha instructs monks on self-reliance and on the need for meditation. After the story of 2–26 has been told, section 27 repeats part of 1, and 28 lists values of ordinary life, juxtaposing to them elements of the ascetic Path as corresponding goods for members of the Monastic Order. But there are many lexical and thematic parallels between these sections and the intervening narrative,[91] which I prefer to call a parable rather than a myth.[92] I read it as a story of decline and revival: it tells of an enormously *longue durée*, from the time of the earliest kings, living as righteous CVs for 80,000 years, through an Armageddon when humans live for only ten years, and back again to a life of 80,000 years at the time of the future Buddha Metteyya. And I interpret this as an elaborate way of giving narrative form to a similar sense of the futility of temporal goods as is expressed in the *Mahāsudassana Sutta*, which is structurally similar to CSS in more than one way: they both state a simple but Buddhistically crucial truth before and after the telling of a long story which illustrates and exemplifies it. CSS depicts life in time, however good or bad, as slightly absurd; and thereby its opposite, timeless nirvana, as the only serious thing in the long run. I suggest that the intention (at least in part) of the long-drawn-out sequence of decline and revival, in all its detailed specificity, numerical and otherwise, and also of the humor and irony of the parable, is to induce in its audiences – or at least to make possible as a reaction for some among them – a sense of detachment from, or at least a (briefly) non-involved perspective on the passage of time.

What follows is an account of both the content and what I see as the structure of CSS (section headings are my own).

[91] The most obvious is the phrase *kusalānaṃ dhammānaṃ samādāna-hetu*, or close variants of it, given in sections 1, 5, 21 and 28; as discussed in detail in Collins (1996), the differences between sections 1 and 27–8 consist in a list of five things in section 28, all of which have lexical and thematic parallels in the intervening story, and some minor changes in the last sentence occasioned by this list.

[92] See Collins (1993c) for similar remarks concerning the *Aggañña Sutta*.

Prologue (section 1)

The Buddha tells monks to make themselves and the Dhamma their refuge; they are not to stray from their customary terrain (*pettika visaya*, literally their "ancestral territory"), which is the Four Foundations of Mindfulness. Māra, god of death and desire, cannot get at them if they stay there. This point is found elsewhere, exemplified by means of animal fables: just as, for example, a quail who strays from her customary terrain can be caught by a falcon, but not if she does not, so monks should concentrate on their own experience (in meditation), where they cannot be caught by Māra.[93] (In CSS it is exemplified by a different kind of fable, where kings who inherit kingdoms from their fathers either do or don't maintain their heritage of Wheel-turning rule.) The context here may also recall that monks are the "Buddha's sons" (*Buddha-puttā*). He concludes *kusalānaṃ dhammānaṃ samādāna-hetu evam idaṃ puññaṃ pavaḍḍhati*, which here, applied to monks, can be rendered "it is by acquiring wholesome states (of mind) that this merit increases," but later will have the lay-oriented sense of "it is by doing Good Deeds . . ." "Wholesome" translates *kusala*, "merit" *puñña*. The semantic fields of these two terms overlap, as discussed in 1.2.b and the Introduction to Part 2, where *kusala* was rendered "skillful." They can be used as synonyms, with an unspecific positive sense, but they can also be distinguished, in that what is in a specific sense meritorious must have a karmic result, but what is wholesome/skillful need not. That is, merit, in the specific sense, is within the realm of rebirth, whereas what is wholesome/skillful need not be: this latter is the category of good deeds and states which are performed or occur without attachment, and so do not entail a karmic result. Thus the concluding sentence in CSS section 1 can be taken as referring both to Good Deeds and good rebirth circumstances, and to deeds and states which, by engendering no result, conduce to the escape from rebirth. The commentary (Sv 847–8) glosses the phrase *evam idaṃ puññaṃ pavaḍḍhati* as *tattha duvidhaṃ kusalaṃ vaṭṭa-gāmi ca vivaṭṭa-gāmi ca*, "here what is skillful is of two kinds, that which leads to rebirth, and that which leads to escape from rebirth." The former refers to mutual love between children and parents, and the latter to the thirty-seven Factors of enlightenment (i.e. monastic practice such

[93] S V 146ff., Ja II 109, cited by the commentary here (Sv 846–7); cp. Mil 367–8.

as the Foundations of Mindfulness). "The highest point [or: end-point] of the Good leading to rebirth in the Human World is the good fortune and wealth of a Wheel-turning King",[94] whereas the end-point of the Good leading to escape from rebirth is the Path, the Fruits (of the Path) and Nirvana. It states that the latter will be dealt with at the end of the *Sutta* (and picks this up in the commentary to section 27), and that the story which begins in section 2 is told to show what happens when children do, or do not follow the advice of their parents.

Act I (sections 2–8) – "Conquest and Government by Dhamma*"*
'Once upon a time there was a king called Daḷhanemi . . ." The name means "Strong-tire," a witty name for a Wheel-turning king. As CV and *dhamma-rāja*, he has conquered the four corners of the earth, and rules over it without the need for punishment or violence. His Wheel-jewel slips from its place in the sky, and he knows he is soon to die, and so he renounces the world and enjoins his son to rule. He remarks, "I have enjoyed the pleasures of human life (*bhuttā . . me mānusakā kāmā*), now it is time to seek the pleasures of life in the heavens" (*dibbe kāme*, D III 59–60) – an enviable attitude to death. He goes forth from home to homelessness, and a week later the Wheel-jewel disappears.

When the son finds out that the Wheel-jewel has disappeared, he is distressed, and makes his distress public. Somewhat pathetically, he goes to ask his father, now a "King-seer" (*rājisi*), what has happened to it.[95] His father tells him that the Wheel-jewel is not his ancestral heritage (*pettika dāyajja*); he must behave like a CV himself. "(You have to) turn in the noble turning (or, the Wheel) of the Wheel-turning king" (*cakkavatti-vatte vattāhi*). The wordplay here is untranslatable: the verb *vattati* can also mean to be, to proceed; *vatta* can mean service, customary duty, so his advice is also to do the customary duty of a CV. There is a pun throughout on the *vatta* of a CV and the round of rebirth, *vaṭṭa*, which he helps to turn, as opposed to *vivaṭṭa*, release from rebirth, which the Buddha is preaching to the monks (by means of this very story).

[94] *Vaṭṭa-gāmi-kusalassa pariyosānaṃ manussa-loke cakkavatti-siri-vibhavo*; there is clearly a play on the words *vaṭṭa*, rebirth, and *vatti*, the Turning of the Wheel-turner.

[95] I assume that the choice, and threefold repetition, of the phrase describing him as "the noble warrior king, who had been duly consecrated" is intended as an ironic contrast to the pathetic air of his feelings and words.

The father then spells out what the duties of the Wheel-turning King's station are, and the son successfully follows his advice, as do the next seven generations.[96] All this takes rather a long time, since we learn in section 14 that each lived for 80,000 years. In the son's rise to CV status, he first follows his father's advice regarding the internal government of his kingdom in section 5, and the Wheel-gem reappears. He sees it and his shock of recognition is expressed with the optative *assaṃ nu kho ahaṃ rājā cakkavattīti.* This must be translated with some modal verb: "I may be a CV king" (= perhaps I am), or probably better, "I must be a CV king!" (= the evidence is undeniable). One is reminded of the Ugly Duckling's more assertive "I am a Swan!"

The CV's manner of extending his kingdom by external conquest in section 6, in a standard passage, is rather remarkable. He sets the Wheel-jewel in motion, and follows it everywhere "along with his fourfold army" (elephants, cavalry, chariots and foot-soldiers). In each of the four quarters, when it comes to rest he makes camp, "along with his fourfold army," as the text takes care to repeat. All the enemy kings[97] come to him and say, "Come, Great King, welcome, Great King, it's yours [i.e. take possession of this territory], great king, give us your orders [or: instruction]." The king recites a shortened version of the standard five Precepts of Buddhist morality: one should not kill, steal, misbehave sexually, lie or drink intoxicants; and he adds "(continue to) govern as you did before."[98] And so "the (enemy) kings become his clients" (*anuyuttā*). A fine piece of deadpan humor: one suspects the realities of ancient Indian warfare probably weren't quite like this, does one not? As two footnotes in Rhys Davids say: "In this parody on the ordinary methods of conquest all the horrors and crimes of war are absent . . . To enjoy this paragraph as it deserves the reader should bear in mind the kind of method of which it is a parody, the laws that would be made, say, by an Assyrian or Hun con-

96 Rhys Davids made an egregious error in translating this section (1921: 62–3), which is repeated, sadly, by both Ling (1981: 117) and Walshe (1987: 397). (It had been correctly translated by Franke 1913: 262.) The text plainly, in simple Pali, has the father tell the son to consult ascetics and Brahmins (*samaṇa-brāhmaṇā*) for religious advice, and to do what they say. The translations reverse this, and have it that the king is to give such advice to them! It is likely that this slip has misled those who rely on translations, both on this particular point and on the general tenor of the text's characterization of the CV.

97 *Paṭi-rājāno*: the prefix indicates that they are facing him, and implies at least potential opposition. It contrasts with the word *anuyuttā*, clients, used after the CV's sermon.

98 For this rendering of *yathābhuttaṃ bhuñjatha* see the note at Appendix 3 section 6.

queror" (1921: 63–4). Tambiah (1976: 46) agrees, though rather less confidently: "one cannot help but wonder whether this account of the rolling celestial wheel is not meant to be at least partly an ironical commentary and a parody of the mode of warfare by force and blood and stratagem practiced by the kings of that time." Indeed. If the *Sutta* were to be performed as a drama in modern dress I would have the king as a Mafia boss along with his sons and a crowd of hit-men, strolling calmly into opponents' territory and asserting his power by carefully worded homilies on Catholicism and family values. The irony here was already introduced in section 2, by juxtaposing a description of the CV as having sons who are "valiant, crushing enemy armies" with the statement that he rules "without punishment or violence." Perhaps too the standard epithet for a CV (found in section 2 and frequently), as "having obtained stability in his [own] country" might be construed in similar fashion as an ironic euphemism.

The commentary to this passage is doggedly but revealingly realist.[99] It pictures the scene as follows: when the CV has camped in the territory of other kings, and they have been told that "the wheel of an enemy (*para-cakka*) has come," they do not gather their troops for a fight, since they know no-one can prevail against him by force of arms. The Wheel-jewel has the name "Enemy-subduer" (*Arindama*), since because of it all the CV's enemies are brought to submission (*arī asesā damataṃ upenti*). The kings come, each with a gift of money appropriate to the wealth of his kingdom, and make obeisance to the CV's feet, declaring themselves to be his servants. The commentary understands the phrase *yathābhuttaṃ bhuñjatha* to concern taxes: after the enemy kings have bid him welcome, the CV "does not say 'bring me annual taxes of such-and-such an amount' (*ettakaṃ . . . anuvassaṃ baliṃ*), nor does he take away (tax-)revenue (*bhoga*) from one (king) and give it to another; rather, with wisdom appropriate to the fact of his being a *dhamma-rājā* he prohibits murder, etc., teaching *dhamma* in a smooth, sweet voice . . ." (i.e. recommends the five Precepts, ending with *yathābhuttaṃ bhuñjatha*). The commentary then asks whether, after the CV's sermon, everyone took his advice, and answers that not everyone takes the advice of a

99 The commentary (Sv 851) refers to that on the *Mahāsudassana* (Sv 620ff. = Ps IV 3219ff.; cp. Mhbv 71–2).

Buddha, so how could everyone take that of a (mere) king? Only the wise did.

Act 2 (sections 9–18) "Paradise Lost"

How to get from the Golden Age to life as we know it, in the present day? By a Fall, naturally: but the story in CSS is completely different from that in the *Aggañña Sutta*. That parable told of mankind's Fall from an immaterial and blissful existence as a celibate community to embodied social life, by means of a series of infractions of the *Vinaya* rule. CSS constructs a story around a slightly elaborated version of the well-known ten Paths of Bad/Good Deeds (*a/kusala-kamma-pathā*). This is appropriate, since they are a set of moral rules for laity; this parable, unlike that of the *Aggañña Sutta*, is exclusively concerned with lay people (from the king down), right up until its last two sections (sections 25–6), when the future Buddha Metteyya arrives and creates a Monastic Order into which the CV king Saṅkha is ordained. The *Aggañña Sutta* mentions the ten Bad/Good Deeds, in sections 5–6, but there they are part of the framing story of the narrated present, not of the parable in the narrated past (in CSS also in the narrated future).

This story seems to me to be intentionally farcical: sections 9–13 depict a king who at first fails to perform the Wheel-turning King's Duty, and then seeks to make up for his error but succeeds only in aggravating the situation, by performing just a part of his Duty. Once the initial move has been made – where this (unnamed) king governs "according to his own ideas" – even well-intentioned actions have bad results. Subsequently, in sections 14–18, once the deterioration has set in, each new generation sees one or more further vices arise to join the others. The logic of the degeneration is very skillfully handled: a close look reveals the Mode 2 Dhamma theme of kingly punishment as bad karma. In section 5 part of the Wheel-turning Duty of a CV is said to be giving money to the poor.[100] In sections 9–10 the miscreant king (the *Vinaya* would call him the first offender, *ādi-kammika*) realizes that his country is not

[100] Just what realism there is here, if any, is a matter for debate. Certainly it is commonly said that kings in premodern, agrarian states attempted to form alliances with "the people" against the mid-level of the ruling, tribute- and tax-extracting class – the "barons" of medieval Europe. Largesse to the poor, or at least the rhetoric of it, could be part of such a strategy.

prospering as it did before, and is then prepared to learn the Wheel-turning Duty from his ministers (not, this time, from his father: perhaps there is an implicit parallel admonition that the monks are not to learn from any teacher other than their "father," the Buddha). But although he subsequently guarantees social order as they prescribe, he fails to give money to the poor. With poverty thus widespread, one of his subjects intentionally steals from others; he is brought before the king, asked if it is true that he stole something, and replies that it is. When the king asks why he did it, the thief replies that he cannot live otherwise. The king then gives him money and urges him to use it to support himself and his family, to start up a business and to give alms to ascetics and Brahmins in order to go to heaven. This is all good Buddhist advice for the laity: the king, one might say, is doing his best at this point. The sequence of events happens again; and in section 12 people start to conclude – with perfect farcical logic – that the way to get money is to steal and have the king find out. A third person is brought before the king because of theft, but now the king's reaction is different. He reasons with himself, somewhat ponderously: "If I give money to whomever commits theft, then theft will increase. How about if I make sure to prevent this man (from doing it again, by) destroying him completely – (by) cutting off his head?" He then orders his men to tie the man's arms tightly behind his back, shave his head, parade him in public on the main road to the sound of drums, and take him outside the city for execution. And so they do. The king here might be taken to be adding, as it were, insult to injury: no king in ancient India, with the possible exception of Aśoka (KRN no. 26), did without capital punishment, but the cruel manner in which it is carried out here perhaps indicates rage (or frustration). At this point the king's recently acquired good intentions are giving way to a partial renewal of his former impetuousness.

The next episode, in section 13, makes sense only in terms of the strictest interpretation of karma in Dhamma Mode 2. It is this which makes it logical – indeed rational, given the suspension of belief required if the whole "Just So" narrative is to work – for others to imitate the king: *not* by taking the law into their own hands and punishing thieves, but by murdering people from whom they steal, to avoid detection. The text gives no indication that their acts of murder are to be evaluated any differently from the king's. Thus they begin to attack villages, small towns and cities (*gāmā, nigāmā, nagarā*) – but prudently, not royal cities, *rāja-dhāni* – and to commit highway robbery. The Buddha's narrative voice offers no judgment on them, but merely brings the episode to a close by stating that because of the sequence of events, from the king's not giving money to the poor down to the inception of murder, the length of life (*āyu*) and beauty (*vaṇṇa*) of these people decreases, and while they live for 80,000 years their children live only 40,000 years.[101] The degenerative process here, as repeatedly in sections 14–19, is expressed in language – notably locative absolutes – reminiscent of other formulations of cause and effect in Buddhism, notably the "short version" of the Dependent Origination (*Paticca-samuppāda*) list: CSS's *adhanānaṃ dhane ananuppadiyamāne . . . pāṇātipāto vepullam agamāsi*, "money not being given to the poor . . . murder flourished," recalls *imasmiṃ sati idaṃ hoti*, "this being, that is" (Collins 1982: 106 and n. 6). Just as in the *Aggañña Sutta* a monastic audience may be thought to have smiled at the text's choice of language recalling their Rule, so here audiences may be thought to have appreciated the wit of placing two things they knew very well, the ten (Paths of) Bad/Good Deeds and the language of causal theory, in a wholly unexpected narrative setting. Members of the Monastic Order would have learned these things by heart at an early age, and they would have figured frequently in sermons.

The logic of the degeneration is particularly subtle in the account of the Ten Bad Deeds (as I call them from now on). Their normal order is: (1) murder (*pāṇātipāta*), (2) theft (*adinnādāna*), (3) misbehavior in sex (*kāmesu micchācāra*), (4) lying (*musāvāda*), (5) harsh speech (*pharusā vācā*), (6) malicious speech (*pisuṇā vācā*), (7) frivolous speech (*sampha-palāpa*), (8) covetousness (or jealousy: *abhijjā*), (9) ill-will (*vyāpāda*), and (10) Wrong View (*micchā-diṭṭhi*) (nos. 1–3 are of the body, 4–7 of voice, 8–10 of mind). So far, (2) has led to (1), by a clear, if farcical narrative logic. In section 14 another thief, in the 40,000-year generation, avoids the king's punishment by the obvious expedient of lying when asked if he had committed theft; thus (2) and (1) lead, "rationally," to (4). In section 15, now in a 20,000-year generation,

[101] The PTS text of section 14, following certain mss., contains a reference to lying, which as the Rhys Davids points out (1921: 67 n. 1) should be omitted; lying is only "invented" in the next generation.

someone reports to the king that another person has committed theft: this report, albeit true, constitutes the arising of malicious speech (6); in section 16 the variation in beauty now evident leads some ugly men to be jealous (8) of those who are beautiful, and so they "commit wrongdoing" with (or: against) the wives of others. (It is not clear whether this is adultery or rape: see the note to Appendix 3 section 16.) The rest of the list now arises, in generations living for increasingly short periods of time. This happens without narrative incident, but careful attention can reveal a design in the sequence. Covetousness (8), in the form of adultery and harsh speech/gossip (5, 7) arises, presumably about the adulterers/rapists; next come covetousness (8, repeated) and ill-will (9) (these often appear as a pair, and the repetition of [8] along with [9] might be taken to be generalizing the vices of adultery/rape and harsh speech/gossip, which were the last two stages); then, perhaps since none of these vices cares much about veracity, Wrong View (10) arises.

At this point, the Ten Bad Deeds have all arisen: we have arrived close to life as we know it, although at this time people are living for 10,000 years. The text then adds some more forms of misconduct: improper desire (*adhamma-rāga* – the commentary [Sv 853] specifies incest), iniquitous greed (*visama-lobha*), and "wrongfulness" (*micchā-dhamma*, said by the commentary to refer to homosexuality, of both genders); then lack of respect for mother, father, ascetics and Brahmins, and for elder members of one's family. In section 18 human life decreases to 100 years, the symbolic (if obviously exaggerated) "full life" assumed in most early Indian texts (Collins 1982: 44–7); and the whole degenerative process is recapitulated in a long sequence of locative absolute phrases. So given the initial act of theft, a representative selection of all human vices arises, beginning with the ten Bad Deeds, in a "falling-domino" sequence.

Act 3 (sections 19–26) "Things will get worse before they get better"

If one wants to pull this text apart and speculate on the separate existence of its constitutive elements, one could say that one such element ends in section 18. A tragicomic Fall story has led, without any one person or stage being wholly to blame, to the present state of humanity. The next part, leading to the arrival of Metteyya, could then be seen as a reworked "separate story" with elements from the "Metteyya saga" as found in Sanskrit and later Pali texts. Our text, however – which is what is before us to interpret, in the first instance as a whole – continues in section 19 with a resolute *bhavissati . . . so samayo*, "There will be a time," clearly intended to parallel the opening word of section 2, *bhūtapubbaṃ*, "Once upon a time." Act 2 portrayed a degenerative sequence analogous to Dependent Origination; here, analogously to its constructive sense (where the cessation of each member is the condition for the non-arising of the next), Act 3 depicts the growth of the Good Deeds which parallel the Bad Deeds of Act 2, arriving back (but forward in time) to a stage where human life lasts 80,000 years.[102] There is a subtle form of realism here, albeit one expressed through a markedly unrealistic narrative. The sequence of vices up to section 18 has brought the tale close to life as we know it. But such a pessimistic account of the present state of things would be by itself inaccurate, unrealistic: for however scarce and fitful, Good Deeds paralleling the Bad do in fact exist amongst us. So in order to reach a nadir where no Good Deeds at all are found, the story has to go beyond the narrated present. And so we are taken to the point I have called Armageddon, where human life lasts ten years and is lived (mixing metaphors from the Bible and Political Science) in the conditions of a Hobbesian "war of all against all."

Gombrich rightly argues against a too-literal intepretation of this *Sutta*: "From the rest of what we know of him, we cannot think that the Buddha believed that one day people would literally be no more than ten years old and go hunting each other like beasts. This casts doubt back on the seriousness of the first half of the myth . . ." (1988: 84). As mentioned earlier, I prefer not to approach such issues by means of speculation about the Buddha as a historical individual. It is certainly true that the character of "the Buddha" in Pali texts is not usually depicted as believing this kind of thing: indeed this particular detail is found nowhere else. What is the text doing here, then? The answer, I think, is something like this: just as the Buddha's parable moves away from the

[102] The arithmetic in both Acts is somewhat impressionistic in places. In some texts (see *Māleyyadevatthera-vatthu*, translated in Appendix 4), the sequence of lengthening lifetimes actually surpasses 80,000, reaching millions of years. But in such circumstances people don't realize the importance of old age and death, and so are negligent in their religious duties; and so the length of life diminishes again, back to 80,000, when Metteyya arrives (Collins 1933: 87).

present, back into the past, to account for the existence of everyday, present human vices, so too it must move away from the present, off into the future, to account for the complete absence and then re-arising of everyday, present human virtues. In a larger perspective this parable has the perfectly serious intention of suggesting that, in the long run, the life of monasticism oriented towards timeless unconditioned nirvana, is the only serious thing: all else, all conditioned life in time, is ultimately madness and mayhem. It seems to me quite normal that a parable expressing that view should depict conditions which are – both in the Golden Age of virtuous CV kings conquering and ruling without violence and in the future Armageddon – altogether unrealistic and "insane." They constitute an impeccably accurate metaphorical representation of the moral chaos of temporality, from which nirvana offers deliverance.

In the projected future when human life lasts ten years, "girls will be ready for marriage at 5."[103] The text mentions the ten Good and Bad Deeds explicitly by name, for the first time, making the wit of Act 2 explicit: the Good will completely disappear, the Bad will "will rage like a great fire." "Even the the idea of '(the) good' will not exist – how will there be anyone who does good?" In section 19 and section 20 the additional Bad Deeds added to the ten in section 17 are mentioned again; no-one will recognize anyone as their mother, etc. (and so presumably have the "improper desire" mentioned earlier) and they will also be violent to each other, like hunters are nowadays to deer: that is, I take it, they will appear to each other not as fellow-creatures but gerundively, as "to-be-killed."

After a seven-day war, the few who have hidden from the violence emerge and reflect that it is "because we have undertaken Bad Deeds" (*akusalānaṃ dhammānaṃ samādāna-hetu*) that they have suffered. This is exactly the same phrase (with the negative prefix *a-*) as the Buddha used in the Prologue (repeated in the positive form in section 22). The survivors then set out to do good, which the text lists in the standard order of the ten Good Deeds given above, with the addition of "respect for one's mother," etc., as before. Thereby "because of their undertaking Good

[103] The term for "marriageable" is *alampateyya*, a word found in the Canon in only two other places, one of which is in section 23 of this text. See discussion below.

Deeds,"[104] their length of life and beauty will increase, until people live for 80,000 years. This part of the story is told simply by cataloging the Good Deeds and enumerating all the increases of age in a numerical list. (Section 22 is translated in full in Appendix 3, to give a sense of its repetitive and enumerative density.) The second chapter of the *Mahāvaṃsa* lists names and numbers without narrative embellishment to induce a sense both of temporal depth and temporal disengagement (3.4.c); something like that is going on here also.

The final sections 23–6 tell of the CV Saṅkha and the future Buddha Metteyya. I comment on just a few of the themes in these sections. When the text reaches the time when people live for 80,000 years, it mentions that "girls" will be marriageable at 500 years of age. This idea is found in the elaboration of the Metteyya story in the *Anāgatavaṃsa* (vv. 34, 130), discussed in 5.2.b. There the emphasis on sensory pleasure and beauty means that this motif (women sexually active for the best part of 75,000 years) has what I called a delicately suggested eroticism. The same thing may perhaps be present in CSS section 23; the idea here parallels that in section 19, of girls being marriageable at five years of age during the worst point of human degeneration. If there is eroticism there, it is bizarre or repellent. A possible nuance is introduced into section 23 by an intertextual reference to the one other place in the Canon where the motif occurs, a short but powerful *Sutta* which deals with a teacher in the past called Araka. (Other texts say that this was a former life of the Buddha; see DPPN s.v.) In his time too, people lived for 80,000 years, with "girls" marriageable at 500.[105] But the burden of Araka's teaching, and that of the *Sutta* as a whole, is that nonetheless life is short: "for those who are born, there is no immortality" (A IV 138). There are seven vivid similes – life is like, *inter alia*, a drop of dew on a blade of grass in the

[104] The phrase here is *kusalānaṃ dhammānaṃ samādāna-hetu*, as in section 1. *Dhamma* cannot strictly refer to a deed, but the reference here is clearly to the ten Good Deeds (section 19 used the phrase *kusala-kamma*); but the text is clearly juxtaposing the Good Deeds leading to rebirth for laity (including Wheel-turning kings) and the wholesome states of mind which for monks lead to nirvana. In this context the reference is to deeds. Buddhist systematic thought regularly interprets deeds in terms of the intentions behind them, which is how karma works: the intention behind an action leaves a trace or seed in the mind, which later comes to karmic fruition in a good or bad experience.

[105] There are other analogies between these two texts: for example, in CSS section 23 there are only three afflictions – desire, hunger and old age – and at A IV 138 only six: cold and heat, hunger and thirst, urination and defecation.

morning, a bubble on water in the rain, a cow being led to slaughter – which would make it, according to the *Visuddhimagga* (237 = VIII 35), an appropriate vehicle for the Meditation on Death. If I am right that the overall point of CSS is to produce a sense of distanciation from the passage of time, then such an intertextual reference, if intended and picked up on by the audience, would be appropriate. The parallel between the nadir of human existence in time, when life lasts ten years and girls marry at five, and the zenith of Saṅkha's utopia, where they live for 80,000 years and "girls" marry at 500, could then be seen to suggest that however much life might be like hell or heaven on earth, in both cases time is short: the turmoil of *saṃsāra*, bad or good, is always a lesser orientation than the peace of nirvana, which passeth all understanding.

There are some nuances of humor and irony in these sections also. In what seems to be a straightforward joke in section 23, in this future utopia the Indian subcontinent will be as full of people as the Avīci hell! (A rather bitter joke from the perspective of the present day.) In section 26 King Saṅkha raises up from underwater the great palace of the former king Mahāpanāda, only to give it away for the use of, *inter alia*, indigents, tramps, and beggars.[106]

There are explicit similarities between kings Daḷhanemi in section 2ff. and Saṅkha in 23–6 (the formulae about the CV's seven Jewels, his conquest and rule without violence, are repeated in section 24 from section 2), and between the Buddhas Gotama and Metteyya. The past of Daḷhanemi and the future of Metteyya are effectively equidistant from the Buddha's narrated present. Both contain the utopia of nonviolent conquest and social order, which the narrated present does not. The similarity between Gotama and Metteyya – individual, finally-nirvanizing Buddhas – is expressed in section 25 by repetitive, chant-like lists of epithets and qualities, thus interweaving non-repetitive and repetitive time, as in the *Buddhavaṃsa* (3.4.b). In some ways, however, the narrated future outdoes both the past and the present. Saṅkha's reign is described in even more utopian terms than Daḷhanemi's. Metteyya's Millennium improves on Gotama's achievement: whereas Gotama's monastic community numbers several

[106] Like the Buddha described in 6.5.a, he will "spit out the sovereignty and fame which are (usually) reckoned to be good fortune" . . . and give no thought to the glory of a Wheel-turning king (Ud-a 24, cp. Bv 283).

hundred, Metteyya will have one of several thousand. Once again, I take the point to be that no matter how good human life was, or how much better it might get, the monks' inheritance (the tradition passed on anew by all Buddhas) is the one they have, now, from the Buddha, in the narrated present: they should not stray from their customary terrain, meditation, into the carnival and carnage of *saṃsāra* but keep their attention focused beyond the temporal domain of past, present and future altogether.

It may well seem odd, indeed unacceptable, to the dour-faced and humorless positivism with which these texts are so often read (despite the Rhys Davids' notes and introductions to their translation), that the earliest text-place where a reference to the future Buddha is found should be a humorous parable whose main burden is to relativize and diminish all temporal goods, past, present and future. But that, I submit, tells us more about modern scholarly vision than it does about the creative possibilities open to the redactors of early Buddhist texts.

Epilogue (sections 27–8)

In section 27 the Buddha repeats word-for-word most of section 1. The commentary here (Sv 857) says that up until the end of section 26 the text has been showing the application of the phrase "it is by acquiring wholesome states (of mind) that this merit increases" to the Good Deeds/wholesomeness/skillfulness which leads to rebirth; now he shows its application to the wholesomeness/skillfulness which leads to escape from rebirth. Section 28 begins with the antepenultimate sentence of section 1: "Keep to your own ground, monks, to your ancestral territory". But in between this and a slightly reworded version of the final two sentences from section 1 comes something else, a list of five qualities or achievements. The transition from what the commentary called the narrative concerning the good which leads to rebirth, in sections 2–26, of which the highest point is the happiness of the CV, back to the admonition to monks concerning the good which leads to the escape from rebirth, with which the *Sutta* began in section 1, is cleverly brought about in section 28 by reinterpreting as monastic practices and virtues these five qualities or achievements, which usually refer to the world of rebirth. They are: length of life (*āyu*), beauty (appearance, *vaṇṇa*), happiness (*sukha*), enjoyment (*bhoga*) and strength (*bala*). The words are all used in one or more episodes of the parable, and they are found together in other texts. Their use here as an ensemble effecting the return from non-monastic to monastic felicity would, as in the earlier cases of the ten Bad and Good Deeds, and the causation syntax of sections 9–18, give pleasure to an audience, at least to one sophisticated and knowledgeable enough to recognize them in an unexpected narrative setting. (The linguistic and textual detail of this section is discussed in Collins 1996.)

At the end of section 28, where the phrase "it is by acquiring wholesome states (of mind) that this merit increases" is repeated from section 1, to bring the *Sutta* to an end, the commentary (Sv 858) explains the words "this merit increases" refer to "the transcendental merit [*lokuttara-puñña*, i.e. what is *kusala*, without attachment and karmic result] which increases as far as the destruction of the Corruptions." "Thus [the Buddha] concludes the application [of the phrase] to the wholesomeness/skillfulness which leads to escape from rebirth, and brings the teaching to an end by means of the high-point [*nikūṭa*, peak or climax] of Arahantship" (cf. 3.3 [i]).

The structure of the *Sutta*, then, as seen by the commentary, whose analysis I have extended, is this: it starts with a standard admonition to monks concerning the practice of the Path. The (deliberate) ambiguity in the sense of the words *kusala* and *puñña* in the sentence concluding the homiletic Prologue – as conducing to good fortune in the world of rebirth and/or to escape from it – allows two things. First, a long story (a drama in three Acts) recounts the tragicomic moral chaos of the world of time and rebirth, from the highest good fortune of the CV to the lowest degradation of human life imaginable (and back up again), in an elaborate parable whose point is to induce distanciation from temporal felicities. Second, the Epilogue reinterprets a familiar list of qualities – temporal goods beginning with "long life" – in such a way that monastic practice, oriented towards timeless nirvana, is seen to be the only really serious thing in the long run (and the *Sutta* certainly gives full expression to the long run of time). CSS does not express a Buddhist social theory: it tells a witty story, by turns pleasantly farcical and fearsomely imaginative, with some familiar doctrinal motifs in unexpected narrative settings; the whole parable being a disbelief-suspending morality tale. *Eheu fugaces.*

Not everyone, now or in the past, would interpret the *Mahāsudassana, Kūṭadanta,* and *Cakkavatti-sīhanāda Sutta*-s in the way I have done. As with the *Aggañña Sutta,* later texts in Pali can easily be found which seem not to know, or at least to ignore the moments of comedy and satire which I (and Gombrich) find in them, and which I see as giving voice to a transcendentalist wisdom oriented towards trans-temporal (and/or timeless) values of asceticism rather than simply stating some "doctrine" or "theory" involving the CV.[107] That is to say, while they can be read – as is usual in modern scholarship despite Rhys Davids' comments, in the best-known modern translation – as imaginatively possible eu-topias, they can also be read as ou-topias which comment, ironically and from a distance, on the actual. An externalist approach, which sees, correctly, that Theravāda ideology was appropriated and promoted by holders of political and military power in premodern Southern Asia but then reads these texts simply as "legitimations" of kingship, underestimates the inside of them. Kings were undoubtedly the greatest powers in this life, and this world: but the imagination can travel beyond this life and this world. The power held by Buddhist ideology, in Dhamma Mode 2, could be wielded both in utopian support of military and political power, and – looking to the real world of violence, the *longue durée* and death – more or less explicitly against it or in one-upmanship contestation of it. Such power derives in great measure from the imaginative limitations of force and the status quo. There is no single and simple "Buddhist" view of society, ideal or actual. Society, one might better say, is a prime site for the work of Buddhist culture, an inexhaustible fund of material on which the antagonistic symbiosis between clerics and kings could draw, to express both sides of the relationship. The ideal of a peaceful, civilized society under a beneficent king could never be without its discontents.

[107] This is obviously not true of all texts: I do not mean to replace one essentialism about "Buddhism and Society" with another. Irony is not to be found in the History of the Future's combined celebration of temporal and timeless felicities; although some minor moments of comedy are found in the *Vessantara Jātaka,* to be discussed next, they are not directed at kingship and the exacting demands of Dhamma, Modes 1 and 2.

CHAPTER SEVEN

The Vessantara Jātaka

The story of Vessantara is popular all over Buddhist Asia.[1] "In the Theravāda Buddhist countries" of Southern Asia, say Cone and Gombrich, "even the biography of the Buddha is not better known."[2] In Burma, "taught to every schoolboy, alluded to frequently in conversation, recounted repeatedly in sermons, and – even more important – regularly enacted in dramatic form as part of the standard fare of the itinerant Burmese repertory groups, the story of Prince Vessantara is probably the best known and most loved of all Buddhist stories" (Spiro 1971: 108). For Keyes, "three texts – or, more properly, several versions of three texts – define for most Thai Buddhists today, as in traditional Siam, the basic parameters of a Therāvadin view of the world."[3] They are the Three Worlds Treatise (General Introduction II.c), the story of the elder Māleyya, (5.2.c and Appendix 4), and the *Vessantara Jātaka*. The story of Vessantara, he says (1987: 181)

is known widely throughout Thailand to this day. It is frequently presented to the populace in the form of a sermon, typically in conjunction with a major festival; the story is also dramatized in folk opera and in

[1] Skt Viśvantara, Tibetan Drimedkundan, etc; also known as Sudāna – there are various Chinese versions of both names: Lamotte (1949: 713–14), Cone and Gombrich (1977: xxxv–xliv, 109–11), Lienhart (1980: 253–5).

[2] (1977: xv), data for Sri Lanka given on pp.xli–xliii; cp. Swearer (1995: 32).

[3] (1987: 179). Keyes wrote this in the mid-1980s; since then, in a rapidly changing, globalizing world, this may well have become less true, especially for those in cities such as Bangkok or Chiang Mai. Fallon (1983: 283ff.) reports ethnographic data from 1976–7 in the rural northeast (Isan), showing that the recitation of VJ was still important there. Gabaude (1991) shows that both criticism and defense of Vessantara – of both traditionalist and modernist forms – have increased in the last few decades, at least among urban and university intellectuals. The political role of the Three Worlds Treatise in modern Thailand is described in Jackson (1993). Cp. Chantornvong (1981) on the Three Worlds – taken to have been written in the fourteenth century – and a fifteenth-century "royal" version of VJ, as "politico-religious literature *par excellence*" in premodernity.

theater; and scenes from it appear in art. In recent years, the *Vessantara Jātaka* has been used as the source of themes in modern fiction and has even been presented in a film version. There is probably no Buddhist in Thailand beyond the age of ten or so who could not give at least a synopsis of the story, and many people especially in villages, can quote passages in the same way English speakers can quote parts of the Bible, or selections from Shakespeare. (1987: 181)

Brereton (1995: 62) states that "in a recent catalog of Lan Na [northern] Thai manuscripts, 396 out of 2,790 (14 percent) were devoted to the *Vessantara Jātaka* [whereas] only 254 contained *Sutta*-s." The General Introduction claimed that this extraordinary story has not been properly appreciated in western scholarship. We need to understand why (for example) it can move Burmese men to tears; and we also need to try to come to terms with the fact that, as Gombrich (1971a: 267) puts it, Vessantara's giving away of his wife and children not only "strikes us as excessive. It strikes the Sinhalese in the same way." The earlier discussion referred to Gellner's idea that ideologies are meant to be offensive (in a special, Kierkegaardian sense) to everyday life and values. This is, I think, a very useful avenue for understanding the Vessantara story, which I use in this chapter; but I prefer to approach the story not in terms of a priori interpretative categories, but through a detailed and close reading of the longer and incomparably more important of the two Pali versions, the prose-and-verse compilation redacted in the canonical *Jātaka* collection. The analysis given here is not intended to apply entirely, or even at all, to other tellings of the tale.[4] Different versions will have different meanings, as is the case in the very much shorter Pali verse version redacted in the canonical *Cariya-piṭaka.* Just as Richman and others (1991) speak of *Many Rāmāyaṇas,* so we might also speak of "many Vessantaras." If generalizing conclusions about "the Vessantara story," separate from particular tellings, are possible at all, they must await careful analysis of as many different versions as can be found.

Cone and Gombrich (77; = CG[5]) give their translation of the *Vessantara Jātaka* (Ja VI 479–593, no. 547; hereafter VJ) the title

[4] I allude here to the highly pertinent discussion of different "versions" of a story in Ramanujan (1991).

[5] The translation is by Cone, and the Introduction by Gombrich, but for convenience I refer to both as CG. As in Chapter 4, I give two page references, one to the Pali text, and the other to Cone's translation.

"The Perfect Generosity of Prince Vessantara", and the subtitle "A Buddhist Epic." The word "epic" in a general sense is accurate.[6] It compares VJ, appropriately, to what are often called the two "Epics" of Brahmanical Hinduism, the *Mahābhārata* (textual links with which in VJ are mentioned by CG: xxviii) and *Rāmāyaṇa* (to which VJ compares itself explicitly), as well as to the *Purāṇa*-s. Although nowhere near as long as the two Hindu epics or most *Purāṇa*-s, VJ is, as CG say (p.xvi), "the longest and fullest literary version known to us" of the many extant versions. As a brief prolegomenon to the reading of VJ, I refer to some remarks by David Shulman on the Sanskrit Epics, which raise some details of relevance here, and also suggest a more general style of interpretation which I find appropriate for VJ. In his "Towards a Historical Poetics of the Sanskrit Epics," he compares the two texts in their attitude to war:

> There is . . . a telling difference in attitude: the Mahābhārata views the battle with persistent doubt, hesitation and ambiguity – its heroes have great difficulty in deciding to fight at all – whereas Rāma, ever the exemplary hero, fights without qualms and achieves a clean, clear-cut victory which ushers in a golden age. In purely personal terms, however, Rāma, too, experiences life as tragic – his unwavering acceptance of his royal duty leads to a final separation from his beloved Sītā – yet this is a tragedy of a very different type from that of the Mahābhārata. The Rāmāyaṇa . . . illustrates the tragedy always consequent on perfection or the search for perfection, just as the work as a whole could be characterized by what I would call the "poetics of perfection." It creates a sustained, lyrical universe peopled by idealized heroes whose very perfection involves them – and the audience – in recurrent suffering. The Mahābhārata's heroes, by way of contrast, are anything but perfect; they are deeply flawed human beings, torn by terrible inner conflicts, confused by reality, and driven by a combination of forces towards ultimate disaster. (1991: 10)

This may perhaps underplay the presence of conflict in Rāma, at least on the level of values (Pollock 1986: 64–73); but for my purposes it usefully introduces the themes of conflict and tragedy on the one hand, and utopian perfectionism on the other, and relates them to each other – all of which is appropriate to VJ. The Vessantara story is both realist drama and allegory: its characters are both realistic representations of human beings going through

[6] OED: "pertaining to that species of poetical composition . . . which celebrates in the form of a continuous narrative the achievements of one or more heroic personages of history or tradition."

a coherent narrative sequence, and textual embodiments of values, emotions and aspirations. VJ not only expresses a wide range of values: it also does not flinch from, indeed to the contrary it highlights and insists on conflicts of value. There is certainly exaggeration in this text, but it is not that of hyperbole and irony, as in the texts discussed at the end of the last chapter. Traditional audiences listening to it, perhaps hoping thereby to be reborn with Metteyya, as in 5.2.c, would have found many of their ordinary and everyday emotions as well as their soteriological aspirations heightened and intensified in the fragile grandeur of Vessantara and his family. The narrative of his fulfilment of the Perfection of Generosity weaves its way through two conflicts: socially, between the ascetic values of renunciation and the mundane need for prudential government; and psychologically, between the aspiration to mental detachment, to a love universalized and depersonalized, and the immediate joys and ties of particular affection, filial, marital and paternal. The two Modes of Dhamma, 1 and 2, are here not overlapping alternatives in a variegated field: they are contrary, sometimes contradictory opposites, and to choose either is necessarily to lose something. The darkness of the tragedy (and melodrama) of these conflicts, however, is shot through with the illumination of every Buddhist felicity, and other kinds of human happiness. For this reason I end the chapter with an account of VJ as a *summa felicitatium.*

The central issue, as has been recognized from the *Milinda Pañha* onwards (Mil 274ff.),[7] is that Vessantara first gives away his children – this, along with their mother's discovery of their absence and her grieving for them, is clearly the story's center of gravity, as CG remark (p.xx)[8] – and then his wife. This is presented as the

[7] Although Nāgasena, the Buddhist spokesman of this text, says that all future Buddhas give away their wife and children (274–5), later he insists on the uniqueness of Vessantara, and of the three earthquakes, the second and third of which occur when he gives away the children and Maddī. Nāgasena's answer to Milinda's charge that the gift was excessive (*ati-dāna*) highlights Vessantara's sufferings; argues that such a painful and difficult gift was given only because Omniscience was dearer than anything to him; and stresses that Vessantara gave the children away only because he knew his father Sañjaya would ransom them.

[8] These sections can also be recited separately: Wells (1939: 80) reproduces an announcement of the dedication of a monastery, which includes "Also from Vessantara will be read the chapters of Madriya [Maddī's lament for the children] and Kumāra [Vessantara's giving away of the children] in the common dialect."

Perfection of Giving, the culmination of the future Buddha's eons-long progress through the ten Perfections necessary for Buddhahood! Two reactions have dominated scholarship: either this is simply an indication of the selfishness (for Spiro, the narcissism) of monastic life and the individual quest for nirvana, or it is simply an expression in myth of the Buddhist values of generosity and renunciation. Both interpretations are mistaken in assuming that the meaning of the story is simple. It is, *inter alia*, a painfully honest confrontation of the difficulties of renunciation, showing that real human goods must, ultimately, be abandoned in the ascetic search for ultimate felicity; and it is the most subtle and successful attempt in Pali literature to infuse ascetic values and soteriological motifs into an ideal image of collective life in an ordinary, productive and reproductive society. This society is only glimpsed at the end of the story, inevitably, since sustained narrative description would falter on the contradictions and paradoxes discussed in the last chapter: just as the fabled *Rāma-rājya*, the utopia which follows Rāma's victory over Rāvaṇa and his consecration as king, occupies only nine verses at the end of Book 6 of the *Rāmāyaṇa*, vv.82–90 in Vaidya's edition (1971: 876–8).

The inescapable distance between the goals of kings and ascetics is preserved in VJ not by irony or one-up-manship, but from the other side, as it were: by the sufferings of Vessantara and his family, and by the fact that he does not and cannot here take the final step of definitively renouncing kinship and kingship. That must remain beyond the text, in other texts and in the Buddhist master-text, in the always-implicit teleology which points to Siddhattha Gotama's final renunciation and nirvana. Vessantara is first *forced* to renounce his own kingdom (the words used in this regard are almost all forms of *pabbajjā*, which is both a standard term for renunciation in general and the technical term for initiation into the Buddhist Monastic Order), but then *chooses* to refuse kingship in another country, to live an ascetic life of chastity, and finally to be parted from his family. If the conflict between renunciatory values and those of what is renounced can in the course of the story reach the level of tragedy, as I think it does, the ending is nonetheless – apparently – a happy one: Vessantara is reunited with his family, and becomes king of a Moral Commonwealth where prisoners are released from jail and the king of the gods rains jewels from the sky. But this is not a static, undynamic resolution, a case of myth blandly reconciling the irreconcilable; the happiness of the ending is encased by the sufferings of Vessantara and his family in the recent past, and the future renunciation of family and kingship by Siddhattha Gotama, who becomes our Buddha. The perfection of Vessantara's Moral Commonwealth, as in the *Rāmāyaṇa* according to Shulman's reading, is accompanied by the tragedy of the sufferings consequent on his ascetic aspirations, an attempt at renunciation to be renewed and brought to completion in the person of Siddattha Gotama.

7.1. THE STORY

A brief outline of the plot was given in 4.3.a, where a number of passages from VJ illustrated "Paradise in the Forest"; and the structure of Birth Stories was explained in 4.3.c, at the outset of the *Kaṇha Jātaka.* This section tells the story, concentrating on:

(i) what the text says about the relationships between Vessantara, his wife Maddī, their son Jāli and daughter Kaṇhājinā, and Vessantara's parents, King Sañjaya and Queen Phusatī;
(ii) how different characters evaluate the actions of Vessantara and King Sañjaya, in relation to "what is right": Dhamma, in both Mode 1 (reciprocal, context-dependent, negotiable) and Mode 2 (absolute, context-independent, non-negotiable); and
(iii) how these evaluations express or reveal attitudes to the problems of kingship, violence and social order with which Chapter 6 was concerned.

In the Story of the Present, the Buddha humbles his proud relatives, the Sākyans, by rising into the air and performing a miracle. After they have all paid homage to the Buddha, a "lotus-leaf shower" rains down on them; that is, "those who wished to be made wet were made wet, while not even a drop fell on the body of anyone who did not wish to be made wet" (479–80/4). This is taken up twice at the end of the Story of the Past, first by an exactly analogous lotus-leaf shower which falls when Maddī and her children are reunited, and everyone faints from emotion, and then by the shower of jewels which Sakka rains down on Vessantara's kingdom.

The Story of the Past opens with an account of some previous lives of Vessantara's mother, Phusatī. In the last one before the narrated present as Phusatī, she is the chief queen of Sakka, king of the gods. When her merit is used up, and so her allotted time in heaven at an end, Sakka offers her ten wishes. She makes them; *inter alia* she wishes to have physical beauty, and to give birth to a child who will become a generous and respected king. The last four are "May my breasts not hang slack, O [Sakka]; may I not go grey. May dust not stick to my body. May I have the condemned set free" (483 v.12/7). She is reborn and becomes king Sañjaya's wife. Sakka is then said to see that nine of her wishes have been fulfilled; one must assume, although the text says only this, that prisoners have been released. (This perhaps suggests that it is a ceremonial one-off gesture, rather than a continuous social policy; Vessantara makes the selfsame wish at the end of the story.) To fulfil the tenth Sakka goes to a god of the Tāvatiṃsa heaven (the future Buddha) and persuades him to be reborn in Phusatī's womb. He does so, and "from the time of the Bodhisatta's conception there was no limit to the king's income, for through the influence of his merit kings from throughout the whole of India . . . sent him presents" (485/8–9).

The child emerges from the womb asking to give gifts; during his childhood he repeatedly gives valuable ornaments his father had made for him to his nurses. At eight he aspires to give "something of [his] very self"; that is, a part of his body, his heart, eyes, flesh, etc. At this there is an earthquake, and other natural marvels, and "Great Brahmā cried "Bravo!"; and all was in tumult right up to the heaven of Brahmā" (486/10). Continuing throughout to give gifts, Vessantara is married to Maddī, and she gives birth to Jāli and Kaṇhājinā. But then he gives away a special elephant. Different tellings of Vessantara's story differ in the extent to which they discuss the significance of the elephant, and as to whether Vessantara gets him back at the end of the story; in the text of the Pali *Jātaka* version he seems not to, although the commentary says that he does (p. 581: see p. 519 below). This version has Brahmins come from Kaliṅga to ask for it, because in that kingdom there is a drought, which has not been alleviated by the king's undertaking the Uposatha Day Precepts and fasting. The people of Kaliṅga have told their king that in the land of the Sivis Prince Vessantara "has a completely lucky white elephant, and wherever it goes, there is rain" (487/11). In one verse, spoken by the Buddha as narrator, the elephant is called "the bringer of prosperity to the kingdom of the Sivis" (489 *bis* / 13–4), an epithet more frequently applied to Vessantara and Sañjaya. When the Kaliṅgan Brahmins have received the elephant, they go through the city on their way out "mocking the crowd with insulting gestures" (489/14). At this some of the Sivis go to the king to complain, saying that Vessantara is "ruining" (*vidhamaṃam,*[9] 490/14) the kingdom, and describing the elephant as "the colossal trumpeter, with tusks like poles, experienced on all battlefields . . . the rutting crusher of our enemies." They warn, "If you do not do what the Sivis tell you, we expect the Sivis will use force against you (*hatthe karissare*) as well as against your son" (490/15)

The text does not specify what punishment the Sivis want Vessantara to undergo. Sañjaya mentions two possibilities, declining to impose either: "Let my country perish, let my kingdom be ruined, I will not, at the command of the Sivis, exile (*pabbajjeyyaṃ*) the prince, innocent (*adūsaka*) as he is, from his own kingdom; for he is my son, dear to my heart . . . I would not harm him, for he is full of noble goodness[10]. It would be shameful for me, and would cause great sin (*pāpa*). How could I slay him by the sword, Vessantara, my own son?" (491/15). The Sivis say that he should be neither killed nor imprisoned, but exiled. Sañjaya agrees to this, but asks that Vessantara be allowed to stay one last night, "to enjoy all pleasures" (*kāme paribhuñjatu*, ibid.). A messenger is sent to Vessantara, to tell him that the Sivis are angry, and that "in a body [they] will banish you." Vessantara asks why they are angry, since "I do not see what I have done wrong."[11] When told why, he at first exclaims that he will not stop giving, even if the Sivis exile or kill him; but then says: "Very well. I shall go by the way taken by criminals, although the citizens banish me for no other crime (*dosa*) than that I made a gift of the elephant." He accepts to go on condition that he be first allowed to make a lavish gift, called "the great gift of the seven hundreds."[12]

[9] The form of this word is a puzzle (see KRN no. 45, pp. 173–4), but the meaning "ruin" is not in dispute.

[10] *Ariyasīlavant.* The choice of word implies for narrator and audience that this is the kind of goodness to which the Buddhist "Noble Path" aspires.

[11] "Wrong" translates *dukkaṭaṃ*, also the word for an offence against the Monastic Code.

[12] This is a gift of 700 elephants, horses, women, slaves, cows and many other things besides. In the famous statues of the Buddha's enlightenment where his right hand is

Vessantara goes to his wife's living-quarters and sits on her bed to tell her that he is to go to the forest. Maddī says that "it is not right" (*n'esa dhammo*) for him to go alone, and that she will accompany him, extolling the delights of the forest, and of life there with the children, which will make him "forget kingship." Phusatī overhears their conversation, and repeats several times to herself and to Sañjaya that Vessantara is "guilty of no crime" (*adūsaka*). She tells Sañjaya not to banish an innocent man, but he replies: although "I banish my own son, who is dearer to me than life itself," in doing so "I act honourably according to my duty" (*dhammass' apacitiṃ kummi*; 499/21); the commentary explains that this is following "the traditional *dhamma* of the kings of old." Later, after the gift of the seven hundreds has been made, in the course of which Vessantara shouts enthusiastically, "Give clothes to those who want them, toddy [liquor] to the drinkers, give food to those who need it, give presents freely!", the recipients of his generosity say that he is "guilty of no crime" (*adūsaka*) (502/24, 25). Brahmins, ascetics and other mendicants say that "it is not right" (*adhamma*) to banish him. When Vessantara takes leave of his parents, the text calls his father the "best of the righteous" (*dhamminaṃ vara*). Vessantara seems to accept, albeit not unambiguously, that he is in some sense wrong ("I have troubled my own people")[13] and at the same time to assert his own superiority as (soon to be) a renouncer. Adopting the Mode 2 Dhamma viewpoint he says that everyone in the past and everyone in the future has and will die "unsatisfied by material pleasures" (*kāma*). "I am doing good [*puññāni*, also meritorious] deeds; you sink in the mud" (505, 506/27). The mud, explains the commentary, is that of desire and its objects (*kāma*).

Next, Maddī asserts that she will go with Vessantara despite the

touching the ground, he is calling the earth to witness this great gift during his battle with Māra; see CG (pp.xviii–xix).

13 The word is *abhisāsiṃ*, which usually refers to verbal violence, insulting or reviling; here it is glossed by the commentary as *pīlesim*, "I have oppressed (them)." Vessantara adds *yajamāno sake pure*, which CG (p. 27) translate "making a sacrifice in my own city." This form of the verb, the middle present participle, was originally used for the patron, usually royal, of a Vedic sacrifice, but came to be used for anyone who gives money to another on a regular basis for religious or other services. I take the point here to be that despite seeming to accept that he is guilty of wrongdoing, Vessantara is also implying that his acts of giving were legitimate acts of patronage, performed in the place, or the station – his own city – where he should, as a member of the royal family, be justified in acting as a generous patron.

hardships of the forest, since the life of a widow is worse; two of her verses here, in aphoristic *nīti* style, say that a widow is as defenseless (*naggā*, literally naked) as a kingdom without a king, and that "a husband gives meaning to a woman" just as "smoke is the sign of fire [and] the king symbolizes the kingdom."[14] Throughout this conversation the happiness the children have brought to Vessantara and Maddī by now, and will do in the future in the forest, is emphasized. Vessantara's last words before leaving are "May all my family [*ñātayo*] be free from sickness!" (511/31). When they are outside the city, Vessantara "turned round, as he longed to take one more look, and because of his longing the area of the earth covered by his carriage detached itself and turned round, so that the carriage faced toward the city, and Vessantara could see his parents' home." He says, "Look, Maddī, see this lovely sight: the home of the best of Sivis, my father's house" (511/32). Here and throughout, the text represents Vessantara as someone with love for his parents, as also for his wife and children, despite his heroic offer (made more than once) to endure exile alone.

During the journey Vessantara gives away his carriage and horses, trees bend down of their own accord to offer their fruit to the children, and deities, out of pity for the children, shorten the journey to a single day. The next scene takes place outside the Cetans' city. The Cetan kings are surprised to see a prince without an army, and ask whether Vessantara has been defeated by enemies. He tells them about his gift of the elephant; "Because of that, the Sivis were angry with me, and my father's mind was distressed. The king banished me" (515/36). "Distressed" translates *upahato*, afflicted, tormented, etc.[15] The Cetan chiefs offer to go and petition king Sañjaya, seeking to win him over (according to the commentary, by convincing him of Vessantara's innocence). Vessantara asks them not to, "for the king is not the power (*issara*) there. The Sivis are haughty, both army and townsfolk, and want

[14] (508/29). "Gives meaning to," "is a sign," and "symbolize" all translate *paññāṇaṃ*, literally "makes known." (Cp. Dhn 264, Ln 115: "a country without a king is empty.")

[15] The commentary glosses this as *kuddho va*, which can mean both "as if (he were) angry," taking *va* as short for *iva*, or "very angry," taking it as short for the emphatic particle *eva*. In either case there is an allusion to the motif that kings who pass judgment in anger (real or assumed) are likely to go wrong. A closely similar phrase, in the negative, occurs at 512/33, where CG have "he was not cast down in spirit"; the commentary there glosses *olīno*, for which CPD gives "depressed, abject, lessened"; and for the verb from which the form derives "waver, hesitate." On the puzzling grammar of the text here see KRN no. 45.

to destroy the king because of me" (516/36). The Cetans suggest that he become king among them; but Vessantara shows that by now he has begun to adopt the pacifist values of Buddhist asceticism. He says "The Sivis, both army and townsfolk, would be displeased if the Cetans were to anoint me as king . . . There would be great dissension between you because of me, and strife with the Sivis. And I do not like war. There would be terrible strife and great conflict. Because of me, one man, many people would be hurt" (517/37). So the Cetans content themselves with accompanying Vessantara and his family to the edge of the forest, and setting a guard there to keep possible enemies at bay. They take their leave of Vessantara by telling him where the "royal ascetics" (*rājisi*) live, describing the beauties of the forest where he should build his ascetic's leaf-hut.

When they arrive at the hermitage built by Vissakamma on Sakka's orders, Vessantara leaves Maddī and the children at the door; he enters, puts on the dress of an ascetic (*isi*, Skt *ṛṣi*), and comes out again holding an ascetic's staff. Later he is said more than once to look "like a Brahmin with his matted hair and garment of animal skin" (e.g. 528/47). "He walked up and down in the covered walk," says the narrative voice, "and then went up to his wife and children, as calm and composed as one who by himself has attained enlightenment" (*paccekabuddha*, 520/40). Later events will show that just as he is in fact a kṣatriya king who only looks like a Brahmin, so his appearance of ascetic prowess here is as much a form of dress – which can be removed – as the ascetic's clothes and staff he found in the hermitage. Maddī's reaction shows that her emotions have not yet fully embraced asceticism: she "fell at the feet of the Great Being [a technical term for a future Buddha] and wept" (ibid.). But then she enters her own leaf-hut, and both she and the children also put on ascetic dress (here *tāpasa-vesa*). She offers to be the one who collects food for the family, while Vessantara looks after the children. He then "asked her a favour. 'Maddī, from now on we are hermits, and a woman is a stain (*mala*) on a life of renunciation [*brahmacariya*, i.e. chastity]. In future do not come to me at an improper time'" (520/40). Later events show that by this he means at night. The text then says that they and animals for miles around began to live in harmony (see Chapter 4 p. 335); and describes the daily routine of the hermit family, as they lived there for seven months.

The text then turns to the Brahmin Jūjaka, and his journey from his home in Kaliṅga to the hermitage. When he arrives at Vessantara's city of Jetuttara, he asks for him but receives a reply which is unexpected, given the earlier events there. The Sivis, or at least some of them, say: "The nobleman (*khattiya*) was undone by too much giving to people like you, Brahmin. He has been banished from his own kingdom and is now living on Crooked Mountain . . . You ruined our king, and yet back you have come. Just you wait here!" They run after him with sticks and clods of earth "but by divine intervention he managed to get on to the road to Crooked Mountain." As he gets closer to the hermitage, an extensive section of the text depicts what Chapter 4 called Paradise in the Forest: it is full of songbirds, perfumed flowers, bathing ponds, etc., and in Vessantara's hermitage "a man knows no hunger, no thirst, no discontent." But then comes a scene in striking contrast with these paradisial surroundings (540–1/54–5). On the night preceding Jūjaka's arrival, Maddī has a dream: "A dark man wearing saffron robes [as do monks, of course] and with red garlands adorning his ears came threatening her with a weapon in his hand. He entered the leaf-hut, and grasping Maddī by the hair dragged her out and threw her flat on the ground. Then, as she shrieked, he dug out her eyes, cut off her arms, and splitting her breast took her heart, dripping with blood." She is frightened and goes to her husband. He asks "Why have you broken our agreement . . . and come here at an improper time?" She says that she has not come because of "improper desires" (*kilesa*, defilements), and tells him of her nightmare; the text calmly reports that Vessantara "understood the dream, and knew that he would fulfil the perfection of giving, and that a suppliant would on the next day come and beg his children from him." He tells Maddī that her nightmare was due to an uncomfortable sleeping position, or an indigestion. And so, we are told, "he deceivingly (*mohetvā*) consoled her, and sent her away." The contrasts between the paradisial description of the forest hermitage, the violence of Maddī's dream, and Vessantara's apparent calmness (and deceit) hang over the next scene: "In the morning, when she had done all her chores, she embraced her two children and warned them to be careful, since she had had a bad dream that night." She leaves "wiping away her tears." Jūjaka then approaches, and "the Great Being came out of the leaf-hut and sat down on a stone slab, looking like a golden statue." One might think that the character Vessantara is slowly being metamorphosed into an icon, an abstract Buddha-image; but the next sentence is astonishing: "There he sat, thinking 'The suppliant will come now,' looking at the path by which he would come, like a drunkard eager for a drink, while his children played at his feet." So the calm exterior of the future Buddha hides strong emotion, which in most cases – of literal or metaphorical drunkenness – would be disparaged in Buddhist ethics.

When Jūjaka arrives Vessantara greets him "in a friendly spirit," and tells him, "We have lived a life of sorrow (*jivasokin*) in the forest for seven months, and you are the first godlike Brahmin with vilva stick and sacred fire and water-pot that we have seen" (542/55). When Jūjaka asks for the children, "the Great Being was filled with happiness, and as if putting a purse of a thousand coins in an outstretched hand he cried out . . . 'I give, I do not hesitate' " (543/56). He suggests that Jūjaka stay for the night, so that Maddī can wash and dress the children; but the Brahmin declines, uttering some misogynist sentiments. No motive is given for Vessantara's suggestion that Jūjaka stay, but in the next exchange he makes another suggestion, and here a motive is implied. He says, "If you do not wish to see my devoted wife, let their grandfather see [the children]. When he sees the children, sweetly chattering in their dear voices, he will be glad and pleased, and delighted to give you much money." Jūjaka again declines, fearing that Sañjaya will punish him; but Vessantara repeats the idea, adding this time that Sañjaya "always does what is right" (*dhamme thito*). Jūjaka again declines, saying "I shall not do what you urge. I shall [instead] take the children as servants for my wife" (545–6/57). The alternatives posed by Jūjaka imply that Vessantara's intention is for Sañjaya to give "much money" as a ransom for the children (as in fact he does): it only makes sense for Jūjaka to put the issue dichotomously in this way if he assumes that by taking the children to Sañjaya it would be impossible for him to have them as domestic servants, as was the original idea.

The children run away and hide, but Vessantara follows them and says to both in turn "Come, my dear [son/daughter], fulfil my Perfection. Consecrate my heart; do what I say" (546/58). They come and collapse at his feet, and their tears fall on his feet while his fall on their backs. The choice of words for the next exchange is particularly striking: then "the Great Being made them get up, and said to comfort them, 'Dear Jāli, do you not know that giving brings me gladness? Help me to realize my aspiration.'[16] And like someone valuing oxen, he put a price on his children just as he stood there." He tells them that "when you wish to be free," Jāli must pay a thousand gold coins; but he sets a price on Kaṇhājinā so high, he says, that only a king could pay it (547/59). There are some textual problems here, concerning the amounts to be given for the children (see CG pp. xxxii–xxxiii); but the text clearly wishes the audience here to think forward to the later scene in which, as they know, the children are to be ransomed by Sañjaya. It seems again to hint that this is Vessantara's intention. But the comparison with valuing oxen is brutal, and would appear deliberately intended to cast a problematic light on both Vessantara's tears and what he says next, that omniscient Buddhahood is a hundred thousand times dearer to him than his children, making both his tears and his aspiration less easy to evaluate unidimensionally.

Jūjaka leads the children away, beating them, but he falls over and they escape and run back to their father. Jāli asks him if they can stay to see their mother, using the intimate terms *ammā* and *tāta*, which CG translate as "mummy" and "daddy" (548/60); "Your heart must be made of stone, or strongly bound with iron," he says. Vessantara says nothing, and the boy then describes how both his parents will weep at losing their children. Jūjaka returns and takes the children away again; as he is being led off, Jāli cries out "Wish our mummy well, and may you be happy, daddy! If you give these toy elephants and horses and oxen of ours to mummy, she will console herself with them . . . she will restrain her grief" (551/62). Of course, as any parent would know, nothing could be less likely to console her. Perhaps Vessantara knows this too, for whereas when he first gave them away he felt "full of joy" (548/60), now "overpowering grief rose up in the Great Being for

[16] Here is a good example of what gets lost, or added, in translation. Rouse, in Cowell et al. (1895: 282), renders the second sentence "So do that my desire may attain fulfilment." Spiro (1971: 347) italicizes "my desire" and makes a direct contrast between it and Vessantara's love for his son, in the service of his psychoanalytic interpretation in terms of narcissism. The Pali word translated as "desire" is *ajjhāsaya*, an emotionally bland word better rendered "intention," "aspiration," etc., and the phrase as a whole, *ajjhāsayaṃ me tāta matthakaṃ pāpehi* means literally "my dear, cause my intention to attain its goal"; *matthaka*, here "goal," can mean the (human) head or the summit of a mountain, and this suggests that for the moment, Vessantara's goal is, for him also, a far-off and lofty one. He is, perhaps, trying to persuade himself as well as Jāli.

his children, and his heart grew hot . . . His feelings unable to bear it, he went into the leaf-hut with eyes full of tears, and wept bitterly" (551/62). He laments the sufferings of the children at Jūjaka's hands, but feels "as helplessly restricted as a fish caught in a net." He considers going after the Brahmin, to kill him and bring the children back; but decides he cannot, because "to wish to redeem a gift once offered . . . is not the way of good men" (552/63; or: "it is not what is right" for them, *sataṃ na dhammo*). The children escape from Jūjaka, but he catches them and leads them off again. Vessantara sees this happen, and as Kaṇhājinā is led away she calls out to her father. "At the sight of his little daughter going off sobbing and trembling, overpowering grief rose up in the Great Being, and his heart grew hot. His breath came from his mouth in gasps, for he could not breathe through his nose, and tears that were drops of blood poured from his eyes. Realizing that such pain (*dukkha*) overcame him because of a flaw in him, his affection [*sineha-dosa*], and for no other reason, and certain that that affection must be banished and equanimity developed, he plucked out that dart of grief by the power of his knowledge, and sat down in his usual position." (554/64–5). Once again, then, Vessantara sits like a golden statue, a Buddha-image, his calm exterior hiding emotional turmoil within, barely mastered.

What the text calls "the section about the children" ends with more verses from Kaṇhājinā lamenting their fate. It is an indication of what is considered important in this telling of the story that although the next section is called the section about Maddī, it does not contain Vessantara's giving her away. That occurs in a short passage called the section about Sakka, which is, as CG remark (p.xx) "rather an anticlimax." The section about Maddī is concerned, at length, with her delayed return to the hermitage, her search for the children, her grief and final acceptance. Again, the text exploits every opportunity to intensify the emotional distress of both Maddī and Vessantara: their suffering presupposes that family affection, albeit a fault from the perspective of soteriology, is nonetheless a source of happiness. The text makes this clear too. Maddī is delayed from returning home by some gods disguised as wild animals. They prevent her returning and running after the children, which would cause her "great grief," and at the same time they keep her safe from real wild animals. She pleads with them to let her pass, describing the scene she imagines at the hermitage:

the hungry children consoled by their father are like babies needing milk or people thirsting for water, since all they have to eat is what she brings home. She recalls how they run to meet her when she returns, like young calves to their mother-cow. Declaring her devotedness to Vessantara to be like that of Sītā to Rāma – and so making explicit the many ways in which this Buddhist epic is comparable to the *Rāmāyaṇa*[17] – she says to the animals "You can see your children in the evening when it is time for sleep. I wish to see my children." "When they heard her pour out her gentle words filled with sadness, the animals moved from her path" (557–8/67).

When she gets home she cannot see the children, and contrasts the now quiet hermitage with the usually happy evening scene. She sees traces of the children in their sandcastles, and their toys dropped on the ground: "My breasts are full, my heart bursts," she says, for "I cannot see the children" (559/68). In a motif repeated five times in the fifteen verses making up this passage she refers to the children's normally being covered with dirt in the evening after their day's play. Charles Hallisey[18] has pointed out that washing children clean is a motif of parental affection found elsewhere, for example in the commentary on the very popular *Maṅgala Sutta*, sermons on which must have been among the most common forms of preaching in traditional Buddhism. The fifth verse of that poem extols aiding one's parents: the commentary says "mother and father are very helpful to children, desiring their welfare and sympathizing (with them), so that when they see their little children who have been playing outside come in with their bodies covered with dirt, they show their affection by cleaning off the dirt, stroking their heads and kissing them all over. And children can never repay a mother and father for that even were they to carry them about on their heads for a hundred years."[19]

17 Gombrich (1985) uncovers specific verbal parallels between VJ and the *Rāmāyaṇa*.

18 Talk delivered at the University of Chicago in May 1992.

19 Pj I 136, translated in Ñāṇamoli (1960: 148). The motif of carrying one's parents is from a canonical text (A I 61–2). The word translated as "stroking (their heads)" is *upasimghāyantā*: CPD s.v. suggests this might be a combination of two verbs, one meaning to sniff or smell, the other to kiss, and hazards "give a sniff-kiss?" as a translation. It cites passages for the causative *upasiṅghāpeti*, where the context demands that it must mean rub, or touch. Skt *upa-ghrā, sam-upa-ghrā* both mean to smell, and might have been changed to *upa-sim*, although *upa-sam-ghrā* is not attested. There is also Skt *upa-śiṅgh*, with the same meaning. Whatever is the correct derivation, the picture here is of parents washing children and putting their face close to their heads, smelling the clean skin and hair, kissing and perhaps stroking them – a vivid sensory image of parental love.

Until now, says Maddī, the hermitage has seemed to her like a fairground; now it is so quiet, even the birds are not singing. She goes to Vessantara, who is "sitting quietly," still presumably in the statue-like immobility he adopted after mastering his distress over the children. She asks him about them, but he at first remains silent. Then, "thinking to stem her grief for her children by harsh words," he scolds her for being late: she is "beautiful and attractive," and the forest is full of ascetics and magicians. "Married women do not behave like this, going off into the forest leaving young children" (561–2/70). The innuendo is harsh and, of course, entirely unfair; it seems impossible not to think that the intention is to cast Vessantara at this moment in an unsympathetic light, for not even the most severely applied values of renunciation would require this kind of slander. She tells him about the animals who blocked her path; but for the rest of the night, during which she searches for the children where they used to play, all the while recalling the joys of the forest and their happiness playing there, he says nothing more except to ask her peremptorily why she is neglecting her domestic tasks, "brooding and doing nothing" (565/72). Perhaps the intention here is not so much to cast Vessantara in an unsympathetic light as to make him seem incompetent: trying to act out what he thinks detachment requires but doing it clumsily.

After searching three times in the same places, she stands in front of him sobbing, until she faints to the ground. At this Vessantara finally reacts, "trembling at the thought that she was dead," thinking that he, alone in the forest, cannot give her the state funeral she deserves. He is still thinking as a king, it would seem; and the next scene shows him still very much thinking as a husband. He gets up from his sitting position, leaving behind him there, one might say, the equanimity of (future) Buddhahood. "He rose to find out how she was. When he placed his hand on her heart he felt warmth, and so he brought her water in a jar, and although he had not touched her body for seven months, the strength of his anxiety forced all consideration of his ascetic state [*pabbajita-bhāva*] from him." Feeling a woman's heart, of course, means feeling under and on her breast. The scene continues: "with eyes filled with tears he raised her head and held it on his lap, and sprinkled her with the water. So he sat, stroking her head and her heart" (566/73). This sitting position makes a rather obvious contrast with his previous Buddha-image posture. Stroking her heart means, again, stroking her breast: but the mood is not sexual – it is rather one of gentle physical intimacy and the concern of a husband for his wife. What is being contrasted here to the ascetic state which Vessantara forgets is not *kāma*, desire, but *sineha*, affection.

Maddī wakes up from her faint, and seems to recognize the meaning of the physical contact. CG render the next sentence "after a little while Maddī regained consciousness and rose, and modestly greeted him thus: 'Lord Vessantara, where have the children gone?'" This is certainly a possible translation of the text,[20] but I think it does not quite catch the force of the words accurately, nor render the precise course of events, which is carefully encoded in the order of words. The specific moment of her regaining consciousness is unexpressed: one can imagine that it is as soon as he sprinkles her with water, *after* which he sits stroking her head and heart. I would translate: "Maddī passed a little time [like this, in his embrace], then, recovering her self-possession,[21] she stood up, and regaining (a sense of) modesty and fear (of blame)[22] she revered [him as a] Great Being and said, 'Vessantara, my husband, your children – where are they?'." Vessantara simply replies "My lady, I gave them as slaves to a Brahmin." The strength of emotion in the exchange is perhaps all the more clearly suggested by the fact that the text is silent about it; this gap in the text allows audiences to react to the scene as they wish. The stark disjunction between individual, celibate detachment, oriented towards an immaterial and future salvation, and the immediate mental and physical joys and consolations of marital and parental love is left unsoftened, with no explicit sign as to how it should be received. To the contrary, indeed, it is emphasized by the contrast between

[20] *Maddī pi kho thokaṃ vītināmetvā satiṃ paṭilābhitvā uṭṭhaya hirottappaṃ paccupaṭṭhāpetva mahāsattaṃ vanditvā sāmi Vessantara dārakā te kuhiṃ gatā ti āha.*

[21] The term used here, *sati*, literally memory, refers to a heightened quality of consciousness, manifested usually in meditative self-awareness and alertness, rather than to the fact of being conscious as opposed to being asleep or in a faint. The point, I think, is that Maddī, feeling the – perhaps at this point conflicting – emotions of a mother and a wife, passes a moment or two being consoled by Vessantara's caresses, but then regains awareness of the ascetic distance which should now lie between them, as the next words show.

[22] *Hiri* and *ottappa* are, like *sati*, virtues which form part of the Buddhist path: CPD s.v. *ottappa* says "*hiri* denotes the subjectively conditioned shame in contrast to *ottappa* which denotes the shrinking from, or fear of the socially conditioned sanctions for transgression and evil-doing."

the delicate sensuality of the earlier part of the scene and the austere tranquillity of its conclusion. Maddī asks why he has not told her before, and he says that he did not want to make her suffer. His next words are revealing: he consoles her by saying that since they are young and healthy, they will be able to have more children in the future. Clearly he does not envisage ascetic chastity lasting all their lives. Of course, the audience knows that he is about to give Maddī away too; but as they also know, that episode is a brief prelude to the denouement of the whole story: recovery of his family and return to kingship. Maddī accepts the situation, agreeing that "children are the best gift," and urges him to be calm. He replies that had he not been calm, the various miracles, such as the earthquake, would not have happened at the moment he gave the gift. In fact, as the text has been at pains to show, he may have finally achieved calm, but it was not without an effort; and even after that, feeling his wife's heart made him forget his "ascetic state." In her conversation with Vessantara after she regains consciousness Maddī uses four words of respectful address to him: in order they are *sāmi*, husband, *deva*, king, *janadhipa*, ruler of people, and *mahārāja*, great king. The sequence indicates that from this point in the narrative he is on his way back to royalty among the Sivis from solitary family life.

Vessantara's gift of the children is the story's center of gravity, but it is not the final act of generosity which brings him to "the peak of Perfection" (568/75). That is achieved by giving away his wife, which occupies the brief "section about Sakka (king of the gods)", which covers only five pages in the Pali text. Sakka disguises himself as a Brahmin and comes to Vessantara to ask for her. Once again, "as if putting a purse containing a thousand gold coins in an outstretched hand," he gives her away. The prose section dismisses the event with "all the miracles of the kind described before happened at that moment also." One verse describes her feelings: "Maddī did not frown at him; she felt no resentment or sorrow. Under his gaze she was silent, thinking 'He knows what is best'." After the very strong, even florid language used to describe events and emotions in connection with the children, here the text's simplicity and directness have their own kind of force: "Wondering how Maddī was feeling, the Great Being looked at her face. She asked why he looked at her, and like a lion roaring she spoke this verse: 'He whose virgin wife I became is my master and lord. Let him give me away or sell me to whomever he wishes; let him kill me!'" (570/77). These are the sentiments, of course, of a patriarchal society; but it is not anachronistic to suggest that a premodern audience, notably the women in it, might be able to infer the existence of trauma in Maddī's silent acceptance and all-too-brave words.

Immediately after this verse Sakka reveals his identity and returns Maddī. He speaks of Vessantara only as a married man and an individual karmic agent: "Just as milk and a conch-shell are alike in colour, so you and Maddī are alike in heart and thoughts . . . Live in peace in a hermitage, so that you may do works of merit by giving again and again." But in their next exchange Vessantara shows that he sees himself as an agent on several planes, and certainly not one confined to the privacy of married life in a forest retreat. Sakka offers him eight wishes, and Vessantara asks for the following things:

- (i) "May my father be glad to see me returned from here to my home. May he call me to take my seat." (As the commentary explains, this means the king's seat, the throne.)
- (ii) "May I consent to no man's execution, even if he has committed a serious crime. May I free the condemned from death."
- (iii) "May the old, the young, and the middle-aged find in me support for life."
- (iv) "May I not go after another man's wife; may I be faithful to my own. May I not be dominated by women."
- (v) "May a son be born to me and may he have a long life. May he conquer the world with justice" (*dhammena*).[23]
- (vi) "As the night grows pale, towards sunrise, may heavenly food appear."
- (vii) "May my bounty never cease. May I never regret a gift I have made."
- (viii) "When I am released from this life, may I go to heaven and reach a higher state, and never be reborn from there" (572–3/78–9).

Just as with Phusatī's ten wishes at the beginning of the story, the fulfilment of Vessantara's wishes is not described explicitly, but can

[23] This is one of the rare occurrences in this text of a motif connected with the Wheel-turning king.

be inferred with certainty. Sakka's immediate reply promising fulfilment mentions only the first, as a synecdoche: "Indeed before long your father will come to see you." The narrative voice ends the episode with "When [Sakka] had granted Vessantara his wishes, he went off to the heavenly assembly". Later, when Sañjaya's army approaches the forest and Vessantara suspects they are his enemies, Maddī sees that it is their own army and tells him "no enemy could overcome you, as fire cannot overcome a flood. Concentrate on that. In this there may be salvation" (583/87). The phrase "in this there may be salvation" translates *api sotthi* [Skt *svasti*] *ito siyā ti. Sotthi* means literally well-being (or felicity), and *ito* can also mean "from here". One can render "there may be salvation from (this place)," meaning that the army's arrival presages a return to the city from the forest, or, taking *sotthi* to refer to all the forms of well being wished for by Vessantara, "in this there may be (all manner of) well being"; that is, all his wishes are about to come true. If one is not attuned to the variety of Buddhist felicities, Vessantara's wish-list may seem oddly heterogeneous. He aspires to righteous monarchy, clemency in administering justice, avoiding capital punishment, personal morality, a Cockaygne-like abundance of celestial food, and soteriological progress.

A note is necessary here about the "soteriological progress" in question. What Vessantara explicitly wishes for is not in accordance with what the narrative voice and audience knows to be his future: and the commentary duly explains that what he really meant was "when I die from the Tusita heaven (in the very next life) and come (again) to the human condition, may I thereafter no longer be subject to rebirth, but may I attain Omniscience." To gloss his words thus is to attribute fore-knowledge to him, as indeed the text might seem to do elsewhere when it has him aspire to Omniscience. But I do not think it is necessary to read the text as assuming here that the character Vessantara has precise fore-knowledge of his future, nor of the Buddhist doctrine that enlightenment can only be attained in a human life.[24] There is no knowledge of the Dhamma in his time, no Buddhist *sāsana*, and so there is no reason why, despite his aspiring to Omniscience, he should know specific details about "his" future – this will be

[24] There are some exceptions to this, such as the "Never-returner" who attains in a human life the certainty of Enlightenment in the next, divine life; but these are not relevant here.

important later (7.3.b), when considering what relation the temporary person "Vessantara" has to the future Buddha Gotama. If an audience has knowledge a character in a play (tragedy or melodrama) does not have, the usual term is dramatic irony: here Vessantara's ignorance of his future is, I suggest, important in distancing him – but not the audience – from the sublime denouement of nirvana. He is suffering, and aspiring to different forms of felicity, as a human being.

The scene now changes to Jūjaka and the children, while "the Bodhisatta and Maddī lived happily in the hermitage." Jūjaka mistreats them, for example by tying them to a bush at night and leaving them to sleep on the ground. But they are cared for by deities; at night two of them, taking on the appearance of Vessantara and Maddī, untie them and wash them (one should recall here the motif of parental love expressed through washing, p. 512 above), feed them and put them in beds; they remove all signs of this in the morning so that it seems to Jūjaka that they have slept on the ground. The children are on their way back to a palatial life from the heroic austerities of forest asceticism, and so they require royal creature-comforts.[25] Thanks also to deities, the three of them travel to Jetuttara, despite Jūjaka's earlier refusal to go there, and finally come into the king Sañjaya's presence. When Jūjaka reveals that he received the children as a gift from their father, the ministers criticize Vessantara: "It would be wrong [*dukkaṭaṃ*] for the king to do this if he were living trustingly in his own home. How could he give away his children when he had been banished to the jungle?" Jāli says that in the forest he had nothing else to give, at which Sañjaya says summarily, "I approve of his gift and do not blame him." He is more concerned with Vessantara's inner state: "When he gave you to the beggar," he asks, "how did he feel in his heart?" Jāli explains how Vessantara suffered: "His heart felt pain and his breath came hot. From my father's eyes, red as Rohiṇī, tears streamed down." He recounts some words Kaṇhājinā had said earlier: "This is not a real Brahmin . . . for Brahmins are good men [*dhammika*]. This is a ghoul [*yakkha*] disguised as a Brahmin" (576/81). Sañjaya then asks what price

[25] Gotama, newly left his palatial household life, where he ate such things as "perfumed sāli-rice kept in storage for three years . . . with various delicacies," found the begged food of an ascetic so disgusting that "his intestines began to turn and were about to come out of his mouth" (Ja I 66; cp. Ap-a 71), Jayawickrama (1990: 88).

Vessantara had set on them, and ransoms the children by giving Jūjaka even more than that. (Jūjaka later dies of overeating, and when no relatives can be found, the wealth given to him reverts to the king.)

Sañjaya then asks about the life Vessantara and Maddī lead in the forest, and Jāli draws a picture with some elements of what Chapter 4 called the good forest, but he emphasizes the qualities of ascetic restraint and hardiness with which they live in Arcadia.[26] Sañjaya now says that he "did a wicked thing" (*dukkaṭa*) in banishing Vessantara, and gives detailed orders for a festive procession out to the forest: he orders "Let puffed rice be scattered and flowers, garlands, perfumes and ointments, and let gifts of hospitality be placed on the road he will travel. Let one hundred jars of toddy and spirits be placed [there]. Let meat and pancakes, cake and junket, together with fish . . . ghee and sesamum oil, curds and milk, panic seed, rice and plenty of toddy be placed [there]. Let there be chefs and cooks, dancers, mimes and singers, players of castanets, of jar-drums and bass-drums; and let there be comedians. Let them play all kinds of lutes . . ." (580/85).

After a short description of Jūjaka's greed and death, the procession to the forest takes place, in an atmosphere like that which 5.2.b called the carnival of life at the time of Metteyya. The verses describing the journey begin with "the [or: a] sixty-year-old elephant of independent will trumpeted forth; while its harness was being tied on, the elephant trumpeted" (581/86). The commentary takes this to be the rain-bringing elephant Vessantara had given away: "After rain had fallen in their country, the Brahmins living in Kaliṅga brought the elephant and gave it back to Sañjaya. He was happy that he was going to see his (former) master and (so) trumpeted." To read the text this way, however, is to ignore the adjective *satthihāyano,* which normally means "sixty-year-old." The elephant Vessantara gives away is born at the same time as

[26] Thus their lives combine what Lovejoy and Boas (1935: 9–11 and *passim*) called soft and hard primitivism. The former is a "Golden Age" of simplicity and comfort in a beneficent natural setting, free of the unnecessary and inhibiting excesses of civilization: "the alluring dream . . . of a life with little or no toil or strain of body and mind." The latter a life of austerity and self-discipline, where people are "inured to hardship, [being] hardy fellows to whom 'Nature' [is] no gentle or indulgent mother. Their food [does] not drop into their laps, they [are] obliged to defend themselves against predatory animals, [etc.]."

him;[27] and he is subsequently married at the age of sixteen (486/11) and is now the father of young children. Unless one takes "in the course of time (*aparabhāge*) Maddī gave birth to a son" (487/11) to refer to the lapse of a very long time, so that Vessantara would now also be sixty years old (which is obviously highly unlikely), or unless *satthihāyano* can be otherwise explained, or unless we simply assume inconsistency here, with a formulaic adjective for large and impressive elephants inappropriately applied, the text here must be referring to another elephant. The issue is of some importance for the moral assessment of Vessantara's gift – from a consequentialist point of view, at least, since getting the elephant back lessens the severity of, perhaps removes, his responsibility for bringing harm to his people – but it cannot be decided: one must simply take this as a source of variation in the tradition of telling Vessantara's tale.

Sañjaya reaches the mountain, and enters the forest to approach Vessantara in his hermitage; "there he saw the prince, who looked beautiful as he sat there in his leaf-hut, composed in concentration, free from any fear." The sitting posture would have been that of the golden Buddha-image, mentioned earlier; the words *samāhitaṃ* and *jhāyantaṃ* used of Vessantara here recall technical terms of Buddhist meditation, and the epithet *akutobhaya*, "free from any fear," is usually used of an enlightened person. Chapter 4.1.b showed that the felicities of meditation are also those of the higher heavens, the Brahma-worlds. But Vessantara's sources of happiness here and now are rather less ethereal: his first words after answering his father's initial question about his well-being are to ask after his children: "If you know anything of the royal children, tell us. Give us relief quickly, as to a man bitten by a snake." When he hears that the children have been ransomed he is "greatly relieved" (585/89). The word for "relief" here is *assāsa*, literally "inhaling," in the sense of breathing freely: thus consolation, solace, etc.[28] This is in clear contrast to the difficulties Vessantara had in breathing when the children were taken from him. Maddī too shows, in the next scene, that she is still very much

[27] The text at 485/9 says that it was born "by reason [*paccaya*] of the Great Being," which seems to involve a confusion giving rise to the elephant's having the name Paccaya (CG pp.xxxiii–xxxiv). Perhaps the confusion over this, and the sixty thousand warriors born on the same day as Vessantara (ibid.), is implicated in the unclarity as to whether the elephant here is the one given away earlier.

[28] See CPD s.v. *assāsa*, MW s.v. *ā-śvas*

an embodied emotional being. This scene was quoted in Chapter 4.3.a, to contribute to a depiction of the forest ascetic life as, from one perspective, an Arcadia of natural abundance; it bears repeating here, to demonstrate the text's insistence on the strength and fecund painfulness of the characters' feelings. "When Maddī saw the children in the distance, and knew they were safe, quivering like the goddess of drink, she sprinkled them with streams of milk from her breasts. She trembled, and with a loud cry fell senseless, and lay stretched on the ground. The children rushed up to her, and they too fell senseless on top of their mother. At that moment two streams of milk flowed from her breasts into their mouths, and if they had not received so much relief, the two children must have perished, their hearts parched" (586/90).

Everyone then falls senseless, and it is at this point that there occurs the lotus-leaf shower, by which the narrative of the Story of the Past now picks up its *point d'appui* in the Story of the Present. When everyone has recovered, the people invite Vessantara to govern the kingdom. He says to Sañjaya, "You and the countryfolk and the townsfolk in assembly banished me from the kingdom, although I was governing the state in accordance with what is right" (*dhammena*) (587/91). Sañjaya once again says that he did a wicked thing (*dukkaṭa*), and begs his son to dispel his grief. The wishes Vessantara made to Sakka have already shown that he wanted to return to the city as king: the text here affirms that he was "willing to govern the kingdom . . . even before this had been said"; and so Vessantara becomes king. He bathes, ceremonially removes his ascetic dress, and has himself shaved: then "he shone . . . with the radiance of the king of the gods" (588/92). Maddī also, as the text says at considerable length (589–91/92–4), is bathed and dressed in royal finery, so that she too "was as beautiful as a nymph in the heaven of the thirty-three gods." She is "blessed with beauty, reunited with her children, [and] was full of joy and delight and happiness." At this point occurs the only note of straightforward irony I can detect in VJ: "being so happy she said to her children . . . 'May you be ageless and free from death!'" (ibid.). I cannot think that any attentive Buddhist audience would miss the point: no amount of non-nirvanic well-being can provide that kind of felicity.

Everyone celebrates the occasion with mountain- and forest-sports for a month, during which time all the animals of the forest live in harmony. When Vessantara departs they all remain silent. He arrives at the city and "an amnesty of prisoners [is] proclaimed"; he has "every creature set free, even the cats" (592–3/96). He reflects that on the next day he will need gifts to give his suppliants; Sakka's seat grows warm, and he sends down a shower of jewels. They fall around the palace to waist-height, and elsewhere to knee-height; on the next day Vessantara, with the orderly and self-interested instincts of a Good King, has the treasure which has fallen "in the grounds of various families [*kula*-s; that is, "good families," the aristocracy] . . . bestowed upon them," while he himself takes the rest to use as gifts in the future. And so he lives happily thereafter, and at death goes to heaven.

"When the Teacher had recited this exposition of the Teaching in the story of Vessantara . . . he gave the key to the jātaka"; that is, he identifies characters in the story with people living in his own time, usually monks and nuns, and his own relatives. Among them are:

Jūjaka = Devadatta (a monk, his cousin and constant enemy)
Sañjaya = Suddhodana (his father)
Phusatī = Mahāmayā (his mother)
Maddī = "the mother of Rāhula" (Gotama's wife, usually referred to thus)
Jāli = Rāhula (his son)
Kaṇhājinā = Uppalavaṇṇā (a nun, one of his two chief female disciples)
"the other attendants" = "the followers of the Buddha"
Vessantara = "myself" (*aham evā ti*).

7.2. WHAT IS RIGHT?

Chapter 6 argued that one can understand why there are conflicting attitudes to kingship and social order in Buddhist texts by seeing that the idea of Dhamma, "what is right," functions on two levels: Mode 1, grounded in the principle of reciprocity, which requires and legitimates violence, when it repays bad with bad in the form of punishment for crime and in self-defense; and Mode 2, where values, including that of nonviolence, are absolute. In VJ too this strategy can help: but one needs to see, here as elsewhere, both that a clear interpretative decision between Dhamma Mode 1 or 2 is sometimes possible and useful, and also that on many occasions it is precisely the connection and slippage between the two senses of the word which allows the narrative to continue with its momentum undiminished by any simple ascription of guilt and innocence, praise and blame. Mode 1 is the default mode of social life (6.1); Mode 2 is a transcendentalist ideology produced by clerics. How far, in VJ, is Mode 1 Dhamma presupposed? And how far can Vessantara's actions, clearly oriented towards Mode 2, be said to "offend against" it?

The adversarial and legal-punitive violence of Mode 1 Dhamma is presupposed on occasion in VJ, most obviously when the Sivis demand that Vessantara be punished, and Sañjaya accedes to their request. Verbally precise occurrences can be found also. Among Phusatī's ten wishes at the start of the story is the hope that she will have a son who would be "honoured by rival kings" (*pūjitaṃ paṭirājehi*); she states that this is the case when she describes Vessantara before his departure to the forest (482/7, 498/21). The prefix *paṭi*, CG's "rival," often has the "well-defined meaning," as PED s.v. puts it, of "back (to), against, towards, in opposition to, opposite." Thus the kings who honor Vessantara are not merely geographical neighbors, but those who, in other circumstances, might be his nearest enemies, those with whom he would be in a relation of mutual – that is, reciprocal – opposition.[29] When the Sivis complain to Sañjaya about the gift of the elephant, they describe it in martial language (489/14, quoted on p. 504 above). The implication of this, as I understand it, is that the loss of the elephant not only removes from the Sivis a magical source of rain, but also an emblem and instrument of military strength. When the Cetans see Vessantara and his family arrive at their city, they assume that he has suffered defeat at the hands of his enemies; and when Vessantara tells them of his gift of the elephant he describes it in the same martial terms as had the Sivis (515/35–6). When the Cetans see him off into the forest, they post guards at its edge "to allay their fears that Vessantara might meet some danger if any enemy of his should seize the chance to harm him" (519/39). When Sañjaya comes with his army to the forest, Vessantara, whom we have just seen oscillating between detached potential Buddha,

[29] It is worth noting that *paṭi-rāja* is relatively rare in canonical texts, and that it most commonly occurs in the account of peaceful conquest by *cakkavatti* kings (cp. 6.5.c, n. 97).

suffering father and affectionate husband, resumes the persona of a worried king, frightened that his enemies have killed his father and are now coming for him. He tells Maddī of this "in fear for his life" (582/86–7). (It makes no difference to my point whether one takes him to imagine that the enemies here are rival kings or the Sivis themselves.) Lastly, the journey back to the city is made with "sixty thousand fine-looking fighting men . . . mahouts and guards, charioteers and foot-soldiers . . . [and] well-armed leather-clad soldiers in skull-helmets" (592/95).

It is against such a background that Vessantara's adopting the Mode 2 value of nonviolence has its force. This is implicit throughout, in the countless depictions of him as perfectly generous. In agrarian societies, as Gellner points out (88: 129, 275, etc.), violence is necessary to protect stores of food and other wealth. The principle of limitless generosity displayed by Vessantara (which is facilitated but not explained by the fact that kings from all over India give his father wealth) is incompatible with this in two ways: imprudent non-storage and nonviolence (to protect stores). The nonviolence is explicit when he goes to the forest and adopts, temporarily, the guise of an ascetic. He declines the Cetan's offer of kingship over them, fearing violence between them and the Sivis (517/37). Among the wishes he makes to Sakka are that he should regain his kingship over the Sivis but avoid capital punishment and release prisoners (as Phusatī had wished also); and that he should have a son who would, like a Wheel-turning king, "conquer the world with justice" (*dhammena*, 572/78). His wishes are granted, and so the final scene of the story, when he returns in triumph to the city and has prisoners and "every creature set free, even the cats" (593/96), is to be taken as inaugurating such a perfectly peaceful moral commonwealth.

Is Vessantara innocent? And if so, did those responsible for his exile, notably his father-king Sañjaya, do wrong? Often the answer to both of these questions seems to be yes: but the issue is not clear-cut. Many characters say straightforwardly that Vessantara is innocent (the word is usually *adūsaka*, one who has done no harm, committed no crime). Sañjaya says so, when the Sivis first complain about the elephant (491/15); moreover, when speaking later to Jāli and then again to Vessantara, he says that "I did a wicked thing [*dukkaṭa*, something ill-done, wrong, an offence], like killing an unborn child, when I banished an innocent man at the command of the Sivis" (579/84; 587/91): on the first of these two occasions the narrative voice comments that he was "confessing his own fault," *attano dosa*: thus he was, in doing this, *dūsaka*, guilty of a crime. Queen Phusatī says repeatedly that her son is innocent (498–501/21–3). Vessantara often protests his innocence (492/16, 493–4/17, 587/91); and his first remarks to Sañjaya when they meet again in the forest imply criticism of him (584–5/88–9). On pp. 502–4/24–6, the textual confusion of the manuscript tradition here (CG: 24–5 and 104 on Ja VI 502/14) matches the confusion which the text seems deliberately to evoke as to who exactly exiled Vessantara (see 7.3.a below); but at one point in this passage one statement is unambiguous: "the Brahmins, the wandering ascetics, and the other mendicants" who receive Vessantara's gift of the seven hundreds say that it is wrong (*adhamma*) that he should be driven from the city (520/25).

If this were all, the story would be simply one of injustice; and as Aristotle said of tragedy, "Good men should not be shown passing from good fortune to bad, since this is not fearsome or pitiable, but repellent."[30] The Sivis, or at least some proportion of them, think that Vessantara's generosity is ruining the kingdom when they threaten violence (490–1/14–15). Sañjaya's first reaction is to protest Vessantara's innocence, but he accedes to their demand. This cannot be seen merely as his giving in to threats: at the very least his decision must be seen as prudentially appropriate; this is what is behind Sañjaya's statement to Phusatī that in banishing Vessantara he is acting "honourably according to [his] duty."[31] When the commentary here explains that he is in this way following "the traditional *dhamma* of the kings of old," even if one does not understand it to be saying that Sañjaya is administering an appropriate punishment for a misdeed, at least one must take the word *dhamma* here to imply the claim that he is acting in a way appropriate to the traditions of kingship at the Mode 1 level. But Vessantara's liberality is something else. As Parry (1986: 468) says (putting the issue, from the point of view of the present context, in reverse), "the more radical the opposition between this world and a world free from suffering to come, the more inevitable is the

[30] *Poetics* XIII 2 (1452b) *ou gar phoberon oude eleeinon touto alla miaron estin.*

[31] *Dhammass' apacitiṃ kummi* (499/21, quoted on p. 505 above), or more literally "showing respect for," or "doing honor to what is right."

development of a *contemptus mundi* which culminates in the institution of renunciation, but of which the charitable gift – as a kind of lay exercise in asceticism – is also often an expression." The point can be made in linguistic terms: the verb *tyaj*, from which is derived the Skt noun *tyāga*, means to abandon or relinquish. This refers primarily to the abandonment of ordinary society by an ascetic; the word *tyāgin*, "one who has abandoned," is a standard term for an ascetic renouncer. It can also refer to the abandonment of wealth in generous giving. The Pali form of *tyāga* is *cāga*; and while this too can refer to ascetic renunciation, its most common sense is that of gift-giving, especially by laity. Thus when Vessantara gives away the elephant "his heart is set on liberality" (*cāgādhimānaso*, 488/12), but the Sivis think that he has reached the point where such a virtue can no longer be practiced in ordinary society, and that this level of *cāga* requires the wholesale abandonment of the social world in renunciation (*pabbajjā*, of the nonvoluntary kind[32]). And Sañjaya, sovereign of the social world, sees their point.

After Vessantara has been told that he is to be exiled, his words to his father and mother include the carefully equivocal remark that he has troubled his own people, as has been seen (505/27; p. 505 and n. 13 above). The narrative voice here chooses a significant epithet for Sañjaya: he is *dhamminaṃ vara*, "best of the righteous" (CG) or "best of those who do [or know] what is right."[33] Although Vessantara's admission of guilt is not unambiguous, the text here certainly does not present him as a hapless victim of injustice; the people have suffered because of his liberality, and so the king, *qua* king, is right to banish him, however much as a father, to whom his son is "dearer than life itself," he does not want to. When Vessantara tells Jūjaka to take the children to see Sañjaya, and perhaps we are to assume that he wants them to be ransomed, he says that his father "always does what is right" (*dhamme ṭhito*, literally "he stands" or "is established in what is right").

So much for Vessantara's giving away the elephant, and subsequent exile. What about his gift of the children? When Jāli and Kaṇhājinā have returned to the city and told Sañjaya that their

[32] For political exile as one of the factors in the cultural background of the third Brahmanical *āśrama* ('stage of life'), forest-dwelling, see Olivelle (1993: 113–17).

[33] There is a v.l. *dhammika*, an adjective: "righteous," "who does (knows) what is right."

father gave them to Jūjaka, the king's ministers, addressing a crowd which has gathered at the palace, criticize or denounce (*garahamānā*) him, saying that this would be wrong, an offence (*dukkaṭa*), even if he had been living as a king at home: how could he have done so, given that he was in exile in the forest? "One could understand his giving away . . . a trumpeting elephant; but how could he give away his children?" (575/81). Their words are said to be a "criticism" (CG) of Vessantara, a denunciation (*garaha*). But both Jāli and Sañjaya have, by this time, ceased to judge Vessantara by the standards of the social world: he is now on the path of soteriology, to which ordinary standards do not apply. Jāli cannot "bear to hear this criticism of his father," and asks Sañjaya what (else) he could have given, since in the forest he had nothing; Sañjaya very briefly expresses his approval of the gift, dismissing the issue in a half-verse, and turns immediately to what is for him a more important issue: he asks how Vessantara felt (literally "how was his heart"). Jāli replies that he suffered greatly.

The text often expresses the enormity (in every sense of the word) of Vessantara's virtuous generosity, when viewed from the perspective of mundane life: as when, for example, it comments that after Maddī's dream, he "deceivingly [*mohetvā*] consoled her" (541/54), when it compares his anticipation of Jūjaka to be like that of "a drunkard eager for a drink" (ibid.), when it compares his setting a ransom price on the children to be "like someone valuing oxen" (546/59), and when it has him cruelly suggest that Maddī's absence from the hermitage on the day he gave away the children is due to a lack of fidelity and modesty, and respond to her sadness over the children's absence by referring to her neglect of domestic duties (562–5/70–2). These kinds of language, simile and incident must be meant to shock, to suggest that while his earlier gifts can be, from any perspective other than that of the Sivis, wholly admirable, the renunciation of family life literally embodied in his giving away/abandoning (*cāga*) the children and Maddī cannot be obviously and indisputably innocuous. Vessantara's liberality conflicts with (offends) Dhamma Mode 1, not by simple criminality, but by following what is right according to Dhamma Mode 2.

Once again, however, the rightness of Mode 2 Dhamma is not a simple thing, even for Vessantara. It is useful to consider his actions and emotions in relation to the five Precepts, the most basic and general expression of Buddhist ethics: the prohibitions on killing, theft, sexual misconduct, lying and drinking intoxicants.[34] It is possible to see him as offending, or thinking of offending, against all of them:

(i) when Jūjaka takes the children for the last, final time, he considers going after him to kill him (552/63);
(ii) at the same time he considers taking the children back by force, but restrains himself with the acknowledgment that it is wrong to take back a gift;
(iii) he does not offend against the third Precept directly, although he does revert to being an affectionate (though not sexually "passionate") husband when Maddī faints (566/73), and he reasons with her that they can have more children later (567/74), which is not appropriate to his then status as an ascetic;
(iv) he deceives Maddī in the matter of her dream (541/54); and
(v) in his longing to give the children away he is "like a drunkard eager for a drink" (ibid.).

A step back from the narrative's realist immediacies of action and emotion will be helpful. As stated earlier, VJ is both realist drama and allegory: Vessantara is both a representation of a human being, with whom audiences can identify in the usual realist way, and a textual figure embodying values, meant not so much as an object of identification and empathetic understanding as a signifying device in a morality play. Second, and looking at the matter from a larger-scale interpretative point of view, an analysis of the text as ideology in Gellner's Kiekegaardian terms is helpful, as has been suggested already. Vessantara's attempts to meet the demands of Mode 2 Dhamma inspire both fear and hope in him, his family, and finally in everyone else. (The fear inspired by Vessantara is of a different kind from that inspired by Jūjaka, the malevolent villain of the piece, but together they contribute to the heightening of emotion in VJ.) The "offensiveness" of his actions is the challenge they offer to mundane sensibilities; and part of the achievement of VJ, as I read it, is vividly to evoke and confront the difficulties of Buddhist ideology's own most cherished values. The character Vessantara cannot be and is not said to be innocent and

[34] I owe this very useful idea to Katherine Ulrich.

admirable, in any and every possible way. To the question "What is right?", in relation to him, to his father Sañjaya and to the other Sivis, one must first respond by asking "in which moral register, Mode 1 Dhamma or Mode 2, the mundane or the ideological-transcendental?" Usually a definite answer is possible, but it is available only in the conditions of detached analysis, not to an audience in the thick of things.

At the end of the story, in the reconciliation scene in the forest, after the Sivis have offered Vessantara the kingdom, he tells his father that when he was banished he was "governing the state in accordance with what is right" (587/91). Here this standard phrase for a Good King must, in Vessantara's case, include what is right by Mode 2 standards. Sañjaya acted according to Mode 1 Dhamma, what is appropriate for kings *qua* kings (the duties of their station), and the ministers obviously had a point in saying that giving away one's children is not the right thing to do for those living in society ("living in a house," they say, using the standard symbol of lay life). But Vessantara represents what the last chapter (6.4.b) called a Mode 2 bonus: as there, in the "Birth Story on Advice to Kings," governing and punishing "justly and equitably," according to the principle of reciprocity, is Mode 1 Dhamma for a king; but still more virtuous is the aspiration to the absolute values of Mode 2. Unlike Brahmadatta in that story, however, Vessantara's supererogatory virtue does not immediately produce a utopia where the law courts stand empty, but leads in the first place to the suffering of exile and the self-imposed anguish of renunciatory generosity taken to its extreme. And this is one reason why the story of Vessantara can be seen as a tragedy as well as a utopian fantasy (or better, a concatenation of utopian fantasies). Shulman's remarks on Rāma are also appropriate to Vessantara: his very perfection – or better, his search for perfection before "he" (or rather, Siddhattha Gotama) is ready – involves both him and the audience in recurrent suffering: this is "the tragedy always consequent on perfection or the search for perfection."

7.3. ELEMENTS OF TRAGEDY

In speaking of VJ, or indeed any Southern Asian text as a tragedy, it is not helpful to enter into definitional niceties. As Mason (1985: 166) puts it, "it is characteristic of the topic of tragedy that, the moment you advance any proposition, you put your foot in it, and if you do not notice what you have done, you plunge even further into a morass." For Buddhism, obviously, the *Vessantara Jātaka* is a *jātaka,* one of the mixed prose and verse stories of Gotama Buddha's former lives, comparable to other prose stories in canonical texts, commentaries and later story collections, to the Pali verse texts called *apadāna*-s, stories of the past lives of various monks and nuns, and to the parallel Sanskrit verse or mixed prose and verse genre of *avadāna*-s. At the start of this chapter I endorsed CG's description of VJ as an epic, intending, as did they, thus to connect VJ with the Sanskrit "Epics." So there are already definitional problems of genre within Southern Asia, without bringing in Ancient Greek and European-American comparisons. But I want to use the word nonetheless: it conveys something of great importance in VJ.

It is certainly true that on a general level, one could object: how can any soteriology be "tragic"? If, as the OED has it, a tragedy is "a play or other work of a serious or sorrowful character, with a fatal or disastrous conclusion," then surely no soteriology can be tragic, since ultimately there can be no disastrous conclusion (even the Christian hell is seen as part of a just universe). Perhaps one could even define soteriologies as ways of avoiding tragedy, in this sense. My own analysis of nirvana as having the syntactic value of closure, providing the sense of an ending in the Buddhist discourse of felicity, clearly makes it impossible for me to speak of there being tragedy in Buddhism in the broadest and most abstract perspective. But this is not the only perspective to adopt; and I think that a focus on the extent to which VJ might be thought of as containing tragic elements not only helps us to see some nuances in this particular text; it also helps to delineate more precisely the civilizational position of the Buddhist discourse of felicity as a whole.

I return to the latter point in the General Conclusion; here I continue to concentrate on a close reading of VJ, using the notion of tragedy to uncover some elements of it which might otherwise be hidden. The OED also elucidates the word "tragedy" in another sense: it is "that branch of dramatic art which treats of sorrowful or terrible events, in a serious and dignified style." As CG remark, in VJ "the giving of the children has pathetic possibilities which are exploited to the full . . . [T]he opportunities for lamentation all cluster round the giving of the children; those opportunities are taken; and the episode becomes the story's centre of gravity, lengthy and heart-rending (p.xx) . . . [VJ] is a fine story, full of pathos and dignity" (p.xxv). I want to address two issues: first, who is responsible for all the suffering in VJ? Second, although in Buddhist doctrinal terms it would be absurd to say, in Aristotelian style, that Vessantara has a "tragic flaw," one might say that for him there is a tragic mismatch between the demands of his soteriological destiny and his immediate feelings. For whose sake does Vessantara suffer?

7.3.a. *Who is at fault? (the inevitability of the avoidable)*

VJ seems to possess what Heilman (1968: 30) sees as a central feature of tragedy: a feeling of "the inevitability of the avoidable." All the characters are in some way responsible for the course of events; with almost everyone there is a feeling of "if only he/she/they had not said/done this . . .". No-one is entirely innocent, and yet no-one is indisputably guilty. The relevant characters here are the Sivis, Jūjaka and his wife, Sañjaya and Vessantara. What was said in 7.2 is perhaps enough in the case of the latter two: Vessantara goes too far, from the point of view of Mode 1 Dhamma, in his enthusiasm for liberality, but no-one could accuse him of committing a crime, given the shared aspiration to Mode 2 soteriological values. Sañjaya, "best of those who do (or know) what is right," does what is appropriate for a king under Dhamma Mode 1, but judged by the Mode 2 moral register he is wrong. What of the Sivis? When Vessantara gives away the mighty rain-bringing, enemy-crushing elephant, they can be assumed to have suffered, or at least to think that they have suffered, a potential material loss, both in battle and in food production (the Kaliṅgan Brahmins came to ask for it because of a drought in their country). The text, however, does not mention this,[35] but offers another reason for their anger, and another cause for their action. The Kaliṅgan Brahmins take the elephant from the south gate to the north, through the center of the town, "mocking the crowd with

[35] Much later in the story, at 585/89, Sañjaya replies to Vessantara's query on the issue by saying that there has been no lack of rainfall in the kingdom. Unless we take the narrative voice here to be, as was said of Homer, "nodding," this detail added at that point helps to show that what Vessantara did had no bad consequences.

insulting [hand-]gestures" (489/14). So the Sivis are humiliated; this in itself is perhaps enough to make them angry, but when they go to the palace to complain they also do so (because, through, on account of, etc.) *devatāvattanena*. CG translate this (ibid.) "by a turn of fate," which I think is misleading. *Devatā* means a deity (or deities); *āvattana* (thus here; also *āvaṭṭana*) is from the verb *ā-vṛt*, to turn around or back, used often with the specific meaning (see CPD s.v.) "enticement, temptation, possession." Thus the Sivis are either literally possessed by a deity (or deities), or if this is too strong, they are at least "influenced" by a supernatural being or beings. As with the actions of gods and goddesses in classical Greek and Latin texts, modern readers may choose to see this as a metaphor for a psychological state: but whether one takes the supernaturalism literally or as a metaphor, the Sivis' fury at the humiliating loss temporarily robs them of the power of self-control and appropriate action.

The Sivis are repeatedly said to be angry at the gift of the elephant (489/14, 492/16 *bis*, 495/518, 515/36): anger, as was seen (6.4.c), is a state in which kings (and others) judge badly. At one point they are said to be *dānena saṅkhubita-cittā*, which CG (490/14) render "incensed by his [Vessantara's] donations." The verb is primarily a physical rather than psychological one (the sea can be *saṅkhubita* by the wind): so perhaps they were just "shaken up, shocked" by his gift. But they are in any case, as Vessantara says when counseling the Cetans against provoking them, a "haughty" people.[36] There is in this a parallel between the Sivis in the Story of the Past and the Sākyans in the Story of the Present. In *Jātaka* stories in general the relationship between the stories of the present and the past can vary: more or less exactly the same incidents can occur, sometimes there is scarcely any relation, and as in this case there can be a structural correspondence between them. Here in the Story of the Present the Sākyans are said to be "proud by nature and stubborn in their pride" (479/3); just as they are subdued by the Buddha with a display of extraordinary physical power (the Miracle of the Pairs, where flames come from one side of his body, water from the other), so in the Story of the Past the anger and haughtiness of the Sivis are subdued, eventually, by the future Buddha with a display of extraordinary moral power.

[36] *Accuggata* (516/37); *ati-uggata*, too high or (CPD) insolent.

Things are often said to happen because of his *tejas*, which means radiance, splendor, glory, as repeatedly at 591/94 where CG translate *Vessantarassa tejena* rather conservatively as "because of the power of Vessantara's character." The showers of rain which are the formal means by which the stories of the Present and Past are tied together, occur in each case after the reconciliation of the (future) Buddha with his people.

So the haughty Sivis are angry because of Vessantara's gift, because they were humiliated by the Kaliṅgans, and because of divine influence or possession. Already one can see that the text is deliberately blurring the issue of their responsibility for what happens. This impression is increased when one asks, who exactly does demand Vessantara's banishment? At the start those who see the Kaliṅgans leaving and complain to the king are said to be city-dwellers (489–90/14); the verses specify that they are "lords and princes, tradesmen and Brahmins, mahouts and guards, charioteers and foot-soldiers"; it was "all the country people [*kevalo* . . . *nigamo*] and the assembled Sivis . . . [who] told the king." At both 492/16 and 493/16–17, in addition to this list, the text refers to "Sivis and countryfolk" (*negamā*); at 493/17 Vessantara says "Let the Sivis, all of them, banish me . . ." But when he makes the gift of the seven hundreds, things become more complex. "As he gave the gift . . . inhabitants of the city of Jetuttara, from all four orders of society, cried, 'Lord Vessantara, those who live in the Sivi kingdom are banishing you because of your gifts, and yet you are giving away even more'" (504/24). Then, "when they had had their gifts, the recipients thought, 'Now that King Vessantara has left us without support and gone into the jungle, to whom shall we go in future?'"; they fall to the ground, "wailing very pitifully" (ibid.). Next (502/25; text as reordered by CG) it is "beggars" who complain that Vessantara is innocent; and further on the same page "old and young, and the middle-aged . . . the overseers, the eunuchs and the women of the king's harem stretched out their arms and cried aloud at the departure of the great king," as did "all the women of the city."[37] Then "the Brahmins, the wandering ascetics, and the other mendicants stretched out their arms and said, 'It is not right . . .'" When Vessantara tells the Cetans the Sivis

[37] The word "all" here is an inference from the Pali syntax, which is possible but not obligatory.

are haughty, he specifies that "both army and townsfolk[38] want to destroy the king because of me" (516/37); but when Jūjaka arrives in the Sivis' city on his way to the mountain, "the people who were congregated there" say that it is Jūjaka's fault, as a Brahmin (525/44). After the children have been ransomed, Sañjaya tells the whole army to prepare to go out to the forest (579/84, 581/86; no account of how, why or when they changed their mind is given); they go, along with an unspecified number of others (587/91: "all the people who had come out together from the kingdom . . ."); and Vessantara tells his father that "you and the country people and the townsfolk in assembly banished me" (ibid.). Finally, by the time he returns to the city in triumph, "the country people and townsfolk crowded together, full of friendship to the prince" (592/95–6).

The moral confusion of Vessantara's banishment is matched by a carefully contrived narrative confusion as to who precisely, among the Sivis, living in the city of Jetuttara and in its environs, threatened Sañjaya with violence and demanded that the prince be exiled; who changed their minds, and who (if anyone) did not. By the time the denouement of the story begins, as Sañjaya comes in procession to the forest, the army and at least some of the Sivis have clearly changed their minds; but by this time, indeed, the evaluative ambience of the action has moved so far to the Mode 2 moral register that one does not need to ask how or why. The sheer force of Vessantara's drama and triumph carries everyone (the Sivis and audiences of VJ) along with it.

What of Jūjaka, his wife and the Brahmin women of Kaliṅga? Here we move away from tragedy, on the surface level: Jūjaka combines two stock characters of comedy or melodrama: the persecuting villain and the buffoon. As CG say (p.xxiv) "at first, in his marital troubles and his hardships on the journey he supplies an element of farce. But ultimately he is a bogeyman pure and simple – as the children point out." For most of the story he is not benevolent at

[38] The word for "townsfolk" is *negama*, translated earlier as "countryfolk"; later (587/91) it is coupled with *janapada*, which must mean country people, and so must there mean "townsfolk." The ambiguity is in the Pali: usually settlements of increasing size are called *gāma*, village, *nigama*, a (market-)town (whence *negama*, those who live in such towns), and *nagara*, a city. As in English, such "townsfolk" can be opposed to either country- or city-dwellers, depending on context. This ambiguity adds further to the confusion as to who specifically insisted on Vessantara's departure.

all, of course, but in the very earliest scenes in which he is introduced there are elements which make him something of a sympathetic character, if simultaneously and increasingly a farcical one. Here too one may see an attempt to spread and dilute responsibility for what happens, making no-one entirely innocent or guilty.

The section about Jūjaka (521–8/41–7) opens with a brief biography of him. He lives in a Brahmin village called *Dunniviṭṭha*, which CG render nicely as Foulstead, in the kingdom of the Kaliṅgans. He is married to a wife much younger than he, whom he received from a family in lieu of some money they owed him. She cares for him very well, so well indeed that other Brahmins complain to their wives that they are not like her. The women resolve to get rid of her, and insult her when they meet at the river. An example of their abuse is given, in sing-song verses whose repeated chorus-line tells her that her family "gave you to a worn-out old man although you are so young," and which are full of sexual innuendo: "there is no fun with an old husband, no pleasure [*rati*, which implies sexual pleasure: see 5.2.b] . . . When a young man and a young woman talk together in private, whatever sorrows lodge in the heart of a woman melt away. You are young and comely, desirable to men. Go and stay with your family. What pleasure will a worn-out old man give you?" Amittatāpanā is upset, and refuses to fetch water any more; Jūjaka consoles her, and offers to get water himself. (I assume that this is intended to portray him as both kindhearted, and – in a patriarchal society [CG p. xxi] – weak.) She is too proud to accept the offer ("I was not born into the sort of family to let you fetch the water"), and tells him to go and procure a slave; she has heard that Vessantara and his family are living in the mountain forest, and suggests he go there. He protests that he is too old for such a journey, and offers again to become her servant, at which now she insults him roundly, saying that if he does not go she will leave him and enjoy herself with other men. At this, "frightened and subject to the Brahmin girl, distressed by his passion" (*attito kāma-rāgena*; i.e. in a state of sexual jealousy), he leaves, "warning her not to go out after dark, but to take especial care until he returned." He is "greedy for his pleasures" (*kāma-giddhimā*), and "unrestrained in his lusting for enjoyment." In place of their earlier marital harmony, now Jūjaka's relationship to his young wife is one of lust and fear of being cuckolded.

In this brief section, clearly, there are already multiple "if only X had not done Y" possibilities, which hover in the background to produce a sense of avoidable but inevitable tragedy. When they are first introduced, Jūjaka and his wife are good, sympathetic characters, the victims of other Brahmins' envy and abuse. A share in the responsibility for the tragedy of Vessantara's children can be attributed to the Brahmin women, for their abuse of Amittatāpana; or further back still, to their husbands, for their envy of Jūjaka and complaints to their own wives. Moreover, the idea that Jūjaka should go to ask for the children is not his, but Amittatāpanā's. In these opening scenes, Jūjaka cuts a pathetic figure, provoking sympathy and ridicule; thereafter, during his journey he becomes increasingly ridiculous, but now also increasingly menacing. To his (partial) responsibility for the tragedy of the children, given in the basic plot of the story, this version has the Sivis add, when he passes through their city, the suggestion that he, as a Kaliṅgan Brahmin, is also responsible for Vessantara's gift of the elephant and subsequent exile. So from being a benevolent, if weak and comic figure, he is transformed, first to a lecherous potential cuckold, comic but now also repulsive (in the physical sense also, as Jāli later points out), and then to the persecuting villain who can be blamed for everything. In the forest he gets lost and is chased by dogs up a tree, where he sings of Vessantara's generosity.[39] These verses are in themselves gentle and pretty; in his mouth they become ironic and painful. The guard whom the Cetans have set to protect Vessantara from his enemies finds him, thinks that "he is up to no good," and at first threatens to kill him. Jūjaka deceives him, and saves his own skin, by pretending to be a messenger come from the Sivis to bring Vessantara back home. There follow the two sections called the Short and Long Description(s) of the Forest, which together cover almost twelve pages of text. Throughout the first, spoken by the Cetan, a sense of Jūjaka's deceit and menace accompanies the idyllic descriptions; as it does also in the second, spoken by a Brahmin ascetic who also suspects Jūjaka's motives but is deceived by him.

In his dealings with Vessantara Jūjaka is by turns polite, deceitful and cruel. Indeed his cruelty to the children makes the evaluation of what he does less easy. When the Cetan guard suspects that

[39] "Sings" literally: this is one of the sections with lines repeated either verbatim or with one word changed (see next section, 7.4).

he wants to ask for the children or Maddī he says "His is no honourable errand; he is up to no good,"[40] but the narrative voice says nothing, as again when the Brahmin ascetic suspects the same thing. But neither during nor after the actual gift does any character, or the narrative voice, condemn the mere act of asking for the children (nor later when Sakka disguised as a Brahmin asks for Maddī). He is blamed by the children, Vessantara and the narrative voice for his cruel words and treatment of the children. It may be implied, but it is not said, that he is in the wrong simply by asking for them. Jāli asks whether he is human or a flesh-eating "ghoul" or "ogre," words repeated by Kaṇhājinā, and again by Jāli when they are about to be ransomed by Sañjaya (*yakkha, pisāca*; 549/61, 554/64, 576/81). On the former occasion, it is Jūjaka's physical repulsiveness which makes Jāli suspect he is not human; on the latter, when Kaṇhājinā says that he cannot really be a Brahmin, since Brahmins are "good men" (*dhammika*), it is his cruelty to them after the gift has been made rather than the gift itself which she gives as a reason. Once again, something is clearly wrong here, but the text takes care not to specify exactly what it is.

Jūjaka goes to Jetuttara with the children despite his earlier refusal to do so, "because of divine prompting" (574/79). Perhaps it is also divine intervention which makes him forget about his wife; or perhaps this is a further way of depicting him as ludicrous: when Sañjaya gives him great wealth and a palace to live in, he goes there and dies of overeating, replacing lust with gluttony (577/82–3, 581/86). No relative of Jūjaka can be found to claim his wealth, so Sañjaya's ransom reverts to him. The scarcely human, lustful and cruel figure who looms over the centerpiece of the story has now become as irrelevant to it as he was at first pathetic and hateful. None of his characteristics, comic or villainous, are appropriate for the atmosphere of reconciliation, festival and peaceable kingship which pervades the happy ending of the story (happy, that is, on the level of represented events).

7.3.b. The character and person (individuality) called "Vessantara"

This section addresses the issue of Vessantara's character from two entirely different points of view: the nature of creativity in relation

[40] *Na kho pan'esa dhamme sudhammatāya āgato.*

to traditional stories or dramas whose plot is – overall – unalterable, and Buddhist attitudes to identity across lifetimes. In relation to the first of these, it is important to remember the constraints imposed on, and the freedoms granted to those who redact and retell traditional stories. The many tellings of Vessantara's story do not seem to display the enormous variation, even in such basic features as plot elements, to be found in different tellings of "the" *Rāmāyaṇa* story across different cultural contexts in South and Southeast Asia (Richman 1991). Certain basic constraints must operate: in any version, for example, Vessantara must be banished from his kingdom, he must give away his children and wife, and he must be reunited with all of them at the end. But even in closely related but variant tellings of the tale, this leaves a great deal of freedom for an individual text to represent other things as it wishes:[41] the feelings and exact words attributed to the characters, minor plot incidents (such as here in the tender scene between Vessantara and Maddī after she faints with emotion), and other such constituents of the narrative. The Pali *Jātaka* version, it seems to me, emphasizes with unmistakable force and certainly at unmistakable length the pain suffered by Vessantara, Maddī and the children. It would be silly, indeed it would be a category mistake, to say that the fixity of the plot of the Vessantara story makes him a hero with a tragic destiny. But one can perhaps say without absurdity that this version takes the giving away of the children as an inevitable, given moment of the story, and chooses to concentrate on it, to heighten the audience's feeling both for the inner turmoil Vessantara suffers before and while doing so – he is at once Everyman in his suffering and Unique Hero in his fortitude – and for the straightforward grief of Maddī afterwards.

The second direction from which I want to approach the idea of Vessantara as tragic hero is Buddhist systematic thought about rebirth. The Introduction to Part 1 (pp. 132–3) spoke of an individual sequence of karmic causal relations as a site for consciousness, which is not in itself a person but a beginningless and (until final nirvana) endless continuum in which narratively coherent

41 I speak here, and hereafter, of a text's having or doing certain things, meaning by this to avoid the clumsy locutions sometimes imposed by the difficulty of using a single word like "author" or "composer" in the context of oral composition, transmission and performance.

persons, beginning and ending in limited stretches of time, appear sequentially, as short stories. Chapter 5.3.a, discussing proper names and ambiguities of reference in relation to the sequence of lives culminating in that of the future Buddha Metteyya, had cause to refer to the account of rebirth and identity in Buddhist systematic thought. This is, once again, that ever-changing, momentary consciousness-events occur in a temporally continuous sequence both within one lifetime, and across different lives. During one lifetime, when a consciousness-series is associated with a body in the psycho-physical particularity called, conventionally, a person, there is not only temporal but also spatial continuity, that of the five constituents of personality, the Aggregates (*khandhā*) taken collectively. One way of referring to this is the term *attabhāva*, the "individuality" of one lifetime; the fact that the body is important in making the sequence of psycho-physical events construable as such an individuality is reflected in the fact that this term can also, and often, refer simply to the body in a physical sense (Collins 1982: 156–60). When such a spatio-temporally continuous individuality or person is seen as an agent to whom the capacity for karmically significant deeds may be attributed, one may ask the question: what is the relationship of that individuality/person to both previous and future individualities/persons? The standard answer in Buddhist texts is that they are "neither the same not different." They are not the "same," because they are spatially discontinuous, separate bodies; but nor are they "different," for they are two segments in one consciousness-series, each segment of which is temporally and causally continuous with those which precede and follow it. Insofar as one chooses to use the language of persons and their deeds in understanding continuity and *karma*, the moral relationship between a present person and future, descendant persons occurring in the same site for consciousness blends what we would normally distinguish as self-interest or prudence and altruism or beneficence (Collins 1982: 186–95; 85). In some ways it makes more sense to call the relation one of altruism, since any knowledge of future persons in a single karmic sequence is subjectively impossible: they are in this sense others.

All this is no doubt as abstruse a topic for most Buddhists as it is for most readers of this book. Moreover, as claimed in 3.4.b and 5.3.a, for certain reasons and in certain respects, it can be narratively advantageous to coalesce past and future persons appearing sequentially in one site for consciousness (at least in the case of those consciousness-series which culminate in a Buddha), either by using one and the same referential device – the pronoun "I" – for both, or by using a proper name such as Metteyya proleptically, to refer not only to a present celestial person but also a future human one. Nonetheless I suggest that the systematic articulation of sameness and difference in sequences of karmically connected lives just given is implicit, or perhaps better potentially available in the quite different cultural context of the telling of a story such as VJ, to a greater or lesser degree, depending on the different levels of sophistication and interest in members of the audience. Perhaps too those who could not themselves articulate the complexities of Buddhist systematic thought might still be able to appreciate the point on an intuitive level, and react to VJ accordingly. Here one might recall, in relation to the analytical point that empirically what gives individuality, *attabhāva*, to a "person" is the body (this is one meaning of the word), that Vessantara's sufferings are all described in strongly physical terms: even without complex articulation of doctrine it is clear that no-body else, so to speak, has to endure what he does. In this light, the name "Vessantara" denotes only the person so designated, the one lifetime about which the narrative is directly concerned. If one asks, as I did earlier, for whose sake does Vessantara suffer, the answer cannot be in any simple sense (and in very few difficult ones) "his own." Vessantara suffers, just as Sumedha made the original aspiration to Buddhahood, for the sake of the future Buddha Gotama and all the beings to whom his salvific message will be brought.

If one puts together the two arguments just made – concerning traditionality and creativity in story plots, and the nature of the spatio-temporal, embodied moral agent called "Vessantara" – one can come as close as is sensible in a Buddhist context to saying that the tragedy consists in this: Vessantara is destined to suffer the pain and torment which the Pali *Jātaka* version of his story ascribes to him at the loss of his children, for the sake of other, future beings. This assertion, taken by itself, is misleading; but it captures something, I venture, of the pathos and dignity which CG rightly perceived in this story. Here recall again what Gellner called the offensiveness of ideology; that is, its non-obviousness, its intrinsic capacity to arouse fear and hope. In imagining oneself into the lived world of a traditional Buddhist audience listening to VJ, one must remember – this is an important issue to which the General Conclusion will return – that people in Buddhist countries are human beings first, and Buddhists (to a greater or lesser degree) second. They are human beings for whom Buddhist ideology, however much they might view or wish to view the world from inside it, nonetheless remains in fact, as Gellner puts it "something *within* the world, and *not* coextensive with it" (1979b: 129–30). VJ has to be understood and appreciated Buddhistically, of course; but not in every conceivable respect and to every conceivable degree. Vessantara is also a (representation of a) human being, in a tale told by and to other human beings. That is to say: from a sophisticated Buddhist perspective the account of "Vessantara's" identity I have given could lead one to speak of altruistic elements in "his" predestined narrative role, and this, I suggest, lends to his story an element of tragedy. From an unsophisticated Buddhist, or a not necessarily (at least never wholly) Buddhist perspective, Vessantara suffers for Gotama's sake, and for those whom Gotama teaches (who include, indirectly, traditional audiences of VJ).

7.4. THE TEXT IN PERFORMANCE CONTEXT

In premodern settings, versions of the Vessantara story would have been for the most part recited aloud and listened to by audiences; and dramatic versions played by actors were frequent.[42] Although we will never have as much knowledge of these performance contexts as we would wish, some inferences about them can be drawn, from the text itself and from the work of modern ethnographers. More ethnographic work is necessary before any safe general conclusions can be drawn; but what exists is enough to begin with.

7.4.a. Songs

CG remark (p.xxviii), apropos the fact that VJ was originally oral literature, "there are long set pieces in which couplets are

[42] Cf. Forbes (1878), cited in the General Introduction; and the works cited in 5.2.c and earlier in this chapter.

repeated with the variation of just one word; these we assume were songs." The action of the story is interrupted, or better the pace of the narrative is set, by a number of shorter or longer descriptive passages in verse, which appear in all sections of the text but one; they are the songs CG refer to and other poetic elaborations which do not in themselves significantly further the action of the narrative. It is in these passages above all that there occur what Chapter 4 called descriptions of the forest, good and bad, the "good" versions of which do much to convey the sense of "Paradise in the Forest." In a traditional recital, one may assume, these would be sung, or at least chanted in a melodious style.[43] These passages are as follows, with the traditional thirteen section headings:[44]

Verses about the ten Wishes
(Future) Phusatī's ten Wishes (482–3/7)

Description of the Himālayas
Maddī's verses on the children playing and the beauties of the forest (496–7/19–20)

Chapter about the Gift-giving
(i) Phusatī's lament on hearing of Vessantara's banishment (499–501/22–3), (ii) lament of the Brahmins and others (502–3/25–6) (this is somewhat obscured by the confusion of the text at this point), (iii) Sañjaya's description of the bad forest (506–7/28), followed immediately by (iv) Maddī's description of the sufferings of widows (507–8/29–30), which is in turn followed by (v) Sañjaya's contrast between the delicate life of the children in the palace and the sufferings they will endure in the forest (510/30–1)

Chapter about entering the forest
Cetans describe the gentle beauty of the forest (518/38–9)

[43] This is also true of other versions: Kingshill (1965: 115) reported that in the early 1950s, a Lanna Thai version of VJ, and other such texts, were "always delivered in sing-song, chanting style"; cf. Kingshill (1991: 229–30).

[44] I include Phusatī's and Vessantara's Wishes, which are not in themselves songs, but are in verse, and they structure the text by the correspondence between them, marking the beginning and the (start of the) end of the story, and setting a general and collective utopian agenda for it.

Chapter about Jūjaka

(i) Brahmin women taunt Jūjaka's wife (521–2/41–2), (ii) Jūjaka describes Vessantara, "while sitting up a tree, besieged by dogs" (Jūjaka calls it a lament) (526/45–6)

Short Description of the Forest

Cetan guard's first idyllic portrait of the forest and ascetic life there (528–30/47–9)

Long Description of the Forest

Cetan guard's second forest idyll, incorporating the encyclopedic cornucopia of botanical terms (4.3.a, pp. 335–6 above) (533–9/51–3; cf. CG's Appendix I, pp. 98–102)

Section about the Children

(i) Jāli's first lament and portrayal of forest beauty (550/61–2), (ii) Vessantara's lament for the children (551–2/62–3), (iii) Jāli's second lament (533/63–4), (iv) Kaṇhājinā's lament (554–5/65)

Section about Maddī

(i) Maddī's first lament, while gathering food (557–8/66–7), (ii) her second lament, on first not seeing the children (559–60/68–9), (iii) her third lament, juxtaposing the beauty of the forest and the children's absence (564/71–2, with two more sets of two verses in the same style at 564–5/72)

Section about Sakka

Vessantara's eight Wishes (572–3/78–9)

Section about the Great King [i.e. Sañjaya]

(i) Jāli's (short) description of the forest (578/83–4), (ii) Sañjaya's instructions for the festival procession to the forest (579–80/84–6)

[Chapter about the Six Nobles: no songs]

End of the Story of Vessantara

(i) Short song of Maddī's happiness (589/92–3), (ii) description of clothes and ornaments given by Phusatī to Maddī (590/93–4), (iii) description of animals in the forest at peace during the sports, and silent at Vessantara's departure (591/94–5), (iv) description of the procession during Vessantara's homeward journey (592/95).

7.4.b. Ritual contexts: meanings and events around the text

Information about the ritual contexts for the Vessantara story is richest in Thailand, where the Pali verses are sometimes recited alone, sometimes with vernacular exegesis, or in an entirely vernacular version; there are also vernacular theatrical representations of it. Chapter 5.2.c explored the use of VJ in rituals expressing, *inter alia*, the aspiration for natural fertility. Here, to suggest how other social meanings and events can cluster around the text in ritual context, I draw on accounts of VJ in context given by Anuman Rajadhon (1961, 1968), S. J. Tambiah (1971), G. E. Gerini (1976 [1892]), B. Brereton (1995) and L. McClung (1975), who builds on Anuman Rajadhon's account and adds a story about a recitation of VJ from "a popular Thai epic-romance," *The Story of Khun Chang and Khun Phaen*, a traditional story first written down during the reign of Rāma II (1809–24)[45].

Tambiah (1970: 180–1) reproduces a photograph of the decorated pulpit which, along with other items in the preaching hall, is intended to represent the forest paradise of Vessantara, complete with wishing-trees (cp. McClung 1975: 198–9). The point I want to stress first, as he does, is the power of the Pali words alone, for the majority of any traditional audience outside institutions – monasteries – of higher learning, who would not understand them; this is a theme which is common in traditional Pali texts.[46] Where only the Pali verses are recited, of course, almost the entire content of this chapter is irrelevant, unless one assumes that audiences would have in their minds at the right moments during the recitation a vernacular version, which seems unlikely, especially given their inattentiveness and coming-and-going, as emphasized by Tambiah. Similar cases are reported from northern Thailand in

[45] I depend entirely on McClung's account. He used a Thai-language edition. In addition to the brief notices he cites, there is a short account of the work in Schweisguth (1951: 205ff., 224ff.) and a more detailed summary and partial translation in Sibunruang (1960).

[46] See Tambiah (1968a, 1968b, 1968c, 1970: Chapter 10 etc.). For the "magical" efficacy of Pali for those – such as animals – who do not understand it, he draws on Wells (1939: 235–6), who recounts a story found in traditional Pali texts (see Collins 1992b).

the 1950s by Kingshill, where on some occasions up to seventeen monks would preach sermons simultaneously; it was explained to him that listening to all seventeen would give seventeen times as much merit (1965: 116). But such inattention to the content of recitations was not always the case, and most often the story is told with Pali verses and vernacular exegesis. Anuman Rajadhon writes that

> [R]ecitation [of "the Gāthā Phan or the Pali Thousand Stanzas"] alone is not popular with the people. Although the hearing of such sacred words recited may give rise to mystical feelings, the people do not understand them and their emotions are not satisfied. The people want something more. They want to hear the voice of their favourite presiding monk, to hear his melodious voice which is familiar to them, for many are able to recite too. They want to live in love and hate, in happiness and sorrow, to be sad or to be in humour, and to raise their imaginative mind to a higher plane and ideal, which the various characters of the story manifest. Hence the reciting of the Pali Thousand Stanzas only, does not appeal to the masses . . . For the contents of the [Pali-with-vernacular-commentary][47] version are more of a secular nature, and in fact in some parts of the story, the reciter has to display his wit and additions of his own are thrown into the recitation which sometimes border on drollery and vulgarity. The orthodox people frown. [He adds that] the traditional [recitation of VJ] is still a living force but the aspect of the merry side is on the wane . . . In order to save this old tradition from being lost altogether, a novel way is introduced in Bangkok today when a theatrical performance of each episode is given just before the recitation of it. (1968: 169–70, 173; cp. Chantornvong 1981: 194)

What exactly he means by "of a more secular nature" is not clear to me. But it is certain that, in Thailand at least, recitation could add elements which an innocent reading of the Pali text or translation, in modern, individual silent form, might not lead one to expect. Brereton (1995: 61), citing Gerini (1976: 25), says that sponsoring a recitation of the whole story is

> a festival of . . . great magnitude [which] requires considerable investment of material resources by the faithful, who are rewarded not only with a wealth of future merit, but also with an evening of entertainment by monks skilled at reading. In the past, certain monks deliberately injected pathos, bawdy humor, and special effects into their recitations to attract large numbers of appreciative listeners. Nowadays, portable movie projectors and giant screens set up next to the preaching hall serve that purpose.

[47] I have added this gloss, which seems to be the logic of his remarks.

"The orthodox people who frown" included those in the government of Rāma I, discussed in the General Introduction: Denis writes,[48] concerning recitations of VJ and the "Story of the Elder Māleyyadeva," with which it is, as has been seen, closely connected:

> These recitations led often to excess. The crowd liked reciters who acted the part of their characters and did not hesitate to make use of comic gestures and tones. A decree of 1801 legislated on the subject: "on the occasion of funerals, the "master of ceremonies" is forbidden to invite monks to recite the P'rah Malai; only the P'rah Aph'ith'amma [the *Abhidhamma*] is to be recited in an ordinary tone, not in the Indian, Chinese, European or Mon tones . . . If there are laypeople who want to recite the P'rah Malay, they may do so, but should avoid a comic tone [*un ton plaisant (drole)*] . . ."
>
> A law of 1782 had already warned monks against reciting the P'rah Malay and similar texts in a theatrical manner . . . "Monks who preach the Law and laity who listen to the [*Vessantara-jātaka*] should use the Pali [text] and the Commentaries; if they want to meet [Metteyya] in the future, they should not use rhyming texts, and the comical, theatrical manner of representing P'rah Malay, which is an offence against the Vinaya."

McClung (1975: 206–17) provides a brief account of a scene in *The Story of Khun Chang and Khun Phaen*, which can be taken as the kind of thing which could happen at a recitation of the Vessantara story. It recounts "the rivalry of two noblemen [the eponymous characters], a rivalry both in their careers in the royal service and over the hand of the heroine, Nang Phim. The tale is set in the early sixteenth century." In one early episode, Khun Phaen is temporarily a novice monk (he later leaves the Order to become a soldier). As a novice he memorizes the text of the Vessantara story, "along with other chants used by the monks on ritual occasions. Not only [does] he know the words perfectly, he [has] a charming voice and a good rhythm as well." He is asked to recite the story on one ritual occasion, of which both Khun Chang and Nang Phim are sponsors; Khun Chang sponsors "the most important and popular" section, on the Children, while Nang Phim sponsors the next section, on Maddī. Khan Chung is a "rich, though bald and ugly merchant [who has] designs on the beautiful young Phim." He dresses up carefully for the occasion, as does Phim: bathing, powdering and oiling herself, she admires her "radiant complex-

[48] From an unpublished thesis, cited in Collins (1993a: 12–13).

ion in the mirror". She puts on a red skirt, "with flame designs of dazzling color . . . an upper garment of soft pink . . . and a shawl of ruby-red, resplendent with flowers embroidered in gold" (a mode of dress which draws her mother's loud disapproval). "Thus attired (interjects the poet) she was a sight to refresh the heart of any man who looked her way."

As the novice entered the pavilion he saw Nang Phim and was immediately dazzled by her beauty. Phim returned his look with amorous glances of her own. Drawing on his knowledge of magical spells [Khun Phaen] focused his gaze intently on Nang Phim and silently muttered incantations which would bind her eyes and heart to him. At that very moment Phim felt a quiver of sexual thrill and desire for the novice sweep over her. [Khun Phaen] kept up his intense stare until the young woman made a slight nod of assent in his direction.

Clearly Khun Phaen's recitation skills are not matched by any great achievements on the path of desirelessness. When his mellifluous recitation reaches the scene where Maddī weeps for the absent children, "the audience, both men and women, were touched with feelings of deep piety, and began exclaiming aloud "sāthu, 'sāthu.' "[49] Nang Phim removes her red shawl, and puts it on the offering tray for the monks, "with prayers and gestures of homage and respect . . . asking that in the future rank, wealth and riches of all sorts might be hers." Khun Chang, irritated and jealous, removes his own outer garment and presents it to the monks, accompanying the gesture with words which both deprecate Nang Phim and express his desire for her. His words anger her: she spits in disapproval, and has her servant pick up her offering tray and carry it disrespectfully over his head. Phim's sister rebukes the servant and urges her sister to go home immediately. "Nang Phim's part of the celebration was thus brought abruptly to an end in disgrace and public humiliation." The unseemly displays put on by both Nang Phim and Khun Chang require as background a quiet and dignified atmosphere, in which everyone recognizes the beauty of the recitation, and feels the pathos of the scenes involving the children and Maddī. This is a story, but it would seem to represent a quite normal situation: ascetic heroism and distressed emotion recollected in festive tranquillity, along with the

[49] More usually spelt *sādhu.* This cry of approval at sermons was mentioned in 3.3, p. 252 and n. 29 above.

continuing agitation and "business" of everyday life. Such would have been a typical *Sitz im Leben* of the Vessantara story.

The evidence given in this section is anecdotal; but it suggests, I hope, that the meanings and values which the text of VJ brings into being could be added to and/or changed by its performative context. The heightening of emotion worked by Vessantara's and Maddī's ordeal could be both diversified and intensified by the elaborate ceremonial decoration of the preaching-place, by the vocal skills of the reciters, by the audience's hopes for future felicity, whether in Metteyya's unprecedented well-being or elsewhere, and above all by the extraordinary way in which the story intersperses into its "tragic" embodiment of the moral dilemmas posed by nirvanic soteriology a panoply of Buddhist felicities.

7.5. SUMMA FELICITATIUM

The Oxford Latin Dictionary gives as meanings for *summa* "the full extent, sum-total," "any complex unity, a whole," and "the crowning stage, culmination, completion"; Du Cange's *Glossarium Mediae at Infimae Latinitatis* has "epitome, synopsis, compendium." To make the medievalist analogy complete one might say VJ is a *summa felicitatium contra* or *adversus dukkham*, though the addition is pleonastic. Buddhaghosa's *Visuddhimagga*, translated by Ñāṇamoli (1975) as *The Path of Purification*, is often called the Theravāda *summa theologica*. That work contains many stories, but they are introduced to elucidate ideas and images in a text which is very firmly a product of systematic thinking. From the perspective of what I would like to think is a comprehensive intellectual and cultural history of Buddhism, VJ has as much reason to stand at the center of attention as the *Visuddhimagga*. VJ gives expression to suffering, drama and value-conflict, but also to the whole gamut of Buddhist felicities, both directly and indirectly. It is, as I hope to have shown, an intricate and tightly woven text, in which the themes abstracted here for analysis do not appear separately but occur together in a continuous and smoothly flowing narrative. The best way to describe the kinds of felicity found in it is to be purely formal, and list them under Davis' types of ideal society; in this way the formalism can be seen to rest in my text, not that of VJ. Although the events and motifs do fit fairly well into

Davis' categories, there will inevitably be imprecisions and overlaps. Once again, this classification of ideal societies and states is used purely as a descriptively convenient device, and as an avenue for comparative connections, for those who wish to make them.

The Land of Cockaygne

(i) The wealth which comes to Sañjaya's kingdom after the birth of Vessantara (485/8–9);

(ii) Vessantara as a wishing-tree (502/25) – compare also Jūjaka's use of tree-images for his munificence (526/45–6);

(iii) Vessantara's wish that "celestial food" appear every night, just before dawn (572/78);

(iv) Maddī's breasts spontaneously giving milk, saving the life of her children (586/90);

(v) Sakka's lotus-leaf shower (ibid.) and his rain of jewels (593/96).

Arcadia

(i) The extensive and continually repeated descriptions of the beauties of the forest, couched in lyrical verse, and sometimes in actual songs (4.3.a);

(ii) Vessantara's and Maddī's living the simple life, by turns that of soft and hard primitivism (see p. 519 n. 26 above) (519/39–592/95 *passim*, and repeatedly before then in anticipation).

Millennialism

(i) Internal to the text, the orientation towards the future Buddha Gotama (see below);

(ii) external to the text, the connection between listening to VJ and seeing the future Buddha Metteyya (5.2.c).

The Perfect Moral Commonwealth

(i) The motif of pardoning prisoners, one of the wishes made by Phusatī (483/7) and Vessantara (572/78);

(ii) the closing scene, Vessantara's entry into kingship, where he offers a Mode 2 bonus to the Mode 1 virtues of the Good King; the problem of scarce resources is solved by the rain of jewels; the problem of punishment is ignored, or perhaps one is to assume that Vessantara's virtue will close the law courts, for lack of crime and litigation (592–3/95–6).

This last point, Vessantara as leader of a Perfect Moral Commonwealth, needs some discussion. Vessantara is addressed as a king throughout the text, although he appears to remain subordinate to his father Sañjaya. At 486/11 Sañjaya wants to hand over the kingship to him, so he has him married to Maddī; next, the text says "he anointed the Great Being in the kingship." Because of subsequent events, CG add in square brackets "as his viceroy." Vessantara is still subject to Sañjaya's command, since he accepts his judgment of exile. Thus while the virtues Vessantara displays can be taken to be relevant to those of an ideal king, before the closing scene he is not fully king, so awkward issues of reconciling his extreme liberality and nonviolence with mundane needs of social order do not arise directly – at least not yet. When he does fully assume kingship, after the reconciliation scene in the forest and triumphal return to the city, the narrative consists solely in a grand (if brief) finale; the audience is left to imagine the nature of his reign, if it so wishes. No doubt, as suggested earlier, he can be seen along the lines of king Brahmadatta in the "Birth Story on Advice to Kings" (6.4.b), who defeats crime and avoids the need for punishment by the strength of his virtue.

As well as the "utopian" fantasies one can classify in terms of Davis' categories, other kinds of well-being are evoked in the text: most obviously, the tenderness between Vessantara and Maddī, along with their love for the children, both as expressed explicitly and as implicit in their sufferings. In both their marital and parental relations affection and pain are expressed in strikingly physical, at times sensual terms. To a certain extent relations among Vessantara's nuclear family are echoed in those between them and his parents, Sañjaya and Phusatī. It is true that all these forms of familial happiness are more often evoked by their absence or rupture than by their presence; but they are nonetheless clearly evoked for that. The striking, sometimes violent language used to depict Vessantara's and Maddī's feelings for their children make it quite obvious that for this text these are not mean, selfish emotions to be discarded by a hero or heroine on the sure march to spiritual eminence: they are affective and physical realities whose renunciation is difficult and painful. Traditional audiences would have found these values of their everyday emotional life valorized in the text, by their being so strongly evoked; the comparison of Vessantara to a drunk, the remark that he put a ransom price on his children like someone valuing oxen, and the like, would have enabled them to feel – though not, indeed, to articulate in this way – that his spiritual heroism is, from the mundane point of view, offensive, in Gellner's Kierkegaardian sense.

When Sañjaya and his company go to the forest, preparations for the procession, the procession itself, and the month-long sports festival held there, all take place in the kind of atmosphere of carnival evoked by the History of the Future, when describing conditions at the time of Metteyya. And indeed the two texts are connected by more than shared themes. As discussed in 5.2.c, the hope that listening to VJ will result in rebirth at the time of Metteyya has been found for centuries in Theravāda countries; and this external millennial relation to the future Buddha Metteyya is paralleled by the orientation toward the future Buddha Gotama internal to VJ. McClung's (1975) doctoral dissertation makes much of this parallel, and I cite his concluding remarks at length here, both to give him credit for an original and creative use of the idea of utopianism, but also to suggest ways in which one can now be more precise, and can take the analysis further.[50] His last two paragraphs, which follow after a discussion of the connection made between listening to VJ and meeting Metteyya, in modern ritual contexts replete with symbolic wishing-trees, are:

> Early in our study we asked the question whether nirvana is in any sense a relevant goal toward which Buddhists strive, or whether it has been subverted as a goal by the hedonistic desire for pleasurable rebirths. Our response to that question in the course of this investigation has been to suggest a third possibility: namely, that these two apparently contradictory goals have been synthesized into a single vision of a utopian society in which the conflict between transcendent and mundane values[51] will completely disappear. The kingdom of the world will merge

[50] McClung (1975: 33) cites a passage in Spiro (1970: 473) which refers in a general way to "the social function of utopian values"; but the specific use of it in relation to VJ is, as far as I know, original to McClung.

[51] For McClung these terms translate *lokottara* and *laukika* (Pali *lokuttara, lokiya*). This dichotomy, though analogous to my use of the terms "transcendent" and "mundane" in the General Introduction I.c, where they have the historical-sociological sense used by Eisenstadt and others, is in the first instance addressed to concerns quite different from that usage. In the last two chapters I have sought to make the sociological use more precise by speaking instead of Dhamma Modes 1 and 2.

with the kingdom of Buddha and all obstacles that separate men will be removed. At that time nirvana will be easily realizable within the world itself; indeed life at that time will be nirvana. Suffering will cease to be a characteristic of human existence; not because desires will be overcome, but because they will be satiated. Desire and grasping will be eliminated from the world along with the elimination of need in that glorious realm in which *lokottara* and *laukika* reality will perfectly coalesce.

The deepest significance of the *Vessantara Jātaka*, we propose, lies in its value as a paradigm for this utopian vision. It portrays a wonderful world of the past, when a righteous and generous monarch was on the throne and all men's desires were fulfilled. That age is now lost. But with the recital of this story its memory is revived and eager anticipation is aroused for the marvelous golden age which lay ahead – a time in which the vision of the way things ought to be will once again become the reality of the way things are. (1975: 232–3)

This is both instructively right and instructively wrong.[52] In part the errors are due to enthusiasm in the Christian style ("the kingdom of the world" and "the kingdom of Buddha"), in part to an impressionistic, associationist logic. McClung runs together reports of modern ethnography and a vague idea of what the History of the Future says about the time of Metteyya,[53] and reads them into VJ. As can be seen from the translation of the History of the Future in 5.2.b, it is wrong to say (as is obvious from the whole structure of Buddhist thought about felicity) that "life at that time will be nirvana." Many people will attain final nirvana then, but some will not. The millennial hope for rebirth with Metteyya is not the aspiration to a history-culminating, *somehow* timeless beatitude. While it will indeed be for some the final life in *saṃsāra*, it will be for some others, as the twelfth-century Burmese king Alaungsithu hoped (5.2.d), a stepping-stone on their own path to future Buddhahood. The majority of the continuing sites for consciousness propelled by karma through *saṃsāra*'s space and time will simply go on as before. As said in 3.2.c, given an infinite number of beings, and an infinity of future Buddhas, there can be no end to history. And however much in any spatiotemporal location – whether Metteyya's millennium or elsewhere – desires may be sati-

[52] It will be clear from my remarks in the General Introduction III.a that I find the language of a pure and original idea of nirvana "subverted . . . by the hedonistic desire for pleasurable rebirths" inappropriate.

[53] He relies (pp. 65–6) for his knowledge of the *Anāgatavaṃsa* on secondary sources, one of which is itself reliant on other secondary sources, which do not describe conditions in the time of Metteyya at all, but those on the island continent Uttarakuru (see 4.2.a).

ated, it flies against all Buddhist psychology and philosophy to suggest that desire can be eliminated, in the long term, by such means. On the contrary, nirvana cannot be attained when life is so good that beings have few desires unfulfilled, as in the heavens or in Uttarakuru: one must wait for rebirth as a human being in Jambudīpa.

McClung is nonetheless right to perceive in VJ (and analogously in the History of the Future and in rituals which associate the two) a coming together of different kinds of imagined felicity; but this coming together is not one of a distinction-obliterating, synthesizing kind. Traditional Buddhists were just as good at making distinctions as we are, and there is no need to assume that in a rush of confused enthusiasm such fundamental ideas and images as desire and its overcoming, conditioning and the Unconditioned, temporality and timelessness, are simply being ignored. One can appreciate the novelty and the achievement of VJ's *summa felicitatium* without changing anything about Buddhism; it is in the interpretative, etic perspective that changes must be made. The most fundamental such change, as stressed throughout this book, is the understanding of nirvana as a syntactic value, implicit in the expression of, rather than being an alternative to the semantic values of narratively imaginable well-being: decentered from the manifest level of "Buddhist thought," but recentered, as in VJ, at the latent level.

In VJ, as outlined here, every kind of Buddhist felicity appears, most of them elaborately expressed. The final, ultimate felicity of nirvana hardly appears on the surface level of the text, with two exceptions. One is in a minor scene at the beginning of the story, where one of two princesses (the other of whom is reborn eventually as Phusatī), is reborn at the time of the previous Buddha Kiki, becomes a nun and attains nirvana (481/5–6). Although a very minor scene in itself, this has the function of establishing at the outset the hierarchy of felicities, with nirvana at its summit. The other is the repeated mention of Vessantara's aspiration to Omniscience, which is in *Jātaka* stories a synonym for the enlightenment of a Buddha.[54] But the final nirvana of the Buddha Gotama is the story's *raison d'être*, everywhere present as the

[54] One might compare this with the use of *bodhi* as a synonym and replacement for nirvana in Mahāyāna texts.

implicit teleology of Vessantara's sufferings. Indeed, the story of the giving away of the children and Maddī's distress, where the text pulls no punches in evoking fear and pity in its audience, can only have its proper effect, and Vessantara's fortitude can only be understood, in the light of that ultimate, transcendental goal. Were it not for that, for traditional Buddhists as much as for anyone else this story would not be "offensive" in the sense in which Gellner attributes the characteristic to all ideologies, but simply offensive in the ordinary sense of the word.

What is so striking about VJ is not any new departure from what is central to the Pali imaginaire as a whole, but the extraordinary grace and economy with which the story both sings its songs of happiness – natural beauty and abundance, Arcadian peacefulness, millennial hope, an ideal society under a king who knows and does what is right (including the Mode 2 transcendental-bonus form), and all along the reassurance and hope engendered by the sense of an ending in Gotama's nirvana – and at the same time cries its lament for the vividly evoked joys and comforts of marital and family life, affective and physical.

In Buddhist systematic thought, time is an epiphenomenon of the conditioning process. In its narrative thought, time is constituted by stories, songs and laments. Other texts make time and temporal duration a principal focus of their attention (3.4); but nowhere else in the Pali imaginaire is the discourse of temporal felicity so richly condensed, or so elegantly and intensely combined with the conflict between everyday happiness and the renunciation required for the felicity of timeless nirvana, as in the *Vessantara Jātaka.* In the abstract perspective of Buddhist systematic thought the real tragedy of everyday happiness is simply to be in time, to be in a story, at all. To narrate felicity, from that point of view, is to adjudge it, ultimately, unsatisfactory. *Sunt lacrimae rerum.*

Conclusion to part 2

IN WHAT SENSE CAN ONE SPEAK OF BUDDHIST UTOPIANISM?

The General Conclusion takes up again the overall sense, introduced in the General Introduction III.d, in which I am using the category of utopia – as eu-topia and ou-topia – in relation to the discourse of felicity in the Pali imaginaire. This conclusion to Part 2 addresses narrower issues concerning the typology of ideal societies taken from Davis (1981) to organize the Buddhist ideas and stories in Part 2. As stated in the Introduction to Part 2, I want these terms to sit lightly on the Buddhist materials: nothing essential to my description or analysis of Pali texts is dependent on these labels and definitions. The aim in using them has been to suggest one avenue for comparative understanding, and invite one kind of comparative reflection. Many others are possible. Even for these purposes, indeed, the typology is not obligatory: other scholars may for their own purposes want to criticize, subtract from and/or supplement Davis' terms. Krishan Kumar, for instance, in a useful textbook (1991: 3–19), differentiates utopia from other "varieties of the ideal society or the ideal condition of humanity": the Golden Age, Arcadia, Paradise, the Land of Cockaygne, the Millennium and the Ideal City. The last has considerable resonance with the Buddhist imagery of nirvana as a city, as also with the city of heaven. (The differences in approach between Kumar and Davis do not rest merely in typology, and I return to them below.)

The minutiae of definitional debate can be exasperating, but the exercise can also be informative.[1] The most general

[1] I thus agree with Kenyon when he says, speaking of *Utopian Communism and Political Thought in Early Modern England*, that "only by advancing stipulative operational definitions can the necessary clarity [for analysis] be attained" (1991: 24). Typologies of utopia are legion: see, *inter alios*, Dawson (1992: 6–7) for ancient Greece, and Eliav-Feldon (1982: 1–5) for the European Renaissance.

interpretation of utopia in recent scholarship is in Levitas (1990: 190–2), who rejects all restrictive definitions in terms of the form, function or content of utopias, and suggests that "the essential element [is] desire – the desire for a better way of being." She distinguishes such desire from "hope for a better world," since utopias need not involve the postulation of alternative and possible worlds. Some utopian dreams may be just dreams, consciously or otherwise, and the better way of being which utopias envisage "does not always involve the alteration of external conditions, but may mean the pursuance of spiritual or psychological states." Such a wide definition is informative within the framework of her discussion, and is in one way welcome to my own. The internal-mental forms of well-being experienced in some celestial realms of Buddhist cosmology, the Brahma heavens, are identical to those attained in states of meditation (4.1.b). Since individual consciousness can take nirvana as its object, at stages of the Path before as well as after enlightenment (1.2.b), nirvana can from this perspective be an element in – more precisely, the "object-condition" (*ārammaṇa-paccaya*) for – what can be called a "spiritual" state. On the other hand, nirvana in itself – more precisely, as an Existent (*dhamma*) with an "essential nature" (*sa-bhāva*) – is external to consciousness (1.2.b, 1.3), albeit that it is certainly not a *world*, in Buddhist terms a Destiny (*gati*) within the universe. If Levitas' definition is applied to nirvana, the English word "desire" immediately runs afoul of Buddhist distinctions between

(i) unwholesome and de-meritorious Craving (*taṇhā*) or Attachment (*upādāna*),
(ii) forms of desire (*kāma*) which can be meritorious and wholesome but which still operate within the samsāric world of Conditioning Factors, and
(iii) the aspiration to nirvana, which must be or become free of Craving and the Corruptions even to discern the real nature of its object, let alone attain it (1.4).

So Levitas' definition is usefully nonexclusive, but it is too broad, and too imprecise when mapped onto Buddhist categories, to be of much value for my purposes.

What value does Davis' typology have, apart from its use as an organizational device? As mentioned in the Introduction to Part 2, and as has been made clear in Chapters 4–7, given Davis' stipulative definition of the word there is no Buddhist utopia. That is, there is no imagined human society of the normal productive and reproductive kind where, in his words, "the collective problem [is solved] collectively, that is by the reorganization of society and its institutions, by education, by laws and by sanctions." "Utopia," in his view, "is a holding operation, a set of strategies to maintain social order and perfection in the face of the deficiencies, not to say hostility, of nature and the willfulness of man" (1981: 37–8). In making this point I do not mean to offer another example of the familiar Orientalist practice of describing a non-western culture in terms of the lamentable absence of some characteristic feature of European-American tradition. The absence of utopias under this definition, I suggest, is on the contrary a sign of good sense on the part of Buddhism, and other traditional ideologies in South Asia: for this kind of ideal society all too often ends, perhaps inevitably ends – and sometimes also begins – as a dystopia of regimentation and the increasingly strict imposition of discipline. As Davis puts it, "Utopia represent[s] an image of triumph over *fortuna*, over the endless play of accident and fate in the lives of men": thus this kind of utopia's "prime aim is not happiness, that private mystery, but order, that social necessity" (1981: 378).

There are many different areas of human behavior where the demands of social order can conflict with the pursuit of happiness; but perhaps the difficulty of organizing society according to a predetermined blueprint is nowhere more evident than in sexual-reproductive relations, where the organizational and institutional form of utopian impulse comes into conflict with what Weber described memorably as "the peculiar irrationality of the sexual act, which is ultimately and uniquely unsusceptible to rational organization" (1963: 238). The eighteenth- and nineteenth-century history of European and (especially) American experiments in communal utopian living which included sexual-reproductive relations amply bears witness to the difficulties. It is not surprising, then, to find that in European tradition, the monastery has been a significant model for utopianism: "many of the early modern utopians [were] drawn to the monastic model, for the monastery in its discipline, structures, rituals and rules of life had sought to subdue sinful nature in servitude to a perfect or holy commonwealth."[2] I argued

[2] Davis (1981: 371); cf. Frye (1965: 333), Séguy (1971), Kumar (1991: 65).

in an earlier article that in European tradition the monastic model also provided, via its use in utopianism, a model for at least some aspects of social thought more generally. This was a model with a number of undesirable features, notably the conception of "society" as something composed of individual adults (males) dissociated from reproductive-kinship ties, entering into associative relations through a rational contract, explicit or implicit (Collins 1988: 115–20). The Buddhist celibate Monastic Order can be seen as an example of a formal organization dedicated to two central aspects of rationality, as Weber defined it: "the kind of rationalization the systematic thinker performs on the image of the world: an increasing theoretical mastery of reality by means of increasingly precise and abstract concepts"; and "the methodical attainment of a definitely given and practical end by means of an increasingly precise calculation of adequate means."[3] But in traditional Buddhism the rationalized organization of the celibate Monastic Order was never taken to be a paradigm form of human society generally. I have tried to show elsewhere (Collins 1994) that premodern Pali texts offer no all-embracing theory of society in general: the only ideal collectivity which defines and thus constitutes agents according to specifically Buddhist principles is the subgroup of the Monastic Order. The monastic milieu of Buddhist agency, to use Frye's (1965: 325) words on "the utopian romance" in general, "does not present [its] society as governed by reason [directly]; it presents it as governed by ritual habit, or prescribed social behavior, which is explained rationally." For ordinary social action Buddhism has been content to adopt whatever local modes of agent-definition happen to have existed (kinship, caste, patron–client matrices, etc.).

Considering Davis' stipulative definition of utopia (dystopia) allows one thus to see more clearly the nature of Buddhist ideology, and the relation between its enunciation of social/cosmic order and "social theory" in European tradition. Although Buddhism offers no example of Davis' category of utopia I think it

[3] Collins (1988, 1994, 1997). The quotations are from Weber (1948: 293); the former was cited in the General Introduction p. 108. The mastery of reality through concepts is most evident, of course, in the systematic thought discussed in Chapter 1; the methodical attainment of ends describes the rationality of the whole of the Buddhist Path, but it may be seen with especial clarity in the textual discussions of the Meditation Levels and the progressive refinement of happiness they provide (4.1.b).

will be evident from the preceding chapters that in the everyday sense of the word quoted from the OED in the Introduction to Part 2 – "a place, state or condition ideally perfect in respect of politics, laws, customs and conditions" – it contains, ignoring some inappropriate senses of the word "perfect," a great deal of utopianism, much more indeed than textbook presentations of Buddhist "doctrine" – that is, its systematic thought – might suggest. In this imprecise sense there is clearly a great deal of Buddhist utopianism. Kumar, whose typology I referred to earlier, prefers a stricter definition of "utopia" than Davis', one which restricts it to European-American tradition. According to him, utopia is "first and foremost a work of imaginative fiction in which, unlike other such works, the central subject is the good society" (1991: 27). This is different from utopian theory as a subcategory of social or political thought: "utopia is not just the conception of the good or perfect society. It is a particular and distinctive way of discussing the good society. It has its own form" (1991: 37). He says:

> When Thomas More coined the word utopia in 1516 he invented more than a word, he invented a new form. His *Utopia* is different from anything that had appeared before in the classical or Christian world. It is also different from anything we find in the non-Christian world . . .
>
> There is no tradition of utopia and utopian thought outside the Western world. (1990: 33)

For Kumar "narrative fiction [is] the defining form" of utopia, and so he disagrees with Davis' suggestion that since political theory deals in fictions such as "sovereignty," "the dialectic," "the general will," and the like, utopianism as a form of such theory can be classed in a single category with works of narrative fiction (1991: 28, citing Davis 1981: 17). He thus prefers to distinguish between utopianism in social and political thought, which he calls "utopian theory" or "utopian thought," and "utopia" proper, which is the specific narrative form invented by Thomas More. He claims that neither utopia nor utopian theory is found outside the West, on the grounds that "nowhere in these societies do we find the practice of writing utopias, of criticizing them, of developing and transforming their themes and exploring new possibilities within them" (1991: 33).

As I said in the Introduction to Part 2, introducing Davis' categories, restrictive definitions of terms which enjoy wider currency in everyday language can only serve the interests, temporarily, of the intellectual project for which they were produced, or for which they are adopted. The definitions of *utopia* offered by Levitas, Davis, and Kumar all seem to me useful for their individual purposes; and I do not want to urge a general acceptance of loose, everyday usage in academic writing. But it would be a shame if such restrictive definitions (in Levitas' case, a broad and Buddhistically imprecise one) should blind us to the quantity and variety of Buddhist cultural production which it seems legitimate to call utopian in an ordinary and easily comprehensible sense. Perhaps a simple distinction between nouns and adjectives might help here. The case of Utopianism is similar to that of other category terms such as Philosophy, History and Autobiography: if one defines these western traditions in terms of a self-conscious and genre-specific relation to ancient Greek or early modern European origins, there cannot be non-western Philosophy, History or Autobiography. But against this must be set an experience familiar to everyone studying non-western culture(s), and one felt also, I hope, by readers of this book: encountering texts and passages within texts, patterns of thought, description, and argument, which are unproblematically called philosophical, historical, or autobiographical.[4] Scholarship in crosscultural epistemology and the history of ideas must indeed acknowledge that nouns such as Philosophy or Utopianism in English very often do refer, in a genre-specific and self-conscious sense, to traditions of intellectual practice in Europe and America, for which precise counterparts outside the west scarcely ever exist. But it is also true – unsurprisingly if one starts from the presumption of a shared humanity – that these *styles* of thought and cultural production are readily visible elsewhere. It is crucial to my comparative point here to note the argument holds in reverse, concerning South Asian categories and European tradition, although it is rarely made in this direction: "what a shame Europe knows no *Purāṇa*-s! But at least we can recognize texts there which have purāṇic elements." In Part 2, I have clothed what are clearly forms of Buddhist utopianism, in an imprecise sense, in the loose-fitting garb of Davis' modes of ideal society. It is not my concern here to argue for any particular position or redefinition within Utopian Studies, considered as a sub-discipline of sociology or social theory, using

[4] For autobiography see Gyatso (1997).

Buddhist materials: were I or others to do so, the presence and distribution of "utopianism" in Buddhism, as a specifiable and definable intellectual practice, would depend entirely on the definitions employed.[5]

Writers in this area commonly agree on the importance of one aspect of utopianism: that it tends to envisage states of collective rather than individual well-being. Levitas shows successfully that all restrictive definitions of utopia, even those which make it necessarily or primarily collective, end up leaving out something or other that can, from some perspective, be seen as legitimately utopian. But her own suggestion – that because it need not assume that what it envisages should be possible "the essential element in utopia is not hope but desire – the desire for a better way of being" – itself runs the risk of being pointlessly wide, welcoming in its capacious embrace what are merely personal whims. If I desire, being incapable of playing the piano at all, to wake up tomorrow able to play like Keith Jarrett, am I being "utopian"? Such a use of the concept seems misplaced.

Of the Buddhist felicities I have described, some are individual and some are not. Nirvana is "to be experienced individually by the wise" (1.1.c). The pleasures of meditation, whether on earth or in the corresponding Brahma-worlds (4.1.a–b) are individual and inward. One can say that some felicities are social but not intrinsically so, such as some of the temporary "Lands of Cockaygne" in 4.2.b: Niggardly Kosiya the Millionaire Miser, for example, would no doubt have very much liked to have access to an entirely private wishing-tree, as do a number of gods in the Deva-heavens (4.1.d). In many of the situations described in Chapters 4 and 5 the forms of well-being are experienced alongside others, but the shared

[5] Had I adopted Kumar's list of "varieties of the ideal society and the ideal condition of humanity," it would have been necessary to define "Paradise," to discuss in what special ways nirvana is an "ideal city" (it is certainly not a "talking picture," travelogue form of narrative), and to say that there is no true myth of a "Golden Age" in Buddhism. Some aspects of the description of the start of the cosmic eon in the "Discourse on What is Primary" (*Aggañña Sutta),* notably the growth of unhusked rice, ready to eat (Appendix 5 section 16), do appear in other utopian contexts (such as the History of the Future: 5.2.b v. 27 and n. 36) and might seem to constitute a Golden Age motif. But even where in the later literature, as arguably not in the *Aggañña Sutta* itself, this state of "beings" is taken to refer, in a straightforward, quasi-historical manner, to a condition occurring at the start of each eon, the motif is too restricted in scope, in my view, to constitute a Buddhist version of the Golden Age.

aspect is not essential to the well-being itself. In the (more or less) Perfect Moral Commonwealths discussed in Chapters 5.2.b, 6 and 7, on the other hand, the very idea of a kingdom over which a good and just king reigns implies collective life. And here, of course, one must acknowledge the oscillation in Buddhist texts between the imagining of such an ideal society and the denial, direct or indirect through irony, that any such thing is possible. In the real, historical world in which the Pali imaginaire was preserved and transmitted, the most anyone could expect from a "Buddhist" king was that he follow the not-specifically-Buddhist recipes for a Good King (6.4). But goodness in the Buddhist Mode 2 *dhamma*, soteriological sense could be for kings a useful bonus to add, in the ou-topia of royal rhetoric. The closest the Pali imaginaire comes to a social utopia is in the image of the Wheel-turning king (cf. Tambiah 1984b), whose beneficent guidance maximizes mundane felicity for all and the possibility of the ultimate felicity of nirvana for some. The best example of such a utopia is the constant carnival of life under the emperor Saṅkha, in Metteyya's millennium.

General conclusion
Buddhism and civilizational history 2 reprise

This General Conclusion returns briefly to the large-scale perspective of the General Introduction, looking to discern structures and processes of Buddhism and civilizational history. I first describe how this book has constructed its argument; and then return to two points of historiographical method: the use of analytical dualism in the attempt to understand Buddhism as a social fact, a phenomenon of civilization, and the endeavor to combine thinking about the inside and the outside of Pali Buddhist texts together.

There have been a number of cycles of argument. The cycle in Part 1 focused on nirvana, trying to offer a multifaceted account of how it appears in the traditional Pali imaginaire as a concept in systematic thought, as an image, and as a moment in narrative, both in narrated time and in the time of narration. I argued that it is important to take account of all three modes of thought, separately and together, and to try to understand both what is said about nirvana and what is left unsaid about it in them, which both contribute to the extensive and concentrated textualization of time, and thus timelessness, to be found in Pali Buddhist texts. Nirvana provides the sense of an ending in both systematic and narrative thought. In the former it does so by providing closure and hence unification to the indigenous ethnography of Buddhism, which, to use Burghart's terms, objectified – i.e made a textual object of – the arena of Southern Asian society. In the latter it does so by providing a satisfactory sense of cessation instead of merely breaking off, as does life: to use Hernnstein Smith's terms, in Buddhist narratives nirvana creates the expectation of nothing which makes stasis, the absence of continuation, the most probable succeeding "event."[1] In both cases closure within the textual object stands in for closure outside it. The Conclusion to Part 1 suggested that imagery can be seen as a bridge between systematic and narrative thought, and argued that these are three modes not only of thought, for an individual, but also of tradition, for collectivities: not merely individual cognition and memory but modes of cultural meaning-construction and social memory.

The cycle in Part 2, asking "what is it like, in the Pali imaginaire, to live in conditions of happiness?", collected together many different Buddhist ideas and stories, or episodes from stories, which answer the question, using Davis' categories of ideal society to sort and present them. Part 2 was directly concerned with Buddhist eu-topias, and its Conclusion addressed briefly the issue of whether and how a comparative utopian studies might be possible. Both Parts 1 and 2 together were concerned to elaborate and exemplify what I mean by "the Buddhist discourse of felicity," aiming to show why I think nirvana should be both decentered and recentered within it: decentered from its manifest semantics but recentered as a latent but necessary syntactic element of all Buddhist aspirations to well-being. This is exactly the position it has in the *Vessantara Jātaka*.

In the cycle of argument of the book as a whole, from the General Introduction through Parts 1 and 2, I have been concerned with what is, for me, a more important sense of the word utopia: the ou-topianism of texts, No-places in history. Soteriologies, both questions and answers, are intrinsically matters of discursive representation; they are essentially textual (oral or written). Thus this book has in more than one sense been about felicities of expression: nice thoughts in a naughty world. I have wanted to extend the usual Weberian analysis of religion in terms of theodicy, to include the production of a discourse of felicity as a necessary element. It is because of this civilizational role of Buddhist felicities – as part of elite cultural traditions centrally involved in the coexistence and conflict of ideological and other forms of power – that I think nirvana must be decentered in the

[1] Quotes are needed because the event of nirvanizing, which is from the point of view of time expressed as a finite verb, is not, as are all other events, followed by more conditioned events, and thus more time.

study of premodern Buddhism, and seen as having had a place within the wider discourse of felicity just as asceticism had its place in the wider *Lebenswelt* of collective cultures.

But there is also a linear argument, along with these cycles, one which begins from the ascetic pinnacle of nirvana and the individual perfection of Buddhas and Arahants, and makes its way towards the Ideal Society (or ideals in society) and the *Vessantara Jātaka.* Books and articles on Buddhism often themselves end with a reference to nirvana, thus producing an analog to the Buddhist use of it to effect closure. But I have wanted to move in the other direction, back from the abstractions of systematic thought, and the a priori moral heroics they make so readily available to the imagination, as if the heroics were simply a matter of extending rationally into the practical domain an array of no-nonsense conceptual dichotomies deriving from that of the Conditioned/ Unconditioned; back, that is, to the lived frameworks of plausibility in which the Pali imaginaire confronted, and did its work of cultural transformation on, the refractory givens, individual and collective, of material, corporeal life. The universal Buddhist *dhamma* had either to inscribe violence within itself (no easy task, given the basic postulates of its soteriology), or to push it outside, and in so doing risk pushing itself outside any sphere of relevance to productive and reproductive communities. The quest for detachment, selflessness and universal love had to coexist with the foul rag-and-bone shop of the heart, in such a way as both to inspire and to leave intact the sexual and familial concerns of the majority. Kingship and kinship were nirvana's ever-present framework. The Buddhist enunciation of order was a civilizational vision which necessarily encompassed the transcendence of order in nirvana, at the same time as it preserved nirvana within its own discourse as the top rung on the ladder of asceticism, which the event of nirvanizing kicks away.

Section II of the General Introduction tried to specify precisely what kind of historiography is attempted in this book. The general picture of history it assumes, which I take to be an empirical hypothesis, is this: the premodern Pali imaginaire was an elite ideology, originally strongest in cities (often with branches in outlying forest regions), which over the course of the second millennium

AD moved, sociologically speaking, downwards and outwards, and at some point before or during the modern period became a "popular" or peasant religion. The reason for using the word ideology is that the Pali imaginaire was, amongst other things, a shared belief- and symbol-system among elites ruling trans-local political formations, paradigmatically in a *maṇḍala* of client-kings around a central monarch, which naturalized the social hierarchy of tribute-givers and tribute-takers. The issues of whether, when, and how far the ideology came to be shared by others than those in the dominant, tribute-taking class at any given time and place may be left open to empirical historical investigation; and variation is to be expected. As every modern ethnography has shown, what we can recognize as "Buddhist" ideas and practices have always and everywhere coexisted with localized supernaturalism (with some exceptions, again urban, in Buddhist modernism).

A recent study of the Shan in Northern Thailand by Tannenbaum (1995) illustrates the sort of approach I have in mind. Section I.a of the General Introduction quoted her contention that Theravāda Buddhism is "a marker of civilized identity [and] a rhetoric of justification," which distinguishes, in her case, lowland Shan from the neighboring hill-tribes, whom they regard as "uncivilized" (1995: 10). She argues, with considerable plausibility, that the fundamental logic of Shan religious practice, both Buddhist and what she calls "animist" (i.e. localized supernaturalist), is a nexus of ideas and practices she labels "power-protection": "Power implies protection. If one has access to power, one is protected; if one is protected, one has the power or freedom to do as one chooses" (1995: 80). This power-protection can be given to people and places by various means: tattoos, reading (or wearing) certain texts, performing certain rituals, keeping the Buddhist Precepts (which, in their stricter forms, is recognized as only rarely possible for ordinary people), and so on.[2] The beings with the greatest power are the five Buddhas of this world-period, including Metteyya; those with least power are beings in the lowest hell. I referred earlier to this nexus of ideas in the Critical Discussion of millennialism, citing Turton's (1991) study of magical invulnerability as an example of Thai "local knowledge." He remarks that "notions of invulnerability [seem] to have had an

[2] See also Bizot (1981), Tannenbaum (1987, 1991), Turton (1991).

important place in ideas and practices within peasant rebellions throughout South East Asia up to recent times . . . regardless of whether the dominant religious traditions were Buddhist Christian, Islamic, etc." (1991: 156). Tannenbaum shows that the Shan understanding and adoption of Buddhism is determined by a fundamental orientation to power-protection: the idea of not-self (*anattā*) as the third characteristic of all conditioned things (along with impermanence and suffering) is translated into Shan as "lack of control." As she recognizes, if perhaps a little belatedly at the end of her book (1995: 209), there is nothing in this which is inimical to the Buddhism of the Pali imaginaire. The argument from lack of control is the first of four arguments for the doctrine of not-self in Pali texts (Collins 1982: 97–8). But she is right to stress that the Shan select and emphasize this aspect of the doctrine, and de-emphasize or ignore other aspects; and right, I think, to suggest that this selection and emphasis are better understood by construing the Shan worldview directly, as a sociocultural phenomenon in itself, than by drawing inferences from what is understood (correctly or incorrectly) about a prior object called "Buddhism." And she is right, furthermore, to insist on the appropriateness for anthropological understanding of this etic, analytical point of view despite the fact that Shan will always identify themselves as "Buddhists," when asked. As she puts it (1991: 79): "An event labeled and identified as Buddhist cannot be interpreted solely within the ethical and moral system scholars have identified as 'Buddhism.'"[3]

To put the matter in my own words: at the particular place and time of her modern *reportage*, what is, as it were, on offer in the Pali imaginaire from the urban centers of civilization – in the modern period carrying for the Shan a specific inflection due to the fact that it is, in Thailand and Burma, and was until recent decades in Cambodia and Laos, a (nation-)state religion – is appropriated in a particular way to blend with local knowledge, and local practices.

[3] Here is a quite different example: recently at the University of Chicago, Professor Chao Huashan of Beijing University gave a slide-lecture on some caves in Central Asia, which had been thought Buddhist but had now been identified (by Professor Chao) as Manichean. The identification was made through an analysis of the iconography in the caves. The argument was convincing, but it struck me that the cave-dwellings and temples, high in the hills in a remote area, had in themselves a very impressive kind of chthonic monumentality, which was prior to and in some ways unaffected by their being either "Manichean" or "Buddhist." See Chao (n.d.).

(Of course, there is more on offer in "Theravāda Buddhism," or "the Pali Cultural Package" than simply the content of Pali texts.) And this, I think, is the way it has always been.[4] To repeat what was said in Chapter 7 (p. 541), people in what are called "Buddhist countries" are human beings first, and Buddhists (to a greater or lesser degree) second. They are human beings for whom Buddhist ideology, however much they might or might not view or wish to view the world from inside it, nonetheless remains, as Gellner put it, "something *within* the world, and *not* coextensive with it." In Northern Thailand – to stay in Tannenbaum's and Turton's ethnographic area – there are clearly elements from the Pali imaginaire both in the Shan worldview and in many of the movements called "millennial." Here, as elsewhere, we can best perceive exactly what they are, what role they play, and how they are related, on the one hand, to the "Buddhism" constructed by scholars (Buddhist and/or western), and to the relevant forms of local knowledge on the other, by treating separately these two aspects of the relevant Cultural System – in Archer's (1988) terminology – and by seeing them as analytically autonomous in relation to Socio-Cultural life in Southern Asia. This Socio-Cultural life has been lived, historically, first in the conditions of premodern agrarian states, and then in the context of modernization, nation-building, colonialism and capitalism referred to in the Critical Discussion in Chapter 5. Most ethnographies and histories do not make such a separation: hence the confusions which that discussion attempted to clarify, or at least to identify.

A vital methodological point can be brought out again here by stressing that the autonomy of the Pali imaginaire, local knowledge, sociocultural and historical context, etc., is *analytical*, not actual; it is a moment within a process of reflective understanding rather than a mode of descriptively accurate ethnography or history. The end result of such an analytical disaggregation should itself involve reintegration of the elements of analysis into a composite but single picture which will be sensitive to the particularities of any given time and place. Here it will be useful to return to Archer's words about the value of an analytical dualism which distinguishes Cultural System(s) from Socio-Cultural life: these two

[4] Compare (and contrast) Mabbett on premodern Champa in the first millennium AD, where various kinds of Buddhism were "part of the Great Tradition of the Court" (1986: 306).

spheres "do not exist or operate independently of one another; they overlap, intertwine and are mutually influential." But this is the point, since one is here "*not* asserting dualism but rather the utility of an *analytically* dualistic approach, the main recommendation for which is the very fact that it allows this interplay to be explored" (General Introduction II.e, p. 79). The point can be expressed in the Buddhist case by looking at some language used by S. J. Tambiah. He criticizes the work of Spiro on Burma, on the grounds that "rather than treat Burmese religion as a totality and a configuration, he wants to sever it into two opposed religions, Buddhism and animism" (1984: 315). In as much as this is true of Spiro, Tambiah is right. But he is wrong to propose a countermethod which aggregates data from a variety of textual, ethnographic and historical primary sources on what he calls "millennial Buddhism," and to characterize the latter as "a totality of beliefs, expectations, practices, and actions" (1984: 319). What is demarcated, sociologically and historically, by the category of "millennial Buddhism" is entirely unclear, without further analysis. The phrase "Burmese religion," on the other hand, refers quite clearly to everything falling under the category "religion" in a more or less specifically circumscribed geographical area.[5] As a descriptive term it includes elements of both Cultural System(s) and Socio-Cultural life, and as such can have neither the logical coherence of what Archer calls a Cultural System, nor the a priori and a posteriori coherence I claim can be found in the Pali imaginaire (my own analytical term).

Part of what Tambiah means by arguing that one should see Burmese religion as a "totality and a configuration" is close to Tannenbaum's suggestion that one look in the first instance for a structure and a logic in people's behavior in its own, local terms. Thus far I am in full agreement. He errs, in my view, in moving from this point to the syncretistic perception of a trans-temporal and unlocated "millennial Buddhism," and more generally in approaching Buddhism, in the style of Marcel Mauss,[6] as a "total

[5] Of course, there may be definitional disputes about what counts as "religion," and it is clearly necessary for historical purposes to realize that the current territory of the modern nation-state of Burma (Myanmar) is historically contingent and unlikely to be of much use in understanding premodern political formations and their relationship to space.

[6] In the next sentence he expresses indebtedness to Dumont; for criticism of Dumont's use of the Maussian search for "total social facts" see Collins (1989).

social fact" (1976: 5): "For me," he says, "Buddhism is a shorthand expression for a total social phenomenon, civilizational in breadth and depth, which encompasses the lives of Buddhist monks and laymen [*sic*], and which cannot be disaggregated in a facile way into its religious, political and economic realms as these are currently understood in the west" (1984: 7). "Religion," "politics" and "economics" are indeed often unlikely to be helpful as analytical terms for premodern Buddhism, and still less likely to be of any value as modes of description; but I do not think that it is helpful to construct a conglomerate called "Buddhism" which encompasses the lives of people for whom in one or more senses we or they find the term "Buddhist" appropriate. The collective life of people in certain areas of Southern Asia has encompassed "Buddhism," which should itself be seen as a scattershot category which regularly hits more targets than need to be aimed at (albeit that it remains indispensable as a shorthand).

I have tried to show that there is sufficient coherence in the Pali imaginaire – at least in the grand matters of time, death, happiness and wisdom with which this book has been concerned – to treat it as a Cultural System in abstraction from its (greater or lesser) imbrication and enmeshment in the Socio-Cultural life of countless millions of people in Southern Asia over countless generations. I have not been concerned here to explore directly the historical interplay between this Cultural System and Socio-Cultural life in any time and place, with two exceptions. The note on the concept of modernity appended to the General Introduction II.c did so briefly in relation to eighteenth- and nineteenth-century Thailand; and the Critical Discussion of millennialism did so in relation to twentieth-century Sri Lanka, Burma and Thailand. But I hope that what has been said about the Pali imaginaire, and its ou-topias in history, will make possible a more nuanced exploration of its changing interplay with human experience and action in different times and places than is possible through the "total social fact" approach. Mauss' idea may perhaps be useful in describing the cultural worlds of so-called "primitive" – i.e., *inter alia*, nonliterate – peoples who do not have objectified, civilizational traditions with autonomous ideological power, preserved by a professional class of clerics. It was characteristic of earlier generations of anthropologists to make a direct contrast between "primitives" (them) and the modern West (us), ignoring historical civilizations such as the

Southern Asian.[7] But in such civilizational contexts a strategy of understanding which first disaggregates elements of Cultural System(s) and Socio-Cultural life, before attempting to recombine them in an empirical-historical manner for particular places and times, seems to me more fruitful. This suggestion is, however, a hypothesis, or a promise, which this book cannot try to confirm, or fulfill, in any detailed way: but what has been said in the General Introduction and here is as close as I can get to a precise statement of the historiographical intentions in terms of which I want it to be read. In the strategy of understanding being proposed, the plurality of voices in the reception-situation of any one book, mentioned in the General Introduction II.e, is crucial. If this book is to be read properly as history it must be read together with other kinds of historiography on Southern Asia, examples of which were cited in the General Introduction II.e.

It is only by keeping the inside and the outside of texts separate in analysis that one can begin to put them together, with both their connections and their disconnections, in one's historical vision. Given the content of many of the texts this book discusses, and its use of the concept of ideology, an unsympathetic critic might say that what it has done is to take a Weberian-theodicy approach to Buddhism and add to it an account of what might be called, blending William James and Marx, "The Varieties of Buddhist Opium." I will plead guilty to the charge, but only if Marx's famous aphorism – that religion is the opium of the people – is seen both in its textual context and under a particular interpretation. (In its historical context, as has often been said, one might just as well say that in many poor urban areas in the early nineteenth-century opium was the religion of the people.) I wish neither to agree nor disagree here with his critical animus against "religion" in general; but a particular way of reading the sentence preceding his aphorism is indeed appropriate for the kind of understanding of traditional Buddhism attempted here: "Religion is the sigh of the oppressed creature, the feeling of a heartless world, the spirit of circumstances without spirit."[8] Some forms of oppression – the

[7] For remarks on the anthropology of India in this respect see Burghart (1985).

[8] English version in Marx (1976). *Die Religion ist der Seufzer der bedrängten Kreatur, das Gemüt einer herzlosen Welt, wie sie der Geist geistloser Zuständer ist* (Marx and Engels 57: 378). The word *Gemüt* has a range of meanings: feeling, heart, sensibility, warmth of character; the

kind Marx was writing about – are contingent and historically produced. But the oppression of passing time and the heartlessness of death constitute an always-already-given stimulus for the work of culture to infuse the spirit of cultural meanings into the material circumstances of particular worlds, particular frameworks of plausibility. If the Pali imaginaire functioned as an ideology of a tribute-taking class, later adopted by the tribute-giving class, it could succeed only if it engaged with genuinely basic features of the human predicament. One of these features is what Chapter 3 claimed is a human universal – the fact of being always and everywhere subject, simultaneously, to both linear/non-repetitive and cyclical/repetitive time.

It is perhaps enough to cite the *Vessantara Jātaka* to refute the charge that Buddhist felicities are wish-fulfilment fantasies in any simplistic or direct sense. It would be wrong to overstress the elements of tragedy in Vessantara's plight, since the final felicity of Gotama's nirvana is vital in making the story also a *summa felicitatium.* But the insistence, in this version of the story, on the sufferings and difficulties consequent on Buddhism's own most cherished ideals bears witness not only to the appropriateness of the text as an emblem of the Buddhist civilizational whole which encompassed the minority goal of asceticism, but also to the fact that, to borrow again LaCapra's phrases about art, "the escapist function of imaginary compensation for the defects of empirical reality" can coexist with "the contestatory function of questioning the empirical in a manner that has broader implications for the leading of life." What Gellner calls the "sex-appeal" of the hypotheses offered by Buddhist ideology – the fact that it is enticing – is not merely that it promises pie-in-the-sky, although it certainly does that. It is also that the spirit which it infuses into the material world of time and death is of such a kind – hierarchized with minority asceticism at its pinnacle – that the majority can only use it to contest the everyday empirical reality of their lived world, since the highest (nirvanic) perspective it offers must put into question any and every kind of felicity in that world[9].

In trying to see Buddhism with double vision – seeing the inside

related adjective *gemütlich* can be translated as "comfortable," and the noun *Gemütlichkeit* as "comfort'; and this might recall Wrigley's remarks about premodern aspirations to comfort, cited in the General Introduction III.a.

9 Conversations with Charles Hallisey have helped me see this point.

and the outside of Pali texts together – the task is not merely to keep in mind both the world of representation and the social, political, economic and other facts of the world it represented. It is also to combine historical realism with a willingness to allow the inside of texts to be susceptible of various interpretations: to allow, for example, that the subtlety of the relations between many of the ideas and stories discussed in Chapter 6 and the world on which they were a comment, and of which they were, in more than one sense, a reflection, is such that they resist being pigeonholed in simplistic categories such as "spirituality" or "legitimation." The *Mūgapakkha Jātaka* (the tale of prince Temīya) and the "Discourse on the Wheel-turning King," for example, can both, in their very different ways, be read as ironic, to a greater or lesser degree, by different people at the same time or by the same people at different times.

At the outset of this book I claimed that an alternative vision of the cultural possibilities of premodernity can be gained through acquaintance with the Pali imaginaire, as an element of Southern Asian Buddhism, itself seen as an element of Southern Asian civilization. That vision is not to be attained only by coming to see that Pali texts had a different way of categorizing the world, a different lexicon of systematic thought, important though it is to make that effort. The categories of Buddhist systematic thought are very thickly descriptive, and it is easy to despair of ever fully translating texts of that kind.[10] I think Hayden White is right to say, however, citing Barthes, that "narrative 'is *translatable* without fundamental damage'" in a way that a lyric poem or a philosophical discourse is not.[11] The "Structuralist Analysis of Narrative" proposed by Barthes is not relevant to the argument of this book, which has focused, rather, on the homologies between narrative, temporality and human experience, on the interplay between linearity/novelty and repetition/familiarity they both require and

[10] C. A. F. Rhys Davids' (1900) version of the *Dhammasaṅgani*, Buddhist Psychological Ethics," shows the problem all too well; more recent attempts, such as those by Ñāṇamoli (1982, 1987, 1991), are a significant improvement – but what can one seriously expect a modern philosopher to do with them, unless he or she is willing to invest a lot of time in studying Buddhism, and Pali language?

[11] White (1987: 1), citing Barthes (1977: 121). The claim can only be a relative one: it would be easy, though scarcely constructive, to argue that in some senses any translation of anything, still less a full translation, is next to impossible.

make possible, in *mimesis* and *poiesis*, and on the capacity of narrative to render intelligible and imaginable certain aspirations to felicity – life in heaven, for instance – which in systematic thought remain abstract possibilities, positions on a chart. But if his point about translatability is correct, it is entirely suitable that the wider eu-/ou-topian discourse of felicity within which I have tried both to decenter and to recenter nirvana, and the alternative premodernity to which that discourse gives access, only become fully visible when one admits narratives, in all their protean diversity, fully into one's understanding of the civilizational history of the Pali imaginaire. At least, that is one of the things this book has tried to propose.

Appendices

(Translated texts)

APPENDIX 1

Selections from the Buddhavaṃsa

Numbered verses are direct translations. The numbers are those of Jayawickrama's PTS edition of 1974, in which Chapter II, vv. 2 and 3 have three lines each; Horner's (1978) translation numbers them as 2–4, each with two lines, and so verses after this point are numbered one higher in her translation than in the text. Passages indented within square brackets are summaries. Gaps between verses indicate a new scene or theme.

CHAPTER 1: THE JEWELED WALKWAY

1.[1] Brahma Sahampati, the Lord of the World,[2] his hands together (reverently, in *añjali*), requested the peerless (Gotama Buddha, in these words): "There are beings in this world who have but little passion; take pity on them and teach the Doctrine (*dhamma*)."

[In vv. 2–5, Gotama agrees to Brahma Sahampati's request, in the first person singular of direct speech; in 6–63, the Redactor's voice depicts Gotama's making of the jeweled walkway, the arrival of large numbers of gods and other supernaturals, and the joyous scene they create, interspersing various remarks of praise addressed by the gods to the Buddha; then describes Sāriputta and other of his important monastic followers, who were present. In vv. 64–70 the Buddha tells of his previous birth in the Tusita heaven, as a god called Santusita, and subsequent rebirth on earth. In vv.71–8 the Redactor describes how Sāriputta (whose words are given in direct speech) asks the Buddha to recount the story of his resolve

[1] The first verse of the first chapter, which begins the narrative *in medias res*, is said by the commentary to have been spoken by Ānanda at the first Council, held immediately after the Buddha's death (Bv-a 11), and the second by the "Recensionists" (*saṅgītikārakehi*) *saṅgītikāle*, which can be translated either "at the time of the (First) Council," or "on the occasion of (each of) the Councils" (Bv-a 13); thereafter various narrative verses are assigned to "the Recensionists," or introduced simply by "so it was/is said" (*tena vuttaṃ*) or a variant thereof. I assign all these simply to "the Redactor." There are some minor difficulties of chronology within the opening story, corrected by the commentary, which need not be discussed here. [2] I.e. the oldest of the Great Brahmā gods (see 4.1).

to become a Buddha, and his acquisition of the Perfections needed for Buddhahood; and then continues:]

79. "By means of his knowledge concerning past lives, for the benefit of the world and its gods he expounded what had been taught about past Buddhas, Conquerors, [as it had been] celebrated and handed down by the lineage of [those] Buddhas.
80. [Gotama Buddha said:] "Listen to me and pay reverent attention [to my exposition], which brings the attainment of all kinds of success, gives birth to rapture and joy, and removes the barbs of sorrow.
81. Follow the Path respectfully, which gets rid of pride, dispels sorrow, liberates [one] completely from rebirth, and destroys all suffering."

CHAPTER 2: THE STORY OF SUMEDHA AND THE VAṂSA OF DĪPANKARA BUDDHA[3]

1. "A hundred thousand [ordinary] eons and four incalculable eons ago[4] there was a beautiful and delightful city called Amara ['Immortal'].
2. It was always filled with the ten sounds,[5] [such as] those of horses, elephants, drums, conch-shells and chariots, and was well provided with things to eat and drink, resounding with the cries of those shouting 'Eat! drink!'
3. It was perfect in every respect, (people there were) engaged in all kinds of work, it possessed the Seven Jewels,[6] was filled with many kinds of people; as opulent as a city of the gods, it was [like heaven] a place where there lived people who had acquired merit.
4. In this city of Amarāvatī [I][7] was a Brahmin called Sumedha, a millionaire owning vast amounts of money and (stored) grain,

[3] Much of this account of Sumedha is repeated in the introduction to the *Jātaka* collection: cf. Jayawickrama's (1990) translation of this text, part of which (= vv.7–14 here) was cited in 1.2.c. The narrative voice throughout Bv from here until the end of Chapter XXVII is the Buddha, a continuation of his words beginning in Chapter I 80. In the text as we have it, the Redactor's voice recommences at Chapter XXVIII 1, speaking of Gotama in the third person singular.

[4] For these eons, see p. 260 n. 42 and Table 4.1.

[5] They are, in Horner's (1975: 9 n. 9) translation: "the sounds of elephants, horses, chariots, drums, chanks, lutes, singing, cymbals, songs, as well as of 'Partake, eat, drink.'"

[6] The commentary explains this as either seven kinds of precious stone (see Horner 1964[MQII]: 251) or the Seven Jewels of a Wheel-turning king, thus indicating that the city was the center of an "empire."

[7] There are no verbs in vv.4–5; all translations I have seen assume that this is a separate sentence, with an unexpressed third person verb, such that Gotama begins speaking of Sumedha here in the third person – "there was a Brahmin called . . ." – and then changes to the first person in v.6. It is possible to take the two verses as a long preliminary to the verb in v.6, in the first person singular, as my translation does. See further n. 9 on v.6, and 39 on v.187 below.

5. [I] was learned, knew the (Vedic) mantras [requisite for the sacrificial ritual] and had mastered the three Vedas; [I] was an expert in the (sciences of) divination and history and the (other, notably ritual) duties of a Brahmin.[8]

6. Seated in private (one day) I[9] thought as follows: "Rebirth and (re)death [literally: the breaking apart of the body] are (forms of) suffering.

7. I, who am subject to birth, old age and ill-health, will seek for the unaging, undying safety and peace[10] [of nirvana].

8. Why don't I cast aside this filthy body, full of all manner of putrescence, and leave (it/here)[11] indifferent and without care (for it)?

9. There is, there must be a Path (to do so) – it cannot not be! I will seek that Path for the sake of liberation from [conditioned] existence.

10. Just as (it is the case that) when suffering is found, happiness is also, so when [conditioned] existence is found one can look for[12] non-existence [= unconditioned existence, *vibhava* in one of its senses: see 2.2.a].

11. Just as when heat is found, so, on the other hand, is coolness, so when the threefold fire [of lust, hatred and delusion] is found one can look for (its) quenching [*nibbāna*].

12. Just as when what is bad exists, what is good ['wholesome,' *kusala*] does also, so when birth is found one can look for that which is without birth.

13. Just as when a person is smeared with excrement, and (though) he or she sees a pool full (of water) does not seek (to wash in) that pool, this is not a fault in the pool,

14. so when the pool of Immortality exists to clean the smearing of defilement, if one does not seek that pool this is not a fault in the pool of Immortality.

15. Just as when someone is surrounded by enemies, and there does exist

[8] The word is *sadhamma* (= Skt *svadharma)*, the "individual duty" of a Brahmin priest.

[9] The commentary (Bv-a 69) here explains that the Buddha, in using the first person "unifies the wise Sumedha with himself." The Pali is *imina attanā saddhiṃ Sumedhapaṇḍitam ekattaṃ karoti.* The term *ekatta* is ambiguous between two meanings: (i) = Skt *ekatva*, "oneness, singleness, unity" (CPD); (ii) = Skt *ekātman*, "of one nature, uniform," etc. (CPD). In neither case is the doctrine of not-self in question here, despite the use of *atta/ātman* in the second (see pp. 264f.). In every *Jātaka* story, at the end the Buddha identifies himself with one character, in the words *tena samayena . . . ahosi:* "at that time I was [so-and-so]." See Collins (1982: 103–4, 152) for a story of a monk-reciter of the *Jātaka*-s misled about the denial of self by this form of words, and sternly reprimanded by the Buddha. [10] *Nibbuti*: see 2.1.a.

[11] That is, both leave the city of Amarāvatī and wander as an ascetic now, and in the long run leave the "city of the body" for the city of nirvana: see 2.3.e.

[12] This is an attempt to translate the pun in the original *icchitabbaka*, which means both "is to be expected" in the logical sense that one quality suggests its contrary or contradictory, and also "is to be desired" in the practical sense of being sought by practice of the Path (cp. the choice of words in Jayawickrama's version given in 1.2.c).

a way to escape, but he or she does not (take it to) run away, that is no fault in the path[13],

16. so when one is surrounded by the Defilements, and there is an auspicious path (by which to escape), but one does not seek that Path, this is not a fault in the auspicious way.

17. Just as when a person is ill, and a doctor is there (to treat him), but he or she does not ask for treatment, this is not a fault in the doctor,

18. so when one is suffering and oppressed by the disease of defilement, (but) does not seek the Teacher, that is not a fault in (that) Preceptor.

19. Just as if a person were to be disgusted at (having) a corpse hung from his neck, and were to free himself (from it) and go away happy, free, and his or her own master,

20. So I will cast aside this filthy body (which is just) a heap of various kinds of putrescence and leave (it/here) [see n. 11 on v.8], indifferent and without care (for it).

21. Just as men and women cast aside excrement in a latrine and go away indifferent and without care (for it),

22. so in the same way I will cast aside this body, full of all manner of putrescence, and go away, as if I had defecated (and gone away from) a toilet.

23. Just as the owners of an old, broken, and leaking boat cast it aside and go their way indifferent and without care (for it),

24. So in the same way I will cast aside this body with its nine holes, constantly dripping, and go my way, like the owners of the broken boat.

25. Just as a person traveling with merchandise and (accompanied by) dishonest men [lit. thieves] might see that there was a danger that the merchandise would be divided up (amongst them), and (so) part company with them and go on his way,

26. So in the same way this body is like a great thief[14] and I will part company with it and go on my way, out of fear that (my store of) what is good might be destroyed."

27. With these things in mind I gave away many millions' worth of wealth, to rich and poor alike, and went off to the Himālayas."

[Gotama then describes, still in Sumedha's first person singular, the various advantages of a well-built meditation walkway, of living in a hermitage, etc.; and recounts his supernatural attainments. He continues:]

34. "While I was thus acquiring (supernatural) attainments, and gaining

[13] The word is *añjasa*, which means "straight, direct path," so there is a comparison here with the "direct Path" to nirvana.

[14] This is because, according to the commentary (Bv-a 74), it plunders one's store of good (*kusala*) through breaking the Precepts, on account of the allure of sense-objects.

mastery in ascetic practice[15], the Conqueror Dīpaṅkara appeared, the Leader of the World.
35. Given over to the bliss of meditation, I did not see the four signs of (Dīpaṅkara's) conception, birth, enlightenment and teaching Dhamma (in the first Sermon).
36. (People) in a border-country invited the Tathāgata (Dīpaṅkara), and delighted by (the thought of) his visit were clearing the road.
37. At that time I went out from my own hermitage, and with bark garment rustling (in the wind) I flew through the air.
38. Seeing the people full of joy, delighted, happy and elated, I came down from the sky and straight away asked them:
39. '(You) people are delighted, happy, elated, and full of joy. For whom is the road[16] being cleared?'
40. They replied to my question: 'A Supreme Buddha has appeared in the world, a Conqueror named Dīpaṅkara, a Leader of the World – (it is) for him (that) the road is being cleared.'
41. When I heard the word 'Buddha' rapture arose in me and I expressed (my) joy, saying 'Buddha, Buddha.'
42. Standing there, happy and thrilled in mind I thought: 'here I will sow the seeds [of future Buddhahood], may my moment not pass (me by)[17]!'
43. [I said to them] "if you are clearing (the road) for a Buddha, give me one place, (so that) I too will clear (his) path."
44. They gave me a place to clear the road, and I cleared it, thinking 'A Buddha, a Buddha!'
45. My section was unfinished when the Great Sage Dīpaṅkara, the Conqueror, entered the path with four hundred thousand excellent, stainless Arahants, who had attained the six Super-knowledges.
46. Many gods and men were on their way to meet him, banging drums, rejoicing and crying 'Sādhu!'[18]
47. Gods saw humans and human saw gods;[19] with hands together (in *añjali*) they followed the Tathāgata.
48. The gods made music on (their) celestial instruments, (as did) the humans on (their) human instruments: (doing so) together, they followed after the Tathāgata.
49. From midway in the sky gods scattered down celestial mandārava flowers, lotuses, and flowers from the Pāricchattaka tree [in the Tusita heaven] in all directions,

[15] The word here is *sāsane*, usually used of a Buddha's teaching; the translation here follows Bv-a 83.
[16] Three additional terms for "road" are given, pleonastically, accentuating the implied allegorical sense here of the Buddhist Path to nirvana.
[17] *Khaṇo ve mā upaccagā*: cp. the similar phrase used in the story of the monk Samiddhi and the temptress goddess, cited in 1.1.c.
[18] On the word sādhu see p. 252 and n. 29.
[19] Normally gods can see humans but not vice-versa.

50. Men on the earth threw aloft flowers from the Campaka, Saḷala, Nīpa, Nāga, Punnāga and Ketaka trees.
51. Loosening my hair[20] I spread out my bark garment and animal skin (right) there in the mud and lay face downwards.
52. 'Let the Buddha and his pupils walk on me; may he not step in the mud – this will be to my benefit.'
53. As I lay there on the ground this thought occurred to me: 'If I wanted to I could burn up my Defilements today.
54. But what's the point (or: use) of my realizing the truth (*dhamma*) here (and now) in disguise[21]? I will attain Omniscience and become a Buddha in (the world) with its gods.
55. What's the point/use of my crossing over, just one person seeing (only my own) strength? I will attain Omniscience and carry (others) across, (in the world) with its gods.
56. By this resolution I have made (in the presence of) he who is unsurpassed among men, I will attain Omniscience and cause many people to cross over.
57. Cutting the stream of rebirth, destroying the three existences,[22] I will board the ship of the Truth (*dhamma*) and carry (others) across, (in the world) with its gods.'
58. Existence as a human being, male gender, the (right) cause[23], seeing a Teacher [= a Buddha], being an ascetic, having the requisite qualities[24], (making a strong enough) resolution[25], the fact of (having strong enough) determination[26]: by putting together these eight things an aspiration [to Buddhahood: *abhinīhāra*] succeeds.

59. Dīpaṅkara, the knower of the world(s) and recipient of (its) offerings, stood at my head and spoke these words:
60. 'Do you see this ascetic, this great matted-hair ascetic? Countless eons from now he will be a Buddha in (this) world.

[20] Sumedha, in this "pre-Buddhist" phase of the story, is being imagined in a standard South Asian ascetic style, with hair grown long and matted, then piled on top of his head.
[21] *Aññātaka-vesena*, for which "incognito" is also a possible translation: a striking thought I have never seen discussed, leave alone explained.
[22] This means the three cosmic realms, of Desire, Form and Formlessness (see 4.1). For the image of "cutting the stream of rebirth" see Collins (1982: 249).
[23] Explained at Bv-a 91, Ja I 14, Pj II 48–9 etc. (see Horner 1978: 132 n. 3 for other references) as meaning only someone who has the ability to attain Arahantship in that same lifetime has "the (right) cause."
[24] Explained, ibid., as the qualities of having attained the Eight Meditative Levels (*samāpatti*) and the Five Super-knowledges (*abhiññā*).
[25] Explained, ibid., as being prepared to sacrifice one's life, as Sumedha had done here by accepting the possibility of being trampled to death by Dīpaṅkara Buddha and his disciples.
[26] Explained, ibid., as being able to swim across the whole world, were it to become a mass of water. For the ambiguities of the idea of "desiring" nirvana ("determination" here is a translation for *chandatā*), see 1.4.

61. One day the (future) Tathāgata will leave a delightful city by the name of Kapila, and will strive the (great) striving, and do what is hard to do;
62. Sitting down at the foot of an Ajapāla tree the (future) Tathāgata will accept (a meal of) milk-rice there, and (then) go to the (river) Nerañjarā.
63. This (future) Conqueror will eat the milk-rice on the bank of the Nerañjarā, and (then) go to the foot of the enlightenment-tree along an excellent, decorated road[27].
64. There he will circumambulate his enlightenment throne[28], and (then) seated at the foot of the Assattha tree that unsurpassed One, of great renown, will attain enlightenment[29].
65. The mother who will give birth to him will be called Māyā, his father Suddhodana; he[30] will be called Gotama.
66. The two chief male disciples will be called Kolita and Upatissa,[31] who will be free from Corruptions, passionless, calm in mind and concentrated.
67. An attendant called Ānanda will serve this/that Conqueror, and the two chief female disciples will be Khemā and Uppalavaṇṇā,
68. who will (also) be free from Corruptions, passionless, calm in mind and concentrated. The enlightenment Tree will be called an Assattha.
69. The two chief male (lay) attendants will be Citta and Hatthāḷavaka; the two chief female (lay) attendants will be Uttarā and Nandamātā.'

70. When they heard these words from the unequaled Great Sage men and gods rejoiced, (saying) 'Here is a sprout (from which will come a) Buddha!'
71. A great outcry was heard, (as) beings and gods (throughout) the ten-thousandfold world-system clapped their hands, laughed, and made obeisance [to Sumedha] with hands together (in *añjali*), (saying):
72. 'If we fail (to profit from) the Teaching of this Lord of the World [i.e. Dīpaṅkara], then at some time in the future may we come face to face with this one [i.e. Sumedha, as Gotama].
73. Just as when people who (are trying to) cross a river (but) fail to reach the opposite bank (at that place, may) reach it further down and so cross the great stream,

[27] As at Ja I 70, the gods decorate the road: cp. 5.3.b on realism and its absence in accounts of a Buddha's enlightenment. The attitude here would seem to be what I call there a "ritual re-enactment," where the characters would seem to be actors in an already-scripted drama.

[28] *Bodhi-maṇḍa.* If this is the same as *bodhi-maṇḍala,* it would seem first to have referred to the ground around the Bodhi tree, and thence to the "throne" of Enlightenment in royal-triumphalist versions.

[29] This renders the verb *bujjhissati,* will awaken. See 2.3.a on the imagery of (En)lightenment.

[30] The demonstrative *ayaṃ* is used, accentuating the blend between "this" Sumedha, visible in the present and "that" Gotama, located in the uncountably distant future. Cp. the similar use of *taṃ* in v.67.

[31] Names of Moggallāna and Sāriputta respectively.

74. in just the same way if we all let slip (the opportunity offered by) this Conqueror [Dīpaṅkara], then at some time in the future may we come face to face with this one [Sumedha, as Gotama].'

75. Dīpaṅkara, the knower of the world(s) and recipient of (its) offerings, praised my deed and raised his right foot (to go).
76. All the sons [= disciples] of that Conqueror made a ritual circumambulation [of my body as it lay there], (while) gods, men and Asuras saluted me and departed.
77. When the leader of the world and his (Monastic) Order had were out of sight, I got up from where I was lying and sat cross-legged [in lotus position].
78. I was filled (to overflowing) with happiness and joy, and sat cross-legged in a state of rapture[32].
79. Sitting cross-legged I had this thought: 'I have mastered (the stages of) meditation, and have attained complete Super-knowledge.
80. There is no sage equal to me in the (ten-) thousandfold world (-system); unequaled in (psychic) Power I have attained such happiness (as this).'

81. As I sat cross-legged all those who dwelt in the ten-thousandfold world-system let out a great shout: 'Assuredly you will be a Buddha!
82. All the portents which appeared when past future Buddhas sat cross-legged [in this way, after making their Resolution], are seen today:
83. Cold disappeared and heat abated (then): these (portents) are seen today – assuredly you will be a Buddha!
84. The ten-thousandfold world-system was quiet and untroubled: these (portents) are seen today – assuredly you will be a Buddha!
85. No great winds blew, rivers did not flow: these (portents) are seen today – assuredly you will be a Buddha!
86. Flowers growing in water and on land all came into flower at that moment: they are all in flower today – assuredly you will be a Buddha!
87. Creepers or trees bore fruit at that moment: they all bear fruit today – assuredly you will be a Buddha!
88. Jewels shone in the sky and on the ground at that moment: they are shining today – assuredly you will be a Buddha!
89. Human and divine musical instruments played at that moment: they are playing today – assuredly you will be a Buddha!
90. Various flowers rained down from the sky at that moment: they appear today – assuredly you will be a Buddha!
91. The great ocean receded, and the ten thousandfold (world-system) quaked: they both resound today – assuredly you will be a Buddha!
92. The ten thousand fires in hell were quenched (*nibbanti*) at that

[32] Literally "I was happy with happiness, joyous with joy, and overflowing with rapture."

moment: these fires are quenched today – assuredly you will be a Buddha!
93. The sun was stainless [i.e. shining brightly] and [nonetheless] all the stars were seen: they are seen today – assuredly you will be a Buddha!
94. Water came up from the earth at that moment, although it had not rained: it comes up from the earth today – assuredly you will be a Buddha!
95. Masses of stars and constellations lit up the whole of the sky; Visākhā is (again) in conjunction with the moon – assuredly you will be a Buddha!
96. (Animals) living in holes and in caves came out from their lairs; today their lairs are empty[33] – assuredly you will be a Buddha!
97. No-one was disconsolate, but (all) were contented at that moment; today all are contented (again) – assuredly you will be a Buddha!
98. Illnesses were cured, hunger came to an end; today these things are seen (again) – assuredly you will be a Buddha!
99. There was little lust, (while) hatred and delusion were destroyed; these things are all absent today – assuredly you will be a Buddha!
100. There was no fear then, and this is seen (again) today; by this sign we know – assuredly you will be a Buddha!
101. No dust was stirred up (then), and this is seen again today; by this sign we know – assuredly you will be a Buddha!
102. Undesirable smells went away, and a divine scent wafted around; that scent wafts around today – assuredly you will be a Buddha!
103. All the gods can be seen, apart from those without form; all are seen today – assuredly you will be a Buddha!
104. Everything was seen at that moment, as far as the Niraya hell; it is (all) seen today – assuredly you will be a Buddha!
105. Walls, doors and rocks were not obstacles then; today they are (again) like (empty) space – assuredly you will be a Buddha!
106. At that (same) moment, there was no dying or being reborn; these things are seen today – assuredly you will be a Buddha!
107. Apply yourself vigorously, don't let (your) energy fail, press forward; we know this: assuredly you will be a Buddha!'

108. When I had heard what was said both by the Buddha (Dīpaṅkara) and by those who dwelt in the ten-thousandfold world-system, I was happy, contented, joyous; and I thought:
109. 'What Buddhas say has but one (sure) meaning; Conquerors do not speak falsely. There is no falsehood in Buddhas – assuredly I ám (to be) a Buddha!
110. As a clod of earth thrown up to the sky is certain to fall back to earth, so too what is said by (the) excellent Buddhas is always certain – assuredly I am (to be) a Buddha!

[33] This is clearly the sense here; and for the possibility of reading *suññā* for *chuddhā*, see Brough (1962: 225).

111. As death is always certain for all beings, so too what is said by (the) excellent Buddhas is always certain – assuredly I am (to be) a Buddha!
112. As when the night is ending the sun always rises, so too what is said by (the) excellent Buddhas is always certain – assuredly I am (to be) a Buddha!
113. As a lion who leaves his den always roars, so too what is said by (the) excellent Buddhas is always certain – assuredly I am (to be) a Buddha!
114. Just as a pregnant woman is sure to be relieved of her burden, so too what is said by (the) excellent Buddhas is always certain – assuredly I am (to be) a Buddha!'"

[In vv.115–65 Gotama, still speaking in Sumedha's first person, says "Now I (will) contemplate the things which make one a Buddha," and goes through the ten Perfections. For each Perfection he begins "In contemplation then I saw . . .", urges himself to action in second person imperatives, and gives a simile. A repeated verse connects each Perfection with the next: "But this is not all there is to Buddhahood . . . I will contemplate other things which ripen to Enlightenment." I translate the first Perfection, and then list the others with a summary version of the self-admonition and simile.]

116. "In contemplation then I saw the first Perfection, that of Giving, the great path followed by the Great Sages of old.
117. 'Be firm! Take up this first, and set off towards the Perfection of Giving, if you want to attain enlightenment!
118. As a pot full of water when turned upside down by anyone discharges its water and keeps nothing back,
119. so you in the same way, when you see a suppliant of low, high or middle standing give gift(s) and keep nothing back, like an upturned pot.'"

[*The Perfection of Morality*: guard morality as a female yak with her tail caught in something will die rather than damage her tail.
Renunciation: see all forms of existence as a prison, and rather than develop desire for it long to escape as does a suffering prisoner.
Wisdom: seek wisdom everywhere as a monk goes for alms to all, without discriminating.
Energy: be energetic in every life as a lion is full of energy in any position, lying down, standing or walking.
Patience: be patient when shown respect or not, as the earth accepts whatever is thrown on it, pure or impure.
Truth: never go beyond the path of the (four) Truths, as the star Osadhī never strays from its path, whatever the time or the season.
Determination: be constantly resolute, as a rock stays in place without trembling, even in high winds.

Lovingkindness: develop lovingkindness (or friendliness, *mettā*) for friend and enemy alike, as water refreshes and cleans good and bad people alike.
Equanimity: remain balanced in happiness or suffering, as the earth remains indifferent to the purity and impurity put on it.]

166. [Gotama continues] "As I [= Sumedha] meditated on these things, (in) their essential nature and their characteristics, through the splendor and power (*tejas*) of the Dhamma the earth and the ten-thousandfold (world-system) quaked.
167. The earth moved and roared like a sugar-cane press when pressure is applied; it shook like the wheel in an oil press.
168. The whole assembly present at the almsgiving to the Buddha (Dīpaṅkara) fell to the ground and lay there, faint and trembling.
169. Many thousands of water-jars and many hundreds of water-pots smashed against each other and were shattered and broken.
170. The people were frightened, full of fear; afraid and staggering, they came together and went to Dīpaṅkara (saying):
171. 'What will there be for the world, (something) good or bad? The whole world is assailed. As one Who Sees, remove this [trouble, fear, etc.].'
172. The Great Sage Dīpaṅkara won them over (by saying) 'Have confidence; don't be frightened by this earthquake.
173. The person of whom today I made the declaration[34] "He will be a Buddha in the world" is contemplating the Dhamma followed by Conquerors of old.
174. While he has been contemplating the Dhamma, the whole ground of Buddhas in its entirety,[35] the earth has, accordingly, quaked in the ten-thousandfold (world-system) along-with its gods.'
175. Their minds were calmed instantly on hearing the Buddha's words; everyone then came to me to do me honor.
176. After undertaking (to acquire) the qualities of a Buddha [= the Perfections], I did obeisance to Dīpaṅkara and got up from my seat.
177. Gods and men both scattered flowers, divine and human, as I got up from my seat.
178. They both, gods and men, made a blessing for safety: 'May you attain the great thing to which you have made an aspiration, as you wish.
179. May you avoid all calamities, may grief and illness be destroyed; let there be no hindrance – be quick to attain the highest enlightenment!
180. As flowering trees flower when the time has come, may you also, great hero, flower with the knowledge of enlightenment!

[34] *Vyākāsiṃ*; i.e. the person of whom he made the declaration, *vyākaraṇa*, as is necessary for that person to be classified as a future Buddha.
[35] The commentary (Bv-a 116) explains this as referring to (all) the Perfections.

181. As all those who were Perfect Buddhas (in the past) fulfilled the ten Perfections, may you also, great hero, fulfil the ten Perfections!
182. As all the Perfect Buddhas (of the past) became enlightened on the throne of enlightenment[36], may you also become enlightened in the Conqueror's enlightenment!
183. As all the Perfect Buddhas (of the past) turned the Wheel of the Dhamma, may you also, great hero, turn the Wheel of the Dhamma.
184. As the moon shines pure on a full moon night, may you also, (your aspiration) fulfilled, shine in the ten-thousandfold (world-system).
185. As the sun, freed from Rāhu,[37] blazes with light[38], may you also, freed from the world, blaze brightly.
186. Just as whatever streams there are flow down to the great sea, may the worlds and their gods flow down to you.'

187. Praised and gladdened by them, taking on the ten (Perfections), he[39] went into the forest to practice them."

CHAPTER 3: THE *VAMSA* OF KONDAÑÑA BUDDHA

1. "Next after Dīpaṅkara there was a leader called Kondañña: his brilliance was endless, his glory unlimited; he was immeasurable and unassailable.
2. His patience was like the earth, his virtue(s) like the ocean, his (meditative) concentration like Mt. Meru, his wisdom like the sky.

[There follow various verses of narrative about and praise for Kondañña, using standard phrases.]

9. At that time I was the warrior-noble Vijitāvī ('Victor'), wielding power from one end of the ocean to the other.[40]
10. I gave excellent food to the millions and millions[41] of faultless Great Sages, along with the Leader of the World.
11. The Leader of the World, the Buddha Kondañña, predicted of me:[42] 'He will be Buddha in the world innumerable eons from now.

[36] See v.64 and n. 28 above. [37] The demon who causes eclipses.
[38] There is an untranslatable pun here on *tapena*, which means both heat/light and ascetic practice: the Buddha Gotama will shine with both.
[39] If *pāvisī* is the correct reading, as it seems to be (there are no variants either here or at Ja I 28 v.197), then, apart perhaps from vv.4–5 above (see n. 7), this is the first and last time Gotama refers to Sumedha in the third person. The first person *pāvisiṃ* would be metrically possible.
[40] That is, as the commentary explains in the standard description, he was a Wheel-turning king. See Chapter 6.5 and Appendix 3.
[41] Literally a hundred thousand times ten million; see Chapter 5 n. 29.
[42] Cp. Dīpaṅkara's words in Chapter II 60ff. above.

12. He will make the (Great) Effort,[43] do what is hard to do, and will attain Complete enlightenment at the foot of an Assattha tree, (and so become) of great renown.
13. The mother who will give birth to him will be called Māyā; his father will be Suddhodana, and he will be called Gotama.
14. Kolita and Upatissa will be his Chief Male Disciples; an attendant called Ānanda will serve this/that Conqueror.
15. Khemā and Uppalavaṇṇā will be his Chief Female Disciples; his Tree of enlightenment will be called an Assattha.
16. The two chief male (lay) attendants will be Citta and Hatthāḷavaka; the two chief female (lay) attendants will be Uttarā and Nandamātā. The life span of this/that renowned Gotama will be a hundred years.'

17.[44] When they heard these words from the unequaled great Seer men and gods rejoiced, (saying) 'Here is a sprout (from which will come a) Buddha!'
18. A great outcry was heard, (as) beings and gods (throughout) the ten-thousandfold world-system clapped their hands, laughed, and made obeisance [to Vijitāvī] with hands together (in *añjali*), (saying):
19. 'If we fail (to profit from) the Teaching of this Lord of the World [i.e. Kondañña], then at some time in the future may we come face to face with this one [i.e. Vijitāvī, as Gotama].
20. Just as when people who (are trying to) cross a river (but) fail to reach the opposite bank (at that place, may) reach it further down and so cross the great stream,
21. In just the same way if we all let slip (the opportunity offered by) this Conqueror [Kondañña], then at some time in the future may we come face to face with this one [Vijitāvī, as Gotama].'
22. When I heard these words my heart grew even more confident. In order to bring that aim [i.e. Buddhahood] to fulfilment I offered my great kingdom to that Conqueror; I gave up my great kingdom and became a renouncer in his presence.
23. I learnt (by heart) the Sutta and Vinaya (*piṭaka*-s), the ninefold instruction of that Teacher, and so illumined the Dispensation[45] of that Conqueror
23. Living there diligently, whether sitting standing or walking, I perfected the (supernatural) Knowledges and (at death) went to the Brahma-world.

25. Kondañña's city was called Rammavatī, the warrior-noble (his father) was Sunanda, the mother who gave him birth was called Sujātā.

[43] In this context this is a technical term for a Buddha's striving: see 5.2.b on Metteyya and Gotama. [44] Cp. II 70–4 above.
[45] Both "instruction" and "Dispensation" here render *sāsana*.

26. He lived the household life for ten thousand years; his three excellent palaces were Ruci, Suruci and Subha.
27. (He had) three hundred thousand attractive women (as wives); his (chief) wife was called Rucidevī and his son was called Vijitasena.
28. He saw the four Sights and left (home) in a chariot; that Conqueror made the (Great) Effort for fully ten months.
29. When he was requested (to preach) by Brahma, Kondañña the Great Hero, the best of two-footed creatures, turned the Wheel (of Dhamma) in the excellent city of the gods.
30. Bhadda and Subhadda were his Chief Male Disciples, Anuruddha was the attendant of Kondañña the Great Sage.
31. Tissā and Upatissā were his Chief Female Disciples; the enlightenment Tree of Kondañña the Great Sage was Sālakalyāṇikā.
32. His two chief male (lay) attendants were Citta and Hatthāḷavaka; the two chief female (lay) attendants Nandā and Sirimā.
33. The Great Sage was eighty-eight feet [literally 'hands'] tall; he shone like the king of the stars [i.e. the moon], (or) like the sun at midday.
34. A (normal human) life span at that time was a hundred thousand years; he lived that long and caused many people to cross [i.e. to the further shore, nirvana].
35. The earth was adorned with faultless Ones whose Corruptions were destroyed; it shone (with their beauty) as the (roof of the) sky (shines) with the stars.[46]
36. Those immeasurable, imperturbable, unassailable nāgas[47] of great renown made themselves look like bolts of lightning when they attained (final) nirvana.[48]
37. That Conqueror's supernatural attainment was unequaled, and his (attainment of) meditation was fostered by wisdom: it has all disappeared: are not all conditioned things worthless?[49]
38. The fine Buddha Kondañña attained (final) nirvana in the Canda park; an ornamented shrine (*cetiya*) was erected there, seven miles high."

CHAPTER 20: THE *VAṂSA* OF VIPASSĪ BUDDHA

1. "Next after Phussa a Perfect Buddha called Vipassī arose in the world, the best of two-footed creatures, endowed with (enlightened) vision.
2. When he had broken through all (forms of) ignorance and attained

[46] The commentary (Bv-a 141) specifies: *tārāgaṇehi gagana-talaṃ viya khīṇāsavehi vicittā ayaṃ medinī . . .*

[47] The word *nāga* is used for many different beings, always large and impressive (notably elephants), and is often used in this way of Arahants and Buddhas.

[48] In a similar way to Dabba (3.3) they rose into the air to the height of seven palm-trees, attained a level of meditation based on the contemplation of fire, and illumined the dark clouds like lightning as they "were completely quenched, like fire with no (more) fuel" (Bv-a 141).

[49] See Chapter 3.4.b n. 45.

the ultimate, Perfect enlightenment he set out for the city of Bandhumatī to turn the Wheel of the Dhamma.

[there follow various verses of narrative about and praise for Vipassī, using standard phrases, similar to those used of Kondañña.]

10. At that time I was a nāga-king called Atula ['Incomparable'], of great supernatural powers, an illustrious maker of merit.
11. I went up to the Most Senior[50] in the world, and surrounded him with many millions of nāgas playing (music) on celestial instruments;
12. Approaching the Perfect Buddha Vipassī, the Leader of the World, I invited the King of the Dhamma to accept my gift of a golden throne inlaid with precious stones, pearls and (other) jewels.
13. Sitting among his monastic community the Buddha predicted of me: 'He will be a Buddha in ninety-one eons from now.'

[Verses 14–21 are almost word-for-word identical with Chapter 2 vv.61–8, translated above, said by the Buddha Dīpaṅkara of Sumedha. The Thai ms. cited by Jayawickrama writes out in full the verses concerning the river of time, as in II 72–4 and III 19–21 above.]

22. When I heard these words my heart grew even more confident. I strengthened yet further my resolution to attain the ten Perfections.

23. The Great Sage Vipassī's city was called Bandhumatī, the warrior-noble (his father) was Bandhumā, his mother was Bandhumatī.
24. He lived the household life for eight thousand years, his three excellent palaces were Nanda, Sunanda and Sirimā.
25. (He had) forty-three attractive women (as wives); his (chief) wife was called Sutanā and his son was called Samavattakhandha.
26. He saw the four Sights and left (home) in a chariot; that Conqueror made the (Great) Effort for fully eight months.
27. When he was requested (to preach) by Brahma, Vipassī the Great Hero, the best of men, turned the Wheel (of Dhamma) in a deer-park.[51]
28. Khandha and Tissa were his Chief Male Disciples, Asoka was the attendant of the Great Sage Vipassī.
29. Candā and Candamittā were his Chief Female Disciples; the enlightenment Tree of the Blessed One was called the Pāṭalī.
30. His two chief male (lay) attendants were Punabbasumitta and Nāga; the two chief female (lay) attendants Sirimā and Uttamā.
31. The Leader of the World was eighty-eight feet tall; his radiance spread out for seven miles all around him.

[50] *Lokajeṭṭha*, literally eldest, but usually glossed as *seṭṭha*, best.
[51] As did Gotama, in Benares.

32. The Buddha's life span at that time was eighty thousand years; he lived that long and caused many people to cross (to nirvana).
33. He released many gods and men from their bonds, and showed the remaining ordinary ones what was the Path and what was not the Path.[52]
34. He showed (people) the light, and taught the Path to the Deathless; blazing up like a mass of fire he attained nirvana [literally "was quenched," *nibbuto*] along with his disciples.
35. (His) excellent supernatural powers, merit, (his knowledge of) the characteristics of (all) four levels[53] – they have all disappeared: are not all conditioned things worthless?
36. Vipassī, the excellent conqueror, the steadfast, attained nirvana in the Sumitta park; right there an excellent seven-mile high Stūpa (was built) for him.

[52] I follow the reading in Bv-a 242, which makes better sense. The idea here is probably that these gods and men attained the level of Stream-enterer or above; the ordinary ones are those below this level.

[53] *Lakkhanaṃ cātubhūmakaṃ*, an obscure phrase (text and commentary have variant readings). It perhaps refers to his consciousness of the three Worlds within *saṃsāra*, of Desire, (Refined) Form and Formlessness, and of nirvana as the "superworldly" (*lokuttara*) fourth, achievable through the Path (cf. Vism 452 = XIV 83). Consciousness with nirvana as its object is nonetheless a conditioned phenomenon (1.2.b).

APPENDIX 2

Chapters 1 and 2 of the Mahāvaṃsa

CHAPTER 1: THE TATHĀGATA COMES (TO SRI LANKA)

1. With a bow to the pure Perfect Buddha, born in a pure lineage (*vaṃsa*), I will speak the *Mahāvaṃsa*, in (full, with) all its varied chapters.
2. The (text) composed by the Ancients[1] is too long in some places and too short in others, and repetitious.
3–4. Listen (now) to this (version), which does not have those faults, and is easy to learn and remember; it has come down (to us) by tradition. (Listen to it carefully) and where (the text) is such as to inspire serene confidence, give expression to (such) serene confidence, and where it is animating, to (such) animation.[2]
5. Our conqueror, long ago, saw the Perfect Buddha Dīpaṅkara and made the Resolution to attain enlightenment, to free the world from suffering.
6–10. Thereafter he paid reverence (in order) to these twenty-four Perfect Buddhas: Kondañña, the sage Maṅgala, Sumana and Revata Buddhas, the Great Sage Sobhita, the Perfect Buddha Anomadassī and the Conquerors Paduma and Nārada, the Perfect Buddha Padumuttara and Sumedha the Tathāgata, the Leaders Sujāta, Piyadassī and Atthadassī, the Conquerors Dhammadassī, Siddhattha, Tissa and Phussa, the Perfect Buddhas Vipassī and Sikhi, mighty Vessabhu, the Perfect Buddhas Kakusandha, Koṇāgamana, and the Happy One Kassapa. He obtained from (each of) them a prediction of his Buddhahood:
11. "When he has fulfiled all the Perfections and attained supreme enlightenment as the supreme Buddha Gotama, he will free beings from suffering."

1 *Porāṇa* – a term for earlier authors and commentators. This verse has been taken to refer to the *Dīpavaṃsa*, but the commentary states that this is a reference to a "Sinhala commentary" version (Norman 1983: 117).

2 "Serene confidence" is *pasāda*, "animation" *saṃvega*. One cannot convey all the nuances of these terms. The first is often said to occur at Buddhist Stūpas; it is a clarity of mind, calmness, and conviction in the religious value of what, or who evokes the feeling. The second is a stronger emotion (from a root meaning to tremble or quiver), and is used when some shock inspires an increase in the intensity of religious feelings and intentions.

12. The Great Sage attained supreme enlightenment at the foot of the Bodhi tree at Uruvelā in Magadha, on the full-moon day of the month Vesākha [May].
13. For seven times seven days he dwelt in mastery[3], enjoying the bliss of release there and showing its sweetness (to others).
14. Then he went to Benares and turned the Wheel of the Dhamma. He spent the Rains there and made sixty (people become) Arahants.
15. He sent those monks out to teach the Dhamma and instructed (a group of) thirty well-to-do friends.
16. The Lord spent the winter at Uruvelā instructing Kassapa and the thousand fire-ascetics and bringing them to maturity [= enlightenment].
17–9. When Uruvela-Kassapa was about to perform a great sacrifice,[4] (Gotama Buddha), destroyer of his enemies,[5] knew that Kassapa did not want him to be present, and so went for alms to Uttarakuru, and ate (what he received) by lake Anotatta. That evening, nine months after his enlightenment on the full-moon day of the month Phussa, the Conqueror came to the island of Lankā to make it pure.
20. The Conqueror knew that the island of Lankā was a place where his Dispensation would shine, and that Lankā was full of spirits [*yakkha*-s] who had to be got rid of.
21–2. He also knew that there was (at that time) a great gathering of the spirits living in the island of Lankā at their battle-ground,[6] which was on a pleasant riverbank in the delightful Mahānāga garden, in the center of the island, (a garden) three miles long and one mile wide.
23–4. The Happy One went to the spirits' gathering, and stood there in midair, right above their heads in the middle of the meeting, at the place of the (future) Mahiyaṅgana Stūpa; and he terrified them (by stirring up) rain, wind and darkness, and so forth.
25. The spirits pleaded with the fearless Conqueror to give them safety from (their) fear and distress; and the Conqueror, the giver of safety, spoke as follows to those terrified spirits:
26. "Spirits, I will take away your fear and suffering (if) you all agree to let me sit down."

[3] *Vasī vasi.* Mhv-ṭ 85 refers to the five forms of (meditative) Mastery, and "all the duties of a Buddha."

[4] According to the Vinaya account (Vin I 27–8) the Buddha's visit to Uttarakuru took place during the winter, before the fire-ascetics had been brought to Enlightenment by the Buddha's third sermon, the Fire Sermon.

[5] This is glossed by Mhv-ṭ 90 as destroying the defilements by the Path; perhaps there is a suggestion that the Buddha could have destroyed Kassapa and his fire-sacrifice had he so chosen.

[6] *Saṅgāma* usually means battlefield; Mhv-ṭ 92 glosses it as *samāgama*, meeting, but I assume from the Buddha's use of *samaggā* in v.26d, where he wants them to "all agree" to give him a seat, and their use of *sabbe*, "all (of us)" in v.27c, that he is preventing a fight, as he does on his second visit.

27. The spirits spoke to the Happy One: "Sir, we will all (together) give you the entire island, (if) you give us safety."
28. He took away their fear and the coldness and darkness, and spread out a leather mat on the ground they gave him; and sat down there.
29. He then made the leather mat spread out (still further), with flames all around (its edges); overcome by the heat, the spirits stood all around the edge (of the mat) in terror.
30. Then the Leader brought here[7] a pleasant island (called) Giridīpa ("Mountain Island"), had the spirits go onto it, and put it back in its own place.
31. The Leader made the leather mat small (again); then gods assembled (there), and in that gathering the Teacher preached the Dhamma.
32. Many millions of beings gained an understanding of the Dhamma, and an incalculable number were established in the (three) Refuges and the (five) Moral Precepts.
33. A lord of the gods (called) Mahāsumana, (who lived) on Sumanakūṭa mountain, attained the Fruit of Stream Entry,[8] and asked him, who is worthy of worship, for something (with which) to worship (him).
34. The Conqueror, the benefactor of living beings, touched (part of) his head, which had bluish-black, pure (hair) and gave a handful of hairs to him.
35–6. He accepted these head-hairs in a fine golden box, placed (them) on a heap of various jewels constructed (to a height and width of) seven *ratana*-s on all sides[9] at the place where the Teacher was sitting[10], covered it in a sapphire Stūpa and made obeisance to it.
37–8. (Later) after the Perfect Buddha's (finally) nirvana, an elder by the name of Sarabhu, a pupil of the elder Sāriputta, took a neck-bone from the funeral pyre, brought it (here) and set it up in this same shrine (*cetiya*), surrounded by (other) monks.
39. He, (a monk) of great (supernatural) power, covered it with gold-colored stones, had a Stūpa built twelve feet high, and departed.
40–2. (Later still) the son of King Devānaṃpiyatissa's brother, Uddhacūḷābhaya saw the wonderful shrine covered it (again) and built it to a height of thirty feet. King Duṭṭhagāmaṇi was there during his war with the Damiḷas, and built a shrine to cover it (which was) eighty feet high. This was how this Mahiyaṅgana Stūpa was established.
43. The Sovereign made the island fit for human habitation in this way, and went back to Uruvelā, a Hero valiant as (are) great (fighting) men.

[7] I.e. to Sri Lankā, where the narrative voice in Mhv is located; the Cambodian ms. version (Ext Mhv I 183ff.) changes the wording to avoid the inappropriate indexical.

[8] The first of the four stages of attainment on the Path. See Glossary s.v. *Sotāpanna.*

[9] *Ratana,* Skt *aratni,* is an arm from elbow to fingertip; Mhv-ṭ 98 says 7 *ratana*-s equal 21 "hands" (*hattha*). I translate the latter in v.39ff. below as "feet," a roughly equivalent English term (cf. Appendix 1, Bv III 33).

[10] Or "had sat." It is not clear whether this happens after the Buddha has left (v. 43) or not.

Here ends (the account of) the Visit to Mahiyaṅgana.

44. The greatly compassionate Teacher, the Conqueror devoted to the welfare of the whole world, lived in the Jetavana (park) for the fifth Rainy Season after his enlightenment.
45–7. He saw that preparations had been made for a battle, over a jeweled throne, between the nāga Mahodara and his nephew Culodara; (and so) the Perfect Buddha, on the morning of the Uposatha day in the dark half of Citta month, took his excellent robe and bowl and went to Nāgadīpa [taken to be in the north of Sri Lankā], out of compassion for the nāgas.
48. This Mahodara was then a king with great (supernatural) powers, (living) in a nāga palace 500 miles (long), under the sea.
49. His younger sister had been given to a nāga-king on a mountain called Kaṇṇā-vaḍḍhamāna, and Culodara was her son.
50–1. His mother's father, a nāga, had given her the superlative jeweled throne and then died; and then the uncle prepared for a battle with his nephew, (whose army consisted of) mountain nāgas with great (supernatural) powers.
52. A god called Samiddhisumana had taken a beautiful Rājayatana (tree) standing in Jetavana (park) as his abode.
53. With the Buddha's permission he held it like an umbrella above the Conqueror as he went (with the Buddha to) to the place (i.e. Nāgadīpa) where he used to live.
54–6. In his previous birth he had been a man in Nāgadīpa, and at the place where the Rājāyatana tree (would, in the future) stand saw some Pacceka-buddhas eating. When he saw them his mind became serenely confident, and he gave them twigs to clean their bowls. Because of this he was reborn in that tree in the delightful Jeta garden, and the tree later (stood) outside (the Jetavana monastery) on the side where the doorway was.
57. The God beyond the gods (i.e. the Buddha) saw an advantage for the god and a benefit for this place (i.e. Sri Lankā), and brought him here along with the tree.
58. The Leader sat there in the sky in the middle of the battlefield, and he who dispels darkness created a darkness which terrified the nāgas.
59. To ease their fear and distress he revealed light (again); they saw the Happy One and joyfully worshiped the Teacher's feet.
60. The Teacher taught them Dhamma on reconciliation, and both (the nāgas) were happy to present the throne to the Sage.
61. The Teacher came down to the ground and sat in a seat while the nāga-kings offered him divine food and drink.
62. The Leader established in the Refuges and Precepts eighty million (of those) snakes (i.e. nāgas), (among) those living in the water and on land.
63–4. The naga-king Maṇiakkhika, the nāga Mahodara's uncle, who was

there to take part in the battle, had heard the Good Dhamma being taught when the Buddha first visited (the island) and had been established in the Refuges and Precepts; now he asked the Tathāgata:
65. "Lord, you have shown great compassion to us in coming here: if you hadn't come, we would (now) be ashes![11]
66. You are very kind – please have compassion for me as an individual, by coming here again to the place where I live, you who are selfless" (*vāsabhūmiṃ mamāmama*).
67. The Blessed One agreed, by remaining silent, to come here again, and right there and then set up the Rājāyatana tree as a shrine (*cetiya*).
68. The Lord of the World gave the nāga-kings the Rājāyatana tree and (his) precious seat, so they could show reverence (to them), (saying)
69. "Nāga-kings, show reverence to this shrine, which (contains objects) I have used[12] – this will be, friends[13], for your benefit and happiness."
70. The Happy One, who has compassion for the whole world, gave the nāgas this and other instructions, and went (back) to the Jetavana (park).

(Here) ends (the account of) the Visit to Nāgadīpa.

71. Three years after this, Maṇiakkhika, sovereign among nāgas, came to the Buddha and invited him (to a meal) with (members of) his Monastic Order.
72–4. In (this) the eighth year after his enlightenment, the Conqueror was living in the Jetavana (park). On the day after (the invitation), the full-moon day of the delightful month of Vesākha, the Leader put on his robe, took his bowl, and went to the Kalyāṇi region (of Sri Lankā), where Maṇiakkhika lived, when the time for the meal was announced, with an entourage of five hundred monks.
75. He sat on a precious seat in a jeweled pavilion which had been made at the site of the (future) Kalyāṇi shrine, along with the monkhood.
76. The king of the nāgas, with his retinue, joyfully served celestial hard and soft food to the king of the Dhamma, with his retinue.
77. Then the teacher preached the Dhamma, and the Leader went up to (the top of Mt.) Sumanakūṭa and placed his footprint (there).[14]
78. He rested for the day, as long as it pleased him, at the foot of this mountain, together with the monks, (then) went to Dīghavāpi.

[11] *Bhasmībhavāmahe*, an indicative middle used as a vivid form of optative counter-factual: "without you, we're done for!" (*-bhāvāma hi* at EM I 702). Mhv-ṭ 109 says that they would have breathed fire on each other.

[12] *Paribhoga-cetiya*, explained on p. 278.

[13] *Tātā* – usually a term of endearment between fathers and sons. Mhv-ṭ 110 says that the shrine will inspire the Nāgas to feel *mettā*, friendship for each other; the Buddha's use of this term is proleptic, to encourage them.

[14] See the discussion of this in 3.4.c (iv), p. 278 and n. 63

79. He sat down there, along with the monks, at the site of the (future) shrine and attained a State of Meditation,[15] so that the place would be worthy of reverence.
80. The Great Sage rose up from that place, and being skilled in (knowing) good and bad places, went to the site of the (future) Mahāmeghavanārāma (monastery).
81–3. The Leader sat down along with his disciples at the site of the (future) Mahābodhi tree and attained a State of Meditation, and (did) likewise at the site of the (future) Great Stūpa, and (did) likewise at the site of the (future) Thūpārāma (monastery). Emerging from that State of Meditation he went with his retinue to the site of the (future) Silā shrine
83. and instructed a crowd of gods who had come with (them). Then the Buddha, who traveled everywhere with his Wisdom,[16] went (back) to Jetavana (park).
84. So the Leader of boundless sagacity looked to the benefit of Lankā in the future, and saw the advantage to the crowds of Gods, snakes (i.e. nāgas) and the like in Lankā at that time. The Light of the World (*lokadīpo*), abounding in compassion, came to the good island (*sudīpaṃ*) three times, and therefore [or: through him] this island (*dīpo . . . ayaṃ*), radiant with the light [or: lamp] of the Dhamma (*dhammadipāvabhāsī*) became highly respected by (all) good people.[17]

(Here) ends (the account of) the Visit to Kalyāṇi.

[End of] the first chapter, called The Tathāgata comes (to Sri Lanka), in the Mahāvaṃsa, composed to bring serene confidence and (religious) animation to good people.

CHAPTER 2: THE LINEAGE OF MAHĀSAMMATA

1. The Great Sage was born into the lineage of Mahāsammata. At the beginning of the (present) eon there was a king called Mahāsammata.

[15] Mhv-ṭ 115 says that this was the Fruit of Arahantship, "with nirvana as its object'.

[16] Mhv-ṭ 116–7 says he has gone with his Omniscience over the whole extent of time, past, present and future.

[17] It is widely said in modern scholarship (e.g. Smith 78a) and in Sri Lankan politics (Kemper 91), that the *Mahāvaṃsa* promotes the idea of Sri Lanka as *dhamma-dīpa*, translated as "island of the Dhamma," meaning that it had been especially selected by the Buddha as the site for the preservation of his Teaching. This verse is the only place the compound appears in the text, and it clearly does *not* mean "island of the Dhamma." The last two lines of the verse contain a play on two senses of Pali *dīpa*, which is equivalent to both Skt *dīpa*, lamp or light, and *dvīpa*, island. In the last line *avabhāsī* can only mean radiant, shining, and so the parts of the compound preceding it must mean "light of the Dhamma." (Guruge's [1989: 496] version, "came to be resplendent as the righteous isle," is a triumph of nationalist sentiment over philological common sense.) Moreover, this line says that it is "therefore," or "through him" (*tena*) that this is the case, referring

2. (Then two called) Roja, and Vararoja, likewise two Kalyāṇakas [i.e. Kalyāṇaka and Varakalyāṇaka], Uposatha and Mandhātā, two (called) Caraka and Upacara,
3. Cetiya and Mucala, one by the name of Mahāmucala, Mucalinda and Sāgara, one by the name of Sāgaradeva,
4. Bhārata and Aṅgīrasa, Rucī and Surucī, Patāpa, Mahāpatāpa and two Panādas,
5–6. likewise two Sudassanās and two Nerūs,[18] and Accimā. His [= Mahāsammata's] sons and grandsons had incalculably long lives; (all) twenty-eight Lords of the Earth [i.e. those listed and Mahāsammata] lived in Kusāvati, dwelling in Rājagaha and Mithilā.
7–11. Then there were a hundred (more) kings, and fifty-six, and sixty, eighty-four thousand, and then thirty-six others; (then) thirty-two and twenty-eight, and twenty-two others, eighteen, seventeen, fifteen, fourteen, nine, seven, twelve, and then twenty-five others, twenty-five and twelve, and twelve and nine more, eighty-four thousand beginning with Makhādeva, and eighty-four thousand beginning with Kālarājanaka, sixteen up to Okkāka – these masses (of kings) occurred in the past, ruling their kingdoms one after the other, in sequence.[19]

back to the third line's use of "Light of the World" as an epithet for the Buddha. To interpret *dīpa* in the compound in the last line as "island," even ignoring the word *avabhāsī*, would sever the connection between the two lines; to take *lokadīpa* in the first verse as "Island of the World" makes no sense. There is a chiasmus (A–B–B–A) in the wordplay on *dīpa*: Light of the World/good island/this island/Light of the Dhamma. This light imagery continues a motif found throughout the chapter: before his first visit (v. 20), the Buddha "knew that the island of Lankā was a place where his Dispensation would shine" (*sāsanujjotanaṭṭhāna*); in the first two visits to the island the Buddha terrifies and pacifies spirits and nāgas by first creating darkness and then dispelling it with light (vv. 24/28, 58/59). It is true that the commentary, Mhv-t 118–9, glosses *dīpa* in both *loka-dīpa* and *dhamma-dīpa* not only as *pajjota-karaṇa*, maker of light, but also, ignoring the word-play, as *patitthā*-(*bhūta*), foundation, basis. In the first case it gives no further exegesis; in the second Lankā is said to be a "basis" for Buddhists (*sāsanikajana*) and for the Buddha himself, through his relics. Pali commentaries, like other Southern Asian exegeses of poetry (*kāvya*), eschew historical accuracy and see as much meaning as possible in the texts they are explicating; this is a version of the ubiquitous practice of giving historically inaccurate but creative "etymologies" (*nirukti*; see Collins 1993c: 316). But even if one were to forget philological accuracy and accept this, the notion that the island is, by *nirukti*, a "foundation" or "basis" for the Buddha's Dispensation does not imply that it has been exclusively so chosen.

I can find the term *dhammadīpa* clearly and unambiguously in the sense of "island of the Dhamma " in no Pali text; no-one familiar with Sinhalese-language sources whom I have asked has been able to find it. The earliest reference (which I owe to Jon Walters) is in 1942, in an article written in English by a western monk, who seems to be attributing it to a speech by Lord Passfield made in the House of Lords: a fine colonial irony. L. A. Perera first used the term, at least in the scholarly world, explicitly introducing it as his own invention: he speaks of "the development of the idea of destiny [which] could be named for convenience here the concept of the *Dhammadīpa*" (1961: 33).

[18] Mhv-ṭ 124 says this means four: Sudassanā and Mahāsudassanā, Nerū and Mahānerū.

[19] Reading *pavuttā* with Mhv-ṭ 130, as p.p.p. from *pra-vṛt* (cp. *pavatte* in II 23). The Pali reads *pavuttā rāsito ime visuṃ visuṃ pure rajjaṃ kāmato anusāsisuṃ*.

12–3. Okkāka's eldest son was the king Okkāmukha. Nipuṇa, Candimā, Candamukha, Saṃjaya (king) of the Sivis, the great king Vessantara and Jālī, Sīhavāhana and Sīhassara – these were his [= Okkāka's] sons and grandsons.
14. Eighty-two thousand sons and grandsons of king Sīhassara were (also) kings, the last one called Jayasena.
15. These were famous Sākyan kings in Kapilavatthu. Jayasena's son of was the great king Sīhahanu,
16–20. Jayasena's daughter was called Yasodharā. In Devadaha there was a Lord of the Earth called Devadahasakka, and then Añjana and Kaccānā were two of his children. This Kaccānā was the chief queen of king Sīhahanu, and this Yasodharā was the chief queen of Añjanasakka. Māyā and then Pajāpatī were two daughters of (king) Añjana, and (he had) two sons called Daṇḍapaṇi and Suppabuddha the Sakiyan. There were five sons and two daughters of Sīhahanu: these five (sons) were Suddhodana, Dhotodana, Sakkodana, Sukkodana, Amitodana, and the two (daughters) Amitā and Pamitā.
21. Amitā was the chief queen of the Sakka Suppabuddha, and she had two children (called) Bhaddakaccānā and Devadatta.
22. Māyā and Pajāpatī were the chief queens of Suddhodana, and our Conqueror was the son of the great king Suddhodana and Māyā.
23. The Great Sage was born in the lineage of Mahāsammata, which had occurred in this way (in an) unbroken (sequence) as the foremost of all warrior-noble (families).
24. The chief queen of the future Buddha when he was a prince was Bhaddakaccānā, and his son was Rāhula.
25. Prince Siddhattha and Bimbisāra were friends, and both their fathers were also friends.
26. The future Buddha was five years older than Bimbisāra; and at the age of twenty-nine he made the Great Renunciation.
27. He strove for enlightenment for six years and in due course attained it; at the age of thirty-five he went to (meet) Bimbisāra.
28–30. Bimbisāra, (a man) of great merit, was fifteen years old when his father consecrated him as king; in the sixteenth year after he became king the Teacher preached the Dhamma to him. He ruled his kingdom for fully fifty-two years, for fifteen years before his meeting with the Conqueror and for thirty-seven years while the Tathāgata was live.
31. Bimbisāra's son, the great traitor Ajātasattu, had him killed and ruled the kingdom for thirty-two years.
32. The Sage attained final nirvana in the eighth year of Ajātasattu's reign, and after that he ruled for twenty-four (more) years.
33. The Tathāgata, who had reached the pinnacle of every (possible) good quality, [although otherwise under the power of no-one in the world] had no power (to avoid) succumbing to the power of imperma-

nence[20]; the person who reflects thus on fearful impermanence will go beyond suffering.

[End of] the second chapter, called The Lineage of Mahāsammata, in the *Mahāvaṃsa*, composed to bring serene confidence and (religious) animation to good people.

[20] This renders what I see as a deliberate play on words in *aniccatā-vasaṃ avaso upāgato.* Pali *avasa*, Skt *avaśa*, can mean both "under the power of no-one" and "having no power." Mhv-ṭ 139 mentions both of these interpretations (my phrase in brackets follows its gloss on the first), but rejects the second, on the grounds that in the Canon (D II 104) the Buddha tells Māra he will not attain final nirvana when the latter encourages him to do so: but it adds that the Buddha attained nirvana and *abhāvaṃ gato* (see 2.2.a p. 205 and n. 14) because of the inherent nature of the Aggregates.

APPENDIX 3

*The discourse (containing) a lion's roar on the Wheel-turning king (*Cakkavatti-sīhanāda Sutta*)*

[Some repetitions in the text are omitted; apart from very minor cases, elisions are marked by brackets and/or ". . .".]

1. Thus I have heard: at one time the Blessed One was staying among the people of Magadha, in (the city of) Matulā. There the Blessed One summoned the monks . . . and said:

"Monks, live with yourselves as an island, with yourselves as a refuge, with no-one else as a refuge. Live with the Dhamma as an island, with the Dhamma as a refuge, with nothing else as a refuge. How does one live [like that]? In regard to this, monks, a (good) monk lives in his body, contemplating (what) his body (is), energetically, aware, mindful, rid of hankering after the world and of melancholy (about it).[1] He lives in (relation to his) feelings [likewise], as also in (relation to his) states of mind and Mental Objects.[2] This, monks, is the way a monk lives with himself as an island, with himself as a refuge, with no-one else as a refuge; with the Dhamma as an island, with the Dhamma as a refuge, with nothing else as a refuge. In your field(s) of movement[3], monks, move (only) in your own customary terrain. When [you do this] Māra [the god of desire and death] can't get an opportunity, can't get anything to latch on to. It is by acquiring wholesome states (of mind) that this merit increases[4]".

2. Once upon a time, monks, there was a king called Daḷhanemi (Strong-tire), a Wheel-turner, righteous, a king of righteousness (*dhammiko dham-*

[1] "World" here is *loka*. The commentary to the *Mahāsatipaṭṭhāna Sutta*, whence this section comes, glosses *loka* as *kāya*, "body'; it usually refers to both the things and the people of the ordinary, non-renunciate world.

[2] The text gives the full formulae in the first and last; the second and third are elided. "Mental objects" renders *dhammesu*, in the plural. In Chapter 1 these are called Existents; the term can also be taken as a shorthand for *dhammāyatanesu*, " (in relation to) objects of the sixth sense, the mind." See Collins (1982: 115).

[3] *Gocare*. Literally "pasture," this can refer, *inter alia*, to places for alms-gathering, or to the "fields" of the senses; the commentary here (Sv 847) explains it as the Four Foundations of Mindfulness, which the text has just referred to. The verb *carati* can be translated "move," "behave" or simply "be"; "own customary terrain" renders *sake pettike visaye*; *visaya* means "range," "scope," etc.; *pettike* is literally "of your father(s)."

[4] This phrase is discussed in 6.5.c.

marāja), a conqueror of the whole world, who had achieved stability in his country and possessed the Seven Jewels. These Seven Jewels [or: 'precious things', *ratana*] of his were as follows: the Wheel-jewel, the elephant-jewel, the horse-jewel, the gem-jewel, the woman-jewel, the householder-jewel, and the advisor-jewel as the seventh. He had more than a thousand sons, who were valiant, of heroic (physical) form, crushing enemy armies. He conquered this earth, surrounded by the ocean, and lived from it, without violence, without a sword, according to what is right [*dhammena*],[5]

3. Then, monks, after the passing of many years, many hundreds and thousands of years, king Daḷhanemi addressed one of his men: 'My good man, (if and) when you see that the celestial Wheel-jewel has slipped down from its place, then let me know.' 'Yes, sir,' the man replied. Then, monks, after the passing of many years, many hundreds of years, many thousands of years, the man saw that the celestial Wheel-jewel had slipped down from its place. [He went to the king and said] 'If it please your Majesty,[6] you should know that the celestial Wheel-jewel has slipped down from its place.'

Then, monks, king Daḷhanemi had his eldest son, the Prince, summoned, and said to him, 'My dear prince, the celestial Wheel-jewel has slipped down from its place. I have heard (it said) that when a Wheel-turning king's celestial Wheel-jewel slips down from its place, the king does not have long to live. I have enjoyed the pleasures of human life, now it is time to seek the pleasures of life in the heavens. Come, my son, take possession of this earth, surrounded by the ocean. I will cut off my hair and beard, put on yellow robes, and go forth from home to homelessness.'

Then, monks, king Daḷhanemi instructed his eldest son the prince thoroughly in (the art of) kingship, cut off his hair and beard, put on yellow robes, and went forth from home to homelessness. Seven days, monks, after he went forth as a Royal Sage the celestial Wheel-jewel disappeared.

4. Then one of the noble warrior king's men went to him, who had (now) been duly consecrated, and said, 'If it please your Majesty, you should know that the celestial Wheel-jewel has disappeared.' Then, monks, the noble warrior king was distressed, and made his distress known (to others).[7] He went to (his father) the King-seer and said, 'If it please your

[5] Adapted from Norman (1992a: 63), as cited in 6.5.a.

[6] This is borrowed from Rhys Davids (1899: 76); see PED s.v. *yagghe*. The PTS text here, and hereafter, inserts a question mark – the idea being, I suppose, to indicate tentativeness: "Does your Majesty know . . .?"

[7] The verb *paṭisaṃvedesi* is causative in form (from *vid*, to know) but it often means simply "felt"; I follow the commentary's (Sv 849) gloss *jānāpesi*, "made known." The verb *paṭivedeti* is always used in the causative sense (cf. variants at Pv-a 6 in Kyaw (1978: 8 n. 17). Taking it this way avoids making the second phrase repeat the first, and contributes to characterizing the new king here as rather pathetic (as argued in 6.5.c): kings

Majesty, you should know that the celestial Wheel-jewel has disappeared.' At these words the King-seer said to the noble warrior king, who had been duly consecrated, 'Don't be distressed at the celestial Wheel-jewel's disappearance, and don't make your distress known. The celestial Wheel-jewel is not your ancestral heritage! Come on (*iṅgha*)! You (have to) behave like a noble Wheel-turning king![8] If you behave like a Wheel-turning king, and on the fifteenth day (of the month), on the Uposatha (Full Moon) day, you wash your head, and as an Uposatha celebrant go up to the top of your fine palace, it is possible that the celestial Wheel-jewel will appear (again), with a thousand spokes (between its) tire and centerpiece.'

8. 'But what is this noble turning of a Wheel-turning king?'

'Well then, my dear: depend on what is right (Dhamma), honor and respect it, praise it, revere and venerate it, have Dhamma as your flag, Dhamma as your banner, govern by Dhamma, and arrange rightful (*dhammika*) shelter, protection and defense for your family, for the army, for your noble warrior client(-king)s, for Brahmin householders, for town-dwellers and countryfolk, for ascetics and Brahmin(-renouncer)s, for animals and birds. Let no wrongdoing take place in your territory[9]; if there are poor people in your territory, give them money. The ascetics and Brahmins in your territory, my dear, who abstain from drunkenness and negligence, who practice forbearance and gentleness, each one conquering himself, calming himself, quenching himself (*ekaṃ atānaṃ parinibbāpenti*) – you should go to them from time to time and ask "What, sir, is good ("wholesome", *kusala*)? What is not good? What is blameworthy, what blameless? What is to be practiced, what not? Doing what would lead to suffering and harm for me in the long run? Doing what would lead to happiness and benefit for me in the long run?" You should listen to them, and avoid what is bad (unwholesome, *akusala*);[10] you should take up what is good and do that.[11] That is the noble turning of a Wheel-turning king.'

Monks, the noble warrior king, who had been duly consecrated, replied, 'Yes, your majesty,' to the King-seer and behaved as a Wheel-turning king (should). [He did so, went to the roof of the palace on Uposatha day, as advised in section 4, and then] the celestial

aren't supposed to complain of depression. Note that, despite the fact that he is "duly consecrated" (*muddhāvasitta*, literally "anointed on the head"), he uses the same subordinate phrase to his father as his servant had said to him: his father is still, for him psychologically, in charge.

[8] Literally "turn in the noble turning of a Wheel-turning king": see the remarks at 6.5.c.

[9] *Mā ca te tāta vijite adhamma-kāra pavattittha.* The verb here echoes the use of *vattati* for the king in section 4.

[10] Avoid it, says the commentary, as if it were excrement, poison or fire (Sv 851).

[11] *Yaṃ kusalaṃ taṃ samādāya vatteyyāsi* – the choice of words ties together the phrases in para. 1, and the plays on words involving *vatta / vaṭṭa*, etc. in regard to the Wheel-turning king in sections 4 and 5 (n. 9).

Wheel-jewel (re-)appeared, with a thousand spokes (between its) tire and centerpiece. When the noble warrior king, who had been duly consecrated, saw this he said 'I have heard it said that when a noble warrior king, who has been duly consecrated, [does all these things, and the celestial wheel appears] he is a Wheel-turning king. I must be a Wheel-turning king!'

6. Then, monks, the noble warrior king, who had been duly consecrated, got up from his seat, put his outer robe over one shoulder, took a pot in his left hand, and with his right hand sprinkled (water from it) on the Wheel-jewel, saying 'Turn (*pavattatu*), honorable Wheel-jewel! Conquer, honorable Wheel-jewel!' Then, monks, that Wheel-jewel rolled (*pavatti*) towards the east, and the Wheel-turning king followed after it with his fourfold army. Wherever the Wheel-jewel stopped, there the Wheel-turning king set up camp, with his fourfold army. The rival kings in the east, monks, came to the Wheel-turning king and said, 'Come, great king, welcome, great king, it's yours [i.e. take possession of this territory], great king, give us your orders [or: instruction, *anusāsa*].'

The Wheel-turning king said, 'No living being is to be killed. What is not given is not to be taken. Misconduct in sexual matters is not to be indulged in. Lies are not to be told. No intoxicant is to be drunk. (Now) continue to govern as you did before'[12]. Monks, those (formerly) rival kings in the east became clients of the Wheel-turning king.

7. Then, monks, the Wheel-jewel plunged into the eastern ocean, came out again and rolled south . . . [where the same things happened; then west and north, where they happened again] . . . Monks, those (formerly) rival kings in the south [west and north] became clients of the Wheel-turning king. Then, monks, after the Wheel-jewel had conquered the (entire) earth, surrounded by the ocean it turned back to the king's

[12] *Yahābhuttaṃ bhuñjatha*; for discussion of this phrase, and previous translations of it, see Collins (1966: 443–4). The term *-bhutta* is from the root *bhuñj*, which can mean to eat, to consume in a general sense, to enjoy pleasures (notably sex), and, for a king, to "enjoy" his territory. When the word is used of kings elements of all these meanings can be present, since they are regularly said to be the husband of the earth they rule over (*bhū-pati, mahī-pati*, etc.). The commentary here understands the situation to concern taxes: after the enemy kings have bid him welcome, the CV "does not say "bring me annual taxes of such-and-such an amount" (*ettakaṃ . . anuvassaṃ baliṃ*), nor does he take away (tax-)revenue (*bhoga*) from one (king) and give it to another; rather, with wisdom appropriate to the fact of his being a *dhamma-rājā* he prohibits murder, etc., teaching *dhamma* in a smooth, sweet voice. . ." (i.e. recommends the five Precepts, and ends with *yathābhuttaṃ bhuñjatha)*. This last phrase is not, as are the five Precepts, imposing or recommending moral rules to the enemy-turned-client kings, but is an example of the Wheel-turning king's own moral behavior. That is, he does not depose the kings he defeats and instal someone else in their stead, which was standard practice among Indian kings; nor does he intend to unseat them and collect taxes directly himself. Of course, direct extraction of taxes of that kind could, in the premodern world, only operate over a small territory: all major kings or "emperors" ruled through other intermediary members of the tribute-taking class.

(capital) city, and came to rest, as though axle-locked[13], in front of the court room by the door of the Wheel-turning king's palace, illuminating [it].[14]

8. The second Wheel-turning king, monks [did the same thing as the first – i.e. became a King-seer at the end of his life and gave sovereignty over to his son], and (likewise) the third . . . fourth . . . fifth . . . sixth . . . seventh. Seven days, monks, after [this seventh king] went forth as a Royal Sage the celestial Wheel-jewel disappeared.

9. Then one of the [eighth] noble warrior king's men went to him, who had (now) been duly consecrated, and said, 'If it please your Majesty, you should know that the celestial Wheel-jewel has disappeared.' Then, monks, the noble warrior king was distressed, and made his distress known (to others). But he did not go to (his father) the King-seer and ask about the noble turning of a Wheel-turning king; rather, he followed his own opinions in governing the country. While he [did so] the country did not (continue to) prosper as it had done before[15] [in the case of] former kings who turned the noble turning of a Wheel-turning king [after their fathers had become king-seers].

Then, monks, his ministers, councilors, chief financial advisers, royal guardsmen, doorkeepers, and magicians[16] assembled (together), went to the noble warrior king . . . and said, 'Your majesty, since you are governing the country according to your own opinions your countrymen are not prospering as they did under former kings who turned the noble turning of a Wheel-turning king. You have in your territory, your Majesty, ministers, councilors, chief financial advisers, royal guardsmen, doorkeepers, and magicians; we, and others, remember what the noble turning of a Wheel-turning king is. Come on (*iṅgha*)! Ask (us) about [it, and we will explain what it is]!'

10. And so, monks, the king had ministers, councilors, etc. called together and asked them about the noble turning of a Wheel-turning king. He listened to [what they said] and arranged rightful shelter, protection and defense – but he did not give money to the poor. [Because of this] poverty flourished. Because poverty flourished, a man intentionally[17] took from others what [they] had not given [him]. People grabbed him, went and showed him to the noble warrior king, saying 'Your Majesty, this man intentionally took from others what [they] had not

[13] *Akkhāhataṃ maññe.* I borrow from Ñāṇamoli (1960: 187); cf. his notes on the Wheel-jewel there.

[14] The commentary (Sv 623–4) says that when this happens for a Wheel-turning king, there is no need for torches or lamps, because the Wheel-jewel's light dispels the darkness at night. The word translated here as "palace," *antepura*, can also mean harem; this perhaps explains in part why the commentary makes the delicate remark that darkness remains, nonetheless, for those who need it.

[15] The text seems corrupt here, but this is clearly the sense (cf. Sv 851–2).

[16] *Mantass' ājīvino,* literally "those who live by mantras." The commentary (Sv 852) Buddhicizes this as "wise men."

[17] *Theyya-saṃkhāta:* see note 20.2 in Collins (1993c).

given [him].' At these words, monks, the king said to the man 'Is it true, as they say, my good fellow, that you intentionally took from others what [they] had not given [you]?'

'Yes, your Majesty.'

'For what reason?'

'I couldn't make a living, your Majesty.'

Then, monks, the noble warrior king . . . gave money to the man, saying 'With this money, my good fellow, you (can) provide yourself with a living, look after your mother and father, your children and your wife, set up a business,[18] establish (regular) excellent gifts for ascetics and Brahmins of the sort that have the happy result of leading you to heaven (after death)'. 'Yes (I will), your majesty,' the man replied . . .

12. Monks, people heard (others saying) 'it seems that the king gives money to those who intentionally [steal] from others. . . . Why don't we [do the same]?'

Then, monks, another man intentionally stole from others. People grabbed him, went and showed him to the noble warrior king, saying 'Your Majesty, this man intentionally stole from others.' At these words, monks, the king said to the man, 'Is it true, as they say, my good fellow, that you intentionally stole from others?'

'Yes, your Majesty.'

'For what reason?'

'I couldn't make a living, your Majesty.'

At this, monks, the noble warrior king . . . thought, 'If I give money to whomever intentionally commits theft, then this theft will increase. How about if I make sure to prevent this man (from doing it again, by) destroying him completely – (by) cutting off his head?' Then, monks, the noble warrior king . . . gave orders to his men: 'Tie this man up tightly with a strong rope, with his hands behind his back, and shave [his head]. Lead him from one high road to another, from one public square to another, with loud drum-beats; take him out to the south of the city, and make sure to prevent him (from doing it again) by destroying him completely – cut off his head!'

'Yes, your Majesty,' they replied [and did as they were told].

13. Monks, people heard (others saying) 'it seems that the king makes sure to prevent thieves (from doing it again) by destroying them completely, by cutting off their heads . . . What if we were to have sharp swords made, and [with them] make sure to prevent people from whom we have stolen [from making it known] by destroying them completely, by cutting off their heads?'

They had sharp swords made, and [with them] started to bring ruin to villages, towns and cities, and to commit highway robbery. They prevented people from whom they stole [from making it known] by destroying them completely, by cutting off their heads.

[18] *Kammante payojehi;* see note 24.1 in Collins (1993c).

14. In this way, monks, money not being given to the poor, poverty flourished; because poverty flourished, theft flourished; because theft flourished, weaponry flourished; because weaponry flourished, murder flourished; because murder flourished, these beings' vitality decreased, as did their beauty; because their vitality and beauty decreased, those who lived for eighty thousand years had children who lived for (only) forty thousand.

When people lived for (only) forty thousand years, monks, a man intentionally stole from others. People grabbed him, went and showed him to the noble warrior king, saying 'Your Majesty, this man intentionally stole from others.' At these words, monks, the king said to the man, 'Is it true, as they say, my good fellow, that you intentionally stole from others?'

"No, your Majesty," he said, consciously telling a lie.

In this way, monks, money not being given to the poor, poverty flourished; because poverty flourished, theft flourished; because theft flourished, weaponry flourished; because weaponry flourished, murder flourished; because murder flourished, telling lies flourished; because telling lies flourished, these beings' vitality decreased, as did their beauty; because their vitality and beauty decreased, those who lived for forty thousand years had children who lived for (only) twenty thousand.

When people lived for (only) forty thousand years, monks, a man intentionally stole from others. Another man went to the noble warrior king and informed him that such-and-such a person had committed theft; [and so, for the first time, someone] spoke maliciously.

16. In this way, monks, money not being given to the poor, poverty flourished; because poverty flourished, theft flourished; because theft flourished, weaponry flourished; because weaponry flourished, murder flourished; because murder flourished, telling lies flourished; because telling lies flourished, malicious speech flourished; because malicious speech flourished, these beings' vitality decreased, as did their beauty; because their vitality and beauty decreased, those who lived for twenty thousand years had children who lived for (only) ten thousand.

When people lived for (only) ten thousand years, some of them were good-looking, some ugly. Then those who were ugly coveted those who were good-looking, and men committed misconduct with other men's wives.[19]

17. In this way, monks, money not being given to the poor, poverty flour-

[19] In the previous phrase, those who are good-looking, and are coveted by those who are ugly, are in the generalizing masculine plural; but this sentence clearly makes men the criminals and women their victims. One could take this as rape rather than adultery, on the grounds that the good-looking women would have no motivation to commit misconduct with ugly men; but some Pali texts do express the misogynist view that women are naturally and indiscriminately promiscuous, and that could be read into this scene.

ished; because poverty flourished, theft flourished . . .[20] . . . misconduct in sexual matters flourished; because misconduct in sexual matters flourished, these beings' vitality decreased, as did their beauty; because their vitality and beauty decreased, those who lived for ten thousand years had children who lived for (only) five thousand.

When people lived for (only) five thousand years, two things (*dhammā*) flourished: harsh speech and frivolous speech. Because these two things flourished, these beings' vitality decreased, as did their beauty; because their vitality and beauty decreased, those who lived for five thousand years had children who lived for (only) two-and-a-half or two thousand.

When people lived for (only) two-and-a-half thousand years, covetousness (or: jealousy, *abhijjhā*) and ill-will flourished; because covetousness and ill-will flourished, . . . those who lived for two-and-a-half thousand years had children who lived for (only) one thousand.

When people lived for (only) one thousand years, Wrong View flourished; because Wrong View flourished . . . those who lived for one thousand years had children who lived for (only) five hundred.

When people lived for (only) five hundred years, three things flourished: improper desire (*adhamma-rāga*), iniquitous greed (*visama-lobha*), and wrongfulness (*micchā-dhamma*).[21] Because these three things flourished . . . those who lived for five hundred years had children who lived for two hundred or two hundred and fifty.

When people lived for two hundred and fifty years these things flourished: lack of respect for one's mother and father, for ascetics and Brahmins, and for the elders of the family.

18. In this way, monks, money not being given to the poor, poverty flourished; because poverty flourished, theft flourished; because theft flourished, weaponry flourished; because weaponry flourished, murder flourished; because murder flourished, telling lies flourished; because telling lies flourished, malicious speech increased; because malicious speech flourished, misconduct in sexual matters flourished; because misconduct in sexual matters flourished, two things flourished: harsh speech and frivolous speech; because these two things flourished, covetousness and ill-will flourished; because covetousness and ill-will flourished, Wrong View flourished; because Wrong View flourished, three things flourished: desire, iniquitous greed, and wrongfulness; because these three things flourished, these things flourished: lack of respect for one's mother and father, for ascetics and Brahmins, and for the elders of the family; because these things flourished, these beings' vitality decreased, as did their beauty; because their vitality and beauty decreased, those who lived for two hundred and fifty years had children who lived for (only) one hundred.

[20] This elision is in the PTS text.

[21] 6.5.c cites the commentary as taking the first and last to be incest and same-sex unions.

19. There will come a time, monks, when the descendants of these people[22] will live for (only) ten years. When people live for (only) ten years, their daughters will be ready for marriage at five. When people live for (only) ten years, these flavors will disappear: (those of) ghee, cream, oil, honey, molasses, and salt. When people live for (only) ten years, the primary[23] food will be (a kind of bad) grain[24]. Just as now, monks, rice, meat and rice porridge are the primary foods, so, monks, when people live for (only) ten years (a kind of bad) grain will be the primary food. When people live for (only) ten years, the ten Good Deeds (*dasa kusala-kamma-patha*) will completely disappear, and the ten Bad Deeds will rage like a great fire. When people live for (only) ten years, the idea of 'good' (*kusala*) will not exist – how will there be anyone who does good? When people live for (only) ten years, those who show lack of respect for their mother and father, for ascetics and Brahmins, and for the elders of their family will be revered and praised. In the same way that now, monks, those who show respect for one's mother and father, for ascetics and Brahmins, and for the elders of one's family are revered and praised, when people live for (only) ten years, those who show lack of respect for their mother and father, for ascetics and Brahmins, and for the elders of their family will be revered and praised.

20. When people live for (only) ten years, [men will not recognize women as] 'mother,' 'mother's sister,' 'mother's brother's wife,' 'teacher's wife,' or 'women of our elders' – the world will become thoroughly promiscuous, just as (it is) now among goats and sheep, fowl and pigs, dogs and jackals. When people live for (only) ten years, fierce mutual violence will arise among these beings, fierce ill-will, fierce hatred, fierce thoughts of murder, in a son for his mother, in a mother for her son, in a son for his father, in a father for his son, in a brother for his brother, in a sister for her brother, and in a brother for his sister . . . Just as now when a hunter sees an animal fierce violence, fierce ill-will, fierce hatred, fierce thoughts of murder arise in him, so when people live for ten years, fierce mutual violence will arise among these beings, fierce ill-will, fierce hatred, fierce thoughts of murder, in a son for his mother, in a mother for her son, in a son for his father, in a father for his son, in a brother for his brother, in a sister for her brother, and in a brother for his sister . . .

21. When people live for (only) ten years, there will be a seven-day period of war, when people will see each other as animals; sharp swords will appear in their hands and they will murder each other, each thinking 'This is an animal.' But some of these beings will think 'Let me kill no-

[22] I.e. the Buddha's contemporaries in the narrated present.

[23] For connections between this text and the "Discourse on What is Primary" (= Appendix 5) see Collins (1996).

[24] It is not known exactly what *kudrūsaka* is. See Horner (1938: 83 n. 4). I gloss "bad" because of the prefix *ku-*.

one, let no-one kill me. Why don't I go to some inaccessible place, in (thick) grass, in a forest, in a tree, by a river where it is difficult to walk, or on a rocky mountain, and eat wild roots and fruit to keep myself alive?' [And they will do so.] After the seven days have passed, they will emerge from their [hiding-places] and embrace one another joyfully, exclaiming[25] to each other 'Wonderful! (Fellow) being, you are alive!'

Then, monks, those beings will think 'It is because we have undertaken Bad Deeds that we have for so long been murdering our (own) relatives. Why don't we start doing good? (But) how do we do good? Why don't we abstain from killing? Let's undertake that good deed and practice it.' They will abstain from killing, undertake this Good Deed[26] and practice it. Because of their undertaking Good Deeds their vitality and beauty will increase, and those who live for ten years will have children who live for twenty.

22. And then, monks, those beings will think 'It is because of undertaking Good Deeds that our length of life and beauty have increased. What if we were to do even more good? Why don't we abstain from taking what is not given; abstain from misconduct is sexual matters; abstain from telling lies; abstain from malicious speech; abstain from harsh speech; abstain from frivolous speech; abstain from covetousness; abstain from ill-will; abstain from Wrong View; abstain from three things: improper desire, iniquitous greed, and wrongfulness; why don't we abstain from lack of respect for one's mother and father, for ascetics and Brahmins, and for the elders of our families?' And they will have respect for their mother and father, for ascetics and Brahmins, and for the elders of their families; undertaking this Good Deed they will practice it.

Because of their undertaking these Good Deeds their vitality and beauty will increase: among these people, increasing with respect to vitality and beauty, those who live for twenty years will have children who live for forty; those who live for forty years will have children who live for eighty; those who live for eighty years will have children who live for a hundred and sixty; those who live for a hundred and sixty years will have children who live for three hundred and twenty; those who live for three hundred and twenty years will have children who live for six hundred and forty; those who live for six hundred and forty years will have children who live for two thousand years; those who live for two thousand years will have children who live for four thousand; those who live for four thousand years will have children who live for eight thousand; those who live for two thousand years will have children who live for four thousand; those who live for eight thousand years will have children who live for twenty thousand; those who live for twenty thousand years will have

[25] As the Rhys Davids point out (1921: 71 n. 3) both text and commentary are difficult to understand here.

[26] I assume that the Buddha's narrative voice is referring to abstention from killing explicitly within the category of Good Deeds (*kusala-kamma-patha*), whereas the beings in his parable simply use the same words.

children who live for forty thousand; those who live for forty thousand years will have children who live for eighty thousand.

23. When people live for eighty thousand years, their daughters will be ready for marriage at five hundred. When people live for eighty thousand years, there will be only three kinds of disease: desire, hunger and old age. When people live for eighty thousand years, this Jambudīpa will be rich and prosperous, with villages, towns and royal cities (so close that) a cock can fly [or: jump] from one to another[27]. When people live for eighty thousand years, this Jambudīpa will be as full of people as the Avīci hell, I should think, (or) like a thicket of reeds or grass! When people live for eighty thousand years, this city of Benares will be called Ketumatī: it will be a rich and prosperous royal city, populous, full of people, and with (more than) enough to eat. When people live for eighty thousand years, in this Jambudīpa there will be eighty-four thousand cities, with the royal city of Ketumatī at their head.

24. When people live for eighty thousand years, in this royal city of Ketumatī there will arise a Wheel-turning king called Saṅkha, righteous, a king of righteousness, a conqueror of the whole world, who will achieve stability in his country and possess the Seven Jewels. These Seven Jewels of his will be: the wheel-jewel, the elephant-jewel, the horse-jewel, the gem-jewel, the woman-jewel, the householder-jewel, and seventhly the advisor-jewel. He will have more than a thousand sons, who will be valiant, of heroic (physical) form, crushing enemy armies. He will conquer this earth, surrounded by the ocean, and live from it, without violence, without a sword, according to what is right.

25. When people live for eighty thousand years, a Blessed One called Metteyya will arise in the world, an Arahant, a Perfectly enlightened Buddha, endowed with (perfect) wisdom and conduct, a Happy One, one who will understand the world, an unsurpassed trainer of those who are to be tamed, a teacher of gods and men, a Buddha, a Blessed One,[28] just as now I have arisen in the world, an Arahant, a Perfectly enlightened Buddha, endowed with (perfect) wisdom and conduct, a Happy One, one who understands the world, an unsurpassed trainer of those who are to be tamed, a teacher of gods and men, a Buddha, a Blessed One. He will understand, realize experientially and proclaim (the true nature of) the world with its gods, its Māras, Brahmas, its ascetics and Brahmins, this world of beings born as gods and men,[29] just as now I understand,

[27] It seems certain that this is the meaning of *kukkuṭa-sampātikā* (cf. Sv 855, giving *sampādikā* as an alternative reading), although the derivation of the second term is uncertain.

[28] This is a standard and very well-known list, in both Theravāda and other kinds of Buddhism: see Ñāṇamoli (1975: 206ff.), Jaini (1986a: xxiii, 84–5, where the first syllables are used as an acrostic), Griffiths (1994: 60–6). In Pali it is chanted, under the title *iti pi so gāthā*; someone reading this text would probably have recited it as a chant.

[29] *Pajaṃ sadevamanussaṃ*; *pajā* means much the same as *loka*, world, from the root *pa-jan*, to be born.

realize experientially and proclaim (the true nature of) the world with its gods, its Māras, Brahmas, its ascetics and Brahmins, this world of beings born as gods and men. He will teach the Dhamma, in letter and in spirit, which is beautiful in the beginning, in the middle, and at the end, and make known (the virtues of) the pure, celibate life, just as now I teach the Dhamma, in letter and in spirit, which is beautiful in the beginning, in the middle, and at the end, and make known (the virtues of) the pure, celibate life. He will have with him a Monastic Order of many thousands, just as now I have one of many hundreds.

26. Then, monks, king Saṅkha will raise up [from underwater] the palace which king Mahāpanāda had built[30] and live in it. He will (then) give it away, let it go, give it as alms (for the use of) ascetics, Brahmins, indigents, tramps, and beggars. In the presence of the Blessed One Metteyya he will cut off his hair and beard, put on yellow robes, and go forth from home to homelessness. He will be a renouncer, alone and secluded, diligent, energetic, self-determined. Living thus it will not be long before in that very life he understands, realizes experientially, takes up and lives (the achievement of) the celibate life, for which sons from good families rightly leave home for homelessness.

27. Monks, live with yourselves as an island, with yourselves as a refuge, with no-one else as a refuge. Live with the Dhamma as an island, with the Dhamma as a refuge, with nothing else as a refuge. How does one live [like that]? In regard to this, monks, a (good) monk lives in his body, contemplating (what) his body (is), energetically, aware, mindful, rid of hankering after the world and of melancholy (about it). He lives in (relation to his) feelings [likewise], as also in (relation to his) states of mind and Mental Objects. This, monks, is the way a monk lives with himself as an island, with himself as a refuge, with no-one else as a refuge; with the Dhamma as an island, with the Dhamma as a refuge, with nothing else as a refuge. In your field(s) of movement, monks, keep to your own customary terrain. When [you do this] your vitality and beauty will increase, as will your happiness, enjoyment and strength.

Monks, what (meaning) is there for a monk in vitality? In this regard a monk develops [i] the Basis of Success (*iddhi-pāda*) that is furnished both with concentration gained by means of desire to act, and with forces of endeavor; and also the Bases of Success that are furnished with concentration gained by means of [ii] strength . . . [iii] mind . . . [iv]

[30] Reading *yo so yūpo* . . . The story of king (Mahā)Panāda (see DPPN s.v.) is told in the *Maitreyāvadāna* of the *Divyavadāna*. The word *yūpa*, which comes to mean "palace" in Pali (Sv 856), originally referred to a sacrificial pole (cf. Norman 1969: 156–8 on Th 163–4); Auboyer (1949: 74ff.) shows how such poles came to refer also to royal thrones, and thence palaces.

investigation, [all with forces of endeavor].[31] By developing these four Bases of Success, by making much of them a monk who wishes to could stay alive for an eon or what remains of an eon[32]. I say that this is what (meaning) there is for a monk in vitality.

Monks, what (meaning) is there for a monk in beauty? In this regard a monk is virtuous (*sīlavā*) restrained by the restraint of the *Pātimokkha* [the Monastic Rule], possessing (proper modes of) conduct and resort,[33] who sees danger in the least wrongdoing, and who takes up and trains himself in the Rules of Training (*sikkhāpada*). This is what (meaning) there is for a monk in beauty.

Monks, what (meaning) is there for a monk in happiness? In this regard a monk, detached from (pleasures based on) desires and from unwholesome states of mind, enters into and remains in the first Meditation Level[34], which is characterized by Applied and Sustained Thought, by Rapture and Happiness. With the calming down of Applied and Sustained Thought he enters into and remains in the second Meditation Level, which is characterized by inner confidence and singleness of mind, which is without Applied and Sustained Thought, but with Rapture and Happiness born of concentration. [Thus also] . . . the third Meditation Level . . . and the fourth. This is what (meaning) there is for a monk in happiness.

Monks, what (meaning) is there for a monk in enjoyment? In this regard a monk suffuses one direction with a mind [or: heart, *citta*] endowed with lovingkindness [or: friendliness, *mettā*];[35] likewise the second (direction), the third and the fourth. Likewise upwards, downwards, and all around, everywhere and equally[36] he pervades the entire world with a mind endowed with lovingkindness, (a mind which is) abundant, extensive, measureless, without hatred or ill-will. He pervades (the entire world) with a mind endowed with compassion . . . sympathetic joy . . . and equanimity, (a mind which is in each case) abundant, extensive, measureless, without hatred or ill-will. This is what (meaning) there is for a monk in enjoyment.

Monks, what (meaning) is there for a monk in strength? In this regard a monk, through the destruction of the Corruptions in this very life

[31] This translation is from Gethin (1992a: 80), who discusses these four Bases of Success at length. In this paragraph and elsewhere in section 28, the elisions are in the text. No doubt when recited what is omitted could be reinserted: monks and nuns would have known most of this section by heart.

[32] This is said of the Buddha in the Mahāparinibbāna *Sutta* (D II 103ff.).

[33] "Conduct" here refers, *inter alia*, to mode of livelihood and "resort" to laity from whom a monk or nun begs: see Vibh 246–7, Vism 17ff. = I 44ff, translated in Ñāṇamoli (1975: 17ff.).

[34] Cf. 4.1.b; Vism 139ff. = IV 79ff., translated in Ñāṇamoli 1975: 144ff.

[35] These are the four Divine Abidings: see Vism Chapter 4, especially 308ff. = IX 44f.; Ñāṇamoli 1975: 333ff.

[36] This is how Vism takes *sabbattatā*, a difficult word which may mean seeing everything as equal to oneself.

understands and realizes experientially the Freedom of Mind and Freedom through Wisdom (which are) without Corruptions; he enters into (them) and lives (in them). This is what (meaning) there is for a monk in strength.

Monks, I do not perceive any other single strength so hard to overcome as the strength of Māra. (But) it is by acquiring wholesome states (of mind) that this merit increases."

The Blessed One said this. The monks were pleased and rejoiced in the Blessed One's words.

APPENDIX 4

Selections from the Story of the Elder Māleyya (Māleyyadevattheravatthu)

These are the parts of this text relevant to this book, with only as many notes as are necessary here. Further notes, textual remarks, etc. can be found in Collins (1993b); and an Introduction in Collins (1993a).

Honor to the Blessed One, the Worthy One, the Fully enlightened One! Bowing to the excellent Buddha, (who is) to be revered by gods and men, to the Teaching which originates from the Happy One, and to the virtuous Monastic Order, I will undertake (to tell) briefly the story of Māleyya, replete with supreme(ly good) advice and edifying for all.

In the past, the story goes, in the island of Tambapaṇṇi, (also) called the isle of Lankā, where the (three) Jewels were established, a certain elder by the name of Māleyyadeva, famous for the excellence of his supernatural power and knowledge, lived in Rohana province supported by (alms given in) the village of Kamboja. The elder repeatedly brought back news of the beings roasting in hell: recounting (this news) to their relatives he inspired them to make merit by almsgiving and the like, and he made them aim for heaven as the result of the merit they acquired and by transferring merit to those (hell-beings). By the force of his supernatural power he traveled to both heaven(s) and hell(s): after seeing the great majesty of laymen and women in heaven who had faith in the Three Jewels, he went to people (on earth) and recounted how such-and-such a layman or woman had been reborn in such-and-such a heaven and experienced great happiness; after seeing the great suffering of miscreants in hell, he went to people (on earth) and recounted how such-and-such a man or woman had been reborn in such-and-such a hell and experienced great suffering. People gained faith in the teaching and did no evil; they dedicated merit (acquired through) almsgiving and the like to their dead relatives, and aimed for heaven as the result of the merit they acquired and by transferring merit to those (dead relatives).

One day the elder got up in the morning, took his robe and bowl and went to the village to collect alms. In the village (lived) a poor man (who) looked after his mother. At the (same) time he went out from the village to bathe; he came to a pond, took his bath, and saw eight blue lotus flowers. He picked them, got out of the pond, and started on his way (back). Then he saw the elder coming (towards him) bowl in hand, (looking) calm, restrained, well controlled, his senses mastered, with perfect bearing. Joy and delight arose in him, and he went up to the elder and greeted him respectfully with his hands in the form of a hollow lotus-bud (made) by putting his ten fingernails together. With great faith he gave the flowers to the elder, and made an aspiration in this verse:

By this gift of flowers, wherever I am (reborn) in a hundred thousand births, may I not be poor!

The elder took the eight blue lotus flowers, and gave thanks in this verse:

Whatever (a person) gives with a faithful mind, whether coarse or choice, has a successful result according to (the donor's) wish.

After giving thanks (thus) the elder (first) reflected, "Where shall I place these eight blue lotus flowers on a shrine – on top of a mountain, at (the place of the Buddha's) final nirvana, at (the foot of) the Great Bodhi-tree or at the place where the Blessed One set in motion the Wheel of the Supreme Law?" Then he thought, "I have worshiped (at) these places seven times (each); what if I were to worship at the Cūlāmaṇi-shrine in heaven?"

Immediately after thinking this, the elder attained the fourth Meditation Level, which is the basis for Supernatural Knowledge; emerging from it he flew along the path of the wind and in the time it takes to snap one's fingers reached the terrace around the Culāmaṇi-shrine in the city of the Thirty-three gods, made beautiful by the (surrounding) land's being adorned with seven precious things; Sakka, king of the gods, had reverently caused (this) delightful sapphire (shrine) to be set up, so that all the gods could worship (there). The Blessed One himself had cut off his top-knot (of hair) with a sword grasped in his cotton-soft, webbed hand, and had thrown it into the air with the aspiration, "If I am to attain enlightenment and become a Buddha may my top-knot not fall to the ground"; it did not fall to the ground, and (Sakka) caught it in a splendid gold casket which he carried on his own head (and then made the shrine for it). (The elder) worshiped (at the shrine) with the eight lotus flowers, walked around it keeping it to his right, paying reverence to the eight directions and with a fivefold prostration, and sat down on the eastern side. Thus it is said:

He attained the fourth Meditation Level, the basis for Supernatural Knowledge, and emerging from it rose up instantly into the sky like a golden swan; in the space of a finger-snap he arrived at the shrine in front of (the) Vejayanta palace, (where he) worshiped and paid reverence.

At that moment Sakka, king of the gods, came with his retinue and worshiped the right tooth of the Blessed One and the Cūlāmaṇi-shrine with various kinds of garlands, perfumes, ointments and the like; seeing the elder sitting down he went up to him, paid reverence and sat down to one side. All the groups of gods paid reverence to the shrine, walking around it keeping it to the right, (and then) paid reverence to the elder and sat down all around (him); so too did all the divine maidens, who paid reverence to the elder with a fivefold prostration. Sakka, king of the gods, asked the elder: "Sir, where have you come from?" "Great king, I have come from the Rose-apple island to pay reverence to the shrine." Then the elder asked Sakka: "Did you have the Cūlāmaṇi-shrine set up?" "Yes, venerable sir, I had it set up to be worshiped by the gods." The elder asked: "King of the gods, these gods did good deeds in the Human World and were reborn here to enjoy divine happiness; why do they make merit now?" "Venerable sir, these gods make merit in the desire to go beyond the world of the gods. Sir, gods who are of little merit do not remain long in heaven, just as a few grains put in a wooden trough are quickly used up; whereas gods who are of much merit remain long in heaven, just as a lot of grain put in a granary remains (there) for a long time and is not used up. Similarly, sir, just as people with little wealth (but) with a lot of skill and knowledge, if they engage in farming, trade and the like make a living without difficulty, gods of little merit who enjoy (its) result (but) then make further merit experience heavenly happiness afterwards. Venerable sir, wealthy people with no skill or knowledge who do not engage in farming, trade or the like, (soon) use up their wealth and afterwards become quite poor: in just the same way gods of much merit who experience (its) result without making further merit afterwards are born in a poor state. Just as poor people with no skill and knowledge who do not engage in farming, trade or the like become (even) poorer, so too gods of little merit who experience (its) fruit without making further merit become (even) poorer; (conversely) just as rich people with a lot of skill and knowledge who engage in farming, trade or the like prosper even more, so too gods of much merit who give alms, practice morality, and so on, go upstream (in the stream of life) and prosper, (even) as far as nirvana."

When the elder heard this he was pleased, and asked Sujā's husband (i.e. Sakka): "Great king, all the gods have come to pay reverence at the shrine of the Blessed One; is the future Buddha Metteyya coming?" "Yes, venerable sir." "When will he come?" "Sir, he has come (in the past) on the eighth, fourteenth or fifteenth days (of the lunar month)." "So – today being the eighth – is he coming (today)?" "Yes, sir." While the elder was thus conversing with Sakka, a junior god came with a hundredfold retinue to worship at the shrine. The elder saw the junior god arrive and asked Sakka: "King of the gods, is this Metteyya?" "No, sir." "Who is it?" "Someone else, sir." "King of the gods, what merit did this junior god make previously in the Human World?" Sakka related his meritorious deed in this verse:

Sir, when born in the human (world) he was a poor grass-cutter who (once) when eating a leaf used for wrapping food gave one piece as an offering to a crow; after doing even so small a meritorious deed he moved on (through life) in the human (realm) which ends in death, and was then reborn (here) because of it.

Therefore it is said:

Whoever gives a gift to an animal such as a crow, as a result of even that gift the giver receives a hundred(fold).

The junior god came, walked around the shrine keeping it to his right, paid reverence to the eight directions, worshiped with garlands, perfumes, etc., and sat down on the eastern side.

[Eleven more junior gods arrive, with retinues of varying sizes. Māleyya asks about each of them, and is told a similar story by Sakka.]

End of the first (section of the) story of Māleyya, dealing with the twelve junior gods.

Then the noble Metteyya, the future Buddha, came down from the Tusita realm to worship at the shrine. He was attended by millions upon millions of junior gods and goddesses, who shone with a light brighter than that of the moon with its thousand rays; he (himself) shone like a full moon in a cloudless autumn sky, surrounded by clusters of stars. They were (all) holding lamps, incense, perfumes and garlands. His celestial radiance filled the whole city of the Thirty-three (gods) with light, gave off a celestial smell, and with his characteristic incomparable grace and charm he came to the shrine-terrace, walked around it keeping it to his right, paid reverence to and worshiped the eight directions, and sat down on the western side. Therefore it is said:

Then the noble Metteyya (came), attended by tens of millions, with a hundred divine young maidens in front, a hundred behind, a hundred to his right and to his left. Metteyya in their midst was like the moon in the midst of stars; everywhere was illuminated by the rays of the divine maidens and of their jewels, like the light from ten million moons.

The elder saw the future Buddha from afar, and asked Sakka: "King of the gods, is this Metteyya the future Buddha?" "Yes, sir." "King of the gods, these divine young girls coming in front of Metteyya, with their (shining) white rays, clothes and jewels – what merit did they make in former lives in the Human World?" Sakka recounted their deeds of merit:

Venerable sir, all these celestial maidens, when formerly born in the human (world), made merit by giving gifts and the like on Uposatha day; they gave white clothes, white garlands, white perfumes and ointments, and white food to the excellent Buddha's monks. Because of these deeds of merit they are coming in front of Metteyya.

On hearing this the elder praised their deeds of merit. [He then asks similarly about the divine young girls to the right and left of Metteyya, and behind him.]

On hearing this the elder praised [the] deeds of merit [of the last group], and again asked Sakka: "What merit did Metteyya make that he should have attained such happiness?" Sakka's capacity to elucidate Metteyya's merit can be compared to a hare (trying to) cross the ocean, or a blind man (trying to) climb a mountain, but he elucidated it briefly (as follows): there are three (types of future Buddha), called those who excel in faith, those who excel in wisdom, and those who excel in energy; Metteyya is one who excels in energy. (All) future Buddhas, by means of the threefold good conduct (consisting in) control of body, speech and mind, accumulated over many ages, fulfil thirty Perfections altogether: ten (ordinary) Perfections, ten higher Perfections, and ten Perfections in the ultimate sense. The Perfection of Generosity comprises the sacrifice of wealth, children and wife [= ordinary Perfection], the sacrifice of (one's own) limbs [= higher Perfection] and the sacrifice of (one's) life [= Perfection in the ultimate sense]; and correspondingly (there are three levels of) the Perfections of morality, renunciation, wisdom, energy, patience, truth, resolution, lovingkindness and equanimity. He spoke these verses:

The merit which Metteyya the future Buddha made over and over again – not (even) the excellent omniscient Buddhas could describe it (all) – cannot be told (even) partially, just as a hare crossing the ocean or a blind man climbing a mountain would not attain (their) goal: in the same way Metteyya's merit is infinite, boundless, (since) he accumulated the necessary conditions (for enlightenment) completely, during many eons. There are three (kinds of) future Buddhas: one is known as he who excels in energy, who fulfils all Perfections during (a period of time lasting) a hundred thousand eons and sixteen uncountable eons and (then) attains supreme Full enlightenment; (the second) is renowned in this human (world) as he who excels in faith, who fulfils all the Perfections during (a period of time lasting) a hundred thousand eons and eight uncountable eons and (then) attains supreme Full enlightenment; (the third) is renowned in this human (world) as he who excels in wisdom, who fulfils all the Perfections during (a period of time lasting) a hundred thousand eons and four uncountable eons and (then) attains supreme Full enlightenment. The future Buddha Metteyya is known as one who excels in energy; he has fulfilled all the Perfections during a hundred thousand eons and sixteen uncountable eons and has been reborn in the Tusita (heaven): when he dies from that body (and is reborn on earth) he will attain Full Enlightenment.

While the elder was conversing thus with Sakka, Metteyya came, walked around the shrine keeping it to his right, paid reverence to the eight directions, worshiped with garlands, perfumes, etc., paid reverence with the fivefold prostration, and sat down on the eastern side. The future

Buddha saw the elder sitting down there, paid reverence to him and asked: "Where have you come from, venerable Sir?" "I have come from the Rose-apple Island, great king." "Venerable Sir, What is happening among the human beings in Rose-apple Island?" The elder answered his question by saying:

Everyonè there lives according to their (past) deeds, rich and poor, happy and unhappy, attractive and unattractive, long-lived and short-lived. The rich are few, the poor are many; the happy are few, the unhappy many; the attractive are few, the unattractive many; the long-lived are few, the short-lived many. Human beings are few, there are more animals; that is why I say that everyone lives according to their (past) deeds.

The future Buddha heard what the elder said (and asked:) "Sir, do the human beings in Rose-apple Island make much merit or demerit?" "Great king, those who make merit are few, there are more who do evil." "Sir, how do they make merit?" He explained "Great king, some human beings in Rose-apple Island give alms, some preserve morality, (or) give the gift of the Truth, keep the Uposatha day(s), make images of the Buddha, build monasteries or residences (for the Order), give rains-residences, robes, alms-food (or) medicine, tend the Bodhi-tree, build stūpas, shrines, parks (for the Order), causeways (or) walkways (for meditation), dig wells (or) canals, give (the monastic) requisites (or) the tenfold gift, look after their mother and father, offer sacrifice for the sake of dead relatives, worship the Three Jewels, have their son enter the Monastic Order (as a novice), or worship the Buddha-image: the human beings in Rose-apple Island do all these deeds of merit, according to their capacity, their strength and their inclination." "Sir, When the human beings in Rose-apple Island make merit in these ways, what wishes do they make?" The elder recounted their aspirations in these words:

Your Highness, when they make even a (small) measure of merit, or cause others to make merit, or rejoice in the merit of others, they make an aspiration for enlightenment (in relation) to you: "By the merit acquired through giving, morality and the like, may we gain sight of the Buddha Metteyya himself, (and) while the Buddha Metteyya is not reborn (on earth, but remains in heaven) worshiped by the gods, may we, moving through rebirths, never go to a hell." In this way the human beings in Rose-apple Island, everywhere and always, make merit and then make an aspiration with regard to you.

The future Buddha, joyful to hear (this) news of human beings in Rose-apple Island, said: "Sir, let everyone who wishes to see me when I have attained Omniscience listen to a complete recitation in one day of the Great Vessantara Birth-story; if they worship with a thousand lamps or a thousand lotuses, a thousand blue lotuses, blue waterlilies, Mandāra-flowers, flax-flowers, a thousand banners, parasols, flags or vehicles, and bring everything to worship the Teaching, they will attain Arahantship along with the analytical insights at the time of my enlightenment (and) in my presence." Then he recounted how evil humans would not attain the sight of his Buddhahood, in these verses:

(Those who) violently mistreat nuns, make a schism in the Order, commit the five actions which bring immediate retribution,[1] destroy a stūpa or Bodhi-tree, murder a future Buddha or take away the peace of the Order: (these) wicked and negligent beings will not be in my presence.

The elder listened to these words and said: "Great king, what you said was good! I will recount (it) to the human beings in Rose-Apple Island. But when will you become Buddha?" "Sir, the Dispensation of Gotama Buddha will last five thousand years and (then) disappear. When it has disappeared there will be an abundance of bad actions in the world. Even the word 'good' will not exist – how much less the occurrence of good (actions)! Gradually human beings will lose (all) conscience and (sense of) shame, breaking (all) rules: they will not consider 'This is my mother, my daughter, my sister or granddaughter,' and will be (as) shameless as goats, sheep, chickens, pigs, jackals, dogs, and the like. Then gradually, because of their abundant bad actions, from (having) a lifetime fixed at a hundred years, human beings will deteriorate and (come to) have a lifetime of ten years. When there is taking and giving in marriage between five-year-old boy(s) and girl(s), then will occur an 'intervening period of the sword.' Men will regard each other as animals; whatever they (can) grasp in their hands will become a weapon like a two-edged (sword) or a single-edged razor, (and) they will kill each other. The wise among them, as soon as they hear of the destruction, will go to the mountains and hide by themselves; all the rest apart from them will attack and destroy each other within seven days. When the seventh day has passed, they will come out, each one from his hiding-place, embrace each other and come into harmony with each other (saying), 'Let us do good, and abstain from killing, from theft, sexual misdeeds, lying, intoxicating drink, speech which is malicious, harsh or frivolous, from envy, ill-will and Wrong Views – let us make merit!' (And so) they will make merit. Those who live ten years will have children who live for twenty; and as human beings make more and more merit, their children will gradually live for thirty, forty, fifty, sixty, seventy, eighty, ninety and a hundred years. Children will gradually live for two hundred years, (then) three, four, five, six, seven, eight and nine hundred years, (and then finally) a thousand. Gradually, the children of those who live a thousand years will live for two thousand; (then) for three, four, five, six, seven, eight, nine and ten thousand. Then human beings will practice religion still more, and will live for a hundred thousand years; as they practice religion still more, there will be those who live for millions and millions of years; practicing religion still further than this, they will live for an incalculable amount of time. Then old age

[1] These are: matricide, parricide, killing an Arahant, causing a Buddha to shed blood, and creating schism in the Order.

and death will not be known among (these) beings; but again they will become negligent, and their length of life will diminish. From (having) an incalculable length of life, men will deteriorate and (come to) have a lifetime of millions and millions of years; from then they will gradually deteriorate (until) they have a lifetime of ninety thousand years; from then they will gradually deteriorate (until) they have a lifetime of eighty thousand years. At that time it will rain (only) in the middle of the night, every fortnight, ten days or five days, increasing the fertility of the earth. The Rose-apple Island will be prosperous (and) continuously filled with flowers, fruits, thickly-clustered garlands, and trees; (it will be) crowded with villages and towns (only) a cock's-flight (apart), free from thieves and robbers, without (any) grasping at (Wrong) Views, (and) blazing with royal cities; (it will be) replete with all treasures, happy, with abundant alms-food and at peace, replete with great amounts of food and drink, hard and soft food, fish, meat and the like, prospering with wealth and possessions. The reservoirs will be everywhere filled with beautifully soft water. Then, sir, husbands and wives will enjoy the pleasures of the five senses without arguments or anger; farmers, traders, and the like will live happily without (needing to) work; men and women will not (need to) spin thread or weave the loom, (but) will wear celestial clothes. Men will be content with their wives, and women with their husbands; restrained, men will not commit adultery nor women make another man their husband, (but) they will be loving and pleasant to one another. No-one will stir up quarrels because of villages, towns, wealth, crops, fields, property or soil; all human beings will be handsome, with beautiful bodies, (and will be) loving and pleasant to each other. Crows will become friendly with owls, cats with mice, deer with lions, mongooses with snakes, lions with deer, and so on: in this way all animals which are (usually) enemies will be friendly to each other. Then, from one grain of self-growing rice (will come already-)husked grains: two thousand two hundred and seventy cartloads will be (for them as easily had as) sixteen *ambaṇa*-measures and two *tumba*-s. Then I will listen to the entreaty of the gods and Brahmas living in the ten-thousandfold world system; I will make the five Considerations, as to time, place, continent, family, and age-limit of the mother; (and) I will come as Buddha to the Human World." When he had said this, in order to praise his own Perfections he said:

During a hundred thousand eons and sixteen incalculable eons I fulfilled the Perfections variously, acting as a future Buddha excelling in energy, and gave gifts: when I attain Omniscience no-one will be deformed. Putting ornaments on my head and ointment on my eyes I gave to beggars for millions and millions of years: when I attain Omniscience no human being will be blind. Ornamenting all parts (of my body) I gave a complete gift: when I attain Omniscience, no-one will be deformed. I told no lies and did not deceive anyone who asked (me for something): when I attain Omniscience, no human being will be dumb. When I heard the Teaching I was glad, and I listened to what supplicant said: when I attain Omniscience, no human being will be deaf. I looked at virtuous supplicants with loving eyes: when I attain Omniscience, no human being will be blind. With upright body I gave gifts and the like at the proper time: when I attain Omniscience no human being will be humpbacked. I gave beings medicine(s) and got rid of the danger (from disease): when I attain Omniscience, then beings will be in good health. I practiced loving-kindness, destroying beings' fear and terror: when I attain Omniscience, then there will be no Māras. In a pleasant way I gave pleasing food and drink: when I attain Omniscience human beings will be prosperous. In a pleasant way I gave pleasing clothes: when I attain Omniscience human beings will be handsome. I gave to supplicants pleasing vehicles, elephants, horses, chariots, palanquins and litters: when I attain Omniscience human beings will be happy. I freed beings from bondage, from hatred and suffering: when I attain Omniscience, living beings will be free. I practiced lovingkindness equally to friend and foe: when I attain Omniscience, the ground will be even. I made supplicants happy with food and wealth: when I attain Omniscience rivers will be full of cool water.

(Then Metteyya said this:)

When they have done any (act of) merit human beings, full of fear of rebirth, aspire to (see) me; I will free them from existence. I will cause (them) to cross to the further shore of the world, (this world) whose fearful origin is ignorance, which is entangled in the net of delusion and carried away by the four floods. I (will) teach the way to liberation to those who are smeared with the dirt of defilement, who follow after the thief (which is) Craving, and have gone astray in (all) the regions of rebirth; I will teach the way to heaven to beings in the hells (called) Sañjiva, Kāḷasutta, Tāpana, Patāpana and Avīci. I will cut from (their) bondage beings who are bound by the ties of ignorance and caught in the net of Craving, and make them attain nirvana. The city of nirvana, without old age or death, has a fence of Wrong Views and a door bolted by the sixty-two views: with the key of the Eightfold Path I will open up (this door) for beings. I will give the medicinal stick of wisdom to beings whose sight is spoilt through being covered with the darkness of lust and hatred, and clean their eyes. I will give the excellent medicine of understanding to beings who are sick with grief, who suffer much, and who are oppressed by old age and death, and (so) cure (them). I will suffuse with the light of understanding (the world) with its gods, asuras and humans, gone astray in the darkness of delusion, and take away the darkness. I will raise from hell those who are falling, helpless and without refuge, into the hells, and show them the way to the further shore.

When he had said this the future Buddha told (the elder): "Sir, recount to human beings what I have said." With his shining hands in the form of a hollow lotus-bud (made) by putting his ten fingernails together, and putting the shining *añjali*-greeting (thus made) firmly to his forehead, (itself) like a well-washed plate of gold, he walked around the delightful sapphire Cūlāmaṇi-shrine, paid reverence to the eight directions and made a fivefold prostration, and took leave of the elder; escorted by millions and millions of junior gods and goddesses, shining like a full moon, risen to the top of the sky freed from masses of dense cloud (and) surrounded by clusters of stars, he went to the Tusita city. So it is said:

Thus the supremely beautiful Metteyya worshiped at the excellent shrine, again paid reverence, and left keeping his face towards (the shrine). And all the celestial maidens worshipped at the excellent shrine, paid reverence to the eight directions and left (likewise). Just as the moon shines on an autumn full-moon night, so the noble Metteyya shone among the gods. Like a lion among deer, a bull among cows, a Garuḍa among birds, so was he among the gods. Like Meru among mountains, adorned with the Seven Jewels, a Wheel-turning king among men, so was he among the gods. The Păricchattaka[2] among trees, the lotus among flowers, beryl among gems, so was he among the gods. Like fire at the top of a mountain, like refined gold, surpassing all the gods he shone with the fire of his beauty. Going to the Tusita realm, surrounded by gods, he experienced divine happiness and caused beings to rejoice for a long time.

The elder (possessed, as if he) was adorned with a multitude of ornaments, unlimited good qualities, such as the four perfect virtues – the supreme virtue of restraint by the Monastic Rule, the virtue of sense-restraint, the perfect virtue of right livelihood and the virtue of dependence (only) on the four requisites (of the monastic life). At the same moment (as Metteyya left) he paid reverence to the Cūlāmaṇi-shrine and took leave of Sakka, king of the gods. He traveled along the path of rebirth[3] which is the origin of sufferings such as birth, old age and death, which have their home in numerous forest thickets crowded with various trees and forest creepers such as the extremely strong (trees, creepers of) lust, Craving and Wrong Views[4]. He shone like a golden swan whose supreme, outstanding body had a head guarding the threefold knowledge, wings of the fourth Meditation Level, two excellent lucky feet of the beautiful, shining bases of supernatural power, and the entire plumage guarding the eight Liberations, the analytical knowledges and the worldly and super-worldly confidences. He descended from the realm of the Thirty-three, came to Rose-apple Island, and with the incomparable grace natural to a disciple (of the Buddha) went for alms in villages, towns and royal cities. So it is said:

Then the elder (Māleyya-)deva took leave of the king of the gods, paid reverence again at the shrine and came down from heaven. He shone like a golden swan as he came again to the human (world) and went for alms in towns and royal cities.

As he returned for alms he announced to the people of Rose-apple Island the news of Metteyya. When they heard what the elder said people

[2] A tree in the Tāvatiṃsa heaven. [3] I.e. he returned to earth from heaven.
[4] There is probably a pun intended here between *vana* as "forest" and *vana* as a synonym for *taṇhā*, "craving." The image is of Māleyyadeva returning from heaven like a swan through a forest, both of which are metaphorically elaborated.

were glad and made merit through giving and the like: at the end of their lives they filled up the divine worlds. The poor man who had given the eight blue-lotus flowers remembered that gift of lotuses all his life; when he died (he went) from the Human World and was reborn in the realm of the Thirty-three, in a blue-lotus palace inlaid with Seven Jewels, crowded with celestial maidens and ringing with the sound of dancing, singing and the five kinds of musical instrument. As he walked lotuses of five colors (appeared to) receive each foot; the odor from his mouth pervaded the entire city of the gods like the perfume of a lotus. The gods and goddesses smelt the lotus-perfume and followed after him; they all saw a lotus receiving each foot, and told Sakka, king of the gods. When he heard their tale he was delighted, and went there (to him) and asked: "God, what deed of merit did you do in the Human World to obtain such happiness?" He listened to what Sakka said and replied: "King of the gods, formerly in the Human World I lived in Mithilā supporting my mother; I was a young man called Piṅguttara.[5] One day I went to a certain pond to bathe. When I had bathed there I saw eight blue lotus flowers; I took them and gave them to a certain elder. Because of that gift of blue lotuses I have been born in a blue lotus palace; as I walk lotus flowers come into existence at each step, my eyes are like blue lotus petals, my body has an odor like that of a blue lotus, and I am born (here) as the junior god named Blue-lotus." When Sakka heard this he became joyful and glad; he took blue lotus flowers and worshiped at the shrine of the Buddha. The junior god Blue-lotus is still there today. So it is said:

To enjoy (the result of) that merit, and divine happiness, in a future birth in the presence of Metteyya – this is the result of a gift of flowers. Therefore the wise man who aspires to be in the presence of Metteyya should practice almsgiving, morality and the like. Whoever remembers the future Buddha's words and does any act of merit, will gain the advantage of seeing Metteyya, and will in the future make an end of suffering; (before then,) moving on through rebirth, that person will not go to hell.

End of the expository account of the Elder Māleyyadeva.

(This) will be a cause of (attaining) nirvana in the future!

[5] J VI 347–9 tells a different story of a young man from Mithila, in north India, with this name; perhaps the *Māleyyadevatthera-vatthu* has borrowed the names, although this is clearly the same person as at the start of the story, in Kamboja village, Rohana, Sri Lanka.

APPENDIX 5

The discourse on what is primary (Aggañña Sutta)

[For Introduction and notes see Collins 1993c.]

1. Thus I have heard. At one time the Blessed One was living in the palatial monastery built by Migāra's mother in the Eastern Park outside Sāvatthi. At that time Vāseṭṭha and Bhāradvāja, aspiring to become monks, were living with the monks there. One evening the Blessed One rose from his solitary meditation, went outside the monastery, and was walking back and forth in its shade, in the open air.
2. Vāseṭṭha saw that the Blessed One . . . was walking back and forth . . . in the open air, and said to Bhāradvāja:

"Friend Bhāradvāja, here is the Blessed One . . . walking back and forth . . . in the open air. Come, friend, let's go to him: perhaps we may get a chance to hear a Dhamma-talk from the Blessed One himself."

"Alright, friend," agreed Bhāradvāja; and so Vāseṭṭha and Bhāradvāja went up to the Blessed One, greeted him, and walked back and forth together with him.
3. Then the Blessed One addressed Vāseṭṭha (and Bhāradvāja):

"Monks, you were (both) born Brahmins, in Brahmin families, (but) you have gone forth from home to homelessness, (leaving your) Brahmin family. Surely Brahmins (must) revile and abuse you?"

"Indeed, sir, Brahmins revile and abuse us fully, completely, with the (sort of) abuse one would expect (from them)."

"How do they abuse you . . .?"

"Sir, Brahmins say 'The Brahmin is the best class (*vaṇṇa*), (any) other class is inferior. The Brahmin is the fair class, (any) other class is dark. (Only) Brahmins are purified, not non-Brahmins. Brahmins are Brahmā's own sons, born from his mouth, born of Brahmā, produced from Brahmā, the heirs of Brahmā. You here have left the best class and gone (over) to an inferior class, since you have become wretched, shaven-headed (pseudo-) ascetics, members of some sect, (no better than) off-spring of our Kinsman's [i.e. Brahmā's] feet. It is not good, it is unseemly, that you have left the best class . . . [and] have become . . . offspring of our Kinsman's feet.' That is how they revile us . . . with the (sort of) abuse one would expect (from them)."

4. "Surely, monks, the Brahmins are not recalling the past when they say [this]. Brahmin women, (the wives) of Brahmins, are seen to menstruate, become pregnant, give birth and give suck; and (so) these Brahmins who say 'The Brahmin is the best class . . . Brahmins are born from Brahmā's mouth . . . heirs of Brahmā,' are (in fact) born from vaginas. They are slandering Brahmā, telling lies, and producing demerit.
5. Monks, there are these four classes: Kṣatriya (warriors/kings), Brahmin (priests), Vaiśya (farmers, merchants) and ¯ūdra (servants). [Take the case where] a particular Kṣatriya is a murderer, a thief, misbehaves in sexual matters, tells lies, speaks maliciously, harshly and frivolously, is envious, malevolent and holds Wrong Views: in this way, monks, those things which are unwholesome, blameworthy, not to be followed, unworthy to be called noble (and known to be all these things), dark with dark (karmic) result, and censured by the wise, are seen here in a particular Kṣatriya. [The same thing is then repeated of individual members of the other three classes.]
6. [Take the case where] a particular Kṣatriya refrains from murder, theft [and all the other things mentioned in 5]: in this way, monks, those things which are wholesome [and the converse of what is said in 5] . . . fair with fair result and praised by the wise, are seen in a particular Kṣatriya. [The same thing is then repeated of individual members of the other classes.]
7. Given that bad and good things, what is censured and praised by the wise, occur mixed up together in these four classes, wise men will not tolerate it when Brahmins say 'The Brahmin is the best class . . . Brahmins are . . . heirs of Brahmā.' Why? Of these four classes, monks, he who is a monk, an Arahant, in whom the Corruptions are destroyed, who has lived the (holy) life, done what was to be done, laid down the burden, attained the true goal, in whom the fetters of existence are destroyed, who is released by Right Wisdom – he is properly called what is primary among them, not improperly (as are the Brahmins). For the Dhamma is the best (thing), monks, in this world, both in this life and in the future.
8. (The fact) that Dhamma is best in this world and in the future, monks, can be understood by the following illustration. The king of Kosala, Pasenadi, realizes 'the ascetic Gotama, who is unsurpassed, has gone forth from a Sākyan family.' The Sākyans are (now) vassals of King Pasenadi of Kosala, monks: they (have to) fall at king Pasenadi's feet in obeisance, salute him respectfully, rise up from their seats for him, do him homage with hands together. Now, all this kowtowing which the Sākyans do before king Pasenadi, king Pasenadi does before the Tathāgata, (thinking) 'Indeed the ascetic Gotama is well-born, while I am ill-born; the ascetic Gotama is powerful, I am not; Gotama is charismatic, I am ugly [or: of bad appearance, *dubbaṇṇo*]; he has great authority, I have little.' It is in reverence, honor, worship and respect for this Dhamma that king Pasenadi falls at the Tathāgata's feet in obeisance,

salutes him respectfully, rises up from his seat for him, and does him homage with hands together. By this illustration, monks, one can understand that Dhamma is the best in the world, in this life and in the future.

9. You, monks, are from various castes, of various names, from various clans and various families, and (yet) you have gone forth from home to homelessness. When asked who you are, acknowledge that 'We are sons of the Sākyan.' When anyone has a faith in the Tathāgata which is firm, rooted, (well-)established and which cannot be disturbed by (any) ascetic, Brahmin, god [or: king, *deva*], Māra, Brahmā, or anyone in the world, that person can fittingly say, 'I am the Blessed One's own son, born from his mouth, born of the Dhamma, produced by the Dhamma, the heir of Dhamma.' Why? (Because) these are epithets of the Tathāgata: 'he who has Dhamma for a body,' 'who has the best body,' 'who is Dhamma,' 'who is the best.'

10. Eventually, after a long time, monks, it comes to pass that the world contracts; as it contracts, usually beings devolve as far as the Ābhassara world. There they remain for a long time, made of mind, feeding on rapture, providing their own light, moving about in the air, glorious. Eventually, after a long time, monks, it comes to pass that the world evolves; as it evolves, usually beings die from their Ābhassara-bodies and come to this world. (Here) they remain for a long time, made of mind, feeding on rapture, providing their own light, moving about in the air, glorious.

11. At that time there is nothing but water, (all) is darkness, (just) deep darkness. It is not possible to discern the moon or sun, the twinkling stars, night or day, months or half-months, seasons or years, men or women. Beings just have the name 'beings.' Then (on one such occasion) an earth-essence spread out on the waters. It appeared in the same way as (does) the spreading out (of skin) on top of boiled milk-rice as it cools down. It had color, smell and taste; its color was like sweet ghee or cream, its taste like fine clear honey.

12. Then, monks, a certain being, greedy by nature, thinking 'What can this be?', tasted the earth-essence with his finger. As he tasted the earth-essence with his finger he was pleased, and Craving came upon him. Other beings imitated that being, tasting the earth-essence with their finger(s). They too were pleased, and Craving came upon them. Then, monks, these beings started to eat the earth-essence taking (big) mouthfuls of it with their hands. As they did so, their self-luminosity disappeared. When their luminosity disappeared, the moon and sun appeared; when the sun and moon appeared, the twinkling stars appeared; when the stars appeared, night and day appeared; when night and day appeared, the seasons and years appeared. Thus far, monks, did the world evolve.

13. Those beings, monks, spent a long time eating the earth-essence, living on it as their food. According to how (much) these beings ate, so

(much did) their bodies become hard, and good and bad looks became known. Some beings were good-looking, others ugly; those who were good-looking despised those who were ugly: 'We are better-looking than they, they are uglier than us!' Because these (beings), proud and arrogant by nature, were proud of their appearance, the earth-essence disappeared. When it had disappeared, they came together and lamented, 'Look (*aho*), the (earth) essence (*rasaṃ*) (has disappeared), look . . . the essence.' So nowadays, when people have tasted something good they say, 'Oh the taste, oh the taste!' (*aho rasaṃ*). They recall the original, primary word(s), but they don't understand what they mean.

14. Then, monks, when the earth-essence had disappeared, a fragrant earth appeared for those beings; it appeared (suddenly) just like a mushroom. It had color, smell and taste; its color was like sweet ghee or cream, its taste like fine clear honey. Then they started to eat the fragrant earth. Those beings, monks, spent a long time eating the fragrant earth, living on it as their food. According to how (much) these beings ate, so to an even greater degree did their bodies become hard, and good and bad looks become known. Some beings were good-looking, others ugly; those who were good-looking despised those who were ugly: 'We are better-looking than they, they are uglier than us!' Because these (beings), proud and arrogant by nature, were proud of their appearance, the fragrant earth disappeared. When it had disappeared, a (kind of) creeper appeared. It appeared like a kalambukā plant. It had color, smell and taste; its color was like sweet ghee or cream, its taste like fine clear honey.

15. Then they started to eat the creeper. Those beings, monks, spent a long time eating the creeper, living on it as their food. According to how (much) these beings ate, so to an even greater degree did their bodies became hard, and good and bad looks become known. Some beings were good-looking, others ugly; those who were good-looking despised those who were ugly: 'We are better-looking than they, they are uglier than us!' Because these (beings), proud and arrogant by nature, were proud of their appearance, the creeper disappeared. When it had disappeared, they came together and lamented, 'We've had it, the creeper has given out on us!' So nowadays, when people are touched by some hardship, they say, 'We've had it, it's given out on us!' They recall the original, primary word(s), but they don't understand what they mean.

16. Then, monks, when the creeper had disappeared, there appeared for those beings rice, growing without cultivation; it was without powder, (already) husked, sweet-smelling and ready to eat. Whatever they gathered in the evening for their evening meal, in the morning had grown back ripe again; whatever they gathered in the morning for their morning meal, in the evening had grown back ripe again: (the work of) harvesting was unknown. Those beings, monks, spent a long time eating the rice which grew without cultivation, living on it as their food. According to how (much) these beings ate, so to an even greater degree

did their bodies become hard, and good and bad looks become known. The female parts appeared in a woman, and the male parts in a man; the woman looked at the man with intense, excessive longing, as did the man at the woman. As they were looking at each other with intense longing passion arose in them, and burning came upon their bodies; because of this burning, they had sex. When the (other) beings saw them having sex, some threw earth (at them), some threw ashes, others cow-dung, (saying) 'Away with you and your impurity, away with you and your impurity!', 'How could a being do such a thing to another being?' So nowadays, people in certain areas, when a bride is being led out, throw dirt, ash or cow-dung. They recall the original, primary (actions), but they don't understand what they mean.

17. Monks, what was thought improper at that time is nowadays thought proper. At that time the beings who took to having sex were prevented from entering either small or larger settlements for a month or two. Since those beings were excessively intoxicated at that period of time by (this) immorality, they took to building houses to conceal it. Then a certain being, lazy by nature, thought, 'Well! Why am I troubling myself gathering rice for my evening meal in the evening, and (again) for my morning meal in the morning? Why shouldn't I gather it just once, for both evening and morning?' And he did so. Then another being came up to him and said, 'Come, being, let's go to gather rice.' 'There's no need! I've gathered rice just once for both evening and morning.' The (second) being thought 'That seems (a) good (idea), my friend,' and imitated him by gathering rice just once for two days. Then another being came up to the (latter) being, and said, 'Let's go to gather rice.' 'There's no need! I've gathered rice just once for two days.' The (third) being thought, 'That seems (a) good (idea),' and imitated him by gathering rice just once for four days. Then another being came up to the (latter) being, and said 'Let's go to gather rice.' 'There's no need! I've gathered rice just once for four days.' The (fourth) being thought, 'That seems (a) good (idea),' and imitated him by gathering rice just once for eight days. Because these beings took to eating rice which they had stored up, powder and husk then covered the grain, cutting without regeneration, and harvesting became known; and the rice stood in clumps.

18. And then, monks, the beings came together and lamented, 'Bad things have appeared for us beings; we were formerly made of mind . . . [they recount their degeneration, concentrating on the succession of food-stuffs, and omitting the etiology of sex and houses. Each disappearance is said to be 'because of the appearance of bad, unwholesome things among us'] . . . and now the rice stands in clumps. Let us now divide up the rice, and set up boundary-lines.' And so, monks, they divided up the rice and set up boundary-lines.

19. Then, monks, a certain being, greedy by nature, while keeping his own portion (of rice), took another portion without its being given, and

ate it. (Other beings) grabbed him and said, 'You have done something bad, being, in that you kept your own portion but took another portion without its being given, and ate it. Don't do such a thing again!' 'Alright,' he agreed. [This happens a second and third time, after which] they hit him, some with their hands, some with clods of earth, some with sticks. From this moment on, monks, stealing, accusation, lying and punishment became known.

20. Then, monks, those beings came together and lamented, 'Bad things have appeared for us beings, in that stealing, accusation, lying and punishment have become known; what if we were to appoint one being to criticize whoever should be criticized, accuse whoever should be accused, and banish whoever should be banished? We will (each) hand over to him a portion of rice.' Then, monks, those beings went to the one among them who was most handsome and good-looking, most charismatic and with greatest authority and said, 'Come, being, (you) criticize whoever should be criticized, accuse whoever should be accused, and banish whoever should be banished; we will (each) hand over to you a portion of rice.' He agreed [and did as they asked]; they (each) gave him a portion of rice.

21. 'Appointed by the people' [*mahājanena sammato*], monks (is what) *mahāsammata* (means): 'Mahāsammata' was the first term (for the Kṣatriya class) which appeared. 'Lord of the Fields' [*khettānaṃ pati*] is what *khattiya* means: 'Khattiya' was the second term (for the Kṣatriya class) to appear. 'He brings joy to others [*paresaṃ . . . rañjeti*] according to Dhamma,' is what *rājā* ('king') means: 'Rajā' was the third term (for the Kṣatriya class) to appear. This was the birth of the Kṣatriya-group, (along) with the original, primary term(s); of just these beings, no others, of similar (beings), not dissimilar, properly and not improperly. For the Dhamma is the best (thing), monks, in this world, both in this life and in the future.

22. Then some beings, monks, thought, 'Bad things have appeared for us beings, in that stealing, accusation, lying, punishment and banishment have become known; let us keep away from (these) bad, unwholesome things.' [And they did so.] 'They keep away from bad, unwholesome things' [*pāpake . . . bāhenti*], monks, (is what) *brāhmaṇā* means: 'Brāhmaṇa' was the first term (for the Brahmin class) to appear.[1] They made leaf-huts in the forest and meditated in them; without coals or smoke (from a cooking fire), pestle (and mortar) set down, they went into villages, towns and royal cities in search of food, in the evening for their evening meal, and in the morning for their morning meal. When they had got their food, they went back again to their leaf-huts in the forest to meditate. (Other) humans saw this and said: 'These beings have

[1] This wordplay shows that an earlier form of this text must have had a different MIA form for *brāhmaṇa*, such as *bamhaṇa*. See KRN no. 84 p. 101.

made leaf-huts in the forest and meditate there; without coals or smoke . . . they go back again to their leaf-huts in the forest to meditate.' 'They meditate' (*jhāyanti*), monks, (is what) 'those who tend a (sacrificial) fire' (*jhāyakā*) (means): 'Jhāyaka' was the second term (for the Brahmin class) to appear.

23. Some of these beings, monks, were unable to maintain (the life of) meditation in forest leaf-huts; they went to the outskirts of villages and towns and lived there making (up) texts. (Other) humans saw them and said, 'These beings are unable to maintain (the life of) meditation . . . they live there making (up) texts. They do not meditate.' 'They do not meditate' (*na . . . jjhāyanti*), monks (is what) Students [or: Reciters] (of the Veda) (*ajjhāyakā*) (means): 'Ajjhāyaka' was the third term (for the Brahmin class) to appear.[2] It was considered a lesser thing at that time, monks; nowadays it is considered the best. This was the birth of the Brahmin-group, (along) with the original, primary term(s); of just these beings, no others, of similar (beings), not dissimilar, properly and not improperly. For the Dhamma is the best (thing), monks, in this world, both in this life and in the future.

24. Some of these beings, monks, practiced sexual intercourse and took up occupations of high repute; 'they practice sexual intercourse and take up occupations of high repute (*vissuta*),' monks (is what) *vessā* means. The term 'Vessa' (thus) appeared. This was the birth of the Vaiśya-group, (along) with the original, primary term; of just these beings, no others, of similar (beings), not dissimilar, properly and not improperly. For the Dhamma is the best (thing), monks, in this world, both in this life and in the future.

25. The beings who were left over led cruel, mean lives; 'they live cruel, mean lives' (*luddācārā, khuddācārā*) (is what) *suddā* (means). The term 'Sudda' (thus) appeared. This was the birth of the Śūdra-group, (along) with the original, primary term; of just these beings, no others, of similar (beings), not dissimilar, properly and not improperly. For the Dhamma is the best (thing), monks, in this world, both in this life and in the future.[3]

26. There came a time, monks, when a Kṣatriya disapproved of his own tasks, and left home for homelessness, in order to become an ascetic. A Brahmin, too, disapproved of his own tasks and left home for homelessness, in order to become an ascetic. So too did a Vaiśya . . . and a Śūdra . . . in order to become an ascetic. This was the birth of the ascetic group, monks, from these (other) four groups; of just these beings, no others, of similar (beings), not dissimilar, properly and not improperly. For the

[2] The wordplay is this: *ajjhāyaka*, Skt *adhyāyaka* (from root *adhi-ī*), "reciter/learner (of the Veda)," is being taken as the negative *a-jjhāyaka*, Skt *a-dhyāyaka* (from root *dhyai*, with the *a* – prefix), "non-meditator."

[3] The wordplay in sections 25 and 26 is not clear (see Collins 1993c). It is not relevant for present purposes.

Dhamma is the best (thing), monks, in this world, both in this life and in the future.

27. A Kṣatriya, monks, who misbehaves in body, speech and mind, and who holds Wrong Views, because of (his) Wrong Views and acquisition of (bad) karma is reborn, after the break-up of the body in death, in a bad destiny, in hell. A Brahmin, monks . . . a Vaiśya . . . a Śūdra . . . an ascetic who misbehaves . . . is reborn . . . in hell.

28. A Kṣatriya, monks, who behaves well in body, speech and mind, and who holds Right Views, because of (his) Right Views and acquisition of (good) karma is reborn after the break-up of the body in death, in a good destiny, in heaven. A Brahmin, monks . . . a Vaiśya . . . a Śūdra . . . an ascetic who behaves well . . . is reborn . . . in heaven.

29. A Kṣatriya, monks, who does both (good and bad) with his body, speech and mind, and whose views are a mixture (of good and bad), after the break-up of the body in death, experiences both happiness and suffering. A Brahmin, monks . . . a Vaiśya . . . a Śūdra . . . an ascetic who does both . . . experiences happiness and suffering.

30. A Kṣatriya, monks, who is restrained in body, speech and mind, by means of (his) cultivation of the seven things which pertain to enlightenment attains nirvana in this very life. A Brahmin, monks . . . a Vaiśya . . . a Śūdra . . . an ascetic who is restrained . . . attains nirvana in this very life.

31. Of these four classes, monks, he who is a monk, an Arahant, who has lived the (holy) life, laid down the burden, attained the true goal, in whom the fetters of existence are destroyed, who is released by Right Wisdom – he is properly called what is primary among them, not improperly (as are the Brahmins). For the Dhamma is the best (thing), monks, in this world, both in this life and in the future.

32. The Brahmā Sanaṅkumāra, monks, spoke this verse:

For those who rely on clan, the Kṣatriya is the best in this world;
(but) the person endowed with wisdom and (good) conduct is the best
in the whole universe.

This verse was well sung by the Brahmā Sanaṅkumāra, monks, not ill-sung, well-spoken not ill-spoken, endowed with meaning not without meaning: I approve of it. I too, monks, say:

For those who rely on clan, the Kṣatriya is the best in this world;
(but) the person endowed with wisdom and (good) conduct is the best
in the whole universe."

The Blessed One said this. Vāseṭṭha and Bhāradvāja were pleased, and rejoiced in the Blessed One's words.

Bibliography

Abercrombie, N., S. Hill and B. S. Turner (1980) *The Dominant Ideology Thesis*. London: George Allen and Unwin.

Abu-Lughod, J. L. (1989) *Before European Hegemony: The World System ad 1250–1350*. Oxford University Press.

Adam, B. (1990) *Time and Social Theory*. Cambridge: Polity Press.

(1955) *Timewatch*. Cambridge: Polity Press.

Alexander, F. (1931) "Buddhistic Training as an Artificial Catatonia," *Psychoanalytic Review* 18: 129–45.

Alheit, P. (1994) "Everyday Time and Life Time: On the Problems of Healing Contradictory Experiences of Time," *Time and Society* 3(3): 305–19.

Allchin, F. R. (1995) *The Archaeology of Early Historic South Asia: the Emergence of Cities and States*. Cambridge University Press.

Allchin, F. R. and K. R. Norman (1985) "Guide to the Aśokan Inscriptions", *South Asian Studies* 1: 43–9.

Almond, P. (1988) *The British Discovery of Buddhism*. Cambridge University Press.

Amin, S. (1976) *Unequal Development: an Essay on the Social Formations of Peripheral Capitalism*. New York: Monthly Review Press. (French original 1973.)

(1980) *Class and Nation: Historically and in the Current Crisis*. New York: Monthly Review Press.

(1989) *Eurocentrism*. New York: Monthly Review Press.

(1991) "The Ancient World-Systems Versus the Modern Capitalist World-System," *Review* 14, 3: 349–85.

Anderson, B. (1990) "Murder and Progress in Modern Siam," *New Left Review* 181: 33–48.

(1991) *Imagined Communities: Reflections on the Origin and Spread of Nationalism* (revised edn.). New York: Verso.

Annas, J. (1993) *The Morality of Happiness*. Oxford University Press.

Anuman Rajadhon, P. (1961) *Life and Ritual in Old Siam*. New Haven: Hraf Press.

(1968) *Essays on Thai Folklore*. Bangkok: Social Science Association Press.

Archer, M. (1988) *Culture and Agency: The Place of Culture in Social Theory*. Cambridge University Press.

Armelin, I. (1975) *Le roi détenteur de la rue solaire en révolution (Cakravartin) selon le Brahmanisme et le Bouddhisme.* Paris: Librairie Orientaliste Paul Geuthner.

Auboyer, J. (1949) *Le trône et son symbolisme dans l'Inde ancienne.* Paris: Presses Universitaires de France.

Aung, S. Z. (1910) *Compendium of Philosophy.* London: Pali Text Society.

Aung Thwin, M. (1979) "The Role of *Sāsana* Reform in Burmese History: Economic Dimensions of a Religious Purification," *Journal of Asian Studies* 38, 4: 671–88.

(1980) "A Reply to Lieberman," *Journal of Asian Studies* 40, 1: 87–9.

(1981) "Jambudīpa: Classical Burma's Camelot," *Contributions to Asian Studies* 16: 38–61.

(1982) "Prophecies, Omens and Dialogue: Tools of the Trade in Burmese Historiography" in D. K. Wyatt and A. Woodside (eds.) *Moral Order and the Question of Change: Essays on Southeast Asian Thought* (Monograph Series no.24). Yale University.

(1983) "Divinity, Spirit, and Human: Conceptions of Classical Burmese Kingship", in L. Gesik, *Centers, Symbols and Hierarchies: Essays on the Classical States of Southeast Asia.* (Monograph Series no.26). Yale University.

(1985) *Pagan: The Origins of Modern Burma.* Honolulu: University of Hawaii Press.

(1990) *Irrigation in the Heartland of Burma.* Northern Illinois University, Center for Southeast Asian Studies, Occasional Paper no.15.

(1991) "Spirals in Early Southeast Asian and Burmese History," *Journal of Interdisciplinary History* 21, 4: 575–602.

(1992) review of Koenig (90), *Journal of the American Oriental Society* 112, 4: 654–6.

(1995) "The 'Classical' in Southeast Asia: The Present in the Past," *Journal of Southeast Asian Studies* 26, 1: 75–91.

Bailey, G. (1985) *Materials for the Study of Ancient Indian Ideologies: Pravṛtti and Nivṛtti.* Turin: Pubblicazioni di "Indologia Taurinensia."

Bakel, M. van et al. (eds.) (1986) *Private Politics: A Multidisciplinary Approach to "Big Man" Systems.* Leiden: E. J. Brill.

Barnes, H. E. (1963) *A History of Historical Writing* (2nd. edn.). New York: Dover.

Basham, A. L. (1954) *The Wonder That Was India.* New York: Macmillan.

Bauman, Z. (1992) *Mortality, Immortality and Other Life Strategies.* Stanford University Press.

Bechert, H. (1966) *Buddhismus, Staat und Gesellschaft.* Frankfurt am Main: Metzner.

(1969) "Zum Ursprung der Geschichtsschreibung im Indischen Kulturbereich," *Nachrichten der Akademie der Wissenschaften in Göttingen, Philologisch-historische Klasse, Dritte Folge, No. 2.*

(1978) "The Beginnings of Buddhist Historiography: *Mahāvaṃsa* and Political Thinking," in B. L. Smith (ed.) *Religion and Legitimation of Power in Ceylon.* Chambersburg: Anima.

(1979) *Burmese Manuscripts Part 1.* (Verzeichnis der Orientalischen, Handschriften in Deutschland.) Wiesbaden: Steiner.

(ed.) (1991) *The Dating of the Historical Buddha.* Part 1 (Symposien zur Buddhismusforschung IV, 1), *Abhandlungen der Akademie der Wissenschaften in Göttingen, Philologisch-Historische Klasse, Dritte Folge, No. 189.* Göttingen: Vandenhoeck & Ruprecht.

(1992) *The Dating of the Historical Buddha.* Part 2 (Symposien zur Buddhismus-forschung IV, 2), *Abhandlungen der Akademie der Wissenschaften in Göttingen, Philologisch-Historische Klasse, Dritte Folge, No. 194.* Göttingen: Vandenhoeck & Ruprecht.

Bechert, H. and H. Braun (1981) *Pāli Nīti Texts of Burma.* London: Pali Text Society.

Bechert, H. and R. F. Gombrich (eds.) (1984) *The World of Buddhism: Buddhist Monks and Nuns in Society and Culture.* London: Thames and Hudson.

Bendix, R. (1978) *Kings and People: Power and the Mandate to Rule.* Berkeley: University of California Press.

Benisti, M. (1971) "Les *stūpa* aux cinq piliers," *Bulletin de l'Ecole Française d'Extrème-Orient* 58: 131–62.

Bentley, G. (1986) "Indigenous States of Southeast Asia," *Annual Review of Anthropology* 15: 275–305.

Benveniste, E. (1936) "Expression Indo-européenne de l''éternité'," *Bulletin de la Société de linguistique* 37: 103–12.

Berger, J (1992 [1979]) *Pig Earth.* New York: Vintage.

Berkhofer, R. F. (1995) *Beyond The Great Story: History as Text and Discourse.* Cambridge: Belknap Press.

Bird-David, N. (1992) "Beyond "The Original Affluent Society": A Culturalist Reformulation," *Current Anthropology* 33, 1: 25–47.

Bizot, F. (1981) "Les Yantras Bouddhiques d'Indochine," *Mélanges Chinois et Bouddhiques* 20: 155–91, vol. I of M. Strickmann (ed.) *Tantric and Taoist Studies in honour of R. A. Stein.* Bruxelles: Institut Belge des Hautes Etudes Chinoises.

(1988) *Les traditions de la pabbajjā en Asie du Sud-est. Abhandlungen der Akademie der Wissenschaften in Göttingen, Philologisch-Historische Klasse, Dritte Folge, Nr. 169.* Göttingen: Vandenhoeck & Ruprecht.

Blair, S. S. and J. M. Bloom (eds.) (1991) *Images of Paradise in Islamic Art.* Dartmouth College: Hood Museum of Art.

Blaut, J. M. (1993) *The Colonizer's Model of the World: Geographical Diffusionism and Eurocentric History.* New York: Guilford Press.

Bloch, M. (1974) "Symbol, Song and Dance or is Religion an Extreme Form of Traditional Authority?", *European Journal of Sociology* 15, 1: 55–81.

(1977) "The Past and the Present in the Present," *Man* (n.s.) 12, 2: 278–92.

(1989) "Literacy and Enlightenment," in K. Schousboe and M. Trolle Larsen, *Literacy and Society*. Copenhagen: Akademisk Forlag.

Bode, M. H. (1909) *The Pali Literature of Burma*. London: Royal Asiatic Society.

Bollée, W. B. (1970) *Kuṇāla-jātaka*. (SBB XXVI) London: Pali Text Society.

(1974) "Buddhists and Buddhism in the Earlier Literature of the Svetāmbara Jains," in L. S. Cousins et al. (eds.) (74).

Bond, G. (1984) "The Development and Elaboration of the Arahant Ideal in the Theravāda Buddhist Tradition," *Journal of the American Academy of Religion* 52, 2: 227–42.

(1988) *The Buddhist Revival in Sri Lanka: Religious Tradition, Reinterpretation, Response*. Columbia: University of South Carolina Press.

Borges, J. (1964) *Labyrinths: Selected Stories and Other Writings*. New York: New Directions.

Brabant, F. H. (1937) *Time and Eternity in Christian Thought*. London: Longmans Green.

Bradley, R. (ed.) (1993) *Conceptions of Time and Ancient Society*. London: Routledge.

Braudel, F. (1969) *Ecrits sur l'histoire*. Paris: Flammarion.

(1972) *The Mediterranean and the Mediterranean World in the Age of Philip*. New York: Harper & Row.

(1980) *On History*. University of Chicago Press.

(1993) *A History of Civilizations*. London: Penguin.

Brereton, B. P. (1995) *Thai Tellings of Phra Malai: Texts and Rituals Concerning a Popular Buddhist Saint*. Arizona State University: Program for Southeast Asian Studies.

Bronkhorst (1986) *The Two Traditions of Meditation in Ancient India* (Alt- und Neu- Indische Studien 28) Wiesbaden: Franz Steiner Verlag.

(1993) "Buddhist Hybrid Sanskrit: The Original Language," in K. N. Mishra (ed.) *Aspects of Buddhist Sanskrit*. Sarnath, Varanasi: Central Institute of Higher Tibetan Studies.

Brookes, J. (1987) *Gardens of Paradise: The History and Design of the Great Islamic Gardens*. New York: Meredith Press.

Brough, J. (1962) *The Gandhāri Dharmapada*. Oxford University Press.

(1980) "*Sakaya niruttiyā: cauld kale het*," in H. Bechert (ed.) *The Language of Earliest Buddhist Tradition*. (*Abhandlungen der Akadmie der Wissenschaften in Göttingen, Philologisch-Historische Klasse; Folge 3, Nr. 117*.) Göttingen: Vandenhoeck and Ruprecht.

Brown, D. E. (1991) *Human Universals*. New York: McGraw-Hill.

Brown, P. (1971) "The Rise and Function of the Holy Man in Late Antiquity," *Journal of Roman Studies*, 61: 80–101, reprinted in *Society and the Holy in Late Antiquity*, London: Faber and Faber.

(1978) "Town, Village and Holy Man," in *Society and the Holy in Late Antiquity*. Berkeley: University of California Press.

(1981) *The Cult of the Saints: Its Rise and Function in Latin Christianity*. University of Chicago Press.

(1985) "The Notion of Virginity in the Early Church," in B. McGinn and J. Meyendorff (eds.) *Christian Spirituality: Origins to the Twelfth Century*. New York: Crossroad.

(1986) "The Notion of Virginity in the Early Church," in B. McGinn and J. Meyendorff (eds.) *Christian Spirituality: Origins to the Twelfth Century* (vol.xvi of *World Spirituality*) London: Routledge and Kegan Paul.

(1988) *The Body and Society: Men, Women and Sexual Renunciation in Early Christianity*. New York: Columbia University Press.

(1992) *Power and Persuasion in Late Antiquity: Towards a Christian Empire*. Madison: University of Wisconsin Press.

(1995) *Authority and the Sacred: Aspects of the Christianization of the Ancient World*. Cambridge University Press.

(1996) *The Rise of Christendom*. Oxford: Blackwell.

Brubaker, R. (1984) *The Limits of Rationality: An Essay on the Social and Moral Thought of Max Weber*. (Controversies in Sociology 16.) London: George Allen and Unwin.

Bruner, J. S. (1986) *Actual Minds, Possible Worlds*. Cambridge: Harvard University Press.

(1987) "Life as Narrative," *Social Research* 54, 1: 11–32.

(1990) *Acts of Meaning*. Cambridge: Harvard University Press.

(1991) "The Narrative Construction of Reality," *Critical Inquiry* 18: 1–21.

Buitenen, H. van (1981) *The Bhagavadgītā in the Mahābhāratā: A Bilingual edition*. University of Chicago Press.

Bunnag, J. (1973) *Buddhist Monk, Buddhist Layman*. Cambridge University Press.

Burks, A. W. (1949) "Icon, Index, and Symbol," *Philosophy and Phenomenological Research* 9: 673–89.

Burghart, R. (1978) "Hierarchical Models of the Hindu Social System," *Man* (n.s.) 13, 4: 519–36.

(1985) "Introduction" to R. Burghart and A. Cantlie (eds.) *Indian Religion*. London: Curzon Press.

Burke, P. (1990) *The French Historical Revolution: the Annales School 1929–89*. Stanford University Press.

Burlingame, E. W. (1921) *Buddhist Legends* (Harvard Oriental Series 28–30.) Cambridge: Harvard University Press.

Butt, J. W. (1978) "Thai Kingship and Religious Reform (18th–19th Centuries)," in B. Smith (ed.) (78b).

Cady, J. F. (1958) *A History of Modern Burma*. Ithaca: Cornell University Press.

Carneiro, R. L. (1970) "A Theory of the Origin of the State," *Science* 169: 733–8.

(1988) "The Circumscription Theory: Challenge and Response," *American Behavioral Scientist* 31, 4: 497–511.
Carr, D. (1986) *Time, Narrative and History*. Indiana University Press.
Carrithers, M. B. (1983) *The Forest Monks of Lanka: an Anthropological and Historical Study*. Oxford University Press.
(1985) "An Alternative Social History of the Self," in M. Carrithers, S. Collins and S. Lukes, *The Category of the Person: Anthropology, Philosophy, History*. Cambridge University Press.
(1992) *Why Humans Have Cultures: Explaining Anthropology and Social Diversity*. Oxford University Press.
Carter, J. R. (1984) "Beyond Good and Evil," in G. Dhammapala et al. (eds.), *Buddhist Studies in Honour of Hammalava Saddhatissa*. Nugegoda, Sri Lanka: Volume Committee Hammalava Saddhatissa Felicitation.
(1993) *On Understanding Buddhists: Essays on the Theravāda Tradition in Sri Lanka*. Albany: State University of New York Press.
Carter, J. R. and M. Palihawadana (1987) *The Dhammapada*. Oxford University Press.
Castoriadis, C. (1987) *The Imaginary Institution of Society*. Cambridge: MIT Press.
Cave, T. (1995) "Fictional Identities," in H. Harris (ed.) *Identities*. Oxford University Press.
Chakrabarti, D. K. (1995) *The Archaeology of Ancient Indian Cities*. Oxford University Press.
Chakravarti, U. (1987) *The Social Dimensions of Early Buddhism*. Oxford University Press.
Chamberlain, J. (ed.) (1991) *The Ram Khamhaeng Controversy: Collected Papers*. Bangkok: Siam Society.
Chandler, D. (1996 [1983]) *A History of Cambodia* (2nd edn., paperback updated). Boulder: Westview.
Chantornvong, S. (1981) "Religious Literature in Thai Political Perspective: The Case of the Maha Chat Kamluang," in T. S. Chee (ed.) *Essays on Literature and Society in Southeast Asia: Political and Sociological Perspectives*. Singapore University Press.
Chao Huashan (n.d.) "Investigation of Manichaeist Cave Temples in Turfan" (ms.).
Chase-Dunn, C. and P. Grimes (95) "World-Systems Analysis," *Annual Review of Sociology* 21: 387–417.
Chase-Dunn, C. and T. D. Hall (1994a) "Forward into the Past: World-Systems before 1500," *Sociological Forum* 9, 2: 295–306.
(1994b) "The Historical Evolution of World-Systems," *Sociological Inquiry* 64, 3: 257–80.
Chatman, S. (1978) *Story and Discourse: Narrative Structures in Fiction and Film*. Ithaca: Cornell University Press.
Chatthip Nartsupha (1984) "The Ideology of the Holy Men Revolts," in Turton and Tanabe (eds.) (84).

Chesneaux, J. (1968) "Egalitarian and Utopian Traditions in the East," *Diogenes* 62: 76–102.

Chutintaranond, S. (1988) "*Cakravartin*: Ideology, Reason and Manifestation of Siamese and Burmese Kings in Traditional Warfare (1538–1854)," *Crossroads: an Interdisciplinary Journal of Southeast Asian Studies* 4, 1: 46–53.

(1990) "Mandala, Segmentary State and Politics of Centralization in Medieval Ayudhya," *Journal of the Siam Society* 78, 1: 89–100.

Claessen, H. J. M. and P. Skalnik (eds.) (1978) *The Early State*. The Hague: Mouton.

Clark, S. (1990) *Paul Ricoeur*. New York: Routledge.

Coedes, G. and C. Archaimbault (1973) *Les Trois Mondes*. Paris: École Française d'Extrême-Orient.

Cohen, P. (1984) "The Sovereignty of Dhamma and Economic Develoment: Buddhist Social Ethics in Rural Thailand," *Journal of the Siam Society* 72, 2: 197–211.

Cohn, N. (1962) "Medieval Millenarism: Its Bearing on the Comparative Study of Millenarian Movements," in S. Thrupp (ed.) *Millennial Dreams in Action*. The Hague: Mouton.

Collins, R. (1990) "Market Dynamics as the Engine of Social Change," *Sociological Theory* 8: 111–35.

(1992) "The Geopolitical and Economic World-systems of Kinship-based, Agrarian-coercive Societies," *Review* 15, 3: 373–88.

Collins, S. (1982) *Selfless Persons: Imagery and Thought in Theravāda Buddhism*. Cambridge University Press.

(1985) "Buddhism in Recent British Philosophy and Theology," *Religious Studies* 21: 475–93.

(1987a) "*Kalyāṇamitta* and *Kalyāṇamittatā*," *Journal of the Pali Text Society* 11: 51–72.

(1987b) "Indian Ideas of the Mind," in R. Gregory (ed.) *The Oxford Companion to the Mind*. Oxford University Press.

(1988) "Monasticism, Utopias and Comparative Social Theory," *Religion* 18: 101–35.

(1989) "Louis Dumont and the Study of Religions," *Religious Studies Review* 15, 1: 14–20.

(1990a) "On the Very Idea of the Pali Canon," *Journal of the Pali Text Society* 15: 89–126.

(1990b) "Introduction," in Wijayaratna (90).

(1990 ms.) "Oral and Written Aspects of Pali Literature."

(1992a) "Nirvāṇa, Time and Narrative," *History of Religions* 31, 3: 215–46.

(1992b) "Oral Aspects of Pali Literature," *Indo-Iranian Journal* 35: 121–35.

(1992c) "Problems with Paccekabuddhas," *Religion* 22: 271–8.

(1993a) "Introduction" to E. Denis, "*Brah Māleyyedevattheravatthuṃ*," *Journal of the Pali Text Society* 18: 1–17.

(1993b) "The Story of the Elder Māleyya," *Journal of the Pali Text Society* 18: 65–96.

(1993c) "The Discourse on What is Primary (*Aggañña Sutta*)," *Journal of Indian Philosophy* 21, 4: 301–93.

(1993ms.) "Notes on Texts of the *Anāgata-vaṃsa* Family."

(1994) "What are Buddhists *Doing* When They Deny the Self?" in F. E. Reynolds and D. Tracy (eds.), *Religion and Practical Reason*. Albany: State University of New York Press.

(1994ms.) "Historiography in the Pali Tradition."

(1996) "The Lion's Roar on the Wheel-turning King: A Response to Andrew Huxley's 'The Buddha and the Social Contract'," *Journal of Indian Philosophy* 24, 4: 421–46.

(1997) "The Body in Theravāda Buddhist Monasticism," in S. Coakley (ed.) *Religion and the Body*. Cambridge University Press.

Collins, S. and A. H. Huxley (1996) "The Post-Canonical Adventures of Mahāsammata," *Journal of Indian Philosophy* 24, 6: 623–48.

Cone, M. and R. F. Gombrich (1977) *The Perfect Generosity of Prince Vessantara: A Buddhist Epic*. Oxford University Press.

Connerton, P. (1989) *How Societies Remember*. Cambridge University Press.

Conze, E. (ed.) (1954) *Buddhist Texts Through the Ages*. Oxford: Cassirer.

Cousins, L. S. (1973) "Buddhist *Jhāna:* Its Nature and Attainment According to the Pali Sources," *Religion* 3: 115–31.

(1983) "Nibbāna and Abhidhamma," *Buddhist Studies Review* 1, 2: 95–109.

(1984) "Buddhism," in J. Hinnells (ed.) *A Handbook of Living Religions*. New York: Viking.

(1992) "Vitakka/Vitarka and Vicāra," *Indo-Iranian Journal* 35: 137–57.

Cousins, L. S., A. Kunst and K. R. Norman (eds.) (1974) *Buddhist Studies in Honour of I. B. Horner*. Dordrecht: Reidel.

Cowell, E. B. et al. (1895–) *The Jātaka or Stories of the Buddha's Former Births*. (6 vols.) London: Pali Text Society.

Cribb, J. (1980) "Kaniṣka's Buddha Coins – The Official Iconography of Śākyamuni and Maitreya," *Journal of the International Association of Buddhist Studies* 3, 2: 79–88.

Crone, P. (1989) *Pre-Industrial Societies*. Oxford: Blackwell.

Dampierre, E. (1961) "Notes sur 'culture' et 'civilisation'." *Comparative Studies in Society and History*, 3: 328–40.

Das, V. (1977) *Structure and Cognition: Aspects of Hindu Caste and Tradition*. Delhi: Oxford University Press.

Da Silva, L. (1978) "Cetovimutti, Paññāvimutti and Ubhatobhāgavimutti," *Pali Buddhist Review* 3, 3: 118–45.

Dauplay, J. J. (1929) *Les terres rouges du plateau des Boloven*. Saigon: Bibliothèque Documentaire Extrême-oriental.

David-Neel, A. (1911) *Le modernisme Bouddhiste et le Bouddhisme du Bouddha*. Paris: Librairie F. Alcan.

Davidson R. (1990) "Appendix: An Introduction to the Standards of Scriptural Authenticity in Indian Buddhism," in R. Buswell (ed.) *Chinese Buddhist Apocrypha*. Honolulu: University of Hawaii Press.

Davis, C. (1994) *Religion and the Making of Society*. Cambridge University Press.

Davis, J. C. (1981) *Utopia and the Ideal Society*. Cambridge University Press.

(1984) "The History of Utopia: the Chronology of Nowhere," in P. Alexander and R. Gill (eds.) *Utopias*. London: Duckworth.

Dawson, D. (1992) *Cities of the Gods: Communist Utopias in Greek Thought*. Oxford University Press.

De, G. D. (1955) *Democracy in the Early Buddhist Saṅgha*. Calcutta University.

Dehejia, V. (1990) "On Modes of Visual Narration in Early Buddhist Art," *Art Journal* 49: 374–92.

De Jong, J. W. (1987) *A Brief History of Buddhist Studies in Europe and America* (Bibliotheca Indo-Buddhica 33). Delhi: Sri Satguru.

Denis, E. (1977) *La Lokapaññatti et les idées cosmologiques du Bouddhisme ancien*. Lille: Atelier reproduction des thèses.

(1993[1963]) "*Braḥ Māleyyadevattheravatthuṃ*," Journal of the Pali Text Society 18: 19–64 (originally a doctoral thesis at the Sorbonne).

Den Uyl, D. and T. R. Machan (1983) "Recent Work on the Concept of Happiness," *American Philosophical Quarterly* 20, 2: 115–33.

Deraniyagala, P. (1954– 5) *Sinhala Verse* (3 vols.) Colombo: Ceylon National Museum.

Deshpande, M. M. (1993) *Sanskrit and Prakrit: Sociolinguistic Issues*. Delhi: Motilal Banarsidass.

De Silva, K. M. (1981) *A History of Sri Lanka*. Berkeley: University of California Press.

De Zoysa, L. (1882) "List of Mss. in the Colombo Museum," *Journal of the Pali Text Society* 1: 46–58.

(1885) *A Catalogue of Pali Sinhalese and Sanskrit Manuscripts in the Temple Libraries of Ceylon*. Colombo: Government Printer.

Dirks, N. (1987) *The Hollow Crown: Ethnohistory of an Indian Kingdom*. Cambridge University Press.

Dover, K. (1974) *Greek Popular Morality in the time of Plato and Aristotle*. Berkeley: University of California Press.

Duby, G. (1980) *The Three Orders: Feudal Society Imagined*. University of Chicago Press.

(1985) "Ideologies in Social History," in J. Le Goff and P. Nora (eds.), *Constructing the Past*. Cambridge University Press.

Dumont, L. (1980) *Homo Hierarchicus: The Caste System and its Implications* (complete revised English edition). University of Chicago Press.

Duncan J. S. (1990) *The City as Text: The Politics of Landscape Interpretation in the Kandyan Kingdom*. Cambridge University Press.

Durkheim, E. (1979) *Les Formes élementaires de la vie religieuse* (6th edn.). Paris: Presses Universitaires de France.
(1995) *The Elementary Forms of Religious Life* (translated by K. E. Fields). New York: The Free Press.
Duroiselle, C. (1916) "The Ari of Burma and Tantric Buddhism," *Annual Report of the Archaeological Survey of India* 1915–16: 79–93.
(1982) *Jinacarita or "The Career of the Conqueror"*. Delhi: Parimal Publications.
Eagleton, T. (1991) *Ideology: An Introduction.* London: Verso.
Eckel, M. D. (1992) *To See the Buddha: A Philosopher's Quest for the Meaning of Emptiness.* San Francisco: Harper.
Eckhardt (1992) *Civilizations, Empires, and Wars: A Quantitative History of War.* Jefferson, NC: McFarland.
(1995) "A Dialectical Evolutionary Theory of Civilizations, Empires and Wars," in S. Sanderson (ed.) *Civilizations and World-Systems: Studying World-Historical Change.* Walnut Creek: Altamira.
Edgerton, F. (1953) *Buddhist Hybrid Sanskrit Dictionary.* New Haven: Yale University Press.
Eisenstadt, S. M. (1981) "Cultural Traditions and Political Dynamics: The Origins and Modes of Ideological Politics," *British Journal of Sociology* 32, 2: 155–81.
(1982) "The Axial Age: the Emergence of Transcendental Visions and the Rise of Clerics," *European Journal of Sociology* 22, 2: 294–314.
(ed.) (86) *The Origins and Diversity of Axial Age Civilizations.* Albany: State University of New York Press.
Eisenstadt, S. N. and L. Roniger (1984) *Patrons, Clients and Friends.* Cambridge University Press.
Elchardus, M. (1988) "The Rediscovery of Chronos: The New Role of Time in Sociological Theory," *International Sociology* 3, 1: 35–59.
Eliade, M. (1954) *The Myth of the Eternal Return* (Bollingen Series XLVI). Princeton University Press.
(1957) *The Sacred and the Profane: the Nature of Religion.* New York: Harcourt, Brace and World.
(ed.) (1987) *Encyclopedia of Religion.* New York: Macmillan.
Elias, N. (1992) *Time: an Essay.* Oxford: Blackwell.
Eliav-Feldom, M. (1982) *Realistic Utopias: the Ideal Imaginary Societies of the Renaissance.* Oxford: Clarendon Press.
Eliot, T. S. (1959 [1944]) *Four Quartets.* London: Faber and Faber. ("Burnt Norton" written 1935.)
(1972 [1940]) *The Waste Land and Other Poems.* London: Faber and Faber. ("Waste Land" written 1922.)
Erdosy, G. (1988) *Urbanization in Early Historic India.* Oxford: BAR International Series 430.
(1995) "City States of North India and Pakistan at the Time of the Buddha," in F. R. Allchin (95).

Ergardt, J. (1977) *Faith and Knowledge in Early Buddhism: An Analysis of the Contextual Structures of An Arahant-formula in the Majjhima Nikāya.* Leiden: E. J. Brill.

Fabian, J. (1983) *Time and the Other: How Anthropology Makes its Object.* New York: Columbia University Press.

Fallon, E. (1983) "The Peasants of Isan: Social and Economic Transitions in Northeast Thailand." Ph.D. thesis, University of Wisconsin.

Feer, L. (1882) "List of Mss. in the Bibliothèque Nationale at Paris," *Journal of the Pali Text Society* 1: 32–7.

(1894) *Saṃyutta Nikāya* IV. London: Pali Text Society.

Fentress, J. and C. Wickham (1992) *Social Memory.* Oxford: Blackwell.

Ferguson, J. P. (1975) "Symbolic Dimensions of the Buddhist Sangha," Ph.D. thesis, Cornell University.

(1977) "The Arahat Ideal in Modern Burmese Buddhism," paper presented at the Annual Meeting of the Association of Asian Studies, New York.

(1989) "Some Historical Arahats of Burma," paper presented at the Annual Meeting of the Association of Asian Studies, Washington.

Ferguson, J. P. and C. B. Johanssen (1976) "Modern Buddhist Murals in Northern Thailand: A Study of Religious Symbols and Meaning," *American Ethnologist* 3, 4: 645–69.

Ferguson, J. and E. M. Mendelson (1981) "The Buddhist Masters of the Occult," *Contributions to Asian Studies* 16: 62–79.

Fernando, C. M. (1908) *Nikāya-saṅgraha* (translation). Colombo: H. C. Cottle.

Filliozat, J. (1992), "Documents Useful for the Identification of Pāli Manuscripts of Cambodia, Laos and Thailand," *Journal of the Pali Text Society* 16: 13–54.

(1993) "The Commentaries to the *Anāgatavaṃsa* in the Pāli Manuscripts of the Paris Collections," *Journal of the Pali Text Society* XIX: 43–63.

Finot, L. (1917) "Recherches sur la littérature Laotienne," *Bulletin de l'école Francaise d'Extrème-Orient* 17: 1–218.

Forbes, C. J. F. S. (1878) *British Burma and its People, Being Sketches of Native Manners, Customs and Religion.* London: John Murray.

Forster, E. M. (1963 [1927]) *Aspects of the Novel.* London: Penguin.

Foucault, M. (1979) *Power, Truth, Strategy.* Sydney: Feral Publications.

Fowden, G. (1993) *Empire and Commonwealth: The Consequences of Monotheism in Late Antiquity.* Princeton University Press.

Frank, A. Gunder (1992) *The Centrality of Central Asia.* Amsterdam: VU University Press.

Frank, A. G. and B. K. Gills (eds.) (1993) *The World System: Five Hundred Years or Five Thousand?* London: Routledge.

Franke R. O. (1913) *Dīghanikāya.* Göttingen: Vandenhoeck and Ruprecht.

Frauwallner, E. (1956) *The Earliest Vinaya and the Beginnings of Buddhist Literature.* Rome: ISMEO.

(1973) *History of Indian Philosophy* (English translation V. M. Bedekar, 2 vols.). Delhi: Motilal Banarsidass.

Freud, S. (1984) *On Metapsychology* (Penguin Freud Library 11). London: Penguin.

Frye, N. (1965) "Varieties of Literary Utopias," *Daedalus* pp. 323–47.

Fytche, A. (1878) *Burma, Past and Present* (2 vols.). London: Kegan Paul.

Gabaude, L. (1991) "Controverses modernes autour du Vessantara Jataka," *Cahiers de l'Asie du Sud-Est* 29–30: 51–72.

Geertz, C. (1973) *The Interpretation of Cultures: Selected Essays*. New York: Basic Books.

(1980) *Negara: The Theatre State in Nineteenth-century Bali*. Princeton University Press.

Geiger, W. (1908) *The Mahāvaṃsa*. London: Pali Text Society.

(1912) *The Mahāvaṃsa* (English translation). London: Pali Text Society.

(1929) *Cūḷavaṃsa*. London: Pali Text Society.

(1960) *Culture of Ceylon in Medieval Times*. Wiesbaden: Harrassowitz.

(1994) *A Pāli Grammar* (revised by K. R. Norman). London: Pali Text Society.

Gellner, D. (1982) "Max Weber, Capitalism and the Religion of India," *Sociology* 16, 4: 526–43.

(1992) *Monk, Householder and Tantric Priest: Newar Buddhism and its Hierarchy of Ritual*. Cambridge University Press.

Gellner, E. (1969) *Saints of the Atlas*. University of Chicago Press.

(1979a [1959]) *Words and Things* (revised edn.). London: Routledge and Kegan Paul.

(1979b) *Spectacles and Predicaments*. Cambridge University Press.

(1983) *Nations and Nationalism*. Ithaca: Cornell University Press.

(1988) *Plough, Sword and Book: The Structure of Human History*. University of Chicago Press.

(1995) *Anthropology and Politics: Revolutions in the Sacred Grove*. Oxford: Blackwell.

Gerini, G. E. (1892) *A Retrospective View and Account of the Origin of the Thet Mahā Ch'at Ceremony (Mahā Jāti Desanā)*. Bangkok: Sathirakoses-Nagapradipa Foundation (reprint 1976).

Gethin, R. (1992a) *The Buddhist Path to Awakening: A Study of the Bodhipakkhiyā Dhammā*. Leiden: E. J. Brill.

(1992b) "The *Mātikās*: Memorization, Mindfulness and the List," in J. Gyatso (ed.) *In the Mirror of Memory: Reflections on Mindfulness and Remembrance in Indian and Tibetan Buddhism*. Albany: State University of New York Press.

Geuss, R. (1981) *The Idea of a Critical Theory: Habermas and the Frankfurt School*. Cambridge University Press.

Ghosh, A. (1973) *The City in Early Historical India*. Simla: Indian Institute of Advanced Study.

Giddens, A. (1979) *Central Problems in Social Theory: Action, Structure and Contradiction in Social Analysis.* Berkeley: University of California Press.

(1981) *A Contemporay Critique of Historical Materialism.* Berkeley: University of California Press.

(1984) *The Constitution of Society: Outline of the Theory of Structuration.* Berkeley: University of California Press.

(1987) *The Nation-State and Violence.* Berkeley: University of California Press.

(1991) *Modernity and Self-identity: Self and Society in the Late Modern Age.* Stanford University Press.

Godakumbara C. E. (1955) *Sinhalese Literature.* Colombo: The Colombo Apothecaries.

(1980) *Catalogue of Ceylonese Manuscripts.* Copenhagen: Royal Library.

Godelier, M. (1986) *The Making of Great Men: Male Domination and Power among the New Guinea Baruya.* Cambridge University Press.

Godelier, M. and M. Strathern (eds.) (1991) *Big Men and Great Men: Personifications of Power in Melanesia.* Cambridge University Press.

Gokhale B. G. (1953) "Dhammiko Dhammarājā: A Study in Buddhist Constitutional Concepts," in *Indica: the Indian Historical Research Institute Silver Jubilee Commemoration Volume.* Bombay: St Xavier's College.

(1966) "Early Buddhist Kingship," *Journal of Asian Studies* 26, 1: 15–22

(1994) *New Light on Early Buddhism.* Bombay: Popular Prakashan.

Gombrich, R. F. (1966) "The Consecration of a Buddhist Image," *Journal of Asian Studies* 27, 1: 23–36.

(1971a) *Precept and Practice: Traditonal Buddhism in the Rural Highlands of Ceylon.* Oxford University Press.

(1971b) "Merit Transference in Sinhalese Buddhism," *History of Religions* 11, 2: 1: 203–19.

(1972) "Buddhism and Society," *Modern Asian Studies* 6: 483–94.

(1974) "Eliade on Buddhism," *Religious Studies* 10: 225–31.

(1975) "Ancient Indian Cosmology," in C. Blacker and M. Loewe (eds.) *Ancient Cosmologies.* London: Allen and Unwin.

(1980) "The Significance of Former Buddhas in the Theravādin Tradition," in S. Balasooriya et al. (eds.) *Buddhist Studies in Honour of Walpola Rahula.* London: Gordon Fraser.

(1985) "The Vessantara Jātaka, the Rāmāyaṇa, and the Dasaratha Jātaka," *Journal of the American Oriental Society* 105, 3: 427–38.

(1988) *Theravāda Buddhism: A Social History from Benares to Colombo.* London: Routledge and Kegan Paul.

(1990) "Recovering the Buddha's Message," in T. Skorupski (ed.) *The Buddhist Forum* vol. I. University of London: School of Oriental and African Studies.

(1992a) "The Buddha's Book of Genesis?" *Indo-Iranian Journal* 35: 179–191.
(1992b) "Why Six Former Buddhas?" *Journal of Oriental Research* (Madras), (Dr. S. S. Janaki Felicitation Volume) 56–7: 326–30.
(1992c) "The Date of the Buddha: a Red Herring Revealed," in Bechert (ed.) (92).
(1993) "Buddhist Prediction: How Open is the Future?" in L. Howe and A. Wain (eds.) *Predicting the Future.* Cambridge University Press.
(1994) "What is Pali," foreword to W. Geiger (94).
Gombrich, R. F. and G. Obeyesekere (1988) *Buddhism Transformed: Religious Change in Sri Lanka.* Princeton University Press.
Gomez, L. (1987) "Buddhist Views of Language," in M. Eliade (ed.) (87).
Gould, J. (1989) *Herodotus.* New York: St. Martin's Press.
Gould, S. J. (1987) *Time's Arrow, Time's Cycle: Myth and Metaphor in the Discovery of Geological Time.* Cambridge: Harvard University Press.
Graham, W. (1987) *Beyond the Written Word: Oral Aspects of Scripture in the History of Religions.* Cambridge University Press.
Granoff, P. (1992) "Buddhaghosa's Penance and Siddhasena's Crime: Remarks on Some Buddhist and Jain Attitudes to Language," in K. Shinohara and G. Schopen (eds.) *From Benares to Beijing: Essays on Buddhism and Chinese Religion in Honour of Prof. Jan Yün-Hua.* Oakville: Mosaic Press.
Graus, F. (1967) "Social Utopias of the Middle Ages," *Past and Present* 38: 3–19.
Green, W. A. (1992) "Periodization in European and World History," *Journal of World History* 3, 1: 13–53.
(1995) "Periodizing World History," in P. Pomper et al. (eds.) *World Historians and Their Critics* (History and Theory Studies in the Philosophy of History Theme Issue 14), Wesleyan University.
Griffiths, E. (1984 ms.) "Breathing Your Last," (Talk given on BBC Radio 3, Sunday September 9, 1984.)
(1984) "Eternal Insomnia?," *The Listener* vol.112, September 13 1984, pp. 14–15.
(1989) *The Printed Voice of Victorian Poetry.* Oxford: Clarendon Press.
Griffiths, P. J. (1981) "Concentration or Insight: The Problematic of Theravāda Buddhist Meditation-Theory," *Journal of the American Academy of Religion* 49: 605–24.
(1986) *On Being Mindless.* La Salle: Open Court.
(1990) "Omniscience in the Mahāyānasūtrālaṅkāra and its Commentaries," *Indo-Iranian Journal* 33, 2: 85–120.
(1994) *On Being Buddha: The Classical Doctrine of Buddhahood.* Albany: State University of New York Press.
Griswold, A. B. (1968) "What is a Buddha Image?" *Thai Culture* new series no.19. Bangkok: Fine Arts Department.

Gunaratna, H. (1985) *The Path of Serenity and Insight.* Delhi: Motilal Banarsidass.

Gunasena, H. M. (1901) *Catalogue of Pali, Sinhalese and Sanskrit Manuscripts in the Colombo Museum Library.* Colombo: Cottle.

Gunawardana, R. A. L. H. (1971) "Irrigation and Hydraulic Society in Early Medieval Ceylon," *Past and Present* 53:3–27.

(1979) *Robe and Plough: Monasticism and Economic Interest in Early Medieval Sri Lanka.* Tucson: University of Arizona Press.

(1987) "Changing Patterns of Navigation in the Indian Ocean and their Impact on Pre-colonial Sri Lanka," in S. Chandra (ed.), *The Indian Ocean: Explorations in History, Commerce and Politics.* New Delhi: Sage.

Guruge, A. (1989) *Mahāvaṃsa.* Colombo: Associated Newspapers of Ceylon.

Gyatso, J. (1997) *Apparitions of the Self: The Autobiographies of a Tibetan Visionary.* Princeton University Press.

Hacking, I. (1983) *Representing and Intervening: Introductory Topics in the Philosophy of Natural Science.* Cambridge University Press.

Hagesteijn, R. (1989) *Circles of Kings: Political Dynamics in Early Continental Southeast Asia.* Dordrecht: Foris.

Halbfass, W. (1991) *Tradition and Reflection: Explorations in Indian Thought.* Albany: State University of New York Press.

Halbwachs, M. (1992) *On Collective Memory.* University of Chicago Press.

Hall, K. R. (1985) *Maritime Trade and State Development in Early Southeast Asia.* University of Hawaii Press.

(1992) "'Economic History of Early Southeast Asia," in Tarling (ed.) (92).

Hallisey, C. (1990) "*Tuṇḍilovāda*: An Allegedly Non-canonical *Sutta*," *Journal of the Pali Text Society* 15: 155–95.

(1992) "Books and Relics as Icons of Longevity," paper presented at the Annual Meeting of the American Academy of Religion, San Francisco.

(1993) "*Nibbānasutta*: An Allegedly Non-canonical *Sutta* on *Nibbāna* as a Great City," *Journal of the Pali Text Society* 28: 97–130.

(1995) "Roads Taken and Not Taken in the Study of Theravāda Buddhism," in D. S. Lopez (ed.) (95a).

Hamilton, S. (1995) *Identity and Experience: The Constitution of the Human Being According to Early Buddhism.* London: Luzac.

Hanks, L. (1962) "Merit and Power in the Thai Social Order," *American Anthropologist* 64: 1247–61.

Hanks, W. (1989) "Texts and Textuality," *Annual Review of Anthropology* 18: 95–127.

Hardy, F. (1993) "Information and Transformation: Two Faces of the Purāṇas," in W. Doniger (ed.) *Purāṇa Perennis.* Albany: State University of New York Press.

Harvey, P. (1986) "'Signless Meditations' in Pali Buddhism," *Journal of the International Association of Buddhist Studies* 9, 1: 25–52.

(1990) *Introduction to Buddhism: Teachings, History, Practices*. Cambridge University Press.

(1995) *The Selfless Mind: Personality, Consciousness and Nirvana in Early Buddhism*. Surrey: Curzon Press.

Hazlewood, A. H. (1987) "A Translation of *Pañcagatidīpanī*," *Journal of the Pali Text Society* 11: 133–59.

Hazra, K. L. (1988) *Constitution of the Buddhist Saṅgha*. Delhi: B. R. Publishing Corporation.

Heesterman, J. (1985) *The Inner Conflict of Tradition: Essays in Indian Ritual*. University of Chicago Press.

Heiler F. (1922) *Die Buddhistische Versenkung*. Munich: E. Reinhardt.

Heilman R. (1968) *Tragedy and Melodrama: Versions of Experience*. Seattle: University of Washington Press.

Helms, M. W. (1988) *Ulysses' Sail: An Ethnographic Odyssey of Power, Knowledge, and Geographical Distance*. Princeton University Press.

Herbert, P. M.(1982) *The Hsaya San Rebellion (1930–32) Reappraised*. Centre of Southeast Asian Studies, Melbourne: Monash University Working Paper no.27.

Hillis Miller, J. (1974) "Narrative and History," *English Literary History* 41: 455–73.

Hinton, P. (1979) "The Karen, Millennialism, and Accommodation," in C. F. Keyes (ed.) *Ethnic Adaptation and Identity*. Philadelphia: Institute for the Study of Human Issues.

Hinüber, O. von (1982) "Pali as An Artificial Language," *Indologia Taurinensia* X: 133–40.

(1983) "Die älteste Literatursprache des Buddhismus," *Saeculum* XXXIV, 1: 1–9.

(1985) "Epigraphical Varieties of Continental Pāli From Devnimori and Ratnagiri," in *Buddhism and its Relation to Other Religions: Essays in Honour of Dr. Shozen Kumoi on his Seventieth Birthday*. Kyoto (n.p.).

(1989) "Origin and Varieties of Buddhist Sanskrit," in C. Caillat (ed.) *Dialectes dans les littératures Indo-Aryens*. Paris: Collège de France.

(1990) Der Beginn der Schrift und frühe Schriftlichkeit in Indien. *Akademie der Wissenschaften und der Literatur, Main, Abhandlungen der Geistes- und Sozialwissenschaftlichen Klasse, Nr. 11*. Wiesbaden: Franz Steiner Verlag.

(1994) *Selected papers*. London: Pali Text Society.

Hodgson, M. (74) *The Venture of Islam*, vol. 1. University of Chicago Press.

(1989) *Rethinking World History*. Cambridge University Press.

Holt, J. (1991a) *Buddha in the Crown: Avalokiteśvara in the Buddhist Traditions of Sri Lanka*. Oxford University Press.

(1991b) "Protestant Buddhism?" (review of Gombrich and Obeyesekere 88), *Religious Studies Review* 17, 4: 307–12.

Horner, I. B. (1936) *The Early Buddhist Theory of Man Perfected.* London: Williams and Norgate.
(1938) *The Book of the Discipline, Part 1* (SBB, x). London: Pali Text Society.
(1940) *The Book of the Discipline, Part 2* (SBB xi). London: Pali Text Society.
(1952) *The Book of the Discipline, Part 5* (SBB xx). London: Pali Text Society.
(1959) *Middle Length Sayings III.* London: Pali Text Society.
(1964) *Milinda's Questions* vol.ii. London: Luzac.
(1974) *The Minor Anthologies of the Pali Canon, Part IV.* London: Pali Text Society.
(1975) *The Minor Anthologies of the Pali Canon, Part III.* London: Pali Text Society.
(1978) *The Clarifier of the Sweet Meaning.* London: Pali Text Society.

Horner, I. B. and P. S. Jaini (1985) *Apocryphal Birth Stories*, vol. I. London: Pali Text Society.

Horsch, P. (1957) "The Wheel: an Indian Pattern of World-Interpretation," in Kshitis Roy (ed.) *Sino-Indian Studies.* Visvabharati Santiniketan: vol.v parts 3 and 4, W. Liebenthal Festschrift.

Howe, L. (1981) "The Social Determination of Knowledge: Maurice Bloch and Balinese Time," *Man* 16, 2: 220–34.

Htin Aung, M. (1967) *A History of Burma.* New York: Columbia University Press.

Hubert, H. and M. Mauss (1898) "Essai sur la nature et fonction du sacrifice", *Année Sociologique* pp. 29–138.

Hundius, H. (1990) "The Colophons of 30 Pāli Manuscripts from Northern Thailand," *Journal of the Pali Text Society* 14: 1–173.

Huntington, S. (1990) "Early Buddhist Art and the Theory of Aniconism," *Art Journal* 49: 401–7.

Huxley, A. H. (1990) "How Buddhist is Theravāda Buddhist Law?" in T. Skorupski (ed.) *The Buddhist Forum, Vol. I: Seminar Papers 1987–1988.* London: School of Oriental and African Studies, University of London.
(1995) "Buddhist Law – The View from Mandalay," *Journal of the International Association of Buddhist Studies* 18, 1: 47–95
(1996a) "The Buddha and the Social Contract," *Journal of Indian Philosophy* 24, 4: 407– 20
(1996b) "When Manu met Mahāsammata," *Journal of Indian Philosophy* 24, 6: 593–621.

Ingold, T. (1993) "The Temporality of the Landscape," in R. Bradley (ed.) (93).

Ishii, Y. (1975) "A Note on Buddhistic Millenarian Revolts in Northeastern Siam," *Journal of Southeast Asian Studies* 6, 2: 121–6.

(1986) *Sangha and State in Thailand.* Honolulu: University of Hawaii Press.

Jackson, P. A. (1988) "The Hupphaasawan Movement: Millenarian Buddhism among the Thai Political Elite," *SOJOURN (Social Issues in Southeast Asia)* 3, 2: 134–70.

(1989) *Buddhism, Legitimation and Conflict: the Political Functions of Urban Thai Buddhism.* Singapore: Institute of Southeast Asian Studies.

(1993) "Re-Interpreting the *Traiphuum Phra Ruang*: Political Functions of Buddhist Symbolism in Contemporary Thailand," in T. Ling (ed.) *Buddhist Trends in Southeast Asia.* Singapore: Institute of Southeast Asian Studies.

Jaini, P. S. (1974) "On the *sarvajñatva* (Omniscience) of Mahāvīra and Buddha," in Cousins et al. (74).

(1986a) *Apocryphal Birth Stories* vol.II. London: Pali Text Society.

(1986b) *Lokaneyyapakaraṇaṃ.* London: Pali Text Society.

(1988) "Stages in the Bodhisattva Career of Tathāgata Maitreya," in Sponberg and Hardacre (88).

(1991) "Is there a Popular Jainism?" in M. Carrithers and C. Humphrey (eds.) *The Assembly of Listeners: Jains in Society.* Cambridge University Press.

Jaspers, K. (1965) *The Origin and Goal of History.* New Haven: Yale University Press.

Jayaswal, K. P. (1967) *Hindu Polity: A Constitutional History of India in Hindu Times.* Bangalore Printing and Publishing Company.

Jayatilleke K. N. (1963) *Early Buddhist Theory of Knowledge.* London: George Allen and Unwin.

Jayawickrama, N. A. (1962) *Inception of Discipline and Vinaya-nidāna.* London: Pali Text Society.

(1968) *Epochs of the Conqueror.* London: Pali Text Society.

(1974) *Buddhavaṃsa and Cariya-piṭaka.* London: Pali Text Society.

(1990) *The Story of Gotama Buddha.* London: Pali Text Society.

Johansson, R. (1969) *The Psychology of Nirvana.* London: George Allen and Unwin.

Johnson, A. W. and T. Earle (1987) *The Evolution of Human Societies: From Foraging Group to Agrarian State.* Stanford University Press.

Johnston, E. H. (1931) "Notes on Some Pali Words," *Journal of the Royal Asiatic Society* pp.565–92.

(1936) *The Buddhacarita: or, Acts of the Buddha.* (reprint Delhi: Munshiram Manoharlal, 1972). Lahore: University of the Punjab.

Jones, J. G. (1979) *Tales and Teachings of the Buddha: The Jātaka Stories in Relation to the Pali Canon.* London: George Allen and Unwin.

Jordan, T. E. (1982) *Texas Graveyards: A Cultural Legacy.* Austin: University of Texas Press.

Kane, P. V. (1973 [1946]) *History of Dharmaśāstra (Ancient and Mediaeval Religious and Civil Law)*, vol. III (second edn.). Poona: Bhandharkar Oriental Research Institute.

Kantorowicz, E. H. (1957) *The King's Two Bodies: A Study in Mediaeval Political Theology*. Princeton University Press.

Kapstein, M. (1987) "Self and Personal Identity in Indian Buddhist Scholasticism: A Philosophical Investigation," Ph.D. thesis, Brown University.

Kasetsiri, Charnvit (1976) *The Rise of Ayudhya: A History of Siam in the Fourteenth and Fifteenth Centuries*. Oxford University Press.

Kasulis, T. (1987) "Nirvāṇa," in M. Eliade (ed.) (87).

Katz, N. (1982) *Buddhist Images of Human Perfection: The Arahant of the Sutta Piṭaka Compared with the Bodhisattva and the Mahāsiddha*. Delhi: Motilal Banarsidass.

Kaufman H. (1960) *Bangkhuad: A Community Study inThailand*. New York: J. J. Augustin.

Kautsky, J. (1982) *The Politics of Aristocratic Empires*. Chapel Hill: University of North Carolina Press.

Kemper, S. (1991) *The Presence of the Past: Chronicles, Politics and Culture in Sinhala Life*. Ithaca: Cornell University Press.

Kenyon, T. (1989) *Utopian Communism and Political Thought in Early Modern England*. London: Pinter.

Kermode, F. (1967) *The Sense of an Ending: Studies in the Theory of Fiction*. Oxford University Press.

Keyes, C. F. (1971) "Buddhism and National Integration in Thailand," *Journal of Asian Studies* 30, 3: 551–68.

(1977) "Millennialism, Buddhism, and Thai Society," *Journal of Asian Studies* 36, 2: 283–302.

(1983) Introduction to C. Keyes and E. V. Daniel (eds.) *Karma: an Anthropological Inquiry*. Berkeley: University of California Press.

(1987) *Thailand: Buddhist Kingdom as Modern Nation-State*. Boulder: Westview.

(1995) *The Golden Peninsula: Culture and Adaptation in Mainland Southeast Asia* (2nd edn.). Honolulu: University of Hawaii Press (originally published 1977).

Keyes, C. F. and E. V. Daniel (1983) *Karma: an Anthropological Inquiry*. Berkeley: University of California Press.

Khantipalo Thera (1970) *The Wheel of Birth and Death*. Kandy: Buddhist Publication Society (Wheel nos.147–9).

King, W. (1980) *Theravāda Meditation: the Buddhist Transformation of Yoga*. University Park: Pennsylvania State University Press.

Kingshill, K. (1965) *Ku Daeng, the Red Tomb* (2nd edn., revised). Bangkok: Church of Christ.

(1991) *Ku Daeng – Thiry Years Later: A Village Study in Northern Thailand*

1954–1984. Northern Illinois University, Center for Southeast Asian Studies, Monograph Series on Southeast Asia Special Report no.26.

Kinnard, J. (1996) "Wisdom Divine: Visual Representations of *Prajñā* in Pāla-period Buddhism," Ph.D. dissertation, Divinity School, University of Chicago.

Kirsch, A. T. (1967) *Phu Thai Religious Syncretism*. Ph.D. dissertation, Harvard University.

(1978) "Modernizing Implications of Nineteenth Century Reforms in the Thai Sangha," in B. Smith (ed.) (78b).

Kloetzli, R. (1983) *Buddhist Cosmology: From Single World System to Pure Land; Science and Theology in the Images of Motion and Light*. Delhi: Motilal Banarsidass.

(1987) "Buddhist Cosmology," in M. Eliade (ed.) (87).

Kloppenborg, M. A. G. D. (Ria) (1982) "The Place of Maitreya in Early and Theravāda Buddhism and the Conditions for Rebirth in his Time," in G. de la Lama (ed.) *South Asia 3*. Mexico: El Colegio de Mexico.

Koenig, W. (1990) *The Burmese Polity 1752–1819*. Ann Arbor: Michigan Papers on South and Southeast Asia no.34, University of Michigan.

Kollmar-Paulenz, K. (1993) "Utopian Thought in Tibetan Buddhism: A Survey of the Śambhala Concept and its Sources," *Studies in Central and East Asian Religions: Journal of the Seminar for Buddhist Studies, Copenhagen and Aarhus* 5/6 (1992–3): 78–96.

Kulke, H. and D. Rothermund (1990 [1986]) *A History of India*. London: Routledge and Kegan Paul.

Kumar, K. (1991) *Utopianism*. Minneapolis: University of Minnesota Press.

Kyaw, U Ba (1980) *Peta-stories* (ed. and annotated P. Masefield; SBB XXXIV). London: Pali Text Society.

LaCapra, D. (1983) *Rethinking Intellectual History: Texts, Contexts, Language*. Ithaca: Cornell University Press.

Ladurie, E. L. R (1979) *Montaillou: The Promised Land of Error*. New York: Vintage.

Lamotte, E. (1949) *Le traité de la grande vertu de sagesse, tome II*. Louvain: Bibliothèque du Muséon vol.18.

(1976) *The Teaching of Vimalakīrti* (SBB XXXII). London: Pali Text Society.

(1988) *History of Indian Buddhism*. Louvain: Peeter's Press.

La Vallée Poussin, L. de (36–7) "Mūsila and Nārada," *Mélanges chinois et bouddhiques* 5: 189–222.

Layton, R., R. Foley, and E. Williams (1991) "The Transition between Hunting and Gathering and the Specialized Husbanding of Resources," *Current Anthropology* 32, 3: 255–63.

Leach. E. (1977) *Rethinking Anthropology*. London: Athlone Press.

Legge, J. (1886) *A Record of Buddhistic Kingdoms*. Oxford: Clarendon Press.

LeGoff, J. (1982) *Time, Work and Culture in the Middle Ages.* University of Chicago Press.

(1984) *The Birth of Purgatory.* University of Chicago Press.

(1985) *L'imaginaire médiéval.* Paris: Editions Gallimard.

(1988) *The Medieval Imagination* (English translation of LeGoff 85). University of Chicago Press.

(1992 *History and Memory.* New York: Columbia University Press.

Lehman. (1987) "Burmese Religion," in M. Eliade (ed.) (87).

Lehrman, J. (1980) *Earthly Paradise: Garden and Courtyard in Islam.* Berkeley: University of California Press.

Leumann, E. (1919) *Maitreyasamiti, das Zukunftsideal der Buddhisten.* Strasburg: Trübner.

Lévi, S. (1932) "Maitreya le consolateur," in *Etudes d'orientalisme publiés par le musée Guimet à la mémoire de Raymond Linossier.* Paris: Librairie Ernest Leroux.

Levitas, R. (1990) *The Concept of Utopia.* Syracuse University Press.

Lieberman, V. (1980) "The Political Significance of Religious Wealth in Burmese History: Some Further Thoughts," *Journal of Asian Studies* 39, 4: 753–69.

(1984) *Burmese Administrative Cycles: Anarchy and Conquest, c. 1580–1760.* Princeton University Press.

(1987) "Reinterpreting Burmese History," *Comparative Studies in Society and History* 29, 1: 162–94.

(1991) "Secular Trends in Burmese Economic History, *c.*1350–1830, and their Implications for State Formation," *Modern Asian Studies* 25, 1: 1–31.

(1993) "Local Integration and Eurasian Analogies: Structuring Southeast Asian History, *c.* 1350–*c.* 1830," *Modern Asian Studies* 27, 3: 475–572.

Lienhart, S. (1980) *Die Legende vom Prinzen Viśvantara.* Berlin: Museum für Indische Kunst.

Ling, T. (1973) *The Buddha: Buddhist Civilization in India and Ceylon.* New York: Charles Scribner's Sons.

Lloyd, G. E. R. (1975) "Le Temps dans la pensée grecque," in P. Ricoeur et al. *Les cultures et le temps.* Paris: Payot (UNESCO).

Lockwood, D. (1964) "Social Integration and System Integration," in G. K. Zollschan and W. Hirsch (eds.) *Explorations in Social Change.* Boston: Houghton Mifflin.

Lopez, D. S. (ed.) (1995a) *Curators of the Buddha: the Study of Buddhism under Colonialism.* University of Chicago Press.

(1995b) *Buddhism in Practice.* Princeton University Press.

Lovejoy, A. and G. Boas (1935) *Primitivism and Related Ideas in Antiquity.* Baltimore: Johns Hopkins University Press.

Low, B. (1920) *Psychoanalysis.* London: Allen and Unwin.

Luce, G. (1969) *Old Burma – Early Pagan,* vol. 1. Locust Valley: Augustin.

Luce, G. and Pe Maung Tin (1920) "The Shwegyugi Pagoda Inscription, Pagan, 1141 AD," *Journal of the Burmese Research Society* 10: 67–74.
(1923) *The Glass Palace Chronicle of the Kings of Burma.* Oxford University Press.
Ludden, D. (1985) *Peasant History in South India.* Princeton University Press.
(1994) "History Outside Civilization and the Mobility of South Asia," *South Asia,* 17, 1: 1–23.
Lupton, J. H. (1895) *The Utopia of Sir Thomas More.* Oxford: Clarendon Press.
McClung, L. (1975) "The Vessantara Jātaka: Paradigm for a Buddhist Utopia," Ph.D. thesis, Princeton University.
MacDannell, C. and Lang, B. (1988) *Heaven: a History.* New Haven: Yale University Press.
MacDonald, J. (1966) "Paradise," *Islamic Studies,* 5: 331–83.
McGill, F. (1997) "Painting the Great Life," in J. Schober (ed.) *Sacred Biography in the Buddhist Traditions of South and Southeast Asia.* Honolulu: University of Hawaii Press.
McGill, V. J. (1967) *The Idea of Happiness.* New York: Praeger.
MacIntyre, A. (1967) *A Short History of Ethics.* New York: Macmillan.
McNeil, W. H. (1990) review of Gellner (88), *History and Theory* 29: 234–40.
Mabbett I. (1977) "The 'Indianization' of Southeast Asia," *Journal of Southeast Asian Studies,* 8: 1–14, 143–61.
(1986) "Buddhism in Champa," in D. G. Marr and A. C. Milner (eds.) *Southeast Asia in the 9th to 14th Centuries.* Singapore: Institute of Southeast Asian Studies.
(forthcoming) "The Indianization of Mainland Southeast Asia: a Reappraisal," in N. Eilenberg (ed.) *Jean Boisselier Felicitation Volume.*
Mabbett, I. and D. Chandler (1995) *The Khmers.* Oxford: Blackwell.
Malalasekara, G. P. (1928) *The Pali Literature of Ceylon.* Colombo: M. D. Gunasena.
Malalgoda, K. (1970) "Millennialism in Relation to Buddhism," *Comparative Studies in Society and History* 12, 4: 424–41.
(1976) *Buddhism in Sinhalese Society 1750–1900: A Study of Religious Revival and Change.* Berkeley: University of California Press.
Mandelbaum, D. (1966) "Transcendental and Pragmatic Aspects of Religion," *American Anthropologist* 68: 1174–91.
Mann, M. (1986) *The Sources of Social Power,* vol. I. Cambridge University Press.
Manuel, F. and F. (1979) *Utopian Thought in the Western World.* Oxford: Blackwell.
Martin, W. (1986) *Recent Theories of Narrative.* Ithaca: Cornell University Press.
Martini, F. (1936) "Dasabodisatta-uddesa," *Bulletin de l'Ecole Française d'Extrème-Orient* 36, 2: 287–413.

Martini, G. (1969) "Pañcabuddhabyākaraṇa," *Bulletin de l'Ecole Française d'Extrème-Orient* 55: 125–44.
Marx, K. (1976) *The German Ideology.* (3rd. revised edn.). Moscow: Progress Publishers.
Marx, K. and F. Engels (1957) *Werke*, vol. I. Berlin: Dietz Verlag.
Masefield, P. (1986) *Divine Revelation in Pali Buddhism.* London: George Allen and Unwin.
(1989) *Vimāna Stories* (SBB xxxv). London: Pali Text Society.
Mason, H. A. (1985) *The Tragic Plane.* Oxford: The Clarendon Press.
Meddegama, U and J. Holt (1993) *Anāgatavaṃsa Desanā: The Sermon of the Chronicle-To-Be* (Buddhist Tradition series, vol. 21). Delhi: Motilal Banarsidass.
Mendelson, E. M. (1960) "Religion and Authority in Modern Burma," *World Today* 16: 110–18.
(1961a) "The King of the Weaving Mountain," *Royal Central Asiatic Journal* 48: 229–37.
(1961b) "A Messianic Buddhist Association in Upper Burma," *Bulletin of the School of Oriental and African Studies* 24: 560–80.
(1963a) "Buddhism and Politics in Burma," *New Society* 38: 8–10.
(1963b) "Observations on a Tour in the Region of Mount Popa, Central Burma," *France-Asie* 179: 780–807.
(1963c) "The Uses of Religious Skepticism in Burma," *Diogenes* 41: 94–116.
(1964) "Buddhism and the Burmese Establishment," *Archives de sociologie des religions* 17: 85–95.
Meyer, R. E. (ed.) (1989) *Cemeteries and Gravemarkers: Voices of American Culture.* Ann Arbor: UMI Research Press.
Minayeff, J. (1886) "Anāgata-vaṃsa," *Journal of the Pali Text Society* II: 33–53.
Mink, L. (1987) *Historical Understanding.* Ithaca: Cornell University Press.
Mitchell, W. J. T (ed.) (1981) *On Narrative.* Chicago University Press.
Momigliano, A. (1977) *Essays in Ancient and Modern Historiography.* Middletown: Wesleyan University Press.
Morton. A. L. (1952) *The English Utopia.* London: Lawrence and Wishart.
Moynihan E. B. (1979) *Paradise as a Garden: in Persia and Mughal India.* New York: Braziller.
Mukhia, H. (1995) "Was There Feudalism in Indian History?", in H. Kulke (ed.) *The State in India 1000–1700* (reprinted from *Journal of Peasant Studies* [1981] 8: 273–310). Delhi: Oxford University Press.
Mumford, L. (1956) *The Transformations of Man.* New York: Harper.
Munn, N. D. (1992) "The Cultural Anthropology of Time: A Critical Essay," *Annual Review of Anthropology* 21: 93–123.
Murdoch, J. B. (1974) "The 1901–1902 'Holy Man's' Rebellion," *Journal of the Siam Society* 62, 1: 47–66.

Mus, P. (1935) *Barabudur*. Hanoi: Imprimerie d'Extrême-orient.
(1939) *La lumière sur les six voies*. Paris: Institut d'Ethnologie.
Nagel, T. (1986) *The View from Nowhere*. Oxford University Press.
Ñāṇamoli, Bhikkhu (1960) *The Minor Readings and Illustrator*. London: Pali Text Society.
(1962) *The Guide*. London: Pali Text Society.
(1964) *Piṭaka Disclosure*. London: Pali Text Society.
(1972) *The Life of the Buddha*. Kandy: Buddhist Publication Society.
(1975) *The Path of Purification*. Kandy: Buddhist Publication Society.
(1982) *The Path of Discrimination*. London: Pali Text Society.
(1987) *Dispeller of Delusion I*. London: Pali Text Society.
(1991) *Dispeller of Delusion II*. London: Pali Text Society.
Nārada Thera (1975) *A Manual of Abhidhamma* (3rd. edn.). Kandy: Buddhist Publication Society.
Narain, H. (1963) "Śūnyavāda: a Reinterpretation," *Philosophy East and West* 13, 4: 311–38.
Nattier, J. (1988) "The Meanings of the Maitreya Myth: A Typological Analysis," in A. Sponberg and H. Hardacre (eds.) (88).
Norman, K. R. (1969) *Elders' Verses I*. London: Pali Text Society.
(1971) *Elders' Verses II*. London: Pali Text Society.
(1983) *Pali Literature* (History of Indian Literature 7, 2). Wiesbaden: Harrassowitz.
(1990–6) *Collected Papers* vols. I–VI. London: Pali Text Society.
(1992a) *The Group of Discourses II*. London: Pali Text Society.
(1992b) "Some Misinterpretations of 'Immortality,'" in T. Skorupski (ed.) *The Buddhist Forum* vol. II. University of London: School of Oriental and African Studies.
Nowotny, H. (1994) *Time: The Modern and Postmodern Experience*. Cambridge: Polity Press.
Nyíri, J. C. (1988) "Tradition and Practical Knowledge," in J. C. Nyíri and B. Smith (eds.) *Practical Knowledge: Outlines of a Theory of Tradition and Skills*. London: Croom Helm.
(1991) *Tradition and Individuality: Essays*. Dordrecht: Kluwer.
Obeyesekere, G. (1966) "The Buddhist Pantheon in Ceylon and its Extensions," in M. Nash (ed.) *Anthropological Studies in Theravada Buddhism*. New Haven: Yale University Southeast Asia Studies, Cultural Report Series No. 13.
(1972) "Religious Symbolism and Political Change in Ceylon," in B. Smith (ed.) (72).
(1976) "The Ayur-Vedic Tradition in Sri Lanka," in C. Leslie (ed.) *Asian Medical Systems*. Berkeley: University of California Press.
(1991) *The Work of Culture: Symbolic Transformation in Psychoanalysis and Anthropology*. University of Chicago Press.
Obeyesekere, R. (1989) *Jewels of the Doctrine*. Albany: State University of New York Press.

O'Flaherty and W. Doniger (1976) *The Origins of Evil in Hindu Mythology.* Berkeley: University of California Press.

(1980) *Karma and Rebirth in Classical Indian Traditions.* Berkeley: University of California Press.

Ogden, C. K. (1922) (translation) [Wittgenstein's] *Tractatus Logico-Philosophicus.* London: Routledge and Kegan Paul.

Olivelle, P. (1992) *Saṃnyāsa Upaniṣads: Hindu Scriptures on Asceticism and Renunciation.* Oxford University Press.

(1993) *The Āśrama System: the History and Hermeneutics of a Religious Institution.* Oxford University Press.

Pagden, A. (1995) *Lords of all the World: Ideologies of Empire in Spain, Britain and France c.1500–c.1800.* New Haven: Yale University Press.

Paranavitana, S. (1970) *Inscriptions of Ceylon,* vol. I. Colombo: Archaeological Survey of Ceylon.

Parry, J. (1986) "*The Gift,* the Indian Gift, and the 'Indian Gift,'" *Man* (n.s.) 21, 73: 453–73.

Parsons, T. (1966) *Societies: Evolutionary and Comparative Perspectives* (Foundations of Modern Sociology Series). Prentice-Hall.

Partin, H. (1987) "Paradise" in M. Eliade (ed.) (87).

Passmore, J. (1970) *The Perfectibility of Man.* London: Duckworth.

Pathak, V. S. (1966) *Ancient Historians of India.* New York: Asia Publishing House.

Pears, D. F. and B. McGuinness (1961) *Wittgenstein's Tractatus Logico-Philosophicus.* Atlantic Highlands: Humanities Press.

Peregrine, P. N. and G. M. Feinman (eds.) (1996) *Pre-Columbian World Systems.* Madison: Prehistory Press.

Perera, L. A. (1961) "The Buddhist Chronicle of Ceylon," in C. H. Philips (ed.) (61).

Perrett, R. (1986) "Regarding Immortality," *Religious Studies* 22, 2: 219–33.

Philips, C. H. (ed.) (1961) *Historians of India, Pakistan and Ceylon.* Oxford University Press.

Pocock, D. (1975) *Understanding Social Anthropology.* London: Hodder and Stoughton.

Polkinghorne, D. E. (1988) *Narrative Knowing and the Human Sciences.* Albany: State University of New York Press.

Pollock, S. (1985) "The Theory of Practice and the Practice of Theory in Indian Intellectual History," *Journal of the American Oriental Society* 105, 3–4: 499–519.

(1986) *The Rāmāyaṇa of Valmīki* vol. II: *Ayodhyākāṇḍa.* Princeton University Press.

(1989) "Mīmāṃsā and the Problem of History," *Journal of the American Oriental Society* 109,4: 603–10.

(1993) "Deep Orientalism? Notes on Sanskrit and Power beyond the Raj," in C. Breckenridge and P. van der Veer (eds.) *Orientalism and the Postcolonial Predicament.* Philadelphia: University of Pennsylvania Press.

(1996) "The Sanskrit Cosmopolis, AD 300–1300: Transculturation, Vernacularization, and the Question of Ideology," in J. Houben (ed.) *The Ideology and Status of Sanskrit in South and Southeast Asia.* Leiden: Brill.

Popper, K. (1975) *Objective Knowledge: An Evolutionary Approach* (reprinted with corrections). Oxford: Clarendon Press.

Potter, K. (1963) *Presuppositions of Indian Philosophy.* Englewood Cliffs, NJ: Prentice-Hall.

Premasiri, P. D. (1976) "Interpretation of Two Principal Ethical Terms in Early Buddhism," *The Sri Lanka Journal of the Humanities* 2: 63–74.

Prince, G. (1987) *Dictionary of Narratology.* Lincoln: University of Nebraska Press.

Pruitt, W. (1987) "References to Pali in 17th-century French Books," *Journal of the Pali Text Society* XI: 121–31

(1988) "The Chronicle of the future Buddha" (*Anāgatavaṃsa* translation), in Tin (88).

Putuwar, S. (1991) *The Buddhist Sangha: Paradigm of the Ideal Human Society.* Lanham: University Press of America.

Quigley, D. (1993) *The Interpretation of Caste.* Oxford University Press.

Rahula, W. (1956) *History of Buddhism in Ceylon.* Colombo: M. D. Gunasena.

(1967) *What the Buddha Taught.* Bedford: Gordon Fraser.

Ramanujan, A. K. (1991) "Three Hundred Rāmāyaṇas: Five Examples and Three Thoughts on Translation" in P. Richman (ed.) (91).

Ray, R. (1994) *Buddhist Saints of the Forest: A Study in Buddhist Values and Orientations.* Oxford University Press.

Redfield, R. (1989 [1956]) *The Little Community and Peasant Society and Culture* (Midway reprint). University of Chicago Press.

Reed, T. J. (1974) *Thomas Mann: The Uses of Tradition.* Oxford University Press.

Reid, A. (1988) *Southeast Asia in the Age of Commerce 1450–1680,* vol. I: *The Lands Below the Winds.* New Haven: Yale University Press.

(1993) [as above] vol. II: *Expansion and Crisis.*

Reynolds, C. J. (1973) *The Buddhist Monkhood in Nineteenth-Century Thailand.* Ph.D. dissertation, Cornell University.

(1976) "Buddhist Cosmography in Thai History, with Special Reference to Nineteenth-Century Culture Change," *Journal of Asian Studies* 35, 2: 203–20.

(1992) "Authenticating Southeast Asia in the Absence of Colonialism: Burma," *Asian Studies Review* 15, 3: 141–51.

(1995) "A New Look at Old Southeast Asia," *Journal of Asian Studies* 54, 2: 419–46.

Reynolds, F. E. (1972) "The Two Wheels of Dhamma," in B. Smith (ed.) (1972).

(1977) "The Several Bodies of the Buddha," *History of Religions* 16: 374–89.
(1985) "Multiple Cosmologies and Ethics: The Case of Theravāda Buddhism," in F. E. Reynolds and R. Lovin (eds.) *Cosmogony and Ethics*. University of Chicago Press.
Reynolds, F. E and M. B. (1982) *Three Worlds According to King Ruang* (Berkeley Buddhist Studies Series 4). Berkeley: University of California Press.
Reynolds, F. E. and C. S. Hallisey (1989) "Buddhist Religion, Culture and Civilization," in J. M. Kitagawa and M. D. Cummings (eds.) *Buddhism and Asian History* (reprinted from Eliade [ed.] 87). New York: Macmillan.
Rhys Davids, C. A. F. (1900) *Buddhist Psychological Ethics*. London: Pali Text Society.
Rhys Davids, T. W. (1899) *Dialogues of the Buddha, Part I* (SBB II). London: Pali Text Society.
(1910) *Dialogues of the Buddha, Part II* (SBB III). London: Pali Text Society.
Richman, P. (1988) *Women, Branch Stories and Religious Rhetoric in a Tamil Buddhist Text*. University of Syracuse, New York: Maxwell School of Citizenship and Public Affairs.
(ed.) (1991) *Many Rāmāyaṇas: the Diversity of a Narrative Tradition in South Asia*. Berkeley: University of California Press.
Ricks, C. (1993) *Beckett's Dying Words*. Oxford: Clarendon Press.
Ricoeur, P. (1984–88) *Time and Narrative*. University of Chicago Press. vol. I (1984), vol. II (85), vol. III (88).
(1992) *Oneself as Another*. University of Chicago Press.
Rimmon-Kenan, S. (1983) *Narrative Fiction: Contemporary Poetics*. London: Methuen.
Robertson, R. (1991) "Social Theory, Cultural Relativity and the Problem of Globality", in A. D. King (ed.) *Culture, Globalization and the World-System: Contemporary Conditions for the Representation of Identity*. State University of New York at Binghampton: Department of Art and Art History.
Rocher, L. (1986) *The Purāṇas* (History of Indian Literature 2, 3). Wiesbaden: Harrassowitz.
Rogers, K. A. (1994) "Eternity has no Duration," *Religious Studies* 30: 1–16.
Rohanadeera, M. (1987) "Telakaṭāhagāthā in a Thailand Inscription of 761 AD," *Vidyodaya Journal of the Social Sciences* 1, 1: 59–73.
Rösener, W. (1994) *The Peasantry of Europe*. Oxford: Blackwell.
Roth, G. and Schluchter, W. (1979) *Max Weber's Vision of History: Ethics and Methods*. Berkeley: University of California Press.
Rouse, W. H. D. (1905) "*Jinacarita*. Translation," *Journal of the Pali Text Society* 5: 33–65.
Rowell, G. (1974) *Hell and the Victorians: A Study of the Nineteenth Century*

Theological Controversy Concerning Eternal Punishment and the Future Life. Oxford: Clarendon Press.

Rowlands, M. (1993) "The Role of Memory in the Transmission of Cultures," in R. Bradley (ed.) (93).

Ruegg, D. S. (1969) *La théorie du Tathāgatagarbha et du Gotra.* Paris: Publications de l'Ecole Française d'Extrême-Orient, vol. LXX.

Ryle, G. (1949) *The Concept of Mind.* London: Hutchinson's University Library.

Saddhatissa, H. (1974) "Pali Literature of Thailand," in L. S. Cousins et al. (eds.) (74).

(1975) *Birth Stories of the Ten Bodhisattas (Dasabodhisattuppatti-kathā).* London: Pali Text Society.

(1976) "The Dawn of Pali Literature in Thailand," in O. H. Wijesekera (ed.) *G. P. Malalasekera Felicitation Volume.* Colombo: Malalasekera Commemoration Volume Editorial Committee.

(1979) "Pali Literature from Laos," in A. K. Narain (ed.) *Studies in Pali and Buddhism.* Delhi: B. R. Publishing Corporation.

(1981) "Pali Literature in Cambodia," *Journal of the Pali Text Society* IX: 178–97.

(1989) *Abhidhammatthasaṅgaha and Abhidhammatthabhāvinī-ṭīkā.* London: Pali Text Society.

Sadri, A. (1992) *Max Weber's Sociology of Intellectuals.* Oxford University Press.

Sahlins, M. (1963) "Poor Man, Rich Man, Big-Man, Chief: Political Types in Melanesia and Polynesia," *Comparative Studies in Society and History* 5: 285–303.

(1972) *Stone-Age Economics.* Chicago: Aldine-Atherton.

Sanderson, S. (1995) *Social Transformations: a General Theory of Human Development.* Oxford: Blackwell.

Sangermano, V. (1966 [1883]) *A Description of the Burmese Empire* (translated by W. W. Tandy). London: Susil Gupta.

Sarkisyanz, E. (1965) *Buddhist Backgrounds to the Burmese Revolution.* The Hague: Martinus Nijhoff.

Scharfstein, B-A. (1993) *Ineffability: The Failure of Words in Philosophy and Religion.* Albany: State University of New York Press.

Schluchter, W. (1979) "The Paradox of Rationalization: On the Relation of Ethics to the World," in G. Roth and W. Schluchter, *Max Weber's Vision of History: Ethics and Methods.* Berkeley: University of California Press.

Schmithausen, L. (1979) "On Some Aspects of Descriptions or Theories of 'Liberating Insight' and 'Enlightenment' in Early Buddhism," in K. Bruhn and A. Wezler (eds.) *Studien zum Jainismus und Buddhismus.* Wiesbaden: Franz Steiner Verlag.

Schneider, J. (1977) "Was there a Premodern World System?" *Peasant*

Studies 6, 1: 20–9; reprinted in C. Chase-Dunn and T. Hall (1991), *Core-periphery Relations in Precapitalist Worlds.* Boulder: Westview.

Schopen, G. (1975) "The Phrase *sa pṛthivīpradeśaś caityabhūto bhavet* in the *Vajracchedikā*: Notes on the Cult of the Book in Mahāyāna," *Indo-Iranian Journal* 27, 3–4: 147–81.

(1987) "Burial *ad sanctos* and the Physical Presence of the Buddha in Early Indian Buddhism," *Religion* 17: 193–225.

(1988) "On the Buddha and his Bones: The Conception of a Relic in the Inscriptions of Nagārjunikoṇḍa," *Journal of the American Oriental Society* 108, 4: 527–37.

(1991) "Archaeology and Protestant Presuppositions in the Study of Indian Buddhism," *History of Religions* 31, 1: 1–23.

Schrader, F. O. (1905) "On the Problem of Nirvāṇa," *Journal of the Pali Text Society* 5: 157–70.

Schwartz, B. I. (1975) "The Age of Transcendence in Wisdom, Doubt and Uncertainty," *Daedalus* (Spring) 1975.

Schweisguth, P. (1951) *Etude sur la littérature siamoise.* Paris: Imprimerie Nationale.

Scott, D. (1994) *Formations of Ritual: Colonial and Anthropological Discourses on the Sinhala Yaktovil.* Minneapolis: University of Minnesota Press.

Scott, J. C. (1975) *The Moral Economy of the Peasant: Rebellion and Subsistence in Southeast Asia.* New Haven: Yale University Press.

(1985) *Weapons of the Weak: Everyday Forms of Peasant Resistance.* New Haven: Yale University Press.

Séguy, J. (1971) "Une sociologie des sociétés imaginées: monachisme et utopie," *Annales E.S.C.* 26: 328–54.

Shanin, T. (1987) *Peasants and Peasant Societies: Selected Readings.* Oxford: B. H. Blackwell.

Sharma, R. S. (1983) *Material Culture and Social Formations in Ancient India.* Delhi: Macmillan India.

Shils E. (1981) *Tradition.* University of Chicago Press.

Shorto, H. L. (1967) "The *Dewatau Sotapan*: A Mon Prototype of the 37 Nats," *Bulletin of the School of Oriental and African Studies* 30: 127–41.

(1978) "The Planets, the Days of the Week and the Points of the Compass: Orientation Symbolism in 'Burma,'" in G. B. Milner (ed.) *Natural Symbols in South East Asia.* London: School of Oriental and African Studies.

Shulman, D. (1985) *The King and the Clown in South Indian Myth and Poetry.* Princeton University Press.

(1991) "Towards a Historical Poetics of the Sanskrit Epics," *International Folklore Review* (London), vol.8, V. Newall (ed.) *Folklore Studies from Overseas.*

Shwe Baw (1955) *The Origin and Development of Burmese Legal Literature.* D.Phil. thesis, University of London.

Sibunruang, J. K. (1960) *Khun Chang, Khun Phăn: La Femme, Le Héros et le vilain.* Paris: Presses Universitaires de France.

Silber, I. F. (1981) "Dissent through Holiness: The Case of the Radical Renouncer in Theravada Buddhist Countries," *Numen* 18: 163–93.

(1985) "'Opting Out' in Theravāda Buddhism and Medieval Christianity: A Comparative Study of Monasticism as Alternative Structure," *Religion*, 15: 251–77.

(1995) *Virtuosity, Charisma and Social Order: A Comparative Sociological Study of Monasticism in Theravada Buddhism and Medieval Catholicism.* Cambridge University Press.

Silburn, L. (1955) *Instant et cause.* Paris: Librarie Philosophique J. Vrin.

Sizemore, R. and D. Swearer (eds.) (1990) *Ethics, Wealth and Salvation.* Columbia: University of South Carolina Press.

Skilling, P. (1992) "The *Rakṣā* Literature of the *Śrāvakayāna*," *Journal of the Pali Text Society* 16: 109–82.

Slater, R. H. L. (1951) *Paradox and Nirvana.* University of Chicago Press.

Smart, N. (1973) "Precept and Theory in Sri Lanka," *Religion* 3: 74–9.

Smith, B. (ed.) (1972) *The Two Wheels of Dhamma: Essays on the Theravāda Tradition in Indian and Ceylon.* Chambersburg: American Academy of Religion.

(1978a) *Religion and Legitimation of Power in Sri Lanka.* Chambersburg: Anima.

(1978b) *Religion and Legitimation of Power in Burma, Thailand and Laos.* Chambersburg: Anima.

Smith, B. H. (1968) *Poetic Closure: A Study of How Poems End.* University of Chicago Press.

Smith, H. (1966) *Saddānīti: la grammaire Pali d'Aggavaṃsa*, vol. II. Lund: Gleerup.

Smith, J. I. and Y. Y. Haddad (eds.) (1981) *The Islamic Understanding of Death and Resurrection.* Albany: State University of New York Press.

Smith, J. Z. (1991) "A Slip in Time saves Nine: Prestigious Origins Again," in J. Bender and D. E. Wellbery (eds.) *Chronotypes: the Construction of Time.* Stanford University Press.

Snellgrove, D. (ed.) (1978) *The Image of the Buddha.* Paris: UNESCO.

Solomon, R. L. (1969) "Saya San and the Burmese Rebellion," *Modern Asian Studies* 3, 3: 209–23.

Somadasa, K. D. (1987–) *Catalogue of the Hugh Nevill Collection of Sinhalese Manuscripts in the British Library*, vol. I (1987), II (1989), III (1990), IV (1990), V (1993), VI (1993). London: Pali Text Society/British Library.

Sorabji, R. (1983) *Time, Space and the Continuum: Theories in Antiquity and the Early Middle Ages.* Ithaca: Cornell University Press.

Southwold, M. (1978) "Buddhism and the Definition of Religion," *Man*, n.s. 13: 362–79.

Spiro M. E. (1966) " Religion: Problems of Definition and Explanation," in M. Banton (ed.) *Anthropological Approaches to the Study of Religion* (ASA Monographs 3). London: Tavistock.
(1971) *Buddhism and Society: a Great Tradition and its Burmese Vicissitudes.* London: George Allen and Unwin.
Sponberg, A. and H. Hardacre (eds.) (1988) *Maitreya, the Future Buddha.* Cambridge University Press.
Starobinski, J. (1993) *Blessings in Disguise; or, The Morality of Evil.* Cambridge: Harvard University Press.
Stavrianos, L. S. (1992) *Lifelines From Our Past: A New World History.* New York: M. E. Sharpe.
Stern, T. (1968) "Ariya and the Golden Book," *Journal of Asian Studies* 27, 2: 297–327.
Sternbach, L. (1969) *The Spreading of Cāṇakya's Aphorisms Over "Greater India".* Calcutta: Oriental Book Agency.
(1974) *Subhāṣita, Gnomic and Didactic Literature* (History of Indian Literature 4, 4). Wiesbaden: Harrassowitz.
(1981) "Indian Wisdom and its Spread Beyond India," *Journal of the American Oriental Society* 101, 1: 97–131.
Story, F. (1971) *The Buddhist Doctrine of Nibbāna.* Kandy: Buddhist Publication Society (Wheel nos. 165–6).
Strong, J. S. (1992) *The Legend and Cult of Upagupta: Sanskrit Buddhism in North India and Southeast Asia.* Princeton University Press.
Stump, E. and N. Kretzmann (1981) "Eternity," *The Journal of Philosophy* 68: 429–58.
Surtz, E. and J. H. Hexter (1965) *The Complete Works of St. Thomas More* (vol.4). New Haven: Yale University Press.
Swearer, D. (1987) "Arhat," in M. Eliade (ed.) (87).
(1995) *The Buddhist World of Southeast Asia.* Albany: State University of New York Press.
Swift, J. (1963) *Gulliver's Travels.* New York: Airmont Books.
Tabata, T. et al. (1987) *Index to the Dhammasaṅgani.* London: Pali Text Society.
Talmon, Y. (1966) "Millenarian Movements," *Archives Européennes de Sociologie* 7: 159–200.
Tambiah, S. J. (1968a) "The Ideology of Merit and the Social Correlates of Buddhism in a Thai Village," in E. R. Leach (ed.) *Dialectic in Practical Religion.* Cambridge University Press.
(1968b) "The Magical Power of Words," *Man* n.s. 3, 2: 175–208.
(1968c) "Literacy in a Buddhist Village in North-East Thailand," in J. Goody (ed.) *Literacy in Traditional Societies.* Cambridge University Press.
(1970) *Buddhism and the Spirit Cults of Northeast Thailand.* Cambridge University Press.
(1976) *World Conqueror and World Renouncer: A Study of Buddhism and*

Polity in Thailand against a Historical Background. Cambridge University Press.
(1984a) *The Buddhist Saints of the Forest: A Study in Charisma, Hagiography, Sectarianism, and Millennial Buddhism.* Cambridge University Press.
(1984b) "The Buddhist Cosmos: Paradise Lost, Gained, and Regained" (review of F. E. and M. B. Reynolds 1982), *History of Religions* 24, 1: 73–81.
Tannenbaum, N. (1987) "Tattoos: Invulnerability and Power in Shan Cosmology," *American Ethnologist* 14: 693–711.
(1991) "*Haeng* and *Takho*: Power in Shan Cosmology," *Ethnos* 56: 67–81.
(1995) *Who Can Compete against the World? Power-protection and Buddhism in Shan Worldview.* Ann Arbor: Association for Asian Studies.
Tarling, N. (ed.) (1992). *The Cambridge History of Southeast Asia*, vol. I. Cambridge University Press.
Taylor, J. L. (1993) *Forest Monks and the Nation-State: An Anthropological and Historical Study in Northeastern Thailand.* Singapore: Institute of Southeast Asian Studies.
Taylor, K. W. (1992) "The Early Kingdoms," in Tarling (ed.) (92).
Teggart, F. J. (1939) *Rome and China: A Study of Correlations in Historical Events.* Berkeley: University of California Press.
Tellenbach, G. (1991) *Church, State and Christian Society at the Time of the Investiture Contest.* University of Toronto Press.
Testart, A. (1982) "The Significance of Food Storage among Hunter-gatherers: Residence Patterns, Population Densities, and Social Inequalities," *Current Anthropology* 23: 523–30.
(1988) "Some Major Problems in the Social Anthropology of Hunter-gatherers," *Current Anthropology* 29: 1–13.
Than Tun (1959) "Religion in Burma 1000–1300, *Journal of the Burma Research Society* 42, 2: 47–69.
Thapar, R. (1984) *From Lineage to State: Social Formations in the Mid-First Millennium* BC *in the Ganga Valley.* Oxford University Press.
Thittila, U (1969) *The Book of Analysis.* London: Pali Text Society.
Thomas, E. J. (1933) *History of Buddhist Thought.* London: Routledge and Kegan Paul.
(1947) "Nirvāṇa and Parinirvāṇa," in *India Antiqua* (Festschrift for J. P. Vogel). Leiden: E. J. Brill.
Thornton, R. J. (1988) "The Rhetoric of Ethnographic Holism," *Cultural Anthropology* 3: 285–303.
Tilly, C. A. (1985) "Warmaking and State-making as Organized Crime," in P. Evans, D. Rueschmeyer, and T. Skocpol (eds.) *Bringing the State Back In.* Cambridge University Press.
Tin, Saya U Chit (1988) *The Coming Buddha Ariiya Metteyya.* Dhammadāna Series 7. Heddington (near Calne), Great Britain: The Sagyagi U Ba Khin Memorial Trust. Reprinted, with some changes, as "The

Coming Buddha Ariya Metteyya," (1992) Kandy: Buddhist Publication Society (Wheel nos. 381–2)

Tiyavanich, K. (1997) *Forest Recollections: Wandering Monks in Twentieth Century Thailand.* Honolulu: University of Hawaii Press.

Toolan, M. J. (1988) *Narrative: A Critical Linguistic Introduction.* London: Routledge.

Trainor, K. (1997) *Relics, Ritual, and Representation in Buddhism: Rematerializing the Sri Lankan Theravāda Tradition.* Cambridge University Press.

Trautmann, T. R. (1995) "Indian Time, European Time" in D. Hughes and T. R. Trautmann (eds.) *Time: Histories and Ethnographies.* Ann Arbor: University of Michigan Press.

Tuck, A. (1990) *Comparative Philosophy and the Philosophy of Scholarship: On the Western Interpretation of Nāgārjuna.* Oxford University Press.

Turner, S. (1994) *The Social Theory of Practices: Tradition, Tacit Knowledge, and Presuppositions.* University of Chicago Press.

Turton, A. (1991) "Invulnerability and Local Knowledge," in M. Chitakasem and A. Turton (eds.) *Thai Constructions of Knowledge.* London: School of Oriental and African Studies.

Turton, A. and S. Tanabe (eds.) (1984) *History and Peasant Consciousness in Southeast Asia.* Osaka: National Museum of Ethnology.

Vaidya, P. L. (1971) *The Yuddhakāṇḍa: the Sixth Book of the Valmīki-Rāmāyaṇa.* Baroda: Oriental Institute.

Ver Eecke, J. (1976) *Le Dasavatthupakaraṇa.* Paris: Publications de l'Ecole Française d'Extrême- Orient.

(1980) *Le Sīhalavatthupakaraṇa.* Paris: Publications de l'Ecole Française d'Extrême-Orient.

Vergati, A. (1982) "Le Culte et l'iconographie du Bouddha Dīpankara dans la vallée de Kathmandou," *Arts Asiatiques* 37: 22–7.

Vetter, T. (1988) *The Ideas and Meditative Practices of Early Buddhism.* Leiden: E. J. Brill.

Vickery, M. (1991) "On Traibhūmikathā," *Journal of the Siam Society* 79, 2: 24–36.

Vogel, J. Ph. (1954) "The Past Buddhas and Kāśyapa in Indian Art and Epigraphy," in *Asiatica* (Festschrift Friedrich Weller). Leipzig: Harrassowitz.

Waldschmidt, E. (1949) *Das Mahāparinirvāṇasūtra. Abhandlungen der Deutschen Akademi der Wissenschaften zu Berlin, Philosophisch-Historisch Klasse.*

Wallerstein, I. (1974) *The Modern World-System,* vol. I. New York: Academic Press.

Walshe, M. (1987) *Thus Have I Heard: the Long Discourses of the Buddha.* London: Wisdom.

Walters, J. (1990) "The Buddha's Bad Karma: a Problem in the History of Theravāda Buddhism", *Numen* XXVII, 1: 70–95.

Warder, A. K. (1971) "The Concept of a Concept," *Journal of Indian Philosophy* 1: 181–96.

(1972) *An Introduction to Indian Historiography*. Bombay: Popular Prakashan.

(1974) *Introduction to Pali* (3rd edn.). London: Pali Text Society.

(1982) "Introduction" to Ñāṇamoli (82).

Warren, H. (1896) *Buddhism in Translations*. Cambridge: Harvard Oriental Series.

Weber, M. (1948) *From Max Weber: Essays in Sociology*. London: Routledge and Kegan Paul.

(1949) *Max Weber on the Methodology of the Social Sciences* (translated and edited by E. A. Shils and H. A. Finch). Glencoe: Free Press.

(1958) *The Religion of India*. New York: Free Press.

(1963) *The Sociology of Religion*. London: Methuen.

Weightman, S. (1978) *Hinduism in the Village Setting*. Milton Keynes: The Open University Press.

Welbon, G. (1968) *The Buddhist Nirvāna and its Western Interpreters*. University of Chicago Press.

Wells, K. E. (1939) *Thai Buddhism in its Rites and Activities*. Bangkok Times Press.

Wezler, A. (1984) "On the Quadruple Division of the Yogaśāstra, the Caturvyūhatva of the Cikitsāśāstra and the "Four Noble Truths" of the Buddha," *Indologia Taurinensia* 12: 289–337.

White, H. (1987) *The Content of the Form: Narrative Discourse and Historical Representation*. Baltimore: Johns Hopkins University Press.

Whitney, W. D. (1885) *The Roots, Verb-forms and Primary Derivatives of the Sanskrit Language*. Leipzig: Breitkopf and Härtel.

(1889) *Sanskrit Grammar* (2nd edn.). Cambridge: Harvard University Press.

Wickremasinghe, D. M. (1900) *Catalogue of the Sinhalese Manuscripts in the British Museum*. London: British Museum.

Wijayaratna, M. (1987) *Le culte des dieux chez les Bouddhistes singhalais*. Paris: CERF.

(1990) *Buddhist Monastic Life: According to the Texts of the Theravāda Tradition*. Cambridge University Press.

Williams, B. (1973) *Problems of the Self*. Cambridge University Press.

Williams, P. M. W. (1981) "On the Abhidharma Ontology," *Journal of Indian Philosophy* 9, 3: 227–57.

(1989) *Mahāyāna Buddhism: The Doctrinal Foundations*. London: Routledge and Kegan Paul.

Wilson, B. (1973) *Magic and the Millennium: Religious Movements of Protest among Tribal and Third-World Peoples*. London: Paladin.

(1982) *Religion in Sociological Perspective*. Oxford University Press.

Wiltshire, M. (1983) "The 'Suicide Problem' in the Pali Canon," *Journal of the International Association of Buddhist Studies* 6, 2: 124–40.

(1990) *Ascetic Figures Before and in Early Buddhism: The Emergence of Gautama as the Buddha.* Berlin: Mouton de Gruyter.

Windisch (191890) "Notes on the Edition of the Udāna," *Journal of the Pali Text Society* 4: 91–108.

Wolf, E. R. (1966) *Peasants.* Englewood Cliffs, Prentice-Hall.

(1982) *Europe and the People Without History.* Berkeley: University of California Press.

Wolters, O. W. (1968) "Ayudhya and the Rearward Part of the World," *Journal of the Royal Asiatic Society,* pp. 166–78.

(1982) *History, Culture and Region in Southeast Asian Perspective.* Singapore: Institute of Southeast Asian Studies

Woodburn, J. (1980) "Hunters and Gatherers Today and Reconstruction of the Past," in E. Gellner (ed.) *Soviet and Western Anthropology.* New York: Columbia University Press.

(1982) "Egalitarian Societies," *Man* n.s. 17, 3: 431–51.

Woodward, F. L. (1935) *The Minor Anthologies of the Pali Canon,* Part Two. Oxford University Press.

Worsley, P. (1968) *The Trumpet Shall Sound.* London: Paladin.

Wrigley, E. A. (1987) *People, Cities and Wealth: The Transformation of Traditional Society.* Oxford: Blackwell.

(1988) *Continuity, Chance and Change: The Character of the Industrial Revolution in England.* Cambridge University Press.

(1992) "Why Poverty was Inevitable in Traditional Societies," in J. A. Hall and I. C. Jarvie (eds.) *Transition to Modernity.* Cambridge University Press.

Wyatt, D. (1982) "The 'Subtle Revolution' of King Rama I," in A. B. Woodside and D. K. Wyatt (eds.) (82) *Moral Order and the Question of Change.* Yale University Southeast Asia Studies, Monograph Series no.24.

(1984) *Thailand: A Short History.* New Haven: Yale University Press.

Young, M. D. (1988) *The Metronomic Society: Natural Rhythms and Human Timetables.* Cambridge: Harvard University Press.

Zysk, K. (1991) *Asceticism and Healing in Ancient India: Medicine in the Buddhist Monastery.* Oxford University Press.

Glossary and index of Pali and Sanskrit words

ārammaṇa-paccaya (nirvana as) object-condition (of Path-knowledge), 165, 556
ariyaphala-rasānubhavana Experience of the Taste of the Noble Fruit (of the Path), 157–158, 160–161
ariya-sacca (four) Noble Truths, 122, 142, 156, 166–167, 185
ārogya health, 201, 229–230
arūpāvacara Formless Sphere, 297–304
asaṃvijjamāna non-existent, 202
asaṃsagga not gregarious, 337
asaṅkhata (used as epithet for nirvana) in which there is nothing conditioned, 147 n. 33, 167–170, 179–180, 202
asaṅkhata (*-dhātu*) (the) unconditioned (element), 28–29, 123–124, 139, 141, 142, 159, 199, 206
asaṅkhata-dhamma (the) unconditioned Existent, 175
asatthena (kings' conquering and ruling) without the sword, 459, 470, 472,
āsava corruption(s) (lit. 'flows' the idea seems to be of bad states of mind flowing in and out of a person in his/her interaction with the world), 145, 149, 151, 152, 154, 155, 160, 187, 188, 200, 229, 311, 583, 590
asura-s anti-gods, demons, 297, 300 n. 4
atakkāvacara inaccessible to (discursive) thought, 97
attabhāva individuality, 539, 540
atthaṃgata set, gone down (like the sun), 162
atthi (verb), exist, 173–174
atthi-bhāva existence, 167, 172
atthi-dhamma, something which really exists, 164
atthitā existence, 173–174 n. 94
ātman (Pali *attā*)- (the) self, 137, 176, 220
atta-suñña empty of self, 142
avacara Sphere (of the universe), 297
avasa powerless/under the power of no one, 601 n. 20
avattabbatā indescribability, 163
avijjamāna-bhāva non-existence (lit.: incapacity to be found), 245
avindeyya (*avindiya*) unfindable, 203
avyākata (1) (morally) indeterminate, 155, 175
avyākata (2) Unanswered Question(s), 218, 221, 244, 249–250
āyatana (1) 'sphere' (used of nirvana), 113, 165–166, 216, 224
āyatana (2) sense-sphere, sense-base (internal and external), 122, 175–176, 184
ayutta illogical, 182–183
āyus (Pali *āyu*) (length of) life, 146 n. 32, 488, 494–495

bala strength, 494–495
bali tax, 460, 479, 485, 605 n. 12
barbara/varvara (=Greek *barbaros*) barbarian, 48
bhagavā Blessed One (used of a Buddha), 474
bhavacāraka, the prison of conditioned existence, 230
bhava-, *vibhava-taṇhā* craving for existence/non-existence, 204
bhoga enjoyment, tax-revenue, 485, 494–495, 605 n. 12
bhuñj (verbal root) enjoy, 145–146, 605 n. 12
bhūmi level (of the universe), 297
bhumma-devatā earth deities, 300–301 (and n. 4)
bodhi awakening, enlightenment, 147 n. 34, 213–214
bodhisatta (Skt *bodhisattva*) future Buddha, 266, 380 n. 77, 381, 383, 392, 459
brahmacariya 'the holy life', celibacy, 145, 320, 338, 507
brahma-loka Brahma-world(s), 105, 298–310
brahman the Absolute, essence of the universe (in the *Upaniṣad-s*), 98, 137, 176, 177
brāhmaṇa (the word) Brahmin, 632
buddha awakened, enlightened, 152, 213–214
Buddha-kicca duties of a Buddha, 379, 381, 412,
Buddha-vacana the Word of the Buddha, 178

cāga (Skt *tyāga*) generosity, renunciation, 196, 290, 526, 527
cakkavatti (Skt *cakravartin*) Wheel-turning king, 5, 28, 29, 66, 82, 89, 214, 290, 315, 398–399, 403, 405, 415, 470–496, 524, 625
caṇḍāla outcast, 460
cātumahārāja-s the Four Great Kings, 301, 320
cetiya (Skt *caitya*) shrine 261, 271, 275, 276, 278–280, 590, 595

cora-geha (king's palace as a) criminal-house, 427 n. 21, 432 n. 87, 434–5

daṇḍa punishment, 448, 453, 459, 470, 472
desānaṃ nitthāpeti to bring a teaching to a close, 251
devaloka World of the Gods, 136, 299–304
devatā deity, 300, 406, 532
dhamma (1) what is right, 342 n. 62, 419–423, 425, 426, 432, 434, 446–447, 449, 450–451, 452, 453, 454, 456, 458, 463, 467, 469–470, 486–488, 502, 505, 509, 511, 521, 522–529, 603
dhamma (2) Existent, 88, 113, 140, 141, 148, 165–166, 175–176, 251, 348, 349, 556, 602 n. 2,
dhammacakka Wheel of Dhamma, 214, 473–474, 591
dhammadhātu, the Mental Data/Object(s)-Element, 176, 184, 188
dhammadīpa 'Light (*not* island) of the *Dhamma* (referring to Sri Lanka), 397 n. 3, 598–599 n. 17
dhammagaṇḍikā (executioner's) block of justice, 422, 459, 464,
dhammakāya (a Buddha's) *dhamma*-body, 245–246, 629
dhammarāja king of the Dhamma/righteousness, 471, 472, 483, 485, 591, 602–603, 605 n. 12
dhammatā the way things are, the nature of things, 348, 351, 389, 413
dhammāyatana the Mental Data/Object(s) Sense-base, 165, 175–6, 184, 188
dhātu (1) element (used of nirvana), 113,
dhātu (2) element (of perception and cognition), 176, 184
dhātu (3) relic(s), 247–248, 277–281
dhātu-parinibbāna the nirvana of a Buddha's relics, 245
diṭṭhe va dhamme here and now, in this life, 159
domanassa sorrow, mental unhappiness, 308
dosa crime, flaw, 504, 511, 525
dukkaṭa wrong, offence, 518, 519, 521, 524, 527
dukkha suffering, unsatisfactoriness, 28, 107, 140, 155–156, 179, 229, 291, 511, 548
  3 forms of *dukkha*, 140, 155, 210–211
  cetasika-dukka mental suffering, 155–156

ekantasukha loka completely happy world, 209
ekatta unity, having the same nature, 265, 579 n. 9

gaṇa-saṅgha-s 'Republics' (of ancient North India), 66, 445
gantha (Skt *grantha*) text, 277
garaha denunciation, blame, 527
gati destiny, 174–175, 361 n. 30, 556
guṇa quality, attribute, 232

hetu cause, 179, 185
hiri modesty, 514

idapaccayatā the fact of (everything's) having specific conditions, 139

janapada-s or *mahājanapada*-s regions or great regions (of ancient North India), 65–66
jhāna, meditation, Meditation Level, 159–160, 208, 209, 227–228, 252, 301, 302, 304–309
jhāna-kīḷita sport of meditation, 342, 358

kāla time, 144–146, 179 n. 113
kāla-kiriyā death, 203
kalaṅkata dead, 217
kāla-vimutta free from time, 144
kāma desire, object of desire, 297, 310, 311 n. 24, 358, 424, 460, 483, 504, 505, 535, 556
kāmāvacara Sphere of Desire, 297–304
kammaṭṭhāna-pāli text of a/the meditation subject, 51
kappa-rukkha wishing-tree, 319, 544, 549
kāraṇa cause, 165–166,
karma (Pali *kamma*) action (and by implication, its results), 14, 29, 109–110, 124, 136, 137, 435, 487, 539, 552
kathāvatthu subject(s) about which one can talk, 161–162
khandhā (five) Aggregates, constituents of personhood, 122, 139, 171, 175–176, 181–182, 188, 201, 210, 212, 253, 539
khandha-(pari)nibbāna nirvana of the Aggregates, 148, 151
khaṇika-maraṇa momentary death, 203
khattiya (Skt *kṣatriya*) nobleman, warrior, 449, 507, 628, 632
khema (*-nagara*) (city of) safety, 207, 226

kilesa defilements, 142, 167, 171, 173, 181, 182, 185, 222, 230, 232, 508
kilesa-(pari)nibbāna nirvana of the defilements, 148, 151
kilesa-vaṭṭa round of defilements, 167
kinnarī-s bird-women, 331
kittimā (Skt *kṛtimā*) artificial (language), 52
kuru-dhamma virtues of the Kurus (=Five Precepts), 461–462, 466,
kusala/akusala wholesome/unwholesome, skillful/unskillful, 154–155, 289–290, 481 n. 91, 482–483, 486, 491, 495, 579, 580 n. 14, 604, 610, 611 n. 26

lobha greed, 309, 311
lokāyatikādiyo, Materialists, etc., 167
lokiya/lokuttara (Skt *laukika/lokottara*) worldly/superworldly, mundane/transcendent, 551–552, 592 n. 53

magga (eightfold) Path, 122, 185
mahābhinikkhamana (the Buddha's) Great Renunciation, 392
mahāpurisa great/big man, 470–476
mahāsatta great being (=*bodhisatta*), 392
majjhima janapadā middle regions (of ancient North India), 48
maraṇa death, 203–204
maraṇa-sati Mindfulness of Death, 203, 493
mātikā (doctrinal) list, 122–123
mettā friendship, loving-kindness, 310, 338, 451, 468, 614
micchā-dhamma wrongfulness, 489, 609
milakkha (Skt *mleccha*) barbarian, 48–49
mokṣa (Pali *mokkha*) release (from rebirth), 96, 230–231
mūla-bhāsā root language (i.e. Pali), 49

nāga snake(s)/human(s), 316–317, 597, (cp. 590 n. 47)
nāma 'name', (the) mental, 175
natthitā non-existence, 173–174 n. 94
na vattabba indescribable, 183
neyyattha whose meaning is to be elucidated, 180
nibbāna-vāṇija trade for nirvana, 380
nibbuta quenched/happy, 192, 231, 279, 393–394, 592
nibbuti peace, happiness, 579 n. 10
nigamana epilogue, 252–253
(ni)kūṭaṃ gaṇhāti to bring (a sermon) to a climax, 251
nipphanna/ anipphanna produced/ unproduced, 159
nirodha cessation, 139, 150
nirodha-samāpatti Attainment of Cessation, 77 n. 96, 157, 158–161, 209–210, 227
nirukti/nirutti (1) dialect, gloss, usage, 47–48, 183
nirukti/nirutti (2) (imaginative) etymology, 599 n. 17
nirvāṇa/nibbāna (the words) 147–148, 191–198
nītattha whose meaning does not require elucidation, 180 n. 116
nivṛtti quiescence, cessation, 174

opapātika spontaneous birth, 303
ottappa fear (of blame), 514

pabbajjā (world-) renunciation, ordination as a Buddhist novice, 501, 504, 526
pabbajita-bhāva ascetic condition, 513
paccakkha (Skt *pratyakṣa*) perception, experience, 178
paccantimā janapadā neighbouring regions (of ancient North India), 48
pacceka-buddha (according to the usual interpretation) a Buddha who does not teach, 471, 507
pada (unmoving) place, site (used of nirvana), 113, 224
padaparama (kind of person) for whom words are the highest thing, 178
padesa-rāja regional king, 472
padhāna effort, 365 n. 43, 393–394, 589 n. 43
pakati (Skt *prakṛti*)- Nature (in the *Sāṃkhya* system), 179, 183
pāli (the word) 46
pamāda-ṭṭhāna (kingship as a) condition conducive to negligence, 425
pamāṇaṃ (na) eti, is within (beyond) reckoning, 162
pañca-lakṣaṇa the five (theoretical) constituent parts of a *purāṇa*, 255
paṇidhi aspiration (for nirvana), 188
paññā wisdom, 153 n. 52, 357
paññatti concept(s), 182–184
paññatti-patha (the) reach of conceptualization, 218–219
pāpa demeritorious, bad, 154–155
paramasuñña ultimately empty, 141
paramātman supreme self, 137
paramattha ultimate meaning, goal, truth, 141, 165, 167

paramattha-suñña empty in the ultimate sense, 142
paraṃ maraṇā after death, 203
pariccāga giving up, renunciation, 196
parinibbuta enlightened and/or (finally) nirvanized, 148
parinirvāṇa/parinibbāna (the words) 147–148, 191–198
paritta protection (verses), 472
pariyāyena/apariyāyena figuratively/literally, 150, 201
pariyosānatthena (in the) sense of an ending, 243 n. 11
pariyosāna-kāla time of the end, 151
pasāda serene confidence, 593 n. 2
paticca-samuppāda Dependent Origination, 139–140,
pātimokkha the Monastic Rule(s), 50
paṭirāja rival/enemy king, 484 n. 97, 523
paṭivedha penetration, 51 n. 64
pāṭiyyekka (existing) separately, 180–181
paṭṭhāna aspiration (for nirvana), 188
peta ghost, 316–319
pettika visaya customary terrain, 482, 602 n. 3
phalasamāpatti Attainment(s) of Fruition (of the Path), 157
pīti rapture, 164, 208, 304–308, 426,
pitṛloka World of the Fathers, 136
pramāṇa (Skt; Pali *pamāṇa*), means of knowledge, 178
pravṛtti action, occurrence, 174
pubbakoṭi earliest point (of *saṃsāra*), 249, 250 n. 23
pūjā veneration, worship, 277
punarjanman rebirth, 146
punarmṛtyu repeated dying, re-death, xi, 136, 146
puñña merit, meritorious (deeds), 154–155, 289–290, 482, 495, 505
purimā koṭi see *pubbakoṭi*
pustaka book(s), 277

rāga passion, 307
rāja-dhammā (ten virtues of a (good) king, 460–461, 466,
ratana (seven) precious things (of a *cakkavatti*), 315–316, 471–472
rati (sexual) pleasure, 358, 424, 535
rūpa form, matter, body, 139, 175, 183
rūpa-kāya (a Buddha's) material body, 245
rūpāvacara Sphere of (refined) Form, 297–304

sabbaññutā-ñāṇa omniscience, 152–153
sabbāpaṇa (the Buddha's) General Store, 290
sabhāva individual/essential nature, 141 n. 14, 159, 167, 184, 216, 556
sabhāva-nirutti 'individual-essence language,' 'natural language' (i.e. Pali), 49–50
sadda, (Skt *śabda*) verbal testimony, 178
saddhā confidence or trust, 'faith,' 188, 357
saddhamma-cakkavatti Wheel-turning king of the Good Dhamma, 274
sādhu Good! Amen!, 253, 581
sāli (Skt *śāli*) rice (grown with transplantation), 67
samasīsī 'equal-headed' (=reaching enlightenment and death at the same time), 151
saṃkhāra see *saṅkhāra*
saṃkhata see *saṅkhata*
sammāsambuddha a Buddha who founds a *sāsana*, 471
sammuti-maraṇa (conventional death) 203
saṃsāra the round of rebirth, xi, 96, 113, 124, 137, 168–169, 170, 223, 248, 443, 493, 494, 552
saṃskṛ to make, construct, 138
samuccheda-maraṇa death as [complete] cutting off, 204
samudaya arising, 139
saṃvega animation, 593 n. 2
sandiṭṭhika (what is) before one's eyes, immediate, 146
saṅgaha-vatthu (four) forms of kindliness (for a king), 461
saṅgīti Council, 258, 577 n. 1
saṅkappa resolve (for nirvana), 188
saṅkhaṃ (na) upeti is within (beyond) reckoning, 162, (cp. 217–218)
saṅkhāra conditioned thing(s)/event(s), conditioning factor(s), 28–29, 123–124, 138, 143, 206, 267
saṅkhata (what is) conditioned, 123–124, 138, 140, 141, 143, 159, 206
saññā perception/cognition, 139, 207
saññāvedayita-nirodha (Cessation of Perception/Ideation and Feeling), see *nirodha-samāpatti*
santilakkhaṇa (nirvana's) characteristic of peace, 184
santuṭṭhi contentment (with little), 337, 342, 423–424
sarvam āyus a full life (=100 years), 136

sāsana a/the Buddha's teaching (as historically instantiated), 88, 282, 348, 416, 589 n. 45, 599 n. 17
sāsava/anāsava with/without corruptions, 187
śāstra (Brahmanical Sanskrit) scholastic treatise, 87
sati mindfulness, 435, 514 n. 21
sa-upādisesa with a remainder of grasping/attachment, 148, 149–150, 151
sīla morality, the Precepts, 416, 457, 468, 614
sineha affection, 393, 511, 514
somanassa joy, mental happiness, 164, 208, 308, 453
sotthi (Skt *svasti*) well-being, 517
stūpa (Pali *thūpa*) shrine containing a relic, 261, 270, 275
sugata one who is in a (particularly) good way (epithet of a/the Buddha), 113, 224
sukha happiness, 166, 179, 187, 207–212, 291, 304–309, 475, 494–495
sundaraṃ ṭhānaṃ gata gone to a good place (i.e. nirvana), 113, 224
suññatā emptiness, 141 n. 25
suti (Skt *śruti*) scriptural authority, 178
suttato 'through (the testimony of) the *Sutta*-s,' 178
svadharma (Pali *sadhamma*) individual duty, 466–469, 579 n. 8
svarga (Pali *sagga*) heaven, 136, 299

taṇhā craving, desire, 187, 195, 556, 625 n. 4, 629
Tathāgata (a name for a/the Buddha: see KRN no.88), 149, 202
tejas radiance, glory, 533
tekālika the three times (past, present, future), 144
ṭhāna place, 199, 224
tilakkhaṇa the three characteristics (suffering, impermanence and not-self), 122, 140–141
tipiṭaka the Three Baskets (i.e. the Pali Canon), 60, 248
tyāga see *cāga*

upādāna attachment, clinging, 187, 556
upalabbhati be found, exist, 165, 173–174
sacchik'aṭṭha-paramatthena upalabbhati 'exists in reality and in the ultimate sense,' 165
upasiṃghāyantā 'giving a sniff-kiss,' 512
upāya means, 179
upekkhā equanimity, 209
uttamattha highest goal, *summum bonum*, 155
utu-pharaṇa refreshment, 308

vaṃsa Chronicle, History, 30, 88–89, 254–281, 360–361
vaṇṇa appearance, beauty, 488, 494–495, 628, 630
vaṭṭa round (of rebirth), 174, 187, 483
vattati 'turn', occur, exist, 174
vedanā feeling, 139, 183, 207, 210–211
vevacana synonym, 198–200
vibhava absence of (conditioned) existence (cp. *abhāva*), 204–205, 579
vijjati be found, exist, 165,
vimāna celestial palace-vehicle, 82, 309, 312–314, 319, 327
vimokkha liberation, 161
vimutti-sukha happiness of release, 207
Vinaya the monastic code of rules, 402, 436, 446–448, 449–450
vinicchaya-dhamma principles of justice, 464
vinicchaya-ṭṭhāna law-court, 452
viññāṇa consciousness, 139, 201–206, 212
viriya energy, 357
visama-lobha improper greed, 489, 609
visesa-hetu special(ly important) cause, 249
vivaṭṭa absence of the round (of rebirth), 174, 187, 483
viya just like, as if, 382, 461, 475
vrīhi rice (grown without transplantation), 67

yakkha-s spirits, 301, 319, 320, 328, 334, 429, 518, 537, 594–595
yathābhūta-dassana seeing things as they really are, 348
yathābhūtaṃ bhuñjatha (non-literally) 'continue to govern as you did before', 484 n. 98, 485, 605 n. 12
yutti (Skt *yukti*) reasoning, 172, 178

Name index

This index contains names of historical people and places (not characters in texts), and of texts which are referred to in the book individually or by genre (not those referred to by abbreviation only). Text titles are cited in Pali (or Sanskrit) or in English, or both, as they are given in the main text.

Subject index

This index contains section headings, and the main discussions of each entry; it does not record every occurrence of all words listed.

Printed in the United States
65178LVS00003B/1-3

9 780521 578424